D0142988

Exploring the Bounds of Liberty

Exploring the Bounds of LIBERTY

Political Writings of Colonial British America from the Glorious Revolution to the American Revolution

❧

VOLUME I

Edited and with an Introduction by
Jack P. Greene and Craig B. Yirush

Latin Translations by Kathleen Alvis

LIBERTY FUND

This book is published by Liberty Fund, Inc., a foundation established to encourage study of the ideal of a society of free and responsible individuals.

The cuneiform inscription that serves as our logo and as the design motif for our endpapers is the earliest-known written appearance of the word "freedom" (*amagi*), or "liberty." It is taken from a clay document written about 2300 B.C. in the Sumerian city-state of Lagash.

Front: "Vintage engraving of Boston Harbour showing the *Dartmouth*, which was one of the ships boarded during the Boston Tea Party, a political protest by the Sons of Liberty in Boston, a city in the British colony of Massachusetts, against the tax policy of the British government and the East India Company, which controlled all the tea imported into the colonies." Used by permission © iStock.com/duncan 1890.

Spine: Library of Congress, dated 1758: "A general map of the middle British colonies in America: Viz. Virginia, Maryland, Delaware, Pensilvania, New-Jersey, New-York, Connecticut, and Rhode-Island: Of Aquanishuonigy the country of the Confederate Indians comprehending Aquanishuonigy proper, their places of residence, Ohio and Tuchsochruntie their deer hunting countries, Couchsachrage and Skaniadarade, their beaver hunting countries, of the Lakes Erie, Ontario, and Champlain, . . . exhibiting the antient and present seats of the Indian nations." Used by permission.

Printed in the United States of America

17 18 19 20 21 22 C 5 4 3 2 1

Library of Congress Cataloging-in-Publication Data

Names: Greene, Jack P., editor. | Yirush, Craig, 1968– editor.
Title: Exploring the bounds of liberty : political writings of colonial British America from the Glorious Revolution to the American Revolution / edited by Jack P. Greene and Craig B. Yirush with an introduction by Jack P. Greene ; Latin translations by Kathleen Alvis.
Description: Carmel, Indiana : Liberty Fund, Inc., 2018. | Includes index.
Identifiers: LCCN 2017026534 | ISBN 9780865978997 (hardcover : alk. paper)
Subjects: LCSH: United States—Politics and government—To 1775—Sources.
Classification: LCC E195 .E97 2018 | DDC 973.3—dc23
LC record available at https://lccn.loc.gov/2017026534

LIBERTY FUND, INC.
11301 North Meridian Street
Carmel, Indiana 46032-4564

Contents

Introduction

When scholars think about early American political writings, they think principally about the *Federalist* or about the writings involving various issues associated with the founding era of the American republic, particularly the debates over metropolitan efforts to tax the colonies after 1764, independence, and the formation of the federal state. The most important of these writings have long been accessible to scholars, many of the principal pamphlets and newspaper writings of the Revolutionary era having been included in the collection edited by Charles Hyneman and Donald Lutz and published by Liberty Fund nearly three decades ago.[1] Several other important collections have republished many of the significant writings for and against the Federal Constitution of 1787.[2] As it has become more widely and easily available and thus familiar to more scholars, this literature has elicited considerable scholarly respect for its political precociousness, learning, and sophistication as well as for its relevance to the ongoing project, so central to the history of the West, of defining the nature of civil liberty and determining how best to cultivate and maintain it. Yet, the impression remains that this literature somehow sprang, phoenix-like, out of the heads of geniuses, the revered founding fathers of the Revolutionary generation.

Geniuses many of the founders may have been, but their achievements in political analysis were built on a long and rich tradition of political writing. Scholars have acknowledged the indebtedness of the founders to the

1. Charles Hyneman and Donald Lutz, eds., *American Political Writing in the Founding Era*. 2 vols. (Indianapolis: Liberty Fund, 1983).

2. See, for instance, Bernard Bailyn, ed., *The Debate on the Constitution: Federalist and Antifederalist Speeches, Articles, and Letters during the Struggle over Ratification* (New York: Library of America, 1993). See also Colleen Sheehan and Gary McDowell, eds., *Friends of the Constitution: Writings of the "Other" Federalists 1787–1788* (Indianapolis: Liberty Fund, 1998); Herbert J. Storing, ed., *The Complete Anti-Federalist* (Chicago: University of Chicago Press, 2007).

great British and European legal and political writers, Edward Coke, John Locke, James Harrington, John Trenchard and Thomas Gordon, Frances Hutchinson, David Hume, William Blackstone, and Baron Montesquieu, to name only the most prominent.[3] What has largely escaped systematic analysis, however, is the rich and extensive political literature produced in and about colonial British America during the century *before* the American Revolution. Already by the 1670s, colonial spokespersons were producing formal writings about political questions, a few of them published in New England, which had the only printing presses then in English America, but most of them published in London. Throughout the colonial era, colonials and metropolitans concerned with colonial questions continued to publish their political writings in London or elsewhere in Britain. However, with the expansion of printing to most of the colonies during the last decade of the seventeenth century and the first three decades of the eighteenth century (part of the expansion of print culture that was taking place throughout the English-speaking world), political polemical literature published in America increased exponentially throughout colonial British America, from Britain's southernmost colony in Barbados to its northernmost colony in Nova Scotia. Indeed, the number of imprints dealing with political questions increased in every decade after 1710 to become, by the 1750s, a veritable flood.

This vast literature was both sacred and secular. Some of it appeared as essays in newspapers, some in sizable volumes, some in sermons, some in poetry, plays, and other belletristic writings, but most of it in pamphlets or short treatises of fewer than a hundred pages. A large proportion of this literature has survived, widely scattered among rare book libraries in the United States, Britain, Canada, and the West Indies. Altogether, between 1670 and 1764 as many as a thousand to twelve hundred explicitly political writings issued from colonial and British presses on matters of moment to the colonial British American world. Because of the ephemeral character of this literature and because it was not associated with a founding national moment, scholars have remained mostly unaware of it.

The obscurity of this literature has meant that an important body of English political writing has been largely ignored. Above all, English people

3. See Jack P. Greene, *The Intellectual Heritage of the Constitution: The Delegates' Library* (Philadelphia: Library Company of Philadelphia, 1986).

thought of themselves as distinct from other peoples because of their successful dedication to liberty and the rule of law, to which even the monarchy had been subjected. English people who migrated overseas to Ireland and to America during the seventeenth and eighteenth centuries took this dedication with them. Liberty and law, they were persuaded, were the essential badges through which they could continue to identify themselves as English people, although living far away in climates and places that bore little physical resemblance to the country they had left behind. Hence, from the very beginning of overseas settlement, colonists made every effort to lay claim to the principles of English law and liberty, to incorporate those principles into the political and legal structures of the communities they were establishing in the New World, and to elicit metropolitan acknowledgment that, by virtue of their national inheritance as English people or the descendants of English people, they were fully entitled to that system of law and liberty. In the 1680s, William Penn, founder of the newest and last of the seventeenth-century English colonies, offered to prospective colonists precisely the sorts of guarantees of their rights to English law and liberties that colonists in the older colonies had long claimed. Thus, when metropolitan officials during the Restoration sought to use prerogative powers to impose a more authoritarian regime upon the colonies, and when in the mid-1680s under James II they sought to amalgamate the New England colonies and New York into the Dominion of New England, a regime that eliminated representative government in those colonies, they encountered widespread and deep resistance.

That resistance was responsible for much of the political literature of colonial British America. The Glorious Revolution in England provided the occasion for the overthrow of seemingly absolutist or Catholic regimes in New England, New York, and Maryland, in the process generating an extensive literature that either justified or opposed the overthrow of existing regimes. In this discussion, apologists for settler resistance widely condemned the Crown's use of prerogative power to stifle or curtail traditional English liberties in the colonies, while their opponents depicted colonial uprisings as violations of the existing political order and invitations, not to liberty, but to licentiousness. At the very heart of these discussions was the question of how English people organized into and living in polities so remote from the parent state could enjoy the traditional liberties of Englishmen, and settler protagonists manifested a powerful determination both to inscribe those liberties into their new polities and to resist any efforts to deprive them of their most valuable inheritance, as they often said, in paraphrase of Sir Edward Coke. At the same time, a significant number of authors in the colonies (many, but not all of them government officials) took the side of the metropolis, defending it against the defiance of colonial protagonists and their alleged encroachments upon metropolitan authority.

During the eight decades following the Glorious Revolution, the same question arose repeatedly, connected to a wide variety of issues. These included the vagaries of colonial justice, abuses of judicial and executive power, the ambiguity of colonial constitutions, the sanctity of colonial charters, the persecution of religious dissenters, the limits and responsibilities of proprietary government, freedom of the press, the enslavement of blacks, the desirability of balanced government, the privileges and powers of colonial legislatures, the efforts of power-seeking politicians to monopolize power, the entitlement of colonial settlers to English laws, and appropriate strategies for economic development. Mostly arising out of local crises, the conflicts over these issues generated a large literature, including formal political tracts, published speeches from legislative debates, political satires, grand jury charges, election tracts and sermons, accounts of political trials, and many other genres. This literature circulated freely around the British world; a pamphlet emanating in Williamsburg might be answered by one written in London, and authors frequently made references to writings produced in disputes in other areas of the colonial British American—or Irish—world. Authors of this literature thus drew upon not just metropolitan political writers but each other. Over time, this body of literature showed an increase in learning as well as in legal, political, and philosophical sophistication, and it produced a body of thought upon which spokespersons for the resisting colonies in the 1760s and 1770s could draw in their defense of colonial liberties from the encroachments of metropolitan power.

For over a century, in formal political writing, they had effectively been testing, defining, and expanding the bounds of liberty in Britain's overseas possessions. In this short general introduction, we can mention only a few of the most impressive examples of this literature. Published by an anonymous Virginian in London in 1701, *An Essay upon the Government of the Plantations in America* (Selection 8), identified most of the tensions between metropolitan power and colonial liberty that would prove to be constant irritants in metropolitan-colonial relations until the American Revolution and, for those polities that remained in the British Empire after 1783, well beyond it. In 1721, Jeremiah Dummer's *A Defence of the New England Charters* (Selection 20) brilliantly argued the colonial case for the sanctity of the charters on which the governments of several of the colonies depended for their immediate legal foundations. Later in the same decade, in *The Right of the Inhabitants of Maryland, to the Benefit of English Laws* (Selection 26), the Maryland lawyer and recent Irish emigrant Daniel Dulany used English jurisprudential thought and natural rights theory to fashion an effective case for the entitlement of Marylanders to the laws and liberties of Englishmen, a subject also canvassed with enormous learning in two New York pamphlets of 1734: William Smith, *Mr. Smith's Opinion Humbly Offered to the General Assembly of the Colony of New-York* (Selection 29), and Joseph Murray, *Mr. Murray's Opinion Relating to the Courts of Justice in the Colony of New York* (Selection 30). In 1748, five anonymous Maryland writers in the Annapolis *Maryland Gazette* (Selection 41), Maryland's only newspaper, subjected that colony's constitution to an elaborate examination in which they explored in detail the relationship between balanced government and liberty and debated the concept of fundamental law. In 1752, the royal officeholder Archibald Kennedy produced *An Essay on the Government of the Colonies* (Selection 42), the best of several tracts attacking the efforts of colonial legislatures to overturn the balance of power that he thought characteristic of the British constitution by vesting all authority in legislative hands. In 1755 and 1756, the Boston printer Daniel Fowle offered two ringing defenses of freedom of the press from legislative control, one of which, *A Total Eclipse of Liberty* (Selection 53), is reprinted here. In 1764, in *A Speech, Delivered in the House of Assembly of the Province of Pennsylvania* (Selection 63), the young Pennsylvania lawyer John Dickinson denounced the efforts of Pennsylvania's proprietary party to exchange its existing government for a royal one as a move that would endanger the colony's existing liberties and privileges. Finally, in 1766, in *The Privileges of the Island of Jamaica Vindicated* (Selection 66), Nicholas Bourke, another Irish emigrant lawyer, in this case to Jamaica, offered the single most impressive defense of parliamentary privilege produced in the English-speaking early-modern overseas world.

This literature has not commanded much scholarly attention. Looking for the roots of American political thought, a few scholars in the late 1940s and early 1950s, notably Clinton Rossiter[4] and Max Savelle,[5] treated this literature seriously. Rossiter and Savelle identified some of the principal writers and sketched out some of the main themes in colonial political discourse. Limited by existing technologies and the scattered nature of this literature, however, they barely scratched the surface. In the 1960s, a few scholars, in particular, T. H. Breen,[6] made careful studies of New England election sermons. At the same time, Lawrence H. Leder[7] and Bernard Bailyn[8] made casual forays into some of the literature without doing justice to its richness, learning, and developing sophistication. Although Jack P. Greene made considerable use of some of this literature in the early 1980s in his analysis of colonial constitutional thought and development,[9] no one seems to have revisited this subject or delved again into these sources until the late 1990s, when Craig Yirush began to read them in preparation for his monograph on selected aspects of colonial political thought.[10]

This work will also be available in an expanded edition of 172 pamphlets.[11] While the present edition includes 75 of the most impressive of the 172 pamphlets, both versions are intended to provide readers with an introduction to this neglected and impressive body of colonial British American political literature. Rather than arranging the selections into modern categories, the editors have chosen to present them in chronological sequence from the earliest in 1688 to the latest in 1774. The choice of a beginning should not be taken to imply the absence of political controversy and political thought

4. Clinton Rossiter, *Seedtime of the Republic* (New York: Harcourt, Brace, 1953).

5. Max Savelle, *Seeds of Liberty: The Genesis of the American Mind* (New York: A. A. Knopf, 1948).

6. T. H. Breen, *The Character of the Good Ruler: A Study of Puritan Political Ideas in New England, 1630–1730* (New Haven: Yale University Press, 1970).

7. Lawrence H. Leder, *Liberty and Authority: Early American Political Ideology, 1689–1763* (New York: Quadrangle Press, 1968).

8. Bernard Bailyn, *Origins of American Politics* (New York: Alfred A. Knopf, 1965).

9. Jack P. Greene, *Peripheries and Center: Constitutional Development in the Extended Polities of the British Empire and the United States, 1607–1788* (Athens, Ga.: University of Georgia Press, 1987).

10. Craig Yirush, *Settlers, Liberty, and Empire: The Roots of Early American Political Theory, 1675–1775* (New York: Cambridge University Press, 2011).

11. Jack P. Greene and Craig B. Yirush, eds., *Exploring the Bounds of Liberty*, ebook edition (Indianapolis: Liberty Fund, forthcoming).

before 1688. From the early work of Herbert Levi Osgood[12] and Charles M. Andrews[13] and many studies of the seventeenth-century history of several colonies, we have long known that the main outlines of both colonial political claims and metropolitan responses to them had been worked out in considerable detail during the years of the English Civil War, the Interregnum, and especially the Restoration. Before the late 1680s, however, few of the important documents arising out of this process found their way into print.[14] The starting point, 1688, acknowledges the beginning of a more extensive resort to print culture and a more consistent pattern of publication during the era of the Glorious Revolution. The tacit ending date, 1764, is a function of the change in the focus of political discussion. Before 1764, the main issue shaping discussions about colonial rights was the extent of the Crown's political prerogative in the colonies. After 1764, Parliament's efforts to tax the colonies shifted to the question of Parliament's colonial authority, a subject already covered extensively in other Liberty Fund publications.

Seven criteria have been used in choosing all 172 selections.

The first criterion was that the selections be secular. Because Ellis Sandoz had already published under Liberty Fund auspices a selection of some of the more important New England election sermons,[15] the editors resolved to limit this collection to secular political writings. They have adopted a fairly generous definition of *secular*, however. Some of the selections address religious issues that spilled over into politics, and some are the work of ministers.

The second criterion was that the selections should cumulatively cover the vast range of issues and concerns that characterized colonial political discourse.

12. Herbert Levi Osgood, *The American Colonies in the Seventeenth Century*. 3 vols. (New York: Columbia University Press, 1904).

13. Charles M. Andrews, *The Colonial Period of American History*, 4 vols. (New Haven: Yale University Press, 1934–38), Vols. 1–3.

14. A. P. Thornton, *West India Colonial Policy under the Restoration* (Oxford: Oxford University Press, 1956); Michael Kammen, *Deputyes & Libertyes: The Origins of Representative Government in Colonial America* (New York: Knopf, 1969); Greene, *Peripheries and Center*, 7–42, and Carla Gardonia Pestana, *The English Atlantic in an Age of Revolution, 1640–1661* (Cambridge, Mass.: Harvard University Press, 2007), provide a more recent gloss on aspects of this subject.

15. Ellis Sandoz, *Political Sermons of the American Founding Era, 1730–1805*, 2 vols. (Indianapolis: Liberty Fund, 1998).

A third criterion was to obtain a broad temporal sweep that would illustrate the changing political landscape over the long period from the 1680s, when colonial political writing first became significant, through the first half of the 1760s, when it began to focus largely upon the issue of Parliament's claims to unlimited authority over the colonies. Many writings from 1764 having already been included in the Liberty Fund collection edited by Charles Hyneman and Donald Lutz, it seemed unnecessary to reprint them here.[16] However, the editors did include eight pamphlets from the post-1764 era that were not part of the pre-Revolutionary debate, but addressed issues of the sort that had traditionally concerned colonial political writings, especially in those British colonies that did not join the thirteen colonies that revolted in 1776. As it stands, the resulting collection will contain eight selections from the 1680s, ten from the 1690s, twelve from the first decade of the eighteenth century, fourteen from the 1710s, twenty-one from the 1720s, fourteen from the 1730s, twenty-six from the 1740s, forty-two from the 1750s, seventeen from the 1760s, and eight from the 1770s. The rising number of selections beginning in the 1720s reflects the expansion of printing facilities and the growing use of the press as a forum for political debate.[17]

The fourth criterion was to produce a collection in which all of the polities that composed a part of Britain's American empire before the conclusion of the Seven Years' War in 1763 would be represented. By that time, Britain had twenty-three American colonies: the thirteen colonies that revolted to form the United States in 1776, plus Nova Scotia, the Atlantic island colonies of Bermuda and the Bahamas, and the West Indian colonies of Barbados, Antigua, Montserrat, Nevis, St. Christopher, Jamaica, and the Virgin Islands (Newfoundland did not have a settled government before the nineteenth century)—all part of the same political culture and most of them contributing extensively and sometimes decisively to the discussion of the bounds of English liberty in the overseas British world of the early modern era. The editors thus sought out pertinent selections not just from the revolting colonies but also from those that remained within the British Empire. They have managed to find at least one selection for each

16. Hyneman and Lutz, eds., *American Political Writing in the Founding Era.*

17. The expansion of print culture lacks a comprehensive study, but a number of essays in Hugh Amory and David D. Hall, eds., *The Colonial Book in the Atlantic World* (Cambridge: Cambridge University Press, 2000) shed considerable light on the subject.

of Britain's older colonies except Bermuda and the Virgin Islands, neither of which had a local printer before 1764 or generated any political writing that saw publication in Britain. The number of selections from each colony varies according to the vigor of its civic life, the extent of political controversy, and the level of its output. With thirty-three, Massachusetts has the most selections, followed by Pennsylvania with thirty-one, New York with twenty-five, Jamaica with twelve, Virginia with eleven, Connecticut and South Carolina with eight each, Maryland and Barbados with seven apiece, New Jersey and Georgia with five apiece, Rhode Island, Delaware, and Nova Scotia with three each, Antigua and Grenada with two each, and the Bahamas, North Carolina, Montserrat, New Hampshire, Nevis, and St. Christopher with one each. Two selections concern Grenada, one of eight new American colonies incorporated into the British Empire after 1763 as a result of conquests made by Britain during the Seven Years' War or ceded to it by the 1763 Treaty of Paris.[18] One selection involving India is included here because it raises issues relevant to the American empire. All 172 selections deal directly with colonial affairs: the 57 published in Britain and the 115 published in the colonies.

The fifth criterion was to include examples of every genre of political discourse. Thus, although the vast majority of selections can be classified as polemical political pamphlets of radically different lengths and orientations, the collection also includes five newspaper essays or exchanges, two essays from magazines, two poems, two plays, three charges to grand juries, three judicial opinions, three trial accounts, four state papers, eleven political speeches, and six analyses of the issue of chattel slavery.

The sixth criterion was that the items had to have been published contemporaneously. To this guideline the editors made two exceptions. Although written as an extended political essay, Gershom Bulkeley's *Will and Doom, Or the Miseries of Connecticut by and under an Usurped and Arbitrary Power,*[19] composed in 1692 as one of the author's several attacks on the rationale for overthrowing the Dominion of New England but not published until the nineteenth century, is certainly the most profound defense of the sanctity of established authority and the dangers of rebellion written in colonial

18. The others were East Florida, West Florida, Quebec, St. John's Island (now Prince Edward Island), Dominica, St. Vincent, and Tobago.

19. Included in the ebook edition only.

British America. Selection 61, the Massachusetts House of Representatives' "Instructions to Jasper Mauduit," sent to the London agent in 1762 but not published until the twentieth century, represented the best statement the editors could find of the colonial point of view of the problems of British imperial governance at the conclusion of the Seven Years' War.

The seventh and last criterion was the quality of the production. For this collection, the quality of a selection was determined principally by the cogency, learning, and originality of the argument and how well the piece illuminates the specific and general issues under consideration and only secondarily by its rhetorical or literary merits.

The editors hope that this collection will help to bring about a deeper understanding of the process of transplanting English liberty to overseas colonies during the first centuries of English colonization, of the ideological context of the American Revolution, and of the formation of the political culture not only of the American nation and the states that composed it but also of those colonies that remained in the British Empire after 1776. Speaking directly to such important general themes in the history of liberty as the nature and source of corporate and individual rights, the importance of due process and the rule of law for the preservation of those rights, the centrality of private property and local autonomy in a free polity, and the ability of people to pursue their domestic happiness, this collection is intended to be a tool for scholars researching and endeavoring to understand the origins and spread of the Anglo-American tradition of political liberty.

Editors' Note

Like the 172 pamphlets and other writings that will comprise the expanded edition of this project,[1] this edition of seventy-five of the very best examples of those writings presents the original text in its entirety, with a brief headnote to set each selection in its contemporary context, place it in its genre, and assess its significance for understanding colonial British American political culture.[2] With the exception of providing translations of Latin and other foreign language passages, the editors have not annotated the selections. Nor have they indicated the original pagination within the selections. With certain exceptions, specified below, we have retained the original grammar, spelling, punctuation, abbreviations (including ampersands), italics, capitals, and footnotes. To make the texts more accessible to the modern reader, however, we have also observed the following conventions:

1. Every sentence begins with a capital and ends with a period.
2. Every long-tailed *ſ* has been converted to a lower case *s*.
3. The initial *ff*, an old form for a capital *F*, has been converted to a capital letter.
4. In cases where *u* and *v*, on the one hand, and *i* and *j*, on the other, have been used interchangeably, as was often the case in seventeenth- and eighteenth-century spelling, modern spelling conventions have been followed.
5. All *th* abbreviations such as y^e, y^t, y^m, and y^n have been expanded to *the*, *that*, *them*, and *then*.
6. Superscript letters in titles have been brought down to the line of text, e.g., *Capt.*, and common words abbreviated by superscript have been expanded on the line of text, e.g., *which* and *your*.

1. Jack P. Greene and Craig Yirush, eds., *Exploring the Bounds of Liberty*, ebook edition (Indianapolis: Liberty Fund, forthcoming).

2. This edition will also appear in ebook format.

7. Except in Spanish words, the tilde has been replaced by the letter or letters it represents.
8. All quotation marks except those at the beginning and end of quotations have been removed.
9. In cases where the printer has omitted punctuation, as is often the case with parentheses, or where new punctuation is required to render texts comprehensible, any added punctuation has been enclosed in curly braces, e.g., {)}. Where the correct placement of missing punctuation is unclear, the editors have included a ?, e.g., {)?}.
10. Obvious typographical errors in spelling have been silently corrected.
11. Corrections in the text specified by errata sections have been silently made and those sections eliminated.
12. With the exception of the current editors' addition of square brackets around an author's name at the beginning or end of a pamphlet to identify a pseudonym or indicate the omission of the author's name in the original, all square brackets found in the original texts derived from the original source; all matter inserted into the text by the editors has been enclosed in braces: { }. Words lost by mutilation, defacement, or illegibility have been replaced by *{torn}*, *{blotted}*, *{illeg.}*, *{undecipherable}*, and braces have also been used to note and explain the absence of missing words, phrases, or lines.
13. Blank spaces in the text have been replaced by *{blank}*.
14. Those marginal or side notes briefly summarizing the content of a paragraph have been eliminated, while those containing substantive additions to the text appear as numbered footnotes.
15. Phrases in Latin and other foreign languages appear as numbered footnotes with the translation in brackets. Phrases that appear multiple times in the same pamphlet are translated only upon their first appearance in that pamphlet.
16. Footnotes from the original texts remain unchanged in location and format.

Finally, because both volume editors contributed in the writing of the headnotes, the initials of the author (J.P.G. or C.B.Y.) appear at the end of each headnote.

Translator's Note

If more of the pamphleteers had anticipated the preservation of their writings, we would probably have had easier access to the assortment of Latin that appears in the pamphlets. That assortment of Latin words and phrases from ancient authors, often uncited, variously spelled, sometimes utterly garbled, of remembered ancient mottos and proverbs and of law Latin terms current to the pamphleteer's day, now a research puzzle for the student of eighteenth-century law, has the patina of much use by that circle of citizen authors.

We modern readers, however, struggle even to distinguish a word meant to be morally uplifting from a law term with its technical meaning sometimes far removed from literal translation. The pamphlet writers assume our familiarity with their law Latin. They freely abbreviate formal descriptions, treat terms humorously, apply Latin mottos in unexpected contexts.

In America, modern law terms sometimes retain similar names but have meanings much changed from those in the 1700s by virtue of the development of law. The exact application of pre-Revolutionary law terms is a question for legal historians. The translations offered here of the legal language employed in the pamphlets are meant to provide a rough practical guide to the general idea of eighteenth-century law, not a scholarly explanation. In spite of the difficulties in translating these various sorts of Latin, the effort seems worthwhile, since the failure and abuses of the execution of laws and court actions narrated in the pamphlets seem to confirm the claim of the colonists that they were being treated as "slaves."

I have translated the Latin and Greek as literally as possible. Latin words, such as *Magna Carta,* that have become familiar in English have been left untranslated. My thanks to my associates David Sweet and Richard Dougherty and to my husband, John, for their helpful suggestions.

Kathleen Alvis

Acknowledgments

To bring a project of this scope and complexity to fruition required nearly two decades and—at every stage—enormous help from a wide assortment of people. When Jack proposed this project to Liberty Fund in the late 1990s, Donald S. Lutz, who with Charles Hyneman had edited a similar Liberty Fund collection on the pamphlets of the American Revolution, strongly supported it, as did William Dennis, G. M. Curtis, Hans Eicholz, and Steve Ealy, all former or current Liberty Fund Fellows. Altogether they had sponsored more than a dozen Liberty Fund conferences that Jack directed, beginning in the late 1980s, on the centrality of ideas of liberty and responsibility in the rich political literature produced by British Americans and their associates during the century before the American Revolution.

Once Liberty Fund had approved Jack's proposal, successive directors of its publication program offered unfailing support in advancing it. When it appeared that financial considerations might require that all 172 selections be published in a digital format only, Liberty Fund management authorized the funding necessary to bring out 75 of the more important pamphlets in this print edition. All of these papers will also be included in the digital edition.

Several of Jack's students helped with this project as research assistants while completing their doctoral studies. James Allegro, Michelle LeMaster, and Paul Tonks gathered photocopies of the selections, while Cathy Cardno and Jessica Roney undertook the tedious, exacting, and time-consuming task of preparing clean copies of the texts. We also wish to thank those members of the Liberty Fund publishing staff and their invaluable freelancers who contributed to the immense, intense effort to get these volumes into print. Without the painstaking work of each of these people, this undertaking could never have come to such a happy conclusion. To all who helped to make these volumes possible, we are profoundly grateful.

J.P.G.
C.B.Y.

Exploring the Bounds of Liberty

· 1 ·

William Penn, The Excellent Priviledge of Liberty and Property (Philadelphia, 1687)

WILLIAM PENN (1644–1718) was a prominent English Quaker and the founder of Pennsylvania. In 1687, he commissioned the printer William Bradford, newly arrived in Philadelphia, to issue *The Excellent Priviledge of Liberty and Property*. Adapting Henry Care's *English Liberties* (1682), Penn intended his compendium to be a guide to English liberties for the colonists in Pennsylvania. From Care's larger collection, Penn included three documents which were central to the seventeenth-century understanding of the English constitution: Magna Charta (1215); Edward I's confirmation of Magna Charta and several earlier charters (1297); and a statute of Edward's limiting his ability to tax his subjects without their consent. Each of these documents was followed by substantial comments, drawn mainly from Edward Coke's *Institutes of the Laws of England*, pointing out their significance for English liberties. In addition to these English legal documents, Penn added an abstract of the patent granted by the King to Penn for founding his colony, as well as a copy of Pennsylvania's second Frame of Government (1683).

Penn's note to the reader and his introduction stressed the importance of the core English rights of life, liberty, and property; the crucial role of consent in checking royal authority via juries and Parliaments; and the idea of law as a limit on royal power. As such, *The Excellent Priviledge* stands as one of the best statements of the jurisprudential understanding of the rights of Englishmen in the early modern Anglo-American world. (C.B.Y.)

The Excellent Priviledge of
LIBERTY & PROPERTY
BEING THE
BIRTH-RIGHT
Of the Free-born Subjects of *England.*

CONTAINING

I. *Magna Charta,* with a learned Comment upon it.

II. The Confirmation of the Charters of the Liberties of *England* and of the Forrest, made in the 35th year of *Edward* the First.

III. A Statute made the 34 *Edw.* 1. commonly called *De Tallageo non Concedendo;*[1] wherein all Fundamental Laws, Liberties and Customs are confirmed. With a Comment upon it.

IV. An abstract of the Pattent granted by the King to *William Penn* and his Heirs and Assigns for the Province of *Pennsilvania.*

V. And *Lastly,* The Charter of Liberties granted by the said *William Penn* to the Free-men and Inhabitants of the Province of *Pennsilvania* and Territories thereunto annexed, In *America.*

Major Haereditas venit unicunq; nostrum a Jure & Legibus, quam a Parentibus.[2]

1. [Literally, "Concerning Taxation That Ought Not to Be Levied"; that is, no tax would be imposed without consent of Parliament.—Tr.]

2. ["From our justice and laws comes to every one of us an inheritance greater than from our parents."]

To the Reader.

It may reasonably be supposed that we shall find in this part of the world, many men, both old and young, that are strangers, in a great measure, to the true understanding of that inestimable Inheritance that every Free-born Subject *of* England *is Heir unto by* Birth-right, *I mean that unparalell'd Priviledge of* Liberty *and* Property, *beyond all the Nations in the world beside; and it is to {be} wisht that all men did rightly understand their own happiness therein; in pursuance of which I do here present thee with that ancient Garland, the* Fundamental Laws of England, *bedeckt with many precious Priviledges of* Liberty *and* Property, *by which every man that is a Subject to the Crown of* England, *may understand what is his Right, and how to preserve it from unjust and unreasonable men: whereby appears the eminent Care, Wisdom and Industry of our Progenitors in providing for themselves and Posterity so good a Fortress that is able to repel the* Lust, Pride *and* Power *of the* Noble, *as well as* Ignorance *of the* Ignoble; *it being that excellent and discreet Ballance that gives every man his even proportion, which cannot be taken from him, nor be dispossessed of his* Life, Liberty *or* Estate, *but by the tryal and judgment of* Twelve *of his* Equals, *or* Law of the Land, *upon the penalty of the bitter Curses of the whole People; so great was the zeal of our Predecessors for the preservation of these Fundamental Liberties (contained in these Charters) from encroachment, that they imployed all their Policy and Religious Obligations to secure them intire and inviolable, albeit the contrary hath often been endeavoured, yet providence hitherto hath preserved them as a Blessing to the* English Subjects.

The chief end of the Publication hereof is for the information and understanding (what is their native Right and Inheritance) of such who may not have leizure from their Plantations to read large Volumns; And beside, I know this Country is not furnished with Law-Books, & this being the Root from whence all our wholesom English Laws spring, and indeed the Line by which they must be squared, I have ventured to make it publick, hoping it may be of use and service to many Free-men, Planters and Inhabitants in this Country, to whom it is sent and recommended, wishing it may raise up Noble Resolutions in all the Free-holders in these new Colonies, not to give away any thing of Liberty *and* Property *that at present they do, (or of right as Loyal English Subjects, ought to) enjoy, but take up the good Example of our Ancestors, and understand, that it is easie to part with or give away great Priviledges, but hard to be gained, if once lost. And therefore all depends upon our prudent Care and Actings to preserve and lay sure Foundations for our selves and the Posterity of our Loyns.*

Philopolites.[3]

Introduction.

In *France,* and other Nations, the meer Will of the Prince is Law, his Word takes off any mans Head, imposeth Taxes, or seizes any mans Estate, when, how and as often as he lists; and if one be accused, or but so much as suspected of any Crime, he may either presently Execute him, or Banish, or Imprison him at pleasure; or if he will be so gracious as to proceed by form of their Laws, if any two Villians will but swear against the poor Party, his Life is gone; nay, if there be no *witness,* yet he may be put *on* the *Rack,* the Tortures whereof make many an innocent Person confess himself guilty, and then with seeming Justice is executed. But,

In *England* the *Law* is both the *measure* and the *bound* of every Subjects Duty and Allegiance, each man having a fixed Fundamental-Right born with him, as to *Freedom of his Person* and *Property in his Estate,* which he cannot be depriv'd of, but either by his *Consent,* or some *Crime,* for which the Law has impos'd such a penalty or forfeiture. For all our Kings take a solmn Oath (1.) At their Corenation, *To observe & cause the Laws to be kept:* (2.) All our Judges take an Oath, wherein among other points they swear, *To do equal Law and Right to all the Kings Subjects, Rich and Poor, and not to delay any person of common Right for the Letters of the King, or of any other Person, or for any other cause:* Therefore saith *Fortescue,* (who was first chief Justice, and afterwards L. Chancellor to K. *Henry* 6.) in his Book *de Laudibus Legum Angliae,*[4] cap. 9. *Non potest Rex Angliae, &c. The King of* England *cannot alter nor change the Laws of his Realm at his pleasure; For why, he governeth his people by Power not only Royal, but also Politick: If his Power over them were only Regal, then he might change the Laws of his Realm, and charge his Subjects with Tallage and other Burthens, without their consent; but from this much differeth the Power of a King whose Government is* Politick; *for he can neither change Laws without the consent of his Subjects, nor yet charge them with Impositions against their wills.* With which accords *Bracton,*

3. ["Lover of citizens." Coined, Greek.—Tr.]
4. ["In Praise of the Laws of England."]

a learned Judge & Law-Author, in the Reign of K. *Henry* the 3d, saying, *Rex in Regno suo superiores habet Deum & Legem;* i.e. *The King in his Realm hath two superiors, God and the Law;* for he is under the *Directive,* tho' not *Co-ercive* Power of the Law.

'Tis true, the Law it self affirms, *The King can do no wrong,* which proceeds not only from a presumption, that so excellent a Person *will do none,* but also because he acts nothing but by *Ministers,* which (from the lowest to the highest) are answerable for their doings; so that if a K. in passion should command *A.* to kill *B.* without process of Law, *A.* may yet be prosecuted by Indictment or upon an *Appeal* (where no Royal Pardon is allowable) and must for the same be executed, such Command notwithstanding.

This original happy Frame of Government is truly and properly call'd an *English mans Liberty,* a *Priviledge* not exempt from the Law, but to be freed in Person & Estate from *Arbitrary Violence* and *Oppression. A Greater Inheritance* (saith Judg Cook) *is deriv'd to every one of us from our Laws than from our Parents;* For without the former, what would the latter signifie? And this Birthright of English-men shines most conspicuously in two things:

1. *PARLIAMENTS.*

2. *JURIES.*

By the *First* the Subject has a share by his chosen Representatives in the *Legislative* (or Lawmaking) Power; for no new Laws bind the People of *England,* but such as are by common consent agreed on in that great Council.

By the *Second,* he has a share in the *Executive* part of the Law, no Causes being tryed, nor any man adjudged to loose Life, Member or Estate, but upon the *Verdict of his Peers* or Equals his Neighbours, and of his own Condition: These two grand Pillars of English Liberty, are the *Fundamental vital Priviledges,* whereby we have been, and are preserv'd more free and happy than any other People in the World, and (we trust) shall ever continue so: For whoever shall design to impair, pervert or undermine either of these, do *strike at the very Constitution of our Government,* and ought to be *prosecuted* and *punished* with the *utmost Zeal* and *Rigour.* To cut down the Banks and let in the Sea, or *to poyson all the Springs* and *Rivers* in the Kingdom, could not be a greater Mischief; for this would only affect the present Age, but the other will Ruin and enslave all our *Posterity.*

But beside these *Paramount Priviledges* which the English are estated in by the *Original Constitution* of their *Government*, there are others more particularly declared and expressed in divers *Acts of Parliament* too large to be inserted in this place.

Magna Charta
or
The *Great Charter* made in the 9th year of King *Henry* the 3d, and confirmed by King *Edward* the 1st in the 28th Year of his Reign.

Edward, *by the Grace of God, King of* England, *Lord of* Ireland, *2nd Duke of* Guyan, *to all Arch-Bishops,* &c.

We have seen the Great Charter of the Lord Henry, *sometime King of* England, *our Father, of the Liberties of* England, *in these Words:*

Henry, *by the Grace of God, King of* England, *Lord of* Ireland *and Duke of* Normandy *and* Guyan, *and Earl of* Anjoy; *To all Arch-Bishops, Bishops, Abbots, Priors, Earls, Barrons, Sheriffs, Provosts, Officers, and to all Bayliffs, and other our faithful Subjects, which shall see this present Charter, greeting; Know ye, that we, unto the Honour of Almighty God, and for the Salvation of the Souls of our Progenitors and Successors, Kings of* England, *to the Advancement of holy Church, and Amendment of our Realm, of our meer and Free-will, have Given and Granted to all Arch-Bishops, Bishops, Abbots, Priors, Earls, Barrons, and to all Free-men of this our Realm, these Liberties following, to be kept in our Kingdom of* England *forever.*

CHAP. I.

A Confirmation of Liberties.

1st, We have granted to God, and by this our present Charter, have Confirmed for us, and our Heirs forever, That the Church of *England* shall be free, and shall have all her whole Right, and Liberties inviolably. (2.) We have granted also, and Given to all the Free-men of our Realm, for us, and our Heirs forever, these Liberties under written, to Have, and to Hold to them and their Heirs forever.

CHAP. II.

The Relief of the King's Tenant of full Age.

If any of our Earls or Barrons, or any other which hold of us in chief, by Knights Service, dye, and at the time of his Death, his Heir be of full age, and oweth his Relief, he shall have his Inheritance by the old Relief, that is to say, The Heir, or Heirs of an Earl, for a whole Earldom, one hundred Pounds; the Heir, or Heirs of a Barron, for a whole Barrony, by one hundred Marks; the Heir, or Heirs of a Knight, for one whole Knights Fee, one hundred Shillings at the most; and he that hath less, shall give less, according to the old Custom of the Fees.

CHAP. III.

The Wardship of an Heir within Age, the Heir a Knight.

But if the Heir of any such be within Age, his Lord shall not have the Ward of him, nor of his Land, before that he hath taken of him Homage. (2.) And after that such an Heir hath been in Ward (when he is come to full Age) that is to say, to the Age of one and twenty years, he shall have his *Inheritance* without Relief, and without time, so that if such an Heir being within Age, be made Knight, yet nevertheless, his hand shall remain in the keeping of his Lord, unto the term aforesaid.

CHAP. IV.

No waste shall be made by a Guardian in Wards Lands.

The keeper of the Land, of such an Heir being within Age, shall not take of the Lands of the Heir but Reasonable Issues, Reasonable Customs, and Reasonable Services, and that without destruction and waste of his Men and his Goods. (2.) And if we commit the Custody of any such Land to the Sheriff, or any other which is answerable to us for the Issues of the same Lands, and he make destruction or waste of those things that he hath in Custody, we will take of him Amends and Recompence therefore. (3.) And the Lands shall be committed to two lawful and discreet men of that Fee, which shall answer unto us for the Issues of the same Land, or unto him whom we will Assign. (4.) And if we give or sell to any man the Custody of any such Land, and he there do make destruction or waste, he shall lose the same Custody, and it shall be assigned to two lawful and discreet men of that Fee; which also in like manner shall be answerable to us, as afore is said.

CHAP. V.

Guardians shall maintain the Inheritance of their Wards, and of Bishopricks.

The Keeper, so long as he hath the Custody of the Land of such Heir, shall keep up the Houses, Parks, Warrens, Ponds, Mills, and other things pertaining to the same Land, with the Issues of the said Land: and he shall deliver to the Heir, when he cometh to full Age, all his Land, stored with Ploughs, and all other things, at the least as he received it; all these things shall be observed in the Custody of Arch-Bishopricks, Bishopricks, Abbies, Priors, Churches, and Dignities vacant, which appertain to us; except this, that such Custody shall not be sold.

CHAP. VI.

Heirs shall be Married without Disparagement.

CHAP. VII.

A Widdow shall have her Marriage Inheritance, and Quarentine: the King's Widdow.

A Widdow, after the death of her Husband, incontinent, and without any difficulty, shall have her Marriage, and her Inheritance. (2.) And shall give nothing for her Dower, her Marriage, or her Inheritance, which her Husband and she held the day of the Death of her Husband. (3.) And she shall tarry in the Chief House of her Husband by forty dayes after the Death of her Husband, within which dayes her Dower shall be Assigned her (if it were not assigned her before) or that the House be a Castle. (4.) And if she depart from the Castle, then a Competent House shall be forth-with provided for her, in the which she may honestly dwell, until her Dower be to her assigned, as it is afore said; and she shall have in the mean time her reasonable Estovers of the Common. (5.) And for her Dower, shall be assigned unto her the third part of all the Lands of her Husband, which were his during Coverture, except she were endowed of less at the Church-Door. (6.) No Widdow shall be distrained to marry her self; nevertheless she shall find surety that she shall not marry without our Lisence and assent, (if she hold of us) nor without the assent of the Lord, if she hold of another.

CHAP. VIII.

How Sureties shall be charged to the King.

We or our Balliffs, shall not seize any Lands or Rents for any Debt, as long as present Goods and Chattels of the Debtor do suffice to pay the Debt, and the Debtor himself be ready to satisfie therefore. (2.) Neither shall the Pledges of the Debtor be distrained, as long as the Debt. (3.) And if the principal Debtor fail in the payment of the Debt, having nothing wherewith to pay, or will not pay when he is able, the Pledges shall answer the Debt. (4) And if they will, they shall have the Lands and Rent of the Debtor, until they be satisfied of that which they before paid for him, except that the Debtor can shew himself to the Acquitted against the said Sureties.

CHAP. IX.

The Liberties of London, *and other Cities and Towns confirmed.*

The City of *London* shall have all the old Liberties & Customs which it hath been used to have: moreover, we Will and Grant, that all other Cities; and Burroughs, Towns, and the Barrons of the five Ports, and all other Ports, shall have all their Liberties and free Customs.

CHAP. X.

None shall distrain for more Service than is due.

No man shall be distrained to do more Service then is due for a Knights Fee, nor for any Free-holder than therefore is due.

CHAP. XI.

Common-Pleas shall not follow the King's Court.

Common-Pleas shall not follow our Court, but shall be holden in some place certain.

CHAP. XII.

Where, and before whom Assizes shall be taken, Adjornments for difficulty.

Assizes of *Novel Disseisin,* and of *Mort d'ancestor,* shall not be taken, but in the Shires, and after this manner, if we be out of this Realm, our Chief Justices shall send our Justices through every County once in the Year, which with the Knights of the Shire, shall take the said Assizes in those Counties (2.) And those things that at the coming of our afore-said Justices, being sent to take those Assizes in the Counties, cannot be determined, shall be ended by them in some other place in their Circuit. (3.) And those things which for difficulty of some Articles, cannot be determined by them, shall be refered to our Justices of the Bench, and there shall be ended.

CHAP. XIII.

Assizes of Darreign Presentments.

Assizes of Darreign Presentments, shall be alwayes taken before our Justices of the Bench, and there shall be determined.

CHAP. XIV.

How men of all sorts shall be amerced, and by whom.

A Free-man shall not be amerced for a small Fault, but after the manner of the Fault; and for a great Fault, after the greatness thereof, saving to him his Contenements. (2.) And a Merchant likewise, saving to him his Merchandize, and any other Alien than ours shall be likewise amerced, saving his

Wainage, if he fall into our mercy. (4.) And none of the said Amercements shall be assessed, but by the Oath of honest and lawful men of the Vicinage. (5.) Earls and Barrons shall not be Amerced, but by their Peers, and after the manner of their Offence. (6.) No man of the Church shall Be amerced after the quantity of his Spiritual Benefice, but after his Lay Tenements, and after the quantity of his Offence.

CHAP. XV.

Making of Bridges and Banks;

No Town, nor Free-man shall be distrained to make Bridges nor Banks, but such as of old time, and of Right have been accustomed to make them in the time of King *Henry* our Grand-Father.

CHAP. XVI.

Defending of Banks.

No Banks shall be defended from henceforth, but such as were in Defence in the time of King *Henry* our Grand-Father, by the same Places, and the same Bounds as they were wont to be in his time.

CHAP. XVII.

Holding Pleas of the Crown.

No Sheriff, Constable, Escheator, Corroner, nor any other our Bayliffs, shall hold Pleas of our Crown.

CHAP. XVIII.

The Kings Debtor dying, the King shall be first paid.

If any that holdeth of us Lay-fee, do dye, and our Sheriff or Bailiff do shew our Letters Pattents of our Summons for Debt, which the dead man did owe to us; It shall be lawful to our Sheriff or Bayliff, to Attach and Inroll all the Goods and Chattels of the Dead, being found in the said Fee, to the value of the same Debt, by the sight and Testimony of

Lawful men, so that nothing thereof be taken away, until we be clearly paid off the Debt. (2.) And the residue shall remain to the Executors, to perform the Testament of the Dead. (3.) And if nothing be owing to us, all the Chattels shall go to the use of the Dead (saving to his Wife and Children the reasonable parts.)

CHAP. XIX.

Purveyance for a Castle.

No Constable, nor his Bayliff, shall take Corn, or other Chattels, of any man, if the man be not of the Town where the Castle is, but he shall forthwith pay for the same, unless that the Will of the Seller was to respit the Payment. (2) And if he be of the same Town, the Price shall be paid unto him within the forty dayes.

CHAP. XX.

Doing of Castle-Ward.

No Constable shall distrain any Knight for to give Money for keeping his Castle, if he himself will do it in his proper Person, or cause it to be done by another sufficient man, if he may not do it himself, for a reasonable cause. (2) And if we do lead or send him in an Army, he shall be free from Castle-Ward, for the time that he shall be with us in Fee in our Host, for the which he hath done Service in our Wars.

CHAP. XXI.

Taking of Horses, Carts, and Woods.

No Sheriff nor Bayliff of ours, nor any other, shall take the Horses or Carts of any man to make Carriage, except he pay the old Price hinted, that is to say, for Carriage with two Horses, 10 *d.* a day, for three Horses 14 *d.* a day. (2.) No Demesne Court of any spiritual Person or Knight, or any Lord, shall be taken by our Bayliffs. (3.) Nor we, nor our Bayliffs, nor any other, shall take any mans Woods for our Castles, or other our Necessaries, to be done by Licence of him whose the Wood is.

CHAP. XXII.

How long Fellons Lands shall be holden by the King.

We will not hold the Lands of them that are convict of Fellony, but one Year and one Day, and then those Lands shall be delivered to the Lords of the Fee.

CHAP. XXIII.

In what place Wears shall be put down.

All Wears from henceforth shall be utterly put down by *Thames* and *Midway,* and through all *England,* but only the Sea-Coast.

CHAP. XXIV.

In what Case a Precipe in Capite[5] *is not grantable.*

The Writ that is called *Precipe in Capite* is not grantable from henceforth to no Person of any Free-hold, whereby any Free-man may lose his Court.

CHAP. XXV.

There shall be but one Measure throughout the Realm

One Measure of Wine shall be through our Realm and one Measure of Ale, and Measure of Corn, that is to say, the Quarter of *London.* (2.) And one Breadth of dyed Cloth, Russets, and Habersects, that is to say, two Yards within the Lists. (3.) And it shall be of Weights as it is of Measures.

5. [A writ whereby the king orders that the sheriff command, *praecipe,* such action as a debt be paid or land given up usually where the demandant claims to hold in chief, *in capite,* the right of ownership of property.—Tr.]

CHAP. XXVI.

Inquisition of Life and Member.

Nothing henceforth shall be given for a Writ of Inquisition, nor taken of him that prayeth Inquisition of Life, or of Member, but it shall be granted freely, and not denyed.

CHAP. XXVII.

Tenure of the King in Socage, and of another by Knights Service, petty Serjeantry.

If any do hold of us by free Farm, or by Socage or Bargage, and he holdeth Lands of another by Knights Service, we will not have the Custody of his Heir, nor of his Land, which is holden of the Fee of another, by reason of that free Farm, Socage or Bargage. (2.) Neither will we have the Custody of such Fee, Farm or Socage, or Bargage, except Knights Service be due unto us out of the same free Farm. (4.) We will not have the Custody of the Heir, or of any Land by occasion of any petty Serjeantry, that any man holdeth of us by Service, to pay a Knife, Arrow or the like.

CHAP. XXVIII.

Wager of Law shall not be without Witness.

No Bayliff from henceforth shall put any man to his open Law, nor to an Oath, upon his own bare saying, without faithful Witnesses brought in for the same.

CHAP. XXIX.

None shall be condemned without Tryal: Justice shall not be sold or defered.

No Free-man shall be taken or imprisoned, or be disseized of his Free-hold, or Liberties, or free Customs, or be out-law'd or exiled, or any otherwise destroyed; nor we will not pass upon him, nor condemn him, but by lawful judgment of his Peers, or by Law of the Land. (2.) We will sell to no man, we will not deny or defer to any man either Justice or Right.

CHAP. XXX.

Merchant strangers, coming into this Realm, shall be well used.

All Merchants, (if they were not openly prohibited before) shall have their safe and sure Conduct to depart out of *England,* as to come into *England,* to tarry in and go through *England,* as well by Land as by Sea, to buy and sell without any manner of evil Tools, by the old and rightful Customs, except in time of War. (2.) And if they be of a Land making war against us, and be found in our Realm at the beginning of the Wars, they shall be attached, without harm of Body and Goods, until all be known unto us, or our chief Justice, how our Merchants be intreated there in the Land making war against us. (3.) And if our Merchants be well intreated there, theirs shall be likewise with us.

CHAP. XXXI.

Tenure of a Barrony coming into the Kings hand by Escheat.

If any man hold of any Escheats, as of the honour of *Wallingford, Nottingham, Boloin,* or of any other Escheats, which be in our hand and our Barronys, and dye, his Heir shall give none other Relief, nor do none other Service to Us, than he should have done to the Barron, if it had been in the Barrons hands. (2.) And we in the same wise should hold it as the Barron held it, neither shall we have the occasion of any Barron of or Escheat, any Escheat, or keeping of any of our men, unless he that held the Barrony or Escheat, otherwise held of us in Chief.

CHAP. XXXII.

Lands shall not be aliened to the Prejudice of the Lords Service.

No Free-man from henceforth shall give or sell any more of his Land, but so, that the residue of the Lands the Lord of the Fee may have the service due to him, which belongeth to the Fee.

CHAP. XXXIII.

Patrons of Abbies shall have the Custody of them in time of Vocation.

All Patrons of Abbies which have the Kings Charter of *England,* of Advowson, or have old Tenure or Possession of the same, shall have the Custody of them when they fall void, as it hath been accustomed, and as it is afore declared.

CHAP. XXXIV.

In what only case a Woman shall have an Appeal of Death.

No man shall be taken or imprisoned upon the appeal of a Woman, for the death of any other than her Husband.

CHAP. XXXV.

At what time shall be kept a County Court, Sheriffs Turn and Leet.

No Country from henceforth shall be holden but from Moneth to Moneth; and where greater time hath been used, there shall be greater (2.) Nor any Sheriff or his Bayliff shall keep his Turn in the Hundred but twice in the year, and no where but in due place, and accustomed, that is to say, once after *Easter,* and again after the *Feast of St. Michael,* without occasion. So that every man hath his Liberties which he had, or used to have in the time of King *Henry,* our Grandfather, or which he purchased since. (4.) The view of Frank-pledge shall be so done, that so our Peace may be kept. (5.) And that the Tything be wholly kept, as it hath been accustomed. (6.) And that the Sheriff seek no occasions, and that he be content with so much as the Sheriff was wont to have for his View-making in the time of King *Henry* our Grand-father.

CHAP. XXXVI.

No Land shall be given in Mortmane.

It shall not be lawful from henceforth, to any, to give his Lands to any Religious House, and to take the same Land again to hold of the same House; nor shall it be lawful to any House of Religion to take the Lands of any, and to lease the same to him of whom he received it: If any from henceforth give his Lands to any Religious House, and thereupon be convict, the gift shall be utterly void, and the Land shall accrew to the Lord of the Fee.

CHAP. XXXVII.

Of Subsidy in respect of this Charter, and the Charter of the Forrest, granted to the King.

Escuage from henceforth shall be taken, like as it was wont to be in the time of King *Henry*, our Grand-father, reserving to all *Arch-Bishops, Bishops, Abbots, Priors, Templers, Hospitalers, Earls, Barrons,* and *all Persons,* as well *Spiritual* as *Temporal, all their free Liberties* and *free Customs,* which they have had in times past. (2.) And all these Customs and Liberties aforesaid, which we have granted to be holden within this our Realm, as well spiritual as Temporal, to Us and our Heirs, We shall observe. (3) And all men of this our Realm, as well Spiritual as Temporal, (as much as in them is) shall observe the same, against all Persons in likewise. (4.) And for this our Gift and Grant of these Liberties, and of others contained in our *Charter of Liberties* of *Our Forrest,* the *Arch-Bishops, Bishops, Abbots, Priors, Earls, Barrons, Knights, Free-holders,* and other our Subjects, have given unto us the fifteenth part of all their Moveables. (5.) And neither We nor Our Heirs shall procure or do any thing whereby the *Liberties,* in this Charter contained, shall be infringed or broken. (6.) And if any thing be procured by any Person, contrary to the Premises, it shall be had of no force nor effect. those being Witnesses, Lord *B.* Arch-Bishop of *Canterbury, E.* Bishop of *London,* &c. We ratifying and approving these Gifts and Grants aforesaid, Confirm and make strong all the same for Us and Our Heirs perpetually. And by the tenure of these presents do renew the same, willing and granting for us and our Heirs, that this *Charter,* and all and singular his Articles, forever shall be stedfastly, firmly and inviolably observed. *In Witness* whereof we have caused these our Letters Pattents to be made, *T. Edward,* our Son at *Westminster* the twenty eighth day of *March,* in the twenty eighth year of our Reign.

The Comment on Magna Charta.

This excellent Law holds the first place in our Statute Books, for though there were, no doubt, many Acts of Parliament long before this, yet they are not now extant; 'tis called *Magna Charta,* or the great Charter, not in respect of its bulk, but in regard of the great importance and weight of the matters therein contained; it is also stiled, *Charta Libertatum Regni,* The Charter of the Liberties of the Kingdom; And upon great Reason (saith *Cook* in his Proem) is so called, from the effect, *quia Liberus facit,* because it makes and preserves the People free. Though it run in the stile of the King, as a Charter, yet (as my L. *Cook* well observes on the 38 chap.) it appears to have passed in Parliament; for there was then a fifteenth granted to the King by the *Bishops, Earls, Barrons, free Tenants* and *People,* which could not be, but in Parliament, nor was it unusual in those times to have Acts of Parliament in a form of a Charter, as you may read in the Princes Case, *Coo. Rep. l.* 8.

Likewise, though it be said here, *That the King hath given and granted these Liberties,* yet they must not be understood as meer Emanations of Royal favour, or new Bounties granted, which the People could not justly challange, or had not a right unto before; for the Lord *Cook* in divers places asserts, and all Lawyers know, that this Charter is for the most part only Declaratory of the principal ground of the Fundamental Laws and Liberties of *England;* No new Freedom is hereby granted, but a Restitution of such as lawfully they had before, and to free them of what had been usurped and encroached upon them by any Power whatsoever; and therefore you may see this *Charter* often mentions *sua jura,* their Rights and Liberties, which shews they had them before, and that the same now were confirmed.

As to the occasion of this Charter, it must be noted, that our Ancestors, the *Saxons,* had with a most equal poize and Temperament, very wisely contrived their Government, and made excellent Provisions for their Liberties, and to preserve the People from Oppression; and when *William,* the *Norman,* made himself Master of the Land, though he be commonly called the *Conqueror,* yet in truth he was not so, and I have known several Judges that would reprehend any Gentleman at the Bar that casually gave him that Title; for though he killed *Harrold* the Usurper, and routed his Army, yet he pretended a right to the Kingdom, and was admitted by compact, and did take an Oath to observe the Laws and Customs.

But the truth is he did not perform that Oath so as he ought to have done, & his Successor *William Rufus,* King *Stephen, Henry* the 1st, & *Richard* likewise made frequent encroachments upon the Liberties of their People; but especially King *John* made use of so many illegal devices to drain them of Money, that wearied with intollerable Oppressions, they resolved to oblige the King to grant them their Liberties, and promise the same should be observed, which King *John* did in *Running-Mead* between *Saints* and *Windsor,* by two Charters, one called, *Charta Libertatum,* The Charter of Liberties (the form of which you may read in *Matthew Paris, fol.* 246. and is in effect the same with this here recited) the other, *The Charter of the Forrest,* Copies of which he sent into every County, and commandeth the Sheriff, &c. to see them fulfilled.

But by ill Council he quickly after began to violate them as much as ever, whereupon Disturbances and great Miseries arose, both to himself and the Realm. The Son and Successor of this King *John,* was *Henry* the third, who in the 19th Year of his Reign, renewed and confirmed the said Charters; but within two Years after cancelled them by the pernicious Advice of his *Favourites,* perticularly *Hubert de Burgh,* whom he had made Lord chief Justice; one that in former times had been a great lover of his Country, and a well-deserving Patriat, as well as learned in the Laws, but now to make this a step to his Ambition (which ever Rideth without Reins) perswaded and humoured the King, that he might avoid the Charters of his Father King *John,* by Duress, and his own Great Charter, and *Charta de Foresta*[6] also, for that he was within Age, when he granted the same; whereupon the King in the eleventh Year of his Reign, being then of full Age, got one of the Great Charters, and of the Forrest into his Hands, and by the Counsel principally of this *Hubert* his Chief Justice, at a Council holden at *Oxford,* unjustly cancelled both the said Charters, (notwithstanding the said *Hubert de Burgh*

6. ["Charter of the Forest."]

was the Primary Witness of all Temporal Lords to both the said Charters) whereupon he became in high favour with the King, insomuch that he was soon after (*viz.* the 10th of *December,* in the 13th Year of that King) created (to the highest Dignity that in those times a Subject had) to be an Earl, *viz.* of *Kent:* But soon after (for Flatterers & Humorists have no sure foundation) he fell into the King's heavy Indignation, and after many fearful and miserable Troubles, he was justly, and according to Law, sentenced by his Peers in an open Parliament, and justly degraded of that Dignity, which he unjustly had obtained by his Counsel, for cancelling of *Magna Charta,* and *Charta de Foresta.*

In the 9th Chapter of this Great Charter, all the Ancient Liberties and Customs of *London* are confirmed and preserved, which is likewise done by divers other Statutes, as 14 *Edw.* 3. Chap. 2 *&c.*

The 29th Chapter, NO FREE-MAN SHALL BE TAKEN, *&c.* Deserves to be written in Letters of Gold; and I have often wondred the Words thereof are not Inscribed in Capitals on all our Courts of Judicature, Town-Halls, and most publick Edifices; they are the *Elixer* of our *English Freedoms,* the Store-house of all our Liberties. And because my Lord *Cook* in the second part of his *Institutes,* hath many excellent Observations, his very Words I shall here Recite.

This Chapter containeth Nine several Branches.

First. *That No man be taken or imprisoned, but* per legem terrae; that is, by the Common-Law, Statute-Law, or Custom of *England;* for these words, *per legem terrae,* being towards the end of this Chapter, do refer to all the precedent matters in this Chapter; and this hath the first place, because the Liberty of a man's Person is more precious to him, than all the rest that follow, and therefore it is great Reason that he should by Law be relieved therein, if he be wronged, as hereafter shall be shewed.

2dly. *No man shall be desseised;* that is, put out of Seisin, *or dispossessed of his Free-hold,* that is, Lands or Livelihood, *or of his Liberties, or free Customs,* that is, of such Franchises and Freedoms, and free Customs as belong to him, by his free Birth-right, unless it be by the lawful Judgment, that is, Verdict of his Equals (that is, of men of his own Condition) or by the Law of the Land, that is (to speak it once for all) by the due Course and Process of Law.

3dly. *No man shall be Out-lawed, made an* Ex lex, *put out of the Law,* that is, deprived of the Benefit of the Law, unless he be Out-lawed according to the Law of the Land.

4thly. *No man shall be Exiled or Banished out of his Country,* that is, *nemo predit patriam,* no man shall lose his Country, unless he be Exiled according to the Law of the Land.

5thly. *No man shall in any sort be destroyed,* (Destruere id est quod prius structum & factum fuit penitus Evertere Ex diruere) *unless it be by the Verdict of his Equals, or according to the Law of the Land.*

6thly. *No man shall be condemned at the King's Suite, either before the King in his Bench,* where the Pleas are *Coram Rege* (and so are the Words, *nec super eum ibimus,*[7] to be understood) nor before any other Commissioner or Judge whatsoever; and so are the words, *nec super eum Mitimus,*[8] to be understood, *but by the Judgment of his Peers,* that is, equals, or according to the Law of the Land.

7thly. *We shall sell to no man Justice or Right.*

8thly. *We shall deny to no man Justice or Right.*

9thly. *We shall defer to no man Justice or Right.*

Each of these we shall briefly explain:

1st; *No man shall be taken,* (that is) restrained of Liberty by Petition, or suggestion to the King or his Council, unless it be by Indictment or Presentment of good and lawful men, where such Deeds be done. This Branch, and divers other parts of this Act, have been notably Explained and Construed by divers Acts of Parliament.

2dly; *No man shall be Disseised,* &c. Hereby is intended that *Lands, Tenements, Goods* and *Chattels,* shall not be seised into the King's hands contrary to this Great Charter, and the Law of the Land; nor any man shall be disseised of his Lands or Tenements, or dispossessed of his Goods or Chattels, contrary to the Law of the Land.

A Custom was alledged in the Town of C. *that if the Tenant cease by two Years, that the Lord should enter into the Freehold of the Tenant, and hold the same until he were satisfied of the Arrearages.* It was adjudged a Custom against the Law of the Land, to enter into a mans Freehold in that case, without Action or Answer.

7. [Literally, "Nor shall we" (the king) "proceed against him." Phrase from *Magna Carta* that prohibits detainment without proper charge.—Tr.]

8. [Literally, "Nor shall we" (the king) "send"; i.e., to arrest him without a trial by jury.—Tr.].

King *Henry* the 6th, granted to the Corporation of Dyers within *London, Power to search,* &c. *And if they found any Cloth dyed with Log-Wood, that the Cloth should be forfeit.* And it was adjudged, that this Charter concerning the Forfeiture, was against the Law of the Land, and this Statute; for no Forfeiture can grow by Letters Pattents.

No man ought to be put from his Livelihood, without Answer.

3dly, [*No man Out-Lawed*] that is, barred to have the benefit of the Law. And note, to this word *Out-lawed,* these words, *unless by the Law of the Land,* do refer [*of his Liberties:*] This word hath three Significations.

1*st,* As it hath been said, it signifieth *the Laws of the Realm,* in which respect this Charter is called *Chartae Libertatum,* as afore-said.

2*dly,* It signifieth *The Freedom the Subjects of* England *have:* for example, the *company* of Merchant-Taylors of *England,* having power by their Charter to make Ordinances, made an Ordinance, *That every Brother of the same Society should put the one half of his Cloaths to be dressed by some Cloathworker free of the same Company, upon pain to forfeit ten Shillings,* &c. And it was adjudged that this Ordinance was against Law, because it was against the *Liberty of the Subject,* for every Subject hath freedom to put his Cloaths to be dressed by whom he will, *&c. sic de similibus.*[9] And so it is, if such, or the like Grant had been made by the Letters Pattents.

3*dly, Liberties* signifie the Franchizes & Priviledges, which the Subjects have of the Gift of the King, as the *Goods & Chattels of Fellons, Out-Laws,* and the like, or which the Subject claims by Prescription, as *Wrack, Waif, Stray,* and the like.

So likewise, and for the same Reason, if a Grant be made to any man, to have the sole making of *Cards,* or the sole dealing with any other Trade, that Grant is against the Liberty and Freedom of the Subject, that before did, or lawfully might have used that Trade, and consequently against this Great Charter.

Generally all *Monopolies* are against this great Charter, because they are against the Liberty and Freedom of the Subject, and against the Law of the Land.

4*thly,* [*No man Exiled*] that is, Banisht, or forced to depart, or stay out of *England,* without his consent, or by the Law of the Land: No man can be exiled, or banished out of his Native Country, but either by Authority of

9. ["Thus in like things."]

Parliament; or in case of Abjuration for Fellony, by the Common-Law: And so when our Books, or any Records, speak of Exile or Banishment, other than in case of Abjuration, it is to be intended to be done by Authority of Parliament, as *Belknap* and other Judges, *&c.* banished into *Ireland* in the Reign of *Richard* the second.

This is a beneficial Law, and is construed benignely; And therefore the King cannot send any Subject of *England* against his Will to serve him out of the Realm, for that should be an Exile; and he should *perdere patriam:*[10] No, he cannot be sent against his Will into *Ireland,* to serve the King or his Deputy there, because it is out of the Realm of *England;* for if the King might send him out of his Realm to any place, then under pretence of Service, as Ambassador, or the like, he might send him into the furthest parts of the World, whom being an Exile, is prohibited by this Act.

5thly, [*No man destroyed*] that is, Fore-judged of Life or Limbs, or put to torture or death, every Oppression against Law, by colour of any usurped Authority, is a kind of Destruction, and the words *aliquo modo,* any otherwise, are added to the verb *destroyed,* and to no other Verb in this Chapter; and therefore all things, by any manner of means, tending to Destruction, are prohibited: As if a man be accused or indicted of Treason or Fellony, his Lands or Goods cannot be granted to any, no, not so much as by *promise,* nor any of his Lands or Goods seized into the Kings hand, before he is attainted: for when a Subject obtaineth a promise of the forfeiture, many times undue means, and more violent Prosecution is used for private Lucre, tending to destruction, than the quiet and just proceeding of the Law would permit; and the party ought to live of his own until Attainder.

6thly, [*By lawful judgment of his Peers*] that is, by his equals, men of his own Rank and Condition. The general division of Persons, by the Law of *England,* is, either one that is *Noble,* and in respect of his *Nobility,* of the *Lords House of Parliament,* or one of the *Commons,* and in respect thereof, of the *House of Commons in Parliament.* And as there be divers degrees of Nobility, as *Dukes, Marquesses, Earls, Viscounts* and *Barrons,* and yet all of them are comprehended under this word *Peers,* and are *Peers of the Realm;* so of the *Commons,* they be *Knights, Esquires, Gentlemen, Citizens* and *Yeomen,* and yet all of them of the *Commons of the Realm.* And as every of the *Nobles* one is a *Peer* to another, though he be of a several degree, so it is of

10. ["Lose his country."]

the *Commons;* and as it hath been said of Men, so doth it hold of Noble Women, either by Birth or Marriage.

And forasmuch as this Judgment by Peers is called *Lawful,* it shews the Antiquity of this manner of Tryal: it was the antient accustomed legal course long before this Charter.

7thly, [*Or by the Law of the Land*] that is, by due Process of Law, for so the Words are expresly expounded by the Statute of 37 *Edw.* 3. Chap. 8. and these Words are especially to be refered to those fore-going, to whom they relate; As, *none shall be Condemned without a lawful Tryal by his Peers,* so *none shall be Taken,* or *Imprisoned,* or *put out of his Freehold, without due Process of the Law;* that is, by the Indictment or Presentment of good and lawful men of the place, in due manner, or by Writ original of the Common-Law.

Now, seeing that no man can be Taken, Arrested, Attached, or Imprisoned, but by due Process of Law, and according to the Law of the Land; these Conclusions hereupon do follow:

1. That the Person or Persons which commit any, must have Lawful Authority.

2. It is necessary that the Warrant or Mittimus[11] be Lawful, and that must be in Writing under his Hand and Seal.

3. The Cause must be contained in the Warrant, as for *Treason, Fellony,* &c. *suspicion of Treason* or *Fellony,* or the like perticular Crime: for if it do not thus specifie the Cause, if the Prisoner bring his *Habeas Corpus,*[12] he must be discharged, because no Crime appears on the return; nor is it in such case any Offence at all, if the Prisoner make his escape; whereas if the *Mittimus* contain the Cause; the escape would respectively be *Treason* or *Fellony,* though in truth he were not Guilty of the first Offence, and this mentioning the Cause, is agreeable to Scripture, *Acts* 5.

4. The *Warrant* or *Mittimus,* containing a lawful Cause, ought to have a lawful Conclusion, viz. *And him safely to keep until he be delivered by Law, &c.* and not until the party committing shall further order.

If a man by colour of any Authority, where he hath not any in that perticular case, shall presume to Arrest or Imprison any man, or cause him to

11. [Literally, "We (the king) send." A writ directing the imprisonment of a person, an arrest warrant.—Tr.]

12. [Literally, "You have the body." A writ directing the sheriff that "you have the body" for confinement and are required to produce a charge in court to justify imprisonment. A bench warrant.—Tr.]

be arrested or imprisoned, this is against this Act, and it is most hateful, when it is done by Countenance of Justice. King *Edward* the sixth did Incorporate the Town of St. *Albans,* and granted to them to make *Ordinance,* &c they made a by-Law upon *pain of Imprisonment,* and it was adjudged to be against this Statute of *Magna Charta;* so it had been, if such an Ordinance had been contained in the Pattent it self.

[*We will sell to no man, deny to no man, &c.*] This is spoken in the Person of the King, who in Judgment of Law in all Courts of Justice is present; and therefore every Subject of this Realm, for Injury done to him *in Bonis, Terris, vel Persona,* in Person, Lands or Goods, by any other Subject, Ecclesiastical or Temporal what-ever he be, without exception, may take his Remedy by the Course of the Law, and have Justice and Right for the Injury done him, *freely* without Sale, *fully* without any denyal, and *speedily* without delay; for Justice must have three Qualities, it must be *Libera,* free; for nothing is more odious then Justice set to sale; *plena,* full, for Justice ought not to limp, or be granted piece-meal and *Celeris,* speedily: *quia Dilatio est quaedam negatio,* Delay is a kind of Denyal: And when all these meet, it is both JUSTICE and RIGHT.

[*We will not deny or delay any man, &c.*] These Words have been excellently expounded by latter Acts of Parliament, that by no means Common-Right or Common-Law should be disturbed or delayed; no, though it be commanded under the *Great Seal,* or *Privy Seal, Order, Writ, Letters, Message,* or *Commandment* whatsoever, either from the King, or any other; and that the Justices shall proceed, as if no such Writs, Letters, Order, Message, or other Commandment were come to them; All our Judges swear to this: for 'tis part of their Oath; so that if any shall be found wresting the Law to serve a Courts turn, they are *Perjured,* as well as *Unjust;* the common Laws of the Realm should by no means be delayed, for the Law is the surest Sanctuary that a man can take, and the strongest Fortress to protect the weakest of all; *Lex est tutissima Cassis,* the Law is a most safe Head-piece: And *sub Clypeo legis nemo decipitur,* no man is deceived whilst the Law is his Buckler; but the King may stay his own Suit; as a *Capias pro fine,*[13] for he may respit his Fine, and the like.

13. [A writ issued after the defendant defaults on the agreement set by the court directing such authority as the sheriff that, literally, "you seize the person in place of the fine" and imprison him until he pays the fine.—Tr.]

All Protections that are not Legal, which appear not in the Register, nor warranted by our Books, are expresly against this Branch, *nulli differemus,*[14] we will not delay any man, as a protection under the Great Seal granted to any man directly to the Sheriff, *&c.* and commanding them, that they shall not Arrest him, during a certain time, at any other man's Suit; which hath Words in it, *Per praerogativam nostram quant nolumus esse Arguendam,* by our Prerogative, which we will not have disputed; yet such Protections have been argued by the Judges, according to their Oath and Duty, and adjudged to be void; as *Mich.* 11 *H.* 7. *Rot.* 124. a Protection granted to *Holmes* a Vintner of *London,* his Factors, Servants and Deputies, *&c.* resolved to be against Law, *Pas.* 7 *H.* 8. *Rot.* 66. such a Protection disallowed, and the Sheriff amerced for not Executing the Writ, *Mich.* 13. and 14 *Eliz.* in *Hitchcock* Case, and many other of latter time: And there is a notable Record of antient time in 22 *E.* 1. *John de Marshalls* case; *Non pertinet ad vicecomitem de protectione Regis Judicare, imo ad Curiam.*[15]

Justice or right] We shall not sell, deny or delay *Justice* and *Right,* neither the end, which is *Justice;* nor the *mean* whereby we may attain to the end, and that is the Law: *Right* is taken here for *Law,* in the same sence that Justice often is so called, 1. Because it is the right *Line,* whereby Justice distributive, is guided and directed; and therefore all the Commissioners of *Oyer* and *Terminer,* of *Gaol-delivery,* of *the Peace, &c.* have this clause, *Facturi quod Justitiam pertinet, secundum legem & consuetudinem Angliae,* i.e. to do Justice and Right, according to the Rule of the Law & Custom of *England;* & that which is called *common Right* in 2 *E.* 3. is called *common Law* in 14 *E.* 3. &c. and in this sense it is taken, where it is said, *Ita quod stat Rectus in Curia, id est Legi in Curia.*[16]

2. The Law is called *Rectum,*[17] because it discovereth that which is *tort, crooked* or *wrong;* for as *Right* signifieth *Law,* so *tort, crooked* or *wrong* signifieth *Injuries,* and *Injuria est contra Jus,* Injury is against Right. *Recta linea est index sui & obliqui,* a right line is both *declaratory of it self and the oblique.*

14. [Translated in next phrase: "We will not delay any man." (From *Magna Carta:* "Nulli negabimus, nulli differemus justitiam": "We will neither refuse nor postpone the administration of justice which is due to any man."—Tr.]

15. ["It does not fall to the sheriff to judge about the protection of the king, but rather to the court."]

16. ["What has been established as right in court, this is as law in court."]

17. ["Right."]

Hereby the crooked Cord of that which is called *discretion* appeareth to be unlawful, unless you take it, as it ought to be, *discretio est discernere per Legem, quid sit Justum,* discretion is to discern by the Law what is just.

It is called *Right,* because it is the best *Birthright* the Subject hath, for thereby his *Goods, Lands, Wife & Children,* his *Body, Life, Honour & Estimation* are protected from Injury & *wrong. Major Haereditas venit unicunq; nostrum a Jure & Legibus, quam a Parentibus,* A greater Inheritance descends to us from the Laws, than from our Progenitors.

Thus far the very words of that Oracle of our Law, the sage and learned *Cook;* which so fully and excellently explains this incomparable Law, that it will be superfluous to add any thing further thereunto.

A Confirmation of the Charters of the Liberties of England, and of the Forrest, made in the 35th Year of Edward the first.

Edward, by the Grace of God, K. of *England,* Lord of *Ireland,* and Duke of *Guyan,* to all those these present Letters shall hear or see, greeting. *Know ye,* that we to the honour of God, and of holy Church, and to the profit of our Realm, have granted for us and our Heirs, that the *Charter of Liberties,* and the *Charter of the Forrest;* which were by common consent of all the Realm, in the time of K. *Henry* our Father, shall be kept in every point without breach. And we will that the same Charter shall be sent under our Seal, as well to our *Justices of the Forrest,* as to others, and to all Sheriffs of Shires, and to all our other Officers, and to all our Cities throughout the Realm, together with our Writs, in which it shall be contained, that they cause the aforesaid Charters to be published, and to declare to the People, that we have confirm'd them in all points. And that our *Justicers, Sheriffs* and *Mayors,* and other Ministers, which under us have the Laws of our Land to guide, shall allow the same Charters pleaded before them in Judgment in all their points, that is to say, the *great Charter* as the *common Law,* and the *Charter of the Forrest* for the Wealth of our Realm.

Chap. 2. And we will, that if any Judgment be given from henceforth contrary to the points of the *Charters* aforesaid, by the Justicers, or any other our Ministers that hold plea before them, against the points of the *Charters,* it shall be undone and holden for naught.

Cap. 3. And we will, that the same Charters shall be sent under our Seal, to *Cathedral Churches* throughout our Realm, there to remain, and shall be read before the People two times by the year.

Cap. 4. And that all *Arch-Bishops* & *Bishops* shall pronounce the sentence of *Excommunication* against all those that by word, deed or council, do contrary to the aforesaid Charters, or that in any point break or undo them. And that the said Curses be twice a year denounced and published by the Prelates aforesaid. And if the same Prelates, or any of them, be remiss in the denunciation of the said Sentences, the Arch-Bishop of *Canterbury* and *York* for the time being, shall compel and distrain them to the Execution of their Duties in form aforesaid.

Cap. 5. And for so much as divers People of our Realm are in fear, that the *Aids* and *Tasks* which they have given to us before time, towards our Wars, and other business, of their own grant, or good will (however they were made) might turn to a bondage to them and their Heirs, because they might be at another time found in the Rolls, and likewise for the prizes taken throughout the Realm by our Ministers, We have granted for us and our Heirs, that we shall draw no such *Aids, Tasks* nor *Prizes* into a Custom, for any that hath been done heretofore, be it by Roll or any other President that may be found.

Cap. 6. Moreover, we have granted for us and our Heirs, as well to *Archbishops, Bishops, Abbots, Priors,* and other folk of holy Church, as also to *Earls, Barons,* and to all the *Commonality of the Land,* that for no business hence-forth, we shall take such manner of *Aids, Tasks* or *Prizes,* but by the common assent of the Realm, and for the common profit thereof; saving the antient Aids and Prizes due and accustomed.

Cap. 7. And for so much as the more part of the *Commonality of the Realm* find themselves sore grieved with the *Maletot of Wools,* that is to wit, a Toll of 40 *s.* for every Sack of Wool, and have made Petition to us for to release the same: We at their Request have clearly released it, and have granted for us and our Heirs, that we shall not take such things, without their common consent and good will, saving to us and our heirs the Custom of *Wools, Skins* and *Leather,* granted before by the *Commonality* aforesaid. *In Witness* of which things we have caused our Letters to be Pattent, Witness *Edward* our Son, at *London* the 10th of *October;* and the twenty fifth year of our Reign.

The Sentence of the Clergy against the breakers of the Articles above written.

In the Name of the Father, the Son and the holy Ghost, Amen. *Whereas our soveraign Lord the King, to the honour of God and of holy Church, and for the common profit of the Realm, hath granted for him & his Heirs forever, these Articles above written;* Robert, *Archbishop of* Canterbury, *Primate of all* England, *admonisheth all his Province once, twice and thrice; Because that shortness will not suffer so much delay as to give knowledge to all the People of* England *of these presents in writing. We therefore enjoyn all persons, of what Estate soever they be, that they and every of them, as much as in them is, shall uphold & maintain these Articles granted by our Sov. Ld. the K. in all points. And all those that in any point do resist or break, or in any manner hereafter procure, counsel, or any ways assent to resist or break those Ordinances, or go about it, by word or deed, openly or privily, by any manner of pretence or colour: We the foresaid Arch-bishop, by our Authority in this writing expressed, do excommunicate & accurse, and from the Body of our Lord Jesus Christ, and from all the Company of Heaven, and from all the Sacraments of holy Church, do sequester and exclude.*

NB. It may be observed that this Curse is left out of our late printed Statute-Books, tho' inserted at large in that printed in 3 Vol. in Q. *Eliz.* days, *anno* 1557. There is likewise another like dreadful, but more full and express Curse, solemnly pronounced before in the time of K. *Henry* 3. which also being omitted in our modern Statute-Book, I shall here add.

The Sentence or Curse given by the Bishops against the Breakers of the *great Charter.*

In the Year of our Lord 1253. *the* 3d *day of* May, *in the great Hall of the K. at* Westminster, *in the presence and by the assent of the Lord* Henry, *by the Grace of God K. of* England, *& the Ld* Richard *Earl of* Cornwall *his Brother,* Roger Bigot *Earl of* Norfolk *and* Suffolk, *Marshal of* England, Humphery *Earl of* Hereford, Henry *Earl of* Oxford, John Earl Warren, *and other Estates of the Realm of* England: W. Boniface, *by the mercy of God Arch-bishop of* Canterbury, *Primate of all* England, E. *of* London, H. *of* Ely, S. *of* Worcester, E. *of* Lincoln, W. *of* Norwich, G. *of* Hereford, W. *of* Salisbury, W. *of* Durham, R. *of* Exeter, M. *of* Carlile, W. *of* Bath, E. *of* Rochester, T. *of St.* Davids: *Bishops appareled* *in Pontificials, with Tapers burning, against the breakers of the* Churches Liberties, *and of the* Liberties *or other Customs of the Realm of* England, *and namely those which are contained in the* Charter *of the* common Liberties of England, *and* Charter of the Forrest, *have denounced the sentence of Excommunication in this form. By the Authority of Almighty God, the Father, the Son and the holy Ghost, and of the glorious Mother of God, and perpetual Virgin* Mary, *of the blessed Apostles* Peter *and* Paul, *and of all Apostles, and of all Martyrs, and of blessed* Edward, *K of* England, *and of all the Sts of Heaven, we Excommunicate, accurse, & from the benefits of our holy Mother the Church, we sequester all those that hereafter willingly & maliciously deprive or spoil the Church of her Right; and all those that by any craft or wiliness do violate, break, diminish or change the Churches Liberties, and free Customs contained in the* Charters *of the* common Liberties, *& of the* Forrest, *granted by our L. the King, to Arch-bps, Bps, and other Prelates of* England, *and likewise to the* Earls, Barons, Knights; *and other* Free-holders *of the Realm: And all that secretly or openly, by deed word or council,* do make Statutes, *or observe them being made, and that bring in Customs, or keep them when they be brought in, against the said Liberties or any of them; and all those that shall presume to judge against them. All and every which persons before-mentioned that wittingly shall commit any of the Premises, let them know, that they incur the foresaid Sentence,* ipso facto.

So zealous were our Ancestors to preserve their *Liberties* from encroachments, that they imployed all the strength of human Policy and religious Obligations to secure them intire and inviolate. And I declare ingeniously, I would not for the world incur this Curse, as every man deservedly doth, that offers violence to the fundamental Freedoms thereby repeated and confirmed.

A Statute made Anno 34 Edw. 1. commonly called de Tallegeo non Concendendo.

Cap. 1. No Tallage or Aid shall be taken or levied by us or our Heirs in our Realm, without the good will and assent of *Arch-Bishops, Bishops, Earls, Barons, Knights, Burgesses,* & other *Free men of the Land.*

Cap. 2. No Officer of ours, or of our Heirs, shall take Corn, Leather, Cattle, or any other Goods of any manner of Person, without the good will and assent of the party to whom the goods belonged.

Cap. 3. Nothing from henceforth shall be taken of Sacks of *Wool,* by colour or occasion of *maletot.*

Cap. 4. We will grant for us and our Heirs, That all Clerks and Lay-men of our Land, shall have their Laws, Liberties and free Customs as largely and wholly as they have used to have the same at any time when they had them best. (2.) And if any Statutes have been made by us & our Ancestors, or any Customs brought in contrary to them, or any manner of Article contained in this present Charter: We will and grant that such manner of Statutes and Customs shall be void and frustrate for evermore.

Cap. 5. Moreover, we have pardon'd *Humphry Bohun,* Earl of *Hereford* and *Essex,* Constable of *England, Roger* Earl of *Norfolk* and *Suffolk,* Marshal of *England,* and other Earls, Barons, Knights, Esquires, and namely *John de Ferrariis,* with other being of their fellowship, confederacy and bond, and also of other that hold 20 *l.* Land in our Realm, whether they hold of us in chief or of others, that were appointed at a day certain to pass over with us into *Flanders,* the rancour and evil will born against us, and all other Offences, [*if any they have committed*] against us, unto the making of this present Charter.

Cap. 6. And for the more assurance of this thing, we will and grant that all *Arch-Bps* and *Bps* forever, shall read this present Charter in Cathedral Churches twice in the year, and upon the reading thereof in every of their Parish Churches shall openly denounce *accursed all those that willingly do procure to be done any thing contrary to the tenor, force and effect of this present Charter in any point.* In witness of which thing, we have set our Seal to this present *Charter,* together with the Seals of the *Arch-Bps, Bps,* which voluntarily have sworn, that as much as in them is, they shall observe the tenor of this present Charter.

The Comment.

The word *Tallage* is derived from the *French* word *Tailler,* to share or cut out a part, & is metaphorically used for any Charge, when the King or any other does cut out or take away any part or share out of a mans Estate; & being a general word, it includes *all Subsidies, Taxes, Tenths, Aids, Impositions,* or other *Charges* whatsoever.

The word *Maletot* signifies an *Evil* (i.e. unjust) *Toll, Custom, Imposition,* or *Sum of Money.*

The occasion of making this Statute, was this, K. *Edward* being injured by the *French* King, resolves to make War against him, and in order thereunto requires of *Humphery le Bohun* Earl of *Hereford* and *Essex,* and Constable of *England,* and of *Roger Bigot,* Earl of *Norfolk* and *Suffolk,* and Marshal of

England, and of all the *Earls, Barons, Knights, Esquires,* and *Freeholders* of 20 *l.* Land, whether they held of him in *Capite,*[18] to contribute towards such his expedition, that is, to go in person, or find sufficient men in their places, in his Army; which the Constable and Marshal, and many of the *Knights* and *Esquires,* and especially this *John Ferrers* taking part with them and all the *Free-men,* stoutly denyed, unless it were so ordained and determined by common consent in Parliament, according to Law. And it seems the Contest grew so hot, that *Bakers* Chronicle, *fol.* 99. relates a strange Dialogue that passed between them, *viz.* That when the *Earl Marshal* told the King, *That if his Majesty pleased to go in Person, he would then go with him, & march before him in the Van-Guard, as by right of Inheritance he ought to do; but otherwise he would not stir.* The King told him plainly, *He should go with any other, tho' he went not in Person. I am not so bound* (saith the Earl) *neither will I take that Journey without you.* The King swore, *By God, Sir Earl, you shall either go or Hang. And I swear by the same Oath* (said the Earl) *I will neither go nor hang.* And so the King was forc'd to dispatch his Expedition without them. And yet (saith my L. *Cook*) altho' the K. had conceived a deep displeasure against the *Constable, Marshal,* and others of the *Nobility, Gentry* and *Commons* of the Realm, for denying that which he so much desired, yet, *for that they stood in defence of their Laws, Liberties and free Customs,* the said K. *Edw.* 1st. who (as Sir *Will. Herle* chief Justice of the Common Pleas, who liv'd in his time, & serv'd him, said in the time of K. *Edw.* 3.) was *the wisest King that ever was;* did after his return from beyond the Seas, not only consent to this Statute, whereby all such *Tallages* and *Impositions* are forbidden for the future, but also passes a *Pardon* to the said *Nobles, &c. of all Rancour, Ill will & Transgressions,* [*if any they have committed*] which last words were added, lest by acceptance of a *Pardon of Transgression,* they should implicitely confess that they had transgressed. So careful were the Lords and Commons in former times to preserve the *Antient Laws, Liberties and free Customs of their Country.*

An abstract of the Pattent granted by the King to William Penn, and his Heirs and Assigns.

We do give and grant (upon divers considerations) to *William Penn* his Heirs & Assigns forever all that tract of Land in *America* with all Islands

18. [Literally, "In chief," i.e., refers to powers delegated by the authority of the king.—Tr.]

thereunto belonging That is to say from the beginning of the fortieth degree of *North Latitude* unto the forty third degree of *North Latitude* whose Eastern bounds from twelve English Miles above *New-Castle* (alias *Delaware Town*) runs all along upon the side of *Delaware-River.*

2. Free and undisturbed use and passage into & out of all Harbours Bays Waters Rivers Isles and Inlets belonging to or leading to the same Together with the Soyl Fields Woods Underwoods Mountains Hills Fenns Isles Lakes Rivers Waters Rivulets Bays and Inlets scituate in or belonging unto the limits and bounds aforesaid Together with all sorts of Fish Mines Mettles, &c. To have & to hold to the only behoof of the said *William Penn* his Heirs and Assigns forever To be holden of us as of our Castle of *Windsor* in free and common soccage paying only 2 Beaver skins yearly.

3. And of our further Grace we have thought fit to erect and we do hereby erect the aforesaid Country and Islands into a Province & *Seigniory* and do call it *Pennsilvania* and so from henceforth we will have it call'd.

4. That reposing special confidence in the wisdom and justice of the said *W. Penn* we do grant to him and his Heirs and their Deputies for the good and happy Government thereof to ordain and enact and under his and their Seals to publish any Laws whatever for the publick uses of the said Province by and with the advice and approbation of the Free holders of the said Country or their delegates so as they be not repugnant to the Law of this Realm & to the Faith & Allegience due unto us by the *legal Government* thereof.

5. Full power to the said *W. Penn,* &c. to appoint Judges Leiutenants Justices Magistrates and Officers for what causes soever & with what Power and in such Form as to him seems convenient also to be able to pardon & abolish Crimes and Offences and to do all and every other thing that to the compleat establishment of Justice unto Courts and Tribunals forms of Judicature and manner of Proceedings do belong And our pleasure is & so we enjoyn & require that such Laws and Proceedings shall be most absolute and available in Law and that all the leige People of us our Heirs and Successors inviolably keep the same in those parts saving to us final Appeals.

6. That the Laws for regulating Property as well for the discent of Lands as enjoyment of Goods and Chattels and likewise as to Felonies shall be the same there as here in *England* until they shall be altered by the said *W. Penn* his Heirs or Assigns and by the Free-men of the said Province or their delegates or deputies or the greater part of them.

7. Furthermore that this new Colony may the more happily encrease by the multitude of People resorting thither therefore we for us our Heirs and

Successors do hereby grant Lisence to all the leige People present & future of us, *&c.* (excepting such as shall be specially forbidden) to transport themselves and Families into the said Country there to inhabit & plant for the publick and private good.

8. Liberty to transport what goods or commodities are not forbidden paying here the legal Customs due to us, &c.

9. Power to divide the Country into Counties Hundreds and Towns to incorporate Towns into Burroughs and Burroughs into Cities to make Fairs and Markets with convenient Priviledges according to the merit of the Inhabitants or the fitness of the place And to do all other thing or things touching the Premises which to the said *W. Penn* his Heirs or Assigns shall seem meet and requisit albeit they be such as of their own nature might otherwise require a more special comandment & warrant than in these presents is exprest.

10. Liberty to import the growth or Manufactures of that Province into *England* paying here the legal Duty.

11. Power to erect Harbours Creeks Havens Keyes and other places of Merchandizes with such Jurisdiction and Priviledges as to the said *W. Penn, &c.* shall seem expedient.

12. Not to break the Acts of Navigation neither Governour nor Inhabitants upon the penalties contained in the said Acts.

13. Not to be in League with any Prince or Country that is in War against us our Heirs and Successors.

14. Power of safety and defence in such way and manner as to the said *W. Penn, &c.* seems meet.

15. Full power to assign alien grant demise or enfeoff of the Premises so many and such parts and parcels to those that are willing to purchase the same as the said *William Penn* thinks fit *to have and to hold* to them the said Persons their Heirs or Successors in fee Simple or fee Tail or for term of Life or Lives or years to be held of the said *Will. Penn, &c.* as of the said *Seigniory* of *Windsor* by such Services Customs and Rents as shall seem fit to the said *W. P.* his Heirs & Assigns and not immediately of us our Heirs or Successors and that the said Persons may take the Premises or any parcel thereof of the said *W. Penn, &c.* and the same hold to themselves their Heirs and Assigns the Statute *Quia emptoroes Terrarum*[19] in any wise notwithstanding.

16. We give & grant Lisence to any of those Persons to whom the said W. P. &c. has granted any Estate of Inheritance as aforesaid with the consent

19. ["Because the buyers of land."]

of the said W. P. to erect any parcel of Lands within the said Province into Mannors to hold Courts Barron & view of Frank-pledge, &c. by themselves or Stewards.

17. Power to those Persons to grant to others the same Tenures in fee simple or otherwise to be held of the said Mannors respectively and upon all further Alienations the Land to be held of the Mannor that it held of before the Alienation.

18. We do covenant & grant to and with the said W. P. his Heirs and Assigns that we will not set or make any Custom or other Taxation upon the Inhabitants of the said Province upon Lands Houses Goods Chattels or Merchandizes except with the consent of the Inhabitants & Governor.

19. A charge that no Officers nor Ministers of us our Heirs & Successors do presume at any time attempt any thing to the contrary of the Premises or in any sort withstand the same but that they be at all times aiding to the said W. P. and his Heirs and to the Inhabitants and Merchants their Factors and Assigns in the full use and benefit of this our Charter.

20. And if any doubts or questions shall hereafter arise about the true sense or meaning of any word clause or sentence contained in this our Charter we will ordain and command that at all times and in all things such Interpretation be made thereof and allowed in any of our Courts whatsoever as shall be adjudged most advantageous and favourable to the said W. P. his Heirs and Assigns so as it be not against the Faith and Allegiance due to us our Heirs and Successors. *In Witness whereof we have caused our Letters to be made Pattents. Witness our self at* Westminster *the fourth day of* March, Anno Dom. 1681.

The Frame of the Government of the Province of Pennsilvania and Territories thereunto annexed, in America.

To all Persons to whom these presents may come;

Whereas King *Charles* the second by his Letters Pattents under the great Seal of *England,* bearing date the fourth day of *March,* in the thirty third year of the KING, for divers Considerations therein mentioned, hath been graciously pleased to give and grant unto me *William Penn,* by the name of *William Penn, Esquire,* Son and Heir of Sir *William Penn* deceased, and to my Heirs and Assigns forever, all that tract of Land or Province called

Pennsilvania in *America,* with divers great Powers, Pre-eminences, Royalties, Jurisdictions and Authorities, necessary for the well-being and good Government thereof. And whereas the Kings dearest Brother *James Duke of York* and *Albany,* &c. by his Deeds of Feoffment under his hand and seal, duly perfected, bearing date the 24th of *August,* 1682. he hath granted unto me the said *William Penn* my Heirs and Assigns all that Tract of Land, lying and being from twelve miles northward of *New-Castle* upon *Delaware* River, in *America,* to *Cape Henlopen* upon the said River and Bay of *Delaware,* southward together with all Royalties, Franchises, Duties, Jurisdictions, Liberties and Priviledges thereunto belonging.

Now *know ye,* That for the well-being and good Government of the said Province and Territories thereunto annexed, and for the Encouragement of all the Free-men and Planters that may be therein concerned, in pursuance of the Right and Powers afore-mentioned, I the said *William Penn* have declared, granted and confirmed, and by these presents for me, my Heirs and Assigns, do declare, grant and confirm unto all the Free-men, Planters, and Adventurers of, in and to the said Province and Territories thereof, these *Liberties, Franchises* and *Properties;* so far as in me lyeth, to be held, enjoyed and kept by the Free-men, Planters and Adventurers of and in the said Province of *Pennsilvania* and Territories thereunto annexed, forever.

Imprimis, That the Government of this Province and Territories thereof, shall from time to time (according to the Powers of the Pattent, and Deed, of Feonment aforesaid) consist of the Proprietary and Governour, and the Free-men of the said Province and Territories thereof in the form of a Provincial Council and Assembly, which Provincial Council shall consist of eighteen Persons, being three out of each County, and which Assembly shall consist of thirty six Persons, being six out of each County, men of most note, for Virtue, Wisdom, and Ability, by whom all Laws shall be made, Officers chosen and publick Affairs transacted, as is hereafter limited and declared.

2dly. There being three Persons already chosen for every respective County of this Province, and Territories therof, to serve in Provincial Council, one of them for three Years, one for two Years, and one for one Year, and one of them being to go off Yearly in every County. That on the tenth Day of the first Moneth yearly forever after, the Free-men of the said Province and Territories thereof, shall meet together in the most convenient place in every

County of this Province, and Territories thereof, then and there chuse one Person, qualified as aforesaid, in every County, being one third of the number to serve in Provincial Council for three Years, it being intended that one third of the whole Provincial Council consisting, and to consist of eighteen Persons falling off yearly, it shall be yearly supplyed by such new yearly Elections, as aforesaid, and that one Person shall not continue longer than three Years; and in case any Member shall decease before the last Election, during his time, that then at the next Election ensuing his decease, another shall be chosen to supply his place for the remaining time he was to have served, and no longer.

3*dly*. That after the first seven Years, every one of the said third parts that goeth yearly off, shall be incapable of being chosen again for one whole Year following, that so all that are capable and qualified, as aforesaid, may be fitted for Government, and have a share of the care and burthen of it.

4*thly*. That the Provincial Council in all cases and matters of moment, as their arguing upon Bills to be past into Laws, or proceedings about erecting of Courts of Justice, sitting in Judgment upon Criminals impeached, and choice of Officers in such manner as is herein after expressed, not less than two thirds of the whole, shall make a *Quorum*, and that the consent and approbation of two thirds of that *Quorum* shall be had in all such Cases or Matters of Moment. And that in all cases and matters of lesser moment, one third of the whole shall make a *Quorum*, the Majority of which shall and may always determine in such Cases and Causes of lesser moment.

5*thly*. That the Governour and Provincial Council shall have the Power of preparing and proposing to the Assembly hereafter mentioned, all Bills which they shall see needful, and that shall at any time be past into Laws within the said Province and Territories thereof, which Bills shall be published, and affixed to the most noted place in every County of this Province and Territories thereof twenty days before the meeting of the Assembly, in order to passing them into Laws.

6*thly*. That the Governour and Provincial Council shall take care that all Laws, Statutes and Ordinances which shall at any time be made within the said Province and Territories, be duly and diligently executed.

7*thly*. That the Governour and Provincial Council shall at all times have the care of the Peace and Safety of this Province, and Territories thereof; and that nothing be by any Person attempted to the Subversion of this frame of Government.

8*thly*. That the Governour and Provincial Council shall at all times settle and order the Scituation of all Cities and Market-Towns in every County, modelling therein all publick Buildings, Streets, and Market-places, and shall appoint all necessary Roads and High-ways in this Province and Territories thereof.

9*thly*. That the Governour and Provincial Council shall at all times have power to inspect the management of the publick Treasury, and punish those who shall convert any part thereof to any other use, than what hath been agreed upon by the Governour, Provincial Council and Assembly.

10*thly*. That the Governour and Provincial Council shall erect and order all publick Schools, and encourage and reward the Authors of useful Sciences, and laudable Inventions in the said Province and Territories thereof.

11*thly*. That One Third of the Provincial Council residing with the Governour, shall with the Governour from time to time have the care of the management of all publick Affairs, relating to the Peace, Justice, Treasury, Trade & Improvement of the Province and Territories, and to the good Education of Youth, and Sobriety of the Manners of the Inhabitants therein, as aforesaid.

12*thly*. That the Governour or his Deputy shall always preside in the Provincial Council, and that he shall at no time therein perform any publick Act of State whatsoever, that shall or may relate unto the Justice, Trade, Treasury or Safety of the Province, and Territories as aforesaid, but by and with the Advice and Consent of the Provincial Council thereof.

13*thly*. And to the end that all Bills prepared and agreed by the Governour and Provincial Council, as aforesaid, may yet have the more full concurrence of the Free-men of the Province and Territories thereof, It is declared, granted and confirm'd, that at the time and place in every County, for the choice of one Person to serve in Provincial Council, as aforesaid, the respective Members thereof at their said Meeting, shall yearly chuse out of themselves six Persons of note, for their Virtue, Wisdom and Ability, to serve in Assembly, as their Representatives, who shall yearly meet on the Tenth day of the third Moneth in the Capital Town or City of the said Province, unless the Governour and Provincial Council shall think fit to appoint another place to meet in, where during eight days, the several Members may freely confer with one another, and if any of them see meet with a Committee of the *Provincial Council*, which shall be at that time purposely appointed to receive from any of them, Proposals for the alteration or amendment of any of the said *proposed* and promulgated Bills, & on the nineth day from their so meeting, the said Assembly, after their reading over of the proposed Bills by the Clerk of the Provincial Council, and the occasions and motives for them being open'd by the Governour, or his Deputy, shall upon the Question by him put, give their Affirmative or Negative, which to them seemeth best, in such manner as is hereafter expressed, but not less than two thirds shall make a *Quorum* in the passing of all Bills into Laws, and choice of such Officers as are by them to be chosen.

14. That the Laws so prepared and proposed, as aforesaid, that are assented to by the Assembly, shall be enrolled as Laws of this Province and Territories thereof, with this Stile, *By the Governour, with the Assent and Approbation of the Free-men in Provincial Council and Assembly met.* And from henceforth the Meeting, Sessions, Acts and Proceedings of the Governour, Provincial Council and Assembly shall be stiled and called, *The Meeting, Sessions, Acts and Proceedings of the General Assembly of the Province of* Pennsilvania, *and the Territories thereunto belonging.*

15. And that the Representatives of the People in Provincial Council and Assembly, may in after Ages bear some proportion with the increase and multiplying of the People, the Numbers of such Representatives of the People may be from time to time increased and enlarged, so as at no time the number exceed seventy two for the Provincial Council, and two hundred for the Assembly; the appointment and proportion of which Number, as also the laying and methodizing of the choice of such Representatives in future time, most equally to the division of the Country, or number of the Inhabitants, is left to the Governour and Provincial Council to propose, and the Assembly to resolve, so that the order of rotation be strictly observed, both in the choice of the Council, and the respective Committees thereof, *viz.* one third to go off, and come in yearly.

16. That from, and after the Death of this Present Governour, the Provincial Council shall together with the suceeding Governour, erect from time to time standing Courts of Justice, in such Places and Number as they shall judge convenient for the good Government of the said Province and Territories thereof; and that the Provincial Council shall on the thirteenth day of the second Moneth, then next ensuing, elect and present to the Governour, or his Deputy, a double number of Persons, to serve for Judges, Treasurers, and Masters of the Rolls within the said Province and Territories, to continue so long as they shall well behave themselves in those Capacities

respectively, and the Free-men of the said Province in Assembly met, shall on the thirteenth day of the third Moneth, yearly, elect, and then Present to the Governour or his Deputy a double number of Persons to serve for Sheriffs, Justices of the Peace, and Coroners for the Year next ensuing, out of which respective Elections and Presentments the Governour or his Deputy shall nominate and commissionate the proper number for each Office, the third day after the said respective Presentments, or else the first named in such Presentment for each Office, as aforesaid, shall stand and serve in that Office the time before respectively limited; and in case of Death or Default, such vacancy shall be supplyed by the Governour and Provincial Council in manner aforesaid.

17. That the Assembly shall continue so long as may be needful to impeach Criminals fit to be there impeached, to pass such bills into Laws as are proposed to them, which they shall think fit to pass into Laws, and till such time as the Governor and Provincial Council shall declare, *That they have nothing further to propose unto them for their Assent and Approbation;* and that declaration shall be a Dismiss to the Assembly for that time, which Assembly shall be notwithstanding capable of assembling together upon the summons of the Governour and Provincial Council at any time during that year, if the Governor and Provincial Council shall see occasion for their so assembling.

18. That all the Elections of Members or Representatives of the People, to serve in Provincial Council and Assembly, and all Questions to be determined by both or either of them, that relate to the choice of *Officers,* & all or any other Personal matters, shall be resolved and determined by the *Ballot,* and all things relating to the preparing and passing of Bills into Laws, shall be openly declared and resolved by the *Vote.*

19. That at all times when the Proprietary and Governour shall happen to be an Infant, and under the Age of one and twenty Years, and no Guardian or Commissioners are appointed in writing by the Father of the said Infant, or that such Guardian shall be deceased, that during such Minority, the Provincial Council shall from time to time, as they shall see meet, constitute and appoint Guardians and Commissioners, not exceeding three, one of which shall preside as Deputy and chief Guardian, during such Minority, and shall have and execute, with the consent of one of the other two, all the Power of a Governor in all publick Affairs and Concerns of the said Province and Territories thereof, according to *Charter;* which said

Guardian so appointed, shall also have the care and over-sight of the Estate of the said Minor, and be yearly accountable and responsable for the same to the Provincial Council, and the Provincial Council to the Minor when of Age, or to the next Heir in case of the said Minor's death, for the Trust before expressed.

20. That as often as any days of the Month mentioned in any Article of this Charter shall fall upon the First day of the Week, commonly called the *Lords day*, the business appointed for that day shall be deferred till the next day, unless in cases of Emergency.

21. And for the Satisfaction and Encouragement of all Aliens, I do give and grant, that if any Alien, who is or shall be a purchaser, or who doth or shall inhabit in this Province or Territories thereof, shall decease at any time before he can well be naturalized, his Right and Interest therein shall notwithstanding descend to his Wife and Children, or other his Relations, be he Testate or Intestate, according to the Laws of this Province and Territories thereof, in such cases provided, in as free and ample manner, to all intents and purposes, as if the said Alien had been naturaliz'd.

22. And that the Inhabitants of this Province and Territories thereof may be accommodated with such Food and Sustenance as God in his Providence hath freely afforded, I do also further grant to the Inhabitants of this Province and Territories thereof, liberty to fowl and hunt upon the Lands they hold, or all other Lands therein, not enclosed, and to fish in all Waters in the said Lands, and in all Rivers and Rivulets in and belonging to this Province and Territories thereof, with liberty to draw his or their Fish to shore on any mans Lands, so as it be not to the detriment or annoyance of the Owner thereof, except such Lands as do lie upon Inland Rivulets that are not boatable, or which are or may be hereafter erected into Mannors.

23. And that all the Inhabitants of this Province and Territories thereof, whether Purchasors or others, may have *the last worldly Pledge of my good and kind Intentions* to them and theirs, I do *give, grant* and *confirm* to all and every one of them *full and quiet Enjoyment* of their respective Lands to which they have any *lawful* or *equitable Claim*, saving only such Rents and Services for the same as are or customarily ought to be reserved to Me, my Heirs and Assigns.

24. That no *Act, Law* or *Ordinance* whatsoever shall at any time hereafter be made or done by the *Proprietary* and *Governour* of this Province and Territories thereunto belonging, his Heirs, and Assigns, or by the *Free-men*

in *Provincial Council* or *Assembly*, to alter, change or diminish the form or effect of this *Charter*, or any part or clause thereof, contrary to the true intent and meaning thereof, without the consent of the *Proprietary* and *Governour*, his *Heirs* or *Assigns*, and *Six parts* of *Seven* of the said *Free-men* in *Provincial Council* and *Assembly* met.

25. And *Lastly*, I the said *William Penn*, Proprietary and Governour of the Province of *Pennsilvania* & Territories thereunto belonging, for my self, my Heirs and Assigns, have solemnly *declared*, *granted* and *confirmed*, and do hereby *solemnly declare*, *grant* and *confirm*, that neither *I*, my *Heirs* or *Assigns* shall procure or do any thing or things whereby the *Liberties* in this *Charter* contained and expressed shall be infringed or broken: And if any thing be procured by any Person or Persons contrary to these Premises, it shall be held of no force or effect. In *Witness* whereof, I the said *William Penn* at *Philadelphia* in *Pennsilvania*, have unto this present *Charter of Liberties* set my Hand and broad Seal this second day of the second Moneth, in the Year of our Lord 1683. being the thirty fifth year of the King, and the third year of my Government.

William Penn.

Indorsed

This within Charter which we have distinctly heard read, and thankfully received, shall be by us inviolably kept at *Philadelphia*, the 2d of the 2d Moneth, 1683.

The Members of the Provincial Council present.

William Markham, Will. Clayton, James Harrison, John Moll, Francis Whitwell, John Hillyard, Christop. Taylor, Will. Clark, Phil. Lehmane, Sec. *Will. Haige, Thomas Holme, John Richardson, John Simcock, William Biles, Richard Ingelo,*

Cl. Concilii.

The Members of the Assembly present;

Casparus Harman, William Fletcher, Robert Lucas, John Darby, John Kipshaven, James Williams, Benjamin Williams, Alexander Molestone, John Blanstone, William Guest, Robert Bracy, John. Songhurst, Valentine Hollinsworth, Tho. Bracy, John Hill, James Boyden, Will Yardly, Nicholas Walln, Benony Biship, John Hastings, Tho. Fitzwater, John Bezor, Robert Wade, John Clows, John Harding, Fr. Hassold, Luke Watson, Andrew Brinkstone, John Hart,

Joseph Phips, Simon Irons, Robert Hall, Dennis Rotchford, Jo. Wood, Robert Bedwell, John Brinklair, John Curtis, William Simsmore, Henry Boman, Daniel Brown, Sam. Dark, Cornelius Verhoof.

John Southworth, Cl. Synod

Some of the Inhabitants of *Philadelphia* then present,

William Howell, *Henry Lewis,*
Edward Warner, *Samuell Miles.*

FINIS.

· 2 ·

[John Palmer], The Present State of New England (Boston, 1689)

JOHN PALMER'S *The Present State of New England* was one of the fullest defenses of the Dominion of New England (1685–89), James II's attempt to augment imperial power in English America by combining all of the northern English colonies into one and ruling them without representative government. Chief judge under the Dominion's royal governor, Sir Edmund Andros, Palmer was jailed after the Boston uprising of April 1689, which put an end to the Dominion.

Responding to a series of pamphlets defending the Boston revolt, Palmer offers an alternate account of the nature of royal authority in English America. According to Palmer, Massachusetts (along with the other English colonies in America) had the same legal status as Ireland: they were conquered dominions "of the Crowne of England" and thus "subject to such laws, ordinances and methods of government as the Crowne shall think fit to establish." As a result, Palmer argues, they "may be Ruled and Governed by such wayes and methods as the person who wears that Crowne, for the good and advancement of those Settlements, shall think most proper and convenient." Building on this argument from conquest, Palmer holds that the Crown had the legal right to revoke the Massachusetts charter and set up the Dominion of New England. In the course of the pamphlet, Palmer also denies the factual basis of many of the complaints against the Dominion. Palmer also draws on both scripture and Hugo Grotius's *Rights of War and Peace* (1625) to deny the legitimacy of resistance to constituted authority. (C.B.Y.)

The Present State of New England *Impartially Considered,* In a *Letter* to the *Clergy.*

Reverend Sirs.

Two Moneths have already past away, since with Astonishment I have beheld the most deplorable Condition of our Countrey; Into what a *Chaos* of Confusion and Distraction have we run our selves? And in what a *Labrinth* of Miseries and Perplexityes are we involved? 'Tis High Time now to make some serious Reflections on the state of our Affairs.

In the First place therefore, 'Twill be Necessary to Examine our selves, and to Consider,

1. *For what Reasons, and to what End did we take up Arms?*
2. *Whether those Reasons be Substantial, and such as carry with them Weight enough to justifie the Act; And whether the proposed End can be obtained by such Methods?*
3. *If* not, *What will be the Event, and whether any way be left open to us for a peaceable and friendly Settlement?*

Although there be some (not of the meanest Capacities) among us, who are of Opinion, that a few persons to gratifie their Malice, Ambition or Revenge have been the *plotters* & *contrivers* of our unhappy Troubles, and the better to carry it on have made use of the deluded Countrey men, as the *Monkey did the Cat's foot to pluck the Chesnut out of the fire;* Yet I shall not lightly be over credulous in that matter, nor give Entertainment to such Suggestions; I shall onely therefore instance such things as Conversation & Report have brought to my Knowledge, or as I shall find obvious in the *Declaration;* the summe of which is,

> That above ten years since, there was an horrid Popish Plot in the Kingdome of *England* in which the Extirpation of the Protestant Religion was designed.

That there was great Reason to Apprehend the Reformed Churches of *New England;* were to be overwhelmed in the same pit of Ruine and Destruction.

That the better to effect it, our Charter (the onely hedge which kept us from the Wild Beasts of the field) was both injuriously and illegally Condemned, before it was possible for us to appear at *Westminster* in the legall Defence of it, and without a faire Leave to Answer for our selves.

That by an illegall Commission we were put under a President and Councill, which was soon superseded by another more Arbitrary and Absolute to Sr. *Edmond Andros,* giving him Power, by the Advice of his Councill, to make Lawes and levy Taxes as he pleased, to muster and imploy all persons resident in the Territory, as Occasion should require, and them to transfer to any English plantation.

That severall Red-Coats were brought over, to support what should be imposed upon us, and more threatned.

That Preferments were principally loaden on Strangers and Haters of the people.

That we were Squeez'd and Oppress'd by a Crew of abject persons from *New-York,* who took and extorted extraordinary and intolerable Fees.

That it was impossible to know the Lawes that were made, and yet dangerous to break them.

That by some in open Councill, and by the same in private Converse, it was affirmed, that the People in *New-England* were all Slaves, and the onely Difference between them and Slaves, was their not being bought and sould; and that it was a Maxim delivered in Open Court, by one of the Councill, That we must not think the Priviledge of English men would follow us to the End of the World.

That we were denied the priviledge of *Magna Charta,* and that Persons who did but peaceably object against raising Taxes without an Assembly, were for it severely fined.

That Juries have been picked and pack'd, and that some people have been fined without a Verdict, yea without a Jury.

That some People have been kept long in Prison, without any Information against them, or being Charged with any Misdemeanour or *Habeas Corpus*[1] allowed.

1. [Literally, "you have the body." A writ directing the sheriff that "you have the body" for confinement and are required to produce a charge in court to justify imprisonment. A bench warrant.—Tr.]

That Jury-men were fined and imprisoned, for Refusing to lay their hand on the Booke, as they came to be Sworn, contrary to the Common Law of *New-England.*

That there was a Discovery made of Flaws in the Titles of our Lands: and that the Governour denied that there was any such thing as a *Towne* among us.

That *Writes of Intrusion* were issued out.

That the Governour caused our Lands to be measur'd out for his Creatures, and that the Right Owners for Pulling up the stakes have been grievously molested.

That more than a few were by Terrours drawne to take Patents at excessive Rates.

That the Forceing of the people at the East-ward thereto, gave a Rise to the late unhappy Invasion by the Indians.

That Blanke Patents were got ready, to be sold at great prices, and severall persons had their Commons begg'd.

That the Governour and five or six of the Councill, did what they would, and that all such who were Lovers of their Countrey were seldome admitted.

That all manner of Craft and Rage was used to hinder Mr. *Mather's* Voyage to *England,* and to ruine his person.

That allthough the King promised Mr. *Mather* a *Magna Charta* for Redresse of Grievances, and that the Governour should be writ unto, to forbeare those Measures that he was upon; yet we were still injured in those very things which were Complained of.

That our Ministers and Churches have been discountenanced.

That we were imbriared in an Indian-Warre, and that the Officers and Souldiers in the Army were under popish Commanders.

That the rest of the English plantations, being alarm'd with just Fears of the *French,* who have treated the English with more than *Turkish* Cruelty, could not but stirr us up to take care for our owne Preservation, lest we should be delivered to the *French,* before Orders could come from His Hig[h]ness the Prince of Orange, and the Parliament of *England.*

That we have for our Example the Nobility, Gentry and Commons of *England,* and above all we esteeme it our Duty to God so to have done.

Thus far have I traced the *Declaration,* and do not know that any one thing materiall is omitted, I shall now mention some other things which have occurr'd.

'Twas credibly reported,

> That *Boston* and all the Inhabitants were to be destroyed, and to that end the *Mahawks* were to be brought down.
>
> That there were severall Fire-workes prepared in the Fort, and Vaults dugg under ground to blow up the Towne.
>
> That the Souldiers at the East-ward were all poisoned with Rumm.
>
> That there were Thirty sail of *French* Frigots upon the Coast.

With severall other things which I cannot recollect.

These are the principall Reasons alledged for our takeing up Arms: now the End can be no other than the Redresse of those evills complained of.

The next thing then to be considered of is, *Whether all or any of the Reasons aforesaid, are sufficient to justifie our Proceedings, and Whether the proposed End can be attained by such Measures.*

First then, That there was an horrid popish Plott, is without doubt, and if *England* at that time had fallen under the Yoak of *Roman* Tyranny and Thraldome, tis as certainly true *New-England* must have undergone the same Fate: but that this should be used or introduced as a Reason or Argument for Vacating our *Charter* is beyond my conception; for Fire and Sword were the designed instruments and ministers of their barbarous and hellish Contrivance: and if they had once prevailed, how weak a Rampart would our *Charter* have been against so cruell and powerfull an Enemy? Would a blood-thirsty and conquering *Papist* have made *Westminster-Hall* the Arbiter? Certainly, No; we must have received our Law from the mouth of the Cannon, and our *Hedge* would have been *broke downe* with a great deal of ease. Is it reasonable to imagine, that after they had waded through the blood of *King* and *Nobles* to their wished-for End in *Old England,* they would make use of Politicks in *New—?* And as preposterous and unreasonable to fancy, That for that end our Charter was called in question, especially when we consider that more than four *Decads* of years have allready past since the *Crowne of England* first thought it not fit for us to hold any longer, and severall years after the *popish Plot* was discovered before the *Scire facias*[2] issued out.

2. That the *Charter* was injuriously and illegally Condemned, without giveing us timely notice of it, or allowing us to Answer for our selves, might bear some weight with it, if true: but it will appeare quite other wise, and that we had opportunity enough to have made defence on behalfe of our Charter, if we had so thought fit, for severall years before the proceedings to the Condemnation thereof. Our late Soveraigne *King* Charles *the Second,* by His Letters signified to us the many Complaints that were made to him of our Encroachments, and ill-Administration of the Government, and commanded that we should send over Agents sufficiently Authorized, to Answer the same, which we at length so far complyed with, as to send Agents, who when they were called to hear and Answer the said Complaints, alwaies excused and avoided the principall parts thereof pretending they were not sufficiently impowered for that purpose; and after, other Agents fully impowered to Answer, but not to submit or Conclude any thing: And when His Majesty was pleased to cause a Writt of *Quo Warranto*[3] to be sued forth, against our *Charter,* and sent over with his Gracious Declaration, and Proposals of such Regulations to be made therein, as might be agreeable with His Majesties Service & the good & well-fare of his *subjects* here, and required an entire Submission from us therein; our *Generall Court* would not submit to, or comply therewith; onely a Letter was sent to the *Right Honourable* Sr. *Lionell Jenkins,* then Secretary of State, dated the 10. of *December* 1683, Subscribed by the Governour & Eight of the Assistants onely; wherein after the acknowledgement of their haveing had a Copy of the *Quo Warranto* and His Majesties Declaration, they say that the major part of the *Magistrates* have for severall Weeks declared their Opinion, and voted to lay themselves at His Majesties feet, by an humble Submission and Resignation of themselves to His Majesties pleasure; not being willing to Contend with His Majestie in a Course of Law, but by the next Opportunity to dispatch their Agents fully impowered to make their submission according to His Majesties said Declaration, but by no means can at present

2. [A writ based upon a record directing the sheriff that literally, "you cause the party to know" the charge brought against him and require him to appear and show cause that the record should not be enforced.—Tr.]

3. [Literally, "By what right." A writ directing a person to show "by what right" he exercises certain powers of office.—Tr.]

obtain the Consent of the *Deputyes* whereby to make it an Act of the *Corporation,* and therefore have agreed with them to a power of Attourney-ship, to save a Default, in hopes that further time will prevail to dispatch their Agents accordingly, and shall earnestly endeavour to give the people a better Understanding before the next Ships saile from hence:

His Majesty by this finding that all the easie meanes He had used could not bring us to any Answer, for the Crimes and Misdemeanours laid to our Charge, nor produce any thing else but Baffles and Delayes, gave Order to His Attourney Generall to sue out a Writ of *Scire facias* out of the High Court of Chancery, against our Governour and Company, which was accordingly done, directed to the Sheriffs of *London &c.* and made returnable in *Easter-Term,* in the 36 yeare of His Majesties Reigne, wherein they were Required to make knowne to the said Governour & Company at *London,* that they appeare in His Majesties High Court of *Chancery* at *Westminster,* on the day of the Returne thereof, to shew cause wherefore the said *Charter* for the Reasons in the said Writt of *Scire facias* mentioned and contained, should not be made void, null, and cancelled, and the Liberties and priviledges thereby granted to the said *Governour and Company* be seized into the King's hands; upon which Writt the said Governour and Company not appearing, another Writt of *Scire facias* of the same Tenour issued forth, Returnable in *Trinity Terme* then next following, when the said Governour and Company appeared by their constituted Attourney and Councill, but refused to plead to the said Writt, onely moved for time to send hither, which not being agreeable with the Rules and Practice of the Court in such Cases, could not be allowed: But in favour to them a Rule was made, that unless they pleaded by the first day of the then next *Michaelmas-Terme,* Judgement should be entered by Default. And in that Terme for Default of pleading, Judgement was enterd on His Majesties Behalfe, and the said *Charter* adjudged to be void, Null, and Cancelled, and that the Liberties and Priviledges of the said Governour and Company be Seized into the Kings hands, which was accordingly done, by the *Exemplification* of the said *Judgement* in the Reigne of King *James* the Second, and by His Majesties Commission to a *President and Councill* to take the Government of this Countrey: All which proceedings are most just and Legall, according to the Rules and practice of the Law of *England,* and agreeable with many Precedents of the like nature, both Ancient and Moderne.

Besides: All Companies, Corporations, or Bodies politick, made or granted by Letters Patents or Charter from His Majesty, for any parts or places beyond the Seas, are by themselves or Agents, to be *always ready* to answer *His Majesty* in any of his Courts at *Westminster*, when He shall think fit to Order any Suite, or Writt to be sued and prosecuted against them; and are supposed to be Resident in or about *London* or *Westminster* for that purpose, as the *East-India, Royall-Affrican, Bermudas,* and *Hudsons-bay Companies* are, who have their Trade, Factories, Colonies and Plantations abroad in *Asia, Affrica,* and *America:* and in the like state and Condition ought the Company and Corporation of the *Massachusetts Bay* in *New-England* to be, According to the Capacities given them by their Incorporation of *Sueing and being sued, Pleading & being Impleaded;* wherein if we have neglected our Duty, as well as exceeded our Powers and Priviledges granted, and would not put our selves into a Condition to be heard when we ought and might, it is not His Majesty nor the Proceedings of His Courts that are to be blamed but our selves.

3. That there was a Commission sent to the *President,* and the successive one to Sr. *Edmond Andross,* are both true, but that they were illegall, is a position a little too confidently asserted by the Penman, who seems to be more a *Clergy-man* than a Lawyer; but because the well clearing up of this point will be of great Service to the subsequent Discourse, 'twill not be amiss that it be throughly considered. I shall therefore lay downe this as a certaine Maxime, both consonant to Reason & the Lawes of the Land: That *Those Kingdomes, Principalities, and Colonies which are of the Dominion of the* Crowne *of* England, *and not of the* Empire *of the* King *of* England, *are subject to such Lawes, Ordinances and Forms of Government as the* Crowne *shall think fit to establish.* That *New-England and all the Plantations are subject to the Dominion of the* Crowne *of* England, *and not to the* Empire *of the* King *of* England: Therefore, *The* Crowne *of* England *may Rule and Governe them in such manner as it shall thinke most fit.* For the proofe of which I shall instance *Wales,* which was once a Kingdome or Territory governed by its owne Lawes, but when it became of the Dominion of the *Crowne* of *England,* either by Submission or Conquest, it became subject also to such Lawes as King *Edward* the first (to whome they submitted) thought fit to impose: as may plainly appeare in the Preamble of the Statute of *Rutland. Leges et Consuetudines, partium illarum hactenus usitatas, coram nobis et proceribus Regni Nostri fecimus recitari, quibus diligenter auditis, et plenius*

intellectis, quasdam illarum de Consilio Procerum predictorum delevimus, quasdam permissimus, et quasdam correximus, et etiam quasdam alias adjiciendas et faciendas decrevimus, et eas de caetero in terris Nostris in partibus illis perpetua Firmitate, teneri et observari volumus, in forma subscripta. In English thus,

> We have caused the Lawes and Customs of those parts hitherto used, to be recited before Us and the Peers of Our Realme, which being diligently heard & more fully understood, some of them, by the Advice of Our Peers aforesaid, We have obliterated, some We have allowed, and some We have corrected, and have also decreed that some others shall be made and added to them; and We will, that for the future they be holden & observed in Our Lands in those parts with perpetual firmnesse, in manner herein after expressed.

Then follow the Ordinances appointing Writts originall and judiciall in many things varying from those of *England,* and a particular manner of proceeding.

And againe in the Close of the said Statute, *et ideo vobis mandamus quod permissa de caetero in omnibus observaetis, ita tantum, quod quotiescunq; et quandocunqe; et ubicunque Nobis placuerit, possimus praedicta Statuta et eorum partes singulas declarare, interpretari, addere sive diminuere pro Nostrae Libito voluntatis prout securitati Nostrae, et Terrae Nostrae viderimus expediri:* "And therefore We Command you that from hence foreward you observe the premises in all things so onely, that as often, whensoever and wheresoever We please, we may declare, interpret, add to and diminish from the said Statutes and every part of them according to Our will and pleasure, so as We shall see it expedient for the safety of Us and Our Land aforesaid."

In the Next place I shall instance *Ireland:* That it is a Conquered Kingdome is not doubted, [*Co. Rep. fol.* 18. *a.*] but admitted in *Calvins* Case, and by an Act of the 11*th,* 12*th,* and 13*th,* of King *James,* acknowledged in expresse words, Viz. *Whereas in former times the* Conquest *of this Realme by His Majesties most Royal Progenitors Kings of* England, *&c.*

That by Virtue of the *Conquest* it became of the Dominion of the *Crowne* of *England,* and subject to such Lawes as the Conquerour thought fit to impose, untill afterwards by the Charters and Commands of *H.* the Second, King *John,* and *H.* the 3. they were entituled to the Lawes & Franchises of *England;* as by the said Charters, Reference being thereunto had, may more fully appeare. I shall onely instance two.

The first is out of the close Rolls of *H. the* 3. Wherein the King, after Thanks given to G. *de Mariscis* Justice of *Ireland*, signifies, That *Himself and all other his Leiges of* Ireland *should enjoy the Liberties which he had granted to his Leiges of* England, *and that he will grant* & *confirm the same unto them:* [Claus. 1. *H.* 3. *dorso* 14] Which afterwards in the 12*th* yeare of his Reigne he did: as followeth, *Rex dilecto et fideli suo* Richardo de Burgo *Justiciar'; suo* Hibern, *Salutem: Mandavimus vobis firmiter praecipientes, quatenus certo die & loco faciatis venire coram vobis, Archiepiscopos, Episcopos, Abbates, Priores, Cometes & Barones, Milites & libere Tenentes, et Balivos singulorum Comitatuum, et coram eis publice legi faciatis Chartam Domini* Johannis *Regis, Patris nostri, cui Sigillum suum appensum est, quam fieri fecit, et jurari a Magnatibus* Hiberniae *de Legibus et Consuetudinibus* Angliae *observandis in* Hibernia. *Et praecipiatis eis ex parte Nostra, quod Leges illas & Consuetudines in Charta praedicta contentas, de caetero firmiter teneant et observent.*

> The King to His faithfull and beloved *Richard de Burg* Justice of *Ireland* Greeting; We have Commanded you, firmly injoining you, that on a certain day and place, you make to come before you, the Archbishops, Bishops, Abbots, Priors, Earles, Barons, Knights, & Free-Holders, and the Baylifs of every County, and before them you cause to be publickly read, the Charter of the Lord King *John* our Father to which His Seal is affixed, and which He caused to be made and sworne to by the Nobility of *Ireland*, concerning the Lawes and Customs of *England*, to be observed in *Ireland*. And command them on Our behalfe, that for the future they firmly keep and observe those Laws and Customs conteined in the Charter aforesaid.

By all which it is evident that after the Conquest, and before the recited Charters, the Inhabitants there, altho' composed of *many free-borne English Subjects who settled themselves among them*, were neither govern'd by theire owne Laws, nor the Laws of *England*, but according to the good pleasure of the *Conqueror:* and if you will take the opinion of Sr. *Edward Cooke* in his Annotations on the *Great Charter*, he tells you plainly That *at the makeing thereof it did not extend to* Ireland, *or any of the King's* forreigne *Dominions*, but after the making of *Poynings* Law, which was in the 11*th* yeare of *H.* the 7*th* (long after the *Great Charter*) it did Extend to *Ireland*.

I have onely one Instance more, and that is *the Usage of forreigne Nations in theire Plantations and Settlements abroad.*

The Government of the *United Provinces* & *Denmarke* are well knowne in *Europe*, and yet in all theire Plantations, their Governments are despoticall and absolute; all the power is in the hands of a Governour & Councill, and every thing is ordered and appointed by them; as is well knowne to those that are acquainted with *Batavia, Surinam, Curasao, New-Yorke* (when formerly in their hands) and the Island of St. *Thomas*.

By which it is evident that *Those Kingdoms and Principalities which are of the Dominion of the* Crowne *of* England, *are subject to such Laws, Ordinances, and Methods of Government, as that* Crowne *shall think fit to establish.*

The next thing then to be proved is, *That* New-England, *and all the English Colonies are subject to the Dominion of the* Crowne *of England,* as *Wales* and *Ireland* are, and not to the *Empire of the King of England,* as *Scotland* is.

'Tis a Fundamentall Point consented unto by all Christian Nations, that the First Discovery of a Countrey inhabited by Infidells, gives a Right and Dominion of that Countrey to the Prince in whose Service and Employment the Discoverers were sent. Thus the *Spaniard* claimes the *West-Indies,* the *Portugals, Brasile,* and thus the *English* these Northern parts of *America;* for *Sebastian Cabott* imployed by King *H.* the *7th.* was the first Discoverer of these parts, and in his name took possession, which his Royall Successours have held and continued ever since, therefore they are of the Dominion of the *Crowne* of England, and as such they are accounted by that excellent Lawyer Sr. *John Vaughan,* in his Reports [*Vaugh. Rep. Craw* versus *Ramsey.*] which being granted, the Conclusion must necessarily be good, and it will follow, That *Englishmen permitted to be transported into the Plantations,* (for thither without the *Kings Licence* we cannot come) *can pretend to no other Liberties, Priviledges* or *Immunities* there, *than anciently the subjects of* England *who removed themselves into* Ireland *could have done:* For 'tis from the Grace and Favour of the Crowne alone that all these flow and are dispensed at the pleasure of him that sits on the Throne: which is plaine in the *Great Charter* it selfe; where after the Liberties therein granted by the King it concludes thus,—*tenendas & habendas de Nobis & Heredibus Nostris in perpetuum,* "To *HAVE* and to *HOLD* of Us and Our Heires for ever," which by the learned Sr. *Edward Cooke* is thus explained: *These Words* (saith he) *are not inserted to make a legall Tenure of the* King, *but to intimate that all Liberties at first were derived from the* Crowne. [*Instit. Pag.* 2. *Fol.* 4.] *Barbadoes, Jamaica,* the *Leeward-Islands* & *Virginia* have their Assemblies, but it is not *sui Juris*,[4] 'tis from the Grace & Favour of the *Crowne* signified by *Letters Patents* under the broad Seale. But these Assemblies have not power to enforce any Act by them made above one year; the King haveing in all the Confessions granted them, reserved unto Himselfe, the Annulling or Continuance of what Laws they make, according to His pleasure.

New-England had a *Charter*, but no one will be so stupid to imagine that the King was *bound* to grant it us: Neither can we without impeaching the prudent Conduct and discretion of our Fore-Fathers, so much as think, they would put themselves to so vast an expence, and unnecessary Trouble to Obtain that which as Englishmen, they thought themselves to have a sufficient right to before: We owe it onely to the Grace and Favour of our Soveraigne, and if we had made beter use of it to promote the Ends for which it was granted the weight of those Afflictions under which we now groan would not have laine so heavy upon us, at least we should have less deserved them.

Besides, The *Parliament of England* have never by any Act of theirs favoured the Plantations, or declared or enlarged their Priviledges; but have all along plainly demonstrated that they were much differenced from *England*, and not to have those Priviledges and Liberties which *England* enjoyed; being in all Acts relateing to the Plantations, Restrained and burthened beyond any in *England*, as appears by the several Acts made for the Encreasing of Navigation and for Regulating and securing the Plantation Trade.

I think I have both by good Authority, Practice & Precedent, made it plaine, that the Plantations are of the Dominion of the *Crown* of *England*, and without any Regard to *Magna Charta*, may be Ruled and Governed, by such wayes and methods, as the Person who wears that Crowne, for the good and advancement of those Settlements, shall think most proper and convenient. Therefore Neither the Commission to the *President*, nor that to Sr. *Edmond Andros* can be said to be illegall.

Since then such an one might lawfully be granted, we have great reason to commend the Moderation of the Gentleman, who was entrusted with it, and so returne thanks to Almighty God for placeing over us a person endued with that prudence & Integrity, that he was so far from *exceeding* his Commission, that he never put in *execution* the powers therein granted him.

4. [Literally, "Of his own right," i.e., legally competent, independent.—Tr.]

Have there been any Taxes laid upon us, but such as were settled by Laws of our owne makeing, any part whereof might be retained & in force after the Condemnation of our Charter that the King thought fit. Who hath been Transferr'd out of this Territory? Or did we ever pay fewer Rates than we have done under him?

And whereas it is also Alledged in the Declaration, that *there were Courses taken to damp and spoile the Trade,* &c. the same is altogether Mistaken, (unlesse by that is meant the irregular Trade, used heretofore with Forreigners and Privateers, contrary to the Acts of Navigation & the Laws of the Land). For the very considerable Advance of His Majesties Revenue ariseing by Customs, doth sufficiently demonstrate that the lawfull Trade of this Territory, was very much encreased under the Government of Sr. *Edmond Andros.*

4. Twill be but time lost to say any thing of the Red-Coats, for no man can be so void of Sence and Reason to think that so many Thousand men, which at this day inhabit this Colony, could be imposed upon by one hundred Red-Coats, and if any body hath been so vain as to threaten us with more, I look upon it an effect of Passion or Folly; for Experience, which certainly is the most convinceing Argument in the world, tells us there is no such thing.

5thly What is meant by Preferments, and who are called strangers and Haters of the People, I must confesse, I cannot easily comprehend, unless to inhabit fourteen or fifteen years within the Territory will make a man such. Is their any one Gentleman of the Councill, that hath either been displaced or put into that station by the Authority here? Which of our Judges are strangers? Were not Three of them brought up amongst us and of our owne Communion? and was not the other in the same Imployment in some part of this Territory at the time of the Annexation? From whome had the Secretary and Collector his Commission? certainly from no body here. Did the Alteration of the Government change our Treasurer? Is it not the same Sr. *Edmond* found here? Is he not a man of estate, good Credit and Reputation, and one of our owne Countrey men? Were not all Officers in the Government, as well Magisteriall as Ministeriall, naturall borne English-men, & Subjects to the Crowne of *England?* How then are Strangers & Haters of the people preferr'd, when there is not one that can reasonably and justly be so term'd in any place of Trust or Office throughout the Dominion?

6. Who are mean't by abject persons from *New-Yorke,* wants an Explanation: for none of the Gentlemen that came from thence now in any Authority, but are well knowne to have liv'd there for a long time in esteem and Reputation enough to merit a better Epethite of all good and honest men; and I believe it will one day appear, that their faithfull Discharge of their Dutyes, their Constancy and Steadiness to the *Church of England,* and unshaken Loyalty & Fidelity to the Crowne was their greatest Crime.

I am not well acquainted what Fees were taken, but this I knowe, that a Committee of the Councill were appointed to make a Settlement of Fees, for all Officers throughout the Government, which was effected, approved of, and sent to *England,* and if any one have exceeded those Limits they deserve to be called to Account: but it ought to be in a due Course of Law. For the personal Miscarriages of a ministeriall Officer, are no sufficient Warrant for an Insurrection; neither ought the Whole Government to be subverted because *Tom,* or *Harry* are ill men. The Authority can but provide good and wholsome Lawes, for the Punishment of evill Doers, and cause those Lawes to be put in Execution against Offenders; but if any one doth me a personall Wrong, for which I have a Remedy by Law, and I will not take it, I ought not to quarrell with the Government, for tis my own Fault, and I might have Redresse if I would. Personall Crimes must be censured personally: and a Government ought no more to be scandalized and aspersed, because an Extortioner is in it, than because there is a Felon or a Traitor.

7. I need not tell you that the Statute Lawes of *England* are printed at large, and that many Abridgements of them are so Likewise, and easie enough to be procured, neither can it be but very well knowne that all the Acts of the Governour and Councill were solemnly publish'd with Sound of Trumpet as soon as made, and authentic Copies afterwards transmitted to the Clerks of each respective county throughout the Territory: why then it should be said, that *It was impossible to know the Laws,* I see no reason, unless by it is meant the *Common Law,* and if so, we may as well quarrell because we do not understand *Euclide,* or *Aristotle;* For the Knowledge of the Law cannot be attained without great Industry Study and Experience, and every capacity is not fitted for such an Undertaking. *Ex quovis Ligno non fit Mercurius.*[5] If this was a Grievance, what a miserable Condition are we in *now,* that instead of not knowing the Law, there is no Law for us to know.

5. ["Not from just any wood is a Mercury made."]

8. What rash or indiscreet Expressions may fall from any single person of the Councill, either in his private or politick Capacity, I will not undertake to justifie; all men are not endued with Qualifications alike, every one in that station ought to give his Opinion, as he himselfe understands the matter; and if any one have unadvisedly uttered words so disagreeable, I know no body injured by it, neither can the Government be justly censured for it.

9. That the Priviledges of *Magna Charta,* & other *liberties of English men* were denied us, is a thing which can never be made appear, however admitting it, I have sufficiently discussed that point in the third Article.

10. By the persons said to be severely fined, for peaceble objecting against raising of Taxes, without an Assembly, I conjecture are meant the *Ipswich* men, who were so far from a peaceable objecting, that they assembled themselves in a *riotous manner,* and by an Instrument conceived in Writing, did associate and oblige themselves to stand by each other in opposition to the Laws of the Government, and by their Example influenced their Neighbours to do the like. And this by the Law is esteem'd an offence of that Nature, That it is next door to *Rebellion,* for which they were Indicted, Tryed, and Convicted, either by Verdict or their owne Confession.

11. I cannot justifie that Sheriffe who doth either pick or pack a Jury, tis both repugnant to the Law and his Oath, and he deserves no Favour that can be guilty of such a Crime, but let him first be known, & the thing proved, for I do not Remember any one that hath been Convicted, nor so much as accused for such an Offence.

12. Judgement upon *Demurrers* and *Defaults* are so practicable and warrantable by the Law, that nothing can excuse the Enumerating them amongst the Grieviances in the Declaration but the Penman's want of Knowledge in that Profession. Tis a Maxim, *Volenti non fit Injuria,*[6] and when both Plaintiffe and Defendant do by a joint Consent submit to the Determination of the Court, or by their owne Negligence make Default; who hath the Wrong? Where is the injury? This hath been a Practice so frequently used in our *former Government,* that no body can be ignorant of it.

13. That any one hath been long imprisoned, without being charged with Crime or Misdemeanour, is an Allegation which I dare be bold to say can never be proved. I have heard an *Habeas Corpus* was in one particular case denied, I will not enquire into the reasons of it, nor pretend to justifie it,

6. ["Injury does not happen to one willing."]

although much may be said in that matter; Admitting the Fact, 'twas but a personall injury, for which the Law gave an effectuall Remedy, and if the party grieved would not make use of such, must the Government be in fault? If we do but consider well *how many persons are now under farr worse Circumstances,* I am sure we cannot but *blush* when we read that part of the Declaration.

14. That Jury men were fined and imprisoned for Refuseing to lay their hands on the Book, I presume is a mistake, probably they may have been fined for their Contempt, and sent to Prison for not paying that fine, which by the Law may be justified; for every Court may fine any man for a Contempt in open Court, and they themselves are Judges of the Contempt.

Whether it be a forceing of Conscience or not, I shall leave to the Casuists, but I am very well satisfied *it is not comprehended within the late Indulgence.*

Yet admit it were, the Judges are sworn to do their duties in their office according to the Lawes of the Land, *Prescription is a good & sufficient Law,* the form of Laying the hand on the Booke hath been the onely *modus* of Swearing, Time out of mind; Therefore the Laying the hand on the Booke in Swearing is a good Law, and the Judges cannot dispense with it *salvo Sacramento,*[7] if they did, a Judgement in such a Case would be erroneous & reversable: and *'Tis dangerous to admit of Innovations.*

The Common Law of *New-England* is brought in to warrant the *Lifting up* the hand; but I take that to be *Rara avis in terris,*[8] for I challenge the whole Territory to produce one Precedent of such a resolved Case: but perhaps by it *Prescription* is intended, if it be, that will as illy serve the turn as the other; for the Colony hath not been long enough settled to claim any Advantage by that Right, or if it had, could it be admitted without apparent Violation of our *Charter,* being absolutely repugnant to the Lawes of *England.*

15. Fully to discuss the question concerning the Titles of our Lands, would be a Subject too copious for this present designe, Therefore I shall onely glance at it as I pass by, being Resolved, when time shall serve to declare my opinion more amply on that Subject; in the mean time let every considering man examine well our *Charter,* which is the very *Basis* of all our Rights, (unless we will set up a power above the Kings) and then let him tell me in whome the Fee Simple of that Tract of Land betwixt *Charles River* &

7. ["With the oath intact."]
8. ["A rare bird on earth."]

Mirrimack remaines: if in the *Grantees* or *their Heires,* how do we derive our Titles from them? If in the *Governour and Company of the Massachusets Bay,* we must enquire whether pursuant to the Directions and powers to them granted, it is by good & sufficient Conveyances in the Law derived unto us, if we find it so, we must not be disturbed with Fears and Jealousies, for nothing can hurt us: if not, we are infinitely obliged to those persons who have made us sensible of our Weakenesses, in a time when by *His Majesties Letters Patents* the *Governour* was impowered to supply all such defects, and not upon Terms either excessive or unreasonable, but upon such as were both easie & *moderate,* which will plainly appear to any man who will but give himself the trouble to peruse the Table of Fees, settled and allowed by the Councill. Yet still every man was at his own Liberty to take a *Patent of Confirmation* or to let it alone, which is Apparent enough by the many Petitions now lying in the Secretaries Office, which although his Excellency was alwayes ready (so far as in him lay) to Grant, yet the more necessitous Affairs of the Government, which both he and all about him ever preferr'd to theire private Advantage, took up so much of his time, that not above Twenty ever past the seale, and I am very well assured, that not one Example can be produced that the least compulsion was ever used in this Case to any man living within this Dominion.

16. *That Writts of Intrusion* were issued out, is doubtlesse true, and the Government would have justly merited a severe Censure, if all Wales should have been free & open for the Subject to attaine his Right, and none left for the *King.* We should think our selves highly injured to be refused a *Capias*[9] or any other Common Writt, and I'm sure the other is as peremptory a one in the Kings Case, and had the Pen man been never so little acquainted with the *Natura Brevium,*[10] or the *Register,* he would have been ashamed to have stuffed up the Declaration with such matter which can be of no other service, than to amuse & deceive ignorant people. Have there been any Writts of this kind dureing Sr. *Edmond*'s Administration, taken out against either *poor* or *ignorant* persons that had neither purses nor brains to defend themselves: hath it not been against such as both for their Estates and Capacities,

9. [A writ directing such as the sheriff that literally, "you seize" the person for imprisonment, usually someone having failed to appear in court as ordered, a bench warrant for arrest.—Tr.]

10. ["The Nature of Writs."]

are sufficiently known to be eminent? And the business of Deer-island was brought on for no other Intent than that Right might be done to the King here, and that the party, if agrieved, might in a Regular way have brought it to the Councill board in *England,* for their determination: and I think if this matter were rightly understood, it would be of excellent Service to the Countrey, for such a Judgement would sufficiently instruct us what we have to trust to;

17. If the Governour did say, there was no such thing amongst us as a Towne, what can be inferred from thence? Tis not to be presumed but his discourse tended onely to a Body Corporate and politick, for we generally call that a Towne in *America,* where a number of people have seated themselves together: yet its very well known, tis so in *name* onely not in fact: I take that Body of People to be a *Towne,* properly so called, who by some Act of Law have been *Incorporated,* and in that sence there is no such thing as a Towne in the Massachusetts, neither was there a power to make such before his Excellencies Arrivall. For *One Corporation cannot make another.* [the case of *Suttons Hospital.* Co Rep.]

18. I am totally ignorant what is meant by *Blank Patents,* for tis the first time I ever heard of such a thing; neither indeed can such a thing be. For he that takes a Patent for his Land, doth it in such a Form as best pleaseth himself, or as he shall be advised to by his Councill, and how any man living can so far know my mind, to prepare such an Instrument for me, I leave the world to judge.

This Notion did arise from one Roll of Parchment onely, brought over by Capt. *Tanner,* and if we do but consider, that all Law process was then in Parchment, it would serve but a little while for that use; for it contains not above sixty sheets.

I am likewise gropeing in the darke, to finde out how the Forceing of the people at the Eastward to take Patents (although I know of no such thing done) gave a Rise to the late unhappy Invasion by the Indians, unless by that means, they were deprived of those Quit-Rents and Acknowledgements, which by a base & dishonourable Agreement the people of those parts some time since submitted to pay them, as their *Lords and Masters.*

19. That our Commons might be begg'd, is not very strange, but that the Governour must be criminall because such a thing is asked of him, is the most wonderfull thing in the world. To whome have they been granted, or for which of his creatures have they been measured out? If Lieut' Col' *Lidget*

be instanced, how came *he* to be the Governour's Creature, that hath so long liv'd among us in Reputation equall to the best of us, and whose Fortunes were not so narrow that he needed a dependancy upon any body, and estate & interest in *Charles-town Lands* equalled if not exceeded any man's there, so his Right to the Grant ought to be preferr'd.

If *Clarks-Island,* (granted to Mr. *Clarke* of *Plimouth*) I must tell you 'tis not within the *Plimouth Patent,* and therefore grantable at the pleasure of the King, which was the Opinion of the Councill in that Case, and neither of the before-mentioned Grants, nor indeed any other, did ever pass without *their Approbation and consent;* and this is all that I know of that can be objected.

20. What an Age do we live in now, and how wonderful a thing is it, that it should be counted a Crime in a land *so well govern'd as once* New-England *was* after a legall Tryal & Conviction, to punish & fine men for a Riot and the Contempt of Authority, in the highest Nature imaginable? For what less was it for the Number of three or more to meet together, throw downe & remove the Land marks sett up by the Surveyor Generall thereunto Authorized by the Governours Warrant? And thus is the Case and no otherwise.

21. That any of the Councill were ever denied Admittance to that Board, is a thing so apparently false, that I'm sure not a man amongst them but must justify the Governour in that point; who was alwaies so far from such a method, that altho there was a certain day appointed for their Meeting every week, *well knowne to them all,* yet it was a frequent thing for him, to send on purpose to *Salem,* and other Neighbouring parts, for the Gentlemen that lived there: and I have seen the Messengers Account, wherein he Chargeth a considerable summe of money for Horse hire on those Errands. 'Tis very well knowne, his Excellency hath waited many houres for several of the Gentlemen that live in Towne, and would never sit, until they came. And as he hath never done, nor ordered the least matter relateing to the Government, without their Advice and Consent, so he never did it without a sufficient Number to make a *Quorum,* which was *Seven.*

22. There was never any other course taken, to hinder Mr. *Mather*'s Voyage to *England,* than what the Law allowes, neither can the Government, without a great deal of Injustice, be charged with any thing relating to that matter, for *none in place knew his errand.*

There was a particular difference between Mr. *Randolph* & him, and I never heard of any other course taken by Mr. *Randolph* than the *ordinary*

Writt in such Cases usual, which was so far from Retarding his Voyage, that an *Attourny's entring a common Appearance* in that Case, would have been sufficient to have discharged him if the Writt had been served.

23. Suppose his Majestie promised Mr. *Mather* a *Magna Charta,* for redress of Grievances, and that his Excellency should be wrote unto, to forbear the measures he was upon, yet no such thing being done, he was Obliged to the Observance of his Majesties Commands, before Signified to him in his Letters Patents, which was a sufficient warrant to him, untill he should receive something subsequent to contradict it.

24. That our Churches and Ministers have been discouraged, is so generall an head, and the rest of the Declaration so particular, that it gives me cause to suspect the Truth of it, and I shall hardly alter my Opinion, until any one of you be instanced who kept himself within his Province, and onely meddled with that which belonged to him.

Tis the Church of *England,* that have most reason to Complain, onley we *cry whore first.* Has not their Minister been publiquely Affronted, & hindred from doing his Duty? What scandalous Pamphlets have been printed to vilify the *Liturgy?* And are not all of that Communion daily called *Papist dogs & Rogues* to their Faces? How often has the plucking down the Church been threatned? One while, it was to be converted to a Schoole, & anon it was to be given to the *French Protestants;* and whoso will but take the pains to survey the Glass Windows, will easily discover the marks of a malice not common. I believe tis the First National Church that ever lay under such great disadvantages, in a place where those that dissent from her must expect all things from her grace and favour.

25. Should I undertake to recount all the particulars of the late *Indian Rebellion,* this would swell to a bulk bigger than ever I designed it, I shall onely tell you, we must look at home for the Reasons of those troubles, which is well knowne began when his Excellency was at *New-York,* and that the Folly and Rashness of the people, drew it on their owne heads. The Governours Conduct in that affair has been so prudent and discreet, that I have no Reason to doubt but the Councill, into whose hands all the Papers relating to that business did fall, are very well satisfyed with it. Things were brought to that pass, that if our unhappy domestic Troubles had not intervened, the War before this time would have been advantageously finished, without any Rates or Taxes on the Countrey, for by His Excellencies good husbandry, the standing Revenue would have defrayed the Charge. Tis true,

We have lost some of our friends and Relations, in that Expedition, but could the *Governour* keep them alive? Are not Diseases in Armies, as fatall to men as the Sword? When Death comes, tis not to be avoided; and we see that all our art & care hath not been sufficient to preserve our dearest friends at home, from the greater Mortality which hath run thro' the Countrey. Did any of them dye Neglected? Which of them wanted any thing to be had in these parts? Did his Excellency lye upon Beds of downe, and fare deliciously every day? No, the same Meat, the same Drink, the same Lodging in their Quarters & Marches, were common to all, only *He* was generally the *last* taken care for. To what a degree of Madness & impiety are we then grown, so *falsely & maliciously* to recriminate a person who hath so generously exposed himself to the *hardships* of that cold & uncomfortable Climate, & the Fatigues of War, against a barbarous and savage people? And certainly if God Almighty hath not *given us over to believe lies*, our eyes must be by this time open, & we cannot but knowe, we have been put-upon, shamm'd and abused. Who are *Popish Commanders* in the Army? Will any man bare-fac'd averr so great an Untruth? It must be confess'd, there was *one* Commander & no more under that Circumstance; but what had he to do with the Forces? His Post was the Command of the *King's* Souldiers & Fort at *Pemaquid*, and was not Commissionated for the Army; besides if he had, hath he not lived long amongst us? Did any one ever question his ability, Courage, Fidelity or Conduct, and ought not that Liberty of Conscience, which has been so hotly preached up, even to the Encouragement of immoral Acts amongst us, to be equally beneficiall to him with other men? Especially when the Gentlemen in the Countrey were so far from offering their Service in the Expedition, that some of the most eminent amongst them have absolutely refused the service. And I have been told, the Governour's proposalls to the Councill, about his going to the *Eastward* met with no Opposition, lest some of the Military men there, should have been bound in Honour to have taken that Employment upon themselves.

26. That some of the *English Plantations* in the *West-Indies*, which are contiguous to the *French*, should be Alarm'd, is no wonder, for they were ever jealous of their Neighbourhood, and always stood upon their Guard; But that *We* should be afraid of being delivered up to the *French*; when there is neither War betwixt the two Crownes, nor any *Frenchmen* that we can yet heare of, to receive us, is one of the most unaccountable things in the world. From what parts must they come? from *Canada* we know they cannot; they

have Reason enough to look to themselves, for they are more afraid than we: *France* have their hands full at home, and its well knowne they cannot spare any from the *West-Indies;* they made their utmost effort against {St.} *E{u}statia,* and by the best intelligence we can get in that Service or War, there was not one *Friggat.* Must they then *drop out of the Clouds,* or do we expect a Fleet from *Utopia?* Certainly this must needs convince any considering man that we have been extreamly abused; and we must be stupid and sencelesse to think that Sr. *Edmond Andros,* and *ten or twelve* men more (for that is all the number said to be concerned in this wonderful plott) could they be guilty of so horrid a wickednesse & impiety) were able to deliver so many Thousand men well appointed, into the hands of a few *Frenchmen,* who from *God knows whence,* were to come the *Lord knows when.*

27. That it was either our Duty to God, or that we had either the Nobility, Gentry or Commons of *England,* for our President, I cannot by any means allow, and I am amaz'd to see *Christians* call that a *Duty,* which God has so remarkably shewed his displeasure against in all Countries and Ages. Is not *Rebellion as the sin of Witchcraft?* Numb. 11. 12, 16. Who was it that sent the *Leprosie amongst the children of Israel for their* Murmurring? *Psal.* 78. Or how came the *Sudden fire with which they were burnt up?* How many *Thousands* perished by the *Pestilence?* Or were they a few that were *flung to death with the fiery Serpents?* Do we not read, that *The earth opened and swallowed up some of their Captaines, with their wives and Children quick,* which horrible destruction fell upon the Israelites for their murmurring against *Moses,* whome God had appointed their *Head & Chiefe Magistrate?* What shall I say of *Absalom?* What of *Achitophel?* Or what of *Sheba?* Holy Writt is so full of Examples of the like nature, that no body can esteem that a Duty which is so often testifyed against. And as it is far from being our duty to God, so there is no parallel between the proceedings of the *Lords Spirituall & Temporall in England* and ours here; for the Designe of establishing *Popery & Arbitrary Government* there, was so evident, that no room was left for the least doubt of it. That there could be a Contrivance to introduce Popery here, is altogether ridiculous, & incredible: For, who was to have effected it? Could these few of the *Church of England,* who with the hazzard of their lives and fortunes so lately opposed it in *Europe,* and that in all Ages have been the onely Bulwark against it? Or were the *Presbiterians, Independants,* or *Annabaptists* to have brought this about? It must have been one of these, for I dare be bold to say, there are not *two* Roman-Catholicks betwixt this

and *New-Yorke;* and I think the others are not likely to accomplish it; which makes it plaine to me there could not be any such designe.

I have sufficiently demonstrated in the third Article, the little Right we have to any other Government in the Plantations, and that we cannot justly call that *Arbitrary,* which by the Law we are obliged to submit to: so that betwixt theire Condition and ours, there can be no *Parity.*

As their Reasons and ours were different, so are the Measures which have been taken: for His late Highnesse the *Prince of Orange,* haveing well weighed and considered the tottering Condition of the *Protestant Religion* all over *Europe,* thought it was high time for Him to take up Arms, as well for His owne Preservation; as that of his Neighbours and Allies. We do not finde, that, notwithstanding the danger that hung over their Heads, the people of *England* took up armes to right themselves, but instead thereof, they became humble suppliants to His Highness for his Favour and Protection, which He was pleased to grant them. Neither do we finde, that the Lords Spirituall & Temporall assumed any Authority, for which they had no colour of Law: as they are *Peers,* they are invested with the highest Authority, are the Grand Conservators of the Peace of the Nation: they never left their Duty and Allegiance to his late Majesty, untill he first left the Kingdome, and all things were transacted in his Name, and by his Authority untill the very minute the *Prince* was proclaimed, who came, not by Force to Conquer and Subject the Nation to a forreigne power, nor to subvert and destroy the Lawfull Government; but to maintaine & support the same in a peaceable manner, by a *Free Parliament,* for which his Majestie issued forth his Writts, and had he thought fit to have stayd untill their sitting, all Grievances might have been redressed: the Prince or Peers never abrogated nor altered any of the lawful powers of the Nation, but strengthened & confirmed all that were capable of bearing Office, by which there was alwaies a due Administration of Justice: The *Sword* was never said to *rule & sway,* and by consequence that Confusion and Disorder avoided which our *Illegall & Arbitrary* Proceedings have precipitated us into.

As to the Fancifull Stories of *Macquaes, Subterranean Vaults, Fireworks, French Friggots, Poisoning the Souldiers to the* Eastward *&c.* they are so apparently *false* & *strangely ridiculous,* that by this time no man in his wits can believe them, and I need no Argument to confute the Credit of those monstrous follies, since time and Experience have sufficiently demonstrated them to be meer *Lyes & Inventions.*

And now I hope all sober thinking men are convinced, That the before-alledged Reasons, are in themselves either absolutely false, or of little moment, and consequently *no sufficient grounds for us to take up Arms.* All that remains on this head therefore, will be to shew,

> 1st. That *If all the Reasons had been true, yet it could not justifie our Proceedings.* And,
>
> 2. *If our Condition had been as bad, and our Grievances really as great as we were made believe, these measures could never Mend the one nor Redress the other.*

The most excellent *Grotius* hath so learnedly wrote upon the first of these, that I shall presume to use no other Argument than his own upon that head, which pray consider.

> Private men may without doubt (saith he) [*Grot. de jure Belli & Pacis*[11] *lib.* 1. *cap.* 4. *Quaest.* 1.] make War against private men, as the Traveller against the Theife or Robber: So may Soveraigne Princes & States, against Soveraign Princes, as *David* against the King of the *Ammonites.* Private men may make war against Princes, if not theire owne, as *Abraham* against the King of *Babylon* and his Neighbours. So may Soveraign Princes against private men, whether they be their owne subjects, as *David* against *Ishbosheth* and his party; or Strangers, as the *Romans* against *Pirates.* The onely doubt is whether any person or persons, publique or private, can make a lawful War against those that are set over them, whether supream or subordinate unto them:

And in the *First* place, "It is on all hands granted, That they that are Commissionated by the highest powers, may make War against theire Inferiors, as *Nehemiah* against *Tobia* & *Sanballat,* by the Authority of *Artaxerxes.*" But whether it be lawful for Subjects to make warre against those who have the supream power over them, or against such as act by, & according to their Authority is the thing in question. It is also by all good men acknowledged, That if the Commands of a Prince shall manifestly contradict, either the Law of Nature, or the Divine precepts, they are not to be obeyed: for the Apostles when they urged that Maxim, (*Act.* 4.) *Deo magis quam hominibus obediendum,* That *God is rather to be obeyed than man,* unto such as forbad

11. ["Grotius, *On the Law of War and Peace.*"]

them to preach in the Name of *Jesus,* did but appeal to a principle of right Reason, which Nature had insculp't in every mans breast: and which *Plato* expresseth in almost the very same words. But yet, if either for this or any other cause, any Injury be offered unto us, because it so please him that hath the Soveraigne power, it ought rather to be patiently tolerated than by Force resisted: *For although we do not owe an active Obedience to such commands of Princes, yet we do owe a passive; though we ought not to violate the laws of God or of Nature to fulfill the Will of the greatest Monarch, yet ought we rather patiently to submit to whatsoever he shall inflict upon us for not Obeying, than by Resistance to violate our Countryes Peace. The best and safest Course we can steer in such a case, is,* Either by Flight to preserve our selves, or resolvedly to undergo whatsoever shall be imposed upon us.

2. *War against* Superiors *as* such, *is unlawful.* And naturally all men have a Right to repell Injuries from themselves by Resisting them (as we have already said) but Civil Societies being once Instituted for the Preservation of the Peace, there presently succeeded unto that Common-Wealth, a certain greater Right over us & ours, so far forth as was necessary for that end. And therefore that promiscuous Right that Nature gave us to *ressist,* the Common-Wealth, for the maintaining of good Order and publick Peace, hath a Right to *prohibit,* which without all doubt it doth; seeing that otherwise it cannot obtein the end it proposeth to it self. For in case that Promiscuous Right of forcible Resistance should be tolerated, it would be no longer a Common-Wealth that is a Sanctuary against Oppression, but a confused Rabble, such as that of the *Cyclops,* whereof the Poet thus,

——— *Where every Ass*
May on his wife & children judgement pass.

A dissolute Company, where *All are speakers and none hearers:* like to unto that which *Valerius* records of the *Bebricii,*

——— *Who all Leagues and Laws disdain*
And Justice, which men's minds in peace retain.

Salust makes mention of a wild and savage people living like Beasts in Woods and mountains, without Lawes and without Government, whom he calls *Aborigines:* and in another place of the *Getuli,* who had neither Lawes, good Customs, nor any Princes to govern them. But Cities cannot subsist without these, *Generale pactum est societatis humanae Regibus obedire;*

All humane societies (saith St. Augustine) *unanimously agree in this, to obey Kings;* So Aeschylus,

Kings live by their owne Lawes, Subject to none.

And *Sophocles,*

They Princes are, obey we must, what not?

To the same Tune sings *Euripides,*

Folly in Kings must be with patience born.

Whereunto agrees that of *Tacitus, Principi summum rerum arbitrium Dii dederunt, &c. Subditis obsequii gloria relicta est; God hath invested a Prince with Soveraign power, leaving nothing to Subjects but the Glory of Obedience.*

And here also,

Base things seem noble when by Princes done;
What they Impose, bear thou, be't right or wrong. [Sen.]

Wherewith agrees that of *Salust, Impune quid vis facere, hoc est Regem esse; To do any thing without fear of punishment, is peculiar to Kings:* for as *Mark Anthony* urged in *Herod's* Case, *If he were accountable for what he hath done as a King, he could not be a King.* Hence it is, that the Majesty of such as have *Soveraign* power, whether in one or more, is fenced with so many and so severe Lawes, and the Licentiousnesse of Subjects restrained with such sharp and exquisite Torments; which were unreasonable, if to resist them were lawfull. If a Souldier resist his Captain that strikes him, and but lay hold on his Partizan, he shall be cashiered; but if he either breake it, or offer to strike againe, he shall be put to Death: For as *Aristotle* observes *If he that is an Officer strike, he shall not be struck againe.*

3. *The Unlawfulness of making War against our Superiours,* is proved by the *Jewish* Law. [*Jos.* 1. 18. 1. *Sam.* 8. 11. *Deut.* 17. 14.]

By the *Hebrew* Law, He that behaved himself contumaciously against either the High Priest, or against him who was extraordinarily by God ordained to govern his people, was to be put to death; and that which in the eighth Chapter of the first Booke of *Samuel,* is spoken of the Right of Kings, to him that throughly inspects it, is neither to be understood of their true and just Rights, that is, of what they may do justly and honestly (for the Duty of Kings is much otherwise described *Deut* 8. 11.) nor is it to be understood barely, of what he will do: for then it had signified nothing that was singular or extraordinary, for private men do the same to private men: But it is to be understood of such a Fact as usurps or carries with it the priviledge of what is right, that is, that it must not be resisted although it be not right; for Kings have a Right peculiar to themselves, and what in others is punishable in them is not. That old saying, *Summum jus, summa injuria,* Extreme right is extreme Wrong, is best fitted to the Case of Kings, whose absolute power makes that seem right, which strictly taken is not so. There is a main difference between Right in this sense taken, and Just; for in the former sence, it comprehends whatsoever may be done without fear of Punishment: but *Just,* respect only things lawful and honest. And though some Kings there be, who are (what *Servius* in *Cicero's Philippicks* is commanded to be) *Magis justitiae quam Juris consulti;* more regardful of their honour and duty than of their power and prerogatives: yet this doth not diminish their Soveraign Right; because if they will they may do otherwise without the danger of being resisted. And therefore it is added in that place of *Samuel* before cited, That when the people should at any time be thus oppressed by their Kings, as if there were no Remedy to be expected from men, they should invoke His help who is the Supream Judge of the whole Earth. So that whatsoever a King doth, tho' the same done by an inferior person would be an Injury, yet being done by him is Right. As a Judge is said *Jus reddere,* to do Right, though the Sentence he gives be unrighteous.

4. *By the Gospel-Law.* When Christ in the New-Testament Commanded to give *Caesar* his due, doubtless he intended that his Disciples should yield as great, if not a greater Obedience, as well active as passive unto the higher power, than what was due from the *Jews* to their Kings: which St. *Paul,* (who was best able to interpret his Masters Words) expounding *Romans* 13. doth at large describe the duty of Subjects; Charging those that resist the power of Kings, with no less Crime than Rebellion against God's Ordinance, and with a Judgment as great as their Sin: For, saith he, *They that do so resist shall receive unto themselves damnation.* And a little after he urgeth the Necessity of our Subjection, *Not altogether for fear but for conscience, as knowing, that he is the minister of God for our Good.* Now if there be a necessity of our Subjection, then there is the same necessity for our *not resisting,* because *he that resists is not subject.* Neither did the Apostle mean *such a necessity of subjection as ariseth, from an apprehension of some worse inconvenience that might follow upon our resistance,* but such as proceeds from the sense of some benefit

that we receive by it, whereby we stand obliged in duty, not unto man onely, but unto God; So that, *He that Resists the power of the supream Magistrate, incurrs a double Punishment* (saith *Plato*) *First from God, for breaking that good Order which he hath constituted amongst men. And Secondly, From the Common Wealth, whose righteous Laws, made for the preservation of the publick peace, are by Resistance Weakned, and the Common-Wealth thereby endangered. For canst thou believe (saith* Plato*) that any City or Kingdom can long stand, when the publick Decrees of the Senate shall be willfully broken and trampled upon by the over-swelling power of some private men, who in struggling against the Execution of the Laws, do, as much as in them lies, dissolve the Commonwealth, & consequntly bring all into confusion.* The Apostle therefore fortifies this Necessity of *publick Subjection* to Princes with 2 main Reasons: First because God had constituted and approved of this order of Commanding and Obeying; and that not only under the *Jewish*, but under the *Christian* Law: Wherefore the powers that are set over us are to be Observed (not servilely, superstitiously, or out of Fear, but with free, rational, & generous Spirits) *tanquam a Diis datae*, as being given by the Gods, saith *Plato*: or as St. *Paul*, *tanquam a Deo ordinatae*, as if ordained by God himself. Which Order as it is Originally God's, so by giving it a Civil Sanction, it becoms ours also: For thereby we add as much Authority to it as we can give. The other Reason is drawn *ab utili*, from Profit: because this Order is constituted for our good, and therefore in Conscience is to be obeyed and not resisted.

But here some men may say, That to bear injuries is not at all profitable unto us, whereunto some men (haply more truly than apositely to the meaning of the Apostle) give this Answer, That patiently to bear Injuries, conduceth much to our Benefit, because it entitles us to a Reward, far transcending our Sufferings, as St. *Paul* testifies. But though this also be true, yet it is not (as I conceive) the proper and genuine sense of the Apostles words, which doubtless have Respect to that Universal Good, whereunto this Order was first instituted, as to its proper end; which was the publick peace, wherein every particular man, is as much concerned, if not much more than in his Private (for what Protection can good Laws give, if Subjects may refuse to yield their obedience to them; whereas, by the Constant observance of good Laws, all Estates, both publick and private, do grow up and flourish together.) [*Plato.*] And certainly these are the good Fruits that we receive from the supream Powers, for which in Conscience we owe them Obedience. For no man did ever yet wish ill to himself. (But he that resists the power of the Magistrate, and willfully violates the Laws established, doth in effect (as far as in him is) dissolve his Countrey's peace and will in the end bury himself also in the ruins of it.) [*Plato.*] Besides, the Glory of Kings consists in the prosperity of their Subjects, When *Sylla* had by his Cruelty, almost depopulated, not *Rome* only, but all *Italy*, one seasonably admonisht him, *Sinendos esse aliquos vivere, ut essent, quibus imperet;* That some should be permitted to live, over whom he might rule as a King. [*Florus. Aug. de civ. Dei. Lib.* 3. *cap.* 28.] It was a common Proverb among the *Hebrews*, Nisi Potestas publica esset, alter alterum vivum deglutiret; *Were it not for the Soveraign Powers, every Kingdom would be like a great Pond, wherein the greater Fish would alwaies devour the Lesser.* Agreeable whereunto is that of *Chrysostome*, *Unless there were a power over us to restrain our inordinate Lusts, Men would be more fierce & cruel than Lions & Tygers, not only biting, but eating & devouring one another. Take away Tribunals of Justice, and you take away all Right, Property and Dominion: No man can say, this is mine House, this my Land, these my Goods or my Servants: but* Omnia erunt Fortiorum,[12] *the longest* Sword *would take all.* [Chrys *de statuis* 6. *ad Eph.*] The mighty man could be no longer secure of his estate than until a mightier than he came to dispossess him; The weaker must alwaies give place to the Stronger: and where the strength was equal the loss would be so too; and this would at length introduce a general Ataxy, which would be far more perilous than a perfect Slavery. Wherefore seeing that God hath Established (and humane Reason upon Tryal approved of) Soveraign Empire as the best Preservative of humane Societies, that every man should yield Obedience thereunto is most rational: For without Subjection there can be no Protection.

Object. But here it will be objected, That *The Commands of Princes do not alwaies tend to the Publique Good, and therefore when they decline from that end for which they were ordained, they ought not to be obeyed.* To which I answer,

That though the Supream Magistrate doth sometimes, either through Fear, Anger, Lust, Coveteousness, or such like inordinate passions, baulk the ordinary path of Justice and Equity, yet are these (hapning but seldome) to be passed over as personal blemishes, which (as *Tacitus* rightly observes) are abundantly recompensed by the more frequent examples of

12. [Literally, "All things will be possessed by the strong." A loose translation is given in the text.—Tr.]

better Princes. (Besides the Lives of Princes are to be considered with some grains of allowance, in respect of those many provocations and opportunities they have to offend, which private men have not; All men have their Failings, we our selves have ours; and in case we will admit of none in Kings, we must not rank them amongst men but Gods. The Moon hath her spots; *Venus* her *Mole;* and if we can find nothing under the Sun without blemish, why should we expect perfection in Kings? He is very uncharitable that judges of Rulers by some few of their evil Deeds, passing over many of their good ones. Seeing therefore that there is in all men's lives, as in our best Coin, an intermixture of good and evil; it is sufficient to denominate a Prince good, if his Vertues excel his Errors. Besides, to charge the Vices of Kings upon the Government, as they usually do who affect Innovation, is but a Cheat: For what is this, but to condemn the Law for the Corruption of some Lawyers: Or Agriculture, because some men do curse God for a Storm? *Si mentiar, Ego mentior, non Negotium; If I do lye,* (saith the Merchant in St. *Augustine) it is I that am to be blamed not my Calling.* And if some Princes do prevaricate in some things, they and not their Function are to be blamed. But as to *Laws,* tho they cannot be so made as to fit every mans Case, yet it sufficeth to denominate them good, if they obviate such disorders as are frequently practised, and so do good to the generality of the People. But as to such cases, which because they rarely happen, cannot so easily be provided against by particular Laws, even these also are understood to be restrained by general Rules. For, though the Reason of the Law being particularly applyed to that special Case, hold not; yet in the *General,* under which special Cases may lawfully be Comprehended, it may. And much better is it so to do, than to live without Law, or to permit every man to be a law to himself. Very apposite to this purpose is that of *Seneca,* [*Lib.* 7. *de Benef.* cap. 16.] *Better is it not to admit of some excuses, though just from a few, than that All should be permitted to make whatsoever they please.* Memorable is that of *Pericles* in *Thucydides,* [Lib. 2.] *Better it is for private men, that the Common-Wealth flourish, though they thrive not in it, than that they should abound & grow rich in their own private estates, and the Common-Wealth pine and Wither: For if the whole be ruined, every private mans Fortunes must needs be ruined with it: but if the Common-Wealth flourish, every private mans estate, though in it self weake, may in time be repaired. Wherefore, since the state if well ordered, can easily support any private mans fortunes, but a private mans estate, though never so well ordered, cannot repair the loss of the publique state: why do ye not rather contribute your utmost care to advance the Publique, than (as ye now do) seek to build your own private Fortunes upon the publique Ruines?* Wherewith agrees that of Ambrose, [*de Off. Lib.* 3.] Eadem est singulorum utilitas, qua Universorum; *The Profit which the Common-Wealth receives, redounds to every private man.* And that also in the Law, *Semper non quod privatim interest ex sociis, sed quod communi societate expedit, servari debet;* Evermore, not that which particularly availeth any one party, but that which conduceth to the Benefit of the Common Society is to be observed. (When the Common people in *Rome* began to Mutinee by reason of some Taxes extraordinarily imposed on them, *Laevinus* the *Consul* exhorted the Senate, to encourage the people by their own example; and to that very end advised every Senator to bring into the Senate-house, all the Gold, Silver and Brass Money he had that it might be delivered to the *Triumviri* for the publick service: adding this reason, If our City overcome, no man needs to fear his own estate; but if it fall, let no man think to preserve his own [*Liv.* 1. 26.]) For as *Plato* rightly observes, *What is common strengthens a city, but what enricheth private families only, weakens and dissolves it: And therefore it concerns both Princes and subjects to prefer the Affairs of the Common-Wealth, before their own either pleasure or Profit*). It is a very true Observation of *Xenophon's, He that in an Army behaves himself seditiously against his General, sins against his own Life.* And no less true is that of *Jamblicus, No man should think himself a Loser by what the Common-wealth gains, for every private mans loss is sufficiently recompensed in the publick profit: For as in the natural body, so doubtless in the Civil,* In totius Salute, Salus est partium; *the well being of every part, consists in the safety of the whole.* But without doubt, among those things that are publick, the chief & principal is that aforesaid Order of well Commanding and well Obeying: which cannot consist where private Subjects assume that Licence of resisting the publick Magistrate: which is excellently described by *Dion Cassius,* whose words sound much to this sense, *I cannot conceive it seemly for a Prince to submit to his subjects, for there can be no safety, where the feet are advanced above the Head, or wher they undertake to govern, whose Duty it is to be governed. What a dismal Confusion would it introduce in a Family if Children should be permitted to despise their Parents or Servants to dispute the Commands of their Masters? In what a desperate Condition is that Patient, that will not be ruled in all things by his Physitian? And what hopes can there be of that Ship, where the Marriners refuse to obey their Pilot? Surely God hath ordained, and humane Reason upon tryal hath found it necessary, that for the preservation of humane Society, some should Command, and some Obey.* To the Testimony of St. *Paul,* we shall add that of St. *Peter,* whose words are these, *Honour the King, Servants, be ye subjects to your Masters with all fear, and not only to the good & gentle, but also to the froward: For this is thank-worthy, if a man for conscience sake toward God endure Grief, suffering wrongfully, for what glory is it, if when ye be buffered for your faults ye take it patiently? But if when ye do well, & suffer for it, ye take it patiently, this is acceptable with God.* 1. Pet. 2. 17, 18, 19. And this he by and by confirms by Christ's own Example, which *Clemens* also in his Constitutions thus expresseth, *The servant that feareth God,* saith he, *will serve his Master also with all faithfulness, yea, though he be impious and unjust.* Whence we may observe two things: First, That under the subjection that servants are in, even to hard Masters, is also couched that of Subjects unto Kings, though Tyrannical. And therefore, as a little before he commanded Subjection to every humane Ordinance; that is, to the Laws and Constitutions of Princes without distinction, (for when that Epistle was written, there were very few Princes that were not Idolaters) yet submit we must, saith St. *Peter,* for all that; and that, *propter Dominum, for the Lord's sake.* So what follows in the same Chapter being built upon the same foundation, respects the Duty as well of subjects as of Servants. And so requires the same Obedience, as well passive as Active; Such as we usually pay to our Parents, according to that of the Poet,

Thy Parents love if good, if bad yet bear.

And also that of *Terence,*

To bear with parents, piety Commands.

And that likewise of *Cicero* in his Oration for *Cluentius, Men ought not only to conceal the injuryes done unto them by their parents, but to bear them with patience.* A young man of *Eretria* that had been long educated under *Zeno* being demanded, What he had learned? Answered, *Meekly to bear his Father's Wrath.* So *Justin* relates of *Lysimachus,* That he endured the Reproaches of the King, with the same calmness of Spirit, as if he had been his Father. [*Lib.* 15.] *Ferenda sunt Reguum ingenia,* The Humours of Kings most be endured: saith *Tacitus:* [*Ann.* 16. *Hist.* 6.] And in another place he tells us, That Good Emperours are to be wished for, but whatsoever they are, they must be obeyed. So also *Livy,* As the Rage of our Parents, so the

Cruelty of our Countrey are no ways to be becalmed, but by patience and Sufferance. For which *Claudius* highly extols the *Persians,* who obeyed all their Kings equally tho' never so cruel.

5. Neither did the *Practice of the primitive Christians* swerve from this Law of God, which is an undeniable Argument that they so understood it. For though the *Roman* Emperours were sometimes the very worst of men, and deadly Enemies to the Christian Faith; yea, though there wanted not such under their Government, who under the specious pretence of freeing the Common-Wealth from Tyranny and Oppression, took Arms against them, yet could they never perswade the Christians to join with them. In the Constitutions of Clemens we read, *Regiae potestati resister: Nefas,* To resist the power of a King is impious. *Tertullian* in his Apology writes thus, *What was that* Cassius *that conspired against the life of* Julius Caesar? *What was that* Poscennius Niger, *that in love to his own countrey, took Arms in* Syria, *as* Clodius Albinus *did in* France & Britain, *against that bloody Emperour* Septimius Severus? *Or What was that* Plautianus, *who to set the Common-Wealth free from Tyranny, attempted the Life of the same Emperour in his own pallace? What was that* AElius Laetus, *who having first poysoned that infamous Emperour* Commodus, *fearing it should not take that effect which he desired, did afterwards hire* Narcissus *a strong* Wrestler *to strangle him? Or What was that* Parthenius, (whose fact Tertullian doth so much detest) *who being* Chamberlain *to that execrable Tyrant* Domitian, *yet killed him in his own Chamber? What* (saith Tertullian) *were all these? Surely not* Christians, *but* Romans. Nay, So abominated they were by Christians, that Tertullian seems to glory in this, that though Christians were every where reproached as Enemies, nay Traitors to the Imperial Crown, yet could they never find any of them, either stained with that Crime, or so much as favouring those Treasonable Practices of either *Cassius,* Niger. or *Albinus.* When St. *Ambrose* was commanded by the Emperour *Valentinus* to give up his Church to be Garrison'd by Souldiers, though he took it to be an injury done, not only to himself and his Congregation, but even unto Christ himself; yet would he not take any advantage of the commotions it made among the People, to make Resistance. [*See* Gratian *c.* 23. *q.* 8.] If the Emperour (saith he) had commanded what was in my power to give, were it mine House, Land, Goods, Gold or Silver, how readily should I obey; Whatsoever is mine I would willingly offer: but the *Temple of God,* I cannot give away, nor can I yield it up to any man: *Cum ad custodiendum, non ad tradendum illud acceperim,* Since it was

committed to mee to defend and to keep, but not to betray. And whereas the people being enraged thereby, did offer their Assistance to repel the Souldiers, he refused it saying, *Coactus repugnare non novi,* Though provoked and compelled thereunto, yet withstand or resist I cannot; grieve and weep, and mourn I can, against Arms, Souldiers and *Goths:* I have no other weapons but Tears: for these are the only Forts and Muniments of a Priest: *Aliter nec debeo nec possum resistere,* Otherwise I neither ought nor can resist. [*Lib.* 5. *Orat. in Anxen.*] And presently after, being commanded to appease the Tumult, he replied, That not to excite them was in his power, but being exasperated and enraged, to appease them was in the sole power of Him, who when He pleased, *could still the ragings of the Seas & the madness of the people.* [*Epist.* 33.] And in another place he writes thus, Will ye hale me to prison, or cast me into chains? I am willing to suffer, neither shall I guard my self with multitudes of people who offer themselves to defend me. Neither would he make use of the Forces of *Maximus,* when offered against the Emperor, though an *Arian,* and a grievous Persecutor of the Church. In imitation of whom, *Gregory* the Great, in one of his epistles confesseth, That if he would have engaged himself in the Death of the *Lombards,* that Nation had at that day, had neither *King, Dukes,* nor *Earls,* but had been reduced into extreme Confusion. [*Greg.* l. 6. Ep. 1.] *Nazianzen* informs us, That *Julian* the Apostate was diverted from some bloody designs he intended against the Church, by the Tears of Christians: Adding withal, That *These are our best Preservatives against Persecutions.* [Naz *Orat.* 1. *in Julian.*] And because a great part of his Army were Christians, therefore his cruelty towards them, would have been not injurious to the Church of Christ only, but would at that time have much endangered the *Common-Wealth.* Unto all which we may also add that of St. *Augustine,* where expounding those places of St. *Paul,* he saith, Even for the preservation of our own Lives, we ought to submit to the supreme Power, & not to resist them in whatsoever they shall take away from us.

6. *Inferior Magistrates ought not to resist the Supream.* Some very learned men there are even *in* this age, who accommodating themselves tho servilely to the times and places wherein they live, to perswade themselves first, and then others, That though this licence of Resisting the Supream power be inconsistent with the Condition of private men, yet it may agree with the Rights of inferior Magistrates; nay, further, that they sin in case they do it not: which Opinion is to be exploded, as seditious. For as in Logick there is a Genus which is called *Sebaltri*{illeg.} which though it be

comprehensive of all that is under it, as a living Creature comprehends both man and Beast; yet hath it a Genus above it, in respect whereof it is but a *Species:* As a living Creature is to a body, which comprehends all sorts of bodies, both animate and inanimate. The like we may say of Magistrates, some are Supream, who rule all, and are ruied by none; others are Subordinate, who in respect of private men, are publick Persons, governing like Princes; But in respect of the Supream Magistrate are but private men, and are commanded as Subjects. For the power or faculty of Governing, as it is derived from the Supream power, so it is subject unto it, And whatsoever is done by the inferior Magistrate, contrary to the Will of the Supream, is null, and reputed but as a private Act, for want of the Stamp of publick Authority. All Order (say Philosophers) doth necessarily relate to somewhat that is first and highest, from whence it takes its Rise and Beginning. Now they that are of this Opinion, that inferiour Magistrates may *resist* the Supream, seem to introduce such a state of things, as the Poets fansied to have been in Heaven before Majesty was thought on, when the lesser gods denied the prerogative of *Jupiter.* But this Order or Subordination of one to another, is not only approved of by Common Experience, as in every Family the Father is the head, next unto him the Mother, then the Children, and after them the Servants, and such as are under them: So in every Kingdom, *Each power under Higher powers are*—And, *All Governours are under Government*—To which purpose is that notable saying of St. *Augustine,* Observe (saith he) the degrees of all humane things: If thy Tutor enjoin thee any thing, thou must do it; yet not, in case the Proconsul command the contrary: neither must thou obey the Consul, if thy Prince command otherwise: for in so doing thou canst not be said to contemn Authority, but thou chusest to obey that which is highest: Neither ought the lesser powers to be offended, that the greater is preferred before them, for *God is the God of order.* [*Grat. c.* 11. *q.* 3, *Qui resistit.*][13] And that also of the same Father concerning *Pilate,* Because (saith he) God had invested him with such a power as was it self subordinate to that of *Caesars.* But it is also approved of by Divine Authority, For St. *Peter* enjoyns us to be subject unto *Kings* otherwise than unto Magistrates: To *Kings as supream,* that is, absolutely, without Exceptions to any other Commands than those directly from God: who is so far from

13. ["Who has resisted (God)."]

justifying our Resistance, that He commands our passive Obedience: But unto Magistrates, as they are deputed by *Kings*, and as they derive their Authority from them. And when St. *Paul* subjects every soul to the higher powers, (*Rom.* 13.) doubtless he exempts not inferiour Magistrates. Neither do we find among the *Hebrews* (where there were so many Kings utterly *regardless* of the Laws both of *God* & *Men*) any inferior Magistrates, among whom, some without all question, there were both pious and valiant, that ever arrogated unto themselves this Right of Resisting by force, the power of their Kings, without an express command from God, who alone hath an unlimited power and Jurisdiction over them. But on the Contrary, What duties inferior Magistrates owe unto their Kings, though wicked, *Samuel* will instruct us by his own Example, who though he knew that *Saul* had corrupted himself, and that God also had rejected him from being *King*, yet before the people, and before the Elders of *Israel*, he gives him that Reverence and Respect that was due unto him. (1. *Sam.* 15. 30.) And so likewise the state of Religion publickly professed, did never depend upon any other humane Authority, but on that of the *King*, and *Sanhedrim*. For in that after the King, the Magistrates with the People, engaged themselves to the true Worship and Service of God, it ought to be understood, so far forth as it should be in the power of every one of them. Nay, the very Images of their false gods which were publickly erected, (and therefore could not but be scandalous to such as were truly religious) yet were they never demolished, so far as we can read of, but at the special Command either of the people when the Government was popular, or of *Kings*, when the Government was kingly. And if the Scriptures do make mention of any Violence sometimes offered unto Kings, it is not to justifie the fact, but to shew the Equity of the Divine providence in permitting it. And whereas they of the contrary perswasion do frequently urge that excellent Saying of *Trajan* the Emperour, who delivering a Sword to a Captain of the *Praetorian Band*, said, *Hoc pro me utere, si recte impero; si male, contra me:* Use this Sword for me if I Govern well, but if otherwise, *against* me. We must know, that *Trajan* (as appears by *Pliny*'s Panegyrick) was not willing to assume unto himself Regal power, but rather to behave himself as a good Prince; who was willing to submit to the Judgment of the Senate and people; whose Decrees he would have that Captain to execute, though it were against himself. Whose Example both *Pertinax* and *Macrinus* did afterwards follow, whose excellent Speeches to this purpose are Recorded by *Herodian*. The like we read of *M. Anthony*, who refused to touch the publick treasure without the consent of the Roman Senate.

7. *Of Resistance in case of inevitable Necessity*. But the Case will yet be more Difficult, Whether this Law of not-Resisting do oblige us, when the Dangers that threaten us be extream, and otherwise inevitable. For some of the Laws of God Himself, though they found absolutely, yet seem to admit of some tacite Exceptions in cases of Extream Necessity: For so it was, by the wisest of the Jewish Doctors, expresly determined concerning the Law of their Sabbath, in the times of the *Hasamonaeans*, whence rose that famous Saying among them, *Periculum animae impellit Sabbatum;* The danger of a man's Life drives away the Sabbath. When the Jew in *Synesius*, was accused for the breach of the Sabbath, he excuseth himself by another Law, and that more forcible, saying, *We were in manifest jeopardy of our lives*. When *Bacchides* had brought the Army of the Jews into a great Strait on their Sabbath day, placing his Army before them and behind them, the River *Jordan* being on both sides; *Jonathan* thus bespake his Souldiers, *Let us go up now & fight for our lives, for it standeth not with us to day, as in times past*. (1. Mac. 9. 43, 44, 45.) Which case of Necessity is approved of, even by Christ Himself, as well in this Law of the Sabbath, as in that of not eating the Shew-bread. And the Hebrew Doctors pretending the Authority of an ancient Tradition, do rightly interpret their Laws made against the eating of meats forbidden, with this tacite Exception: Not that it was not just with God to have obliged us even unto death, but that some Laws of His are conversant about such matters as it cannot easily be believed that they were intended to have been prosecuted with so much Rigour as to reduce us to such an Extremity, as to dy rather than to disobey them, which in humane laws doth yet further proceed. I deny not, but that some Acts of Vertue are so strictly enjoyned, that if we perform them not, we may justly be put to Death: As for a Centinel to forsake his Station. But neither is this rashly to be understood to be the Will of the Law-giver. Nor do men assume so much Right over either themselves or others, unless it be when, & so far forth as extreme Necessity requires it. For all humane laws are so constituted, or so to be understood as that there should be some allowance for humane Frailty. The right understanding of this Law of *Resisting or not-Resisting* the Highest powers in cases of inevitable Necessity, seems much to depend upon the Intention of those who first entered into Civil Society, from whom the Right of Government is devolved upon the persons governing: who had they been demanded,

Whether they would have imposed such a yoke upon all Mankind as death it self, rather than in any case by force to repel the Insolencies of their Superiours; I much question whether they would have granted it, unless it had been in such a case, where such Resistance could not be made without great Commotions in the Common Wealth, or the certain Destruction of many Innocents, for what Charity commends in such a case to be done, may, I doubt not, pass for an humane Law. But some may say, that this rigid Obligation, To dye rather than at any time to Resist Injuries done by our Superiours, is not imposed on us by any Humane, but by the Divine Law. But we must observe, That men did not *at first* unite themselves in Civil Society, by any special Command from God, but voluntarily, out of a sence they had of their own impotency to repel force and Violence whilst they lived solitarily, and in Families appart; whence the civil power takes its Rise. For which cause it is that St. *Peter* calls it an humane Ordinance, although it be elsewhere called a Divine Ordinance, because this wholesome Constitution of men was approved of by God Himself. But God in approving an humane Law, may be thought to approve of it as an humane law, & after an humane manner. *Barkly* (who was the stoutest Champion in defending Kingly Power) doth notwithstanding thus far allow, That the People or the Nobler part of them, have a Right to defend themselves against cruel Tyranny, and yet he confesseth, that the whole Body of the people is subject unto the King. [*Barkley. Lib.* 3. *contra. Monarchomach. c.* 8.] Now this I shall easily admit, That the more we desire to secure any thing by Law, the more express and peremptory should that Law be, and the fewer exceptions there should be from it; (for they that have a mind to violate that Law, will presently seek shelter, and think themselves priviledged by those Exceptions though their Cases be far different;) yet dare I not condemn indifferently either every private man, or every, though lesser part of the people, who as their last Refuge, in cases of extream Necessity, have anciently made use of their Arms to defend themselves, yet with respect had to the Common Good. For *David,* who (saving in some particular Facts) was so celebrated for his integrity, did yet entertain first four hundred, and afterwards more armed men; to what end unless for the safeguard of his own person, against any violence that should be offered him? But this also we must note, That *David* did not this until he had been assured, both by *Jonathan,* and by many other infallible Arguments, that *Saul* sought his life; and that even then, he never invaded any City, nor made an offensive Warr against any but lurked only for his own security, sometimes in Mountains, sometimes in Caves, and such like devious places, and sometimes in forreign Nations, with this Resolution, to decline all occasions of annoying his own Countrey-men. A Fact parallel to this of *David's,* we may read in the *Maccabees:* For whereas some seek to defend the Wars of the *Maccabees* upon this ground, That *Antiochus* was not a King, but an Usurper; this I account but frivolous: for in the whole Story of the *Macabees,* we shall never find *Antiochus* mentioned by any of their own party, by any other Title than by that of *King;* and deservedly: For the Hebrews had long before submitted to the *Macedonian* Empire, in whose Right *Antiochus* succeeded. And whereas the Hebrew Laws forbad a Stranger to be set over them, this was to be understood by a voluntary Election, and not by an involuntary Compulsion, through the Necessity of the times. And whereas others say, That the Maccabees did act by the peoples Right, to whom belonged the Right of Governing themselves by their own Laws, neither is this probable: For the Jews being first conquered by *Nebuchadonosor,* were by the Right of War subject unto him, and afterwards became by the same Law subject to the Medes and Persians, as successours to the Chaldeans, whose whole Empire did at last devolve upon the Macedonians. And hence it is, That the Jews, in *Tacitus* are termed *The most servile of all the Eastern Nations;* neither did they require any Covenants or Conditions from *Alexander* or his successours, but yielded themselves freely, without any Limitations or Exceptions, as before they had done unto *Darius.* And though they were permitted sometimes to use their own Rites, and publickly to exercise their own Laws, yet was not this due unto them by any Law that was added unto the Empire, but only by a precarious Right that was indulged unto them by the Favour of their Kings. There was nothing then that could justifie the Maccabees in their taking of Arms, but that invincible Law of *Extream Necessity* which might do it so long as they contained themselves within the bounds of Self-Preservation, and in imitation of *David,* betook themselves to secret places, in order to their own security; never offering to make use of their Armes unless violently assaulted. In the mean time, great Care is to be taken, that even when we are thus enforced to defend our selves in cases of certain and extream danger, we spare the person of the King; for they that conceive the carriage of *David* towards *Saul,* to proceed not so much from the Necessity of Duty, as out of some deeper consideration, are mistaken: for *David* himself declares, that no man can be innocent that stretcheth forth his hand against the Lord's Annointed:

(1. *Sam.* 26. 9.) Because he very well knew that it was written in the Law, *Thou shalt not revile the Gods,* that is the Supream Judges: *Thou shalt not curse the Rulers of thy people.* (*Exod.* 22. 28.) In which Law, special mention being made of the Supream power; it evidently shews That some special Duty towards them is required of us. Wherefore *Optatus Melevitanus* speaking of this Fact of *David,* saith, *That God's special Command coming fresh into his memory, did so restrain him, that he could not hurt* Saul, *though his mortal enemy.* Wherefore he brings in *David* thus reasoning with himself, *Volebam hostem vincere, sed prius est Divina praecepta observare,* Willingly I would overcome mine Enemy, but I dare not transgress the Commands of God. [*Lib.* 2.] And *Josephus* speaking of David after he had cut off Sauls Garment, saith, *That his heart smote him:* So that he confessed, *Injustum facinus erat Regem suum occidere,* It was a wicked act to kill his Soveraign. And presently after, *Horrendum Regem quamvis malum occidere, poenam enim id facienti imminere constat, ab eo qui Regem dedit,* It is an horrid act to kill a King, though wicked, for certainly He, by whose providence all Kings reign, will pursue the Regicide with vengeance inevitably. To reproach any private man falsely is forbidden by the Law, but of a King we must not speak evil, though he deserve it; because as he that wrote the Problems (fathered upon *Aristotle*) saith, He that speaketh evil of the Governour, scandalizeth the whole City. So *Joab* concludes concerning *Shimei,* as *Josephus* testifies, *Shalt thou not dye, who presumest to curse him whom God hath placed in the Throne of the Kingdom?* The Laws (saith *Julian*) are very severe on the behalf of Princes, for he that is injurious unto them, doth wilfully trample upon the Laws themselves. [*Misopogoris*][14] Now if we must not speak evil of Kings, much less must we do evil against them. *David* repented but for offering violence to *Saul's* Garments, so great was the Reverence that he bare to his person, and deservedly: For since their Soveraign power cannot but expose them to the General Hatred, therefore it is fit, that their security should especially be provided for. *This,* saith *Quintilian, is the face of such as sit at the Stern of Government, that they cannot discharge their Duty faithfully,*

14. [It seems likely that "Misopogoris" is a misspelling of the Greek "Misopogon," meaning "beard hater." It is the title of a publication by the emperor Julian in A.D. 323, written during an economic crisis at Antioch. The exchange became insulting; the Antiocheans mocked the emperor's scruffy appearance. The essay is a self-satire in which Julian makes fun of himself as a philosopher but implicitly ridicules the nonphilosophical Christians in Antioch around him.—Tr.]

nor provide for the publick safety, without the envy of many. (And for this cause are the persons of Kings guarded with such severe Laws, which seem, like *Draco's*, to be wrote in blood,) as may appear by those enacted by the *Romans*, for the security of their Tribunes, whereby their persons became inviolable. Amongst other wise Sayings of the *Esseni*, this was one, That the persons of Kings should be held as sacred. And that of *Homer* was as notable,

His chiefest care was for the King,
That nothing should endanger him.

And no marvel: For as St. *Chrysostome* well observes, *If any man kill a sheep, he but lessens the number of them, but if he kill the Shepherd, he dissipates the whole flock.* The very Name of a King, as *Curtius* tells us, among such nations as were governed by Kings, was as venerable as that of God. So *Artabanus* the Persian, *Amongst many and those most excellent Laws we have, this seems to be the best, which commands us to adore our Kings as the very image of God who is the Saviour of all.* And therefore as *Plutarch* speakes, *Nec fas, nec licitum est Regis corpori manus inferre,* It is not permitted by the Laws of God or man, to offer violence to the person of a King. But as the same *Plutarch* in another place tells us, *The principal part of valour is, to save him that saves all. If the eye observe a blow threatening the head, the hand, being instructed by nature, interposeth it self, as preferring the safety of the head (whereupon all other members depend) before their own.* Wherefore, as *Cassiodore* notes, He that with the loss of his own life, Redeems the Life of his Prince, doth well; if in so doing he propose to himself the freeing of his own soul, rather than that of another mans body, for as conscience teacheth him to express his fidelity to his Soveraign; so doth right Reason instruct him to prefer the life of his Prince, before the safety of his own body. But here a more difficult question ariseth; as namely, Whether what was lawful for *David* and the *Maccabees*, be likewise lawful for us Christians: Or whether Christ who so often enjoins us to take up our Cross, do not require from us a greater measure of patience? Surely, where our Superiours threaten us with Death upon the account of Religion, our Saviour advised such as are not obliged by the necessary Duties of their Calling to reside in any one place, to flee, but beyond this, nothing. St. *Peter* tells us, That *Christ in his suffering left us an example, who tho' he knew no sin, nor had any guile found in his mouth, yet being reviled, reviled not again, when he suffered, he threatned not, but remmitted his cause to him that judgeth righteously* (1. *Pet.* 4. 12, 13, 14, 15, 16.) Nay he adviseth us to give thanks unto God, and to rejoice when we suffer persecution for our Religion: and we may read how mightily Christian Religion hath grown and been advanced by this admirable gift of patience, wherefore how injurious to those ancient Christians (who (living in or near the times of either the Apostles themselves or men truly Apostolical) must needs be well instructed in their Discipline, and consequently walked more exactly according to their Rules, yet suffered death for their faith) how injurious I say, to these men, are they, who hold that they wanted not a Will to resist, but rather a power to defend themselves at the approach of death? Surety *Tertullian* had never been so imprudent, nay, so impudent as so confidently to have affirmed such an untruth, whereof he knew the Emperor could not be ignorant, when he wrote thus unto him, *If we had a will to take our private Revenge, or to act as publick Enemies, could we want either numbers of men, or stores of warlike Provisions? Are the* Moors, Germans, Parthians, *or the people of any one Nation, more than those of the whole World? We, though strangers, yet do fill all places in your Dominions; your Cities, Islands, Castles, Forts, Assemblies, your very Camps, Tribes, Courts, Palaces, Senates; only your Temples we leave to your selves: For what war have we not alwaies declared our selves fit and ready, though in Numbers of men we have sometimes been very unequal? How cometh it then to pass, that we suffer* Death *so meekly, so patiently, but that we are instructed by our* Religion, *that it is much better to be killed than to kill? Cyprian* also treading in his Masters steps, openly declares, *That it was from the principles of their Religion, that Christians being apprehended, made no Resistance, nor attempted any revenge for injuries unjustly done them, though they wanted neither numbers of men, nor other means to have resisted, but it was their confidence of some divine Vengeance that would fall upon their persecutors, that made them thus patient, & that perswaded the innocent to give way to the nocent.* [Lib. 5.] So Lactantius, *We are willing to confide in the Majesty of God, who is able, as well to revenge the contempt done to Himself, as the injuries and hardships done unto us: Wherefore, though our sufferings be such as cannot be expressed, yet we do not mutter a word of discontent, but refer our selves wholly to him who judgeth righteously.* And to the same tune sings St. Augustine, *When Princes err, they presently make Laws to legitimate their errors, and by those very laws they judge the innocent, who are at length crowned with Martyrdom.* [Ep 166.] And in another place, *Tyrants are so to be endured by their subjects, & hard Masters by their servants, that both their temporal lives (if possible) may be preserved, and yet their eternal safety carefully provided for:* Which he illustrates by the examples of the primitive Christians, *Who though they then sojourned upon earth as Pilgrims, and had infinite numbers of nations to assist them, yet chuse rather patiently to suffer all manner of torments, than forcibly to resist their persecutors: Neither would they fight to preserve their temporal lives, but chose rather not to fight, that so they might ensure unto themselves an eternal. For they endured Bonds, Stripes, imprisonment the Rack, the Fire, the Cross; they were flead alive, killed, and quartered, and, yet they multiplied; they esteemed this life not worth the fighting for, so that with the loss of it they might purchase what so eagerly they panted after, a better.* Of the same opinion was *Cyril,* as may appear by many notable Sayings of his upon that place of St. *John,* where he treats of *Peter's* Sword. The *Thebean* Legion, we read, consisted of 6666. Souldiers, and all Christians, who when the Emperour *Maximianus* would have compelled the whole Army to sacrifice to Idols, first removed their Station to *Agaunus,* and when upon fresh orders sent after them, they refused to come, *Maximianus* commanded his officers to put every tenth man to Death, which was easily done, no man offering to resist: At which time *Mauritius* (who had the chief Command in that Legion, and from whom the Town *Agaunus* in *Switzer-land* was afterwards called St. *Mauritz,* as *Eucherius,* Bishop of *Lyons,* records) thus bespake his fellow souldiers, *How fearful was I lest any of you under the pretence of defending your selves (as was easie for men armed as ye are to have done) should have attempted by force to have rescued from death those blessed Martyrs? which had you done, I was sufficiently instructed by Christs own example to have forbidden it, who expresly remanded that Sword into its sheath, that was but drawn in his own defence; thereby teaching us that our Christian Faith is much more prevalent than all other arms.* This tragick Act being past, the Emperor commanding the same thing to the survivours, as he had done before to the whole Legion, they unanimously returned him this answer, *Tui quidem,* Caesar, *milites sumus, &c. We are thy Soldiers, O* Caesar, *we took arms for the defence of the* Roman Empire; *we never yet deserted the war, nor betrayed the trust reposed in us; we were never yet branded with fear or cowardise, but have alwaies observed thy commands, until being otherwise instructed by our Christian Laws, we refuse to worship the devil, or to aproach those altars that are polluted with blood. We find by thy commands, that thou resolvest either to draw us into Idolatry, or to affright us by putting every tenth man of us to death: make no further search after those that are willing to lye concealed; but know that we are all of us*

Christians, all our bodies thou hast indeed under thy power, but our souls are subject only to Christ our redeemer. Then *Exuperius* being the Standard-bearer to that Legion thus bespeak them, *Hitherto, Fellow-Soldiers, I have carried the Standard before you in this secular war, but it is not unto these arms that I am now to invite you, it is not unto these wars that I now excite your valour, for now we are to practise another kind of warfare; for with these weapons ye can never enforce your way into the kingdom of heaven.* And by & by he sends this Message to the Emperor, *Against thee, O* Caesar, *Desperation it self (which usually makes even Cowards valiant) cannot prevail with us to take arms. Behold, we have our weapons fixt, yet will we not resist; because we chuse rather to be killed by thee than to overcome thee, and to dye innocents, than to live rebels to either God or thee.* And a little after he adds, *Tela projicimus, &c. We abandon our arms, O Emperour, & will meet thy messengers of death with naked breasts, yet with hearts strongly munited with Christian Faith.* And presently after followed that general Massacre of the *Thebean* Band, whereof *Eutherius* gives this Narrative, *It was neither their Innocence nor their Numbers, that could exempt them from death, whereas in other more dangerous tumults, a multitude though offending, are rarely punished.* The same story in the old Martyrology we find thus recorded, *They were every where wounded with swords, yet they cryed not out, but disdaining the use of their Arms, they exposed their breasts naked to their persecutors: It was neither their numbers nor their experience in war, that could perswade them to assert the equity of their cause by their swords, but placing His example alwaies before them, who was led to the slaughter dumb, and like a lamb to be sacrificed, opened not his mouth; they also in imitation of Him; like the innocent flock of Christ, suffered themselves to be worried and torn in peices by an herd of persecuting wolves.* Thus also do the *Jews* of *Alexandria*, testifie their *innocency* before *Flaceus, We are, as thou seest, unarmed, and yet we are accused unto thee as publick enemies to the state: these hands which nature hath given us for our defence, we have caused to be pinnacled behind us, where they are of little use, & our breasts we expose naked to every man that hath a mind to kill us.* And when the Emperor *Valens* cruelly persecuted those Christians, which according to the Holy Scriptures, & the Traditions of the Ancient Fathers, profest Christ to be ομχσιον, that is, *Co-essential with the Father,* though there were every where great Multitudes of them, yet did they never attempt by arms to secure themselves. Surely, wheresoever Patience in times of persecution is commended unto us, there we find Christ's own example held out unto us (as we read it was to the *Thebean* Legion) for our imitation. As therefore His patience, so ours, should have no bounds nor limits but death it self. And he that thus loseth his life, is truly said by Christ Himself to find it.

Secondly. These measures could never *better our Condition,* nor *redress our Grievances,* unless we should be so vain to imagine our selves capable of waging war with the Crown of *England,* and all its Allies. Is the KING so petty and inconsiderable a Prince that He should be forced? Or can we think that the noise of our *Thousands and Ten Thousands* will frighten *Him* into a Compliance? Without doubt if we do, we shall too late find our mistake, and a woful experience will quickly teach us, that the sole want of *Their Majesties* Protection, will in a very short time reduce us to the most miserable & deplorable condition in the world.

But perhaps we may fancy that this action of ours hath extremely obliged Them, and that all things now are become justly due to the merits of our services: 'twill do very well if it be so understood, but I cannot see the least probability of such a Construction; for we have sufficiently manifested in our *Declaration,* that *Self-interest* was the first and principal motive to our Undertaking, and our Progress doth plainly demonstrate, that we have only made use of Their Names, the better to effect our own Designs; whilest every thing that hath any Relation to Them, lies neglected & unregarded, without any recognition of Their Authority over these Dominions, or the least Acknowledgment of our *Submission* to such orders as should come from Them; saving what particularly related to some *few ill men* (as we call them) whom we have imprisoned & detained *without* any *Law* or *Reason;* so that we have rashly & imprudently adventur'd our *All* upon a chance, (not an *equal* one) whether it will be well, or ill taken: if well, we can expect nothing more than what we should have had by sitting still & quiet, unless it be a vast Charge, Trouble & Expence, which we have inevitably brought upon our selves: if ill, what will be the Event?

In the first place our Countrey, which hath been so remarkable for the true Profession and pure Exercise of the Protestant Religion, will be termed a Land full of Hypocrisie, *REBELLION,* Irreligion, and what not, and we our selves a degenerate, wicked people, that have fallen from the practises of our Fore-fathers, and the purity of our first principles.

2. In all our Pamphlets and Discourses, we have so magnified our Action, and boasted of the vast numbers we can bring into the Field, that it must be of great import to the Crown of *England* to *curb* us & in *time* to reduce us to

our former obedience; & no body will imagine it consistent with the *interest* of that *Crown*, any more to trust Government in the hands of a people, so ready & so able upon all occasions to set up for themselves, and the stronger we are, the more need there will be to keep us under.

3. And lastly, We shall realy endure and undergo all those Miseries & Calamities which we *fancied* to our selves under the late Government; and become the Scorn and By-word of all our Neighbours.

What then *remains*, but that *whilst it is yet called to day*, we should *endeavour* to settle our selves in such a Posture, as may at least *mitigate*, if not wholly prevent the before-mentioned inconveniences. If our Charter be restored such a Condition cannot hurt us; but the *want* of it may; for we are *accountable* for every Action & every false Step we make after the date of it, & render our selves lyable to be Questioned & *Quo-Warranto'd* for our Male-feazance whensoever the Supream Authority shall think it meet; if not, it must be of great service to us to be found in a submissive and humble posture, fit & ready to receive Their Majesties Commands; lest while we value our selves too much, upon our own merits, we become unworthy of Their Favour in a most gracious pardon, without which (think what we will) we never can be safe & secure from the severity of the Laws, which we have indisputably violated, in matters of the highest nature & consequence imaginable.

I hope every good man will seriously & impartially consider the foregoing Discourse, and suffer himself to be guided by the Dictates of Reason, and not of Humour or Prejudice, and then I am well assured, it will be evident enough, that we have mistaken our Measures, and that a timely recess, will more Advantage us than an obstinate and wilful perseverance & that nothing but such a Remedy can restore our almost-perishing & undone Countrey, to a lasting Peace and happy Settlement: Which that GOD of His mercy would grant us, shall ever be the hearty prayers of

F. L.

Postscript

I was principally induced to direct the precedent Discourse to you, Gentlemen, because I would rightly be understood, which I'm sure I can never fail of by persons of your Learning and Worth, and I hope you will be so kind to me & so just to your Countrey, to let me know in the most *publick manner* you can, wherein I have *mistaken* the matter either in point of Fact or Judgment; but if I have been so fortunate to Convince you, that wrong measures have been taken, and that the people had no reason for what they have done, nor no bottom for what they are yet doing; let me tell you, tis your duty, not only to admonish them but to reduce them to such a temper as becomes pious men & good Christians, for which you will have the praise and God the Glory.

FINIS.

· 3 ·

Gershom Bulkeley, The People's Right to Election (1689)

ശ

IN THE AFTERMATH OF THE FALL of the Dominion of New England (1685–89), colonists in Connecticut debated whether to resume their old charter government, or wait for instructions from the new monarchs, William and Mary. Gershom Bulkeley (1636?–1713), a Connecticut minister, a physician, and a justice under Royal Governor Sir Edmund Andros, was adamant that a unilateral resumption of the charter was unjustified.

In *The People's Right to Election or Alteration of Government*, Bulkeley argued that all political power was divinely sanctioned, flowing from God to the King, with none residing in the people. For Bulkeley, it followed from this that Connecticut had no legal standing to reconstitute any kind of political authority in the absence of royal assent. Only the King could restore Connecticut's old political institutions. As Bulkeley put it, "For Subjects in *private* Capacity to take upon them to set up and exercise Government as they see cause, is direct Rebellion and Treason." Although Bulkeley held that he was not "an Enemy to our ancient Charter priviledges," he adamantly maintained that, despite whatever injustices or violations of rights had happened under Andros, "The Government is changed and taken into his Majesties hands." Although he continued to oppose the colony's stance, Bulkeley was ultimately unsuccessful in his opposition to the resumption of the charter. In 1694, after much lobbying in London, Connecticut received royal recognition of their charter government. (C.B.Y.)

The PEOPLE's RIGHT TO ELECTION.

Or *ALTERATION* of *GOVERNMENT* in *Connecticott,*

ARGUED

In a LETTER;

By *Gershom Bulkeley* Esq; one of their Majesties Justices of the peace In the County of *Hartford.*

Together with a Letter to the said *Bulkeley,* from a Friend of his in the BAY.

To which is added, The *Writing* delivered to *James Russell* of *Charlestown* Esq; warning him and others concerned, not to meet to Hold a Court at *Cambridge,* within the county of *Middlesex.*

By *Thomas Greaves* Esq; Judge of their Majesties Inferior Court of Pleas and one of their Majesties Justices of the peace within the said County And also his ANSWER to Mr. *Broadstreete* and the Gentlemen mett at the *Town-house* in *Boston* concerning the same.

Published for the Information & Satisfaction of their Majesties loyall (but abused) Subjects in NEW ENGLAND.

Philadelphia, Printed by Allignes of *William Bradford,* Anne 1689.

To the honourable Robert Trent Esq; *and to the Worshipfull* James Bishop, William Jones & James Fitch, *and other the Worshipful Justices of the severall Counties: and any other whom it may concern, assembling at* Hartford: *To advise concerning Holding of a Court of* Election *by Virtue of and according to the late Patent.*

Sirs, I Am at this time (by reason of bodily Infirmity) unable to wait upon you in a suitable manner, or to maintain discourse as this Occasion may require, or indeed to write much, yet (considering the Exigency of the case) I will do what I can, & apply my selfe to you as followeth.

And to prevent all prejudice against what I have to say, I shall premise thus much, *Viz.* That tho' I was no free-man of the Colony, yet I never was, nor am an Enemy to our ancient Charter-priviledges, and could they now be regularly Recovered, I should rejoice in it, and if I knew any thing whereby to justify the present proceeding, I should not conceal it; but we must not do evil that good may come of it.

I am not at all ambitious of keeping my place, it is a Burthen and no Benefit to me; an orderly discharge will be very welcome, and the sooner the better; if I could absolve my self from my oath, it had not been to do now; so that I am under no Temptation on these accounts. Tis onely the Trust reposed in me, and my reall desire of the Common good which puts me on, very well knowing, that nothing but ill Will is like to be my reward.

Further, I am sensible of mine inability to wade in those great Affaires, and would not abound in my own sence, nor in any sort take upon nor go about to teach those of whom I had need to learne; yet, *Plus vident oculi quam oculus.* Many eyes see more than one: and a weak eye may chance to see that which a better over-looks. And I having with others, (tho much against my own Inclination) received his Majesties Commission as a Justice of the Peace for the County of *Hartford,* and having at that time taken the Oaths of Supremacy and Obedience, as also that of a justice, for keeping of the Law, the Conservation of the Peace, and the quiet and good Government of the people, it did concern me to Consider the Duty by these meanes so strangly bound upon me, and accordingly I have since that time done my poor endeavour to inform my self in the Laws, that I might discern between Right and Wrong for the good of the people.

Therefore, in sence of my duty to God, the King, your selves, and all his Majesties good people here (for I am debtor to you all, and am embarqued in the same Bottom with you; and do account it my Duty to seek the peace of the place where I live) therefore (I say) I shall not (and I think, I ought not) be wholly silent at this time, but according to that little which I have learned and observed, I shall modestly, and yet freely & plainly, offer a few Considerations to you which respect the present Affaire, desireing you neither to accept nor reject what I say, because it comes from me, but according to its own merit; for the matter in hand seems to me to be of very great Weight, and I beseech you to consider and ponder it throughly before you engage in it, forasmuch as an Irregularity in this Preceeding, may be the beginning of great Calamity and Woe to this people.

The present Motion seems to me to be not only illegall, needless & unprofitable, but indeed very criminal dangerous and hurtful to us, and that upon these Considerations.

First, Before you can Regularly (or by Virtue of and according to your late Patent) hold a Court of Election, you must be first Restored to your former politick Capacity, whereby you were under the Name of His Majesties Governour and Company of the English Colony of *Connicticott,* Persons able & capable in the Law to plead and be impleaded &c; and to Have, Take, Require and possesse Lands and other Hereditaments &c. of which, that Priviledge of *Government* was a principall one given by your Patent.

For I reason thus, If you do now assume the Government, and proceed to Election, you do it either in a private and personal Capacity, or in a publick and politik Capacity, I suppose you do not pretend to the First, for that is not to do it according to your patent, and besides it is criminall.

For Subjects in *private* Capacity to take upon them to set up & exercise Government as they see cause, is direct *Rebellion* & Treason. Therefore you must do it in a publick and politick Capacity, but this you cannot do but you are restored to such a Capacity, in which indeed you once were, but now are not: which I thus prove from the Patent it self.

Our late Soveraign King *Charles* the Second, did in the year 1662 by his Letters Patents for himself his Heires and Successours, Ordaine & Constitute the therein named Patentees, & the then present & future Freemen &c. One Body politick and Corporate in fact and Name, by the name of, *His Governour and Company of the English Colony of Connecticut in New-England in America;* and that by the same Name they and their Successours shall and may have perpetuall Succession, and shall & may be persons able & capable in the law to plead & be impleaded, to Answer & be Answered unto, to defend & be defended in all Suits, Causes, Quarrels, Matters Actions and things of what kind and nature soever. And also to Have, Take, Possesse, Acquire and Purchase Lands, Tenements and Hereditaments &c. This is the expresse Letter of that Clause of the Patent, whereby you were constituted one body politick and Corporate, able and capable in the Law as aforesaid; and whereby also, you were by the name of Governour and Company to have perpetuall Succession, or to be perpetuated by annuall Election, at least, as the Patent afterwards shews, and upon this Clause do all the priviledges afterwards granted depend.

But now you are not such a Body politick and Corporate capable in Law as aforesaid, for you know, that by the late Transaction between his Majesty and his then Governour and Company of the late Colony of *Connecticut*, the Government is changed and taken into his Majesties hands, and the late Colony of *Connecticot* annexed to the Bay, the Governour and one of the Assistants made and sworn Councellours and Judges under this new Government, the late Deputy-Governour and the rest of the Assistants, made & sworn Justices in the severall Counties under the same new Government, and this a year and a half agone: How legall these proceedings were we need not now dispute; but this it is in fact: Hence there is no such thing in fact and name as the Governour and Company of the Colony of *Connecticut*. And hence the Corporation is dissolved and made incapable in the law to plead and be impleaded &c. or to have and take or possesse any Hereditaments; and consequently incapable to Take, Erect and Exercise Government. For neither the Governour alone, nor the Company alone is the Corporation, nor capable to plead or be impleaded as such, but the Governour and Company together. If they Claime or Take, they must Claime or Take together, if they Sue, they must Sue together, and if they be sued, they must be sued together and not apart. Besides, by the meanes aforesaid the Succession is interrupted and broken off, for by the same name of the Governour & Company of &c. you were to have perpetuall Succession, and that Succession to be perpetuated by annuall Election of the Governour, Deputy-Governour &c. which hath not been. Therefore in your present state you are not Successours of the former Corporation; and consequently cannot take the priviledges untill restored to your former politick Capacity: and (to add that) you cannot restore your selves to it, for that is inconsistent with your Subjection to the Supreame power.

By all this it doth appeare, That as there is no Governour, or Deputy-Governour to give Order for the Assembling of the Company, (without which their Assembling for such an end is unlawful) so there are no Freemen capable of choosing or of being chosen; for if there be not a Corporation capable, there cannot be capable Freemen of that Corporation: And if in this state you proceed to Election, there is no Freeholder or free Subject of *England* belonging to this Late Colony, but hath as good a Right, & is as capable of Choosing as any of you, because there is nothing to hinder it, and this the people see. Also there are now no Assistants enabled by lawfull Authority (without which none may do it) to take the Oath of the Governour or Deputy Governour when Chosen; all which things the Patent doth expresly require.

All this seems necessarily to follow from the very words of the Patent, and how it can be avoided I cannot see: but that I may not seem to vent my own Notions onely, I shall briefly give the words of Sir *Edward Coke* as sound a Lawyer and as great a friend to the *English* Subjects Libertyes as ever *England* knew. *In the Case* (saith he) *of Mayor & Commonality* (which is the same in effect as Governour and Company) *Where there is no Mayor the Commonality cannot make claim; because they have neither ability nor Capacity to take or sue any Action.* [*Coke* upon *Lit.* pag. 203.] so that without a Governour or Deputy Governour you cannot so much as Claime the Government by Law, much lesse enter upon it. And therefore we see that in the Patent, the King doth not Constitute onely a number of Freemen, and make them immediately capable to take such and such priviledges, and give them power rudely to run together whensoever some factious spirits shall make a bustle, and so in a tumult to choose them a Governour & Magistrates; No, but he first creates them a Body politick consisting of Governour and Company, and by that name makes them capable in Law to take the priviledges which he thereafter gives. And he himselfe nominates and appoints the first Governour or Deputy Governour for the time being, to give order for the Assembling of the Company upon all occasions (whether for Election or otherwise) and in such orderly manner gives them leave to assemble as often as need requireth.

Secondly, (Which doth also confirm the former) Before you can hold a Court of Election according to the Patent, you must have a General Court or Assembly constituted according to the Patent: the reason is, because the Patent doth ordaine, that the Governour, Deputy-Governour, and

Assistants &c. be annually chosen, not without, but in the said Generall Court: concerning this matter the King in his Patent, ordains three things.

1. That every second Thursday in May and October (or oftner if need be) there shall be a Generall Assembly. 2. That this Generall Court or Assembly consist of the Governour or Deputy Governour, and at least six of the Assistants, and of the Freemen or their Deputyes. 3. That at least once in every year (Viz) on the second Thursday in May, the Governour Deputy Governour & Assistants of the said Company and other Officers &c. shall be in the said Generall Court and Assembly to be held from that day or time newly chosen for the yeare ensueing &c. Thus saith the Patent expresly: But you have now no Governour, Deputy Governour, nor Assistants, therefore can have no such Generall Court or Assembly; therefore can hold no Court of Election by virtue of or according to your Patent. Examine the Patent and see &c.

From these two Considerations it appears, that if you do proceed to Election in your present state, you will but deceive your selves and trouble the Country to no purpose: all that you will do, will be void in Law: the Government you think to set up will be but an imaginary Government, a shadow without a substance, Magistrates without Authority, for you can give them none, neither does the Patent give them any. A Government that cannot determine the Present Government, nor vacate the Commissions that have been given out from the King, and are still in force, nor exercise any Authority to effect: for their Authority may justly (yea, ought to) be denied by every one, and they cannot enforce it, without Lawlesse Usurpation & Tyrannie. 2. You will but trouble your *selves,* for you will be immediately liable to a *Quo-Warranto,*[1] and can give no account by what Authority you do these arbitrary things.

Thirdly, The Government is now in the Kings hands, (and here, that no person may cavill, the word *King* may be understood indefinitely for the King his Heires & Successours, for the Heir or Successour is King, when the Time of Succession is come. But I say, The Government is now in the Kings hands, and it will be wisdome to proceed in a regular way, if you desire to recover it. For in regard of the dignity of his person, the King has by Law a Prerogative above the Subject for the keeping of what he hath.

1. [Literally, "By what right." A writ directing a person to show "by what right" he exercises powers of office.—Tr.]

Hence, a man may not enter upon the King as he may upon his Fellow subject; much lesse may he enter upon the King by Force. I do not now enter upon that Question, *How far those that are by and under the King entrusted with publick Power and Office, for the defence of the Lawes and the Libertyes of the Subject, may, in case, use force for that end; and the people under them at their Call and Command;* This is another Question, and not our case, and those that desire satisfaction, may consult those that have written weightily upon that Subject. It is one thing to defend the Lawes and Liberties of the Subject. This some think *some* may do, and this defends the Government: But it is another thing to subvert & change & take possession of the Government it self, this none may do. And tho' some may say, *But the Government is illegally taken into the Kings hand, and it is one of our great Liberties:* I shall say something to that by and by.

Therefore to let that Question passe untoucht. I said that the Subject may not enter upon the King with force: now you cannot enter upon the King in point of Government, but it is with force, for all power of Government implies force antecedent, for the setting of it up, and concomitant for the Support and Defence of it, and partly because you cannot do it in this way of Election without Multitude which is *Force* in the judgment of the Law, as well as *Manus armatae,* or Force of Armes, so that if you do it, it must necessarily be done with force; now to enter upon the King in point of Government with Force, what is it but to invade the Crown? And Kings do account their Heads & Crownes to be very neare each to other; and that he that attempts against the one, attempts against the other.

This Affaire therefore doth touch the Crowne, and nearly concerne your Allegiance, and is worthy to be well considered, for it is of dangerous consequence; 'tis dangerous to those that shall Choose, and be Chosen, and Accept; dangerous to all that shall any waies contrive, counsell, abett or conceale, (tho here is hardly room for Concealing, (*A Citty set on a Hill cannot be hid,* and these things cannot *be done in a Corner*) 'tis dangerous to your selves and Posterity, yea dangerous to us all, and doth require more skill in Law and state affaires than is very common among us, to make the way plain to a safe proceeding in it; for I cannot find that the Law doth use any softer Language concerning such Actions, than that of *Tumults, Insurrections, rebellios Riots, Sedition, Rebellion, Treason &c.*

Gentlemen, I hope you will be carefull to keep at a due distance from such things which are wont to be *Bitternesse in the end.* 'Tis an easy matter to run too farr; And the worst is wont to be made of such things when they come to Tryall.

Fourthly, You may here consider that the Government was not taken into the Kings hand without your own Submission, and some sort (at least) of Consent; whence possibly there was not so much illegality in that proceeding as some do imagine. I was not personally acquainted with those Transactions, and therefore cannot undertake much in this; but this I suppose will not be denied, that if parties be at Law (whether King and subject, or subject and subject) and instead of standing a Tryal, they agree upon Conditions, and the Conditions are performed, and so the Action be let fall, this is not illegall: and if afterwards either party be sensible of inconveniency, will it be fair and honest for him to say it was illegall, & thereupon breake his Agreement? The *Inhabitant of the Holy Hill swears to his own hurt, and changeth not.* You were at Law with the King, and its like you thought it would be a great Charge to maintaine the Action, and it might go against you at last, & you should be annexed to *Yorke;* and hereupon you submit to the Kings Wisdome and pleasure, begging that you may be annexed to the *Bay;* the King performs this condition, and lets fall his Action, Demands the Government, and you yield it up to him; if now you finde it prejudiciall, you must *lay your hand upon your mouth,* and not take it again by force. We must not think to leave and take when we please.

Fifthly, None are allowed by the Law to be Judges in their own Case, no not the King himself: But if you proceed in this manner, you take upon you, in your own case to judge the King, to condemn and take possession, which in reason will never be borne, for Princes are as tender of their Prerogative as Subjects can be of their Liberties.

But to abate the Force of these Considerations, some say, *We heare there is no King, Regall Power is Extinct, &c.* I answer, tis no pleasant Objection or Subject to speak to, but yet the Necessity of the present time seems to require a word or two to prevent these unwise and unwary speeches which do not become Subjects. Therefore I say first, That Rumours are but a sandy foundation to ground such assertions, or to change & build Government upon, we have yet nothing of Record concerning the King. 2 This doth not help our case at all, for if it were indeed so, that *the Sceptre were departed,* you have then nothing to do with the Patent; Tis onely the *King's* Governour and Company that hath Interest in the Patent, and the King grants it onely for Himself, his Heires and Successours, if there be none of these, your Patent and Estate in it are expired without any more to do. But, 3*ly*. The King is a Royall Body politick which hath Succession whereby the Crown passeth not onely to heires by *Blood*, but to Successours also; in which respect it is said, That in Judgement of Law, *The KING never dyes*. There is therefore allwaies a King.

But others say, *What shall we do? there is no Government; the Governour who is the Head of it is imprisoned, and hath Surrendred his Government*. I answer, It is a very great Errour and proceeds from ignorance to think that *there is no Government*, & it containes so many *inconveniencies* & *mischiefs* in it, as it is not safe to mention them; so long as there is any supream power, there must needs be a Government. 2. The Governour is not the Head of the Government but the *King*. And the Government is not his properly and originally but the *King's*. The Governour is but a Minister of the King in the Government, which Ministry it is said he hath surrendred to be secured and be disposed of by Orders that shall be received from the Crown of *England*. It will not become us to present these Orders and dispose of the Government otherwise our selves; but to acknowledge our Subjection to that Crown, as our Neighbours would do well to do. 3. The Commissions of the Judges and Justices of the severall Counties (the Execution whereof is no small part of Government) are granted by the Governour (its true) but not from the Governour, but from the *King*, & are derived from the Crowne; it is not from an inferiour but from a Supreame power, and they do still continue in force, notwithstanding the *imprisonmen*t or Surrender of the Governour; for they are matters of Record under the great Seale of the Dominion, & cannot be countermanded without matter of Record of as high a nature. You may take one instance from *Charles* the first his time, He was indeed the head of the Government; but yet notwithstanding the great Breach and long Warrs between him and his Parliament, and his long imprisonment after that, {(?} both together) from 42. to the end of 48. there was still a Government, and it was his Government, and exercised by the Kings Commissions as long as he lived, for they were not changed nor superseded till a year after his death, as the Histories of those times shew. So that notwithstanding all the Rumours we have had from abroad, and the Overtures at home, there is a Government still, to which we ought to submit; and that for Conscience sake. Let us not have cause to say, that *there are none that will be governed*.

Sixthly. I may desire you to consider those honoured Gentlemen who had the Rule over you under the former Government, and are now also in place under this Government, who I believe would hardly have accepted any Commission under the present Government, but for this end, that you might not be so much Ruled by strangers as otherwise you might have been, and to prevent the miseries that might follow thereupon: I am sure that this was one principall Argument that they used with me, when they saw me so averse as I was to Accept, and I think the end has been so far attained, as that you ought with Thankfullness to acknowledge, that by this meanes you have escaped the greatest part of those grievances which others complain of, and not now (you think you have the staffe in your hand) to ride over their Consciences who are under Oath (from which neither they nor you can absolve them to execute their Commissions, and to tread them down as mire in the streets: The measure that you mete may be measured to you again. 'Tis a golden Rule, That which you would that others should do to you, do you the same to them; & do not recompence evil for good.

Some I know reflect hard upon them for giving up the former Government, much like those that reflect upon old father *Adam;* but I will so far apologize for them, as to desire you to reflect upon your selves, for have you already forgotten that you (I mean the people) were divided in your opinions; many grudged at the charge of that Affaire, whence it was hard (if possible) for them *seasonably* to *raise mony* to maintaine the suite (I my self know who were then as hot against the raising of money for that Purpose (and cry'd out it was illegall) as now hot for the Patent, and ready to cry out upon the losse of that as illegall; but I will not prejudice any man) Others were so affraid of being annexed to *Yorke,* that they thought it the best way to submit without more a doe so that they might be annexed to the Bay. Surely you cannot forget these things, by which (comeing from the people by their Deputyes) it is reasonable to think that the Generall Assembly was moved to make that Submission to the King, and in all Reason it was much better so, than for want of money, to have had a Judgement given against us upon a *Nihil-Dicit,* or Contempt, and it is possible, that if those who reflect so hard upon them had been under the same Circumstances, they would have done the same thing or worse. Therefore methinks they might be a little considered, and not made the scorn of the people.

Seventhly. Consider your Profession, we are all Protestants, I hope there is not a Papist in our Limits, I know not any: and we professe to believe (rejecting humane Traditions) That the word of God is the onely and sufficient Rule of Faith and Manners. And do we not there finde that *Sure word of Prophesie, to which we may do well to take heed, as to a light that shines in a Dark place*, which doth direct and counsell us, *To fear the Lord and the King*, and *not to meddle with those that are given to change*, To *Keep the Kings Commandment, and that in regard of the Oath of God*, To *Give unto Caesar the things that are Caesar's, and to God the things that are God's*, To *Study to be quiet, and to be subject to Principalities and powers* (*because they are of God*) *and to obey Magistrates*, To *submit our selves to every ordinance of man for the Lord's sake, whether it be to the King as supreame, or unto Governours as unto those that are sent by him for the punishment of evil doers and the praise of them that do well, for so is the will of God, that with well doing, we may put to silence the ignorance of foolish men*, &c. and, *Not to despise Government, nor to speake evill of Dignityes?* These are sound Doctrines, and will well consist with the protestant Religion (else we had reason to be ashamed of it) and it were to be wished, That these among us who *are the salt of the earth* & *Light of the world* would season the people by putting them in mind (as *Paul* commands *Titus*) of those great Duties so necessary for these perilous days, wherein men are (as was prophecied they would be) so apt to be Traiters, heady & high minded, and to despise Government. Therefore before we proceed in this Affaire, consider what our Religion will gain by it, an Ornament or a Blott and whether we shall not give Occasion to adversaries (that seek occasion) to blaspheme the name & speake evill of the waies of God amongst us.

Eighthly, Consider the time and state of affaires in the Christian world. If any thing be true of that which comes to us it seems, it is a time wherein there is a strong engagement to root out the Protestant Religion. *Europe* is upon this account in flames, the Ax is laid to our own Root, if it be so, it is a time wherein we had need to *strengthen the things that are weake*, to join heart and hand together against French and Pagan Force and Cruelty, and to unite heaven and Earth if possible, for the preservation of our selves and posterity, and for the Defence of the cause of God and his Truth with us; surely this is no time to fall to Faction and parties, to tread down the Government that is left, (too weak already) to disturb and obstruct the Course of Justice, To confound the Militia, that no man shall know whome to Command nor whome to Obey, and to promote private interests, and therefore set every man's hand against his Brother, unlesse we designe to ruine all. I wish there be not some Jesuit that has foisted in this Project amongst them in the Bay and us here, as the most probable way to ruin us at this time; for it is the old trade of that Diabolical sort of men by their plausible crafty Counsells, to make protestants destroy themselves, by stirring up, and fomenting divisions among them; and promoteing any thing which tends thereto, the which, how naturally & necessarily they will flow from this proceeding is easy to shew: but it is better to be silent than by speaking to shew men the way which they are too ready to run into.

Ninethly. More might be said, but the last Consideration that I shall offer (and which I think may satisfy any reasonable man) is, That it is known the Countrey is in daily Expectation of Orders from the Crowne of *England* for the Settleing and Regulating of the Government, those Orders will either contradict or overthrow your Election, or else countenance and Encourage it:

If they overthrow it, to what end is it to hold a Court, (if we could hold a Court) to make Election, to change and turn things up-side down, and hereby put the Countrey (which is poor enough allready) to unnecessary Charge, and know not how to defray it when we have done, and to run the hazzard of displeasure from the supreame power abroad, and of making Division and Mischief at home, and all for an imaginary Government, which may possibly last for a week or a moneth. *Sapiens incipit a Fine.*[2]

If the Orders that shall come do countenance and encourage to an Election, they will be such as will enable us to it, and so we shall preserve a good Aspect abroad, and Unity and Peace at home; what need then of such Haste? These things cannot be spoken against. And the Town-Clerke of *Ephesus* could say, that these things being so, *you ought to be quiet & do nothing rashly.*

But some say, We shall loose our day if we do not proceed now. I Answer, There is nothing in that, for if you have sufficient Warrant from the Crowne of *England*, to enable you to the thing, you will be enabled as to a Day, and Persons, and what else is needfull which now you are not, as before was said.

But say others, If we have an Election before these Orders come, we shall be in a Capacity to capitulate, and so obtain the better termes, &c. I answer this is a great mistake, It will be a mighty Disadvantage; for it will be a wonderfull thing if you be not look'd upon and dealt with as Criminalls.

2. ["A wise man begins from the end."]

Again, Whome do you mean to Capitulate with? Surely it will be good manners for us to Aske, and not to Command; to Follow our Leaders and not to go before them.

But some think; These are small matters that will be over-look'd, and easily pardoned, we need not stand upon such nicetyes.

But I Answer how small they are will be best seen afterwards, and it is better not to need a pardon, than to presume upon getting one.

From all these Considerations I conclude, that our strength is to sit still, and therefore do advise

That instead of moving towards an Election, the Judges and Justices in the severall-Counties, considering their Commissions which they have received and the Oathes which they have taken, for the faithfull Execution of them, and Remembring that the Judgement is not man's but God's who is with them in the Judgement, they take Courage and do it; and in Order thereto Unanimously Declare, that they will Maintain and Exercise the Government (in their Degree) according to their Commissions, in Conformity to the Lawes which are the Rules of their Commissions, & the true and propper Bulwarks of the Subject's just Libertyes, being carefull to do nothing contrary thereto, to the best of their understanding: & that the good People here do willingly & cheerfully submit & yield obedience to the severall Officers in their Respective places, as their Duty is, untill such time as sufficient Warrant shall come from the Crown of *England* for other Orders. And in the meane time, we all with one consent *Lift up our hearts with our hands to God in the Heavens* for a happy Composure of these Commotions in *England* and those other Kingdomes, for the Restitution, Security and propagation of the Gospell, true Religion and Worship of God, and for the preserving and establishing of the peace and liberty of his people there and here, and else-where throughout the world to the glory of God.

This Course is regular, innocent, offensive to none, and most safe for our selves and ours: but if the people will not be advised, I very much fear that the Issue will not be like a Tree of Life, or the desire satisfied, else truly I should not at this time have given you or my selfe this trouble.

The Opinion, and Resolution of the other Justices I know not, but for my part, I am plaine, and I must declare & protest against an Election at the present, as that which is justly offensive to the supreame Power, in whose hands soever it is, or shall be, and pernicious to our selves; and if the people should willfully proceed to it, it will remaine for the Justices to consider whether the Law and their Oathes don't require them to make a Record of it, and Certifie it into the Chancery, &c. But I hope there will none enforce to such things, and I pray that you may all Act under the Influence of the God of peace and order. And in Testimony that this is my Opinion and Advice, I have hereunto set my hand, on the eighth day of May 1689.

Gershom Bulkeley.

Pacem te poscimus omnes.[3]

Peace is the Tranquillity of Order, therefore Order is the onely right Way to Peace

A Letter to Gershom Bulkeley Esq; (one of their Majesties Justices of the Peace in the County of Hartford*) from a friend in the Bay.*

Sir,

I have seen your Letter referring to the Government of *Connecticut Colony* Directed unto Col. *Trent* and other Gentlemen there, and being very well acquainted with the papers and passages you refer to and the Truth of them severally: I earnestly expected the Answer, as extreamely necessary for the Vindication of the assumed Government in your parts, if at least they mean to continue their Allegiance and Dependance upon the Crowne of *England,* or to hold their Majesties Subjects in those parts in Obediance to them. But for that I heare nothing in their Defence, I must be allowed to guesse, that either those Gentlemen have Orders from their Majesties unknowne to any, thus to advance themselves, or that they mean to cast off their Dependance & Obedience to the Crown of *England.* The first of these is dishonourable to suppose, the latter will end in the utter Ruin of the English interest here, and *leave us a prey to all Nations, when the wild beast shall passe by and tread down the Thistle.*

But whatsoever be the Opinion or Resentment of your Gentlemen, I will assure you Sir the good people here (that are so far quitt of the fright and hurry of the late and present confusion in these parts) wish that the men of *Sechem* had *hearkened* unto *Jotham,* that *God might have hearkened unto them;* and fear lest the proceeding here as well as with you, being plainly represented at home, should alarm a just and wise Prince, to take some

3. ["We all beg you for peace."]

severe method to keep the people of these Colonies in a more strict Obedience to the Crowne of *England* than will agree with our present licentious & ungovern'd frame; there being amongst us men not of the least interest that daily say, they will not be shuffled out of their Allegiance.

When it shall be seen and understood that the Noise of a French PLOT, and a Maqua's PLOT, A Plot to BURN the TOWN of BOSTON and to MASSACRE the PEOPLE, neither have nor ever had the least shadow of truth, but a pure *Malicious Invention* onley, to perswade the Common-people into an ill Opinion of those appointed to rule & Govern them, and whom in Duty & Conscience they ought to obey, and being in that manner amused were pushed and hurried into such a Rising and Convulsion of the Government, without ever considering the effect.

And when it shall be told (as now too truly it may) that the Effect of these changes, are the totall Subversion of their Majesties Government, the Losse of the Garrison at *Pemaquid,* the County of *Cornwall,* the *Province of Main* and other parts, Severall hundreds of their Majesties subjects, the Fishery and Lumber trade, the Running away of many of our people, who turn Pirates and do their Countrymen and neighbours the same Mischiefs that the *Algerines* do upon the Coasts of the Christians, whilst their Majesties Ship of Warre is dismantled and made uselesse, the most injust, long & cruell Confinement and imprisionment of the Governour, (who was both capable and active on all occasions for the publick good and safety of the Countrey) severall of the Councill, and other persons imploy'd in publick Office in the Government, (an Act, for which the *American* world can shew no example or Parallell) and the Committing of the greatest Routs and Riots, even on the Sabbath day, and many other inconveniencies that duly grow upon us surely all sober and thinking men cannot but see the Folly and Errour of these things, and wish that day had never been, which has occasioned so great mischiefs and miseryes, of which we all see the Beginning, but none can tell the end.

Amongst the many and false *Rumours and Aspersions* cast upon his *Excellency* the *Governour,* and spread abroad to bring him into Disreputation with his *Prince,* and make him odious to the Common People, I finde one (not of the least) taken notice of by you {(?} very well answered and made of no Weight) which doubtless Influenced some and was a meanes to withdraw & delude others, but do not perceive by your Writeing that you were satisfied in the Falsity as well as the Weaknesse of that Assertion.

Therefore that you may be rightly informed in that perticular, I must tell you, That the Peoples takeing to Armes, was wholly a Surprise to *His Excellency*, and that untill they were actually so, he had not the least Advice or Intimation thereof, and used no other meanes, but by the force of his Authority endeavoured to Satisfie them; And to that end Hearing that many of the Councill were at the Councill-Chamber, where (it being the ordinary Councill Day) they were to meet, (and some perticularly by him sent for from *Salem* and other parts to be there) *His Excellency* went to them, and desired their Assistance to pacifie the people then in Armes, offering on his part to do what might be proper for His Majesties Service and the Good and Wellfare of His Subjects here: but severall others of the Cheife of the Towne and Magistrates in the late Government being designedly met there, instead of Complying with *his Excellencies* Proposalls, and to *Support and Maintaine the Government*, they *lent the Croud their arme to shake the Tree*, and made *his Excellency* a Prisoner in the Councill-Chamber, and soon after some of the *Councill* and other Officers that waited on him: An Act much like that of *Brutus* to *Caesar*, abating the difference of the Person, and that they did not *stab* him; but kept him a Prisoner to undergoe worse Miseryes.

After *his Excellency* was *thus Confined*, he was often pressed with *Threats* to give Order for the Surrender of the *Fort* and *Castle*, which he absolutely *Refused*, and never gave any Order for the Surrender of either, but they were *Forced from the Officers* that had the Command of them: If this be a *Surrender of the Government*, you and all prudent men may judge: I am sure (as you have well observed) the Law gives it a quite other Terme.

His Excellency had sufficient Authority and Orders from the Crowne of *England* to secure the *Government*, which (no doubt) he would have done, had all those in place discharged their Duties, and the People continued their Obedience and Subjection: He wanted not further Orders from *England* for that purpose, nor had he occasion to appoint Trustees, the *King* had appointed and intrusted such as He thought were sufficient. But it was Wonderfull to see, with what a *Strong Delusion* the people were possessed at that time; and thought they had with their *Thousands* obtained a mighty Victory over *Ten* or *Twelve naked persons*, and therein *done God good Service*. The Strength of Government consists in the Obedience of the People, and when that Duty is not Regarded the Government is soon Overthrowne, and all turned into *Anarchy* and Confusion; of which we have now a sad

Example: for what between an *Imaginary Government* & the *Fury* of the *Mobile* it is hard to *know who is uppermost.*

I have alwaies considered the Ministry of this Countrey as that which the people came into this Wilderness *to see,* and I hope it shall never be *a Reed shaken with the wind,* and their present influence in all parts of the Countrey to move the people to bethink themselves of their Causelesse & unaccountable Prejudices, Wrath and Rage, their ungodly deeds, and hard Speeches one against another; and to dispose them to their Dutyes and Obedience to their Majesties Government as established and appointed over them from the Crown of *England,* and that they would prove themselves to be *Children that will not lye,* that God may become their Saviour; is humbly offered as a great part of their Province.

I am ignorant whether from any in these parts you have been written unto since your letter was made publick here, but I am sure your Reasons will be found true, agreeable to Religion and Law, and what you have said against an Election, is as true against an Assumption; and what is true of the Avoidance of the Charter of Connecticut, is much more true of that of the Massachusetts; and how a dependant part of the English Nation can legally come at Government, at least the Coercive part of it, without a Grant from the Crowne, being not to be found in the ordinary Readings of the Law; may be enquired for at *Delphos.*

We often say, that *every man has a pope in his belly,* but I hope nobody pretends to have a *King* there, whatever Soveraignty men take to themselves of opinions in Religion, the Government expects by private persons to be treated with more Distance & Difference, and will certainly be obeyed.

Sir I have Known you long a true Lover of your Countrey, of Integrity and Service in your Place and Station, and account your plainnesse to your Countreymen in this great Affaire, as the best Service you could offer them, and am deeply sorry if any other Opinion be taken thereof amongst the people, however I perceive you have what you expected: and the Rewards of Vertue and public Service are not so soon nor easily gotten.

That all these things may have a happy Composure, and *Their Majesties* Subjects in this their Dominion a due & true Sence of their Duty & Allegiance (which can onely make these Plantations happy & flourish) I am very sure is your desire as well as of (Sir) your Friend and Servant *&c.*

The Writeing Delivered to *James Russell* of *Charlestowne* Esq; by *Thomas Graves* Esq; Judge of their Majesties Inferiour Court of pleas, and one of their Majesties Justices of the Peace, within the County of *Middlesex*.

To *James Russell* of *Charlestowne* Esq; to be communicated to any others that are in like manner with your self concerned herein.

Sir, *Forasmuch as I am credibly informed, that your self with some other pretended Magistrates do intend on the first Tuesday in October next, to meet together at* Cambridge *to keep a pretended Court of Judicature, not having any lawful authority from our Soveraigne Lord and Lady King* William *& Queen* Mary *enableing you so to do, I therefore considering the obligation lyeing upon me, by the Commission of the Peace for this County of* Middlesex, *as also by a Commission to be Judge of the inferiour Court of Pleas in said County, both from the Crowne of* England; *neither of which (altho I have by the late Tumults (not yet stilled) been hindred from executing the power therein to me committed) is yet legally vacated, or superseded: I can do no lesse to shew my Loyalty to the Crowne of* England *than to signify unto you, that any such Meeting can be look'd upon no otherwise than as contrary to the peace of our Soveraigne Lord & Lady King* William *& Queen* Mary *their Crowne & Dignity: and therefore I must on their Majesties behalfe warne you, that you presume not to assemble at* Cambridge *or any other place within this County, for any such unlawfull purpose aforesaid; but that you do at all times bear good Faith & Allegiance to their sacred Majesties, as you will answer the contrary at your perill.*

Dated in Charlestowne this 21st day of September in the first yeare of the Reigne of our Soveraigne Lord and lastly King WILLIAM *and Queen* MARY Annoq *Dom. 1689.*[4]

The Answer of *Thomas Greaves* Esq. to Mr. *Broadstreete* & the Gentlemen met at the Town-house in *Boston* concerning the aforesaid Writing.

Mr. Thomas Greaves *being Summoned to make his appearance at Boston, on the 24 of Septemb. 1689. at which time Mr.* Broadstreete *produced a paper which was shewed Mr. Greaves, demanding if he knew it, (who answered he did)*

4. ["In the year of our Lord 1689."]

it was proposed for a Reading, but Mr. Greaves *made answer,* They need not give themselves that Trouble, for he fully knew the Contents and owned it to be his Act. But it was Read; after the Reading Mr. *Broadstreete* made a Speech to Mr. *Greaves,* in fine saying, He would say no more till Mr. *Greaves* made Answer; which he had ready prepared in *Writing,* as followeth *Viz.*

> *As to the paper delivered to Mr. James Russell I judge I did but my duty in it, & therefore cannot in conscience recede from it, & I shall be ready to answer King William & Queen Mary whensoever they or any authorized from them shall call me to account for the same. I am sworne to the Crown of England, & your selves have proclaimed King* William *& Queen* Mary *to be the rightfull Soveraigns of the Realmes and Territories belonging thereunto; Therefore I cannot own any Lawfull* Authority *in any untill I be legally informed that they have Commission from their Sacred Majestyes.*
>
> Thomas Greaves.

FINIS.

· 4 ·

[Edward Littleton], The Groans of the Plantations (London, 1689)

During the closing decades of the seventeenth century, Barbados was the most heavily peopled and most valuable colony in English America. Having been the first English colony to produce sugar successfully, to develop a plantation agricultural system, and to make extensive use of African slavery, it quickly developed an articulate elite that did not hesitate to express its political opposition to measures emanating from metropolitan authorities in London. Edward Littleton was a successful planter, and his pamphlet offered a powerful critique of post-Restoration England's commercial policy toward its colonies. The immediate spur for the pamphlet was a new supplementary duty imposed by Parliament upon West Indian sugar imports into England. But Littleton seized the occasion also to express Barbadian discontent with the older duties and to spell out the pernicious effects of English trade laws, in particular those regulations that confined West Indian sugar to English markets, upon Barbados's economic welfare. In the course of developing this protest, Littleton provided a detailed portrait of the nature of the colonial sugar industry as it had developed over the previous fifty years and its declining profits, of the colony's dependence on enslaved labor and the high cost of defending the settlers from the numerically superior black population, and as a generator of English wealth, both by its exports and by its extensive consumption of English goods.

But the principal subject of the pamphlet was the nature of the relationship between England and the colonies. Attributing the offensive measures to "projectors" who had misled the government about their certain consequences, Littleton dilated upon the injustice of improving the plantations "to the advantage of England" at the expense of the colonies. Arguing that "equal justice" and "the equal distribution of publique Burdens" were the essence of every political society and the hallmarks of English governance, he condemned the duties for subjecting the planters to a condition worse than that of foreigners. For English subjects overseas, he observed in passages that would become a central theme in colonial political writings about the structure of the emerging empire, England was the "*Center* to which all things tend." He emphasized the settlers' pride in their English heritage, articulated their sense of themselves as English people with full entitlement to English liberties, enunciated their wish to be treated as "a part of *England*" and to be "cherish[ed] . . . as *English* men," and pleaded for treatment equal to other English people. (J.P.G.)

THE GROANS of the PLANTATIONS:

OR

A True ACCOUNT

OF THEIR

Grievous and Extreme Sufferings

By the Heavy

IMPOSITIONS

UPON

SUGAR,

And other HARDSHIPS.

Relating more particularly to the

ISLAND of *BARBADOS*.

LONDON, Printed by *M. Clark* in the Year MDCLXXXIX

The Groans of the Plantations.

You have here the Case of the Plantations presented to your view: which you will find to be most lamentable. You will find, that as the Old Duties upon Sugar did fleece *us, so the Addition of the New doth* flea *us. And you will likewise perceive, that when we treat of these Matters, our Minds are sometimes under great disturbances. There are some things that make even wise Men mad, and therefore We, who do not pretend to that high attainment, must not be wondered at; if in the Anguish of our Souls we let fall some Expressions, that seem little better than* Ravings. *However we thought it concern'd us to lay open our Condition in any manner, that so the World may know, by what cruel Methods, and by what fatal Degrees, the once flourishing English Colonies have been brought to ruine. But our chief end is to get Relief which if it cannot be had, (as God forbid but it should); it will yet be some Comfort in our Miseries, if we obtain Compassion.*

In former times we accounted our selves a part of *England:* and the Trade and Entercourse was open accordingly so that Commodities, came hither as freely from the Sugar Plantations, as from the Isles of *Wight* or *Anglesey.*

But upon the King's Restauration we were in effect made Forainers and Aliens: a Custom being laid upon our Sugars amongst other Forain Commodities. And this was in higher Proportion than others; that is, above the common Poundage of Twelve Pence in the Pound. For eighteen pence a Hundred was laid upon *Muscovadoes,* and five Shillings upon *Whites:* the common price of the *Muscovado* Hundred being little above twenty Shillings, and the *Whites* under fifty.

At the same time the Duty of four and a half *per Cent.* was extorted from us in *Barbados,* full sore against our Wills. For it may well be imagined, that we had no mind to burden our own Commodities. The uses of this Duty were pretended and express'd to be; For support of the Government, and for the publick Services of the Island. But the Duty was soon farmed out for Money payable in *England.* Which Money hath been here paid, and none of the Uses performed, nor any thing allowed towards them. And all the Applications that we have made for it, have been without success. So that we make and repair our Forts and Brest works, we build our Magazines, we buy our great Guns and Ammunition; and are forced to lay great Taxes upon our selves, for defraying these and all other publick Charges. Moreover this *four and a half* is collected in such manner, that in the Judgment of all that have tryed it, the Attendance and Slavery is a greater burden than the Duty.

Upon the laying these Impositions (the one in *England*, the other in *Barbados*) the price of Sugar continued the same: nor could we in the least advance it, either then or any time since. So that we find plainly, that we the poor Planters bear the whole burden of these Duties: and whatever we pay, year after year, by occasion of them; is the same thing in effect, as a Land-Tax upon our Estates.

Let us now consider the proportion of this Tax: and first, what it comes to in *Muscovadoes*. We will suppose that four pound and an half of this Sugar (which is the *Barbados* Duty) is there worth but six pence. This, with the eighteen pence paid in *England*, makes two Shillings. Since therefore we reckoned a Hundred of *Muscovado* at about twenty Shillings; you will say the Duties lie upon the Planter, as a Land-Tax of two Shillings in the Pound.

But this is not a true Reckoning, for if you will reckon right, you must consider; not what is the full Value of such a Hundred of Sugar, but what is the clear Profit. For out of this Profit the Planter pays the Duties: that is, by the payment of them his clear Gains are the less by two Shillings in each Hundred. The ordinary clear Profit of a Hundred of *Muscovado* may be about five Shillings: or hardly so much for, for one Hundred that yields it, three or four fall short. However, that we may a little flatter and deceive our selves, we will suppose this clear Profit to be six Shillings, and then the Duties draw two Shillings out of six, and are as a Land-Tax of a Noble in the pound. But if the Sugar yield only two and twenty Shillings, the Duty swallows up the whole Profit; if it yield but twenty, the Planter pays the Duty out of his Pocket and must live by the loss, and there is many a hundred of Sugar sold under twenty.

We have truly said, that the ordinary Profit of a *Muscovado* Hundred is but five Shillings since to clear so much, the Sugar must be sold for five and twenty: which is a full price. For it stands the Planter in twenty shillings: that is, ten the making, and ten the transporting. That the Cask, Fraight, and other Charges of the Transportation, come to ten shillings, for every hundred that comes to *England;* is known to all Merchants and Factors that use the Trade. And it is as well known to all Planters, that whoever makes

Sugar for ten shillings a Hundred, shall not get a Groat a day for his *Negroes* labour: though he reckon nothing for his Land, nor for his great and chargeable Buildings. And these *Negroes* stand him in near thirty pound a Head, by that time they are seasoned. So that they cannot in truth be afforded, to work at such low and miserable Wages.

Thus we see that it is a great Mistake to think, that the old Duties upon Sugar, are but as a trifling Land-Tax of two shillings yearly in the pound. Though even this, in *England,* would not be accounted a Trifle: it being more than the Tax of seventy thousand pounds a Month, made perpetual. For that monthly Tax, take one place with another, doth not amount to more than eighteen pence in the pound for the whole year. Where as our old Duties, as it hath been made out, a regular constant Land-Tax of a Noble: in the pound: and shear from us in third part of our Estates.

If the Impositions be thus heavy upon *Muscovado* Sugars, they are much worse upon *Whites:* which pay more than treble the Duty, and seldom reach double the price. Though in reason, it must be confess'd, their price should be treble: considering the Room and the Time they take in Curing, together with the Labour and the Waste. But there is no disputing: we must take for them what we can get.

It was some ease to us for a while, that though our Sugars were so burden'd in *England,* yet they came free to our Northern Plantations in *America.* But this did not long continue. For it pleased the Parliament of *England* to stretch forth their Hands, and to lay them upon us in those remote Parts, they having made an Act, which is dutifully obeyed, That all Sugars that go to the Plantations aforesaid, shall pay the said Duty of eighteen pence and five shillings, at the Places from whence they are exported. So that now we have no way to avoid any part of the Burden. Which also is a grievous Clog to our Commerce with those Plantations.

The Burden of the Duties paid before Exportation is then most sensible, and seems to press hardest upon us, when the Goods for which we have paid them are lost at Sea. Which sometimes happens before our faces, if the *Hurricane* catch the Ships before they sail. We therefore thought it not unreasonable to expect the same favour, that Merchants (in the like case) have in *England* and other places, to Ship off the like Quantity Custom-free. And we prepared and pass'd an Act for that purpose: which we also transmitted to *England* humbly hoping, that we should find no difficulty in obtaining the Royal Assent. But by it we incurr'd very great displeasure: and our Act was not only disallowed, whereby it became of no effect, but we were commanded expresly to repeal it, which we did, with Hearts full of Sorrow.

Moreover there are divers things, whereby our Condition is made worse than it was in former Times, and which make us less able to bear these Impositions. Of which Things I shall name some few.

Heretofore we could Ship off our Goods at any Port, or Bay, or Creek; and at any time, either by day or by night. But now since the Kings Restauration we must do it at those Times and Places only, at which the Collectors of the Customs please to attend.

Heretofore we might send our Commodities to any part of the World. But now we must send them to *England*, and to no Place else. By which means the whole Trade of Sugars to the *Streights*, (to say nothing of other Places), is lost both to Us and to the *English* Nation. For by multiplying our Charge, others can undersell us. We hear of a certain old Law in *Scotland*, which obliged the Fishermen to bring their Fish into the *Scottish* Markets, before they might Ship them off. And surely if they had studied seven years, for a Law to destroy their Fishing Trade, they could not have found one more effectual. In the like manner it may be truly affirmed, that the bringing all Sugars to the *English* Market, hath gone a great way in destroying that Trade. As for confining the Plantation Trade to *English* Ships and *English* Men, though it be to our particular Loss, (for the *Dutch* were very beneficial to us); yet we took it in good part, in regard our great and dear Mother of *England* hath by it such vast Advantages. But that *English* Ships and *English* Men should not be permitted to trade to their best convenience and profit, is a thing we cannot understand. The great End and Design of Trade, as to the Publick, is to get the foreign Money: and such means should be used, as do most conduce to that End.

Heretofore the things we wanted were brought to us from the Places where they might best be had. But now we must have them from *England*, and from no other Place. Had we been confined to *England* only, for those Things that *England* doth produce, we should have been well contented. But that we must fetch from *England* the Things that are produced elsewhere, seems very hard. We are sure it makes the Prices excessive to us.

Heretofore we might send to *Guiney* for *Negroes* when we wanted them and they stood us in about seven pound a Head. The Account is short and plain. For they cost about the value of forty shillings a Head in *Guiney*; and their freight was five pound, for every one that was brought alive, and could go over the Ship side. But now we are shut out of this Trade: and a Company is put upon us, from whom we must have our *Negroes,* and no other way. A Company of *London* Merchants have got a Patent, excluding all others, to furnish the Plantations with *Negroes:* some great Men being joyned with them, with whom we were not able to contend. But those great Men might have had some better Exercise for their Generosity, than the pressing too hard upon (we must not say, oppressing) industrious People. And now we buy *Negroes* at the price of an Engross'd Commodity: the common Rate of a good *Negro* on Ship board being twenty pound. And we are forced to scramble for them in so shameful a Manner, that one of the great Burdens of our Lives is the going to buy *Negroes.* But we must have them; we cannot be without them and the best Men in those Countries must in their own Persons submit to the Indignity.

There never want fair Pretences for the foulest Monopolies. But what do they pretend for this? They will tell you, that (to the common Good and Benefit of the *English* Nation) they can deal with the People of *Africa* to much better advantage, by being a Company. And so they might, if they could shut out other Nations. But since the *Dutch, French, Danes, Swedes,* and others, trade thither, and they can shut out none but the poor *English;* their being a Company, as to their dealing with the Natives, signifies nothing. And it plainly appears, that 'tis not upon the People of *Africa,* but upon the *English* Planters in *America,* that they make their advantage. They will also tell you of the necessity of Forts and Garrisons, and that a Company was therefore necessary. But these might have been made and maintain'd without a Company, by an Imposition upon *Negroes* sold, or some such Tax, to which the Plantations would cheerfully have submitted.

It may well be imagin'd, (no, it cannot be imagin'd), how the Company and their Agents Lord it over us, having us thus in their power. And if any offer at the Trade beside themselves, they make such Examples of them, that few dare follow them. If they catch us at *Guiney,* they use us down right as Enemies. And at home we are drag'd into the Admiralty Courts, and condemned in a trice, there is not such speedy Justice in all the World. And the word is, that we are found Prize; or condemn'd as Prize as if we were Forrainers, taken in open War.

They have got a trick of late, to bring *Interlopers* within the Acts of Navigation or Trade: which are the severe Acts about Plantations. But even in this case we are brought into the Admiralty, what ever the Law says to the contrary. Nor doth it avail us to plead, that all Offences against Statutes must be tryed by Jury.

The Forfeitures of the Acts before named (which are never less than Ship and Goods) are given to the King, the Governour, and the Informer. The Governour, in these Matters, sits chief Judge of the Court: I am sure *Dutton* did in his time. The Company's Agents, who are the Informers, (or some Servant in their behalf) sit with him, and as soon as Sentence is given, they divide the Spoyle. And what ever becomes of the Kings share, we may be sure the Pains takers will not lose theirs. But the while the Kings Subjects in those Parts are in a blessed Condition.

They contemn the Laws against Monopolies: and they tell us, that the Laws of *England* are not in force among us in this Matter, though they are in all things else, save only where our own Special Laws do make some difference.

Of all the Things we have occasion for, *Negroes* are the most necessary, and the most valuable. And therefore to have them under a Company, and under a Monopoly, whereby their prices are more then doubled, nay almost trebled; cannot but be most grievous to us. Many an Estate hath been sunk, and many a Family hath been ruin'd, by the high prices they give for *Negroes*. One would think, that while we were under such a Company, there were little need of Impositions to undo us.

These Duties and these Hardships we have lain under, during the Reign of King *Charles* the Second. And we have born them as well as we could. But some were not able: and sunk under the Weight, being put out of all Capacity, to pay these Debts, and provide for their Families. For having so many Pressures beside, they could not undergo those Impositions, by which a third part of their Estates was lop't off. Where a Man had threescore pound a year in all the World, and found it little enough, and too little; it was too hard upon him to pay twenty pound a year out of it. Also if a Planter be in debt (as most of us are), so that not a fourth part of his Estate comes clear to him, above the Interest he paies; how is he able to pay a third part in Taxes?

Upon the coming of King *James* to the Crown, a Parliament being called, We were preparing a Complaint against the Commissioners of the Customs. Who had taken a liberty of late, to our grievous prejudice, to call that *White* Sugar, which had never been accounted such before, and which was far from that Colour. And whatever They pleased to call *Whites*, must pay the Duty of five shillings the Hundred.

But we were soon forced to lay aside these Thoughts, to provide against a new Storm that threaten'd. For we were told, to our great Astonishment, that a Project was set on foot to lay more Load upon us: no less then seven Groats a Hundred more upon *Muscovado,* and seven shillings upon Sugars *fit for Use* for that was now the word. We saw this tended plainly to our destruction. but the thing was driven on furiously by some *Empsons* and *Dudleys* about the late King; who did not care how many People they destroyed, so they might get Favour and Preferment for themselves.

Since we were put into the Heard of Forrainers, and paid Duties with them; we hoped we should fare no worse than other Forrainers did. But that the Plantations should be singled out, as the hunted Deer; and the burden upon their Commodities should be doubled and almost trebled, when all others were untoucht; was matter of Amazement and Consternation. We humbly moved, that if the whole Tax must be laid upon Trade, it might be laid upon all Commodities alike. We said that a small advance upon all the Customs, might serve every purpose, as well as a great one upon some and that this might be born with some ease, there being so many shoulders to bear it. But they would hearken to nothing of that kind: being resolved and fixt to lay the whole burden upon the Plantations. Which could not but seem very strange to us.

But here lay the Mystery. The Projectors consider'd, that if other Forrainers were hardly used in *England,* they would carry or send their Commodities to other Places. But we poor *English Forrainers* are compell'd to bring all Hither, and therefore they thought they could hold Our Noses to the Grind stone, and make us pay what they pleased.

However they told us, that this new Duty should do us no hurt: in regard it was to be paid by the Buyer. But this we knew to be a meer Mockery (the Mockery seem'd almost as bad as the Cruelty.) For if an Impost be laid upon the Sugar, who ever pays it, the Planter is sure to bear it. VVhat avails it though the Buyer pays the Duty, if the Seller must presently allow it in the price?

The Brewer hath a certain price for his Beer: and he adds the Excise or Duty to his price: and the Customer pays it. But where the price is uncertain, and a bargain is to be driven, and a Duty yet to be paid; the first word of this bargain will be, who must pay the Duty? And 'tis not the Appointment of Law, but the Agreement of the Parties, that must decide the question. In Our case, the Buyer will naturally be at this lock: If you clear the Duty, I will give you so much for a Hundred of your White Sugar; if I must pay it, you must have seven shillings less. Which is as broad as long.

The Buyer, they say, must pay the Duty, but sure the Seller may pay it if he please. And he will please to pay it, rather then not sell his Sugar. If He will not, there are enow beside that will.

This Duty upon Sugar is the same thing in effect, as a Duty of twelve pence a Bushel would be upon Corn. Though it be said that the Buyer shall pay this, yet the Seller or the Farmer would be sure to feel it, and it would be a heavy Tax upon the Land.

These plain things notwithstanding, and what ever else we could say, the *Projectors* stood stoutly to it in the Parliament house, that the New Tax upon Sugars should not burden the Plantations. But this was esteemed such barbarous Nonsense, that there was little fear of their prevailing, had not the late King (to our great unhappiness) been so strangely earnest for this Tax. Which yet that Parliament, who then denied him nothing, had never granted, but that some Privy Councellors assured them, in the Kings name and as by his Order; that if the Duty proved grievous to the Plantations, it should be taken off, and be no longer collected.

So the Act passed, and the Plantations are ruin'd. For now we feel, what we certainly foresaw, that the whole Burden of this new Duty lies upon the Plantations. No Chapman will meddle with our Sugars, unless we clear the Duty. Which when we have done, we are so far from being able to advance the price, that it is rather lower than ever it was before. 'Tis not Impositions, but Plenty and Scarcity that rules the Market. And it is found by constant Experience, That where an Impost is laid upon a Commodity in demand, there the Buyer may be brought to bear some part of it. But if the Market be glutted, and the Commodity be a Drug, (as Ours is, and for ever will be); in this case the Buyer will bear no part of the Duty, but the Seller must pay it all.

It hath been said before, that the cleer Profit of a Hundred of *Muscovado* Sugar, take one with another, may be about five shillings: or to reckon largely, about six. And you have seen that the old Duties upon that sort are two shillings; and the new, two shillings four pence. So that the Duties do now take four shillings four pence out of six shillings. Which sweeps away above two thirds of our Estates, and lies upon us as an effectual Land-Tax of fourteen shillings in the pound.

To make the Computation another way; We find that what we pay yearly in Duties, is much more then the whole Rent of our Lands. And if this be true (as it is most true) in *Barbados,* where we reckon our Land at twenty shillings an Acre; it goes to a greater degree in the other Plantations, where Land is much cheaper. But by this means we are wholly stripp'd of our Lands and Freeholds, and are made worse then Rack-Tenants. For we have not the whole profit of our Stocks to live upon; since a good part even of this, must go help to pay our Taxes.

The ordinary midling price of *Muscovado* Sugars, hath been reckoned at six and twenty shillings a hundred at most. For as it hath been said, many are sold under twenty. And on the other side if they rise to thirty shillings, they will be adjudged *fit for Use:* many under that price being so adjudged. In which case they must pay seven shillings a Hundred for the new Duty, beside the old Duties which come to two shillings. If we do but Sun-dry our Sugar, to keep it from running away in its passage home; this pitiful stuff will be adjudged *fit for Use,* and must pay the seven shillings. But if the Sugars will reach five and thirty shillings, they are sure to be adjudged *Whites.* And then they pay seven shillings for the new Duty, and five shillings for the old beside the Duty in *Barbados,* which in such Sugar comes to neer eighteen pence. Which makes in the whole above thirteen shillings: and for the most part is more then the whole Gains of that Sugar.

Whereas we talk of Sugars adjudged *fit for Use,* and others adjudged to be *Whites;* You will ask, where and in what Court are these things adjudged? I answer, In the Court of the High Commissioners. You will say, the Court of High Commissioners is damned. Why then, to speak plainly, we mean the Commissioners of the Customs: those are Our High Commissioners. And 'tis They that adjudge these Matters, at their discretion.

I know it doth not become us, considering our Condition, to jest at these Matters. But our Miseries make us savage: they make us forget all Rules of Decency.

All other Duties are put in certainty: and so might Ours too. But We only are thought fit to be left to discretion. But how should the Duties upon Sugars be made certain? By letting them be according to the value of the Sugars. And if the Officer, or any for him, had liberty to take the Sugars at ten *per Cent* under the price given in, no man would give an under value.

In *Barbados,* we can get but little by making Sugar (though it had none of these Burdens) except we improve it: that is, purge it, and give it a Colour. Others can live by making plain Sugar: We must live by the improved. This is all the help we have, against the disadvantages we ly under: in this we are willing to take Pains, and content to take Time; and in this lies the Planters chiefest Skill. But the Duties fall so terribly upon our improved Sugars, that it doth quite discourage and confound us. Our Ingenuity is baffled, and our Industry cut up by the roots: here they have us, and there they have us; and we know not which way to turn our selves.

We can make shift sometimes to put off our fine Sugar to some little Profit, above the Charges and the Duties. But our *Course-Clayed* (and much of our Sugar is such, for all will not be fine) is quite beaten out of the Pit. We cannot sell it in *England* but with so great Loss, that it would turn us suddenly a begging. We are therefore forced to Ship it off for Forrain Markets: half the old Duty (I mean that in *England*) being allowed us back. But then new Cask must be bought, and new Fraight must be paid, and there are all the Charges of unshipping it and shipping it again, and the half Duty still lyes upon us. So that we are upon very unequal terms with those Sellers of other Nations, who are suffer'd to come directly to those Markets. Whereas we are compell'd to bring these Sugars first to *England*, where we cannot sell them, which makes our Condition most lamentable. Moreover the Forrain Markets are glutted as well as Ours: and there also we meet with new Duties and Impositions. For other People have learn'd by the Example of *England*, to load us without Mercy. Upon the whole Matter; the Sugars we thus Ship off, do turn for the most part to a poor and miserable account.

The *Projectors* did pride themselves in the drawing of the New Act: as a thing of great Art and Skill, whereas of all that ever were drawn, it is the most foolish. This is not spoken, to reflect upon the Wisdom of the Parliament that past the Act, but upon the Projectors Folly that drew it. Their Folly lies in this, that they make so much ado about nothing. So many confounded turnings and windings, Bonds to be given and taken up again, other things to be done and undone; and all to make an appearance of obliging the Buyer to pay the Duty, which is not effected in any measure, nor ever can be. But in the mean while, all these things lick Money from the Planter. For the Officers will have their Fees for every thing they do. And if any thing should be ordered to be done without Fee, it would never be done. Also by this means the Facture is made so uneasy, so troublesome, so vexatious and slavish; that none care to meddle with our Commissions. Heretofore our Commissions were courted: but now they go a begging. One good thing there is in the *Projectors* Contrivances, that by means of them we have some Time for payment of the Duties. But if they had given us the Time, and kept all the rest to themselves, leaving us to pay the Duty directly and the plain way, without so much as naming their Consumptioner; they had done us a Courtesy.

These heavy Duties have been exacted from us, not only with extremity of Rigour, but also with manifest Injustice and Oppression. As we can particularly make it out, when ever we are called to it.

We have been in the hands of Men without Mercy: who delighted in the Calamities of the People; and who would willingly have seen the whole Kingdom of *England,* in the same miserable Condition that the Plantations are in. Our Sufferings were but a Prelude to the *French* Government: Or, as a leading Card. Of which Government it is an essential part, that People in general pay all they are worth in Taxes.

We made our humble Applications several times to the late King, and laid our Distresses before him. But he was not pleased to take off our Burdens or any part of them, nor to give us the least Ease or Mitigation. One time we were referr'd to the Commissioners of the Customs: amongst whom (to our comfort) we might find our Friends the Projectors. Another time we were told by a Great Minister of State (who was a principal Projector likewise, and who was to give us our Answer) *That it was very undecent, not to say undutiful, to tax the King with his Promise.* When as we had only said in our submissive Petition, That we had been encouraged to Address to his Majesty, by the gracious Expressions he had been pleased to use in Parliament, concerning his Plantations.

We cannot now be at the Charge to procure and keep White Servants, or to entertain Freemen as we used to do. Nor will they now go upon any terms to a Land of Misery and Beggery. So that our *Militia* must fall: and we shall be in no Capacity to defend our selves, either against a Forrain Enemy, or against our own *Negroes.*

In the mean time our poor Slaves bear us Company in our Mones, and groan under the burden of these heavy Impositions. They know that by reason of them, They must fare and work the harder. And that their Masters cannot now allow them, and provide for them, as they should and would.

It is no wonder if Planters break (as now they do every day) since they ly under such heavy Burdens. We send our Bills to *England,* designing they should be paid out of the produce of the Sugars we send with them. But the clear Profit of our Sugars being swallowed up by the Impositions; Our Bills are not paid, but come back Protested; and our Debts remain and increase upon us. And at last our Estates are torn in pieces to pay them, and will not do it.

Most of Us Planters are behind hand, and in debt. and so we were, before the Impositions gave us their helping hand. For there is no place in the World, where it is so easy to run into debt, and so hard to get out of it. But now these heavy Impositions do so disable us, that we can by no means contend with Interest, but must sink under it. Heretofore we endeavour'd to work out our Debts; but now we must work to pay our Taxes.

Many that had good Estates four years ago, are now worse then nothing, and in a starving Condition: these heavy Impositions having quite undone them. It were a Mercy to take away our Lives, rather then leave them to us with so much bitterness. They that have Puppies or Kitlings, more then they are willing to keep; choose rather to drown them, then to let them perish miserably for want of Sustenance. And those poor little Creatures find so much pity, that when they must live no longer, People take care to give them an easy Death. But we poor Planters cannot have that favour. It is our hard lot to live, depriv'd of the Comforts and Supports of Life.

What have we done, or wherein have we offended, that we should be used in this manner? Or what strange Crime have we committed, to make us the Object of so great Severities? And how have we incurred the displeasure of *England*, our great and dear Mother? The very Sense of our dear Mothers displeasure (though the direful Effects had not followed), and the very Thought that we are grown hateful to her, is worse then death it self. Had we been in the hands of our Enemies, and They had set themselves to crush and oppress us; it had been in some measure to be born, because we could expect no better, but to be ruin'd by those, by whom we hoped to be cherish't and protected, is wholly unsupportable.

These things notwithstanding, our Hearts continue as firm to *England*, as if all were well with us. Nor can any Usage lessen our Obsequious Devotion to our dear and native Country. We renounce the Doctrine of *Grotius*, That Colonies owe an Observance to their Mother Country, but not an Obedience. It is Obedience as well as Observance, that we owe eternally to *England*; and though our dear Mother prove never so unkind, we cannot throw off our Affection and Duty to her. We had rather continue our Subjection to *England*, in the sad Condition we are in; then be under any others in the World, with the greatest Ease and Plenty. No Advantages can tempt us to hearken to any such thing: nor can move in the least our stedfast

Loyalty. In this matter we shall stop our Ears, even to the wisest Charmers. Nor shall we only not affect such a Change, but we shall likewise oppose it to the uttermost of our power. Upon such an occasion, we shall cheerfully expose our selves to hardships and dangers of every kind; and fight for our Drudgery and Beggery, as freely as others do for their Liberties and Fortunes. Nay though it were represented to us, that our setting up for our selves were never so feasible and beneficial; yet we should loathe that Liberty, that would rob us of our dependence upon our dear native Country.

We, and those under whom we claim, have (without any Assistance from the Publick) settled these Plantations, with very great Expence and Charge, with infinite Labour, with Hazards innumerable. and with Hardships that cannot be exprest. And now when we thought to have had some fruit of our Industry, we find our selves most miserably disappointed. Our Measures are broken, and our Hopes are confounded, and our Fortunes are at once ruined, by Pressures and Taxes which we are not able to bear. Is all our Care and Pains come to this? and is this the End and Upshot of all our Adventures? Have we gone so many hundred Leagues, and hewed out our Fortunes in another World; to have the Marrow suck'd out of our Bones by Taxes and Impositions? Had these things been foreseen, it had cool'd the Courage of our most forward Adventurers. They would never have gone so far, to be made Rogues of by those that staid at home. They would have thought it more advisable to sit by the Fire side, and to sleep in a whole Skin.

Many of us have our Estates by purchase: and we thought we had purchased Estates, but now they prove just nothing, though most commonly we laid out upon them all we had, and all that we could borrow.

Some of the Plantations, 'tis true, came to *England* by Conquest. But must the Conquerors themselves be look't upon as a conquered People? It were very strange, if those that bring Countries under the Dominion of *England*, and maintain the possession, should by so doing lose their own *English* Liberties.

In former daies we were under the pleasing sound of Priviledges and Immunities, of which a free Trade was one, though we counted That, a Right and not a Priviledge. But without such Encouragements, the Plantations had been still wild Woods. Now those things are vanisht and forgotten: and we hear of nothing but Taxes and Burdens. All the Care now is, to pare us close, and keep us low. We dread to be mention'd in an Act of Parliament; because it is alwaies to do us Mischief.

We hear that the People of *Carolina* go upon the making of Silk: which surely is one of the best Commodities in the World, and the Design seems very hopeful. But it were but fair to let them know before hand, That when they have brought their matters to any perfection, there will be ways found to leave them not worth a Groat; and to make them miserable Drudges and Beggers, even as We are. It will then be time for them, to be improved to the advantage of *England*.

The Improvement of the Plantations to the advantage of *England* sounds so bravely, and seems to the Projectors a thing so plausible; that they would have it believed to be their chief Aim and End, in all that they do against us. And then they think they talk very wisely, when they talk of Improving the Plantations to the advantage of *England*. Just as a Landlord would improve his Mannor, by racking his Lands to the utmost Rent, or as the Masters of Slaves, improve and contrive their Labour to their own best advantage. But it is our misery and ruin to be thus improved. And so it would be to the Counties of Wales, or any *English* Counties, to be improved to the advantage of the rest.

The certain Charges of a Sugar-work are so great, and the Casualties so many; that it were no easy matter to bear up against them, though there were no other Pressure. The very hanging of our Coppers and Stills is a great constant Charge. It comes often to be done; and every one of them that is new hang'd, doth cost us one way or other at least three pound. Beside, they are perpetually burning out and spoyling: and the buying of new ones comes to a great deal of Money.

We must have yearly some hundred pairs of Sugar-Pots and Jarrs. Every hundred pair doth cost neer ten pound; and we must fetch them several Miles upon *Negroes* Heads.

The Wear of our Mills (to say nothing now of the Tear, which is casual) is also a continual Charge to us. And if a Mill be to be new built, and made perfect in all its parts, it costs neer five hundred pound.

The Fraight of every Servant that we have from *England* is five pound: and their Cloths and other Necessaries come to little less. Which Fraight and Charges the Masters of Ships will be allowed for them, if they are brought over upon the Ships account. Their Time may not be above five years, and is commonly but four.

We must have a great many Horses, and (in *Barbados*) we scarce breed any. The Fraight of a Horse from *England* (with his Hay and Water) is ten pound, and a great hazard of losing him by the way.

He that hath but a hundred *Negroes,* should buy half a dozen every year to keep up his stock. And they will cost, as it hath been noted, about twenty pound a Head.

A good Over seer will have a hundred pound a year. Some give a great deal more. There are others also that must have great Salaries, and we cannot be without them.

The ramassing the vast quantities of Dung we must use, the carrying it to the Field, and disposing it there; is a mighty Labour, which in effect is Charge. An Acre of ground well dress'd, will take thirty load of Dung: and he that hath two Wind mills, must plant yearly neer a hundred Acres.

We carry Mould and Cane-Trash, or any thing that is proper, into our Cattle-Pens, and into our Still-Ponds; to turn all into Dung. We take all ways and means for the raising of Dung; and we rake and scrape Dung out of every Corner. Some save the Urine of their People (both Whites and Blacks) to increase and enrich their Dung.

We make high and strong Walls or VVears to stop the Mould that washes from our Grounds: which we carry back in Carts or upon *Negroes* heads. Our *Negroes* work at it like Ants or Bees.

Moreover the Charge of our *Militia* is exceeding great upon us. In *Barbados,* every twenty Acres must find a Footman, and every forty Acres a Horseman. So that an Estate of five hundred Acres sends five Horsemen and fifteen Foot, which is more then is done here by the greatest Peer in *England.* Perhaps this may seem incredible; but it is most true, for our Law is expresly so, and it is strictly executed. Also every one that keeps a Horse, must serve on Horseback; and every other Housekeeper must serve on foot. Otherwise our *Militia* could not rise (as it doth) to six Regiments of Foot and two Regiments of Horse; beside a Life-Guard for the Governour, of a hundred Gentlemen. and all this, in a Place no bigger then the Isle of *Wight.* It must be added, that the other Plantations have as great a Share of this Burden: that is to say, in proportion to the value of their Estates though not to the Quantity of their Land. And we are forced to be thus upon our Guard, and to strain our selves in this manner; our All lying at stake, our Enemies being near us, and our Friends (if we have any) being far from us. But we in *Barbados* have a Charge extraordinary in this Matter, for all that serve in Our *Militia* must appear in Red Coats. This was put upon us by *Dutton* when he was Governour. He would have it; and made us insert it in our Act of *Militia*. And it hath driven many a poor House keeper from off the Island.

If the constant Charge of a Plantation is terrible, the Casualties do not come behind. For let a Planter be never so careful, he must ly open to many and various Accidents: and like *Job*'s Messengers, one in the neck of another, his People will bring him Tidings of continual Losses and Disasters.

We cannot say that Horses and Cattle are much more casual with us, then they are in other places, only our loss is the greater, in regard they cost us much dearer. But our Canes, on which we rely and which are our Estate, are too often burnt down before our faces when they are ready to cut. They are then like Tinder: and if a Fire get amongst them, a whole Field of them is consumed in a few Minutes. Also our Boyling-houses and Still-houses are very subject to Fire.

Sometimes we suffer by extreme Droughts, and sometimes by continual violent Rains. And a sudden Gust will tear or maim our Windmills. But if a *Hurricane* come, it makes a desolation: and puts us to begin the World anew. The damage it does the Planter is sometimes so great, that the profit of divers years must go to repair it.

Our Negroes, which cost us so dear are also extremely casual. When a man hath bought a parcel of the best and ablest he can get for money; let him take all the care he can, he shall lose a full third part of them, before they ever come to do him service. When they are season'd, and used to the Country, they stand much better, but to how many Mischances are they still subject? If a Stiller slip into a Rum-Cistern, it is sudden death: for it stifles in a moment. If a Mill-feeder be catch't by the finger, his whole body is drawn in, and he is squeez'd to pieces. If a Boyler get any part into the scalding Sugar, it sticks like Glew, or Birdlime, and 'tis hard to save either Limb or Life. They will quarrell, and kill one another, upon small occasions: by many Accidents they are disabled, and become a burden: they will run away, and perhaps be never seen more: or they will hang themselves, no creature knows why. And sometimes there comes a Mortality amongst them, which sweeps a great part of them away.

When this happens, the poor Planter is in a hard condition: especially if he be still indebted for them. He must have more Negroes, or his Works must stand, and he must be ruin'd at once. And he cannot procure them without contracting new Debts; which perhaps he shall never be able to work out.

These are some of the Charges and Casualties that attend Plantations. It would be too tedious to number them all; and they are hardly to be numbered.

If out *Empsons* and *Dudleys* had duly consider'd these things, they would have laid aside their inhumane Project against the poor Plantations. But they consider nothing, but how they may do most mischief.

These are the Men that will perswade Princes, that it is a more glorious Conquest to crush their own Subjects, then to subdue an Enemy.

These Men seem to be trying Conclusions, whether they can so far provoke us, as to make us desperate. And as much as in them lyes, they would make the very Name of *England* hatefull to us. But there is no danger. For we shall bear whatsoever is laid upon us, with the most submissive patience; and nothing can make us forget or lay down our love, to the *English* Name and Nation.

They would make our Great and Dear Mother, *England*, to be so cruel and unnatural, as to destroy and devour her own Children.

They would put us in the dismal Condition of those that said, being opprest by a hard Master; *Subjectos nos habuit tanquam suos, & viles ut alienos. We are commanded as Subjects, and we are crusht as Aliens.* Which Condition is the most dismall and horrid, that people can be under.

They would use us like Sponges: or like Sheep. They think us fit to be squeezed and fleeced; as soon as we have got any Moisture within us, or any Wooll upon us.

These *Egyptian* Tax masters would bring us into the State of *Villenage*. They would make us the Publique *Villeins*. They would have us work and labour, to pay the Publique Taxes, as far as it will go.

They would make meer *Gibeonites* of us: hewers of Wood, and drawers of Water. And tho these things must inevitably bring us to desolation and destruction, what do the Projectors care?

But although we are designed by the Projectors to be made perfect *Villeins*, yet they should remember, that even *Villeins* must not be misused too much. We are told out of old Law Books, that *'tis Wast for the Tenant to misentreat the Villeins of the Mannor, so that they depart from the Mannor, and depart from their tenures*. And in another place; *Destruction of Villeins by tallage is adjudged Wast*. In which Cases the Writ says; *Quod fecit Vastum, destructionem, & exilium.*[1] Surely in our Case; there is a plain destruction by Tallage.

The names of old *Empson* and *Dudley* are infamous and odious to this day. And they were hang'd for their Villianies. Yet they ruin'd men but singly,

1. ["That has made waste, destruction, and exile."]

and one by one. How much higher Gibbets, and how much greater detestation, do these men deserve, that have destroyed whole Countreys?

A Quack pretending great Skill, makes a Woman give her Child Arsenick: he facing her down, that Arsenick is not poyson. The Child is kill'd, and the Quack is hang'd. Even so our dear Mother hath seen a Cup of deadly Poyson, given to her Children the Plantations: these men (who would be thought great Quacks in Trade) giving the highest assurances that the Drench should do no harm: by which means the Plantations are murder'd and destroyed. And shall not these Men be hang'd? Some think they deserve it better, then all that have been hang'd at Tyburn this twice seven years.

The Projectors might think, in the Naughtiness of their hearts, that many would favour this Project against us, for their owne Ease: and would be willing, or at least content, to have the Plantations bear the whole Burden. Not caring how heavy the burden lay upon others, so they could shift it off from themselves. But this is a thing of so great baseness, that we are very confident, it cannot enter into the heart of any English man, the Projectors themselves excepted. At least there is no English Parliament but will put it far from them. They know that they are entrusted to do equal and righteous Things. They know that the raising of Money is one of the most important things in a State. If it be done equally, though the burden be heavy, yet it is born with cheerfulness. If otherwise, it occasions furious Discontents, and at last brings all to Confusion. When a Government falls once to shifting and sharking, (pardon the expression, I hope we are not concern'd in it); it is a great sign that that Government will not stand. No Society of Men can stand without equal Justice, which is the Lady and Queen of all the Vertues. If the equal dividing the common Booties, be necessary to Pirates and *Buccaneers;* the equal distribution of publique Burdens, is much more to a State.

But it is the Projectors base sharking Principle to make Inequality in these Matters: and to get Ease to themselves by laying the burden upon others. The Writer of these Papers heard one of them say (it was, after that the late Parliament had been so liberal: I forbear his Name, I would not put that Brand upon him): but he said Vauntingly, in his drink; *We have given the King several Millions of Money, and I shall not pay six pence towards it.* And yet he was a great landed Man, which also made the saying the less become him.

The *Projectors* chief skill is to fall upon the weakest, and make Them pay all. But then why do not they persuade the *Western* men, since they can out-vote the *Northern,* to make them pay all the Taxes, themselves paying nothing? Or why do they not single out a few Counties, which by the combining of the rest against them, may be made to pay Taxes for all the rest? The six *Western* Counties (for now the Dice are turn'd against Them) are in value above two Millions yearly. So that a Tax of two thirds (such as the Plantations now bear) would amount yearly to thirteen hundred thousand pounds. And if this were kept constantly upon them, all the rest of the Kingdom needed to pay nothing. But perhaps these things might cost a great deal of Noise. They might therefore, to go a smoother way, direct their Projects against Widows and Orphans, and Heirs within age. If these were tax'd, well towards the value of their Estates, it would be a great Ease to the rest of the Kingdom.

But our Masters the *Projectors* think they have a great advantage over us, in regard we have none to represent us in Parliament. 'Tis true, we have not: but we hope we may have them. It is no disparagement to the Kingdome of *Portugall*, rather it is the only thing that looks great; that in the assembly of their Estates, the Deputies of the City of *Goa* have their place, among their other Cities. But at present we have them not and what follows? Must we therefore be made meer Beasts of burden? It is not long, since the Bishoprick of *Durham* had any representatives in Parliament. But we do not find, that before they had this Priviledge, they were in the least over-laid with Taxes. Also there are now divers Counties that have but few Members in comparison. *Essex* hath but eight: whereas *Cornwall*, which is of much less value, hath above forty. But because they have not half their proportion of Members, must an advantage be taken against them, to make them pay double their proportion of Taxes?

They have a Saying Beyond Sea of Us English Men, that we will not let others live by us. The Saying is false: but if it were never so true, sure it would not hold among our selves, but is only in relation to Strangers. To be cruel to and among our selves, would be a Cruelty without Example. Even Wolves and Bears spare their own Kind; nor is there to be found so fell a Monster in Nature, as to deny his Brother Monsters their Means of living. What do the Projectors take us to be? Are we not of your own number? are we not English Men? Some of us pretend to have as good *English* Bloud in our Veins, as some of those that we left behind us. How came we to lose our Countrey, and the Priviledges of it? Why will you cast us out?

Suppose a Quantity of Land were gain'd here out of the Sea, by private Adventurers, as bigg as two or three Counties. (Never say that the thing is impossible; for we may suppose any thing.) Suppose also, that people went by degrees from all parts of *England,* to inhabit and cultivate this New Country. Would you now look upon these people as Forrainers and Aliens? Would you grudge at their Thriving and Prosperity, and ply them with all the methods of Squeezing and Fleecing? Would you forbid them all forrain Trade; and so burden their Trade to *England,* that their Estates should become worth nothing? Would you make them pay the full value of their Lands in Taxes and Impositions? It cannot be thought that you would do these things. Rather you would esteem the Country a part of *England,* and cherish the People as *English* Men. And why may not the Plantations expect the like Kindness and Favour? If the thing be duly weighed, They also are meer Additions and Accessions to *England,* and Enlargements of it. And our case is the very same with the case supposed. Only herein lies the difference, that there is a distance and space between *England* and the Plantations. So that we must lose our Country upon the account of Space. a thing little more then imaginary: a thing next neighbour to nothing.

The Citizens of *Rome,* though they lived in the remotest Parts of the World then known, were still *Roman* Citizens to all Intents. But we poor Citizens of *England,* as soon as our backs are turn'd, and we are gone a spit and a stride; are presently reputed Aliens, and used accordingly.

It is a great wonder that these Projectors never took *Ireland* to task. They might there have had a large Field for their squeezing and fleecing Projects. And they might have found out wayes, to skim the Cream of all the Estates in *Ireland.* But what is it they could have done in this Affair? The answer is, that they might have thought of several good things. In the first place, Nothing to be brought to *Ireland,* or carried thence, but in English Ships, navigated by English Men. The next thing had been, to consider, what things those People had most occasion for: and to put those Things under a severe Monopoly, which also must be in the Conduct and Management of a Company here in *England.* Then care should be taken, that what ever is carried out of *Ireland,* be brought directly to *England* and to no place else: and what ever that Country wants, be had only from *England.* By which means, *England* would be the Staple, of all the Commodities imported thither, or exported thence. There is also another thing, which is by no means to be forgotten: and that is, That the Commodities they send into *England* may be under such Impositions, as may drink up the whole Profit.

These are some of the VVaies for Improving *Ireland* to the advantage of *England.* Nor can any thing hinder their Execution; in regard those People are in our power, as well as the Plantations, and subject to the Laws of *England* when we please to name them. But you will say; These things make up such a Devillish Oppression, as is not to be endured. Truly it must be confesst, that the things may seem something hard. But yet there is no Oppression in the case. For all these things, and divers more of the like nature, do the Plantations ly under.

The Projectors think they have been very merciful to us, in that the new Duties are to continue but eight years. They might tell a Man as well, that in pity and tenderness to him, they will hold his head under water but half an hour, or keep him but a Week without Victuals: that is, long enough to destroy him. For the Plantations will be certainly ruin'd within that time, if these Burdens ly upon them: some few perhaps excepted, who had Money beforehand, or have Estates in *England.* And these also must be involved in the general Ruine.

Hitherto we have given some account of our deplorable Condition. But to afflict us yet more, we are told that we deserve no better usage, in respect of the great hurt and damage we do to *England:* as all new Colonies do. But then it had been more prudent, and likewise more just and merciful, rather to prevent the settling of the Plantations, then to ruine them now they are settled. The least signification that they were not pleasing, would have kept people at home. People would never have ventured their Estates and Lives, and undergone such Labours; to get the ill will of those, whose Favour they valued. Had this been the opinion alwaies concerning Colonies, it might pass for a Mistake in Judgment. But when We, who had all encouragement at first, shall as soon as we have got something, be accounted pernicious to our Country; we have reason to doubt, that this is only a pretence to oppress us, and not a real belief or sentiment.

If a new Country should now offer, no question but free leave would be given to make a Settlement, and all due Encouragements granted. We must not say that the People in this case would be decoyed and trapann'd and chous'd and cheated; these are not fit words to be here used, but they would find, that they had miserably deceived themselves. For by that time they were warm in their Houses, and had got things about them; the Projectors would be upon their bones: and these new Favourites would be esteemed pernicious, and used accordingly, as well as the rest of the Plantations.

But we are very sure, that this Opinion concerning us (if any be really of it) is a great Mistake: and that the Plantations are not only not pernicious; but highly beneficial and of vast advantage to *England.*

We by our Labour, Hazards, and Industry, have enlarged the *English* Trade and Empire. The *English* Empire in *America,* what ever we think of it our selves, is by others esteemed greatly considerable.

We employ seven or eight hundred *English* Ships in a safe and healthy Navigation. They find less danger in a Voyage to our Parts, then in a Voyage to *Newcastle.* And as the Ships come safe, so the Men come sound. Whereas of those that go to the *East-Indies,* half the Ships Company (take one Ship with another) perish in the Voyage.

It did the Seamens hearts good, to think of a Plantation Voyage: where they might be merry amongst their Friends and Countrymen, and where they were sure of the kindest Reception. While we had it, we thought nothing too good for them. But now their beloved Navigation is gone. For by destroying the Plantations, it could not be, but that the Navigation to them must be destroyed likewise: or at least made good for nothing. Which, to them, is the same thing as destroying. We are so pinched our selves by the Impositions, that we are forced to pinch all those, with whom we are concern'd. And our Trade is become so hard and so bare a pasture, that it starves every thing that relates to it. And in particular, we cannot now afford the Seamen, that liberal Fraight which we did formerly. We would willingly do reason to our good Friends the Seamen, and give them a fair and full price for the transportation of our Goods; but we are not able.

The Seamen did well foresee, that they should feel the ill consequence of our new Burdens. And we have good Assurance, that while the thing was brewing, they had thoughts of making humble and earnest Addresses to keep them off. But the swiftness of the Projectors motion prevented their design.

And what followed upon the laying the new Taxes? Truly such a flight of the *English* Seamen in the late Reign, as never was known. They plainly deserted the *English* Service. Of which there was no cause so visible, as the spoiling that Navigation which was most dear to them. So that it plainly appears, that by the Sufferings of the Plantations, the Navigation doth highly suffer; whereas while they are permitted to be in a tolerable Condition, they are a great advance to the Navigation of *England.*

Let us now consider the further advantages of Trade, though the building, repairing, fitting and furnishing so many Ships, and the finding Cloths and Victuals for the Seamen, is a considerable Trade of it self. But moreover, there is hardly a Ship comes to us, but what is half loaden at least (many of them are deep loaden) with *English* Commodities.

Several Scores of Thousands are employed in *England,* in furnishing the Plantations with all sorts of Necessaries, and these must be supplied the while with Cloths and Victuals, which employs great numbers likewise. All which are paid, out of Our Industry and Labour.

We have yearly from *England* an infinite Quantity of Iron VVares ready wrought. Thousands of Dozens of Howes, and great numbers of Bills to cut our Canes. many Barrels of Nails; many Sets of Smiths, Carpenters, and Coopers Tools; all our Locks and Hinges; with Swords, Pistols, Carbines, Muskets, and Fowling Pieces.

VVe have also from *England* all sorts of Tin-ware, Earthenware, and VVooden-ware: and all our Brass and Pewter. And many a Serne of Sope, many a Quoyle of Rope, and of Lead many a Fodder, do the Plantations take from *England.*

Even *English* Cloth is much worn amongst us; but we have of Stuffs far greater Quantities. From *England* come all the Hats we weare; and of Shoos, thousands of Dozens yearly. The white Broad-cloth that we use for Strainers, comes also to a great deal of Money. Our very *Negro* Caps, of Woollen-yarn knit, (of which also we have yearly thousands of Dozens) may pass for a Manufacture.

How many Spinners, Knitters, and Weavers are kept at work, here in *England,* to make all the Stockings we wear? Woollen Stockings for the ordinary People, Silk Stockings when we could go to the price, Worsted Stockings in abundance, and Thread Stockings without number.

As we have our Horses from *England;* So all our Saddles and Bridles come from *England* likewise, which we desire should be good ones, and are not sparing in the price.

The Bread we eat, is of *English* Flower: we take great Quantities of *English* Beer, and of *English* Cheese and Butter: we sit by the light of *English* Candles; and the Wine we drink, is bought for the most part with *English* Commodities. Ships bound for the Plantations touch at *Madera,* and there sell their Goods, and invest the Produce in Wines.

Moreover we take yearly thousands of Barrels of *Irish* Beef: with the price whereof those people pay their Rents, to their Landlords that live and spend their Estates in *England.*

'Tis strange we should be thought to diminish the People of *England,* when we do so much increase the Employments. Where there are Employments, there will be People: you cannot keep them out, nor drive them away, with Pitchforks. On the other side, where the Employments faile or are wanting, the People will be gone. They will never stay there to starve, or to eat up one another. Great numbers of *French* Protestants that came lately to *England,* left us again upon this account. It was their Saying; We have been received with great Kindness and Charity, but here is no Imployment.

However it is charged upon the Plantations (and we can be charged with nothing else), that they take People from *England.* But doth not *Ireland* do the same? It may be truly said, that if the *American* Colonies have taken thousands, *Ireland* hath taken ten thousands. Yet we cannot find, that people were ever stopp'd from going thither, or that ever it was thought an Inconvenience. You will say the Cases are different: in regard the *Plantations* are remote; whereas *Ireland* is neer at hand. and our people that are in *Ireland* can give us ready Assistance. In answer hereunto it is confess'd, that where Colonies are neer, the Power is more united. But it must be confess'd likewise, that where the Colonies are remote, the Power is farther extended. So that These may be as useful one way, as Those are another way. It concerns a Generall to have his Army united, but may he not detach part of it, to possess a Post at some distance, though it be of never so great advantage? It is plainly an advantage, to have a Command and Influence upon remote Parts of the World. Moreover the remote Colonies of *America* are much more advantageous to *England* in point of Trade, then is this neer one of *Ireland.* For Ireland producing the same things, takes little from us, and also spoiles our Markets in other places. Nor doth it furnish us with any thing, which before we bought of Forrainers. But the *American* Plantations do both take off from *England* abundance of Commodities; and do likewise furnish *England* with divers Commodities of value, which formerly were imported from forrain Parts, which things are now become our owne: and are made Native. For you must know, and may please to consider, That the Sugar we make in the *American Plantations* (to instance only in that) is as much a native *English* Commodity, as if it were made and produced in *England.*

But still you will say, that we draw People from *England.* We confess we do, as a Man draws Water from a good Well. Who the more he draws in reason, the more he may: the Well being continually supplied. *Anglia puteus inexhaustus,*[2] said a Pope of old in another sense, that is, in matter of Money. But in matter of People it is likewise true; That *England* is a Well or Spring inexhausted, which hath never the less Water in it, for having some drawn from it.

You will say yet further, that the Plantations dispeople *England.* But this we utterly deny. Why may not you say as well, that the *Roman* Colonies dispeopled *Rome?* which yet was never pretended or imagined. That wise and glorious State, when ever there was a convenience of settling a Colony, thought fit to send out thousands of people at a time, at the Publick Charge. And wise Men are of opinion, That as the *Roman* Empire was the greatest that the World hath yet seen; so it chiefly owed its Grandeur to its free emission of Colonies.

And whereas the Kingdoms of *Spain* may seem dispeopled and exhausted by their *American* Colonies; if the thing be well examin'd, their Sloth and not their Colonies hath been the true Cause. To which may be added the Rigour of their Government, and their many Arts and Waies of destroying Trade.

But what will you say to the *Dutch?* for They, we know, have Colonies in the *East-Indies.* Do these exhaust and depopulate *Holland,* or at least are they a Burden and an Inconvenience? The *Dutch* themselves are so far from thinking so, that they justly esteem them the chief and main foundation of their Wealth and Trade. Their *East-Indy* Trade depends upon their *East-Indy* Colonies; and their whole State in effect, that is, the Greatness and Glory of it, depends upon their *East-Indy* Trade. Moreover as their Wealth and Trade increases, their People increase likewise.

They have also some Places in the *West-Indies:* which they prize not a little. How do they cherish *Suranam,* though it be one of the basest Countries in the World? And their Island of *Quaracoa* (*Carisaw* we pronounce it) they are as tender of, as any man can be of the apple of his Eye. Also their repeated Endeavours to settle *Tabago* do sufficiently evince, that they would very willingly spare some of their People, to increase their share in the Sugar Trade. But for a further proof of their Sentiment in these Matters; we may remember, that in the heat of their last War with *France,* they sent their Admiral *De Ruyter* with a great Force, to attempt the *French* Sugar Islands in *America,* which they would not have done, had they not thought them

2. ["England is an unexhausted well."]

highly valuable. But the *French* King was as mindful to keep his Islands, as they were to get them: and he took such order and had such Force to defend them, as render'd the *Dutch* Attempts ineffectual. Thus the *French* and *Dutch*, while all lay at stake at home, were contending in the *West-Indies* for Plantations; which our Politicians count worth nothing, or worse then nothing. You'll say, this same French Court, and these Dutch States, are meer ignorant Novices, and do not know the World. Perhaps not so well as our Politicians: But however something they know.

Many have observed that *France* is much dispeopled by Tyranny and Oppression. But that their Plantations have in the least dispeopled it, was never yet said nor thought. And That King sets such a value upon his Plantations, and is so far from thinking his People lost that are in his Plantations; that he payes a good part of the Fraight, of all those that will go to them to settle: giving them all fair Encouragements besides.

If Colonies be so pernicious to their Mother Country, it was a great happiness to *Portugall*, that the *Dutch* stripp'd them of their *East-India* Colonies. And surely they feel the difference: but it is much for the worse. *Lisbon* is not that *Lisbon* now, which it was in those days. And did not the recovery of *Brasile* (though that Trade be now low) in some measure support them, with the help of *Madera*, the *Western Islands*, and some other Colonies; *Portugall* would be one of the poorest places upon Earth.

But still you persist in the opinion, that the Plantations do more hurt then good, and are pernicious to *England*. Truly if it be so, it were your best way to shake them off, and cleerly to rid your hands of them. And you must not be averse to this motion. For if you cry out that the Plantations do hurt, and yet are not willing to part with them, it cannot be thought that you are in earnest. You will say, this should have been done sooner. But if 'tis fit to be done, 'tis better done late then not at all. Have the Plantations robbed you of your People already? Let them rob you no more. A man will stop a leake in his Vessell, though some be run out.

We of the Plantations cannot hear the mention of being cast off by *England*, without regrett. Nevertheless if it must be so, we shall compose our Minds to bear it, and like Children truly dutifull, we shall be content to part with our dearest Mother, rather than be a burden to her, But though we must part with our Country, yet we would not willingly part with our King: and therefore, if you please, let us be made over to *Scotland*. We are confident that Scotland would be well pleased to supply us with People, to have the sweet Trade in Exchange. And we should agree well with them: for we know by Experience that they are honest Men and good Planters. They would now be as busy as Bees all *Scotland* over, working merrily for the Plantations. And *England* the while might keep her People at home: to pick strawes, or for some such other good work, though some of them, 'tis doubt, would make the Highway their way of Living. And now *Scotland* would be the Market for Sugar: where our Friends of *England* would be welcome with their Money. We should be glad to meet them there, and should use them well for old acquaintance. But what would be the Effect of these things? The Effect would be; that in a very few years, the value of Lands in *England* would fall a fourth part, if not a third: and the Land in *Scotland* would be more than doubled. It were therefore better to acknowledge, according to truth, that the Plantations are greatly beneficial; and to keep the Plantations.

There is one main advantage by the Plantations which hath not been sufficiently explained: and that is, that we have now divers good Commodities of our own, which before we had not, which doth very much conduce to the enriching of *England*. For it is agreed by all that pretend to understand Trade, that a Country doth then grow rich, and then only, when the Commodities exported out of it are more in value then those that are imported into it. This proportion between the *Importation* and the *Exportation* is called the *Balance of Trade*, and there is no way in the World for a Country to grow rich by Trade, but by setting this Balance right, and by sending out more than it takes in. Some other Tricks and shifts there are, which make shew of doing great Matters: but they prove idle and frivolous, and signifie just nothing. A Country, in this respect, is in the same Condition with a private Man that lives upon his Land. If this Man sells more than he buys, he lays up money. If he buyes more than he sells, he must run in debt, or at least spend out of the quick stock. And where the Bought and the Sold are equal, he hath barely brought both Ends together.

It is therefore most evident, that the increasing of Native Commodities brings in Riches and Money. since it makes the Exportation greater, or at least the Importation less. And it is as evident, that the Plantations give *England* a great increase of Native Commodities. *Cotton, Ginger, Indico,* and *Sugar,* (to omit other things) are now the Native Commodities of *England*. We may insist a little further upon Sugar, as being the most considerable. Heretofore we had all our Sugars from *Portugall:* and it is computed, that they cost us yearly about four hundred thousand pounds. Now that great Leak is stopp'd: and we hardly buy any *Portugall* or *Brasile* Sugars, being plentifully supplied by our own Plantations. But moreover; beside what we use our selves, we export as much Sugar to other Countries, as brings us in yearly near the same summe. So that the Plantations; by this one Commodity, do advance near eight hundred thousand pounds a year, (the one half in getting, the other in saving), to turn the scale of Trade to the advantage of *England*.

Why should *England* grudge at the prosperity and wealth of the *Plantations;* since all that is Ours, She may account her own? Not only because we are really a part of *England* (what ever we may be accounted) as it is taken largely; but also because all comes to this Kingdom of *England* properly so called, these two and fifty Shires. By a kind of *Magnetick* Force *England* draws to it all that is good in the Plantations. It is the *Center* to which all things tend. Nothing but *England* can we relish or fancy: our Hearts are here, where ever our Bodies be. If we get a little Money, we remit it to *England*. They that are able, breed up their Children in *England*. When we are a little easy, we desire to live and spend what we have in *England*. And all that we can rap and rend is brought to *England*. What would you have? Would you have more of a Cat than her Skin?

We have made it out, in the former parts of these Papers, what Multitudes of People the Plantations employ here in *England*. It is easily said, that if there were no such thing as Plantations, those People might be otherwise employed. And some Men will talk of the Fishing Trade, and the Linnen Trade, and other projects of the like nature. But they would do well to contrive a way, how the People imployed in them may make wages. For unless they do that, they do nothing. There is nothing more easy then to find out unprofitable Employments. But those that are profitable are already overstock't: and people can hardly live one by another. And therefore the Plantations ought in reason to be valued, since they give *profitable* Employments to so many thousands of People whereas the Fishing Trade and the Linnen Trade will not turn to profit.

It is now time that we put an end to this sad Discourse Having made it appear, that the Plantations are brought to a miserable and ruinous Condition; and that they have not deserved this hard Usage, considering the many and great Advantages they bring to *England*.

We have laid before you such a *Series* of Calamities, as are not easy to be parallell'd. And we think our patient Submission under them is almost without Example. But we must beg pardon of all good Men, if we cannot be in Charity with those cursed Projectors, by whom our Livelyhoods (which is in effect our Lives) have been torn from us with so much Inhumanity.

But hath our dear Mother no *Bowels* for her Children, that are now at the last Gasp, and ly struggling with the pangs of Death? Will She do nothing to deliver us from the Jaws of Death? We cannot despair, but that she will yet look upon us with an Eye of Mercy. However we desire it may not be ill taken, that we have eased our Minds by recounting our Sorrows. Let us not be denied the common liberty and priviledge of Mankind, to groan when we dy. Let not our Complaints seem troublesome and offensive; but be received with Compassion, as the Groans of dying Men.

FINIS.

· 5 ·

[Edward Rawson], The Revolution in New England Justified (1691)

AFTER THE OVERTHROW of the Dominion of New England in April of 1689, there was a wide-ranging debate about the legitimacy of the uprising against royal authority in Massachusetts. In response to John Palmer's defense of the Dominion (see Selection 2), Edward Rawson, longtime Secretary of Massachusetts (1650–86), defended the right of the settlers in New England to representative government.

To Palmer's claim that the settlers in New England had been conquered, Rawson replied that they had purchased the land from the Native Americans and then "at vast charge of their own conquered a wilderness, and been in possession of their estates forty, nay sixty years." Rawson also insisted that there had been a contract between the original settlers and the king, in which he had promised them that in return for risking their lives to expand the empire they would be guaranteed the privileges granted in their charters. And he added that even if their charter had been taken away legally, the settlers "did not cease to be Englishmen," and were thus entitled to all the same rights as their fellow subjects at home. Finally, Rawson pointed out that in resisting Governor Andros the settlers in New England had done no more than their fellow subjects in England had done when they rose up against James II. What's more, the New Englanders had not opposed the Dominion precipitately; rather, they had waited to resume their charter rights until they knew that William and Mary had taken the throne and saved England from popery and slavery. (C.B.Y.)

The REVOLUTION IN New England JUSTIFIED,

And the People there Vindicated From the Aspersions cast upon them By Mr. *JOHN PALMER*, In his Pretended Answer to the Declaration,

Published by the Inhabitants of *Boston*, and the Country adjacent, on the day when they secured their late Oppressors, who acted by an Illegal and Arbitrary Commission from the Late King *JAMES*.

Printed for *Joseph Brunning* at *Boston* in *New England*. 1691.

To The Reader.

It is not with any design or desire unnecessarily to expose the late Oppressors of that good Protestant People which is in New England, *that the Authors of the ensuing* Vindication *have published what is herewith emitted. But the* Agents *lately sent from thence could not be faithful to their Trust, if when the People whom they Represent are publickly (as well as privately)* aspersed, *they should not (either by themselves, or by furnishing some other with materials for such an undertaking)* vindicate *those who have been so deeply injured.*

As for Mr. Palmer *his Account which he calls* Impartial, *he has wrong'd* New England *thereby, in some other particulars besides those insisted on, in the subsequent* Apology. *For he does endeavour to make the World believe that the* Massachusetts *refused to answer to the* Quo Warranto[1] *prosecuted against their* Charter: *Than which Misrepresentation nothing can be more untrue or injurious. An Account concerning that matter hath formerly (and more than once) been made publick, in the which it is most truly affirmed,*

> *That when the* Quo Warranto *was issued out against the Governour and Company of the* Massachusetts *Colony in* New England *in the year* 1683. *the then King did by his Declaration enjoyn a few particular persons to make their Defence at their own Charge, without any publick Stock; which shew'd that there was a Resolution to take away that Charter: Yet the Governour and Company appointed an Attorney to answer to the* Quo Warranto; *but the Suit was let fall in the Court of* Kings-Bench, *and a new Suit began by* Scire facias[2] *in Court of* Chancery, *where time was not allow'd to make Defence. The former Attorney for that Colony brought several Merchants to testifie that in the time allow'd (which was from* April 16. *till* June 18.) it *was impossible to have a New Letter of Attorney returned from* New England. *The then Lord Keeper* North *replied, That no time ought to be given. So was Judgment entred against them before they could possibly plead for themselves.*

By this the Impartial Reader may judge what Ingenuity and Veracity is in Mr. Palmers *Account.*

1. [Literally, "By what right." A writ directing a person to show "by what right" he exercises powers of office.—Tr.]

2. [Literally, "You cause the party to know." A writ based upon a record directing the sheriff that "you cause the party to know" the charge brought against him and require him to appear and show cause that the record should not be enforced.—Tr.]

There is lately come forth another Scandalous Pamphlet, *called* New England's Faction Discovered. *The Author has not put his Name to it: But it is supposed to be written by a certain person known to be a Prodigy for Impudence and Lying. The Reflections in it not only on* New England *in general, but on particular persons there as well as in* England, *are so notoriously and maliciously false; as that it must needs be much beneath a great Mind to take notice of such* Latrations, *or to answer them any otherwise than with contempt. When we are treated with the Buffoonry and Railery of such ungentiel Pens, 'tis good to remember the old Saying,* Magnum Contumeliae remedium, Negligentia.[3]

As for what Mr. Palmer *does in his Preface insinuate concerning the* New-Englanders *being* Commonwealths-men, Enemies to Monarchy, and to the Church of England, *that's such a* Sham *as every one sees through it.*

There are none in the World that do more fully concur with the Doctrine *of the Church of* England *contained in the* 39 *Articles, than do* the Churches in New England, *as is manifest from the Confession of their Faith published in the year* 1680. *Only as to* Liturgy and Ceremonies *they differ; for which cause alone it was that they, or their Fathers transported themselves into that* American Desert, *as being desirous to worship God in that way which they thought was most according to the Scriptures. The* Platform of Church Discipline *consented unto by the Elders and Messengers of the Churches Assembled in a General Synod at* Cambridge *in* New England *in the year* 1647. *sheweth that they are as to* Church-Government *for the* Congregational way. *The judiciously Learned Mr.* Philip Nye *has long since evinced, that no Form of Church-Government (no not that which is Episcopal) is more consistent with Monarchy, or with the King's Supremacy, than that of the* Way-Congregational, *which some will needs call* Independent. *But there are a sort of men, who call those that are for* English *Liberties, and that rejoyce in the Government of Their present Majesties King* William *and Queen* Mary, *by the name of* Republicans, *and represent all such as Enemies of Monarchy and of the Church. It is not our single Opinion only, but we can speak it on behalf of the generality of Their Majesties Subjects in* New England, *that they believe (without any diminution to the Glory of our former Princes) the* English *Nation was never so happy in a* King, *or in a* Queen, *as at this day. And the God of Heaven, who has set them on the Throne of these Kingdoms, grant them long and prosperously to Reign.*

E. R.
S. S.

3. ["A great remedy of abuse, Negligence."]

The Revolution in *New England* justified.

The Doctrine of *Passive Obedience* and *Non-Resistance*, which a sort of men did of late when they thought the World would never change, cry up as Divine Truth, is by means of the happy *Revolution* in these Nations, exploded, and the Assertors of it become ridiculous.

No man does really approve of the *Revolution* in *England*, but must justifie that in *New England* also; for the latter was effected in compliance with the former, neither was there any design amongst the *People in New England*, to reassume their Antient *Charter-Government*, until His present Majesties intended descent into *England*, to rescue the Nation from *Slavery* as well as *Popery*, was known to them (for indeed to have attempted it before that would have been madness.) They considered that the men then usurping Government in *New England* were King *James*'s Creatures, who had invaded both the *Liberty and Property of English Protestants* after such a manner as perhaps the like was never known in any part of the World where the *English* Nation has any Government: And the *Commission* which they had obtained from the Late King *James* was more Illegal and Arbitrary, than that granted to *Dudley* and *Empson* by King *Henry* 7th. or than it may be was ever before given to any by King *James* himself, or by any one that ever swayed the *English* Scepter, which was a Grievance intolerable; and yet they desired not to make themselves Judges in a case which so nearly concerned them, but instead of harsher treatment of those who had Tyrannized over them, they only secured them that they might not betray that Countrey into the hands of *the Late King*, or of King *Lewis*, which they had reason enough to believe (considering their Characters and Dispositions,) they were inclined to do. They designed not to revenge themselves on their Enemies, which they could as easily have done as a thousand men are able to kill one, and therefore when they secured their Persons, they declared (as in their *Declaration* Printed at *Boston* in *New England* is to be seen) that they would *leave it to the King and Parliament of* England, *to inflict what punishment they should think meet for such Criminals*. Their seizing and securing the Governour, was no more than was done in *England*, at *Hull*, *Dover*, *Plimouth*, *&c*. That such a man as Mr. *John Palmer* should exclaim against it, is not to be wondred at, seeing he was one of the Governours Tools, being of his Council, made a Judge by him, and too much concern'd in some Illegal and Arbitrary Proceedings: But his Confidence is wonderful, that he should publish in Print that neither himself nor Sir *Edmund Androsse,* nor others of them who had been secured by the People in *New England, had any Crimes laid to their charge,* whereas the foresaid Declaration emitted the very day they were secured, doth plainly set forth their Crimes. And in the Preface of his Book he hath these words; *viz.*

"*We appeared at the Council-Board where the worst of our Enemies, even the very men who had so unjustly imprisoned and detained us, had nothing to say or object against us*—" By these Enemies he speaks of, we suppose he means those who were lately sent as *Agents* from *Boston* in *New England;* He hath therefore necessitated us to inform the World, that the following Objections (tho' not by his Enemies, yet) by those *Agents* presented at the Council-Board.

Matters objected against Sir Edmund Androsse, *Mr.* Joseph Dudley, *Mr.* Palmer, *Mr.* Randolph, *Mr.* West, *Mr.* Graham, *Mr.* Farewell, *Mr.* Sherlock *and others, as occasions of their Imprisonment in* New England.

It is objected against Sir *Edmund Androsse,* that he being Governour of the *Massachusetts* Colony after notice of His present Majesties intention to land in *England,* issued out a Proclamation, requiring all persons to oppose any descent of such as might be authorized by him, endeavourd to stifle the News of his Landing, and caused him that brought this Kings Declaration thither to be imprisoned as bringing a Seditious and Treasonable Paper.

2. That in the time of his Government, he without form or colour of legal Authority made laws destructive of the Liberty of the People, imposed and levied Taxes, threatned and imprisoned them that would not be assisting to the illegal Levys, denied that they had any Property in their Lands without Patents from him, and during the time of actual War with the *Indians,* he did supply them with Ammunition, and several *Indians* declared, that they were encouraged by him to make War upon the *English,* and he discountenanced making defence against the *Indians.*

3. As to all the other persons imprisoned, they were Accomplices and Confederates with Sir *Edmund Androsse,* and particularly Mr. *Dudley,* Mr. *Randolph,* and Mr. *Palmer* were of his Council, and joined with him in his Arbitrary Laws and Impositions, and in threatning and in punishing them who would not comply. Mr. *West* was his Secretary, and guilty of great Extortion, and gave out words which shewed himself no Friend to the *English.* Mr. *Graham* was his Attorney at one time, and

> Mr. *Farewell* at another, both concerned in illegal proceedings destructive of the Property of the Subject. Mr. *Farewell* prosecuted them who refused to comply with the Illegal Levies, and Mr. *Graham* brought several Writs of Intrusion against men for their own Land, and Mr. *Sherlock*, another person imprisoned, though not named in the Order, acted there for some years as an High Sheriff, though he was a stranger in the Countrey, and had no Estate there, during his Shrievalty he impannelled Juries of Strangers, who had no Free-hold in that Countrey, and extorted unreasonable Fees.

These particulars were not only presented at the *Council-Board*, but there read before the Right Honourable the Lords of the Committee for Foreign Plantations, on *April* 17, 1690. when Sir *Edmund Androsse*, Mr. *Palmer*, and the rest concerned were present, and owned that they had received Copies thereof from Mr. *Blaithwaite*. It is true, that the Paper then read was not signed by the Agents aforesaid, for which reason (as we understand, nor could it rationally be otherwise expected) the matter was dismissed without an hearing: Nevertheless the Gentlemen who appeared as Counsel for the *New England* Agents, declared, That they were ready to prove every Article of the Objections; which shall now be done.

1. That Sir *E. A.* with others whom the People in *New England* seized and secured, did, *after notice of His present Majesties intended descent into* England *to deliver the Nation from Popery and Arbitrary Power, to their utmost oppose that glorious design*, is manifest by the *Proclamation* Printed and Published in *New England, Jan.* 10. 1688. signed by Sir *E. A.* and His Deputy Secretary *John West*, in which K. *James*'s Proclamation of *Octob.* 16. 1688. is recited and referred unto. Sir *Edmunds* Proclamation begins thus;

> Whereas His Majesty hath been graciously pleased by His Royal Letter bearing date the 16th of *October* last past, to signifie that He hath undoubted Advice that a great and sudden *Invasion from Holland*, with an armed Force of Foreigners and Strangers will be speedily made in an hostile manner upon His Majesties Kingdom of *England*, and that although some false *Pretences relating to Liberty, Property and Religion, &c.* And then he concludes thus—All which it is His Majesties pleasure should be made known in the most publick manner to His Loving Subjects within this His Territory and Dominion of *New England*, that they may be the better prepared to *resist any Attempts* that may be made by His Majesties

> Enemies *in these parts,* I do therefore hereby charge and *command all Officers Civil and Military, and all other His Majesties Loving Subjects within this His Territory* and Dominion aforesaid, to be vigilant and careful in their respective places and stations, and *that upon the approach of any Fleet or Foreign Force, they be in readiness, and use their utmost endeavours to hinder any Landing or Invasion* that may be intended to be made within the same.

2. And that they used all imaginable endeavours *to stifle the News of the Prince's Landing in England,* appears not only from the Testimony of the People there, and from the Letters of those now in Government at *Boston,* but from the deposition of Mr. *John Winslow,* who affirms that being in *Nevis* in *Feb.* 1688. a Ship arrived there from *England* with *the Prince of Orange's* Declaration, and intelligence of the happy change of Affairs in *England,* which he knew would be *welcom News in New England,* and therefore was at the charge to procure a written Copy of that Princely Declaration with which he arrived at *Boston* about a fortnight before the *Revolution* there. He concealed the Declaration from Sir *Edmund,* because he believed if it came into his possession, he would keep the people in ignorance concerning it; but intimation being given that Mr. *Winslow* had brought with him the Declaration, he was therefore committed to Prison (though he offered two thousand pound Bayl) for bringing into the Country *a Treasonable Paper.* For the satisfaction of such as are willing to be informed in this matter, Mr. *Winslow*'s testimony as it was given upon Oath before a Magistrate in *New England* shall be here inserted. It is as follows.

> *John Winslow* aged 24 years or thereabouts, testifieth and saith, that he being in *Nevis* some time in *February* last past, there came in a Ship from some part of *England* with the Prince of *Orange*'s Declarations, and brought news also of his happy proceedings in *England* with his entrance there, which was very welcome News to me, and I knew it would be so to the rest of the people in *New England;* and I being bound thither, and very willing to carry such good news with me, gave four shillings six pence for the said Declarations, on purpose to let the people in *New England* understand what a speedy deliverance they might expect from Arbitrary Power. We arrived at *Boston* Harbour the fourth day of *April* following, and as soon as I came home to my house, Sir *Edmund Androsse* understanding I brought the Prince's Declarations with me, sent the Sheriff to me; so I went along with him to the Governours house, and as soon as I came

in, he asked me why I did not come and tell him the news. I told him I thought it not my duty, neither was it customary for any Passenger to go to the Governour when the Master of the Ship had been with him before, and told him the news; he asked me where the Declarations I brought with me were, I told him I could not tell, being afraid to let him have them, because he would not let the people know any news. He told me I was a Saucy fellow, and bid the Sheriff carry me away to the Justices of the Peace, and as we were going, I told the Sheriff, I would choose my Justice, he told me, no, I must go before Doctor *Bullivant, one pickt on purpose* (as I Judged) *for the business;* well I told him, I did not care who I went before, for I knew my cause good, so soon as I came in, two more of the Justices dropt in, *Charles Lidget* and *Francis Foxcroft,* such as the former, *fit for the purpose,* so they asked me for my Papers, I told them I would not let them have them by reason they kept all the news from the people, so when they saw they could not get what I bought with my money, they sent me to Prison for bringing *Traiterous and Treasonable Libels* and Papers of News, notwithstanding, I offered them security to the value of two thousand pounds.

Boston in *New England, Feb.* 4. 1689. sworn before *Elisha Hutchinson* Assistant.

John Winslow.

By these things it appears that it was absolutely necessary for the people in *New England* to seize Sir *E. A.* and his Complices, that so they might secure that territory for their present Majesties King *William* and Queen *Mary.*

3. That Sir *E. A.* &c. did *make Laws destructive to the liberty of the Subjects,* is notoriously known, for they made what Laws they pleased *without any consent of the People, either by themselves or representatives,* which is indeed to *destroy the Fundamentals of the English,* and to *Erect a French Government.* We cannot learn that the like was ever practised in any place where the English are Planters, but only where Sir *E. A.* hath been Governour: For whereas in *New-England* by constant usage under their Charter Government, the Inhabitants of each Town did assemble as occasion offered to consider of what might conduce to the welfare of their respective Towns, the relief of the poor, or the like, Sir *E. A. with a few of his council,* made a Law prohibiting any Town meeting, except once a year, *viz.* on the third Monday in *May.* The Inhabitants of the Countrey were startled at

this Law, as being apprehensive the design of it was to prevent the people in every Town from meeting to make complaints of their Grievances. And whereas by constant usage any person might remove out of the Countrey at his pleasure, a Law was made that no man should do so without the Governours leave. And all Fishing Boats, Coasters, *&c.* were to enter into a thousand pound bond, whereby Fees were raised for himself and creatures. This Law could not pass at *Boston,* because many of Sir *Edmund's* Council there opposed it; but then a *Juncto*[4] of them meeting at *New-York,* passed it; and after that Law was made, how should any dissatisfied persons ever obtain liberty to go for *England* to complain of their being oppressed by *Arbitrary Governours?*

4. But besides all this, They made Laws for the *Levying Moneys without the consent of the People either by themselves or by an Assembly;* for in order to the supporting of their own Government, they did by an Act bearing date *March* 3. 1686. raise considerable sums of Money on the Kings subjects in that part of his dominions, *viz.* a penny in the pound on all Estates personal or real, twenty pence *per* head as Poll Money, a penny in the pound for goods imported, besides an Excise on Wine, Rum and other Liquors.

It hath indeed been pleaded that all this was but what the Laws of the Countrey before the change of the Government did allow. But this is vainly pretended; for there was no such Law in force at the time when these sums were levied, the former Laws which did authorise it, were repealed *Octob.* 10. 1683. some years before Sir *E. A.* and his complices had invaded the Rights and Liberties of the people there. Moreover, in those, parts of the Countrey where there were never any such Laws in force, particularly in *Plymouth* Colony, this Money was levied, which they heavily complained of. Yet further, in another Act dated *Feb.* 15. 1687, they did without any colour of antient Law make an additional duty of Impost and Excise, which raised the duty, some ten shillings, some twenty shillings *per* Pipe on Wines, and so on other things. Nay they levied Moneys on *Connecticot* Colony contrary to their Charter, which was never vacated, than which nothing more Illegal and Arbitrary could have been perpetrated by them.

5. They did not only act according to these Illegal Taxes, but they did *inflict severe punishment on those true English men who did oppose their Arbitrary*

4. [A group of men assembled together for a purpose, a self-selected group; also "junto."—Tr.]

proceedings, as shall be made to appear in many instances. When the Inhabitants of *Ipswich* in *New England* were required to choose a Commissioner to tax that Town, some principal persons there that could not comply with what was demanded of them, did modestly give their reasons, for which they were committed to Gaol, as guilty of high misdemeanours, and denied an *Habeas Corpus*,[5] and were obliged to answer it at a Court of *Oyer & Terminer* at *Boston*. And that they might be sure to be found guilty, *Jurors* were picked of such as were no Freeholders, nay of Strangers; the Prisoners pleading *the priviledges of English men* not to be taxed without their own consent, they were told that *the Laws of* England *would not follow them to the end of the Earth*, they meant the priviledges of the English Law, for the penalties they resolved should follow them *quo jure quaque injuria*.[6] And why should they insist on, and talk of the priviledges of English men, when it had been declared in the Governours Council, that *the Kings Subjects in* New England *did not differ much from Slaves, and that the only difference was, that they were not bought and sold?* But to go on with the matter before us; In as much as the Prisoners mentioned had asserted their English Liberties, they were severely handled, not only imprisoned for several weeks, but fined and bound to their good behaviour; Mr. *John Wise* was fined fifty pound besides costs of Court, deprived of the means of his subsistance, and gave a thousand pound bond for good behaviour. And Mr. *John Appleton* was fined fifty pound and to give a thousand pound bond for good behaviour, and moreover declared incapable to bear Office, besides unreasonable Fees. After the same manner did they proceed with several others belonging to *Ipswich*. Likewise the Towns men of *Rowley, Salisbury, Andover*, &c. had the same measure. And the Kings Subjects were not only oppressed thus in the *Massachusetts* Colony, but in *Plymouth*. For when *Shadrach Wildboar* the Town Clerk of *Taunton* in *N.E.* did, with the consent of the Town. Sign a modest Paper signifying their not being free to raise money on the Inhabitants without their own consent by an assembly, the honest man was for this committed close Prisoner, and after that punished with a Fine of twenty Marks and three Months Imprisonment, and bound to find sureties

5. [Literally, "You have the body." A writ directing the sheriff that "you have the body" for confinement and are required to produce a charge in court to justify imprisonment; a bench warrant.—Tr.]

6. ["By any sort of right or wrong." (Terence)—Tr.]

by Recognizance to appear the next Court, and to be of the good behaviour. As to the matter of fact, the persons concerned in *these Illegal and Arbitrary Judgments* will not have the face to deny them; if they do, there are *Affidavits* now in *London* which will evince what hath been related whenever there shall be occasion for it.

It is a vanity in Mr. *Palmer,* to think that he hath answered this by affirming, but not proving, that the *Ipswich-men* assembled themselves in a *riotous manner;* for that saying of his is very false. The World knows that *New England* is not the only place where honest men have in these late days been proceeded against as guilty of *Riots,* when they never deserved such a censure any more than these accused by Mr. *Palmer.* But the truth of what hath been thus far related is confirmed by the following *Affidavits.*

Complaints of great wrongs done under the Ill Government of Sir *Edmund Androsse* Governour in *N.E.* in the year 168–.

We *John Wise, John Andrews senior, Robert Kinsman, William Goodhue junior,* all of *Ipswich* in *New England,* in the County of *Essex,* about the 22d day of *August,* in the year above named, were with several principal Inhabitants of the Town of *Ipswich* met at Mr. *John Appletons,* and there discoursed and concluded that it was not the Towns Duty any way to assist that ill method of raising Money without a general Assembly, which was apparently intended by abovesaid Sir *Edmund* and his Council, as witness a late Act issued out by them for such a purpose. The next day in a general Town-Meeting of the Inhabitants of *Ipswich;* We the above named *John Wise, John Andrews, Robert Kinsman, William Goodhue* with the rest of the Town then met (none contradicting) gave our assent to the vote then made.

The ground of our trouble, our crime was the Copy transmitted to the Council, *viz.* At a Legal Town meeting *August* 23. Assembled by vertue of an Order from *John Usher.* Esq. Treasurer for choosing a Commissioner to join with the Select men, to assess the Inhabitants according to an Act of his Excellency the Governour and Council for laying of rates; the Town then considering that the said Act doth infringe their Liberty, as free born English Subjects of His Majesty by interfering with the Statute Laws of the Land, by which it was Enacted that no Taxes should be Levied upon the Subjects without consent of an Assembly chosen by the Freeholders for assessing of the same, they do therefore vote that they are not willing to choose a Commissioner for such an end without said priviledge; and moreover consent not that the Select men do proceed to lay any such rate until it be appointed by a general Assembly concurring with the Governour and Council. We the complainants with Mr. *John Appleton* and *Thomas French* all of *Ipswich* were brought to answer for the said vote out of our own County, thirty or forty Miles into *Suffolk*, and in *Boston* kept in Gaol, only for contempt and high misdemeanours as our *Mittimus* specifies, and upon demand, denied the priviledge of an *Habeas Corpus*, and from Prison over ruled to answer at a Court of *Oyer* and *Terminer* in *Boston* aforesaid. Our Judges were Mr *Joseph Dudley* of *Roxbury* in *Suffolk* in *New England*, Mr. *Stoughton* of *Dorchester*, *John Usher* of *Boston* Treasurer and *Edward Randolph*. He that officiates as Clerk and Attorny in the case is *George Farwel*.

The Jurors only twelve men and most of them (as is said) Non-freeholders of any Land in the Colony, some of them Strangers and Forreigners, gathered up (as we suppose) to serve the present turn: In our defence was pleaded the repeal of the Law of Assessment upon the place. Also the *Magna Charta* of *England*, and the Statute Laws that secure the Subjects Properties and Estates *&c*. To which was replied by one of the Judges, the rest by silence assenting, that we must not think the Laws of *England* follow us to the ends of the Earth, or whither we went. And the same person (*John Wise* abovesaid testifies) declared in open Council upon examination of said *Wise*; Mr. *Wise* you have no more priviledges left you, than not to be sold for Slaves, and no man in Council contradicted. By such Laws our Trial and Trouble began and ended. Mr. *Dudley* aforesaid Chief Judge, to close up the debate and trial, trims up a speech that pleased himself (we suppose) more than the people. Among many other remarkable Passages, to this purpose, he bespeaks the Jury's obedience, who (we suppose) were very well pre-inclined. *viz*. I am glad, says he, there be so many worthy Gentlemen of the Jury so capable to do the King service, and we expect a good Verdict from you, seeing the matter hath been so sufficiently proved against the Criminals. Note the evidence in the case as to the substance of it, was that we too boldly endeavoured to perswade our selves we were English Men, and under priviledges: and that we were all six of us aforesaid at the Town meeting of *Ipswich* aforesaid, and as the Witness supposed, we assented to the foresaid Vote, and also that *John Wise* made a Speech at the same time, and said we had a good God, and a good King, and should do well to stand for our Priviledges.—Jury returns us all six guilty, being all involved in the same Information. We were remanded from Verdict to Prison, and there kept one and twenty days for Judgement. There with Mr. *Dudley*'s approbation, as Judge *Stoughton* said, this Sentence was passed, *viz. John Wise* suspended from the Ministerial Function fine fifty pound money, pay cost, a thousand pound bond for the good behaviour one year.

John Appleton not to bear Office, fine 50 *l.* money, pay cost, a thousand pound bond for the good behaviour one year.

John Andrews not to bear Office, fine 30 *l.* money, pay cost, five hundred pound bond for the good behaviour one year.

Robert Kinsman not to bear Office, fine twenty pound money, pay cost, five hundred pound bond for the good behaviour one year.

William Goodhue not to bear Office, fine twenty pound money, pay cost, five hundred pound bond for the good behaviour one year.

Thomas French not to bear Office, fine 15 *l.* Money, past cost, 500 *l.* bond for the good behaviour one year.

The Total Fees of this case upon one single Information demanded by *Farewell* abovesaid amount to about a hundred and one pound seventeen shillings, who demanded of us singly about sixteen pound nineteen shillings six pence, the cost of Prosecution, the Fines added make up this, *viz.* Two hundred eighty and six pounds seventeen shillings money.

Summa Totalis[7] 286 l. 17 s.

To all which we may add a large account of other Fees of Messengers, Prison charges, Money for Bonds and Transcripts of Records, exhausted by those ill men one way and another to the value of three or fourscore pounds, besides our expence of time and imprisonment.

We judge the Total charge for one Case and Trial under one single Information involving us six men abovesaid in expence of Time and Moneys of us and our Relations for our necessary Succour and Support to amount to more, but no less than 400 *l.* Money.

Too tedious to illustrate more amply at this time, and so we conclude. *John Wise, John Andrews* Senior, *William Goodhue* Junior, *Thomas French,* these four persons named, and *Robert Kinsman.*

7. ["Total amount."]

These four persons first named appeared the twentieth day of *December,* and *Robert Kinsman* appeared the one and twentieth day of *December,* 1689. and gave in their Testimony upon Oath before me *Samuel Appleton* Assistant for the Colony of the *Massachusetts* in *New-England.*

6. That those who were in confederacy with Sir *E. A.* for the enriching themselves on the Ruins of *New-England,* did *Invade the Property* as well as Liberty of the Subject, is in the next place to be cleared, and we trust will be made out beyond dispute. When they little imagined that there should ever be such a *Revolution* in *England* as that which by means of His Present Majesty this Nation is Blest with, they feared not to declare their Sentiments to the inexpressible exasperation of the people whom they were then domineering over. They gave out that *now their Charter was gone, all their Lands were the Kings,* that themselves did Represent the King, and that therefore Men that would have any Legal Title to their Lands must take *Patents* of them, on such Terms as they should see meet to impose. What people that had the Spirits of Englishmen, could endure this? That when they had at *Vast Charges of their own conquered a Wilderness,* and been in possession of their Estates Forty, nay Sixty years, that now a parcel of Strangers, some of them indigent enough, must come and inherit all that the people now in *New-England* and their Fathers before them, had laboured for! Let the whole Nation judge, whether these Men were not driving on a French design, and had not fairly Erected a French Government. And that our Adversaries may not insult and say, these are words without proof, we shall here subjoyn the Testimonies of the Reverend Mr. *Higginson* and several other worthy Persons, given in upon Oath, concerning this matter—

Being called by those in present Authority to give my Testimony to the Discourse between Sir *Edmund Androsse* and my self, when he came from the Indian War, as he passed through *Salem* going for *Boston* in *March* 1688–89, I cannot refuse it, and therefore declare as followeth, what was the substance of that Discourse. Sir *Edmund Androsse* then Governour being accompanied with the Attorney General *Graham,* Secretary *West,* Judge *Palmer,* the Room being also full of other people, most of them his Attendants, he was pleased to tell me, he would have my judgment about this question; *Whether all the Lands in* New-England *were not the Kings?* I told him I was surprized with such a question, and was not willing to speak to it, that being a Minister, if it was a question about a matter of Religion, I should not be averse, but this being a State matter, I did not look upon it as proper for me to declare my mind in it, therefore entreated again and again that I might be excused. Sir *E. A.* replied and urged me with much importunity, saying, Because you are a Minister, therefore we desire to know your judgment in it, then I told him, if I must speak to it, I would only speak as a Minister from Scripture and Reason, not medling with the Law. He said, the Kings Attorney was present there to inform what was Law. I then said, I did not understand that the Lands of *N.E.* were the Kings, but the Kings Subjects, who had for more than Sixty years had the possession and use of them by a twofold right warranted by the Word of God. 1. By a right of just Occupation from the Grand Charter in *Genesis* 1st and 9th Chapters, whereby God gave the Earth to the Sons of *Adam,* and *Noah* to be subdued and replenished. 2. By a right of purchase from the Indians, who were Native Inhabitants, and had possession of the Land before the English came hither, and that having lived here Sixty years, I did certainly know that from the beginning of these Plantations our Fathers entered upon the Land, partly as a Wilderness and *Vacuum Domicilium,*[8] and partly by the consent of the Indians, and therefore care was taken to Treat with them and to gain their consent, giving them such a valuable consideration as was to their satisfaction, and this I told them I had the more certain knowledge of, because having learned the Indian Language in my younger time, I was at several times made use of by the Government, and by divers particular Plantations as an Interpreter in Treating with the Indians about their Lands, which being done and agreed on, the several Townships and proportions of Lands of particular Men were ordered, and setled by the Government of the Countrey, and therefore I did believe that the Lands of *New-England* were the Subjects Properties, and not the Kings Lands. Sir *E. A.* and the rest replied, That the Lands were the Kings, and that he gave the Lands within such limits to his Subjects by a Charter upon such conditions as were not performed, and therefore all the Lands of *New England* have returned to the King, and that the Attorney General then present could tell what was Law, who spake divers things to the same purpose as Sir *E. A.* had done, slighting what I had said, and vilifying

8. [Literally, "Residence-empty," i.e., land uninhabited and available.—Tr.]

the Indian Title, saying, They were Brutes, *&c.* and if we had possessed and used the Land, they said we were the Kings Subjects, and what Lands the Kings Subjects have, they are the Kings, and one of them used such an Expression, *Where-ever an Englishman sets his foot, all that he hath is the Kings,* and more to the same purpose. I told them that so far as I understood, we received only the right and power of Government from the Kings Charter within such limits and bounds, but the right of the Land and Soil we had received from God according to his Grand Charter to the Sons of *Adam* and *Noah,* and with the consent of the Native Inhabitants as I had expressed before. They still insisted on the Kings right to the Land as before, whereupon I told them, I had heard it was a standing Principle in Law and Reason: *Nil dat qui non habet;*[9] and from thence I propounded this Argument; he that hath no right, can give no right to another, but the King had no right to the Lands of *America* before the English came hither, therefore he could give no right to them. I told them, I knew not of any that could be pleaded but from a Popish Principle, that Christians have a right to the Lands of Heathen, upon which the Pope as the Head of the Christians had given the *West Indies* to the King of *Spain,* but this was disowned by all Protestants. Therefore I left it to them to affirm and prove the Kings Title. They replied and insisted much upon that, that the King had a right by his Subjects coming and taking possession of this Land. And at last Sir *E. A.* said with indignation, Either you are Subjects or you are Rebels, intimating, as I understood him according to the whole scope and tendency of his Speeches and Actions, that if we would not yield all the Lands of *N.E.* to be the Kings, so as to take Patents for Lands, and to pay Rent for the same, then we should not be accounted Subjects but Rebels, and treated accordingly. There were many other various replies and answers on both sides, but this is the sum and substance of that discourse—

John Higginson aged seventy four years.
Stephen Seawall aged thirty two years.

John Higginson Minister in *Salem* personally appeared before me, *Dec.* 24. 1689. and made Oath to the truth of the abovesaid Evidence—

John Hathorne Assistant.

9. ["He who does not possess a thing gives nothing."]

Captain *Stephen Seawall* of *Salem* appeared before me, *Dec.* 24. 1689. and made Oath to the truth of the abovesaid Evidence.

John Hathorne Assistant.

Joseph Lynde of *Charles-towne* in the County of *Middlesex* in *N.E.* being fifty three years of age, testifieth and saith, That in the year 1687. Sir *Edmund Androsse* then Governour of *New-England* did inquire of him the said *Lynde* what Title he had to his Lands, who shewed him many Deeds for Land that he the said *Lynde* possessed, and particularly for Land that the said *Lynde* was certainly informed would quickly be given away from him, if he did not use means to obtain a Patent for it. The Deed being considered by Sir *E. A.* he said, it was worded well, and recorded according to *N.E.* custom or words to the same purpose. He further enquired how the Title was derived he the said *Lynde* told him, That he that he bought it of had it of his Father-in-law in Marriage with his Wife, and his said Father from *Charles-towne*, and the said Town from the General Court grant of the *Massachusetts* Bay, and also by purchase from the Natives, and he said, my Title were nothing worth if that were all. At another time after shewing him an Indian Deed for Land, he said, that their hand was no more worth than a scratch with a Bears paw, undervaluing all my Titles, though every way legal under our former Charter Government. I then petitioned for a Patent for my whole Estate, but Mr. *West* Deputy Secretary told me, I must have so many Patents as there were Counties that I had parcels of Land in, if not Towns, finding the thing so chargeable and difficult I delayed, upon which I had a Writ of Intrusion served upon me in the beginning of the Summer 1688, the Copy whereof is in *Charles-towne*'s Mens complaint, and was at the same time with that of Mr. *James Russel*'s, Mr. *Seawall*'s, and Mr. *Shrimpton*'s, it being for the same Land in part that I shewed my Title unto Sir *E. A.* as above, being my self and those I derived it from possessed, inclosed, and improved for about Fifty years, at which time I gave Mr. *Graham* Attorney General three pounds in Money, promising that if he would let the Action fall I would pay Court charges, and give him Ten pound when I had a Patent compleated for that small parcel of Land, that said Writ was served upon me for, which I did because a Quaker that had the promise of it from the Governour, as I was informed in the Governors presence should not have it from me, the said *Lynde*, having about seven Acres more in the same common Field or Pasture, about a Mile from this forty nine Acres near unto the Land that the said Governour gave unto

Mr. *Charles Lidget,* of divers of my Neighbours, which I concluded must go the same way that theirs went, and therefore though desired to be patented by the said *Lynde* with the forty nine Acres, he could not obtain a Grant for it. About the same time Mr. *Graham* Attorney General asked the said *Lynde* what he would do about the rest of his Land, telling him the said *Lynde* that he would meet with the like trouble about all the rest of his Lands that he possessed, and were it not for the Governours going to *New-York* at this time, there would be a Writ of Intrusion against every Man in the Colony of any considerable Estate, or as many as a Cart could hold, and for the poorer sort of people said Sir *E. A.* would take other measures, or words to the same purpose. The said *Lynde* further saith, That after Judgments obtained for small wrongs done him, tryable by their own Laws before a Justice of the Peace, from whom they allowed no Appeals in small Causes: he was forced out of his own County by Writs of false Judgment; and although at the first superiour Court in *Suffolk,* the thing was so far opposed by Judge *Stoughton* as illegal, as that it was put by, yet the next Term by Judge *Dudley* and Judge *Palmer,* the said *Lynde* was forced to answer *George Farewell* Attorney aforesaid, then saying in open Court in *Charles-town,* that all Causes must be brought to *Boston* in *Suffolk,* because there was not honest men enough in *Middlesex* to make a Jury to serve their turns, or words to that purpose; nor did *Suffolk,* as appeared by their practice, for they made use of Non-Residents in divers cases there. I mention not my damage, though it is great, but to the truth above-written I the said *Lynde* do set to my hand—

Boston the 14th of *January,* 1689–90. *Juratus coram me*[10] *John Smith* Assistant.

Joseph Lynde.

And that the practices of these men have been according to their Principles, *destructive to the Property of the Subject,* is now to be declared. It is a thing too well known to be denied, that some of Sir *Edmunds Council* begged (if they had not had secret encouragement no man believes that they would have done so) those Lands which are called *The Commons* belonging to several Townships, whereby *Plymouth, Lyn, Cambridge, Road Island, &c.* would have been ruinated, had these mens Projects taken effect. And not only the *Commons* belonging to Towns, but those Lands which were

10. ["Sworn before me."]

the Property of several particular persons in *Charles-town,* were granted from them. And *Writs of Intrusion* were issued out against Coll. *Shrimpton,* Mr. *Samuel Seawall,* and we know not how many more besides, *That their Lands might be taken from them, under pretence of belonging to King* James. An Island in the possession of *John Pittome* antiently appropriated to the maintenance of a *Free-School,* was in this way seized. How such men can clear themselves from the guilt of *Sacrilegious Oppression,* they had best consider. Mr. *Palmer* swaggers and hectors at a strange rate; for he hath these words, (*p.* 29.) "*I should be glad to see that man who would bare-faced instance in one particular grant of any mans Right or Possession passed by Sir* E. A. *during his Government.*—" And what if we will shew him the men; that dare affirm as much or more than that? what will he do?

Me me adsum qui feci, in me convertite Ferrum.[11]

We will produce those that have said (and sworn as much as all this comes to. For *John Pittome* hath upon Oath declared, That *James Sherlock,* Sir *Edmunds Sheriff,* came on *Dear Island* on the 28th of *January* 1688. and turned him and his Family afloat on the Water when it was a snowy day, although he was Tenant there to Coll. *Shrimpton,* and that the said *Sherlock* put two men (whom he brought with him) into possession of the said Island (as he said) *on behalf of King* James *the Second.* Let him also know, that Mr. *Shepard* and Mr. *Burrill* of *Lyn,* and *James Russell* Esq; of *Charles-towne* in *New-England* have declared upon Oath as followeth.

> *Jeremiah Shepard* Aged forty two years and *John Burril* aged fifty seven years, we whose names are subscribed being made choice of by the Inhabitants of the Town of *Lyn* in the *Massachussetts* Colony in *New England* to maintain their right to their properties and Lands invaded by Sir *Edmund Androsse* Governour, we do testify that (besides Sir *Edmund Androsse* his unreasonable demands of Money by way of Taxation, and that without an assembly, and Deputies sent from our Town according to ancient custom, for the raising of Money or levying of Rates) our Properties, our honest and just and true Titles to our Land were also invaded, and particularly a great and considerable tract of Land called by the name of the *Nahants,* the only secure place for the Grazing of

11. ["Kill me, *me.* I am present who have done this, turn the sword against me." Emphasis added.—Tr.]

some thousands of our Sheep, and without which our Inhabitants could neither provide for their own Families, nor be capacited to pay dues or duties for the maintenance of the publick, but (if dispossessed of) the Town must needs be impoverished, ruined, and rendred miserable, yet this very tract of Land being Petitioned for by *Edward Randolph*, was threatned to be rent out of our hands, notwithstanding our honest and just Pleas for our right to the said Land, both by alienation of the said Land to us from the Original Proprietors the Natives, to whom we paid our Moneys by way of purchase, and notwithstanding near fifty years peaceable and quiet possession and improvement, and also inclosure of the said Land by a Stone Wall, in which tract of Land also two of our Patentees were interested in common with us, *viz.* Major *Humphreys*, and Mr. *Johnson*, yet *Edward Randolph* Petitioning for the said Land, Sir *Edmund the Governour* did so far comply with his unreasonable motion, that we were put to great charges and expences for the Vindication of our honest rights thereto, and being often before the Governour Sir *Edmund* and his Council for relief, yet could find no favour of our innocent cause by Sir *Edmund, notwithstanding our Pleas of Purchase, antient Possession, Improvement, Inclosure, Grant of the General Court, and our necessitous condition,* yet he told us all these Pleas were insignificant, and we could have no true Title unless we could produce a Patent from the King, neither had any person a right to one foot of Land in *N.E.* by vertue of Purchase, Possession or Grant of Courts, but if we would have assurance of our Lands, we must go to the King for it, and get Patents of it. Finding no relief (and the Governour having prohibited Town Meetings, we earnestly desired Liberty for our Town to meet, to consult what to do in so difficult a case and exigency, but could not prevail. Sir *Edmund* angrily telling us that there was no such thing as a *Town* in the Country, neither should we have Liberty so to meet, neither were our Antient Town Records (as he said) which we produced for the vindication of our Titles to said Lands worth a Rush. Thus were we from time to time unreasonably treated, our Properties, and civil Liberties and Priviledges invaded, our misery and ruine threatned and hastned, till such time as our Country groaning under the unreasonable heavy Yoke of Sir *Edmunds* Government were constrained forcibly to recover our Liberties and Priviledges.

Jeremiah Shepard.
John Burril.

Jeremiah Shepard Minister, and *John Burril* Lieutenant, both of *Lin*, personally appeared before us, and made Oath to the truth of this Evidence, *Salem. Feb.* 3. 1689–90.

John Hathorn.
Jonathan Corwin. } Assistants.

James Russel Esq; on the behalf of the Proprietors of the stinted Pasture in *Charlestown*, and on his own personal account, declares as followeth.

That notwithstanding the answer made to Sir *E. A.* his demand by some Gentlemen of *Charlestown* on the behalf of the Proprietors, which they judged satisfactory, or at least they should have a further hearing and opportunity to make out their Rights, there was laid out to Mr. *Lidget* adjoining to his Farm in *Charlestown* a considerable tract of Land (as it is said one hundred and fifty Acres) which was of considerable value, and did belong to divers persons, which when it was laid out by Mr. *Wells* there were divers bound marks shewed by the Proprietors, and some of them, and I had Petitioned for a Patent for my particular Propriety, yet the whole tract was laid out to the said *Lidget*, who not only did cut down Wood thereon, without the right owners consent, but Arrested some for cutting their own Wood, and so they were deprived of any means to use or enjoy their own Land. And notwithstanding there was about twenty Acres of Pasture Land and Meadow taken from the said *Russel*, and given to Mr. *Lidget;* yet afterwards there was a *Writ of Intrusion* served upon a small Farm belonging unto the said *Russel*, unto which the aforesaid Pasture Land did belong, and had been long improved by *Patrick Mark* his Tenant, (and others good part thereof) above fifty years, so that to stop Prosecution, the said *Russell* was forced to Petition for a Patent, he having a Tenant who was feared would comply in any thing that might have been to his prejudice, and so his Land would have been condemned under colour of Law, and given away as well as his Pastorage was without Law. Further the said *Russel* complains, that he having an Island in *Cascobay*, called *Long-Island*, which his honoured Father long since bought of Mr. *Walker*, and was confirmed to *James Russell* by the General Court, and improved several years by Captain *Davis*, by mowing as Tenant to the said *Russell*, and the said *Russell* hearing it was like to be begged away, caused his Writ to be entred in the Publick Records in Mr. *West's* Office, which he paid for the Recording of; notwithstanding Sir *E. A.* ordered Capt. *Clements* (as he said) to survey the same, and he shewed me a Plat thereof, and said, If I had a Patent for it, I must pay three pence *per* Acre, it being 650 Acres. He was further informed, That if the said *Russell* would not take a Patent for it, Mr. *Usher* should have it—

Per James Russell.

Jan. 30. 1689–90. *James Russell* Esq; personally appeared before me, and made Oath to the truth of what is before written—

William Johnson Assistant.

Had not an happy *Revolution* happened in *England,* and so in *New-England,* in all probability those few ill men would have squeezed more out of the poorer sort of people there, than half their Estates are worth, by *forcing them to take Patents.* Major *Smith* can tell them, that an Estate not worth 200 *l.* had more than 50 *l.* demanded for a Patent for it. And if their boldness and madness would carry them out to oppress the Rich after such a manner as hath been shewed, what might the Poor look for? Nevertheless, their Tyranny was beyond any thing that hath been as yet expressed: For if men were willing to bring their Titles to their Possessions to a Legal Tryal, they were not only threatned, but fined and persecuted, and used with barbarous Cruelty. When some Gentlemen in *Boston* resolved in a Legal way to defend their Title to an Island there, Sir *Edmund's Attorney* threatned that it might *cost them all that they are worth, and something besides,* as appears by the following Affidavit.

The Deposition of Captain *Daniel Turel,* and Lieutenant *Edward Willis* Sworn say, That upon *a Writ of Intrusion* being served on *Deer-Island* belonging to the Town of *Boston,* and let unto Colonel *Samuel Shrimpton* by the Select Men of the said Town, the Rent whereof being of long time appropriated towards the maintenance of a Free School in the Town, we the Deponents two of the select Men of the said Town, do testifie, That meeting with Mr. *James Graham* upon the Town-house, and telling him, that if Colonel *Shrimpton* did decline to personate the case of the said Island, we the select Men would. The said *Graham* said, Are *you* the Men that will *stand Suit against the King?* We the Deponents told him we would answer in behalf of the Town. The said *Graham* replied, There was no Town of *Boston,* nor was there any Town in the Countrey; we made answer we were a Town, and owned so to be by Sir *Edmund Androsse* Governor, in the Warrant sent us for the making a Rate; then the said

> *Graham* told us, We might stand the Tryal if we would, but *bid us have a care what we did,* saying, *it might cost us all we were worth, and something else too,* for ought he knew, and further these Deponents say not—
>
> *Jan.* 30. 1689.
>
> *Daniel Turel.*
> *Edward Willis.*
>
> Captain *Daniel Turel* and Lieutenant *Edward Willis* appeared personally before me, and made Oath to the truth of what is above written.
> *William Johnson* Assistant.

One of Sir *Edmund*'s Council and Creatures, Petitioned for an Island belonging to the Town of *Plymouth,* and because the Agents of the said Town obtained a voluntary Subscription from the Persons concerned to bear the charge of the Suit; they were treated as Criminals, and against all Law, Illegally compelled to answer in another County, and not that where the pretended Misdemeanours were committed. And Mr. *Wiswall* the Minister of *Duxbury* having at the desire of some concerned transcribed a Writing which tended to clear the right they had to the Island in Controversie, and also concerning the abovesaid voluntary Subscription, both Transcribed in the Winter 1687. A Messenger was sent to bring him to *Boston* on the 21th *June* 1688. He was then lame in both Feet with the Gout, fitter for a Bed than a Journey, therefore wrote to the Governour, praying that he might be excused until he should be able to Travel, and engaged that then he would attend any Court, but the next Week the cruel Officer by an Express Order from Sir *E. A.* forced him to Ride in that condition, being shod with Clouts instead of Shoes; and when he came before the Council he was there made to stand till the anguish of his Feet and Shoulders had almost overcome him; after he was dismissed from the Council, the Messenger came and told him, he must go to Gaol, or enter into Bonds for his appearance at the next Superior Court held in *Boston,* and pay down 4 *l.* 2 *s.* in Silver. His Sickness forced him to decline a Prison, and to pay the Money. At the next Superior Court he appeared in the same Lame and Sick condition, and the extremity of the Weather cast him into such a violent Fit of Sickness, that he was in the judgment of others nigh unto death, and he himself thought that he should soon be out of their Bonds, and at liberty to lay his Information against his Oppressors before the Righteous Judge of the whole World. After all this having been forced a third time out of his own County and Colony near Forty Miles, he was delivered from the Hands and Humours of his Tyrannical Oppressors, who had exposed him to great difficulties, charges, and to 228 Miles Travel in Journeying to and from *Boston,* directly opposite to the place where he ought to have been tryed, had he been guilty of any of the *pretended Misdemeanours,* none of which his worst Enemies ever had the Face to read in open Court, or openly to charge him with to this day. Now shall such Men as these talk of *Barbarous Usage* who have themselves been so Inhumane?

Quis tulerit Gracchos de seditione querentes![12]

7. As for Sir *E. A.* his *supplying the Indians with Ammunition in the time of actual War with them,* the following Testimonies confirmed the people of *N.E.* in the belief of it.

Lenox Beverley aged about twenty five years being Sworn, saith, That he being Souldier at *Pemyquid* the Winter time 1688. where was Captain General Sir *E. A.* Knight, there came to the Fort where Sir *E. A.* then was, two Squaws, the one *Madocowandos* Sister, and the other *Moxis* Wife (as was said,) and two other Indian Women that went along with them; they were in the Fort with Sir *Edmund* two days, and when they came forth they seemed to be half drunk, this Deponent and *Peter Ripley* was commanded to Guard these Squaws from *Pemyquid* to *New Harbour,* being in distance about two Miles, and as we passed on the way *Madocowandos* Sister laid down her Burden in the Snow and commanded the Deponent to take it up, whereupon the Deponent looked into the Basket, and saw a small Bag which he opened, and found it to be Gunpowder, which he judged five pounds weight, and a Bag of Bullets of a greater weight and the weight of the Basket I took up, was as much as the Deponent could well carry along, and the other three Squaws had each one of them their Baskets, which appeared rather to be of greater than lesser burden, than that the Deponent carried, which were all of them loaden, and brought out of the Fort, and *Madocowandos* Sister said she had that Powder of Sir *Edmund,* and added, that she was to come again to him within four days—

Boston, Aug. 17. 1689. Sworn in Council. Attests *Is. Addington* Secretary.

Lenox X Beverley his mark.

12. ["Who would tolerate the Gracchi complaining about sedition!"]

Gabriel Wood of *Beverly* aged about twenty four years, testifies, That being one of the Souldiers that was out the last Winter past, *Anno* 1688. in the Eastward parts, and under the command of Sir *Edmund Androsse*, and being then at *Pemyquid* with him, was commanded by him the said Sir *E.* together with so many more of the Souldiers as made up two Files to Guard and safely Conduct three Indian Women from *Pemyquid* aforesaid to *New Harbour*, which said Indian Women were all laden, and to my certain knowledge one of the said Women had with her in her said Journey a considerable quantity of Bullets, which she brought with her from *Pemyquid* aforesaid, and to my best apprehension, she had also a considerable quantity of Powder in a Bag in her Basket, but I did not see that opened, as I did see the Bullets, neither dared I be very inquisitive; the rest of the Souldiers in company with me seeing the Indians so supplied with Ammunition (as we all apprehended they were by our Governour and Captain General Sir *E. A.* aforesaid) *we did very much question amongst our selves, whether the said Sir* E. *did not intend the destruction of our Army, and brought us thither to be a Sacrifice to our Heathen Adversaries*—

The mark of *Gabriel* [A] *Wood*.

Gabriel Wood of *Beverley* in the County of *Essex*, personally appeared before me at *Salem* in *N.E. Jan.* 29. 1689–90. and made Oath to the Truth of the above said Evidence.

John Hatherne Assistant.

8. *That the Indians declared they were encouraged by Sir* E. A. *to make War upon the English*, is most certainly true, although the Lying Author of that *Scandalous Pamphlet*, called *New-Englands Faction discovered*, has the impudence to say, that it is *certainly false*. Two Indians, *Waterman* and *David*, testifie that the *Maquas* Indians sent a Messenger to *Pennicock*, to inform that Sir *E. A.* had been tampering to engage them to fight against the English. Another Indian called *Solomon Thomas*, affirmed, that Sir *Edmund* gave him a Book, and that he said that Book was better than the Bible, that it had in it the Picture of the Virgin *Mary*, and that when they should fight at the Eastward, Sir *Edmund* would sit in his *Wigwam*, and say, *O brave Indians!* Another Indian named *Joseph* (who was in hostility against the English) bragged that the Governour had more love for them than for the English. Another Indian named *John James*, did of his own voluntary mind declare to several in *Sudbury*, that Sir *E. A.* had hired the

Indians to kill the English: The men to whom he thus expressed himself, reproved him, and told him that they believed he belied Sir *E. A.* and therefore they secured him, and complained to a Justice of Peace, by which means he was brought to *Boston*, but Sir *E.* instead of punishing, was kind to the Indian, when as both the Justice and the *Sudbury* man had (to use Mr. *Palmers* phrase) *horrible usage*, by means whereof an Alarm and Terrour ran through the Countrey, fearing some mischievous design against them. That this Relation is not a feigned story, the ensuing Testimonies make to appear.

The Testimony of *Waterman*, and *David*, Indians, saith, That the *Maquas* sent a Messenger to *Pennicock* to inform, that Governour *Edmund Androsse* hired the *Maquas* to fight the English, and paid down to them one Bushel of white Wompon, and one Bushel of black Wompon, and three Cartloads of Merchants goods, trucking Cloath and Cotton Cloath, and Shirt Cloath, and other goods. The *Maquas* said, That the English were their good Friends, and said, they would not fight them, for the English never wronged them, but the *Maquas* took the pay on account of the *Maquas* helping the English to fight their Enemies the last War.

Witness our hands { *Davids* X mark.
Watermans Q mark.

Test.
Cornelius Waldo senior,
Moses Parker,
Thomas Read.

The two Indians above-mentioned *Waterman* and *David*, appeared the 4th day, of *May* 1689. and to the Council then sitting owned the above-written to be truth;

Isa. Addington Secretary.

Rochester in the King's Province, *Sept.* 16. 1688.

Samuel Eldred junior of *Rochester* came before *Arthur Fenner* and *John Fones* Esq; two of His Majesties Justices of the Peace, and did declare upon Oath, that on the Evening before an Indian whom he had seized, by name *Joseph*, did in an insulting and vaunting manner say, There was 500 at *Martins Vineyard,* 700 at *Nantucket,* and 400 at *Chappaquessot,* all very well armed, and in a better manner than him the said *Samuel Eldred,* and that our Governour did not dare to disarm them, for that the Governour had more love for them, the said Indians, than for His Majesties Subjects the English. The said Indian being brought before us, and examined, did confess the greatest part of what was sworn against him, and owned that he was one of them that were in hostility against the English in the late Wars, upon which the said Indian was committed to Gaol.

Per Arthur Fenner,
John Fones.

The Testimony of *Joseph Graves* aged 46 years or thereabout, and *Mary Graves* about 30 years, of *John Rutter* aged about 40 years, witness that on the 2d day of *January* 1688. *Solomon Thomas* Indian, being at the house of *Joseph Graves,* in the Town of *Sudbury,* said, that when the Fight at the Eastward should be, if the Indians had the better of it, as the English did retreat, the Friend Indians were to shoot them down, but if the English get the day, we say nothing, and that in the Spring *French and Irish would come to Boston,* as many, and all won Indians, for that was the first place that was to be destroyed, and after that the Countrey Towns would be all won nothing. And further, the said *Solomon* said, that the Governour had given him a Book, which said Governour said, was better than the Bible, and all that would not turn to the Governours Religion, and own that Book, should be destroyed. In which Book he the said *Thomas* said was the Picture of our Saviour, and of the Virgin *Mary,* and of the Twelve Apostles; and the Governour said, when we pray, we pray to the Virgin *Mary;* and when the Fight should be at the Eastward, the Governour would sit in his Wigwam, and say, *O brave Indians!* Whereupon *John Rutter* told the Indian, that he deserv'd to be hanged for speaking such things, but the Indian replied, it was all true. Upon the hearing this discourse, we resolved to come to *Boston,* and acquaint Authority with it, but by reason of the sickness of *Jos. Graves,* we could not presently, but as soon as conveniently we could, we accordingly appeared at *Boston* with our Information, which the said *Joseph Graves* carried to Mr. *Bullivant* a Justice of the Peace.

Joseph Graves,
John X *Rutler signum.*
Mary Y *Graves* mark.

Boston, Jan. 28. 1689. *Joseph* and *Mary Graves* came and made Oath to the truth above-written,

Before me *William Johnson* Assistant,

That when the English secured some of the Indians mentioned, and brought them before Sir *E. A.* Justices, they were basely & barbarously used for their pains, the following *Affidavits* shew.

Sudbury in *New-England, March* 22. 1689–90

Thomas Browne aged about Forty four years, and *John Goodenow* aged about Fifty four years, *John Growt senior*, aged near Seventy years, *Jacob Moore* aged about 44 years, *Jonathan Stanhope* aged about 57 years, and *John Parmiter* aged about 50 years, all Inhabitants of the Town of *Sudbury* aforesaid, do witness that we heard *John James*, Indian, of his own voluntary mind, say, That the Governour was a Rogue, and had hired the Indians to kill the English, and in particular, had hired *Wohawhy* to kill Englishmen, and that the Governour had given the said *Wohawhy* a gold Ring, which was his Commission, which gold Ring the said *Wohawhy* sold to *Jonathan Prescott* for two shillings in money: Whereupon we replied, Sirrah, you deserve to be hanged for what you say. *John James* the Indian replied, What you Papist, all one Governour. I speak it before Governours very face. This discourse of *John James* Indian, was at the place, and on the day above-written.

Thomas Browne,
John Goodenow,
Jacob Moore,
Jonathan Stanhope,
John Parmiter.

Thomas Browne and *John Goodenow*, two of the Subscribers above, having received this Declaration from *John James* the Indian, we thought it our duty forthwith to inform Authority, and did with the Indian presently go to *Water-town* to Justice *Bond* where the said *John James* did voluntarily give his Testimony before the said Justice *Bond*, which after he had taken, the said Justice *Bond* ordered us the said *Thomas Browne* and *John Goodenow* to make our appearance before the Governour Sir *E. A.* or one of the Council with the Indian, which accordingly we did, when we came to the Governours house; after long waiting in a very wet and cold season, we were admitted unto the Governours presence, where we were detained until eleven or twelve a Clock at night, and after a very unkind Treat, we humbly prayed his Excellency, he would please to discharge us of the Indian, but he told us no, and joaked us, saying, we were a couple of brave men, and had the command, one of a Troop of Horse, and the other a Company of Foot, and could we not know what to do with a poor Indian? Further, he asked us what money we gave the Indian to tell us such news, and commanded us still to take care of the Indian till his pleasure was to call for us again, and this as we would answer it. Thus being severely chidden out of his presence, we were forced with the Indian to seek our quarters where we could find them. The next morning we were preparing to go home again to *Sudbury* (being 20 miles or more) being *Saturday*, we were again sent for by the Governour by a Messenger, to wait on the Governour with the Indian, which we did, and waited at the Exchange or Council-house in *Boston*, from nine a Clock in the morning till three of the Clock in the afternoon, where in the face of the Countrey we were made to wait upon the Indian with many squibs and scoffs that we met withal; at last we were commanded up before the Governour and his Council, where we were examined apart over and over, and about the Sun setting were granted leave to go home, it being the Evening before the Sabbath.

Thomas Browne,
John Goodenow.

On Munday Morning following being the 25th of *March*. 1689. *Jacob Moore, Joseph Graves, Joseph Curtis, Joseph Moore, Obadiah Ward,* were by *Thomas Larkin* as a Messenger fetched down to *Boston,* where after Examination, *Jacob Moore* was committed to close Prison. *Joseph Moore, Joseph Graves, Joseph Curtis,* and *Obadiah Ward* were sent home again, paying the said *Larkin* twelve shillings *per* Man. On the next Monday Morning after, being the first day of *April* 1689. *Samuel Gookin* the Sheriff of *Middlesex* and his Deputy came up to *Sudbury,* and commanded *Thomas Browne, John Goodenow* Senior, *John Growt* Senior, *Jonathan Stanhope, John Parmiter,* forthwith to appear at *Boston,* at Collonel *Page's* House, but it being a Wet and Cold Day, we were detained at Judge *Dudleys* house at *Roxbury,* where after long waiting, had the kindness shewn us, to have an examination every man apart before Judge *Dudley,* Judge *Stoughton,* Mr. *Graham* and others, and were bound over to answer at the next Superiour Court to be held at *Boston,* what should there be objected against us upon his Majesties account. *Thomas Browne, John Goodenow* Senior, *John Growt* Senior, were each of them bound over in three hundred pound Bonds, and each man two sureties in three hundred pound Bond a piece. *John Parmiter* and *Jonathan Stanhope,* were bound in a hundred pound a piece, besides the loss of our time and hindrance of our Business, the reproach and ignominy of Bond and Imprisonment, we shall only take the boldness to give a true account of what money we were forced to expend out of our own Purses as followeth, to the Sheriff and other necessary Charges.

	l.	s.	d.
Thomas Browne.	2	00	00
J. Goodenow Senior.	2	00	00
J. Growt Senior.	0	10	00
J. Rutter Junior.	3	05	00
Joseph Curtis.	0	17	00
Jacob Moore.	3	00	00
Jonathan Stanhope.	0	15	00
John Parmiter.	0	15	00
Joseph Graves.	3	15	00

Boston the 21st. of *Decemb.* 1689. *Jurat. cor. Isaac Addington* Assistant.

Thomas Browne.
John Goodenow.
Jacob Moore.
Jonathan Stanhope.
Joseph Curtis.
John Parmiter.

Altho no man does accuse Sir *Edmund* meerly upon Indian Testimony, yet let it be duly weighed (the premises considered) whether it might not create suspicion and an astonishment in *the People of New England,* in that he did not punish the *Indians* who thus charged him, but the English who complained of them for it. And it is certain, that some very good and wise men in *New England* do verily believe that he was deeply guilty in this matter, especially considering what might pass between him and *Hope Hood* an Indian, concerning which Mr. *Thomas Dantforth* the present Deputy Governour at *Boston* in *New England*, in a Letter bearing date *April* 1. 1690. writeth thus—

> The Commander in chief of those that made this spoil (*i.e.*) the spoil which was made in the Province of *Maine* on the 18th of *March* last, is *Hope Hood* an Indian, one that was with sundry other Indians in the summer 1688 seized by some of Sir *Edmunds* Justices and Commanders in the Province of *Maine*, and sent Prisoners to *Boston*, Sir *E.* being then at the Westward, where he continued absent many weeks; upon his return finding the Indians in Prison, fell into a great rage against those Gentlemen that had acted therein, declared his resolution to set them at liberty and calling his Council together, was by some opposed therein, and among others, one Gentleman of the Council accused this *Hope Hood* to be a bloody Rogue, and added that he the said *Hope Hood*, had threatned his Life, and therefore prayed Sir *E.* that he might not be enlarged, but Sir *E.* made a flout and scorn of all that could be said. At the same time some of the Council desired Sir *E.* that this *Hope Hood* might be sent for before the Council, to which he replied, that he never had had a quarter of an hours conference with any of them, and that he scorned to discourse with any Heathen of them all, yet all this notwithstanding, at the same time whilst the Council was thus met, did Sir *Edmund* privately withdraw himself, and repair to the Prison where this *Hope Hood* was Prisoner, and did there continue with him two or three hours in private, the truth of what is above related is attested by sundry Gentlemen that were of Sir *Edmunds* Council, and were then Ear Witnesses and likewise by others that saw Sir *E.* at the Prison; *and it is now verily believed that at that very time he consulted the mischief that is now acted by the said* Hope Hood and Company. Thus Mr. *Dantforth.*

9. That Sir *Edmund Androsse discountenanced making defence against the Indians*, is complained of by five Gentlemen who were of his Council, and much concerned at his strange actings in that matter as in the account annext to this *Apology* is to be seen. It is also confirmed by the *Affidavits* of two honest men—

> *Henry Kerley* aged about fifty seven years and *Thomas How* aged thirty five years or thereabouts, both Inhabitants of the Town of *Malborough*, do both testifie that in the Fall of the year, 1688. When Sir *Edmund Androsse* came from *New-York* to *Boston*, sometime after the Indians had

killed some English men at *North-field* in *New England*, coming through our Town of *Malborough*, the said Sir *E. A.* examined this Deponent *Henry Kerley* by what Order we did Fortify and Garrison our Houses, I answered it was by order of Captain *Nicholson*, the said Sir *E.* then said, he had no power so to do. He the said Sir *E.* examined what Arms we made use of, and carried with us on the Watch, and what charge was given us, answer was made by the Deponent; they carried Fire Arms, and the charge was to keep a true Watch, to examine all we met with, and secure suspicious persons that we met with, the said Sir *E.* said what if they will not be secured, and what if you should kill them, answer was made by the Deponent, that if we should kill them, we were in our way, then Mr. *Randolph* being there in the company said, you are *in the way to be hanged*. Sir *E. A.* said further that those persons that had left their Houses to dwell in Garrisons, if they would not return, others should be put in that would live there.

Boston the 27th of *Decemb.* 1689. *Jur. Henry Kerley*, and the 2d of *Janu.* 1689. *Jur. Thomas How. Cor. Is. Addington.* Assistant.

Henry Kerley.
Thomas How.

That Sir *Edmunds High Sheriff was a Stranger in the Country, and one that had no Estate there* needs no proof, and that *Strangers who had no Freehold, were Impannelled for Jurors* is notoriously known. So it was in the case of the *Ipswich-men* as hath been noted, and when that Reverend person Mr. *Charles Morton*, was causelesly and maliciously prosecuted, he was not only compelled to answer (contrary to Law) in another County, and not in that wherein the good Sermon they found fault with, was Preached, but that if possible, they might give him a blow, there was summoned to serve as a Jury man, one *John Gibson* no Householder nor of any Estate or Credit, and one *John Levingsworth* a Bricklayer, who lived in another Colony two hundred Miles distance. When those in Government will use such *base Artifices* as these to accomplish their pernicious designs, how should any mans Estate or Life be secure under them?

11. That the persons objected against, were some of them *guilty of great extortion* is manifest from what hath been related, and may yet be further proved, for (as by some instances we have already seen, and shall now hear more) they *compelled men to take Patents for their own Lands*, which they, and their Fathers before them, had quietly possessed till these covetous Creatures

became a *Nusance* to the Country, and it may be none more Criminal, as to this particular, than Mr. *Palmer* and Mr. *West.*—A Friend of their own *viz.* Mr. *Randolph* does in several of his Letters bitterly complain of them upon this account. In a Letter of his of *August* the 25th 1687. he writeth thus.

> I believe all the Inhabitants in *Boston* will be forced to take Grants and Confirmations of their Lands, as now intended, the Inhabitants of the Province of *Maine* which will bring in *vast profits to Mr. West,* he taking what Fees he pleases to demand. I shall always have a due Honour and Respect for his Excellency, but I must buy his Favour at three or four hundred pound a year loss. And in another to the same, *June* 21. 1688. he hath these words. I went to one *Shurte,* Town-Clerk of *Pemyquid* to know what Leases were made lately, and by whom, and for what quit Rent, he told me that above a year ago Captain *Palmer,* and Mr. *West* produced to them a Commission from Collonel *Dungan,* to dispose of all their Lands to whoever would take leases at five shillings the hundred Acres quit Rent. They let there and at a place called *Dartmouth* twelve or sixteen Miles distant from *Pemyquid* about one hundred and forty Leases, some had eight hundred or ten hundred Acres, few less than a hundred, some but three or four Acres, and all paid 2 l. 10 s. for passing their Grants of 100 Acres of Wood Land, with twenty Acres of Marsh where ever it could be found, but this bred a great mischief among the People; few or none have their Land measured or marked, they were in haste, and got what they could, *they had their Emissaries amongst the poor people, and frighted them to take Grants,* some came and complained to the Governour, and prayed him to *confirm their Rights, which he refused to do,* the Commission and whole proceeding being Illegal, having notice they were to be under his Government, they resented it, but it served their turn. *The poor have been very much oppressed here,* the Fort run all to ruine, and wants a great deal to repair it, Captain *Palmer* and Mr. *West* laid out for themselves such large lots, and Mr. *Graham* though not there, had a Childs Portion, I think some have eight thousand or ten thousand Acres. *I hear not of one penny rent coming in to the King, from them who have their Grants confirmed at York,* and the five shillings an hundred Acres was only *a Sham* upon the People: at our return we saw very good Land at *Winter Harbour,* enough to make large settlements for many people. The Governour will have it first measured, and then surveyed, and then will dispose of it for settlements, Mr. *Graham* and his Family are setled at *Boston,* he

> is made *Attorney General, and now the Governor is safe in his* New-York *Confidents,* all others being Strangers to his *Council.* 'T was not well done of *Palmer* and *West* to tear all in pieces that was setled and granted at *Pemyquid* by Sir *E.* that was the Scene where they *placed and displaced at pleasure and were as Arbitrary as the great Turk. Some of the first setlers of that Eastern Country were denied Grants of their own Lands, whilst these men have given the Improved Lands amongst themselves,* of which I suppose Mr. *Hutchinson* hath complained. In another, *May* the 16th 1689. he says; I must confess there have been *ill men from New-York* who have too much studied the disease of this people, and both in Courts and Councils, they have not been *treated well.*

Thus does *Edward Randolph,* a Bird of the same Feather with themselves confess the truth, as to this matter, concerning *his Brother* Palmer *and* West.

And that *Oppressive Fees have been extorted by Indigent and Exacting Officers* is declared by Mr. *Hinckley* the present Governour of *New-Plymouth* in his *Narrative of the Grievances and Oppressions of Their Majesties good Subjects in the Colony of* New-Plymouth *in* New-England *by the Illegal and Arbitrary Actings in the Late Government under Sir* E. A. which *Narrative* is too large to be here inserted, but it is possible it may be published by it self, whereby it will appear that every corner in the Countrey did ring with complaints of the Oppressions, and (to speak in Mr. *Palmer's* phrase) *horrible Usages* of these ill Men. Some passages out of Mr. *Hinckley's Narrative* respecting this matter, we shall here Transcribe whose words are these which follow.

> The Bill of Cost Taxed by Judge *Palmer* seems also to be the greatest Extortion ever heard of before, as thrice twenty Shillings for three motions for Judgment at the same Term, (and was it not their courtesie they did not move ten times one after another at the same rate) and Taxed also, *five pound for the Kings Attorney, and one and twenty Shillings for the Judges, and ten Shillings for the Sheriff,* and other particulars as by the said Bill appeareth, and that which makes it the greater Extortion is, that the whole Bill of Cost was exacted of every one of them, which each of them must pay down, or be kept Prisoners till they did, though all seven of them were jointly informed against in one Information. Thus Mr. *Hinckley.*

The cry of poor Widows and Fatherless is gone up to Heaven against them on this account; for the Probate of a Will and Letter of Administration above fifty Shillings hath been extorted out of the hands of the Poor, nay they have been sometimes forced to pay more than four Pounds, when not much above a Crown had been due. Let *Andrew Sergeant* and *Joseph Quilter* among many others speak if this be not true, who were compelled to Travel Two Hundred Miles for the Probate of a Will, and to pay the unreasonable and oppressive Fees complained of—

Besides these things, under Sir *Edmund's* Government they had wicked ways to extort Money when they pleased. Mr. *William Coleman* complains (and hath given his Oath accordingly) that upon the supposed hired Evidence of one Man he sustained Forty Pound damage in his Estate. And there were complaints all over the Countrey that Sir *Edmund's Excise-men* would pretend Sickness on the Road, and get a Cup of Drink of the Hospitable People, but privately drop a piece of Money, and afterwards make Oath that they bought Drink at those Houses, for which the Innocent Persons were fined most unreasonably, and which was extorted from them, though these Villanies were declared and made known to those then in Power. *William Goodhue, James* and *Mary Dennis* might be produced as Witnesses hereof, with many more. Some of Sir *Edmund's* Creatures have said, That such things as these made *his Government to stink.* Also *John Hovey* and others complain of sustaining Ten Pound damages by the Extortion of Officers, though never any thing (they could hear of) was charged upon them to this day, *John* and *Christopher Osgood* complain of their being sent to Prison nine or ten days *without a Mittimus,*[13] *or any thing laid to their charge,* and that afterwards they were forced to pay excessive charges—It would fill a Volume, if we should produce and insert all the *Affidavits* which do confirm the truth of these complaints.

In the time of that unhappy Government, if the Officers wanted Money, it was but Seizing and Imprisoning the best Men in the Countrey for no fault in the World, and the greedy Officers would hereby have Grist to their Mill. Thus was *Major Appleton* dealt with. Thus Captain *Bradstreet.* Thus that worthy and worshipful Gentleman *Nathaniel Salstonstal* Esquire was served by them and *barbarously prosecuted,* without any Information or Crime laid to his charge; for he had done nothing worthy of Bonds, but it was the pleasure of Sir *E.* and some others thus to abuse a Gentleman far more Honourably descended than himself, and one concerned in the

13. [Literally, "We (the king) send," i.e., a writ directing the imprisonment of a person, an arrest warrant.—Tr.]

Government of *N.E.* before him, but (to his Eternal Renown) one who refused to *accept of an Illegal and Arbitrary Commission,* when in the Reign of the Late K. *James* it was offered to him—

We have now seen a whole Jury of complaints which concur in their Verdict against Sir *E. A.* and his Confederates. Were these things to be heard upon the place, where the Witnesses who gave in their *Affidavits* are resident, they would amount to legal proof, as to every particular which was by *the Agents of the Massachusetts Colony in* N.E. objected against Sir *E. A.* and others Seized and Secured by the people there.

Moreover, there are other matters referring to Sir *E. A.* which caused great, and almost Universal Jealousie of him. For, 1. His Commission was such as would make any one believe that a Courtier in the time of the Late King *James* spoke true, who said Sir *E. A. was sent to* New-England *on purpose to be a Plague to the people there.* For he with three or four more (none of them chosen by the people, but rather by that *Implacable Enemy who prosecuted the* Quo Warranto's *against their Charters,* had power given them to make Laws, and raise what Moneys they should think meet for the support of their own Government, and he had power himself alone to send the best and most useful Men a Thousand Miles, (and further if he would) out of the Countrey, and to Build Cities and Castles (in the Air if he could) and demolish them again, and make the Purses of the Poor people pay for it all. Such a Commission was an unsufferable grievance, and no honest Englishman would ever have accepted of it, or acted by it—

Secondly Jealousies were augmented by his involving the Countrey in a War with the Indians, by means whereof he hath occasioned the Ruine of many Families and Plantations; yea the Death, or Captivity of we know not how many Souls. *For he went (with the* Rose *Frigat, and violently seized, and took, and carried away, in a time of peace all the Houshold Good; and Merchandises of* Monsieur Casteen *a Frenchman at* Penobscot *who was Allied to the Indians,* having Married the Daughter of one of their *Princes* whom they call *Sagamores* or *Sachems;* and when this was done, it was easie to foresee, and was generally concluded that the *French* and *Indians* would soon be upon the English, as it quickly came to pass. After the Flame was kindled, and Barbarous Outrages committed by the Indians, Sir *Edmund's* managery was such as filled the Countrey with greater fears of an *horrid design.* For Bloody Indians whom the English had secured, were not only dismissed, but rather courted than punished by him.

3. It cannot be exprest what just and amazing fears surprized the People of *New-England,* when they had notice of the Late *King James's* being in *France,* lest Sir *E. A.* whose Governour and Confident he was, should betray them into the Power of the *French King,* other circumstances concurring to strengthen these fears. The *Mohawks* and other Indians were in hostility against the *French,* and it was very advantagious to the English Interest to have it so, but Sir *E. caused them to make a Peace with the French,* whereby the French Interest in those parts was strengthened, and the English weakened. Mr. *Peter Reverdy* (a French Protestant) in his *Memoirs* concerning Sir *E. A.* complains of this.

After that Sir *E. A. and his Complices* were secured such reports and informations came to hand, as made *New-England* admire the Divine Providence in accomplishing what was done against the late Oppressors. They then saw the persons from whom they suspected the greatest danger, were now incapable of betraying them—

If an unaccountable Instinct and Resolution had not animated the Inhabitants in and about *Boston,* to seize on those few men, the People there believe *N.E.* would have been in the hands not of *King William* but *King Lewis e're this day:* For in *Sept.* 1689. several Vessels belonging to *N.E.* were taken near *Cansir* in *America* by some French Men of War. The Prisoners since at liberty, inform, that the French told them, that there was a Fleet of Ships bound from *France* directly for *Boston* in *N.E.* but some of them were taken by the *English* Ships of War, and three or four of them lost at *New-found-land,* and that Sir *E. A.* had sent to the French King for them to come over, and the Countrey should be delivered up. And the Lieutenant of a French-man of War professed, that if Sir *E. A.* had not been imprisoned, they would then have gone to *Boston.* This shews what a good Opinion the French had of him, and such reports so testified made a strange impression on the spirits of the People throughout the Countrey: And that the World may see we do not write Fictions of our own, the subsequent *Affidavits* are produced and here inserted.

> *John Langford* of *Salem* testifieth, That he being in the Ketch *Margaret* of *Salem, Daniel Gygles* Commander, they were taken by the French Ships off of *Tarbay* in *America* near *Cansir* on *Tuesday* the 17th day of *September* last past, and being put on board of the Admiral, *viz.* The *Lumbuscado,* and in the said Ship carried a Prisoner to *Port Royal,* and then did hear several of the Company on board the said Ship say, that they came

directly from *France*, and that there was ten or twelve Sail of them Ships of War that came in company together, but some of them were taken upon the Coast of *France*, and some were lost since, and that they were all bound directly for *N.E.* and that Sir *E. A.* late Governour of *N.E.* had sent to the French King for them to come over, and the Countrey should be delivered up into his hands, and that they expected that before they should arrive, it would have been delivered into the hands of the French.

John Langford.

Benjamin Majery of *Salem Jersey-man* also testifieth, That he being taken the same day, and at the same place in the *Ketch Diligence, Gilbert Peters* Commander, as is abovesaid in the Evidence of *John Langford*, he heard the same related, by several of the company on board the other French Ship of War that was in company with the *Lumbuscado;* viz. *The Frugum*, so called, that there was ten Sail of them came out directly from *France* together; that Sir *E. A.* late Governour of *N.E.* had sent to the King of *France* for them to come over, and he would deliver the Countrey into their hands, and that they were bound directly for *Boston* in *N.E.* but had lost most of their Ships coming over.

The mark M of *Benjamin Majery.*

John Langford and *Benjamin Majery* both made Oath to the truth of these their respective Evidences in *Salem, Novemb.* 23. 1689.

Before me *John Hathorne* Assistant.

Joshua Conant testifieth, That he being Commander of the Ketch, *Thomas* and *Mary* of *Salem*, he was taken by three French Ships off from *Tarbay*, near *Cansir*, upon *Tuesday* the 17th of *September* last, two of which were Ships of War, the other a Merchant-man, and being put on board the Admiral, *viz.* the *Lumbuscado*, and therein carried to *Port-Royal*, a Prisoner, Mr. *Mero* told me that the French on board told him, that there was ten Sail of them Ships of War came out in company together from *France*, and that they came directly from *France*, and were bound to *Boston* in *N.E.* and that Sir *E. A.* had sent to the French King for them, and that the Countrey was to be delivered up into their hands; but having lost several of their Ships in their Voyage, and hearing that Sir *E. A.* was taken, and now in hold, should not proceed at present, but threatned what they would do the next Summer.

Joshuah Conant.

Joshuah Conant personally appeared before me, and made Oath to the truth of the abovesaid Evidence. *Salem, Novemb.* the 23d. 1689.

John Hathorne Assistant.

Phillip Hilliard of *Salem, Jersey-man* testifieth, That he was taken by the French in a Ketch belonging to *Salem;* viz. *The Thomas* and *Mary, Joshua Conant* Commander off from *Torbay* near *Cansir,* this Autumn *Septemb.* 17. and being carried on board the *Lumbuscado,* did on board the said Ship hear several of the company say, that there was about twelve Sail of them Ships of War, came out in company together from *France,* and were bound directly for *Boston* in *N.E.* and that Sir *E. A.* the late Governour there had sent into *France* for them to come over.

The mark 8 of *Phillip Hilliard.*

Phillip Hilliard personally appeared before me, and made Oath to the truth of the abovesaid Evidence. *Salem, Novemb.* the 23. 1689.

John Hathorne Assistant.

James Cocks of Salem Mariner testifieth, That he was taken by the French in the Ketch *Margaret of Salem, Daniel Gygles* Commander on *Tuesday* the 17th of *September* last past off from *Tarbay* near *Cansir* by two French Ships of War, who had one Merchant-man in company with them, and he being carried on board their Admiral, *viz.* the *Lumbuscado,* he there met with a man he had known in *London,* one of the said Ships Company, who was a *Biscay* born, named *Peter Goit,* who told him that there was thirteen Ships of them came out of *France* in company together, and that they were bound directly for *Boston* in *New-England,* expecting that the Countrey was before, or would be at their coming delivered up to the King of *France,* and told him, before they could get clear of the Coast of *France,* several of their Ships were taken by the English Ships of War, and the rest of their Fleet taken or dispersed and lost about *New-found-land.*

The mark SS of *James Cocks.*

James Cocks personally appeared before me, and made Oath to the truth of the abovesaid Evidence. *Salem, Nov.* 23. 1689.

John Hathorne Assistant.

But as to one of the Crimes objected against Sir *E. A.* and his Arbitrary Complices, *Habemus confitentem reum.*[14] Mr. *Palmer cannot deny but that*

14. ["We have the defendant pleading guilty."]

they levied moneys on the King's Subjects in New-England, *contrary to the fundamentals of the English Government,* which doth not allow the imposition of Taxes without a *Parliament.* The *New-Englanders* supposed that their late Oppressors had been guilty of no less than a capital Crime by their raising Money in such a way as they did; and we are assured that one of them after he received, and before he acted by vertue of his illegal Commission from the Late King, professed, that *if ever he had an hand in raising a penny of Money without an Assembly, his neck should go for it;* and yet no man that we know of had a deeper hand in it than this person had. But Mr. *Palmer,* for the justification of this so foul a business, laies down several Positions which he would have no man deny; One of his Positions is, *That it is a fundamental Point consented to by all Christian Nations, That the first discoverer of a Countrey inhabited by Infidels, gives a right and dominion of that Countrey to the Prince in whose service and employment the discoverers were sent.* These are his words, *p.* 17. We affirm, that this *fundamental Point* (as he calls it) is not a *Christian,* but *an unchristian Principle.* It is controverted among the School-men, *an dominium fundatur in gratia.*[15] *Papists are* (as Mr. *Palmer* is) for the *affirmative,* but the *Scripture teaches us to believe* that {all} the Heathen Nations, *and the Sons of Adam,* and not *the Children of Israel* only, have a right to the Earth, and to the Inheritance which God hath given them therein, *Deut.* 32. 8. When Mr. *Palmer* hath prov'd that *Infidels* are not the *Sons of Adam,* we shall consent to his notion, that Christians may invade their Rights, and take their Lands from them, and give them to whom they please, and that the *Pope* may give all *America* to the *King of Spain.* But let him know, that the first Planters in *New-England,* had more of conscience and the fear of God in them, than it seems Mr. *Palmer* hath. For they were not willing to *wrong the Indians in their Properties;* for which cause it was that they purchased from the Natives their right to the Soil in that part of the World, notwithstanding what right they had by vertue of their Charters from the Kings of *England.* Mr. *Palmer's* Position is clearly against *Jus Gentium & Jus Naturale,*[16] which instructs every man, *Nemini injuriam facere.*[17] He that shall violently, and without any just cause take from Infidels their Lands, where they plant, and by which they subsist, does them manifest injury. And let us know of Mr. *Palmer* if *Christian* Princes have power

15. ["Whether dominion is founded upon grace."]
16. ["*The Law of Nations* and *The Natural Law.*"]
17. ["That he do injury to no one."]

to dispose of the Lands belonging to *Infidels* in the *West-Indies*, whether they have the like Dominion over the Lands belonging to the *Infidels in the East-Indies*, and if these *Infidels* shall refuse to consent that such *Christians* shall possess their Lands, that then they may lawfully *Vi & Armis*[18] expel or destroy them, as the *Spaniards* did! We may send Mr. *Palmer* for further instruction in this point to *Balaam's Ass*, which ingenuously acknowledged that her Master (though an Infidel) had a Property in, and right of Dominion over her, *Numb.* 22. 30. but this *Gentleman* hath some other *Assertions* which he would have us take for *postulata*,[19] and then we shall be his *Slaves* without all peradventures. He tells us in page 17, 18, 19. that the *English Plantations* (*in particular* New-England) *are no parts of the Empire of* England, *but like* Wales *and* Ireland, *which were Conquered, and belong to the Dominion of the Crown of* England, *and that therefore he that wears the Crown, may set up Governments over them, which are Despotick and Absolute, without any regard to* Magna Charta, *and that whereas in* Barbadoes, Jamaica, Virginia, *&c. they have their Assemblies, that's only from the favour of the Prince, and not that they could pretend Right to such Priviledges of Englishmen.*

And now we need no further *discovery of the man*. Could the people of *N.E.* who are zealous for English Liberties ever endure it long, that such a person as this should be made one of their *Judges*, that so by squeezing them, he might be able to pay his *Debts?* And can any rational man believe, that persons of such Principles did not *Tyrannize* over that people when once they had them in their cruel Clutches, and could pretend the Authority of the late King *James* for what they did? In our opinion Mr. *Palmer* hath not done like a Wise man thus to expose himself to the just resentments and indignation of all the *English Plantations*. If ever it should be his chance to be amongst them again, what could he expect but to be lookt on as *communis Hostis*,[20] when he thus openly declares that they have no English Liberties belonging to them?—That worthy Gentleman Sir *William Jones* (who was *Attorney General* in the Reign of King *Charles* the second) had certainly more understanding in the Law than Captain *Palmer*, and yet Captain *Palmer* (we suppose) is not ignorant that when some proposed, that *Jamaica* (and so the other Plantations) might be governed without an

18. ["By force and arms."]
19. ["Necessary or self-evident assumptions as a basis of reasoning."]
20. ["The common enemy."]

Assembly, *that excellent Attorney* (not like Captain *Palmer* but like an Englishman) told the then King, *That he could no more Grant a Commission to Levy Money on his Subjects there without their consent by an Assembly, than they could discharge themselves from their Allegiance to the English Crown;* and what Englishmen in their right Wits will venture their Lives over the Seas to enlarge the Kings Dominions, and to enrich and greaten the English Nation, if all the reward they shall have for their cost and adventures shall be their being deprived of *English Liberties,* and in the same condition with the *Slaves* in *France* or in *Turky!* And if *the Colonies of* N.E. *are not to be esteemed as parts of* England, *why then were the* Quo Warranto's issued out against the Government in *Boston* as belonging to *Westminster* in *Middlesex!* Are the English there, like the *Welsh* and *Irish* a Conquered people? When Mr. *Palmer* hath proved that, he hath said something. They have (through the Mercy of God) obtained Conquests over many of their Enemies, both *Indians* and *French,* to the Enlargement of the English Dominions. But except Mr. *Palmer* and the rest of that Crew will say, That his and their *domineering* a while was a *Conquest,* they were never yet a *Conquered People.* So that his alledging the case of *Wales* and *Ireland* before English Liberties were granted to them, is an impertinent Story. Besides, he forgets that there was *an Original Contract* between the King and the first Planters in *New-England,* the King promising them, if they at their own cost and charge would subdue a Wilderness, and enlarge his Dominions, they and their Posterity after them should enjoy such Priviledges as are in their Charters expressed, of which that of not having Taxes imposed on them without their own consent was one. Mr. *Palmer* and his *Brethren Oppressors* will readily reply, Their *Charter* was condemned. But he cannot think, that the Judgment against their Charter made them cease to be *Englishmen.* And only the Colony of the *Massachusetts* had their Charter condemned. And yet these Men ventured to Levy Moneys on the Kings Subjects in *Connecticott Colony.* For the which *Invasion of Liberty and Property* they can never answer. Indeed they say the Corporation of *Connecticott surrendred their Charter.* But who told them so? It is certain, that no one belonging to the Government there, knoweth of any such thing; and how their Oppressors should know that *Connecticott* made a Surrender of their Charter when the Persons concerned know nothing of it, is very strange. We can produce that written by the Secretary of that Colony with his own Hand, and also Signed by the present Governour there, which declares the contrary to what these Men (as untruly as boldly) affirm. Witness the words following.

> In the Second year of the Reign of King *James* the Second, we had a *Quo Warranto* served upon us by *Edward Randolph*, requiring our appearance before His Majesties Courts in *England*, and although the time of our appearance was elapsed before the serving of the said *Quo Warranto*, yet we humbly petitioned His Majesty for his Favour, and the continuance of our Charter with the Priviledges thereof. But we received no other favour but a second *Quo Warranto*, and we well observing that the *Charter of London* and other considerable Cities in *England* were condemned, and that *the Charter of the Massachusetts* had undergone the like Fate, plainly saw what we might expect, *yet we not judging it good or lawful to be active in surrendring what* had cost us so dear, nor to be altogether silent, we empowered an Attorney to appear on our behalf, and to present our Humble Address to His Majesty, but quickly upon it as Sir *E. A. informed us*, he was empowered by His Majesty to Receive *the Surrender of our Charter*, if we saw meet so to do, and us also to take under his Government. *Also Colonel Thomas Dungan* His Majesties Governour of *New-York*, laboured to gain us over to his Government. *We withstood all these motions*, and in our reiterated Addresses, we Petitioned His Majesty to continue us in the free and full enjoyment of our Liberties and Properties, Civil and Sacred, according to our Charter. We also Petitioned that if His Majesty should not see meet to continue us as we were, but was resolved to annex us to some other Government; we then desired that in as much as *Boston* had been our old Correspondents, and a people whose Principles and Manners we had been acquainted with, we might rather be annexed to Sir *E. A.* his Government, than to Colonel *Dungans*, which choice of ours was *taken for a resignation of our Charter, though that was never intended by us for such, nor had it the Formalities in Law to make it such*. Yet Sir *E. A.* was Commissionated to take us under his Government, pursuant to which about the end of *October* 1687. he with a Company of *Gentlemen and Granadeers* to the number of Sixty or upwards came to *Hartford* the Chief Seat of this Government, *caused his Commission to be read, and declared our Government to be dissolved*, and put into Commission both Civil and Military Officers throughout our Colony as he pleased. When he passed through the principal parts thereof, the good people of the Colony though they were under a great sense of the

injuries sustained thereby, yet chose rather to be silent and patient than to oppose, being indeed surprized into *an involuntary submission* to an Arbitrary Power—

Hartford, June 13. 1689.

Robert Treat Governour.
John Allen Secretary.

Thus did Sir *E. A.* and his Creatures, who were deeply concerned in the Illegal Actions of the Late Unhappy Reigns, contrary to the Laws of God and Men, commit a Rape on a whole Colony; for which Violence it is hoped they may account, and make reparation (if possible) to those many whose Properties as well as Liberties have been Invaded by them—

Captain *Palmer* in the close of his *partial account of N.E.* entertains his Readers with an *harangue* about the *Sin of Rebellion,* and misapplies several Scriptures that so he might make the World believe that the people of *N.E.* have been guilty of wicked *Rebellion* by their casting off the Arbitrary Power of those ill men who invaded Liberty and Property to such an intolerable degree as hath been proved against them. But does he in sober sadness think, that if when Wolves are got among Sheep in a Wilderness, the Shepherds and Principal men there shall keep them from Ravening, that this is the Sin of Rebellion condemned in the Scripture? How or by whose Authority our *Lawyer* comes to play the *Divine* we know not. But since he hath thought meet to take a Spiritual Weapon into his hand, let him know that the Scripture speaks of a lawful and good *Rebellion,* as well as of that which is unlawful. It is said of good *Hezekiah that he Rebelled against the King of Assyria and served him not,* 2 *Kings* 18.7. Indeed reviling *Rabshakeh* upbraided him, and said as in *verse* 20. *thou Rebellest* (not unlike to Captain *Palmer*) saying to *N.E. thou rebellest. Hezekiahs* predecessours had basely given away the Liberties of the people, and submitted to the *Arbitrary Power* of the *Assyrians,* and therefore *Hezekiah* did like a worthy Prince in casting off a Tyrannical Government, and asserting the Liberty of them that were the Lords People, and God did signally own and prosper him in what he did, and would never permit the *Assyrian* to regain his Tyrannical Power over *Jerusalem* or the Land of *Judah,* though for their tryal he permitted their Enemies to make some Devastations among them. The like (we hope) may be the happy case of *New England.* Mr. *Palmer* tells us, that *N.E. hath valued it self for the true profession and pure exercise of the Protestant Religion,* but he intimates that they will be *termed a Land full of Hypocrisie and Rebellion, Irreligion, and a degenerate wicked people, p.* 39. And is this the *Sincerity and Christian Moderation* which he boasts himself of in his Preface? Surely these are the *Hissings of the Old Serpent* and do sufficiently indicate whose Children the men are that use them. Since he will be at Divinity, let him (if he can) read the *Apologies* written by *Justin Martyr,* and *Tertullian* and there see if *Pagans* did not accuse *Christians* of Old just after the same manner, and with the same Crimes that he wickedly upbraids that Good and Loyal People with. Who are they that use to call the Holiest and most Conscientious men in the World, *Hypocrites, Liars, Rebels, and what not?* but they that are themselves the greatest *Hypocrites, Liars, and Rebels* against Heaven that the Earth does bear? It is hard to believe that Captain *Palmer* does not rebel against the light of his own Conscience, when he affirms as in Page (38) that in *N.E. every thing that hath any relations to their Majesties is neglected, and unregarded without any recognition of their Authority over those dominions.* He cannot be ignorant of the humble *Addresses* which the people in *N.E.* have from time to time made to their present Majesties, acknowledging their Authority. He knows that on the first notice of their Majesties being proclaimed *King* and *Queen* in *England,* both those now in Government in *N.E.* and the body of the people with them, did (without any command) of their own accord, with the greatest Joy proclaim their Majesties in *N.E.* he knows that their Majesties have no subjects more cordially and zealously devoted to them than those in *N.E.* are, or that do with greater fervour pray for their long and happy Reigns, or that are more willing to expose themselves to the utmost hazards in their service, and yet this man that knoweth all this, to cast an *Odium* on that Loyal and Good people, insinuates as if they were *Rebels,* and *disaffected* to the Present Government, and designed to set up an *Independant Common Wealth,* and had *no regard to the Laws of God or Men.* After this lying and malicious rate hath he exprest himself—What Rational Charity can be extended so far as to believe that 'tis possible for him to think that what himself hath written is true? When *Sanballat* wrote that *Nehemiah* and the Jews with him *intended to Rebel,* did he believe what he had written? no, he did not, but *feigned those things out of his own heart.* The like is to be said of those *Sanballats* that accuse the people of *N.E.* with thoughts of Rebellion. And so we have done with Mr. *Palmer.* What hath been said is sufficient to *justify* the *Revolution* in *N.E.* and to *vindicate the People* there from the Aspersions cast upon them by their Enemies. Several

Worthy Gentlemen have under their hands given an account concerning some of Sir *Edmund's Arbitrary proceedings*, which is subscribed by five (and more would have concurred with them had there been time to have communicated it) of those who were of Sir *Edmunds* Council during his Government there, and for that cause their complaints carry the more weight with them, which shall therefore as a Conclusion be here subjoined.

Reader,

There is such Notoriety *as to Matter of Fact in the preceding* Relation, *that they who Live in* New-England *are satify'd concerning the Particulars contained therein. If any in* England *should Hesitate, they may please to understand that Mr.* Elisha Cooke, *and Mr.* Thomas Oakes (*who were the last Year sent from* Boston *to appear as Agents in behalf of the* Massachusetts Colony) *have by them Attested Copies of the* Affidavits (*at least wise of most of them*) *which are in this* Vindication *published, and are ready* (*if occasion serve*) *to produce them.*

FINIS.

·6·

John Montague, Arguments Offer'd to the Right Honourable the Lords Commissioners (1701)

THE DECADES following the Glorious Revolution in British America were characterized by an ongoing uncertainty about the rights that the colonists were entitled to as subjects outside the realm. But in contrast to the violent overthrow of the Dominion of New England in 1689, legal appeals to the Crown and lobbying in London became the preferred method for expressing colonial grievances. War with the French also shaped the politics of the empire in these years as royal officials came to see colonial autonomy as inimical to imperial defense. These officials were particularly concerned that the colonists' desire for land not alienate the Native Americans whose support was vital in the long conflict with New France. Because of its proximity to both the French and to the strategically important Five Nations (the Iroquois confederacy), New York was at the center of both military and political conflict in the post–Glorious Revolution empire.

John Montague's *Arguments Ofer'd* is a product of the fraught politics of New York in the new transatlantic political world of the late 1690s and early 1700s. Montague was a London lawyer retained by prominent New Yorkers who sought to prevent the royal confirmation of three acts passed in 1699 by the legislature at the behest of the new governor, Lord Bellomont. The most important of these acts overturned several grants of Mohawk land made by the previous governor, Benjamin Fletcher. Because Bellomont had been sent to New York to strengthen the defenses of the northern colonies against the

French, he wanted to mollify the Mohawks (one of the powerful Iroquois confederacy) and thus got the council and the legislature to annul Fletcher's grants. In addition to preserving their claim to Mohawk land, Montague's clients were also concerned about the jailing of two excise collectors, as well as the removal of a minister, Godfrey Dellius, from his post at Albany (Dellius was one of the recipients of Mohawk land).

In opposing these acts, Montague expressed a growing settler concern about the prerogative power of royal governors in the colonies. As he told the Lords Commissioners, in jailing the two excise collectors without due process, Bellomont had acted in an "arbitrary" fashion and had violated "that Liberty whereto every *English Subject* is entitled." Montague also accused Bellomont of using his powers of appointment to influence the composition of the legislature in order to get these acts passed, thereby placing "the Liberties and Properties of the People of this Province" at "the will & pleasure of the Governor." In addition to defending the idea of a balanced constitution, Montague also argued that the Indians had a natural right to the lands in question which they had then transferred to his clients. Indeed, Montague went so far as to argue that these lands were "never the Possessions . . . of the Crown." Moreover, he held that his clients, having purchased the land from the Indians, had made "Improvements" which increased its value and which had also "enlarged the Dominions and Territories of the *Crown of England*." To now "wrest these Lands out of the hands of the Grantees" would, he argued, be both "Unjust" and "Unreasonable." And, in what may be the earliest use of Locke's ideas in British America, Montague also argued that "People" leave the "state of Nature" and "unite themselves into Politick Societies" in order to render their property more secure. Montague drove this point home by quoting directly from the *Second Treatise* to argue that neither the executive nor the legislature could therefore take property arbitrarily (and in a somewhat transparent attempt to influence the commissioners, he added that Locke "lately had the honour to sit at this Board").

Although Montague was initially successful in preventing the confirmation of Bellomont's acts, the case dragged on unresolved for several more years, its indeterminate status exemplifying the tensions inherent in an empire where royal authority competed with the desire of settlers to exercise rights to property and self-government irrespective of the claims of non-Europeans and the imperatives of imperial defense. (C.B.Y.)

ARGUMENTS

Offer'd to the Right Honourable the

Lords Commissioners

FOR

Trade & Plantation

Relating to some Acts of Assembly past

at *New-York* in *America.*

Printed in the Year 1701.

Arguments, Etc.
To the Right Honourable the Lords Commissioners for Trade & Plantations.

The humble Memorial of John Montague *of* Chancery-Lane, London, *Gent. on behalf of several hundreds of Land Owners and principal Inhabitants of his Majesties Province of New York, touching some Acts (now before your Lordships) of the Assembly (or pretended Assembly) of that Province, beginning the 2d of March, 1698, and ending the 16th of* May *following.*

May it please your Lordships;

Having received several Instruments from *New-York,* under the Hands of several Hundreds of the Gentlemen and others of that Province, to impower me to act for them against the said Acts, and in other Matters, I did on their behalfs present my humble Petition to your Lordships, praying to be heard by Council, against several of the said Acts; and have in answer thereto, received from Mr. *Popple* your Lordships Commands to lay before your Lordships in writing what I have to offer upon this Subject.

In obedience whereto, I shall with all humble Submission to your Lordships, attempt to say something against some of these Acts, in such a manner (tho' with much less advantage) as I can suppose Council would have done, had it been your Lordships pleasure first to have heard my Clyents by their Council.

And (*My Lords*) if the Consideration of my Duty to my Clyents, regard to the Trust I am favour'd with by so great a Number of People, and the apprehensions I have conceived of the weight of the Concern, shall occasion me to speak of things too high for me, rather than omit any thing I can in my small Capacity think of, that may be fit for Consideration upon this subject, I hope your Lordships will Pardon my so doing, together with the Prolixity thereby occasioned.

And I beseech your Lordships to believe, that nothing but the Considerations before-mention'd induced me thus to wander above my Sphere.

My Lords, I shall trouble your Lordships with particular Objections but against three of these Acts. And the first that I shall mention is that entitled, *An Act for committing* Ebenezer Willson *and* Samuel Burt (*Farmers of the Excise on the Island of* Nassaw) *for their contemptuous refusing to render an Account of what they farm'd the same for, to the respective Towns, Counties and Mannors on the said Island for the last year.*

This Act recites, That the Governour and Council had required the Farmers of the Excise to lay before the House of Representatives, upon Oath, the most plain and perfect Account they could give, of what they had let the Excise for, of the several Towns, Mannors and Jurisdictions within the Island of *Nassaw,* the last year of their Farm. And that Mr. *Burt* and Mr. *Willson,* without giving any sufficient Reason, in contempt of his Majesties Authority, wherewith (says the Act) the House, in the Quality they were then sitting, was invested, wilfully & stubbornly had done, and did refuse to give such Account as was required. And therefore enacts That Mr. *Burt* and Mr. *Willson* should be committed into safe Custody, without Bail or Mainprize, until they should exhibit under hands, upon Oath, the Account required, &c.

The Case (as I am inform'd, and as I presume will not be denyed) of these two Gentlemen was thus: They are Traders, and were Farmers of this Excise: They lost by the Farm, and were unwilling such loss should be made publick, lest it should prejudice their Credit, & so damnifie them in their Trade. The Governour sends for them, and [*extra judicially*] requires them to give an Account upon Oath (which Oath he likewise would have extrajudicially administred to them) of what they had made of their Farm. They refuse to take this Oath, & the Governour therefore was so rash as to commit them. After they had lain several days in Prison, then is this Act procur'd to be past.

Now, *My Lords,* with humble submission, either these Gentlemen were obliged by Law (antecedent to this Act) to give the Account required, or they were not. If they were obliged to it by Law antecedent to this Act, then there was no occasion for this Act, nor ought this Act to have been made; for they ought then to have been compell'd to do it by the Executive Power in the ordinary course of Justice; and the Legislative Power ought not to have been made Executive to compell them to it.

If these Gentlemen were not obliged by Law antecedent to this Act to give the Account required, Then, with humble submission, the Governour in committing them was guilty of a very arbitrary proceeding, and a great Violation of the Law; and then this Act is made to countenance or excuse an Illegal Act of the Governors; and with submission, the Governour's Commitment was illegal, even although they had been obliged to give such Account by Law antecedent to this Act; for in that case the Governour could not compell them thereto extrajudicially, but they would even in that case have been compellable thereto (only) in the ordinary course of Justice.

And they were guilty of no manner of Offence in refusing to take the Oath the Governour thus arbitrarily and illegally tendered to them.

When the Excise was farm'd in *England*, there was, as I am inform'd, a Covenant on the part of the Farmers, to give an Account, like what was demanded in this case, which (if there needed any) is an argument they could not, without such Covenant, have been compell'd to it. And it would, with humble Submission, have been thought a very strange and arbitrary proceeding here in *England*, and a great Instance of Infringement of the *English Liberties*, for the King to have sent for the Farmers of the Excise and tendered them an Oath to give such Account, and upon their refusal immediately to have committed them, such a Commitment would, without doubt, have been illegal, and against the Letter and meaning of *Magna Charta;* and therefore in his case neither the Governour, nor the House could (antecedent to the Act) be invested with any Authority to commit these Gentlemen, nor to require (especially in an extrajudicial manner) any Oath from them touching what they had made of their Farm. And yet this Act punishes them for an Offence, as such, antecedent to the Act, and does not first make it their Duty by enacting, That they should do it within a limitted time after the passing of the Act, & that in default thereof they should be committed for the breach of the Law after it was made, but enacts, *That they should be forth-with committed*, as having been guilty of an Offence before the Act made.

My Lords, therefore, with humble submission, to confirm this Law, will be either to countenance an illegal Act, and a violation of the Law by the Governour, in derogation of that Liberty whereto every *English Subject* is entituled, or else it will be to declare, That Mr. *Willson* & Mr. *Burt* were guilty of an Offence against the Law in refusing the Oath extrajudicially tendered to them before the making of this Act, when there was no Law to oblige them either to give the Account or take the Oath required; and the very tendring the Oath to them was illegal.

The Complainers therefore against these Acts think their Liberties much concern'd in this matter, and humbly hope your Lordships will think so illegal and Arbitrary a Proceeding of the Governour's, as the tendring such an Oath extrajudicially, and afterwards committing these two Gentlemen only for refusing to take it, ought not afterwards to receive the Countenance, much less the Affirmance of the Legislative Power; & that your Lordships will so far discourage a Governour's acting arbitrarily and illegally and upon any slight occasion making use of the Legislative Power, as Executive in a particular case, to countenance his illegal Proceedings; or (as it may happen) to gratifie his Revenge, by making a Law to punish that as an Offence, which was not so before, nor at the time it was committed. They hope your Lordships will at least so far discountenance things of this Nature, as to advise his Majesty to reject this Act, which they apprehend to be a President of dangerous Consequences to the Laws and Liberties whereto they are very well assured your Lordships will, at all times, and upon all occasions, have a very tender regard.

My Lords, the next of these Acts that I shall beg leave to object to, is that entituled, *An Act for the vacating, breaking and annulling of several Grants of Land, &c.* Which is complain'd of not only as great Injustice to the Grantees and divers others, but also as a thing of dangerous Consequence, and that renders the Property of all Lands within this Province incertain and precarious, and perfectly at the will of the Governour and fifteen, fourteen, or a less number of Men. But before I speak to the vacating of the Grants in Question by this Act, and divesting the Grantees of them, I must not omit to take notice of a Clause that is very strangely thrust into this Act, and more strangely into the Preamble of it, among the Recitals of the Grants there said to be Extravagant, in these words.

> That it having appear'd to the house of Representatives conven'd in general Assembly, That Mr. *Godfrey Dellius* has been a principal Instrument in deluding the *Mahaque Indians* and illegally and surreptitiously obtaining of said grant, that he ought to be, and is hereby suspended from the Exercise of his ministerial function in the City and County of *Albany.*

My Lords, What is here meant, by deluding, and what by surreptitiously *obtaining this Grant,* is so uncertain that nothing can be more, had the Act specified how and in what the *Indians* were *deluded,* and how Mr. *Dellius* was *Instrumental* in that, what facts Mr. *Dellius* did to *delude* the *Indians,* and what he did to *obtain* this *Grant,* then his Majesty and your Lordships might have been able thereby to judge whether Mr. *Dellius* had been guilty of an Offence, of what nature and Quality the Offence was, and what punishment it ought to receive, and whether it were an Offence that was worthy the consideration of and punishment by the Legislative Power, But to attaint and punish a man by the Legislative Power, and not to specifie and describe plainly in the Act of attaint, the Offence for which he is so punished, is, with submission, a Method altogether strange and unusual, and very unbecoming the Justice and Wisdom of a Legislative Power to use. It is very well known, that Mr. *Dellius* has been very Instrumental in converting the *Mohaques* and other *Indians* to the *Christian* and *Protestant Religion,* and thereby keeping them from the *French* and uniting them to the *English Interest;* And (for ought appears by this Act) that may be the deluding there meant.

The punishment is very severe, yet uncertain too; he is disgraced by an Attaint by the Legislative Power, and is suspended from the Exercise of his Ministerial Function in the City and County of *Albany,* where he has been (with considerable Reputation) a Minister for above fifteen years. He is stript at once of his livelihood, and no body knows (nor can learn by this Act) for how long he is suspended, nor when or how he shall be restored. Nor does it (as has been said) appear by this Act what he has done to deserve so severe a punishment. More might be said against this clause: But I shall only, with submission, add at present, That at least your Lordships will think That before his Majesty gives his Authority for the inflicting so severe a Punishment on a particular Person (especially a Minister) as the publickly disgracing him, and utterly stripping him of his Livelihood, his Majesty will be better satisfied of the crimes laid to his charge, than he can be by the incertain, general and ambiguous Terms used in this Act, for the reasons why he is thus punished.

My Lords, As to the principal part and design of this Act, to wit, the vacating Grants of Land and divesting the Owners of them, (for which no other reason is assign'd but that the Legislators are pleased to think them Extravagant, or at least to call them so) there seems to be so many things of weight to be objected to it, that the difficulty is not to find out Exceptions to, and Reasons against it, but rather which to begin with.

The Gentlemen who have attempted to be advocates for this Act have endeavoured to represent it as a thing done pursuant to the Lords Justices Instructions, and to be like an Act of Resumption of Crown Lands here in *England.*

As to the Lords Justices Instructions, They were to *break the Grants by legal means;* which term of [*Legal*] is a Relative Term, and must relate to the Law then in being, and not to a New Law after to be made; And therefore these Instructions cannot, with Submission, be construed to intend any thing but to vacate them by a proceeding in the Ordinary Course of Justice.

And whose Representation from this Province, and Solicitation gave occasion to these Instructions, (or rather procured them,) is, I presume, not unknown to your Lordships.

My Lords, with Submission, This Act is not at all in the Circumstances or Reason of an Act of Resumption of Crown Lands in *England.* For *First,* All that have any Lands in this Province, have a Grant from the Crown of them, so that to disturb these Grants, is to disturb the Titles of the Lands of an whole Province. 2*dly,* Most of the Lands in Question, (and particularly those comprized in the Grants to Mr. *Dellius* and Coll. *Bayard,*) were by the Grantees purchased of the *Indians,* and afterwards Grants were taken of them from the *Crown of England,* under small Quit-Rents, by way of Acknowledgment, to fix the Tenure and Soveraignity of them in this Crown, and put them under it's Protection; and so as to these Lands, the Revenues of the Crown are not diminished by the Kings Grants, but the Territories and Dominions of the Crown are inlarged by the Subjects purchase.

My Lords, I will endeavour to reduce, at least, the greatest part, I have to say to this Act, to these two heads.

1st. *That it is Unreasonable and Unjust.*

2dly. *That it tends not only to the discouraging and Interruption of all planting and improving of Lands within this Province but even to the subversion of Government, and reducing things to disorder and Confusion.*

My Lords, with humble Submission, this Act is *Unjust* and Unreasonable, and that for these Reasons.

1st. Because the Grantees are by this Act divested of the Lands granted, and several of them have been at considerable Charges in Buildings and Improvements, and several of them have made Leases and Conveyances of the granted Lands to others, who have made Improvements thereon; and yet by this Act there is no manner of provision made to Reimburse the Grantees the charges they have been at about the Lands it arbitrarily divests them of; nor any provision made for, or care taken of those who have (upon the Credit of the Grants in Question, and his Majesties Declaration, *That they should be good against his Majesty, his Heirs and Successors*) taken Leases or other Conveyances, and made Improvements under these Grants. In case it could be made out to be just for the Legislative Power to take the Lands in Question away from the Grantees (as for reasons which I shall mention hereafter I presume your Lordships will think it never can) yet certainly (with Submission) the Grantees and those that have taken Leases &

Conveyances under these Grants, ought in all Reason and Justice at least to be satisfied all Charges and Expences they have been at about these Lands. It cannot (with humble Submission) but be thought a very strange proceeding in a Government, first, to grant these lands to particular Persons, & incourage them to be at Charge about them, and others and also to be at Expence about the Lands comprized in such Leases and Conveyances; and afterwards (by an Act of the Legislative) arbitrarily to wrest these Lands out of the hands of the Grantees, and all claiming under them, without any manner of Consideration for the Charges they have been at about them. This, with humble Submission, is so manifest an Injustice, That it plainly seems (if there were no other) a sufficient reason for rejecting this Act.

But, *2dly*, This Act is Unjust and Unreasonable, Because it seizes into the Kings hands, and divests several Persons of Lands, that were never the Possessions or Rights of the Crown, but purchased by these Persons so divested (or those under whom they claim) of the *Indians*. That this is the case at least of a very great (if not the far greatest) part of the Lands in Question, I presume the advocates for this Act will not deny; If they do, 'tis ready to be proved. Nor will it be deny'd I believe but the *Indians* had possession of at least a great part of the Lands in Question, till they sold them to the Persons who are divested of them by this Act. Nor that those Persons had Lycences from the Government to purchase them of the *Indians*. If the *Indians* had possession of them, then, with Submission, they had a Right to them by preoccupancy, by the Law of Nature; and by all other Laws, a Right by Possession against every one but he that could shew a better Right. The discovering and possessing these Lands, might give the English a Right against any others, but the Natives; But that which gave them a Right before others (not being the Natives, *viz* Possession and Preoccupancy) gave the Natives a Right against them, until the Natives by free agreement should part with such their Right.

The advantage any Nation has over another, in Might and Power, in true Religion, or in the Arts of Government, War or Improvements, or other Arts or Sciences, does not, (with humble Submission) give the Nation that has those Advantages, in ever so great a Degree, a Right to the possessions of another People, be they ever so Weak, and Unable to defend them, ever so Ignorant and Irreligious, ever so salvage and Barbarous. Nor is it pretended that these Indians are in a state of War with *England*, for they have been treated with as Friends, and the granting Lycences by the Government to purchase Lands of them, admits them to have a Right to sell them; which 'tis not to be doubted but they once had, and (with humble Submission) I do not see how they have lost it; unless their being Weak and Unable to defend themselves, or unskill'd in Religion, Policy and Arts, can alter matter of Right, upon the Principles of Natural Justice; I shall therefore say no more at present as to this, until I have learn'd from the advocates for this Act, what Title the Crown had to the Lands purchased by Coll. *Bayard* and Mr. *Dellius,* and others respectively of the *Indians,* (and of which Lands they are divested by this Act) before they were so purchased; Only that the Owners on such Lands by or under such purchases, do humbly insist and rely upon it, that by such purchases they have a full Right and Property in the Lands so purchased; And that I am inform'd that it was formerly thought for the Interest of the Crown of *England,* that as much Lands as could, should be purchased from the *Indians;* And also that all Incouragement was given to People to make such purchases, for that the Territories of the *Crown of England* are thereby inlarged.

But, *3dly* This Act has the Misfortune to be most manifestly Unjust and Unreasonable upon its own principles. The Fundamental Principle upon which this Act proceeds, is, *That the Grants in Question are Extravagant,* but the Deduction it makes from that principle will by no means, in Justice or Reason, follow from it.

For, (for ought appears by this Act) all the Grants in Question, (except one of the two Grants to Mr. *Dellius*) were duly and legally made. But they are *Extravagant;* Admitting them to be so, then, with humble Submission, The proper and reasonable Measure is, not to take all the granted Lands from the Grantees, but such parts only, as would reduce the Extravagancy of the Grant to reasonable and moderate Limits: If a Grant be *Extravagant,* It is because more is granted than ought to have been, and then it will follow, that some part ought not to have been granted; But it will not from thence follow, that no part ought to have been granted, or that all ought to be taken from the Grantee.

Had the Act in taking notice of the Grant of Ground of fifty foot long to Mr. *Caleb Heathcote,* declared it to be *Extravagant,* because it granted him too much by Twenty five foot in length; and had divested him of twenty five foot of this ground, and left him the other twenty five. And in the last clause (which is introduc'd with these words, *To the intent it may not be in the Power of any of his Majesties Governours or Commanders in Chief, for the time being, hereafter to make any such Extravagant Grants.* And how little this Clause answers its own introductory words, I humbly submit to your Lordships Consideration) had enacted, That no body should hereafter have had Grants of Lands in this Province exceeding twenty five foot in length; This, with submission, would have made the Act much more coherent than now it is.

But, *My Lords,* with humble submission, to say, that because a Subject has too much, therefore all ought to be taken from him, deserves the Name of a gross Absurdity; and whether the former be not the very Principle this Act goes upon, and the latter the very deduction it makes from that Principle, is humbly submitted to your Lordships Consideration.

My Lords, The other Objection I humbly proposed to make to this Act, is, *That it tends not only to the Discouraging and Incorruption of all Improvements of Lands within this Province, but even to the subversion of Government, and reducing things to Disorder and Confusion.*

I have already observed to your Lordships, That all Persons who have any Lands in this Province, have Grants from the Crown for them, although purchased from the *Indians,* which is to fix the Tenure and Soveraignity of such Lands (so purchased) in the Crown of *England,* and put them under its Protection.

I must now beg leave to observe two things more.

1st. By how few Persons the Acts of the Assembly of this Province may pass. The Assembly consists but of Twenty one Men, after the addition that the present Governour has made of Members to it, and so Eleven makes a Majority in a full House. And the Governour may displace all the Council, and take seven of his own chusing (and this Governour has done so, as I am informed) and of these seven, five or six may act, and so three or four, at the most, make a Majority in the Council.

2dly, That the Lands in question are taken away, by this Act, from the Grantees, because they are *Extravagant;* and yet here is no Rule or Measure (either expressed in the Act, or that can be collected from it) whereby it can be Known what is *Extravagant,* and what not, in the sence of these Legislators. A Grant of Lands of fifty Miles long is said to be *Extravagant,* and so is a Grant of a piece of Ground that is but fifty Foot long. A Grant in Fee is there said to be *extravagant,* and so is a Grant for a small Term of years, even so small as that of *seven years,* altho' it be for publick Use to support the Charge of a Church for the service of Almighty God; so that upon the whole, that is *Extravagant* which a Governor and fourteen or fifteen Men (I mean the Majority of the Council and Assembly) shall please to call so.

My Lords, It is well known to your Lordships, that the Governors of this Province have been by their Commissions impowered to make Grants of Lands, under such moderate Quit-Rents and Acknowledgements, as the Governor (with the advice of his Council) should think fit or reasonable; and the King thereby declares, That such Grants shall be good and effectual against his Majesty, his Heirs and Successors.

This Declaration & Assurance was, without doubt, design'd to encourage People to accept these Grants, and Leases and Conveyances under them, and to settle, plant and improve the Lands granted, for he that builds on, or plants or improves Lands, does it with a prospect that he and his shall enjoy it; who then will settle, build on or improve Land, when his Property therein is altogether incertain and precarious? when a Governour and fourteen or fifteen Men may call the Grants of such Lands *Extravagant*, (though actually made according to the afore mentioned Power) and arbitrarily take them (with the Improvements) away from the Proprietors?

An Act therefore of the Legislative Power, that arbitrarily divests men of their Lands, for no other Reason, but that they have *too much*, (and without ascertaining what is too much in the sence of the Legislators) makes Property altogether incertain and precarious, and is the most effectual way to discourage and stop all manner of Improvements of Land, and not only so, but tends even to the Dissolution and Subversion of Government, and reducing things into Disorder and Confusion.

For, *My Lords*, with humble submission, it is a true Maxim, That Interest Governs the World. The great motive and inducement to People to unite themselves into Politick Societies, and to submit to Government, was the Preservation & Protection of their Properties, and rendering them more certain and secure than they could be in a state of Nature, without any publick Regiment. And this is the great Motive and Incouragement to People to contribute their endeavours for the Support and Defence of that Government, whereby they are protected in their Properties.

A settled Rule of Property, steadily observed, and impartially applied, is the great Legament of Government; and when Property is made uncertain and precarious, this Legament is broken, and the Society in danger of running into Disorder and Confusion.

If Grants of Lands, in these Circumstances, shall be vacated, because a Governour and eleven, or a less number of Men (who if he does not chuse, he has at least a very great Influence in the choice of them) and three or four Men (absolutely of his own chusing) are pleased to call them *Extravagant* who can tell what they will call *Extravagant?* No man can be at any reasonable Certainty of his Title. At this Rate, a Governour and three or four Men, whom he may chuse himself, and eleven, or a less number of other Men (in whose choice he has at least a great Influence) may share and divide all the Lands of this Province among them & their Relations: 'Tis but saying, those that have them have *too much,* That their Grants are *Extravagant* & then (according to the excellent reason and justice of this Act) they may take them all from the present Owners, *Divest them of all;* and then the Governour has Power (with the consent of his Council) to grant them to whom he pleases: He may grant to his eleven Men in the Assembly, and three or four Men in the Council, such parts as [perhaps] they have privately bargain'd for before they gave their Votes, and the rest to others of his own Creatures, and [it may be] in trust for himself.

Should (therefore) this Act be confirm'd, it will put all the Province into Confusion. Who knows but the Governour, and his fourteen or fifteen Men in the Council & Assembly, will call any Grant *Extravagant,* when they or their Friends shall have a mind to have another Mans Estate, with the fruits of his Expence, Care and Labour, to wit, the Improvements made upon it? For if this Act be confirmed, the People of this Province may, with reason, fear, that this Assembly will, at the next meeting, take away some more of their Lands, with their Improvements; and another Assembly, more after that [for by the same Measures of this Act, they are all now become Tenants at Will to their Governour & his fourteen or fifteen Men] And what an effect must such Apprehensions have? No Body will lend any Money upon a Mortgage of any of these Lands, nor accept long Leases or Conveyances, or make Improvements under these Grants [for the fate of those that have taken Leases and Conveyances, and made Improvements under the Grants in Question, will be too fresh in Memory] nor will any Body accept them in Settlements upon Marriage, because they know not but the Governour and his fourteen or fifteen Men, will some time or other, (and how soon they know not,) think the Lands too much for the Owners, and by their Legislative Power, arbitrarily divest the Owners of them; nor will any Body, for the same reason, make further Improvements on their own

Lands, for improving them will advance their value, & that will occasion the Governour and his fourteen or fifteen men to call them *Extravagant*, and take them away.

My Lords, I beg leave upon this occasion, further, humbly to put your Lordships in mind of the dangerous Consequence of the *Legislative Power* acting as *Executive* in this Province.

It is the happiness of our *English Constitution*, that the *Legislative* and the *Executive Powers* act distinctly, in distinct Capacities, and by several Agents. The former to make Rules and Laws, the latter to apply those Rules and Laws to particular cases. Where this is so, the individuals of the Legislative are cautious of making ill Rules or Laws, lest they should themselves suffer by them: And the latter stands in awe of punishment for mis-applying the Law in particular Cases. Hereby the true and great end of Government is answered, *viz.* None are without Check, and all sorts of Mankind are kept from injuring one the other.

But when the *Legislative Power* (who are too great to be punished) act as *Executive* in particular Cases, they are then without check, for they give no general Rules to fear the effects of themselves, and yet act without any prescribed Rules.

And when this is done in a Country where the Number of Men that compose the Legislative Power is so small, and where the Governour may have the choice of so great a part of them, & so great an Influence and Power towards getting his own Creatures to be return'd and sit in the other part, in a Country that is so remote from the Fountain of Justice [the place of their Princes Residence] To how great and how arbitrary Injustices and Oppressions the unhappy People of such a Country, where this is so practised, are liable, is not difficult to be conceived.

I beseech your Lordships to consider what two fatal strokes here are made by the two Acts I have here particularly mentioned the one at the Liberties, and the other at the Properties of the People of this Province, if the measures and methods of these two Acts be countenanced and practised, then are the Liberties and Properties of all the People of this Province wholly at the will of the Governour and fourteen or fifteen Men at the most. And if the Governour may displace the whole Council, and chuse another: then three or four of these fourteen or fifteen are of his own chusing. And if the Sheriffs (who are of his own chusing) shall be instrumental in undue Elections, and shall make false Returns of Members to serve in the

Assembly, and those Members assembled stand by such undue Elections & false Returns, and are the Governours Creatures, Then will the *Liberties* and *Properties* of the People of this Province be at the will & pleasure of the Governour; for they will then be without Remedy, otherwise than by complaining of such undue Elections in *England;* and in things of so great a Complication, and to be proved by so many Witnesses, as the facts about Elections are, it will be too chargeable to send Witnesses hither; and that Magistrates or Courts will not take the Depositions or Affidavits of Witnesses that are touching Elections, where the Governour favours the contrary side is, (as I am informed) found too true by very late Experience; & besides few dare appear as Witnesses against the frowns of a Governour; howbeit some Affidavits have been gotten and sent over, touching the undue Elections & Returns of several Members who served in this Assembly, that made these two Acts, which I shall beg leave to lay before your Lordships when I have them.

My Lords, With humble Submission, should an Act of Parliament be made in *England,* that should say such a one had an Estate of 50000*l.* a year, another 5000*l.* another 500*l.* and another 50*l. per ann* and that these are *Extravagant Estates,* and for that reason divest the Owners of them; would not other Owners of Land have but too much reason to think themselves altogether insecure of their Properties, and to fear their Turns might be next? What a Discontent and Confusion such an Act would make in *England,* I humbly submit to your Lordships Considerations.

To shew further the Inconsistency of this Act with the Fundamental Principles and Ends of Government, and how unjust it is, and fit to be rejected, I will beg leave to cite the words of a very worthy and learned Author that but lately had the honour to sit at this Board.

> The Supream Power (saith he) cannot take from any Man any part of his Property without his own consent; for the Preservation of Property being the end of Government, and that for which Men enter into Society, it necessarily supposes and requires, that the People should have Property, without which they must be supposed to lose that by entering into Society, which was the end for which they entered into it, too gross an Absurdity for any Man to own. Men therefore in Society having Property, they have such a Right to the Goods which by the Law of the Community are theirs, that no body hath a Right to take them, or any part of them from them, without their own consent, without this they have no

> Property at all. For I have truly no Property in that which another can, by Right, take from me when he pleases, against my Consent. Hence it is a Mistake to think that the Supream or Legislative Power of any Common Wealth can do what it will, and dispose of the Subjects Estate arbitrarily, or take any part of them at pleasure.[1]

> And again, afterwards, *fol.* 274.

> But Government, into whatsoever hands it is put, being, as I have before shewed, intrusted with this Condition, and for this end, that Men might have & secure their Properties. The Prince or Senate (however it may have Power to make Laws for the regulating of Property between the Subjects one amongst another, yet) can never have a Power to take to themselves the whole or any part of the Subjects Property without their own consent; for this would be, in effect, to leave them no Property at all.

My Lords, I will beg leave to mention one thing that I have hinted at before, and that is, That in Commissions to Governours of this Province, there is this Clause, *viz.*

> And We do likewise give and grant unto you full Power and Authority, by and with the advice and consent of Our said Council, to agree with the Inhabitants of our Province and Territories aforesaid, for such Lands, Tenements and Hereditaments, as now are, or hereafter shall be in Our Power to dispose of, and them to grant unto any Person or Persons for such Terms, and under such moderate Quit-Rents, Services and Acknowledgements to be thereupon reserved unto Us, as you, by and with the Advice aforesaid, shall think fit; which said Grants are to pass and be sealed by our Seal of *New-York,* and (being entered upon Record by such Officer or Officers as you shall appoint thereunto) shall be good and effectual in Law against Us, Our Heirs and Successors.

My Lords, (with Submission) the Resolutions and Declarations of a Prince, are the Fruit of great Wisdom, Advice and Deliberation, and ought to be steadily pursued, and not lightly altered; for that will be apt to put too slight a value on them, and much lessen that esteem and credit they ought to have among the People, and that relyance and dependance which 'tis necessary Subjects should have upon the Declaration of their Prince.

1. Two Treatises of Government, fo. 273. —Margin note in the original.

His Majesty might (if He had so pleased) have restrained this Power so granted to his Governours; but having not thought fit to do it, whether it be convenient to undo any thing afterwards that has been done pursuant thereunto, is humbly submitted to your Lordships Consideration.

His Majesty has, in a most solemn manner declared, under his great Seal, That the Grants made by his Governours, should be good and effectual against His Majesty, His Heirs and Successors; and his Subjects have believed and depended on such His Majesties Declaration, and in confidence of it have been at considerable Pains and Expences in treating with and purchasing Lands of the *Indians,* in suing for, and obtaining and passing these Grants, and in Improvements, & otherwise, about the granted Lands: And whether afterwards to confirm (or permit to remain in force) an Act that is made in manifest Contradiction to this Declaration, will not do the Publick more Mischief by far, than all the Lands in question are worth (*viz.* by discouraging Improvements of Lands, and by lessening the Esteem and Credit of his Majesties Declarations to his Subjects, and Powers granted to his Governours, and hindering that Relyance and Dependance upon them, which 'tis absolutely necessary his Majesties Subjects should have) is also humbly submitted to your Lordships consideration; as also, whether (if there were no other reason) this Consideration alone might not be a sufficient Motive for rejecting this Act.

But, *My Lords,* When your Lordships consider not only this, but that this Act proceeds upon such incertain Principles as have been mentioned, and is (even upon its own Principles) plainly and demonstrably Unjust and Unreasonable, in taking away all the Lands compriz'd in each Grant, from the Grantees; whereas it ought (even according to its own Principles) to have taken away only a part, when it arbitrarily takes away Lands from those who have honestly purchased them from the *Indians,* and by such Purchases justly and quietly enlarged the Dominions and Territories of the *Crown of England;* and inflicts a most severe Punishment, an endless Suspension, on a Minister of the Gospel, in an extraordinary manner, without setting out what he has done to deserve it, so that any one can discern whether he hath been guilty of any Crime or not; when (with submission) this Act is most plainly inconsistent with its own fundamental Principles, and contrary to the true fundamental Principles of Government.

When your Lordships consider it to be a thing done by so few Persons, and upon such uncertainty of Reason, as may be applyed to any man's case, that has any Lands within this Province, whose Lands may be taken from him by the same, or the like small number of Persons, upon the same Principle, and in the same manner, and that manner liable to so much Corruption, as has been mentioned.

When your Lordships consider, That therefore this Act (if permitted to remain in force) will discredit the Titles of the Lands of an whole Province, discourage all Improvements, spoil all Credit that might be raised on the Lands by the Owners, and endanger a Confusion & Disorder among the People of this Province, and probably the Ruin of it.

The Complainers against this Act rest assured, That your Lordships will (upon these Considerations) advise his Majesty to reject this Act.

My Lords, The other of the said Acts that I must beg leave to object to, is that, entituled, *An Act for granting unto his Majesty the Sum of two Thousand Pounds, fifteen hundred Pounds whereof to be allowed to his Excellency* Richard *Earl of* Bellomont, *and five hundred Pounds to Capt.* John Nanfan, *Lieut. Governor.*

And as for this Act, your Lordships have already given such just & excellent Reason against such Presents (in general) that I will not trouble your Lordships with any about this Act, but what are particular.

And the Complainers against these Acts doubt not but your Lordships, upon consideration of your own excellent Reasons in general, and of the Undue Elections of the Representatives, (or at least some of them) that sate in this Assembly & voted for this Act and the two former, and of the ill Company this Act comes in (I mean, the other two Acts) will advise his Majesty to reject this Act, or at least to direct, That the Moneys thereby raised shall be applyed to the Publick Uses of the Province, and in case of future Taxes.

I cannot but believe my Lord *Bellomont* so just a Person, that if the Heat of his Pursuit would have permitted him to have stood still and considered, he would have been so far from promoting two such Acts as the two former are, as that he would himself have given the Negative Voice against them, and especially against that for vacating Grants, and still believe that his Excellency upon Re-consideration, will desire those Acts should be rejected.

And when his Excellency shall appear to have rectified these Mistakes, and some other that are thought to be such by the Complainers against these Acts, they will (I hope) be very willing to make his Excellency a generous

Present; but till that be done, and a new House of Representatives fairly and duly elected and returned, they humbly hope that his Excellency and his Lieutenant shall rest contented with their Sallaries, and other Profits of their Government; and that all Moneys that is or shall be raised by Act of Assembly as a Present, shall remain in the Publick Treasury of the Province, for the publick Uses thereof.

My Lords, If the Advocates for these Acts shall undertake to defend them, I humbly desire they may also do it in writing, without Delay, and that I may have the favour of a Copy of it.

And if what I have offered be not sufficient Reasons for rejecting these Acts, I must still be an humble Suitor to your Lordships (on behalf of my Clyents) to hear them by their Council.

My Lords, I shall add no more at present, but humbly to beg your Lordships Pardon for troubling you so long, and for what failings I have been guilty of in this matter, humbly to beseech you to understand every thing I have presumed to say, to be with the greatest submission to your Lordships, and to take this opportunity of doing my self the Honour of subscribing,

Your LORDSHIPS
Most Obedient and most Humble Servant.

· 7 ·

[Thomas Hodge], Plantation Justice, London (1701)

THE PRIMITIVE CHARACTER of colonial systems of justice was a common complaint among those associated with colonial ventures. Published in London in 1701 and written by Thomas Hodge, an English merchant who had extensive dealings with the colony of Barbados, this pamphlet provides the classic expression of metropolitan merchant discontent with the delivery of justice in the colonies. Contending that an English merchant could get "better and more speedy Justice in the most distant Provinces of the *Ottoman* Dominions from their Bashawa, than they do in some of the *American* Colonies," he condemned Barbados for its "most corrupt and dilatory Course of Justice," spelled out the partial, interested, and inexpert behavior of the local judges, whom he regarded as yet another example of "arbitrary Government in the Plantations," and asserted that local power holders co-opted royal governors by giving them monetary presents and thereby prevented the careful enforcement of the Navigation Acts, which, he reported, "the Planters generally think it their Right, as well as Interest, to evade." If Barbados, "the best model'd of the Plantations," exhibited such problems, he observed, "the Condition of the rest may thereby be conjectured." Pointing out the extraordinary economic benefits England derived from the single colony of Barbados and how the prosperity of the nation had come to depend "in a great measure on the good Government of the Plantations, and regular Administration of Justice there," he advocated the creation, presumably by the English Parliament, of "a due and regular Administration of Justice in the Plantations," with independent and knowledgeable judges appointed from London. As colonial justice systems became more sophisticated during the eighteenth century and as the Crown, for patronage purposes, assumed a larger role in the appointment of judges, critics like Hodge found colonial justice far more satisfactory. But Parliament never acted to reform the colonial justice systems, which largely remained instruments of settler authority and power. (J.P.G.)

Plantation Justice,

Shewing the Constitution of their Courts, and what sort of Judges they have in them.

By which Merchants may see the occasions of their great Losses and Sufferings in the Plantation Trade {and} Lawyers may see such a Model of Justice as they could not have thought of; and Others may see how those Parts of the World are governed.

LONDON, Printed for *A. Baldwin* in *Warwick-lane.*

1701.

The Present state of Justice in the American Plantations, and particularly in the Island of Barbados; which being the best model'd of the Plantations, the Condition of the rest may be thereby conjectured.

On the first Settlement of the Plantations the Inhabitants were few, and found their mutual Interest in a good Correspondence; and when any Controversy hapned amongst them (which was but seldom) it was decided in a summary way by some of the principal among them, who were thereunto commissioned by the King. Under this Administration they continued some years; and being thereby under no Necessity of spending much time in Litigating, they could the better attend their several Trades and Plantations.

But in process of time, as the Plantations and their Trade increased, Controversies multiplied, and some Cases were found too intricate to be decided in a summary way: Whereupon Courts were erected in imitation of those in *England*. This in the Island of *Barbados* was done in the Year 1661. by an Act of the Governour, Council, and Assembly of that Island: The Island was divided into five Precincts, and it was declared that each Precinct should have a Court of Common Pleas, consisting of a Judg, and four Assistants, who were to be appointed by Commission under the Hand and Seal of the Governour, giving them, or any three of them, power to determine all Civil Causes in their several Precincts; the said Commissions to continue during the Pleasure only of the Governour. An other such Act was made, declaring *the Governour and Council to have the whole Power of Petitions in equitable Causes, and to hear and determine all Writs of Error.*[1]

Under this Model the Administration of Justice was at first much more tolerable than after the same had some continuance, because Suits were in the beginning fewer, and less intricate; the Forms used both in Law and Equity were plain and short; Niceties in pleading were neither understood nor attempted among them: by their natural Reason only, those Judges and their Assistants did commonly guess at the right of a Cause, and the Matters then controverted were seldom so considerable as to give a sufficient Temptation to injustice; and if wrong were done to any, it was their good fortune to

1. *These are the words of the Act.*—Margin note in the original.

have it done soon, and without that great expence of Money and Time (as at present is used there) by which such a misfortune is doubled; it being certain that in many Cases speedy Injustice is less grievous than dilatory Justice.

But as Suits[2] grew more numerous and important, incouraged by Profit, and compelled by Necessity, many Clerks, and other such small dealers in the Law, went thither from *England,* who tho ignorant of the Law, yet had so much knowledge of the Forms, as to be able to perplex, delay, and confound all the Business of the Courts there; by reason that the Judges there, and their Assistants were wholly ignorant of the Forms, as well as of the Law it self, and thereby incapable of regulating the said Disorders, which multiplied, and do still multiply every day: Nor can any other be expected of the Judges and their Assistants, who always were, and still are made of the Planters, Merchants, Customhouse Officers, Shopkeepers, or other Inhabitants of the Island, who were never bred to, or otherwise versed in the Law. From hence proceeds the Custom in that Island, to influence their Courts by the written Opinions of Council sent over out of *England;* and the Custom, that if any Authority of Law be urged to the Court, out of a Latin or French Book, the Interpreter is immediately sworn to interpret the same to the Judg and his Assistants.[3]

One reason why they are no better furnished with Judges is, That no Salaries are allowed them, only some small Perquisites;[4] insomuch, that the place of Provost Marshal, or Jaylor of the Island, is esteemed to be worth more than the income of all the said Judges put together. Another reason is, because they hold their Places during the pleasure only of the Governour. Those Places therefore being so precarious and unprofitable, the meanest Clerk that goes over will not accept of them, but chuses to depend on the certainty of his own Practice.

Writs of Error[5] on Judgments given by those Judges, are brought before the Governour and Council, who in the said Island are called the Court of Errors: This Council consists of twelve Gentlemen[6] of the Island, who decide, by majority of Votes, all the Business of this Court, as well as of the *Chancery.* But

2. *There were lately above a thousand Causes depending at one time in the Courts of that Island, and some of them for above ten thousand Pounds.*—Margin note in the original.

3. *This Rule may have some Exceptions.*—Margin note in the original.

4. *Which Perquisites may be increased by delaying Causes, or diminished by dispatch of them.*—Margin note in the original.

5. *No Error lies under* 300 l. *value, by the Governor's Instructions.*—Margin note in the original.

6. *Most of these are interested in many Suits depending in the Courts where they sit Judges.*—Margin note in the original.

how worthy soever they may be in other respects, they cannot be proper and fit Judges in such Cases where the greatest Niceties of Law are handled, unless they had some knowledg of the Rules by which they are to proceed; for want of which infinite Hardships have been suffered, and many gross and most unwarrantable Judgments have been (without any colour of Law) there given, to the great Oppression of his Majesty's Subjects, as in many instances may appear. One Person has lately lost above five thousand nine hundred Pounds by such a Judgment in that Island, tho the same has been since reversed by his Majesty in Council; some of the Defendants dying during the dependance of the Appeal, and their Estates descending according to former Settlements; others have imbezeled, or so covered their Estates, that he has now lost not only his Debt, but likewise in the Charge and Trouble of many Years Suit, and of bringing his Cause by Appeal from thence to *England.*

It is the happiness of his Majesty's Subjects, that such Judgments and Decrees in that Island are not final, and that Persons grieved may have relief by Appeal to his Majesty in Council:[7] Yet when it is considered, that in regard of the great distance of the said Island, and the great Charge, Delay, and Trouble of such long Voyages, the Remedy which Persons grieved have by Appeal, is in small Causes (and if often repeated in great ones) almost as grievous as it would be to suffer under such Injustice; there seems to be a much greater Necessity for a due and regular Administration of Justice in the Plantations, than there would be if they were nearer to the Place to which they are to appeal.

And whereas the Governours of that Island (as in the other Plantations) are both Chancellor and Chief Justice, it is a great Misfortune to the People there, and to all others who deal with them, that the same Commission which gives them their Power, cannot give them some Skill for the Execution of so great a Trust as is thereby reposed in them; by which they would be inabled to administer Justice in their own Courts, and regulate the Proceedings of inferior Courts, which are under their Inspection. But the said Governors being usually unacquainted with the Rules of Law, and altogether Strangers to the Forms thereof, are forced to direct all their Proceedings by the Advice of some Person in the Island professing the Law, who is usually called *Attorney,* or *Solicitor-General,* who seldom fails of being concerned of one side in the

7. *No Appeal is allowed, unless the Sum or Value appeal'd for exceeds* 500 l. *and the Appeal be made within fourteen days after Sentence, which is frequently impossible.*—Margin note in the original.

Cause, and therefore cannot be supposed a proper Director of the supream Justice of the Island; but the Governors cannot avoid it, being put upon Business which it is impossible for them (of themselves) to understand.

It may deserve Consideration, whether in so small an Island, the number of Thirty nine of the Inhabitants at one time in judicial Places, does not introduce many Partialities, especially where Suits are carried on for Inhabitants of *England*, against those in the Plantations; and whether the Acts of Trade and Navigation are like to be best executed to the Advantage of *England* under such a Model, since the Planters generally think it their Right, as well as their Interest, to evade those Laws.

The Custom of making yearly Presents[8] to the Governours by the Assembly, amounting commonly to two thousand Pounds a Year, sometimes more, and this raised by an Excise on Liquors imported into that Island by *English* Merchants, may likewise deserve Consideration; and whether it would not conduce more to his Majesty's Service, and the good of his People,[9] that the Profits of all Plantation-Governments were made more certain: The present practice having been found by Experience to produce many Partialities, and other Irregularities, disadvantageous to his Majesty, and extreamly prejudicial to many of his People; for the Plantation-Inhabitants are always indebted to those of *England*, and the latter are much mistaken if such large Presents made by their Debtors, do not conduce much to the difficulty they find in recovering their just Debts. And whether the Acts of Trade and Navigation are not the worse executed in some Colonies, in regard of such Presents, may be worthy of inquiry.

It may likewise deserve Consideration, Whether the Measures of Government, and Administration of Justice used in the Plantations at their first Settlements, when they were but thin of People, and of little importance to this Nation are fit to be still continued, when they make so considerable a part of his Majesty's Dominion, the small Island of *Barbados* alone (about twenty five Miles long, and half so broad) by a reasonable Computation produce to *England* in its Trade above five hundred thousand Pounds *per Annum*, one Year with another, to his Majesty; by Customs in *England*

8. *At the same time these Presents are given, the King is importuned by Petitions in* England, *to consider the sad and defenceless Condition of the Island for want of Money to repair their Fortifications, and supply their Magazines.*—Margin note in the original.

9. *Governors of small Places, when justly complained of, are sometimes turned out with disgrace; but against the greater Governors, who receive large Presents, and are able to give the like, it is so commonly in vain to complain.*—Margin note in the original.

about 20,000 *l. per Annum,* and by the Duty of four and a half *per Cent* (as paid in the Island) about 1000 *l. per Annum,* besides the great number of Ships they imploy, and many thousands of hands in English Manufactures.

The Plantation Trade is now acknowledged to be the most advantageous this Nation enjoys; and it is no less certain that the prosperity thereof depends in a great measure on the good Government of the Plantations, and regular Administration of Justice there. It would seem then very strange, if when such diligence is used in all other parts of his Majesty's Service, that in the meanest and most mechanick part thereof no Man is imploy'd to do any thing to which he was not bred, or which there is not reasonable ground to believe he understands, the Administration of Justice in the Plantations should be thought the easiest part of his Service, which any one may perform, and on the miscarriage of which little depends.

It has been hitherto the principal Objection against any regulation of Justice in the Plantations, that they were first peopled, and continue still to be supplied by numbers of indigent persons who escape thither to be easy from their Creditors; that the difficulty of having Justice in the Courts there, is their chief Security, and that if they do not find such Protection there, it will ruin the Plantations.

To this it is answered, That the arbitrary Government in the Plantations does hinder many Persons from going thither, or staying when they are there: And tho it may be reasonable perhaps by an express Law, to exempt all Persons from Imprisonment in the Plantations, or to give them other certain and known Privileges, who are imployed in planting, or other bodily Labour, or who have not sufficient to answer their Creditors; yet to continue a most corrupt and dilatory Course of Justice, on pretence of favouring such poor Debtors, and thereby to exempt those of great Estates (several Planters having now two or three thousand Pounds *per Annum*) from Law and Justice, is so far from encouraging the Plantation Trade, that no one thing does contribute more to the discouragement thereof. On the first Settlement of the Plantations, particularly in the Island of *Barbados,* they planted Tobacco, Ginger, and Cotton; and then any Man that had Instruments for digging and clearing the Ground, could manage a small Plantation himself, without any Stock or other help; and then a Relaxation of Justice might be some incouragement to carry such People thither: But since the setting up of Sugar-works in that Island (about fifty Years since) the planting of Tobacco, Cotton, and Ginger, is in a great measure disused as unprofitable, and no Sugar-work can be managed without a considerable Stock: Such a Work with Negroes, and other things sufficient to imploy one Windmil only (which is the smallest sort of Sugar-work) will not cost much less than 5000 *l.* Sterling. Since therefore the Plantation of Sugar cannot be managed without imploying great Sums therein, whatsoever is done to secure the certain possession of Purchasers, or reimbursements of Sums advanced by Adventurers, would best promote that Trade, which like all others, must in a great measure be carried on by Credit; for want of which Security nothing is more evident, than that the Plantation Trade has suffered more than it did even by the double Imposition formerly laid on their Sugar in *England:* for the Planters wanting necessary Credit in *England* for carrying on their Trade, where they are trusted, they are now made to pay very dear for it, because of the great difficulty of having Justice against them, if they fail of payment. Several *English* Merchants have heretofore imployed great Sums on Plantations in that Island, but many of them have been great Sufferers, and many others ruined for want of Justice in the Island; and the Children of others after their Parents death, having been miserably used there, and defrauded of great Estates (insomuch that few Instances can be given, where Children under Age have not been so used there) the Merchants of *England* are grown too cautious to venture much in a Trade, which for want of Justice proves so pernicious to them: Whereas if Justice was strictly administered there, great Sums would be imployed in so beneficial a Trade, to the great Advantage of this Nation. And tho it may seem incredible to those who are not rightly informed, nothing is more certain than that the English Merchants find more security, and better and more speedy Justice in the most distant Provinces of the *Ottoman* Dominions from their Bashaws, than they do in some of the *American* Colonies, tho under the Dominion of their own Prince;[10] and of this the Merchants are so sensible, that they will trade to the first for a much less Profit than to the last. Whether this ought to be reformed, is submitted to those whose Province it is to judg of it.

When the Laws, not only of *England,* but of all Nations, agree in giving more speedy Justice in matters of Trade, than in any other, and that with design to advance Traffick, it is very strange that it should now be thought of ill Consequence to the Plantation-Trade.

10. *The truth of this is known to all Merchants that have traded to these Places.*—Margin note in the original.

It is grown a Proverb with the English Merchants, that tho a Man goes over never so honest to the Plantations, yet the very Air there does change him in a short time: And it is certain they have too much ground to complain of the universal Corruption of Justice among them; for the Judicature of that small Place being in the hands of thirty seven of the Inhabitants, it introduces many Partialities, *&c.* for there can scarce be any Suit of moment in the Island that some of these Persons, or their nearest Relations, are not concern'd in. From hence proceed the great disappointments that Merchants and others meet with from Factors and Agents, whom they imploy to sell Goods, or recover Money in that Island: For if such Agents, by prosecuting, do disoblige those who have Power without Appeal in all Cases under 500 *l.* value, and who by forcing them to an Appeal on greater Sums in their own Causes, may send them a Voyage of many thousand Leagues to *England,* and back again, to the loss of a Year or more time from their Business; it is plain, that unless such Factors and Agents are content to sacrifice their own Interest to serve others, they cannot do what is expected of them: And many are encouraged to betray their Trust, and defraud those that imploy them, by the great difficulty of having Justice against them in the Plantations. Many hundred instances can be given where Factors have laid out all the Effects of others (with which they have been intrusted) in purchasing Plantations for themselves; and then by proper Applications to Governours there, and to others in *England,* they are put into the Judicatories of the Places they live in;[11] and those that entrusted them, can have no Justice against them, but what comes through their own hands; which discourages Merchants from imploying greater Sums in that Trade. And nothing is more plain, than that their depravity proceeds only from thence; for let them send Factors, Agents, or Servants, into any other part of the World, *Italy, Turkey, Muscovy,* or the *East-Indies,* they are no where found to degenerate so much from their original Honesty, and to give those that imploy them so much Cause to complain, as in the Plantations.

From what has been observed it may appear, That the principal Root and Foundation of most Grievances in that Island, and the other Colonies, is, That Governours are not appointed capable of holding the said Courts, or that some other Persons fitly qualified are not appointed, only or principally

11. *Overseers of other Mens Plantations have been recommended by Governours, and their Masters rejected who sued for the same.*—Margin note in the original.

depending on the King, and not subject to be removed at the pleasure of the Governours, by whom Justice might be administred, and matters of War and State might be the proper Province of Governors and their Council; which Judges, or Civil Magistrates, might on extraordinary Occasions be controuled by the Governour and Council, as is practised in the Colonies of all other Nations.[12]

That such Regulation may be lawfully made, and without any new Charge to his Majesty, or his People, to the great Advantage of the Plantation Trade, and Benefit of his Majesty's Subjects, both in the Plantations, and in *England*, might easily be demonstrated; but since the printing of such a Scheme would prevent its being practised, and since Reformation is the Province of others, this matter is submitted to their Consideration.

FINIS.

12. *Even the* French *Islands have Civil as well as Military Governours, and no Nation is without them but the* English.—Margin note in the original.

· 8 ·

"An American" [Benjamin Harrison], An Essay upon the Government of the *English* Plantations on the Continent of America (London, 1701)

THIS PAMPHLET is perhaps the best overall critique of the structure and operation of the English empire produced by any colonist before the 1760s. Published anonymously, it was probably the work of Benjamin Harrison, a prominent tobacco planter and public figure in Virginia, the oldest English colony in America. Because Virginia would not have a printing press for another thirty years and because Harrison wrote it for a metropolitan audience, he published it in London. As he explains in a lengthy preface, the occasion for its publication was the publication by Charles D'Avenant, a prominent English economic writer, of a "Discourse on the Plantation Trade." For Harrison, D'Avenant's tract was prejudicial against royal colonies like Virginia and an illustration of the fact that "Plantation Affairs" were "not so well understood [in England] as they ought to be." This ignorance, he observed, enabled "Arbitrary Governours" and "some Evil Ministers about Court" to promote schemes "whereby the Plantations" had "been very much injured and oppressed, and the Interest of *England* very much prejudiced." To remedy this situation he proposed that each colony keep an agent in England and that the Crown appoint a commissioner with broad powers of inquiry to travel to each colony and produce a comprehensive report on its governance, relations with Indians, system of justice, revenues, religious composition, trade, and grievances.

But Harrison's main objective was to lobby for the establishment of "a Just and Equal Government" so that the colonists, as he put it, could "enjoy their Obscurity, and the poor way of living which Nature is pleased to afford them out of the Earth, in Peace, and be protected in the Possession thereof, by their lawful mother *England*." Pointing out that England had never supplied the colonies with "a good Constitution of Government," he objected strongly to recent metropolitan contentions that "the Plantations should be under an unlimited Government," denying that "the King should be more Absolute in the Plantations than he is in *England*" and arguing for the "settling of a free Constitution of Government in the Plantations." Such a constitution, he went on to explain in impressive detail, would place colonial governors under proper restraints, clarify the extent of legislative authority in colonial representative bodies by acknowledging both the extensive jurisdiction they had long exercised over land, justice, and administration and their capacity even to "make Laws disagreeable to the Laws of *England*, in such Cases, where the Circumstances of the Places are vastly different," clarify the extent of Parliamentary authority over the colonies, and establish a "good Constitution of Courts of Judicature" in the colonies in which colonial judges, like English judges after the Glorious Revolution, would hold their offices during good behavior and not at the pleasure of the Crown.

He also recommended that the government of all the colonies be annexed to the Crown, that the Crown confirm all land titles in the colonies, that Parliament revise the trade laws to take a smaller share of the colonial planter's profits, that every colony be guaranteed "an Equal Liberty of Trade" from one to another, that the colonists be guaranteed the same degree of religious toleration as established by the Toleration Act in England, and that the English government assist the poor to emigrate to the colonies and forcibly transport petty criminals there. "The true Interest of *England*," he concluded, was "to have the Plantations cherished, and the poor People encouraged to come hither, every Man here being of great Value to *England*."

The English government largely ignored these recommendations. Six decades after Harrison wrote, it had done little to remedy the many "Mismanagements," grievances, and ambiguities that he identified. (J.P.G.)

AN
ESSAY
UPON THE
GOVERNMENT
OF
The *English* Plantations
ON
The Continent
OF
AMERICA

Together with some Remarks upon the Discourse on the Plantation Trade, Written by the Author of the Essay on Ways and Means, and Published in the Second Part of His Discourses, on the Publick Revenues and on the Trade of *England*.

By an AMERICAN

LONDON, Printed for *Richard Parker* at the *Unicorn*, under the *Piazza* of the *Royal Exchange*.
1701.

[The Preface]

SIR,

I herewith send you a Transcript of that imperfect Essay upon the Government of the *English* Plantations on the Continent of *America,* which I shewed you when you were in these parts, and which you laid so many obligations on me to let you have.

It was at first designed for private view only, and accordingly it was drawn for that purpose, as you may easily perceive by many Passages in it, neither is it (in my Opinion) at all fit for the Publick; but since you have desired it so earnestly, I give it up intirely to you, to be disposed of according to your Discretion, only I must enjoyn you to conceal my Name, that I may not of necessity be engaged in a Pen and Ink War three Thousand Miles from home.

In pursuance of your request, I have (as carefully as my time and health would permit) once more perused the Discourse on the Plantation Trade, written by the Author of the Essay on Ways and Means; and I am still of the same Opinion that I told you; I take that Gentleman to be a Man of good Parts, but in this Discourse, I think he hath gone beyond his Province, for it appears pretty plain to me, that he went on blindfold, having an intire dependance upon the knowledge and integrity of those from whom he received his Informations; this I am obliged to believe, for certainly a Person of that Authors Abilities could never have written so incoherently and inconsistently upon a Subject that himself had any knowledge of.

I shall not trouble you with a particular Examination of every Paragraph of that Discourse; but I shall apply my self to the consideration of the most general of his Notions and the Principles he proceeds upon, and if the Foundation appears to be deceitful, I suppose the Superstructure will fall of course; but in the first place, it will be necessary to observe to you how very irregular, that Discourse is, and how incoherent the several Parts of it are one with another.

In some Places (p. 225, 226, 230, 231), he tells the World *the great advantage* of New-England, Mary-Land, Pensilvania, Carolina, *&c. Furnishing the Southern Colonyes with Provisions, which he confesses may be had from* England *and* Ireland, *but not so cheap.*

In another Place (p. 232), he says, *It cannot be for the Publick good of a Kingdom to furnish Colonies out of it, with People, when the Product of such*

Colonyes is the same with the Kingdoms, and so Rivals the Kingdom both in its Navigation and in its Product, at the Market where such Product is vended; neither can it be the Interest of a Country to suffer its People to make settlements of several Plantations that yeild one and the same Commodity.

In another place (p. 233), he is *for having some method proposed of Collecting within a narrower Compass, the scattered Inhabitants of the Continent, by inviting some to cultivate the* Islands, *where their labour is certainly most profitable to* England, *and by drawing the rest if possible to four or five of the Provinces, best scituate and most Productive of Commodities not to be had in* Europe.

In other Places (p. 244, 245, 250, 251, 283, 284), he argues very strongly for the *Proprieties and Charter Governments being restored to the several forms of Government, by which they were first encouraged at their great Expence, &c. to discover, cultivate and plant remote places, &c. and since they have a worse Soil to improve* (than the other Colonies) He is for *having them recompenced in Property and Dominion.*

In another place (p. 236), he finds fault that *the Servants bred up (in Virginia) only to Planting, are forced into other Colonies, where their Labour is not so profitable either to the Crown, or People of* England, *as it would be in a province not producing Commodities that are of* English *growth.*

Now Sir, please to lay these several Parts of that Discourse together and observe the strength of the Arguments.

You may perceive throughout his whole Discourse that he is a great Friend to the *Proprieties* and *Charter-Governments,* and often pleads for their having great Liberties and Encouragements; and for that purpose his Arguments are very convincing.

It is not the Interest of any Kingdom to furnish Colonies out of it with People, when the Product of such Colonies is the same with the Kingdoms (p. 232).

But the Product of the Colonies of *New England, Mary-Land, Pensilvania, Carolina,* &c. (being Proprieties) are the same with the Product of the Mother Kingdom of *England* (p. 225, 231).[1]

Ergo, those Colonies should be encouraged.

Again, *It cannot be the interest of a Countrey to suffer its People to make settlements of several Plantations that yeild one and the same Commodity.*

1. *The Product of these Colonies is Provisions of several sorts, and the Colonies can sell cheapest.*—Margin note in the original.

But *New England, Rhode Island, New York,* the *Jerseys, Pensilvania, Carolina* (and according to our Author *Maryland*)[2] yield one and the same Commodity. *Ergo,* all those colonies are to be encouraged.

Once more let us try our Logick.

Those Provinces are to be encouraged, *that are most Productive of Commodities not to be had in* Europe (p. 233).

But the *Islands, Virginia,* and *Mary Land,* are most Productive of Commodities not to be had in *Europe* (p. 233, 236).

Ergo, New England, Pensilvania, Carolina, &c. are to be encouraged (because their Product is the same with that of *England*).

Is not this an excellent way of arguing? But it is very difficult, even for so Ingenious a Gentleman as this Author, to engage in a bad cause, and not to be sometimes detected of false reasoning: He seems to doat upon the Proprieties, but he cannot find one good Argument to use on their behalf.

All his long Cant of the *temperance, sobriety, and seeming Vertuous living of the Dissenters in the Northern Colonies* (p. 227, 229, 230, 247), is nothing to the purpose; and if it were, it is not true; I could give convincing Proofs of the contrary, but I can't think it worth my while.

And all that he urges in favour of the Proprieties, because of their furnishing the *Islands* with Provisions, when they cannot have it from *Europe*—will not much strengthen his Arguments; for if it appears that the supplying those *Islands* be for the interest of *England,* the Tobacco Plantations may be made sufficient for that purpose, without diminishing the quantity of Tobacco that is now made.

All the Arguments that Gentleman uses to evince the Advantage of the Plantations to *England,* I agree with him in; nor do I condemn him for his smart reflections, upon the Evil Governours in these Parts, I am so far from it, that for the sakes of the poor Old *English* Men that groan under the burthen, I could wish, I had a competent Portion of Gall, and knew where to find words sufficient, to give a lively Representation of the truth in those Cases; however, I doubt it may be a peice of ill service to deter every body from coming to the Plantations, and therefore I will not endeavor at it, but by the way I must observe to you, that the Governours of some Proprieties are as bad as the Kings Governours.

2. *Tho our Author speaks of* Mary-Land, *as furnishing the* Islands *with great quantities of Provisions, he is very much mistaken, for 'tis not so.*—Margin note in the original.

I come next to his Considerations, for a more safe and lasting settlement of the Colonies in *America,* which are as follows,

First, without doubt, the negligence of former times has suffered a greater Number of Plantations upon the Continent, than do well consist with the Navigation and other Interests of the Mother-Countrey (p. 232, 233).

Secondly, it cannot be for the Publick good of a Kingdom, to furnish Colonies out of it with People, when the Product of such Colonies, is the same with the Kingdoms, and so Rivals the Kingdom, both in its Navigation, and its Product, at the Markets where such Product is vended.

Thirdly, it can hardly be the interest of a Country to suffer its People to make settlement of several Plantations that yeild one and the same Commodity, for Inhabitants thus dispers'd, are neither so useful to each other in time of Peace, nor strong enough to defend themselves in time of War, so that their Mother-Kingdom is usually at a great Charge for their defence, whereas if they lay in a more compact and less extended Territory, they could be more ready to give each other mutual help, and not be exposed as they are, to every little strength, and insult of an Invader.

Fourthly, as many Empires have been ruined by too much enlarging their Dominions, and by grasping at too great an Extent of Territory, so our Interest in America *may decay, by aiming at more Provinces, and a greater Tract of Land, than we can either cultivate or defend: upon which account, it may perhaps be sometime or other worth the consideration of the State, whether a way might not be proposed of Collecting within narrower Compass, the scatter'd Inhabitants of the Continent, by inviting some to cultivate the* Islands, *where their Labour is certainly most profitable to this Kingdom, and by drawing the rest, if possible, to four or five of the Provinces best scituate and most Productive of Commodities, not to be had in* Europe; *but this is to be done with great deliberation, with a due regard to property, by degrees, and by good Encouragement.*

Fifthly, former times have not only been faulty in suffering too many Provinces to be erected, but in the Repartition of the Land taken in, there are Corruptions conniv'd at very prejudicial to the Plantation Trade, and to the Kings Customes from thence arising.

To all which I answer that, if all these Parts of the World, had been so intirely at the disposal of the *English,* that no other Nations dared to have settled here without their leave, then indeed it might have been more prudent to have settled only two or three Colonies on the Continent of

America in such places as would best have suited the Interest of the Mother-Kingdom: But the Case was otherwise, for when the *English* were settled both to the *Northward* and *Southward*, we know the *Dutch* came and settled at *New York*, and would not leave their possession, till they were beaten from it; further *North* the *French* have settled themselves and become Masters of *Canada* River [the St. Lawrence]; and on the *South* the *Spaniards* press so hard upon us, that they did more than once attempt to hinder the *English* settling at *South-Carolina*.

These particular instances will not give us leave to doubt but that, if we had neglected seating any considerable part of the Continent, some other Nation would have stepped in, and taken possession of it, and would either have kept it, or perhaps have ventured a War with *England* for it.

We have certain Information, that the *French* are now settling upon the Mouth of the River *Meschasipe* [Mississippi], if so, and some speedy care be not taken, No one can (I think) foretel the fatal consequences that may follow to all the *English* Colonies on the Continent.

The two great Rivers of *Canada* and *Meschasipe*, run a long way up into the Continent, one on the *North*, and the other on the *South* side of all the *English* Plantations, that on the *South* side extends it self far *North*, and that on the *North* side extends it self very far *South*, when it comes up within the Land, and from the Heads of these two Rivers without much difficulty may be had a Communication, with all those vast Lakes, that lye to the *Westward* of all the *English* Colonies, which will make the *French* Masters of a great and profitable Trade with the *Indians* living upon those Lakes; and in Case of another War with *France*, will give them great opportunities by themselves and the *Indians* in League with them, to destroy the Inhabitants on the *Western* Frontiers of all the *English* Colonies; therefore instead of Proposing to invite the Inhabitants to leave any of the Plantations on the Continent, I should rather advise the establishing a Company, with a joynt Stock of about 15000£. or 20000£. *Sterl.* to settle a Trade with the *Indians* beyond the Mountains, which Trade that Company should have exclusive of all others, for one and twenty years next coming after their settlement; such a Company under a due regulation and management, would gain a Trade of considerable advantage to the *English*, and would settle two or three small Factories with about thirty or forty Men each, to take possession of the Lakes in behalf of the *English*, which Trade and Settlements would both disappoint the designs of the *French* in their Trade, and keep the *Indians* in Amity with the *English,* and by that means be a good defence to the *Western* Frontiers of our Colonies.

This Sir, I do assure you is no *Romantick* Fiction, for I have made inquiry into the true State of those Affairs, and am well informed, that we in *Virginia* lye many hundreds of Miles nearer to those *Indians* than any of the *French* settlements do, and consequently can furnish that Trade cheaper than any others; if the Duties upon the Exportation of Woollen out of *England* be not too heavy; for that is the Principal Commodity for such a Trade.

I must further observe to you, that I think it strange, the Gentleman should in this place find fault with there being so many Plantations upon the Continent of *America,* and propose the inviting them off into the *Islands;* when in another Chapter of the same Book he seems to be in great fear of the *French,* if they should possess themselves of the River *Meschasipe* and the Lakes to the *Westward;* and if I can guess any thing at his meaning, he is for having the *English,* get the first possession there; but take his own words (p. 116, 117), *should the* French *settle at the Disemboguing of the River* Meschasipe, *in the Gulph of* Mexico, *they would not be long before they made themselves Masters of that rich Province which would be an Addition to their strength very terrible to* Europe. *But this would more particularly concern* England; *for by the opportunity of that Settlement, by erecting Forts along the several Lakes between that River and* Canada, *they may intercept all the Trade of our* Northern *Plantations.*

And here again, I cannot but take notice that this Gentleman is very little acquainted with these Parts of the World, as appears by his saying, *they may intercept all the Trade of our* Northern *Plantations,* for our Plantations have no Trade with any body in those Parts, (except a little from *New York,* and that very uncertain, being already well near deprived of it by the *French* from *Canada*) what Trade we have, is with the *Indians* on this side the Mountains, and all the Lakes lye beyond them; but the danger is, that if the *French* make Settlements in those Parts, they may discover a Considerable new Trade, not yet enjoyed by any body, and thereby they (with the help of the *Indians*) will also be enabled to destroy the Inhabitants on the *Western* Frontiers of all our Colonies upon the Continent; and against such Incursions from the *Indians,* we shall not be able to make any effectual defence, because of the vast Woods in those Parts, which we are little acquainted with, and they know very well; Therefore my Proposition in this matter is, that this new Trade may be discovered and enjoyed by the *English,* who lye more convenient for it, than the *French*, by which means also the Frontiers will be much better secured, than otherwise they can be.

It is said (p. 233, 234), that *in the Repartition of the Land, taken in, there are Corruptions connived at very prejudicial to the Plantation Trade, and to the Kings Customs from thence arising;* and he goes on to give an Example of this in *Virginia*, which seems to me to be the strangest Part of all the Story; if he had talked of the abuses that have been in *New England, Pensilvania, Carolina* and the rest of the Proprieties, he had done something, but to fall upon *Virginia* at such an unmerciful rate as he has done, and to dwell upon it for three or four pages together, and to pretend to tell matter of fact exactly, and yet to Misrepresent (or falsify if you please) every part of it, this Sir, if I were as angry with him, as I perceive he is with some People, would make me speak very hard words, but I will not quarrel with the Gentleman, because I believe it to be only a sin of Ignorance and too much Credulity. In the Essay which I send you herewith, *p.* ______ I have Answered most of what he says about *Virginia*, and therefore in this place, I shall only let you know, that whereas, *p.* 234, He says, *all the Land here is taken up, except what lyes at the utmost bounds of the Colony, the Seating upon which often furnishes matter for War with the Indians;* I have examined into the matter of fact, and I find that between the twenty seventh of *October*, 1697, (About which time this Gentleman writ his Book) and the tenth of *May*, 1700, There issued Patents under the Seal of the Colony of *Virginia*, for 157667. Acres of Land, several Parcels of which are in some of the Counties best Inhabited, and notwithstanding all this Gentleman alledges, 'tis very probable from many reasons, which I could give, that before the tenth of *November*, 1701, Patents will issue for 150000. Acres more, and not all to the Council and their favourites neither; as to the *furnishing matter for War with the Indians*, that is such a fiction, that I think no one of a duller Invention, than the *Northern* Proprietor, who I suppose gave this Gentleman his Instructions could have thought of it. There are no *Indians* now in being, that have pretentions to any Lands near us, except some few of our tributaries, who are always in perfect Friendship with, and Obedience to us, and when any Foreign *Indians* come into these Parts, are ready upon all occasions, to give us what help they can, which indeed is but very little, the most considerable Nation of them all not having fifty Men, and some of the others not above ten, and some sixteen or twenty, these tributaries are descended from the Nations, who Inhabited not only the Land we now live upon, but all for many Miles, beyond the utmost of our Settlements, and 'tis a very likely matter that they should be able, or have any occasion, to make War with us about these Lands.

I agree with the Gentleman in what he says, *p.* 232, that *it cannot be for the Publick good of a Kingdom to furnish Colonies out of it with People, when the Product of such Colonies, is the same with the Kingdoms, and so Rivals the Kingdom both in its Navigation, and in its Product, at the Markets where such Product is vended, and that it can hardly be the Interest of a Country to suffer its People to make Settlements of several Plantations that yeild one and the same Commodity*—And I desire the favour of him to reconcile these Passages, with those in *p.* 244, 245, 250, 251, 283, 284, where he talks of *letting the* Northern *Colonies* (whose Product is the same with that of the Mother Kingdom *England*) *find their Recompence in Property and Dominion; having Liberty to choose their own cheif Magistrates; having their Original Charters kept inviolable;* and many more such like matters.

I would not be mistaken, as if I was an Enemy to Liberty, but since the Product of those *Northern* Proprieties is the same with that of *England* (the Mother Kingdom) I would gladly be informed whether according to this Gentlemans own Principles, it is not more for the interest of *England,* that the Kingdom should appoint them Governours, who would take care that they duely observed the Acts of Trade, then that such Power and Dominion should be given them, as in time to make them grow prejudicial to the Interest of *England,* as most certainly they will, if some better care be not taken, than hath been formerly.

By taking better Care, I do not mean new fangled Contrivances and Orders of People, that know little or nothing of the matter, where perhaps a whole Society may be managed by one Man, that knows as little as any of them, only happens to have a little more Modest assurance than his Brethren: But the best way to manage Affairs at so great a distance from home, is to call in the advice and assistance of Persons of known Abilities and Truth, and such as are acquainted with the true State and Circumstances of Places, Persons and things, and some who have been Eye-Witness, and have endeavoured to inform themselves in such matters, these are Men fit to be imployed on such occasions; not that I think every Man that hath been in the Plantations capable to do much Service; for I know some at this day in *London,* that have lately been in *Virginia* some years, and others that have been born here, and yet neither one nor the other of them have so much knowledge or integrity as to give a true State of the Country;[3] which makes it seem strange to me, that some Men (by many People esteemed very knowing in Plantation Affairs) should take so much notice of them; but Interest and Revenge have strange Operation sometimes upon Gentlemen about Court.

And here Sir, let me observe it to you once for all, that tho we have many Acts of Parliament, Publick Orders, and Instructions for the Management of Trade and Plantations, and tho these seem most of them to be drawn with a great deal of care and advice, yet there are so many defects and doubts and ambiguities in them, that it is almost impossible from them to draw any regular, practicable and effectual method for the Management of those Affairs; some things of no use and in themselves utterly impracticable, being enjoyned with the greatest rigour; and other things very necessary and easie never being so much as once required; from whence it happens, that in some places upon several occasions, without any manner of advantage or service, there is abundance of puzzle and hurry and confusion about no one knows what; and in other places where good care and application is really wanting, nothing at all is done, and yet perhaps neither of these People are guilty of the Breach of any Law now in being; from all which I conclude, that the Plantation Affairs are not so well understood as they ought to be.

The Propositions, *p.* 237, I purposely pass over, there being nothing material in them, but what I have already taken as much notice of as is necessary.

As to the Scheme of a Council of Trade proposed, *p.* 238, 239, I shall say nothing concerning it, only that I should be very glad to see such a free Council for those Affairs Established, as would answer the ends proposed.

The several Propositions made in *p.* 253, 254, 255, require not much to be said to them, the first would never have been put in that place, only I perceive the Author hath met with a Misrepresentation of a difference that happened some time since, between the Government of *Mary Land* and the Proprietor of *Pensilvania*, and so he hath made an Article of Reformation

3. *I have lately seen some Proposals to the Commissioners of Trade, by a Gentleman who is thought by some, to know these Parts very well: wherein he pretends to argue the reasonableness of Seating the* French Refugees *in the Kings Colony of* Virginia, *rather than in a new Propriety in Lower* Norfolk; *whereas* Norfolk *is one of the Counties of* Virginia; *and (being but a very little one) is already well Seated by the* English, *under the Kings Government, without any dependance upon Proprietors.*—Margin note in the original.

of it. The rest of them, I shall not make any remark upon; because some are not of any great use, and the others I do not find much amiss.

I agree very heartily with what is said, *p.* 246, that it is prejudicial, that the Offices and Places of trust in the Colonies, should be granted by Patent to Persons in *England,* with liberty to execute such Imployments by Deputies; but above all things, I admire his Comparison, *p.* 247, where *the Hans Towns* (I suppose) represent *the Proprieties;* and *those under Arbitrary Princes,* are put for *the Kings Colonies;* this is a mighty fine Story indeed, but the Misfortune of all is, that there is nothing in it but Story; for I think no one will say, that the Propriety of *Mary Land* is better settled, and the People more Industrious in Trade, than they are in the Kings Colony of *New York;* or that there is any Comparison between the Propriety of *North-Carolina,* and the Kings Colony *of Virginia.* As to the Government being Arbitrary, that indeed is somewhat too true, and if this Paragraph were inserted here with a design to have that remedied by the Parliament, we should have owned the obligation to him; but it appears plainly that he only intended it to Cast a blemish upon the Kings Colonies, and invite People over to the Proprieties, otherwise he might have mentioned them all as Arbitrary Governments; for without much Inquiry, Instances may be given that Governours have usurped more Authority than belonged to them, as well in the Proprieties as in the Kings Colonies.

The next thing I shall take notice of is, the Scheme for the general Government of the *Northward* Plantations, mentioned, *p.* 259, 260, 261. In the Essay, which I send you herewith, I have said something concerning this Scheme (*Essay, p.* ______), therefore I shall add but very little about it here; but I cannot forbear observing to you, that according to this Gentlemans Propositions, that Assembly will be very well modelled, with respect to the Interest of *England;* for you may perceive all along, that he is for having the Proprieties and Charter Governments restored, and then of all the ten Provinces he mentions to send Members, to the National Assembly, he proposes; none but *Virginia* and *New York* will be under the Kings Government; so that the plain tendency of this Scheme, is to put the Government of all the Continent of *America* under the Proprieties; for they will have sixteen Voices in twenty, in that National Assembly; which will be much for the Interest of *England;* since the almost intire dependance of seven of these Proprieties is upon Provisions of several sorts; and Woollen Manufactures, and without doubt in all their proceedings, they will have a little regard at least to their own Interest, which of necessity must be prejudicial to *England*, even according to our Authors own Doctrine, *p.* 232.

'Tis true, the High Commissioner having a Negative in all their Acts, may prevent any Notorious Injuiries, but where there is only a Power to prevent Injustice, and not an Interest to procure Justice, there will be little good done by such a Government.

It is proposed that this Assembly should meet at *New York*, and the reason given is, because that is a Frontier; if the Gentleman means that the *Western* bounds of *New York*, are the Frontiers of *New York*, he is in the right indeed; but if he means that the Province of *New York* is a Frontier to *Virginia*, *Mary Land* or *Carolina*, he is very much mis-informed, for it is quite otherwise; I know during the Late War, the *New York* Men made a great noise, that they defended all our Frontiers, and therefore ought in reason to be assisted by the Neighbouring Colonies, but the truth of the matter was, they only defended themselves and their own Trade with the *Indians*.

Whoever observes, the Scituation of the Colonies on the Continent, may easily perceive that to the *Eastward*, they are bounded by the Sea; on the *Northward*, and *Southward*, they border upon each other; and on the *Westward*, they are all open to the *Indians*; who can come in upon the *Western* Frontiers of any Colony they please, and *New York* can by no means in the World hinder it.

This Scheme of Government may be made useful, if the Governments of the Proprieties were taken into the Kings hands, and some other Alterations were made, which I have proposed elsewhere, and therefore I shall not say anything further of it here (*See Essay p.* ______).

I have already declared my Opinion for Liberty of Conscience in the Plantations, and therein I find this Gentleman and I do not differ; and for his long Digression about Moral Vertue; and his Practical Ethics (as he calls them) I shall not trouble my self or you with repeating any part of them; because I do not find they concern the matter in hand, nor can I see any Reason, why they might not have suited any other Subject as well as this, and perhaps have been more properly put in a distinct Chapter by themselves; under the Title of a Lecture against the Court, or any thing else you please; I perceive the Gentleman is very angry with every body (about Court especially) but the King; to whose Character he endeavours (now and then by fits) to do Justice; upon which I can only say, that great is our *Caesar*, since even *Brutus* vouchsafes to extol him; and for the Courtiers, I doubt all his Lashes are in vain, for they know better things than to mend upon Good Advice only.

Thus Sir, I have given you my thoughts of that Discourse, as well as the shortness of my time, my late want of health, and my other Affairs would permit and rough as it is, I was willing to send it to you by this Ship, because it will be the last for this year.

I had once Proposed to have troubled you, with an Essay on the Enlargement of Trade with the *Indians*, and on the most probable means, to secure the *English* Plantations on the Continent from such Inconveniences and prejudices, as they may hereafter be lyable to, in Case of another War with *France;* wherein I intended to have given a more particular and exact account of those Affairs than hath been hitherto given; and also I designed to have laid open the unheard of Practices of some Arbitrary Governours, and the mischievous contrivances of some Evil Ministers about Court, whereby the Plantations have been very much injured and oppressed, and the Interest of *England* very much prejudiced; but these being matters that require some time and expence, I have not been able to perfect them at this time, neither am I very willing to engage in a War upon my own strength alone; however if hereafter I find the Publick service requires it, I shall venture to strike one bold stroak, in such a Cause, without being in the least frighted, either by the Greatness or Power of those Persons, whose Gaudy Tinsel Pomp I despise, as much as I should their mean base Spirits, if I found them in Lower Stations.

I am
SIR, &c.

An ESSAY upon the GOVERNMENT of the *English* Plantations on the Continent of *AMERICA*

As of late many Controversies have arisen in the *English* Nation; so 'tis observable, that the two great Topicks of Trade and Plantations have had their Parts in the Dispute; and indeed it must be confess'd, that (considering the present Circumstances of the World) they are of the greatest importance to all Nations, but more especially the *English.*

Almost all that hath been hitherto written concerning the Plantations hath had a more peculiar Relation to their Trade, and accordingly the several Advocates either for their Freedom, or binding them to a more strict Dependance upon the Crown of *England,* have framed their Arguments so as they thought might best answer those Purposes; from whence it may be very naturally inferr'd, that some By Ends of their own have had a great Influence over many of them, and that private Interest was the great *Diana* for which they contested.

The Design of these Papers

The Design of these Papers is not to treat of the Trade, but the Government of the Plantations; not how to make them great, and rich, by an open free Traffick, but happy, by a Just and Equal Government; that they may enjoy their Obscurity, and the poor way of living which Nature is pleased to afford them out of the Earth, in Peace; and be protected in the Possession thereof, by their lawful Mother *England.*

I am sensible the *English* Plantations may be rendred very serviceable and beneficial to their Mother Kingdom, and I do not in the least doubt she will make the best Advantage of them she can; 'tis what others would do if they were in her place; and therefore I shall not complain of any Hardships in Trade, neither shall it be mentioned but as it comes in the way, in pursuit of the main Design I have laid down.

The Countries under the *English* Government on the Continent of *America* are healthy and fertile, and very well situate both for Pleasure and Profit, especially *Virginia* and *Maryland,* which, as they are the best and most advantagious to the Crown of *England;* so likewise is the Air and Climate of them most agreeable to the *English* Constitutions of Body, the Land richest, the Rivers most commodious, and naturally the whole Countries far excelling any part of the Continent either on the North or South of them.

The chiefest Thing wanting to make the Inhabitants of these Plantations happy, is a good Constitution of Government; and it seems strange, that so little care hath been heretofore taken of that, since it could not be any Prejudice, but of great Advantage even to *England* it self, as perhaps may appear by what shall be offered hereafter.

'Tis true, many Propositions have been made for regulating the Governments of particular Plantations, several of which are now extant; but being mostly calculated by Persons who seem to be biassed by Interest, Prejudice, Revenge, Ambition, or other private Ends I dare not rely on them: Some there are which I shall make bold to use some Parts of, as I find them for my Purpose.

Objections against this Discourse

But before I proceed further, it is necessary to answer some Objections that may be made against my self, and the Work I am going about.

It hath been alledged by some that the Plantations are prejudicial to *England;* but this is already so well answered by Sir *J. Child* in his New Discourse of Trade, from Page 178, to Page 216, by the Author of the *Essay upon Ways and Means,* in his Discourses on the Publick Revenues and the Trade of *England,* Part II. p. 193, to 209. and several other Writings which have been Published, that I cannot think it needful to say any thing more about it.

The Objections I shall take notice of, are these following:

1. It may be objected, that I being an Inhabitant of the Plantations, may probably be too much biassed to their Interest, and therefore am not to be relied on.

2. That the Plantation Governments are already setled well enough; and it may be dangerous to make any great Alterations in them.

3. That it is necessary the King should be more Absolute in the Plantations than he is in *England:* And consequently,

4. That the setling a free Constitution of Government in the Plantations will be prejudicial to the King's Service.

Answer to those Objections

In answer to all which, I beg leave to offer the following Considerations.

1. That, let the Author be what he will, the most material Thing to be respected, is the good or evil Tendency of the Work. If his Majesty's Service seems chiefly aimed at, and no private Interest mixed with it, then I hope that Objection is removed: And for my self, I can with a great deal of Truth and Sincerity affirm, that I have not the least Thought or Design of any thing but his Majesty's Interest and Service, and therein of the Good of all his Subjects in general; but whether the Means I shall propose, may be any wise conducive to those Ends, is humbly submitted to those who have the Honour to be intrusted with the Charge of those Affairs.

The Plantation Governments never well setled

2. If the Governments of the Plantations are already well setled, there needs not any Alteration, (that, I think, every good Man will grant:) But if upon inquiry, it appears, that none of them have ever been well setled; that the present Method of managing them is inconvenient and prejudicial; and that much better Ways may be found: If, I say, these things can be shewn, why should they not be received: If, being considered, they are not approved, they may be rejected, no Alteration will be made, nor any harm done; but rather Good: For my Attempt may set some better Hand to work on the same Subject; and being instructed by others Observations on my Errors, may be more capable to make Amendments: But this, I think, may be safely said, that if any Alterations in the Government of the Plantations are necessary, they may be much more easily done now they are in their Infancy, than hereafter when they grow more populous, and the Evils have taken deeper Root, and are more interwoven with the Laws and Constitutions of the several Colonies.

The King ought not to have a more absolute Power in the Plantations than in England

3. It may perhaps be said that it is necessary the King should have a more absolute Power in the Plantations than he hath in *England.* I know this hath been said, and pretended to be asserted by Argument; and to make it more passable, it hath been framed into a sort of a *Syllogism,* thus: All such *Kingdoms, Principalities, Dominions, &c. as are dependent on the Crown of* England, *and are not a Part of the Empire of the King of* England, *are subject to such Laws as the King is pleased to impose on them; But the* English *Plantations in* America *are dependent on the Crown of* England, *and are not part of the Empire of the King of* England: Ergo, *they are subject to such Laws as the King shall please to impose.* Now it is observable, that the main Stress of this Matter depends upon the Distinction between the *Crown of* England, and the *Empire of the King of* England: And if there is no such Distinction (as possibly there may not) the whole falls to Ground: But if there be such a Distinction, then the clear Tendency of the Argument, is to lay the Plantations intirely at the King's Feet, for him to do what he pleases with them; and the Parliament are not at all concerned in the Business, only upon

sufferance. This I take to be the clear Consequence of the Argument, which no King ever yet pretended to; and for which the Lords and Commons of *England* are very much obliged to the Inventer.

But tho' the King's Right and Prerogative are pretended in the Argument, there were other Reasons for inventing it; and that will appear, if it be remembered that it was first made use of upon the following Occasion. In former times a certain Gentleman was made Governour of one of the *English* Plantations, and had a large Commission for his Office, which he put in Execution after such a manner, that the People were not able to forbear shewing the highest Resentments of such Usage; and at last had recourse to Arms.

And hereupon to vindicate the Governour's Proceedings, it was thought necessary to start this Argument of the King's absolute Power in the Plantations, thereby to lay the Odium of an ill Governour's wicked Actions upon the King.

By the ancient known Laws of the Land the King's Power is sufficient to make himself a great Prince, and his Subjects a happy People; and those very Men that raise these strange Arguments for Absolute Power do not aim at the King's Service in it: But they know, that if they make the King Absolute, his Lieutenant will be so of course; and that is their chief Design.

Thus the King's Power is pretended to be made great, whilst in reality his Interest is destroyed, and so is the Interest of *England* too: for these are the true Reasons that many People who are poor and miserable at home, will not come to the Plantations because they know they shall be ill used.

From what is said, I think it appears very plain, that it is not for the Interest or Service either of the King or Kingdom of *England*, that the Plantations should be under an unlimited Government: the true Interest of *England*, is to have the Plantations cherished, and the poor People encouraged to come hither, every Man here being of great Value to *England*, and most of those that come, are not able to do much good at home.

Whatever Power the King hath in the Plantations must be executed by his Lieutenants: and if it should so happen that the King be mistaken in the Man, and send one who would aim more at his own Interest than the King's Service; and by Extortion, Bribery, and other the like Practices (too often complained of in some Places) should so distract the People, that they make Commotions or Insurrections against him: The King cannot possibly know this till it is too late; and then he will be obliged to inflict the severest

Punishments upon some of the most considerable Offenders, to the Ruin of them and their Families, who otherwise might have done his Majesty good Service.

Neither is this all; for by such Commotions the Product of one Year at least will be lost in that Colony where they happen, which will be a greater Prejudice to *England* than the best Governour will ever be able to make amends for; the Loss of the Tobacco made in one Year in *Virginia*, considering the Customs and the Merchants Damage, by their shipping and Stock being unimployed, will amount to at least 500000£. prejudice to the King and Kingdom of *England*.

I know it will be said, that all this proceeds either from groundless Jealousies of I know not what Dangers to happen, no one knows when; or else, that I am very much prejudiced against some of the present Governours of the Plantations; to which I answer: That it is not to be supposed such things should happen every Day; but since they have been heretofore, it is probable, they may be again, and the Consequence being so very dangerous, the more Reason there is to endeavour the Prevention of them: And for the other Imputation, I can with a great deal of Truth say, that I have the Honour of being known but to two of the King's Governours, and for both of them, I have the most profound Respect and Regard imaginable; nor can I believe that either of them will find fault with me for endeavouring to prevent those male-Administrations in others, of which they will never be guilty themselves.

A free Constitution of Government in the Plantations not prejudicial to the King's Service

4. The other Objection to this Work is, That the setling a free Constitution of Government in the Plantations may be prejudicial to the King's Service. To this I answer, That by a free Constitution of Government, I mean, that the Inhabitants of the Plantations may enjoy their Liberties and Estates, and have Justice equally and impartially administred unto them; and that it should not be in the power of any Governour to prevent this. Now by enjoying Liberty, I understand, the Liberty of their Persons being free from Arbitrary, illegal Imprisonments; not that they should have great Liberties of Trade, or any other Liberties or Priviledges, that may be thought prejudicial to the King or Kingdom of *England*; for my Design is not to complain of our

Subjection, or any thing of that Nature; but to shew as well as I can, what may be done for the Interest and Service both of *England* and the Plantations.

It is no advantage to the King, that his Governours should have it in their Power to gripe and squeeze the People in the Plantations, nor is it ever done, for any other Reason, than their own private Gain. I have often heard Complaints made, that the Governours and their Officers and Creatures, have been guilty of ill things to raise Estates for themselves, or to gratify their own Revenge, or some other Passion; but I never heard, that any of the Plantations were oppressed to raise Money for the King's Service, and indeed I think it is past Dispute, that the King's and Plantations Interest is the same, and that those who pretend, the King hath, or ought to have an unlimited Power in the Plantations, are a sort of People, whose Designs make their Interests run counter to that both of the King and Plantations.

Thus having briefly answered those Objections which perhaps may be made to what I shall offer: I proceed to the main Design, which is to shew several things, which I must beg leave to say, I conceive are amiss, and to propose some Methods for redressing those Grievances.

The Heads of the following Discourse

The Particulars which I shall treat of may properly enough be ranked under these several Heads, *viz. Religion, Laws, Trade, People, Relation* of *one Plantation* to *another, Governours, King.*

Grievances relating to Religion

The present Inconveniencies relating to Religion, in short are these. 1. That there is not a good free Liberty of Conscience established; but generally whatever Religion or Sect happens to be most numerous, they have the Power over all the rest; thus the Independants in *New-England,* and the Quakers in *Pensylvania,* abuse all Mankind that come among them, and are not of their Persuasion; and in *New-York* it is as bad, or rather worse; for there the contending Parties are pritty near equal; from whence it follows, that (sometimes one, and sometimes the other prevailing,) those who happen to have the best Interest and most favour in the Government, exert their utmost Skill and Industry to ruin the others.

In our Government of *Virginia* we are, or pretend most of us to be of the Church of *England;* some few Roman Catholicks amongst us, some

Quakers, who at present seem to be greatly increasing; and about two or three Meetings of Dissenters, and those in the out-parts of the Countrey, where at present are no Church of *England* Ministers, nor can any be put well there, no sufficient Provision being made for their Maintenance; all the Ministers Salaries are paid in Tobacco, which in those places is of so small value, that they cannot well subsist upon the Salary allowed by Law.

But notwithstanding the Church of *England* is so generally established here, yet there is scarce any sort of Church Government established amongst us; the Laws indeed do direct building of Churches, and have ascertain'd what Salaries shall be paid to the Clergy, but it is not well determined who are Patrons of the Parishes, what Right of presentation they have, in what Cases the King, or the Bishop may present *jure devoluto*,[4] and many other Defects of that Nature there are, as yet unprovided for; here also I may add, that there is no established Court for the Punishment of Scandalous Ministers, nor any Care taken to prevent Dilapidations, neither are there any Courts where Incestuous Marriages, and other Causes of the like nature are properly triable.

In some places no care at all is taken, either of the Religion or Morality of the Inhabitants, as particularly, *North-Carolina*, and in this almost all the Proprieties and Charter-Governments are to blame.

I shall not take upon me to offer much towards remedying these Grievances of Religion, because I think it is an improper Subject for me; but it is to be wish'd, that some Care were taken to instruct the People well in Morality, that is, what all Perswasions either do, or pretend to desire.

Grievances on Account of their Laws

The Inconveniences the Plantations labour under, on Account of their Laws, are very many.

It is a great Unhappiness, that no one can tell what is Law, and what is not, in the Plantations; some hold that the Law of *England* is chiefly to be respected, and where that is deficient, the Laws of the several Colonies are to take place; others are of Opinion, that the Laws of the Colonies are to take first place, and that the Law of *England* is of force only where they are silent; others there are, who contend for the Laws of the Colonies, in Conjunction with those that were in force in *England* at the first Settlement of the Colony,

4. ["With the right transferred."]

and lay down that as the measure of our Obedience, alleging, that we are not bound to observe any late Acts of Parliament made in *England*, except such only where the Reason of the Law is the same here, that it is in *England;* but this leaving too great a Latitude to the Judge; some others hold that no late Acts of the Parliament of *England* do bind the Plantations, but those only, wherein the Plantations are particularly named. Thus are we left in the dark, in one of the most considerable Points of our Rights; and the Case being so doubtful, we are too often obliged to depend upon the Crooked Cord of a Judge's Discretion, in Matters of the greatest Moment and Value.

Of late Years great Doubts have been raised, how far the Legislative Authority is in the Assemblies of the several Colonies; whether they have Power to make certain Acts or Ordinances in the nature of by-Laws only; or, whether they can make Acts of Attainder, Naturalization, for setling or disposing of Titles to Lands within their own Jurisdiction, and other things of the like Nature; and where Necessity requires, make such Acts as best suit the Circumstances and Constitution of the Country, even tho' in some Particulars, they plainly differ from the Laws of *England*.

And as there have been Doubts made concerning the Enacting of Laws with us, so likewise there have been great Controversies concerning the Repeal of Laws made here: The Assemblies have held, that when any Law made by them, and not assented to by the King in *England* is repealed by them; such Repeal doth intirely annul and abrogate, and even (as it were) annihilate the former Law, as if it never had been made, and that it cannot by any means be revived, but by the same Power that at first enacted it, which was the Assembly; but the Governours have held, that tho' the King hath not assented to the first, yet he hath the Liberty of refusing his Assent to the repealing Law, and by Proclamation may repeal that, and then the other is revived of course: This Dispute, and others of the like Nature, ran very high in the late Reigns.

It is also to be observed as a great Defect, that no one of these Colonies on the Continent, have any tolerable Body of Laws; all of them have some sort of Laws or other; but there is not any such thing amongst them all, as a regular Constitution of Government, and good Laws for Directions of the several Officers, and other Persons therein, with suitable Penalties to enforce Obedience to them.

This seems to have been a Fault in the Beginning; for then it was put into bad Hands, and hath been little mended since: One notorious Instance may be given in *Virginia*. This Colony was at first given for the Encouragement of it to a Company of Adventurers, who by Charter from King *James* the first, were constituted a Corporation, and they set up a sort of Government here, the Chief Magistrates whereof were called Governours and Council; and they (I suppose) as the chief Members of the Corporation, constituted the highest Court of Judicature; afterwards this Countrey was taken into the King's Hands, and the same Constitution of Governor and Council remained; and they to this Day continue to be the highest Court of Judicature in the Countrey; tho' we have no Law to establish them as such, neither have they ever had any Commission for that purpose, and till *April* 1699, were never sworn to do Justice, but being made Counsellors, they took their Places as Judges of Course.

From hence it may be observ'd, that no great Stress is to be laid on any Argument against Alterations in the Plantations, barely because Changes may be dangerous, for (it seems) a Regular Settlement hath never yet been made, and therefore 'tis time to be done now.

Courts of Judicature

After what has been said concerning the Defects in the Legislative Authority, and the Laws of the Plantations; It is not to be thought strange, that the Establishment of the Courts of Judicature is defective also, that being the Superstructure and the other the Foundation.

Grievances relating to Trade

The next thing to be consider'd, is the Trade of the Plantations on the Continent of *America;* and herein I shall not pretend to calculate the Advantage that may be made to *England* thereby; I think no Body at this time of day is ignorant of that, neither shall I pretend to plead for the Plantations having great Liberties of Trade allow'd them; But I hope it may be thought reasonable, that the Colonies under the King's more immediate Protection, and which are by far the most profitable to *England,* should at least be as much encouraged as the Proprietors and Charter Governments, who are almost so many People lost to *England.*

The King's Plantations are governed by Persons appointed by the King, and they generally take all possible Care to prevent illegal Trade, and Frauds, and Abuses in the Revenues; but it is otherwise in the Charter

Governments, for there the Parties concerned, find it their Interest to connive at (if not assist) those Practices; and to excuse themselves in it, they say, they are obliged to give all reasonable Incouragement for People to come and live with them.

Nor are these all the Injuries that the King's Governments suffer by the Proprieties, for they being under no obligation but their own Advantage, have many other ways to serve themselves to the Prejudice of their Neighbours.

There is almost a constant Intercourse of Trade and Commerce from *New-York*, and the other Northern Colonies to *Madagascar*, and other parts of *India*, from whence are brought Muslins, and other *Indian* Goods, which are privately run into the Colonies under the King's Government: The last Summer, one *Shelley*, a *New-York* man, brought about sixty Pyrates, (Passengers) with great quantities of Goods from those Parts; and lay at Anchor off Cape *May*, at the Mouth of *Delaware*, till he had disperst most of them into *Pensylvania*, the *Jersey's* and other neighbouring Colonies; these Practices are prejudicial to the Plantation Trade, contrary to the Act of Parliament for settling the *India* Trade, and tend to the ruin of all Trade in the World; and yet I think *Shelley* went into *New-York* afterwards and was never questioned about it.

Nor is this one Instance only of such Practices amongst them; but it is notorious in this Part of the World, that Pyrates and Privateers have been very much harboured by them, especially to the Northward; and those People bringing in great quantities of Money, and other rich Goods, all the Seamen in the adjacent Plantations run thither, and many of them take up that Trade, and being acquainted with the Coasts, are the more capable to commit Robberies, and to take and plunder Ships sailing in and out, between the Capes of *Chisapeak* Bay, on their Voyages between *England* and *Virginia* and *Mary-Land:* This is a great Prejudice to the Trade of those Places, and not only so, but to the King's Revenues.

We in the King's Governments look upon the Pirates and Privateers to be Robbers and Thieves; but the good People of *Pensylvania* esteem them very honest Men for bringing Money into their Countrey, and encouraging their Trade.

The King's Governours in the Colonies are strictly bound up by their Instructions, that they cannot give their Assent to any Laws for ascertaining the Value of Coin, in their Governments; but the Proprieties not being tyed up to this Rule, they are always at Liberty, either to raise or lower the Value of Money, as their Interest and present Occasions require; by which means they have dreined almost all the Ready Money out of *Virginia* and *Maryland,* the two Colonies, that (considering their Value to *England*) 'tis presum'd, may reasonably expect at least as much Favour and Protection as any of their Neighbours.

Grievances particularly relating to the Trade of Virginia *and* Mary-Land

All that hath been observed hitherto, hath had relation more or less to all the Colonies on the Continent; what follows under this Head of Trade, will more particularly have regard to the Plantations of *Virginia* and *Mary-Land;* which as they are the most Considerable, and of greatest Consequence, so they seem (and perhaps with some Reason) to apprehend themselves to be under harder Circumstances than any of their Brethren.

The Duties upon Tobacco, the only Produce of those Places, are very high and burthensom; those they cannot expect to be eased from, untill the Crown of *England* is in better Condition to afford it; but it seems modest enough to wish, that those Duties were laid upon them in the easiest manner.

When the 3 *d. per lib.* was first laid upon Tobacco, it was paid in the nature of an Excise, by the first Buyer in so many Months, and not by the Importer; but now that 3 *d.* and all the rest of the 6 *d.* is paid by the Importer as a Custom, which is extreamly grievous and burthensom to the Inhabitants of these Plantations.

The manner of Trade between *England* and these Plantations is thus; either the Tobacco is bought from the Planters by the Merchants of *England,* and by them shipped, or else it is shipped by the Inhabitants of the Countrey, and consigned to their Correspondents in *England,* and by these Inhabitants or Planters in *Virginia,* we may reasonably compute that 20000 *Hogsheads* of Tobacco a Year are sent for *England,* which weighing one with another about 500 *Net.* Tobacco, the whole amounts to 10,000,000 of Pounds of Tobacco.

Upon all Tobacco's sold in *London* there are certain Allowances called *Clof* and *Tret,* amounting to about 4 *per Cent.* which are made to the Buyer: Now when the Importer paid only the two Pence, and the Buyer the rest, that Allowance was but of four times two Pence in every Hundred Weight of Tobacco; but now the Importer pays the whole six Pence, that Allowance comes to four six-pences in every Hundred Weight of Tobacco; so that the Importer loses just 4 *per Cent.* upon the last four Pence.

The Factor in *London* takes 2 *l.* ½ *per Cent.* to himself as Commission for the Sale of the Goods, and when the Importer paid only the 2 *d.* the Factor had Commission only upon that; but now he charges it upon the whole, which is a further Damage to the Importer of 2 *l.* ½ *per Cent.* upon the last 4 *d. per lib.*

Now these two Articles alone, which are so little, they are hardly taken notice of, are yet so considerable as to amount to very near a Tax of 10*s. per Pole* on all the Tythables in *Virginia;* for they are not above 22,000. and this comes to 10833 *l.* 6 *s.* 1 *d.* ½ which I compute thus, the 4 *d. per lib.* on 10,000,000 *lib.* of Tobacco amounts to 166,666 *l.* 13 *s.* 4 *d.* upon which Account

	l.	*s.*	*d.*
4 *per Cent. Clo.* and *Tret* is	6666.	12.	09.½
2½ *per Cent.* Commission to the Factor is	4166.	13.	04.
	10833.	06.	01.½

This Sum to so great a Kingdom as *England* is not worth speaking of; but to so poor a Handful of People as we are, is very considerable, and the more, because it is paid anew every Crop that is made.

When the Importer paid only the two Pence *per lib.* it was at the peril of the Factor in *London,* to see that he sold the Tobacco to such Men as were capable to pay the remaining four Pence, because he was answerable to the King for it: But now the Planter is answerable for the whole six Pence; and if by any Omission of the Factor, the Tobacco is sold to a Man that breaks, and cannot pay for it, the Planter loses not only the first Cost of his Goods, but all the Duties besides, which perhaps all he hath in the World will not make Good, and so he is ruined by his Factor's Neglect.

And moreover, the Duty being so very great, the Importer is necessitated to sell his Goods in a short time, at such a rate as he can get, because he is not able to let so vast a quantity of Money lie dead upon his Hands, to wait for a better Market.

These particular Circumstances afore-mentioned, make the Condition of the Planter very hazardous and difficult, even in Comparison of what it was, under the former Method of paying the Duties; and since the King's Interest is not touched, it would be a great deal of Charity to relieve us, if possible; it is the Product of our Labour, we run the Risque of the Sea, and of the Market; the Buyer runs no Hazard, neither doth the Factor; and yet it very often happens, that he gets more for his Commission of Selling, than the Planter doth for the first Purchase; nay, sometimes he loses the whole, and is brought in Debt for the Charges, when the Factor gets very considerably for his Commissions, and the Buyer makes very profitable Returns.

Running Tobacco in England

The great Abuse of running Tobacco in *England*, and defrauding the King of his Customs, is of very ill Consequence to the Plantations, for all that is run must be sold at under Rates, and that beats down the Price to the fair Trader; this hath been endeavoured to be prevented by an Act made the last Session of Parliament, to prohibit the Importation of Bulk Tobacco into *England*, and peradventure that Act may be of great use, but Practice only can tell that.

Act against the Importation of Bulk Tobacco, defective

However, by the way it is to be noted, that that Act is somewhat defective, for no Penalties on the Breach of it can be recovered but in the Courts of *Westminster*, when in Truth the Officers in the Plantations, are the proper Persons to prevent the Abuse; and they cannot make a Voyage for *England* to prosecute; neither is it plain, that the Penalty becomes due, till the Breach is detected in *England*; and if so, the Masters of Ships and their Mariners are only obliged to put it on Shore before it is found, and then they are safe.

Grievances with relation to the People in the Plantations

In the fourth Place I come to discourse of the People in the Plantations: And here it is extreamly to be lamented, that such a vast Tract of Land, so Pleasant, so Fruitful, so Healthy, so Capable of all sorts of Improvement, for the Support and Encouragement of the Inhabitants; so well furnish'd with all sorts of Beasts, Birds, and Fruits; and so conveniently situate for Traffick, by many commodious navigable Rivers, and those so well stored with Fish of all sorts; I say it is a very melancholy Consideration, that so great a part of the World, by Nature so rich and improveable, should lie almost wholly rude, and uncultivated for want of People.

It hath been said by some, that the Plantations drawing People from *England* are prejudicial to it; but this will appear to have very little Weight in it, if it be consider'd, that not many come hither who are capable of doing much for their Countrey's Service at home. In the first Settlements indeed, many worthy good Men adventured themselves hither, with Expectations to raise their Fortunes, but most, if not all of them, were disappointed in their Hopes: Also in the late Civil Wars, and other unquiet Times in *England*, many Persons of good Character and Reputation fled to the Plantations, for the Enjoyment of that Protection, which was denied them at Home; and when *England's* Misfortunes cast her again into the like unhappy Circumstances, 'tis reasonable to believe, more such People will be constrain'd to leave their own Country for the Plantations (which is yet far better than to go into Foreign Princes Dominions) but without some such Accident happen, very few, or none will come to inhabit there, but such poor miserable Wretches, as not being able to get Bread at home, are forced to submit to be Servants four or five Years, to defray the Charge of their Transportation; and surely it is a great Service to *England*, that the Plantations take off, and Imploy very much to her Benefit, those Persons, who otherwise must Beg, Starve, or perhaps be dispatched by the Cord of Justice, for using unlawful Means, to procure a mean Subsistance. The Governments of the Plantations not being well setled, and the Want of an Impartial Administration of Justice, are great Discouragements to those that otherwise would come hither, or being here, would stay.

The late Act of Parliament incapacitating Foreigners to purchase Lands, to bear Offices, or to be upon Juries, is a great Discouragement to those People from coming hither.

Grievances of one Plantation to another

5. The Inconveniences and Prejudices that one Plantation receives from another, are very considerable, and under the present Management, are almost impossible to be prevented; but above all, the Proprieties and Charter

Governments, do ever prove ill Neighbours to such of the King's as lye next them; especially *Carolina* and *Pensylvania,* to *Virginia* and *Mary-Land;* the two first being continual Receptacles for Servants and Debtors, that run from the two latter, to the great Detriment of their Masters and Creditors.

Another Master Policy of the Proprieties hath been to raise, and encourage Faction in their Neighbouring Colonies; as well knowing the weakest Party must fly to them for Shelter.

I have already under the third Head mentioned the Prejudices, the King's Plantations lie under, from the Proprieties, in Point of Trade, and Coin, and by harbouring Pyrates.

Remarks on the Author of the Essay on Ways and Means

And here I cannot but take notice, what I find written by the Author of the *Essay on Ways and Means,* in his Discourses on the *Publick Revenues,* and on the *Trade of England,* in the second Part of that Work, concerning the Plantation Trade.

I would not be thought so fond of my own Abilities, as to believe my self sufficient to enter the Lists of Controversy with that Gentleman, who seems to be a Man of good Parts, and to have taken a great deal of Pains in that Discourse; but being himself unacquainted, and very badly informed by others, 'tis not to be thought strange, that he has managed his Business very lamely: I shall not at this time take upon me to controvert any of his Reasonings and Arguments, (tho' perhaps liable to many Objections) but wholly confine my self to matter of Fact, in which he has been very much misinform'd, and considering the Particulars, it is not hard to guess, That a certain Northern Proprietor had a great Hand in it.

I shall not mention any thing for Argument's sake only; but I shall remark some Particulars, wherein the Truth is misrepresented, and so leave them barely, to shew, that if I write any thing contrary to what that Gentleman hath offer'd, 'tis not thro' Inadvertency of what he has done, but because I think I am better able to give a true Account of the Matter of Fact. P. 240, 245, 250, 251, 283, 284. I observe he is often finding Fault, that the Charters to the Proprieties are not kept inviolable, and asserting that to be the best way to encourage those Plantations: Whether it would encourage them or not, I know not; but sure I am, that if the Proprieties are let alone to entertain Pyrates and Privateers, and to carry on a Course of Illegal Trade, as of late Years hath been practised amongst many of them, the Consequences thereof to *England* will be too fatal not to be taken notice of.

But to take off any Imputations of this Nature, it is said, (Page 250) that in those Colonies which by Charter are not governed from *England,* as to all Duties belonging to the Crown Revenue, the King has as immediate an Influence by having an Officer of his own upon the Spot, as in other Places; but with Submission I would ask him, What such an Officer signifies under a Charter Government: The King thought fit lately to erect a Court of Admiralty in *Pensylvania;* but the great Opposition the Judge and other Officers have met with, and the many Tricks and Contrivances that have been used to ruine some of them, do sufficiently evidence what they would be at.

P. 229. It is urged in favour of the Proprieties, That the Dissenters living there, are a sober temperate People, which is the Cause of their Increase of Inhabitants; But under Favour I take it that their Pyracy and Illegal Trade have drawn more People to them, than their Sobriety and Temperance have increased.

'Tis true, they will not all of them swear and be drunk so publickly as is usual in some other Places, but their other Morals are no better than those of their Neighbours; perhaps not so good, if they were, whence should spring that Tenet of theirs, That every Man is bound to believe a Professor upon his bare Affirmation only, before another Man upon Oath; Whence hath proceeded the great Opposition they have made to the Court of Admiralty lately erected by his Majesty's Authority, whence their Pretence of making Laws for the Management of their Trade, without Regard to the Acts of Parliament of *England;* and whence their Esteem of the Pyrates as honest Men, bringing Money into their Countrey: Are Knavery, and Injustice, and Disobedience, and Rebellion, and Pyracy, and Robbery such commendable Morals? Much more may be said on this Occasion; but at present I pass it by.

P. 234. It is said the Reasons why *Virginia* hath thriven no better, are, That the Planters and Inhabitants have been, and at this time are discouraged from Planting Tobacco in that Colony; and Servants are unwilling to go thither, because the Members of the Council and others having an Interest in the Government, have from time to time procured Grants for large Tracts of Land, so that none is left to be cultivated by Servants coming in at this time; and to render the thing as ill as may be, P. 236, it is represented, that the Quit-rents for those Lands are seldom paid; and instead of Building and Stocking, they fell a few Trees, and throw up a little Hut covered with Bark, and put three or four Hogs into the Woods: And by these means it comes to pass, that many hold twenty or thirty Thousand Acres of Land apiece, and that largely survey'd; some Patents including double the quantity of Land that was intended to be granted: And hence (saith he) it proceeds, that many hundred thousand Acres are taken up but not planted; which Practice drives away the Inhabitants and Servants bred up only to Planting, and forces them into Colonies where there Labour is not so profitable either to the Crown or Kingdom of *England*. This is the Substance of what he asserts, and of this he saith, he hath certain Information. To all which I say, That true it is, that in some Places great Quantities of Land have been taken up, and not very well seated, by reason the People have been driven off by the *Indians*, that is by Foreign *Indians*, not those that pretend any Right to the Land: And some other Tracts of Land have been Patented, and but just so much Seating and planting upon them as the Law directs; which perhaps upon better Consideration may not be thought sufficient; but that ever throwing up a Hut of Bark, or putting three or four Hogs into the Woods was accounted Seating a Tract of Land, I do positively deny, and am very sure no Man can give one Instance, that ever it has been so adjudged.

That the Council and other Persons having Interest in the Government, and not others as well as they, gained great Tracts of Land is an entire Fiction: That was not the Cause of such extravagant Grants; but the Government always esteem'd it the King's Interest, that the Land should be taken up, because it increased the Quit-rents, and therefore they were willing to give it to any one that would take it: I do not say, that this Management of former Governours may not be thought an Oversight, but certainly it will not bear the Colour that Gentleman seems to put upon it; for he represents it as a piece of downright Knavery in the great Men, to advance themselves and their Friends; tho' I believe, it will be difficult for any one to shew, that it was ever attempted to parcel the Land out amongst the Favorites, till about five or six years ago, some Lands that were valuable in *Pamunkey Neck*, (lying at the Head of *York* River) were granted to particular friends; but upon a dispute arising about a Tract of Land in that Neck, given by the King's Charter to the College, those Grants were surrendred, and so the Project fell.

The Quit-rents of all the Lands held of the King in *Virginia*, are constantly paid, except perhaps some few that escape by Fraud; but of them there are not many, and those by the Negligence of Officers.

There are not above three or four Men in the Countrey, that have each of them 20,000 Acres of Land in Possession, and the most valuable of them holds the greatest part of his by Marriage with a Widdow, as Guardian to an Orphan, and in right of his Children now *Minors:* And excluding the Lord *Fairfax's* Propriety in the Northern Neck, there is not one Man that holds 30,000 Acres of Land in the whole Colony; and it is further to be observed, that the best landed Men in the Country came to those Estates either by Descent or Purchase, and not by those Extravagant Grants as is suggested. The large Measure allowed by Serveyors in old Times, is as disingeniously narrated as any Part of the Story, for it is put in just after he mentions the great Quantities of Land some Men hold, so that he seems to insinuate, as if they held 40 or 60 instead of 20 or 30 thousand Acres; but he mistakes the Case, for here and there indeed some small Tracts are overmeasured; but the great ones have most of them been servey'd of late, and where the old Patents fell short, new ones have been taken out more exact.

I am sensible many Instances may be given of the Impolitic Methods of managing the Land in *Virginia,* and if they had been mention'd only as such, without any Air of Design and Abuse cast over the whole, as this Gentleman has done, I should not have taken upon me to contradict any thing he had said; but I think him ill used by those that have given him these Informations, and that much to the Prejudice of the King's Plantations; for the whole Discourse seems to be calculated as a Commendation of the Proprieties, and to bring Disgrace upon the King's Plantations, that People may be discouraged to come hither, and induced to go thither; and this Art of getting and keeping People from us, is a piece of very ill Neighbourhood in them.

Great Notice is taken of Lands being wanting in *Virginia,* when there is really good Land not yet granted, sufficient to satisfie many thousands of People; but nothing is said of the great numbers that have been decoyed over into a certain Northern Propriety, and how they bought large Tracts of Lands of the Proprietor in *England,* and when they came to seat it, there was not a sixth Part of what they bought to be found: Such Proprietors are like to teach pure Morals no doubt.

By what is said P. 249, 250, of the petty Emulations, or private Interests of Neighbour Governours, and the Petitions of hungry Courtiers at home, prevailing to discourage those particular Colonies, who in a few years have raised themselves by their own Charge, Prudence and Industry, to the Wealth and Greatness they are now arrived at, without Expence to the

Crown, &c. and by what is proposed P. 253, 254, that no Province should obstruct or clog the Passage of any Ship or Goods coming from England to it, with any Custom or Duty, &c. I say, by these two Passages in that Discourse, it is easie to tell who gave the Author of it the greatest Part of his Information; tho' I must confess I am somewhat at a loss for his Meaning in the Words, *Petitions of hungry Courtiers at Home,* unless they have relation to such Grants as the King hath been pleased to make of Wrecks, Prizes, Goods of Pyrates in those Parts, or some such things; for I know no other Petitions of or Grants to Courtiers, that could give the least colour for such a Reflection. But to leave Controversy I proceed.

One other great Inconveniency that the Colonies suffer from one another, is, that the Inhabitants of one Government go into that which is adjacent, and contract Debts, or commit Breaches of the Laws, and return home, and by reason that no proper Method is yet setled, one cannot be compelled to satisfie his just Debts, nor the other brought to condign Punishment for his Offences.

Grievances with Relation to the Governours

6. The next concerning Governours is a tender Point, and must be touched with clean Hands; and when I profess that I do not design to expose any particular Person now in Office, I hope Liberty may be allowed me, to remark some Grievances that the Plantations have, and may have Cause to complain of, if they knew where.

And herein I shall but lightly mention some things, part of which at least, perhaps it may be necessary to reform hereafter, not accusing any Person for what is past.

Some Governours either through Weakness or Prejudice, have contributed very much to raise Factions in the Colonies under their Command, by making use of, and encouraging some one particular Sort or Sett of Men, and rejecting all others, and these Favourites being oftentimes of mean Education and base Spirits, cannot bear their good Fortunes, but thinking absolute Command only is their Province, either for private Interest, or to gratifie their Ambition, Revenge, or some other Passion, they hardly ever fail to run all Things into Confusion; and of these Actions by Favourites, Instances are not wanting.

The King's Governours in the Plantations either have, or pretend to have very large Powers within their Provinces, which together with the Trusts reposed in them, of disposing of all Places of Honour and Profit, and of being chief Judges in the Supream Courts of Judicature, (as they are in many Places, if not all) render them so absolute, that it is almost impossible to lay any sort of Restraint upon them.

On the other side, in some of the Proprieties, the Hands of the Government are so feeble, that they cannot protect themselves against the Insolencies of the Common People, which makes them very subject to Anarchy and Confusion.

The chief End of many Governours coming to the Plantations, having been to get Estates for themselves, very unwarrantable Methods have sometimes been made use of to compass those Ends, as by engrossing several Offices into their own Hands, selling them or letting them out at a yearly Rent of such a part of the Profits, and also by Extortion and Presents, (or Bribery) these things have been heretofore, and in ill Times may be done again.

And here I must beg Leave to say, that I am of Opinion, the Court of *England* hath hitherto gone upon wrong Principles, in appointing Governours of the Plantations; for those Places have been generally given as the last Rewards for past Services, and they expecting nothing after that, were almost necessitated, then to make Provision for their whole Lives, whereby they were in a manner forced upon such Methods (whether good or evil) as would compass those Ends.

Another very considerable difficulty the Plantations lie under from their Governours, is, that there is no way left to represent their evil Treatment to the King; for nothing of that Nature can be done without Money, no Money can be had without an Assembly, and the Governour always hath a Negative in their Proceedings, and not only so, but if he fears any thing of that Nature, he can let alone calling one, or (being called) can dissolve them at pleasure.

King unacquainted with the true State of the Plantations

7. But the last and greatest Unhappiness the Plantations labour under, is, that the King and Court of *England* are altogether Strangers to the true State of Affairs in *America,* for that is the true Cause why their Grievances have not been long since redress'd.

The present Establishment of the Lords Commissioners for Trade and Plantations is very necessary and expedient for that Purpose, and perhaps may be rendred much more so, but they being Strangers to the Affairs in these

Parts, are too often obliged to depend on the Relation of others who pretend to be better acquainted. Misrepresentations in those Cases may be very dangerous, and cannot well be prevented, there not being as yet any Method setled for them to gain certain Information of the true State of the Plantations.

Remedies for the aforementioned Grievances

Hitherto I have taken notice of some of the most material Inconveniencies attending these Plantations: Now I must beg Leave to offer such Remedies to Consideration as with Submission I conceive may prevent the like Grievances for the future.

To propose Schemes of Government, I know, hath always been esteemed a difficult Task, and the more, because the Proposer is look'd upon as obliged to answer all Objections that shall be made against them, and it is not impossible to raise many Objections against the best Government in the World, tho' perhaps it would be difficult to make any real Amendments.

I do not pretend to assert, that what I offer is of necessity to be approved, and that better cannot be done; I shall only presume to offer some few Generals to consideration; if they are well accepted, I have my Reward, if not, many Men of much greater Abilities than I am, have lost their Labours in such Cases, and therefore I shall be contented.

And as I began to lay open the Inconveniencies and Grievances of the Plantations, in order as they came under the General Heads set down in the beginning, so I shall likewise endeavour to propose the Remedies in the same Method; and,

Remedies for the Grievances of Religion

1. For Religion; I have already said, I take it to be improper for me to offer much upon that Subject, and therefore, I shall only presume to mention two things, which I take to be of necessity, for the Maintenance and Support of the Civil Government.

Liberty of Conscience

1. That sufficient Provision be made for all People, to enjoy the same Liberty of Conscience in the Plantations, that is indulged to them in *England,* upon the same Terms, and not otherwise; and as Dissenters should be sure

of this Liberty, so likewise good Care should be taken that they may not abuse it; particularly, it is necessary to make such a Settlement, that no one may find it his Interest to leave the Church of *England;* as now in Virginia every Housholder is obliged by Law to provide himself with Arms and Ammunition, and to go to Musters of the *Militia;* if they fail, they are to pay such a Fine: But the Law for imposing it being somewhat defective, and therefore the Fines not duly levied, many People (who have no great Sense of any Religion,) turn Quakers, chiefly to save the Expence and Trouble of providing Arms and Ammunition, and of going to Musters, and also by professing themselves Quakers, they are eased of being Constables, Church-wardens, and all such troublesome Offices, which other People are obliged to execute.

Against Immorality

2. Tho' perhaps it may not be convenient to force all People to be of one Religion, yet it may be requisite to oblige every one to profess and practise some sort of Religion or other: to this end I humbly propose, that severe Laws be made against Blasphemy, Prophaneness, Cursing, Swearing, Sabbath-breaking, &c. with suitable Penalties to enforce the Observation thereof, and that all possible Diligence be used by the Governours, and other principal Officers of the Plantations to put those Laws in Effectual Execution within their respective Provinces.

Remedies for the Grievances relating to the Laws

2. For remedying of the Grievances mentioned under the Head of Laws, I humbly propose,

1. That some Rule be established, to know what Laws the Plantations are to be subject to, and particularly, how far the late Acts of Parliament do affect them, where they are not expressly mentioned.

Legislature

2. That it be agreed how far the Legislature is in their Assemblies; whether they have Power of Naturalization, Attainders of Treason, Illegitimating of Heirs, cutting off Intails, settling Titles to Lands, and other things of that nature; and whether they may make Laws disagreable to the Laws of

England, in such Cases, where the Circumstances of the Places are vastly different, as concerning Plantations, Waste, the Church, &c.

Courts of Judicature

3. That a good Constitution of Courts of Judicature be established in the several Plantations, as shall be most agreeable to their respective Forms of Government, and other Circumstances.

That the Judges of the Supream Courts in every Province hold their Offices *quam diu se bene gesserint*,[5] and that Provision be made to ascertain what shall be adjudged Misbehaviour in them, or at least, that care be taken, that it be not absolutely in the Governour's Breast, to displace any Judge at pleasure, without shewing his Reasons for the same, together with the Judge's Answer thereto.

That the last Resort of Justice may not be to the Chief Governours and Council here, and thence to the King and Council in *England*, as is now practised in most places; but that from the Judges commissionated as aforesaid, an Appeal directly to *England* may be allowed to such People as think themselves injured, in any Sum exceeding the Value of five hundred Pounds *Sterl.*

Lands to be confirmed by the King

4. That in the King's Colonies, his Majesty would be graciously pleased to confirm all Lands to the several Possessors, (where any privat Persons Interest is not concerned) as was done by King *Charles* the second in his Charter to *Virginia*, of which also Care should be taken, that it be not infringed, as heretofore it hath been.

Tenants of the Proprietors to be secured in their Lands

And that by some Law for that purpose, good and wholsom Provisions be made, for the setling and adjusting the Inhabitants Titles to those Lands they hold of Proprietors, that those People may not be continually obliged to a servile Dependance upon their Landlords, and thereby be sometimes necessitated either to behave themselves disrespectively and disobediently to the Governour, acting by the King's Authority there, or to be in danger of

5. ["As long as they will have conducted themselves well," i.e., good conduct.—Tr.]

losing their Lands, being forced to pay extravagant Fines for Confirmation of their Titles, or of being some other way liable to suffer under the Proprietors, or their Agents Displeasure.

I am very far from desiring, that the Right of the Proprietors in their Lands should be injured, therefore (for Explanation) I add further, that I do not propose, that the Proprietors shall be compelled to part with their Land at any set Price; in that let them make such reasonable Terms as they can; but whatever the Terms are, let the Inhabitants be secured by good Laws from any Tricks or Designs, which may be put upon them thereafter, for that will certainly cause Disorders and Mutinies, which are publick Inconveniencies and by no means to be tolerated for any private Man's Advantage; or if the People find themselves so far in the Proprietors Power, that they are of Necessity obliged to submit to him, then all that Interest will most surely be employed in prejudice of the King's Government there; and of this an Instance may be given, but it is an Invidious Task to tell Men of their Faults, and therefore I shall not mention them.

Remedies for the Grievances of Trade

3. For Remedy of the Grievances mentioned under the Heads of Trade, I humbly propose,

Equal Liberty of Trade in all the Plantations

1. That sufficient Care be taken to establish an Equal Liberty of Trade in all the Plantations on the Continent of *America,* as well as the Proprieties as the King's Colonies, and that the Inhabitants of all the Plantations be obliged to buy and sell by the same Weights and Measures; in which several Abuses have been complained of in some Places.

Some Acts of Parliament about Trade not well calculated

And here I must beg leave (with all Submission and Deference imaginable to that great and Illustrious Council of the Nation) to say, that some of the present Acts of Parliament relating to the Plantation Trade, seem to be faulty in the Contrivance of them, for they are mostly calculated for all the Plantations in general, whereas the different Circumstances of the Several

Places make many particular Provisions necessary for some Colonies, which are not so in others: This I presume to mention not as an Instance of Neglect or Mismanagement, but as an Argument, that it is necessary the Court of *England* should be better acquainted with the true State of the Plantations, than hitherto they have been.

Standard of Coin

2. That one certain Standard for all sorts of Coin be setled in all the Plantations on the Continent, which Standard I humbly conceive should be as near the Intrinsick Value of *Sterl.* as may be.

But here perhaps it will be objected, that bringing the Standard of Money to the Intrinsick Value, will be very injurious to Proprieties, who have always set a higher Value upon their Money: And that,

These Plantations are in great Want of Money, and the readiest way to make it plenty among them, is to enhance the Value. To the first of these Objections I answer: That tho' indeed we ought as near as may be, to accommodate all Laws, and other publick Transactions, to the Interest of every Individual Party concerned; yet when some must suffer, it is reasonable to steer that Course which seems most equitable, and hath the greatest Tendency towards the Welfare of the Whole. And if it appears to be the Interest of *England* and the Plantations, (taken generally together,) as well hereafter as at present to ascertain the Standard of Coin as near as may be to the Intrinsick *Sterl.* Value, then I think this Objection will be sufficiently answered.

2. To the second Objection I answer, that it is probable, enhancing the Value of Coin may bring in Money for the present; but what will be the Consequences of that? Will it not confound the Method of our Trade? Will it not destroy our Exchange? and how many, and how great Evils will follow upon that, no one can I think pretend to foresee. 'Tis possible many Arguments may be drawn from the present Necessity, and it may be urged, that extraordinary Diseases must have the like Cures: But I cannot perceive the Weight of such an Allegation, nor can I apprehend the Advantages that may be proposed; We here are but a handful of People, and have no other Trade, but plain Barter between *England* and us, and amongst our Neighbouring Plantations, and certainly the best way for us, must be to keep the Standard of our Coin, which is the Measure of Trade and Traffick, as near as may be, to equal the Real Value set upon it by the Prudence of our Common Mother, lest by making Alterations in it,

we give Opportunity to some sharp *English* Merchants to put such Tricks upon us, as we cannot foresee; they have great Advantages of us, if their Inclinations tend that way; they are skilful in Trade and Exchange, which we cannot pretend to; they have much the larger Purses, and can outdo us at any thing, whenever they please; and besides all this, they have daily Opportunities of looking abroad in the World, and may have many Prospects of Advantage, which we that are shut up in *America* know nothing of.

Reasons for setling the Standard of Coin

For the further Answer to both these Objections, I beg leave to offer the following Particulars to Consideration.

1. That it is not necessary for the Plantations to have more Money, than just so much as is sufficient to manage their Trade; and that, they will have in a few Years, when Trade and the Coin is setled upon an Equal Foot.

2. That it is not expedient for *England* to give the Plantations Opportunities of laying up great Banks of Treasure among themselves.

3. That if enhancing the Value of Coin, should bring great quantities of it into these Northern Plantations, more than the carrying on of Trade requires, it would be just so much Loss to *England;* for none can come hither, but that which otherwise would have gone thither.

4. That the Difference of Coin would cause great Difficulties in making up Accounts of publick Revenues, and give great Opportunities of defrauding the King of the Exchange.

5. It would be very discouraging to all Officers in the Colonies, who have certain yearly Salaries established, especially Governours and Lieutenant-Governours, for they could not possibly remit any Money to *England,* for their necessary Occasions, without great loss by the Exchange.

'Tis true, these two last mentioned Inconveniencies may be remedied, but not without more than ordinary Trouble.

Pyrates to be suppressed

3. In the next place, I humbly propose, that all possible means be used to suppress Pyrates and Sea-Rovers in these Parts of the World.

And perhaps no way will be more effectual to that End, than a Proclamation of general Pardon for all that will submit in so many Months, and to keep three or four of the new fifth Rate Frigates along this Coast, and let a good

Reward be established by Law in the Plantations, for every one that shall apprehend a Pyrate, and if one would discover and convict the other, let him have his Pardon, and the Reward also; and if besides all this, they be terrified in the *East-Indies* with about twelve or fourteen good Ships of War, doubtless most, if not all of them, will be glad to come in and accept of their Pardons.

The Customs on Tobacco to be paid as formerly

4. If it might be done without the Imputation of too much Presumption, I would humbly propose, That for the Incouragement of the Tobacco-Planters, (the most beneficial Slaves that pay Obedience to the Crown of *England,*) his Majesty and the Parliament would be pleased to enact, That for the future, the great Duties upon Tobacco, might be paid in the same manner as was usual before the late Act, by which his Majesties Revenues would not be lessened, and yet the Planters greatly eased.

Remedy for the Grievance of want of People

4. In part to remedy the Grievances mentioned under the fourth Head, Of want of People in these Plantations.

Strangers to be encouraged

It is humbly proposed, 1. That all necessary Encouragement be given to Strangers to come hither, and to this End perhaps it may be necessary to revise the late Act of Parliament prohibiting Strangers to buy Land, &c. in the Plantations, and upon this Subject many Particulars are worthy Consideration, which cannot well be incerted here.

But tho' I would have Strangers encouraged to come amongst us, yet I would not have them seated in particular Towns or Parts of Provinces by themselves; but they should be dispersed amongst the other People, that by Marriages and other Obligations of Interest, they may be bound to study the Welfare of the Place of their Habitation.

Smal Offenders to be sent to the Plantations

2. That all Persons convicted of small Offences in *England,* be sent to these Plantations: By small Offences I mean Petty Larcenies, and all other such Offences as are generally punished with Whipping or the Pillory, (except

for Forgery;) and also such dissolute idle Persons as generally are punish'd with the House of Correction; but they should be sent hither upon the first Conviction, before they grow hardened in their Wickedness.

Objections against this

To this it may be objected, 1. That these People of evil Lives and Conversations, will be apt to stir up the Slaves and Servants, who being very numerous, may make a dangerous Rebellion against the Government.

2. That such People will very much destroy Morality in the Plantations.

3. That the idle Vagabonds may be employed in Workhouses at home, to better Advantage than they can be sent abroad.

Answer to these Objections

To all which I answer, 1. That the Servants and Slaves are not so numerous on the Continent: In the Islands it is true, there may be danger; but in these parts it is not very difficult to contrive such Laws against Servants and Slaves, wandring from their Masters Plantations without Leave, as will effectually preserve the Government against any Insurrections, that such People will be able to make, especially if those Laws be well executed.

2. That in these Parts they will not have Opportunity to pilfer and steal as they have in *England;* there it is easy to turn every thing immediately into Money, here they cannot do so, but it must be detected; neither can they find Things to steal here, so easily as they may there; and it is to be remembred, that there many People are forced oftentimes to steal that they may not starve; for they cannot get an Employment to live by: Here the Case is quite otherwise, for every one that will, may always live by his Labour, and need never sit idle.

And for the prevention of all other kind of Immorality, as Fornication, Drunkenness, &c. the Laws in those Cases provided, may be much more easily put in execution here, than in *England;* and that it is possible to reform the most vitious Persons, by good Laws well executed, I presume, no one will doubt that considers the History of the old *Romans,* who from the vilest and most wicked People living, by good laws became the most Virtuous that ever were.

But let us reckon at the worst, suppose these People should continue their Wicked Inclinations, it is plain, they cannot put their evil Desires in Practice, so that at the most, they can be but intentionally ill, and they may have many good Children, that may be of great Service; whereas if they were let alone in *England*, after scandalous and vitious Lives, they must almost of necessity come to shameful Deaths.

3. It is most certain, that *England* hath never yet employed the idle Vagabonds at home in Work-houses, to any purpose, till very lately, and that but in some few Places; nor perhaps is it possible, they ever can do it throughout the whole Kingdom; for there is a vast difference in the Circumstances relating to this particular Affair between *England* and *Holland*, which is so often proposed for a Pattern to be imitated.

The *Dutch* have but a small Space of Territory, and consequently but few poor; and being a place of extraordinary Trade, have many Manufactures set up amongst them, and these things employ their Poor; but *England* is a large Tract of Countrey, many Poor in it, and not near so many Manufactures in proportion as in *Holland*, and consequently not so much Work for the Poor; from whence it will follow, that the Poor cannot all be set to work, so as to maintain the Charge of themselves and their Work-houses; and if the Employers must be Losers, those Work-houses will never be built, neither will all the Poor in *England* ever be employ'd.

Since then it seems reasonable to believe, that those People cannot be employed at home, why should they not be sent to the Plantations, where they will certainly be beneficial, and *England* eased of the Burthen of maintaining so many useless People.

For the better and more certain and expeditious transporting these People hither, some small public Stock may be setled to begin it, and afterwards it would bear its own Charge, for they might be sold here as Servants for more Money than their Transportation would cost.

Remedy of Grievances that one Plantation is to another

5. To redress the Grievances that one Plantation may suffer by another, some Things have been already proposed under the Head of Trade; as particularly, the Setling an equal Liberty of Trade, and the same Standard of Coin throughout all the *English* Plantations on the Continent; the Reasonableness of which, I suppose, is already so clearly evinced, that I think it needless to say any thing more to it here.

For a further Redress to these Grievances, it is humbly proposed, That by some General Law, to be binding to all the Colonies on the Continent, a certain Method be established, 1. To decide all Controversies between

Colony and Colony. 2. To bring Persons to condign Punishment, who commit Offences against the Laws of one Colony, and then fly into another, or who living in one Colony, go into another, and commit Offences, and then return to their own Habitation. 3. To compel Fugitive Debtors to pay their just Debts, and run-away Servants and Slaves, to be returned to their Masters living in other Colonies. 4. To adjust all Disputes concerning Trade or Commerce in the several Colonies, and all other Matters whatsoever relating to the general Benefit of them all.

General Assembly of all the Provinces proposed by the Author of the Essay on Ways and Means

And here I must beg leave to take notice of a Scheme, for the General good Government of these Northern Plantations, set down in the aforementioned Discourses of the Publick Revenues, &c. Part 2*d.* Page 259. which Scheme with some little Alteration (the Government of the Colonies being rightly constituted) will perhaps prove the most effectual Remedy for all Grievances of this Nature, that can be proposed; but under the present Management, or whilst so many Colonies are governed by Proprietors, perhaps nothing can be proposed more prejudicial to the Interest of *England.*

The first Contriver of that Scheme was a Person not well acquainted with the State of every particular Colony here, and therefore no wonder if he hath committed an Error, in proposing an equal number of Deputies for the several Provinces, when they are so vastly different, for numbers of People, extent of Territory, and of the Value of them in their Trade, especially that to *Europe.*

Therefore with submission I conceive, that those Deputies would be more equally proportion'd in manner following, *viz. Virginia* four, *Mary-Land* three, *New-York* two, *Boston* three, *Connecticut* two, *Rhode Island* two, *Pensylvania* one, the two *Carolina's* one, each of the two *Jersey's* one.

And as angry as the Gentleman seems to be with *Virginia,* I think he cannot find fault with allowing one Deputy more for that, than for any of the rest, because it hath the most Inhabitants, is the eldest and most profitable of all the *English* Plantations in *America;* and if at such a Convention, we should pretend to take place of all our Neighbours, perhaps they may not give any good Reason to the contrary.

It is there proposed that these Deputies may always meet at *New-York,* and that the Chief Governour there for the time being, shall preside as High

Commissioner amongst them; this was well designed no doubt by the Proposer: But under favour I presume it would be much more convenient and useful too, if they met by turns, sometimes in one Province, and sometimes in another; and the chief Governour in the Province where they meet, being commissionated by his Majesty, may preside as Commissioner in manner aforementioned.

The Court of the *Amphictiones*, in Imitation of which this is proposed, did not always meet in one place, but sometimes at *Pylae*, and sometimes at *Delphi*, and without question there were a great many Reasons for their so doing; but in this Case I conceive there are more.

1. It is necessary that those Deputies should be well acquainted with the true State of the whole Continent, which at present they know little of, and no way more proper to instruct them in it, than by holding these Conventions, sometimes at one place, and sometimes at another; which in time would make the most considerable Persons of every Province, become personally acquainted; for the better sort of People would look upon it as a piece of Gentile Education, to let their Sons go in Company of the Deputies of the Province to these Conventions.

2. It seems a little unreasonable, that the Province of *New-York*, and consequently the Governour thereof for the time being, should be so much advanced in Dignity above the rest of the Colonies and their Governours; some of the other are more considerable, the Governments more valuable, are more immediately depending upon the King, and by far the more profitable to *England*.

3. It is unequal that *New York* should have such an Opportunity of drawing so much Money to it every Year from all the other Colonies.

To obviate these and many other Objections of this nature which may be made, it is humbly proposed, That the whole Continent be divided into five Circuits or Divisions, thus, 1. *Virginia*. 2. *Mary-Land*. 3. *Pensylvania*, and the two *Jersey's*. 4. *New-York*. 5. *Boston*, *Connecticut*, and *Rhode Island*; in each of which Division, let it be held by turns one after another, in a certain Order.

Remedy of the Grievances from the Governours

4. The next general Head is as much as may be to remedy the Grievances that may happen to the Plantations by their Governours.

Under the Head of Laws it is already proposed, That the last Resort of Justice in any Province, may not be to the chief Governour there; the Reason is plain, to wit, it is very dangerous to establish any Judicature, which cannot be called to Account for male-administrations; and that the Governours of the Plantations are so, is already made appear in the Grievances before complained of under this Head.

The Government of all the Plantations to be annexed to the Crown

For the better Regulation and Management of these Plantations, it is humbly proposed, That the Government of them all may be annexed to the Crown by Act of Parliament, for without that, it will be impossible to keep them upon an equal Foot; but some Tricks or other will be plaid by the Charter Governments, let their Pretentions be never so fair. Without question *New-England* Men pretend, that they would not entertain Pyrates upon any account in the World, and yet it is observable, that tho' they have long used those Parts, none of them have been taken till of late, since the Government of the Earl of *Bellamont,* who may properly be called the first Governour of the *English* Interest in that Province.

I am not ignorant that many Persons whose Interests are concerned, will look upon this as a very unjust Proposition, and object the great Injustice of such an Action, as very much tending to the Destruction of Property, and the like; to all which I shall make but little Answer, and that in this manner.

That in the beginning, *Virginia* was planted by a Company, who had a Charter for their so doing; and afterwards (the good of the whole so requiring) not only the Government, but the very Property of the Land was taken into the King's Hands, and so remains at this Day.

The Government of *Mary-Land,* is now in the King's Hands, and yet the Lord *Baltimore* enjoys his Property in the Land as he did heretofore, and not only so, but all other Revenues that were setled on him by the Assembly of that Province.

The Government of *New-England,* is now in the King's Hands; and if the Publick Welfare required it, why should not the Proprieties of *Pensylvania,* the *Jersey's* and the *Carolina's* be likewise governed in the same manner?

2. The Propriety of the Soil may remain to the Proprietor, as heretofore, and need not be prejudiced by the King's appointing Governours in those Parts: And if this be not satisfactory, but they still pretend to have the Governments intirely in their own Hands, I beg leave to admonish them

to consult with their Counsellors at Law, how far the King hath Power to grant the Supream Government of the Plantations, to any Person or Persons, and their Heirs, without the assent of the Parliament.

I shall say no more to this Point at present; tho it may very reasonably be urged, that in times of Danger, *England* must be at the Charge to defend them all, which cannot well be done without taking the Government.

That it is necessary for all the Colonies to be united under one Head, for their common Defence; and that it will be much more so, if the *French*, or any other Nation, possess themselves of the River *Messachippe*, and the Lakes to the West-ward.

That in case of a War with *Spain*, nothing could tend more to the Advantage of *England*, than having all these Colonies under the Crown, to give such Assistance as should be necessary towards any Design upon the *West-Indies*, which would never be done by the Proprieties, unless they saw some extraordinary private Advantage by it.

I say, all these Considerations may reasonably be urged, but Time permits me not to examine them at present.

Representations in England *of the State of the Plantations*

A true Representation in *England* of the State of Affairs in the Colonies, would very much conduce to the keeping of the Governours in good order, or at least from notorious Transgressions, for fear of being complained of at Home; therefore with Submission, I shall by and by propose such Methods, as seem most feasable to procure such Representations to be made.

Against Governours engrossing Offices, Bribery, &c.

It hath already been complained of, as a Grievance, that sometimes Governours do engross into their own Hands several Offices, and others they let out for such a part of the yearly Profits: And for the prevention of the like Practices, and of all sorts of Bribery, Extortion, and other Misdemeanours, for the future, perhaps no Method will prove more effectual than by laying severe Injunctions upon the King's Governours, that they do not presume to keep any Place vacant, more than such a space of Time as shall be thought requisite, and that they do not take any manner of Present or Gratuity for the bestowing of any Office, that they do not upon any Pretence whatsoever take any manner of Gift, Reward, or Perquisite; that they be not any ways concerned in Trade.

Encouragements to Governours to behave themselves well

And that none of the Governours may pretend a necessity of minding something besides their Offices, to get their Living by, their Salaries may be so much enlarged, as will make them sufficient for their Maintenance, and to spare.

For a farther Encouragement to them to behave themselves well in their Governments, it seems reasonable to contrive it in such manner for the Future, that such good Behavior may recommend them to farther Rewards at Home, (and not that these Governments be given as formerly, for Rewards of past Services, and so the Governours be obliged to make the best of it they can, because they expect nothing to come after.) To this end it may perhaps be found convenient, to provide that hereafter all Governours behaving themselves well in the Plantations, and having been there above three years, shall obtain the King's leave to resign, without any Mismanagements laid to their Charge, may have a yearly Pension allowed them, (after their return Home) of a fourth part of the value of the Established Salary in the Governments they left, which Pensions should be duly paid, till some other Preferments were bestowed on them, to the value thereof: And if after all these Encouragements, any Governour dare offend, let him fall without Mercy.

The King and Court of England *unacquainted with the State of the Plantations*

7. The last and greatest Grievance I mentioned, is, that the King and Court of *England* are very much unacquainted with the true State of Affairs in the *American* Plantations, for the Redress whereof it is humbly proposed.

Remedy for this Grievance

1. That every Colony have an Agent constantly residing in *England,* to give an account from time to time, as he shall be thereto required, of all the Affairs and Transactions of the Plantation he is authorized by; and lest this Agent be corrupted and wrought upon, to give wrong Informations, as a check upon him,

2. Let one Person be commissionated from *England*, to travel through all the Plantations, to make enquiry into, and give a true Representation of the State of their Affairs; and these two Persons being Checks one upon the other, would both of them be obliged to speak the Truth.

That this last Proposition may be the better understood; I beg leave to set it down somewhat more particularly.

1. Let one Person, thereunto commissionated by his Majesty, travel through all the Colonies on the Continent.

And the better to enable him to do Service, let him have Power to sit in the Councils of every Colony where he cames: Let him have free access to all Records, Council-Books, Publick Accounts, and all other Books and Papers relating to the Government, or any Office of Trust or Profit. Let him have Authority to inquire into, and examine the State of all the Colonies where he comes; and for his better Guidance and Direction herein, a Scheme of material and pertinent Queries may be drawn up and given him; as particularly to enquire 1. Concerning the Legislature in the Plantations, In whom it is invested, What Powers they have, What their Priviledges, Methods of Proceedings, And how often they are conven'd.

2. Concerning the Civil Government: What the Governours Power? What the Councils? How many of them there are? How they are made? What Offices they hold, and what Value those Offices are of? &c.

3. Concerning the public Offices of the Government; How many there are? Of what Value? In whose Gift? How executed? What Estates they have in them?

4. Concerning the *Militia;* What numbers of them? How armed? How commanded? In how long time they may be ready for service?

5. Concerning the *Indians;* How many Nations are tributary to the Crown of *England?* What their Number and Strength? Where scituate? What *Indian* Enemies most dangerous? What Trade with them may be most profitable? What the best Method of Defence against them?

6. Concerning Courts of Justice; How many there are? Where held? Who Judges? What their Jurisdiction? What Commissions they have? How Justice is administred? How long Causes are generally depending?

7. Concerning the Revenue; What particular Branches there are? How Collected? What the Charge of Collection? Who keeps the Public Money in Bank? How much every particular Branch brings in, and to what Uses applied? What Money in Bank? Or, what Debts, and how contracted?

8. Concerning Religion; What Religion most numerous? What established by Law? What number of the Church of *England?* What Provision made for the Clergy? What Ecclesiastick Authority?

9. Concerning Works of Piety and Charity; What Foundations for Learning? What Maintenance for Poor? By whom founded? By what Authority? How endowed? How the Primitive Institutions are observed?

10. Concerning Trade; What the Product of the Countrey for Exportation? Whither carried? What usually imported, and from whence? What Ports? What Towns? What their Privileges? How governed? What Manufactures? Whither carried? What number of Ships and Vessels? What Trade they are imployed in? How the Trade is managed? Whether by Money or Barter?

11. Concerning Money; How plenty Money is? What Coin most current? At what Value? What the Exchange of remitting Money to *England?*

12. Concerning Grievances; What the greatest Grievances? What the Cause of them? How they may be redressed?

I might add many more Queries, as concerning the number of People, the Value of Lands, the Scituation of Places, the Conveniencies of Offence or Defence, the King's Rents, the Proprietors Interest, the Wealth of the Inhabitants, &c. But I purposely omit them for Brevity sake, the Particulars before mentioned, being sufficient to make the Method clearly apprehended.

These Queries (together with such other as shall be thought necessary,) being proposed in the Plantations to the Governours, Councils, General Assemblies, Courts of Judicature, Lawyers, Clerks, Clergymen, Magistrates, Merchants, &c. their Answers will give a great Light into the true State of Affairs in these Parts; and also such a Persons own Observations might be of great Use, if carefully made.

And that no one may be fearful to answer the Truth to the aforementioned Queries, let both Queries and Answers be kept secret, till they are laid before the Commissioners of Trade in *England,* and if they find any thing material, let them send Orders for a more particular Inquiry, and let Care be taken, that no Man suffer for speaking the Truth in these Cases.

The main Thing in this Proposition to be consider'd, is, whether the Advantage of it will be greater than the Charge, for such Inquiries cannot be made without some Charge, tho' that need not be much; if a very great Man be employed in such a Service, then indeed the Cost will be great also; but if one that is not above the Business, who will be active and industrious, be employed, a Salary of five hundred Pounds a Year (with an Allowance of ten Shillings a Day, whilst he is travelling from Place to Place) will be sufficient; if he behave himself well, he will be thereby recommended to further Favour at his Return home; if otherwise, that is more than he deserves.

And perhaps it may not be convenient to let any one enjoy this Office above five years, and so as one returns, another may be sent.

Now if this Commissioner be obliged to give the best Account he can, of the State of those Colonies through which he travels, if the several Governours be directed to represent the State of their respective Provinces, if the Convention of the whole Continent aforementioned, remonstrate the Affairs of them all, and if the Agents of every Colony residing in *England*, be required from time to time, to give a true and impartial Relation of the Constitution and Transactions of their respective Colonies; I say, if all these Persons be obliged to give their several Representations of the State of these Colonies, it is reasonable to believe, they will be necessitated both to enquire after, and to represent the Truth, lest they contradict one another.

By these means it is probable, the King and Court of *England* may be made thoroughly sensible of the true State of Affairs in this remote Part of the World, which it is presum'd, will be the first and greatest Step towards remedying any former Mismanagements.

FINIS

· 9 ·

[William Penn], The Allegations Against Proprietary Government Considered (1701)

ꟹ

THE COLLAPSE of the Dominion of New England in the late seventeenth century did not end the attack on chartered governments in America. Two long wars against the French led the new Board of Trade to call for the annulment of the charters of all the proprietary and corporate colonies in the early 1700s on the grounds that they were not contributing money and men to imperial defense and were violating the Navigation Laws by trading illegally and harboring pirates.

The main target of the board was Pennsylvania, a Quaker colony founded by William Penn in the early 1680s, whose pacifist leaders were reluctant to contribute to imperial wars, and whose major city, Philadelphia, was, royal officials contended, a haven for smugglers. The board succeeded in removing the colony's charter in 1692 only to have it reinstated in 1694 due to lobbying by Penn in England. However, the return of the charter did not stop the colony's enemies from continuing to send damning reports to London in which they cataloged its resistance to imperial edicts. Concerned that he would lose his charter again, Penn returned to the colony in 1699. He initially sought greater compliance with royal authority, but then took the side of Quaker elites who had long opposed his authority. In late 1701, Penn again crossed the Atlantic to assert his rights after news reached him that Parliament was about to pass a Bill revoking the charters of all of the corporate and proprietary colonies.

On Penn's instructions, his allies in London published *The Case of William Penn* in 1701. Penn also issued a four-page leaflet, *The Allegations Against Proprietary Government Considered,* in which he denied that the proprietary colonies were independent of Crown, even conceding that they were bound by imperial trade regulations as long as these regulations did not "Fundamentally Invade their Charters." Penn also denied that these colonies harbored pirates and called for a royal inquiry into the matter. But even if these charges were true, Penn maintained that dissolving the charters would be too harsh a punishment for any offence less than "Absolute Dis-Allegiance to the Crown." Penn also contended that the colonial charters were "of a higher Nature than those of our Corporations at home," for they were granted as "a Condition or Encouragement to Plant and Cultivate a Remote Wilderness." And without such a guarantee for their rights the colonists would not have undertaken such a hazardous enterprise. To the claim that the charters would be annulled by Parliament and not the Crown, Penn reminded his readers that parliaments in the past have only taken away property "as wise Physitians do Blood, for the Preservation and Security of the Patient." Penn also objected to the argument that he would be able to keep his property rights in the colony, only surrendering the powers of government, by claiming that "any Man, who at an extraordinary Expence has made a country" should not be stripped of his "Civil or Religious Priviledges." In any case, Penn argued that the king did not grant the original colonists the land in America. Rather, all he gave them was "a Right of Pre-emption," after which they had to purchase the "Savage Soil" from the Native Americans, and add all the value to it by their own labor. Penn concluded his brief for the American charters by pointing out that royal governors were often venal, that proprietors save the king the expense of governing the colonies directly, and that the chartered colonies have expanded the trade and thus the wealth and power of England.

Penn's tireless lobbying paid off as the Board of Trade failed to get Parliament to introduce legislation abrogating all the American charters in either 1701 or 1702, though not before Penn, hedging his bets, had also offered to sell his proprietary rights. (C.B.Y.)

Allegations Against Proprietary Governments Considered, and Their Merit and Benefit to the Crown Briefly Observed.

Since some endeavour to Recommend themselves to the Government, by being more *Officious* than Useful, in their Accounts of Proprietary Governments abroad: It will not, I hope, be made a Fault to set that Matter in a better Light.

The first Allegation is, *That they have absolute Powers of Government, and* [*are*] *consequently Independent of the Crown.*

Answer. This is by no means true; since all Proprietary Governments pay a *Fee Farm* to the Crown, and are *Concluded* by the War and Peace that the Crown makes, and are also Subject to the *Laws of Trade and Navigation,* and yield *Obedience* to such Regulations, from time to time, as do not *Fundamentally* Invade their Charters. But particularly some of them express a nearer Dependency upon the Crown, since the King has therein Reserved to himself a Negative to their Laws, and *Final Appeals* in Judgment from their Superiour Courts: So that in Effect, the *Legislation* and *Jurisdiction* of such Colonies *Ultimately* Center in the Crown. And we must take leave to say, That some of them have Performed the Part of a King's Governour, with the best Skill and Zeal they could, at their own Cost, and not upon his Salaries.

It is farther humbly offered to Consideration, That no Government can be call'd *Independent of the Crown,* where the Officers of its *Revenue* and *Admiralty* may Exercise the *same* Authority and Jurisdiction that they do in the Kingdom of *England.*

The Second Objection against Proprietary Governments is, *The Entertainment of Pirates, and the Connivance at forbidden Trade.*

To which we humbly Answer, That we know of no such Encouragement that has been given to one or other. On the contrary, some of us have not only made Laws as Nicely as we have been able to prevent such Evil Practices; but have Endeavoured, all that in us lay, to Enforce their Execution. And we should think our selves very Happy, as well as that it seems but Just, that this mighty Cry against Proprietary Governments, on those Accounts, might have a *Royal Commission of Enquiry* (which has several Presidents) to Inspect, *upon the Spot*, their Conduct, and the Merit of those Clamours. The Plantations Claim it, and think they Deserve it; since they were not made by the Crown, but by Themselves, and are of that Benefit to it. However, since the King has his own Officers there, it must needs lessen the Force of those Imputations upon those Governments.

We will not say that some private Persons, for their *own Advantage*, may not have been sometimes *Faulty;* but that ought no more to be Charged upon the Governments, than a Merchant or Brewer, by their *Vicious* Trading, should be a Reason sufficient to *Change* the Commissions of the Customs or Excise.

And that which yet renders the Design less Reasonable against the Proprietary Governments, is this, that the King's are notoriously more Culpable in the very *same* Things the others are accused of; and how making them King's Governments will *Cure* them of that Malady, is submitted to the Judicious.

But if what is alledged were as True as it is Fabulous, and a Contrivance of none of the best People to serve an Ill Turn upon those deserving Colonies; we hope *English-Men*, that went so *far* to be Easie and Free, and are *so manifestly Beneficial to the Trade and Crown of England*, shall never fall below the Liberties of the Great Charter thereof, which says, *That no Man shall be Fined above the Nature of his Offence;* and whatever be his Miscarriage, there is a *Salvo contenimento Suo*[1] to be observed by the Judge. And we must beg their Pardon, who do not seem to favour Proprietary Governments, if we say we cannot tell how to think that Dissolving those Charters which were the *Condition*, as well as *Encouragement* and *Authority* upon which those Chargeable and Hazardous Adventures have been made, can bear *any Proportion* with the Offence objected; or that they are Dissolvable on any other Account than that of an *Absolute Dis-Allegiance* to the Crown.

For we take this sort of Charter to be of a higher Nature than those of our Corporations at home; since these were granted to a People Seated upon Improvements already made, and were rather of the Nature of a Recompence, than a Condition or Encouragement to Plant and Cultivate

1. ["With his own means of support intact."]

a *Remote Wilderness;* and Enlarge, by the Addition of fresh Colonies, the English Trade and Empire abroad.

It is that without which the Adventurers would never have undertaken a Voyage so many Thousand Miles from their own Country (being neither *Criminals* nor *Necessitous*) nor have run so many Risks, expended so much Money, exposed themselves to such Hardships, and have undergone the extream Labour, to which their Enterprize subjected them. And if it was a Fault in the two last Reigns to *Quo Warranto*[2] and Dissolve so many Charters, instead of Punishing the Faults complain'd of, (if real) by Fines *proper* and *proportionable* to the Nature of the Offence; can this sort of Treatment of the *American* Charters admit of a Justification? If we forget not, this very Case was an *aggravating Argument* towards our late Revolution, and therefore a *Fundamental Article* in our *New* Contract.

But it is alledged, *That it is fit to be done for Reason of State:* An odd Argument in *England.* Pray is it not Incomprehensible how *Reason of State* should be pleaded in opposition to *Property,* in plain English, especially at this time of Day?

But perhaps it may be urged, by such as seek the Dissolution of these Charters, *That they intend to proceed in a* Parliamentary way, *against which there can be no Exception.*

We humbly Answer, That *Parliaments* may be *surprized,* and have been more than once *mis-led;* tho' we do not think so of this. But if we look back, and nicely Survey the Course of Parliaments, we shall generally find that they have taken away *Property* only as wise Physitians do Blood, for the *Preservation* and *Security* of the Patient. Nor do they ever strike their Launce into a *vital* part, as the Heart, Liver, or Lungs, but some more *remote* and external Member, where there is little Pain, and no hazard to the Party.

If it should be said, *Nothing is intended against the Property of Proprietaries, or their Freeholders; that part of their Respective Charter shall stand: It is the Government granted in them that we would Re-annex to the Crown.*

We pray that our Answer may not be mistaken or offensive; our only aim by it, being an humble Vindication of our hard Case, which we apprehend is not well understood. For we take the *Powers* of our Patents to be *as much* our Property from the Crown as the *Soil,* if not more; since 'twere vain to

2. [Literally, "By what right," i.e., a writ ordering a person to show "by what right" he exercises powers of office.—Tr.]

think of undertaking to Plant a Country, *without Power to Govern it;* and so the very Grants themselves express: And it must seem unaccountable afterwards to be deprived of it, when Government was the very Condition and Requisit of the Adventure.

But that any Man, who at an extraordinary Expence has made a Country, should have another Person set over him, under the King, to give Rule to him in his own House, for so it is, *Proprietarily* speaking, is something so odd and severe, that we would humbly hope such an Unnatural President in Property shall never be made upon us.

We pray that it may be Considered, that the Lands granted us in *America,* were not a *Vacuum Domicilium* (Uninhabited of Mankind) and that the Crown of *England* did neither *Conquer* nor *Purchase* it for us of the Natives; so that the Grant, as to the Soil, must rather be of a Right of *Pre-emption,* than the Thing it self; with Powers, when we have Bought it, to Govern them that Seat it. But suppose the Crown had Bought, or Conquered it, Pray let us Value the Land there by an *American,* and not an *European Scale* (for an *Inch* of This is more than an *Ell* of That) and we shall find the *vast Difference* there is in Property.

Indeed an Acre there, is as *big* as an Acre here; but That is *Ruff, Sower* and *Incumbred* with unprofitable Woods, and This Clear and Cultivated: That Acre worth, to be Sold, but One Shilling, when This perhaps may fetch Twenty Pounds: That then which will render the Values Parallel, must be *Time* and the Extraordinary *Labour* and *Expence* of the Undertakers. And 'tis certain, that even *now* it self the *Labour* and *Charge* of the Present Planter, bears the Proportion of *Forty Nine* Parts in Fifty, if not *Ninety Nine* in an Hundred, to the Intrinsick Value of the Savage, and Incumbred Soil. And to say true, those Parts were but *bare Creation* to the First Planters, and their Labour like the *Beginning of the World:* So that making the best of it, the Property Granted was not of Lands of Improved Value or Rentable; nor of Lands Free, without Purchasing of the Natives, and being made such by our Improvements: And the Keeping of those Lands, so dearly Cultivated, is all the Share, it seems, that these Gentlemen would do us the Favour to leave us, that are so Solicitous to recommend themselves to the Government at Home, by endeavouring to get ours Abroad.

On the contrary, we take leave to say That the Crown granted us so little besides the Government, that even with it (our extream Labour and Charge considered) together with a Thousand Difficulties that attended us thither, and there, during the first Years of our Settlement (to say nothing of other Discouragements we labour'd under) we cannot think a *full* Enjoyment of our Charters an *Immoderate* Consideration: Tho' we always must the Loss of it, if we should be so Unhappy as to Feel it.

I take the Comparison between the Savage Soil, and the Powers of Government, to be that between the Ring and the Diamond; the Ring is worth forty Shillings, but the Diamond a Thousand Pounds: And we cannot see how a Man may be said to have his Ring, and lose the Stone that is so much the more valuable Part of it.

But perhaps this Argument may be turned against us, *That if the Government be so Valuable, it is the King's Interest* (or some Body's else at least) *to look after it.* No, we mean not *Money,* but *Freedom.* The Liberties we *went thither for,* and were by our Grants Enabled to give our selves in our Respective Constitutions, as a Security against all Encroachments upon our Civil or Religious Priviledges, and which we have little Reason to hope may be continued if the Charters are once Dissolved, and the Administration put into other Hands than theirs that made the Countries: Especially if we consider the Condition some People are *already under* in other Colonies, and the vehement Endeavours of a sort of Men that cannot think themselves Happy or Easie, while those of *differing Sentiments* are not an *intire Property* to them.

But it will be further alledged *That the King's Revenue,* and the *Trade of the Kingdom* will be much better Secured by Governours of the King's Nomination than by *Proprietary Ones.*

Answ. Were this true, 'twould weigh more with us to a Surrender than any Thing that has been urged upon us: But when the contrary is more reasonable we must beg their Pardon if we cannot suffer it to pass upon us.

For 'tis then that the King's Governours must excel, when their Interest and Obligations are greater to Improve the Colonies than *Theirs* whose Propriety they are; and when such Temporary Governours have a better Caution, or Security to Give to the Crown for their Integrity and Conduct, than the Value of the *Provinces* of Proprietary Governours. And lastly, when it is more the King's Interest to Improve and Govern Colonies at his own Cost, than at the Charge of the Respective Proprietaries and their Sub-Undertakers.

But it is not that time of Day with those Governments, whatever some may please to insinuate, to *decline* their Obedience to the King's Authority for the *Good* of their *Mother Country. Let England Live,* or they can never Subsist; but let not them be under any Discouragements, that have so considerably Contributed to her *Wealth* and *Greatness;* since the King may as well Govern them by their *Proper Governours and Officers,* as he doth his other Colonies by those of his own Nomination: That so those who have had the Merit to lead Colonies into that *Remote* Part of the World, and thereby to Augment the English Dominions, may be allowed to Reap the Fruit of their *own Labours,* whereby the *Royal Faith* Plighted in their *Grants* to them, may be preserved, and the Adventurers under them Encouraged to *Enlarge* their Improvements; where it is no News to say, That every Man's Labour is worth to *England Thrice* the Value he could be to her at Home, as well by Consumption of her Growth, as the Returns of his Labour: To say nothing of the great Increase of Navigation, so much the *Strength* and *Benefit* of the English Nation.

For Conclusion, They only Wish to be *better* understood, and to be *Cherished,* as well as Chid or Commanded, and by such as are able to *Mend,* as well as find Faults: Who can *Instruct* their Genius, and *Direct* their Industry, by being *Expert* in Trade, and *Conversant* in Government: But especially that are *Masters* of *American* Affairs; The *Situation, Growth, Commerce,* the *Ballance* of Trade, the *Genius* of the People, with a proper Method both to Amend and Improve them: And *America* cannot fail in time to make *England* the Glory and Mistriss of *Europe.*

· 10 ·

Reflections on the Printed Case of William Penn, Esq., in a Letter from Some Gentlemen of Pensilvania (1702)

As William Penn lobbied to keep his charter in the spring of 1702, a pamphlet appeared in London rebutting the arguments that Penn's friend had made on his behalf in *The Case of William Penn*. The anonymous authors represented the Lower Counties of Pennsylvania, which had joined the colony in an Act of Union in 1682 following the grant of their land to Penn by the Duke of York. Despite consenting to this legislative union, these counties, which were largely non-Quaker, resented the dominance of the Quaker elites in the colonial assembly. The lower counties supported Governor Fletcher of New York in the early 1690s when he was briefly the royal governor of Pennsylvania after the colony's charter was taken away. By 1699, when Penn returned to the colony, the lower counties were openly in favor of royal government, even engaging Robert Quary, Penn's nemesis, to make their case in London. Under pressure from London and his fellow Quakers in Pennsylvania, Penn reluctantly granted the lower counties legislative independence in 1701 just before he returned to London to try to stop Parliament from annulling his charter.

The arguments put forward in the *Reflections on the Printed Case of William Penn* intended to undermine Penn's efforts to defend his charter in London. Its anonymous authors pointed out that Pennsylvania was not, as Penn insisted, an uninhabited wilderness when he arrived, for the Swedes and the Dutch had been there long before he founded his colony. Nor was Penn's claim to have bought the land directly from the Native Americans tenable, for this would have led to the creation of "a vast number of Principalities and Independent Governments" not subject to English law or the sovereignty of the Crown. Contrary to Penn's claim that proprietary governments benefit the empire, the gentlemen from the lower counties contended that a royal government which respects the rights of all subjects will increase the number and industry of the inhabitants. After all, it is individual colonists who create wealth and not the proprietor. Maryland, they pointed out, has prospered since it became a royal colony, while under Penn's rule non-Quakers are forced to "groan under the Oppression of Quaker governments" As for Penn's claim that royal governors are rapacious, the authors pointed out that Penn has levied excessive quit rents and taxes on the colonists, has sheltered pirates, and has refused to crack down on illegal trade. They concluded the pamphlet by insisting that the lower counties will be better off under royal government as they will enjoy all the rights of English subjects, including protection from the king's enemies in time of war; and that the Anglicans among them will no longer be mistreated by Quakers. Appended to the pamphlet is a copy of an address that the members of the assembly from the lower counties sent to Penn in the fall of 1701 complaining of the expense of attending the colonial assembly, the injustice of some recent bills, and the danger they would face from the French in the West Indies should war resume.

The arguments of the lower counties in favor of royal government did not prevail in London. Penn was able to keep his charter, and for the rest of the colonial period these counties remained under his rule, though governed by their own assembly. (C.B.Y.)

REFLECTIONS

ON THE

Printed Case

OF

William Penn, Esq;

IN A

Letter from some Gentlemen of *Pensilvania,*

to their Friend in *London.*

Together with

A True Copy of the Address

OF THE

Members of the Assembly

of the three Lower Counties,

to Mr. *Penn,* the 10th of *October* 1701.

LONDON, Printed: And Sold by the Booksellers.

1702. *Price* 3 d.

Reflections on the Printed Case of William Penn, Esq; In a Letter from some Gentlemen of Pensilvania, to their Friend in London.

SIR,

We shall not detain you by any preambular Discourse, but immediately address to the Business: And,

I.

Observe, That Mr. *Penn* endeavours to Impose upon the World, by telling them, That the Province Granted to him by the King's Letters Patents, was an unknown and uninhabited Wilderness: whereas it was settled for more than Forty Years before his Grant; first, by the *Swedes,* under the Government of Queen *Christiana,* Daughter to *Gustavus Adolphus;* afterwards under the Government of the *Dutch,* and by them deliver'd, together with the Province of *New-York,* to the Crown of *England,* in Exchange for *Suranam.* The Truth of which doth fully appear by Mr. *Penn*'s Grant, wherein there is care taken to preserve the Rights of all the first Settlers; which we have too much cause to fear he hath most unjustly violated in very many Instances.

II.

'Tis true, we cannot much blame his Industry in magnifying his Father's Merits, which we are not willing to dispute with him; and provided the *Hispaniola* Expedition be not reckon'd as one of them, we will allow them considerable: yet 'tis presumed the Crown hath made sufficient Recompence, besides the vast Advantage of this Charter, the Particulars of which shall in this Paper be made appear, notwithstanding which Mr. *Penn* is pleas'd, after a most disingenuous and ungrateful manner, to lessen and undervalue the King's great and generous Bounty, by insinuating to the World, that he could have bought that vast Tract of Land from the Natives for a very inconsiderable matter. Certainly Mr. *Penn* must needs know better than to think that private Subjects, without the King's Letters Patents, may purchase Provinces from the Natives, and by vertue of that Title erect Governments: if so, we should quickly have in *America* a vast number of Principalities and Independant Governments; and perhaps if the Arbitrary and Illegal Actions of his Government were set in a true Light, it would look as if he thought himself Absolute and Independant from the Crown of *England;* and that the Grant of *Pensilvania* was not restricted to the Laws of his Native *England.*

III.

Upon a strict View of the King's Patent to Mr. *Penn,* we find that his Majesty has no way distinguish'd his Subjects by their Religious Perswasions; neither did Mr. *Penn,* by his Prints for the Encouragement of his Colony, confine himself to his own Friends the *Quakers,* but generally invited all Perswasions (as well Foreigners as Subjects) who have been no less industrious than the *Quakers* in the Improvements of the Country and Trade. Nor can we find in the Grant any Clause that countenances any Form or Mode of Government repugnant to the Laws of *England;* and therefore to expect otherwise, is to strain the Patent beyond the true Design and Intent of it. All which duely consider'd, we can see no reason why all Government and Power must Be engrossed and confined to the *Quakers,* and all other his Majesty's good Subjects excluded and denied the Benefit of the King's Laws and the Rights of Subjects. Which is most humbly submitted to the Consideration and Wisdom of the Right Honourable the Lords Commissioners for *Trade* and *Plantations.*

IV.

We cannot but admire that so ingenious a Man as Mr. *Penn* is, should not distinguish betwixt the Rights of Mannors and Lordships, and the Power pretended to by him; to wit, Levying Men and Money, Calling Assemblies, Power of Life and Death, and all the other *Regalia*'s of Government: which we humbly conceive are inseparable from the Crown, and widely distinguishable from the other.

V.

We are not of Mr. *Penn*'s Opinion, that it is the Interest of the Crown to countenance and keep up Proprietary Governments, but the quite contrary. His Argument run thus: 1. Owners of Soil will improve it, and thereby augment the King's Revenue: Whereas temporary Governours squeeze Provinces, and make the most they can of them during their time. In Answer to the first part we say; that it is not the Proprietors that do improve the Soil, but the Inhabitants, and nothing would more increase their Number and Industry, then to live under a Government where they might have Protection, and enjoy securely the Rights and Liberties of *English* Subjects; all which, under Mr. *Penn*'s Government, they are denied, and indeed those that improve the King's Revenue in that Province, by planting Tobacco, are very few of them *Quakers*, but such as at present are forced to groan under the oppression of the *Quaker* Governments. And as to the latter part of his Argument, we must believe it was only design'd as a general Reflection on all the King's Governours to throw an Odium on them by insinuating their oppression, *&c.* and thereby to possess the King's Subjects with prejudice against them. But if it be consider'd what Sums have been rais'd since Mr. *Penn*'s late Arrival in his Government, it will be found that he hath squeez'd the Inhabitants sufficiently; exacting, under the Colour of Law, upwards of 2000 *l.* besides his Quit-Rents and other Taxes that amount to nigh 1000 *l. per* 3 Months; which is more than any of his Majesties Governours ever attempted. We could give Instances of several other Proprietory Governments that have oppress'd, squeez'd, and tyraniz'd over the King's Subject to the highest degree imaginable; but we shall confine our selves only to the Government of *Pensilvania.*

VI.

What Satisfaction Mr. *Penn* hath given to the House of Lords, in Relation to Piracy, is best known to their Lordships: but how shall we discriminate him from those that acted under him, since, by his own Argument, he is answerable for their Faults; and that they have notoriously sheltred Pirats, and encouraged illegal Trade, is so obvious, that we presume it will scarce be denied, the Particulars whereof would rather require a Volume, than be contracted in the compass of a Sheet or two. Mr. *Penn* is pleased to say, that the consideration of the Proprietors having most to Loose, is a sufficient caution to them against indirect Practices; but it is notoriously evident, that

that Consideration hath not been able to awe them from carrying on illegal Trade to *Holland, Scotland* and *Curasoe* as is evident by the many Complaints of the Kings Officers home to the Commissioners of the Customs and Councel of Trade, and Violating all Laws relating thereunto: which is demonstrable not only from Mr. *Penn's* Government, but likewise from all the other Propriety-Governments.

VII.

Mr. *Penn* has but little Reason to complain of any hardship in Relation to his Property, since it was never designed to be invaded, or taken from him; but on the Contrary, there is all the care imaginable taken to preserve and secure it, by the Bill that was brought into the Parliament: all that is designed Principally by that Act, was only to re-assume Regal Government, which widely differs from Property, as has been before observed.

VIII.

We cannot but observe, that Mr. *Penn* is pleased to lay a great stress on that Clause of the Act of the 7th and 8th of this Reign, which Impowers his Majesty to approve of the Proprietory Governours. We had good Reason to think, that both he, and his Governours, were altogether Strangers to that Act, by their affronting of it, and making Laws repugnant, and in opposition to it, which is matter of Fact ready to be produced: as also, by his, and Leiutenant Governour's neglecting, or rather refusing to quallify themselves according to the Directions of that Act, even to this very Day; and yet have executed all the Powers of Government to the very highest degree, in defiance and contempt of an Act of Parliament. So that now let the World judge, how far the End of that Act hath been answer'd, which is humbly submitted to the Honourable the high Court of Parliament.

IX.

Mr. *Penn* is pleas'd to say, that it hath cost him 20000 *l.* to settle his Plantation; and that he hath not as yet receiv'd 500 *l.* If he means, that it hath cost him a great deal of Mony in Building and Improvements, it is easily answered, that he receives the benefit and advantage of it. But he ought to have spoke plain *English,* that it hath cost him a vast Sum to defend the Extravagant and illegal Acts and Proceedings of his Government: and to what account that Charge ought to be brought let the World judge. But that he actually has received about 40000 *l.* is true; and that besides this vast Sum, that he and his Posterity is advanced and bettered by the King's Grant at least 40000 *l.* more, is matter of Fact, and thus demonstrable. *Viz.* The first 100 Purchasers paid him 10000 *l.* in *England,* and other Purchasers there since upwards of 5000 *l.* His 18 Years Quit-Rents, by a modest computation, amount to 10000 *l.* all which he hath either receiv'd or sufficiently Secured; besides which he hath reserved and secured 8 or 10 Manners of 10000 Acres each in the Heart of the several Counties, which are worth 2000 *l.* a Mannor one with another. The next thing to be consider'd is the Over-plus Land upon a Re-survey, which will amount to more than 5000 *l.* Then there is all his Liberty-Lands and Town-Lots, one of which he hath lately dispos'd of for 2400 *l.* Next is the Bank or Front of the City, on which there is a 100000 *l.* Improvement; the third part of the Yearly Rent whereof is, after the Expiration of the Lease, to be paid to him and his Heirs forever. The said Leases were for 40 Years, and almost 20 of that time is expired; but how unjustly he extorted that Front-Land from the first Purchasers, We leave them to tell their own doleful Story. We had almost forgot to mention all the Imposts, Taxes, Fines, Forfeitures, Esscheats, Licenses: and besides all this, there is the remaining parts of all his Province undispos'd off, which will amount to a vast Sum and yet, notwithstanding all these vast Profits and Advantages, which far exceeds what we first propos'd for him, to tell the World in Print that he has not received 500 *l.* is monstrously strange and unaccountable: We are altogether Strangers to his Father's Merits; but how far all this may compensate for it we leave the World to judge.

X.

And now, as a finishing stroke, Mr. *Penn* is pleased to assert, That the King's taking that Government into his own hands, will depopulate the Colony, discourage Men of large Enterprizing Minds, and sink the Propriety *Cent. per Cent.* The reverse of all which is certainly true; nor need we go far for a lively and pregnant Instance thereof. Let us but look into our next Neighbour, the Province of *Maryland,* and there we shall find, that since that Government hath been in the King's Hand, the value of Land is very much advanced, and more valuable; the Country is grown far more populous; Trade and Industry vastly improved; and thereby the King's Revenue augmented, the Inhabitants very easy, satisfied and contented, and all this without the least Injury to my Lord *Baltimore*'s property but on the contrary his Lordship's property is the better secured, and Interest much advanced and improved, and why all this, and more, may not reasonably be expected in *Pensilvania,* we know not especially if we consider that we shall receive far greater Advantage by such a Change than the People of *Maryland* did; for they enjoyed under my Lord *Baltimore*'s Government, the Priviledge of a Subject, the Benefit of the King's Laws, Protection and Defence against Enemies from abroad and from *Indians* at home, all which we want and are denied. But notwithstanding all this, we very well know, that no Arguments or Consideration will prevail with Mr. *Penn* and his Friends, to part with their beloved Darling, Arbitrary Government.

What Satisfaction or Justice he designs the Church of *England,* may be guessed at by his Treatment of her Members hitherto, and we shall give you a fuller account of, by the Addresses that are sending here to the Lords of *Trade* and *Plantations* on that Head. And now, Sir, We hope that we have fully replyed to Mr. *Penn*'s Case, and set his dark Steps in a true Light. We beg continuance of your Advice and Correspondence with us, and that you would give us Leave to subscribe our Selves,

SIR,
Your assured Friends.

An Address of the Members of Assembly for the Lower Counties, to the Honourable William Penn, Proprietor and Governour.

May it please your Honour,

We the Representatives of the Lower Counties, in this Assembly, with great Reluctancy lay before your Honour the Burthen those Counties have laboured under by attending no less than five Assemblies since your last Arrival, at the Expence of above Six Hundred Pounds, besides the Funds raised for Support of Government.

We cannot but with Grief observe, that instead of reaping the designed Security by the Laws past at *Newcastle,* we find the most Essential have not yet been sent for His Majesty's Allowance or Approbation, especially such as nearest concern us and our Estates, *viz.* the Acts for Qualification of Magistrates and Juries, and those for Establishing Property, and Raising Money; the Reasons whereof we are yet to seek.

That the Powers of Government of the Lower Counties by your Honour, being, as we are informed. under debate at home, and question'd by some here; we thought our selves concerned to Address your Honour in so important a Point: and therefore did it by desiring a sight of your Deeds of Feoffment. But instead of your usual healing and condescending way, *we met with the Threats of a Gaol without Bail till the King's Pleasure was known.* Your Honour's Return or Deliverance by the Mobb (in case we had not then been in Assembly) which we took to be harsh Language, having not presumed to examine the requisite Qualifications of your Honour as Governour by the late Act of Parliament.

We are likewise under a necessity to lay before your Honour the Danger the Secretary of State cautions these Colonies of (as we apprehend) from the *French* Squadrons now in the *West-Indies* (if the War break out); and we have reason to fear will fall on us naked and defenceless, being without Militia, Fort, Powder, or Shot, though we are the Frontiers of this River, and Heart of the Main, where the Enemy may Land without Bloodshed: and as we have heretofore alledged, not unvaluable to the Crown of *England* in the Product of our Tobaccoes. On this Head we have made Application to your Honour several times before, therefore say less at present.

Notwithstanding these Difficulties, and many more, we have been willing, for the publick Peace, to join with the Members of the Upper Counties in any thing that might conduce thereto. But the House now requiring us to Confirm the Laws so solemnly passed at *Newcastle,* gives us ground to believe they suspect their Validity in being made there; and awakens us to review what we have been doing so many Years past: And besides our Reasons given in the House against that Act, we do conclude, before we make any farther Progress therein, to go home to our Counties, and consult with them what Steps are proper in this Affair. We Conclude.

Philadelphia, Oct. 10. 1701.

Kent.	Newcastle.
John Brinckloe.	*Richard Halliwell.*
William Rodeney.	*John Donaldson.*
John Walker.	*Adam Pieterson.*
William Morton.	*Jasper Yeates.*

Sussex County.
Luke Wattson, Jun.

FINIS.

· 11 ·

Anonymous, A Letter from a Merchant at Jamaica to a Member of Parliament in London (London, 1709)

Because English people placed so much emphasis upon civil liberty, regarding it as the most essential component of their national identity, historians have been puzzled that they slipped so easily into the use of chattel slavery in the colonies and during the early eighteenth century became the primary carriers in the African slave trade to America. Scholars have not found significant published protests against English participation in slavery and the slave trade until after 1760, when a burgeoning antislavery literature began to appear in England. But this tract, published in London in 1709 by an anonymous writer calling himself a "Merchant at Jamaica," indicates that long before the emergence of an antislavery movement, at least a few English people found the slave system that had spread from elsewhere in the Atlantic world into English America disagreeable. The author mainly concerned himself with attacking the inhumanity of the slave trade and the evils of giving planters such wide latitude in the governance of their slaves. But his inclusion of a long speech, allegedly delivered by a black slave in the French sugar colony of Guadeloupe but probably written by the author himself or at least by some person thoroughly familiar with the philosophy and conventions of English law, questions the entire rationale and legal foundations for European enslavement of non-European peoples. It provides an early example of awareness of the incongruities between English professions of their own liberty and their denial of that liberty to other human beings. (J.P.G.)

A

LETTER

FROM A

Merchant at JAMAICA

TO A

Member of Parliament in LONDON,

Touching the AFRICAN TRADE.

To which is added,

A SPEECH made by a BLACK of *Gardaloupe*,

at the Funeral of a Fellow-Negro.

LONDON, Printed for *A. Baldwin*. MDCCIX.

Price 2*d*.

A Letter from a Merchant at Jamaica to a Member of Parliament in London, touching the African Trade.

SIR,

Hearing from *England*, that there's like to be a Struggle next Session of Parliament between the *African* Company and the other Traders thither; I take the freedom to send you a Speech made by a *Black* at *Guardaloupe*, a *French* Island, upon the Funeral of a Negro, kill'd by his Master for taking a small Loaf of Bread as he pass'd thro the Kitchin: From which, and what I shall add, you may perhaps collect more of the Iniquity of that Trade, and see more of the Cruelty wherewith the poor Wretches the Negroes are used, than either the Planters or Merchants, the Company or Traders, will think it their Business to shew, or for their Credit or Interest to have known.

The Acquaintance I had the honour to have with you, whilst I was in *England*, gives me reason to believe you so great a Lover of Justice and Humanity, and that you have so much at heart the *just Rights and Libertys of Mankind*, that I persuade my self you will take pleasure in doing what in you lies for the *Relief and Ease* of so many *miserable Men*, who are really *treated worse than Brutes*. Your God-like Mind, I'm sure, knows the *Joy of doing Good*. And a greater Good can hardly be imagin'd, than to help and relieve so many *Thousands of miserable Men*, who groan under the *Weight* of an insupportable *Tyranny* and *Oppression*.

The *Black* seems to have so fully argu'd the Justice and Injustice wherewith they are acquir'd, that I need say little upon that Head: But I shall give you two or three Instances of the Usage they meet with after they are brought to *America*; with my Thoughts in general.

A Ship being arriv'd at a certain Plantation, a Planter goes on board to buy; he casts his eye upon a stout jolly young Fellow: *Captain*, says he, *what shall I give you for that Man?* Sir, says the Captain, he has a Wife; if you have him, you must take the Cow too. ——— *Which is she?* ——— This. ——— *D———n her*, says the Planter, *she's an ill-thriven Jade; I'll not meddle with her: Prithee let me have the Fellow alone.* ——— He's very fond of her: you'l have no good of him without her. ——— *I'll venture that*, says the Planter: *Come, set your own Price*. By this time the Black perceiv'd they were treating about him; and fearing they meant to separate him from his Wife, steps to her, takes her in his Arms, looks upon her with all the Passion and Fondness of a loving Husband; then goes to the Planter, points to his Wife, then to himself, and by his Looks and Actions seem'd to signify he beg'd the Planter would buy them both; and that if he did, it would be the greatest Obligation in the World, and he might expect a Return in good Services.

The Planter, to please and delude the poor Wretch, signify'd by Looks and Signs he would. But the Captain sets his Price; the Planter strikes him: And now the matter is, how to decoy the poor Man from his Wife. The Planter signifies to him, that he had bought them both; and that they were to go immediately on shoar. The overjoy'd Negro falls upon his knees, kisses the Planter's hands, and is almost transported. Both Man and Wife are brought to the Ship-side; the Man goes down into the Boat, the Woman still in the Ship; the Boat, as order'd, strait puts off. The Negro seeing himself thus deluded, and ready to be rent from what *Nature* had so closely *join'd* him to, snatches up an Oar, and knocks the Rowers down, returns to the Ship-side, and ascends with all the Resentment and Fury, that so base and inhuman an Action cou'd produce; runs to his Wife, clasps her in his Arms, looks with Anger and Indignation upon the Planter and Captain, and draws his Finger along his Throat; meaning he'd cut that if they parted him from his Wife. The Planter seeing the Constancy and Resolution of the Man, and what he was to expect if he did not take the Wife too; and having set his mind upon the Fellow, vouchsafed in his great Goodness to buy them both. So much for our Traffick.

The next Instance is of the Usage of our Negroes, when we have bought them. Tis this ——— On a Sunday a Planter taking a Tour about his Plantation, finds a Stranger Black Woman with one of his Black Men in the Negro's Hutt. *Hussey!* says the Planter; *who are you? To whom do you belong?* And, without staying for an Answer, falls a caning her. His Negro beseech'd him to spare her, for that she was his Friend. *Why, Sirrah!* says he, *what Friends have you? If you want a Woman, have not I Women enou for you? You Dog you! Sirrah, whose is she?* and began to maul him. Sir, says the Negro, for God's sake forbear: I'll tell you.—*Out with't then, you Dog.*—Why, Sir, she's such an one's Servant in the Town.—*But, you Rascal, what does she here? I'll teach you to bring other Peoples Servants upon my Plantations.* (Then falls on him again) *And for you, Hussey! I'll teach you better manners than to come here again. Here!* (calling to his Servants) *strip this W——re; tie her to yonder Tree, and let her have forty sound Lashes with the Cat-of-nine-tails.* The poor trembling Woman, scar'd almost out of her wits with this dreadful Sentence, falls upon her knees, and in the most humble and earnest manner beseeches his Mercy; for that she meant no harm. *Why, you d——'d B——ch,* says he, *what came you here for then?* To tell you true, says the poor thunder-struck Creature, I'm your Servant's Wife. *Are you so?—Then let her have forty Lashes more; and as for the D——g, I'll sacrifice him for daring to meddle with any Women but mine.* The Negro takes to his heels, and hides himself. The Woman's stript, unmercifully lash'd, and let go. Some time after, the Negro comes into his Master's Presence, hoping the Storm was blown over: But so far had the Spirit of Rage and Cruelty the ascendant; that tho the Fellow was better worth than 50*l. per ann.* to him, in looking after the boiling of Sugars and other things; yet the most earnest Requests and Intreatys of the Planter's Wife and other Friends present were all little enough to dissuade him from Killing him; and with *difficulty* he was *restrain'd from* imbruing his Hands in the poor Man's *Blood.*

The last Instance I shall trouble you with, is, of the Manner and Measure of some of our Punishments.

At a principal Town of a considerable Island in this part of the World, a Woman Negro-Servant had stole a Silver Cup, or some such small thing, from her Master; (probably to buy some little Necessarys for the Child she went with.) Now he might either correct her in his own House, or order her to be chastiz'd in the open Market by the hands of the common Whipsman. He chose the latter. Out she's led to the Whipping-Post in the Market Place; and tho she was so big with Child, that she seem'd near her Delivery, yet she was stript stark naked, her Hands ty'd in a Rope, by which she was hoisted till she stood on tip-toe, and all her Parts so distended, as one would have thought a Blow must have made 'em crack and fly asunder. Thus naked, thus distended, thus big with Child, the Executioner of Cruelty comes to her with a Whip made of Wires; and falls on so unmercifully, you would have thought each following Lash would sure have made the Child spring from her Body: yet still her cruel Master's Eye pity'd not; nor did the Beadle's Hand spare her. Thus stood this miserable Spectacle in the face of the Sun and of the World, whipt and scourg'd so long, so cruelly, till to the *shame* of those who call themselves *Men, good-natur'd Men,* and *Christians,* till to their lasting shame the poor Wretch felt such Pains and unspeakable *Agonys,* as made her sweat even *Drops of Blood;* whilst all her Back and hind Parts were so gaul'd and flay'd; that they no longer look'd like human Body, but all appear'd one Piece of mangled Flesh with reeking Gore. The poor Creature, enduring all these racking Torments with an invincible Patience, did not so much as open once her mouth. The cruel Execution ended (if it may be said to be so when so much Smart's to follow) her furrow'd Back and bleeding Wounds were wash'd with Salt and Water. A sharp Remedy, you'l say—But yet, you'l think it mild, compar'd with what they do in some Plantations.—Sometimes, if they think Scourging and such-like too gentle Punishments, forgetting all Humanity, they will with a Knife lay open the *Flesh* of a Slave's Limbs *in long Furrows,* and then pour a *hot Liquor,* made of Pitch, Tar, Oil, Wax, and Brimstone, or such-like Ingredients into the *Green Wounds.*

Thus, Sir, I have given you just a Taste of our *Humanity:* for to attempt the recounting all our Methods of dealing, and our many Ways of punishing those miserable Creatures, were as endless as what *Avarice* and *Iniquity* can suggest, or what the *Caprice* and *Cruelty* of Men, *bounded by no* Fences of *human Law,* can invent and execute.

Yet this is the Case of those Wretches, whom were the D——l himself to torment, and yet profit by or expect their Labour, I do not easily see how he could make them more miserable.

Why they should be thus treated I cannot imagine. The most of them are taken in War, and by the Custom of those barbarous Nations the Captors are reputed to have Right or however they have got the Power, to kill or do what else they please with their Prisoners. The Custom of Servitude, as it was at first introduc'd by Men, who would not forbear one Cruelty, except they exercis'd another not much less; so was it not every where, or at all times receiv'd. *Gro. de jure B. & P*[1] *l.* 3. *c.* 7. §. 8. Whatever cruel Barbarians may think or practise, 'tis plain all the Christian, I might perhaps say all the Civiliz'd World, account it barbarous and inhuman to kill a Prisoner, or treat him ill after you have given him Quarter; and they have intirely laid aside the Custom of Slavemaking, as being against all Rules of Charity: *Gro. Vol.* 1. §. 9. For the end of all just War being Peace, *i.e.* a quiet Enjoyment of Life and Property, what occasion is there to kill a Man I have disarm'd, and from whom I have nothing to fear, and who perhaps had no Malice, but fought against me only because his Prince or Captain would have tuckt him up if he had not? And if in such Case it be inhuman to take his Life, it

1. [*Gro. de jure B. & P*: "Grotius, *On the Law of War and Peace.*"]

is almost as bad to take from him the Liberty of a rational Creature, and to spare his Life no longer than he blindly submits his Understanding; and all his Facultys both of Mind and Body, to the imperious Dictates of my Will, how unreasonable and extravagant soever. But then even among those who allow'd of *Servitude,* yet it was upon supposition of a *just War;* for otherwise the Conquerors were so far from having a Right to kill, that if they knew the War to be unjust, it was Murder if they did; and by consequence also they could have no Right to enslave or sell, or so much as keep their Prisoners. So sensible were the *Romans* of this that *Grot. c.* 10, §. 6. gives several Instances of their making *Restitution* of what they had took in *unjust Wars;* so that they even sold Lands bought with the Price of Captives, and *rebought* whom they had *before sold, and set them at liberty.* And *Grotius, Vol.* 1. is clearly of Opinion, that if one *possess Goods* taken in an *unjust War,* tho he had no hand in the taking them, or did it innocently, yet he is *bound to restore* them. But admitting we had as good a Right in our Slaves as we are willing to imagine, yet still they are Men. And tho *the Law* has a great while indulg'd or conniv'd at *our being Judges in our own Cause;* yet it seems but a piece of natural *Justice and Equity,* that no Man should be so in matters of any moment, where a more *impartial Judg* may be found: Or, however, if the *Law* thinks fit to allow them this, yet it would seem but reasonable that, like *all other Judges,* they should *forfeit* their *Office,* if they be ever guilty of *abusing it.*

These unhappy Mortals, the Negroes, make a great part of the *African* Trade, about which there is like to be so great a Bustle. Let them take it for me that like it: Let them study Ways and Means to preserve and increase it. It has never yet throve, nor do I believe ever will, till 'tis manag'd with more Justice and Humanity both in the first and after Buyer. We have had many publick Calamitys in this Island, and many of our Neighbours have smarted too. I do not wonder, I rather admire the Divine Goodness and Forbearance.

It must be own'd our Plantations are of great Consequence to both Us and *England.* They are work'd and cultivated mostly by the hands of Negroes, and it would be hard to do it by any others. But it does not therefore follow, that those poor Wretches, by whose Labour we are enrich'd, must not be treated with Humanity and Reason; or if they are ill us'd, that the Law should give them no Protection or Redress. 'Tis very hard, that whilst they help to make us some of the happiest People in the World, we should in return make them the most unhappy, the most wretched and miserable part of the Creation. No, Sir, you well know no Advantage can legitimate Injustice and Inhumanity. Whatever Advantages are built upon such false, such rotten Foundations, however they stand for a time, will surely end in Ruin and Destruction. I make no Apology for my long Letter: I know you will excuse it. I heartily pray Heaven may incline your wise Senate to do somewhat for the Relief and Ease of so many, who are basely opprest, and inhumanly treated by their unjust and cruel Masters. It would be an Act worthy of so August an Assembly. It would be laying so good a Foundation of Power and Riches, as might probably outlast human Expectation. Certain 'tis, it would render them the Delight of all good Men. Heaven would look down on so becoming an Action, and all Generations would call them blessed.

I am with great Respect and Affection,
SIR,
Your most humble Servant.

Octob. 10. 1708.

A Speech made by a Black of Gardaloupe, at the Funeral of a Fellow-Negro.

The great and beneficent *Creator,* the *Best* of *Beings,* as Reason tells, and as our Master's Books assure us, when he had form'd this Speck of Earth, was pleased to crown the Work, by making Man, on whom he stamp'd the Image of Himself. All he expected in return, was but a just and grateful sense of the kind Maker's Bounty, and an honest Care to copy after the Divine Original in doing good; that is, in other words, promoting his own and others *Happiness.* The good and wise *Maker* had sufficiently furnish'd Man with Facultys necessary to so kind and glorious a Design. He gave him the Powers of Perceiving, Deliberating, Judging: He implanted in him a strong Desire of preserving his own Being and Happiness, and gave him unexpressible Tendernesses towards others. And as God made of the same *common Mold all People,* so whilst he subjected the inferior Animals to these little Vice-Roys, he left *them* all *free* to use and follow the *Conduct* of that *Divine* Ray of *Reason;* whereby they were shew'd and taught that reasonable Service which he requir'd. He made them, I say, free to follow this bright and faithful Guide, so soon as they should grow up to Man, and their Eyes were strong enough to bear the Light: that so the Creator might have the Glory of a free and chearful Service, and the Creature the Reward of Virtue, and an unconstrain'd Obedience. But, alas! how far is Mankind fallen? How much degenerated from the pure and happy State in which God created them? Sin introduc'd Sloth in some, Wantonness and Luxury in others. These were tempted to affect Command over, and Service from others; while those were again inclin'd to a base Submission and Dependence, rather than be at the Pains of exerting those Powers the wise Author of Nature had given them; which were abundantly sufficient to all the Purposes of Life; and so they; like the profane *Esau* whom we read of in our Master's Books, sold their Birthright and Inheritance for a poor Mess of Pottage. Thus fond Mankind forsook the Divine Light plac'd in their Breasts, and by first becoming Servants to their own Lusts and Appetites, became Servants to each other. It had been well, comparatively speaking, had Matters stop'd here; for hitherto there is no Wrong, no Violence: Besides, the Infirmitys of Nature made it a necessary and even prudent Charity to serve their Neighbour in time of want, whose Assistance they again in their Turn might need and expect.

And if any set so little Value on the Gem of Liberty, as quite to part with it for a little Bread, which they might have reap'd and made with their own hands, they were to thank themselves for so foolish a Bargain, and had nothing to complain of but their want of Industry and Wit. But still this extended no farther, than their own Consent had carry'd it; and the Agreement being mutual, they were no longer bound by it than their Masters perform'd their part, and treated them fairly. But the Lust of Dominion and the Desire of possessing, seizing Mens Brains, they grew fierce and raging, broke thro the Ties of Nature and Humanity; and upon slender, or only pretended Causes, made War upon their weaker and more innocent Neighbours. Hence is the Source of all our Woes and Miserys; to these we owe our Captivity and Bondage; to these we must lay the innocent Blood of our Brother who lies murder'd, barbarously murder'd, before us. Good God! what have we done? What Right have these cruel Men thus to oppress, insult, and inhumanly butcher their Fellow-Creatures? Let us examine all their Title, and see what it amounts to; and then we shall the better know, whether their Usage of us, or our Complaints, are the more just. They say, they bought us with their Mony.—Confess'd; but who had Power to sell? We were it may be condemn'd by colour of Law, that is, the Will of some Great Map, to be sold by way of Banishment for some suppos'd Crime.—But how did the Buyer know there ever was a Crime committed, or that the Sentence was just? or if he did, what Right can this confer? 'Tis plain, I think, it gives him only Right to carry us whither he pleas'd, and make us work till we repaid him by our Labor what we cost, with other Charges.

It may be we were taken in War; what Right then had the Conqueror? or what did he transfer? Suppose the War against us was just, and that our Buyers knew 'twas so; yet they likewise know, that 'tis barbarous and cruel to take a conquer'd Enemy's Life, when the Injur'd can be safe without it; and that 'tis still more barbarous and inhumane for another to take it away, to whom he has sold and deliver'd his Prisoner; since by the Sale and Price receiv'd he seems to have taken the Mony for his Security, and upon that Consideration runs the Hazard of the other's setting him at liberty if he thinks fit. So that 'tis plain, this gives them no such Right over our Lives, as any Man that has the least Tenderness or Humanity (I might, I think, say Justice) would make use of. And as for perpetual Slavery—it must be cruel Justice, that for so small a Sum, so soon repaid, wou'd purchase and exact what makes his Fellow-Creature, from whom he has nought to fear, so miserable for Life. If they contend for this as a Right which they are fond of, let them shew it, and let them take it and the sole Glory of it. But who told our present Lords the War was just? Do Victory and Right go always hand in hand? No, our Masters by Experience know they don't. This then at best can give but a dark doubtful Right, which never can defeat that natural and undoubted one the God of Nature has bestow'd on Men, to have, to own, no other Lord but *him*.

It may have happen'd we were sold to pay our Debts: What will this give them? In Equity they have at most hereby a Right to so much Service as will pay the Debt and Charges of transporting us. The first was all the Creditor could ask. But do they know what this Debt was? No, they never so much as once enquir'd or ask'd to be inform'd. We were perhaps bought of some unkind unnatural Father. Be it so. What have they got by this? Can a Father transfer what he has not? or have they what he neither did or cou'd possibly give them? surely no. A Father has Power indeed, and ought to help and feed his young and tender Offspring; as all Creatures do, but not to cast them out into the Fields, or sell them wantonly to a base Servitude. God gave him Power to beget and become a Father of Men, not Slaves. A Father, as 'tis fit, has Power too to guide and steer his Childrens Actions while Reason's weak; and if by Age, or otherwise, he's brought to want their help, they are oblig'd by Nature, and by Gratitude, to give their helping hand and best Assistance. But still they are not his Slaves or lasting Property; for when wise Nature has fitted them to propagate and educate their Kind, Reason requires, and Nature loudly tells they are at Liberty, they then are Men. It's true, we seem oblig'd to our Lords, that they were pleas'd to take us off the Hands of cruel Conquerors, or such wanton and unnatural Parents as begot us only for their Pleasure; either of which might likely have destroy'd, if they cou'd not have sold us. But it wou'd be remember'd, no Benefit obliges further than the Intention. Was it then for our sakes, or for their own, our Masters built such mighty Ships in which they plow the Main? Was it for us they laid out so much Wealth? Or was it to save our Lives, they so much ventur'd and expos'd their own? Alas! the Answer is too obvious? Our hard Labour, and harder Fare, but most of all, our cruel Punishments, and perpetual Bondage; but too plainly shew for whose sake all this was done. But besides, 'tis certain many Wars are made, many Children parted with, only because there are so many Buyers. So that all we have to thank them for, is, that they sought to serve themselves; and doing so, they sav'd us from those first of Ills their Avarice had wrought. Further, Many of us, it may be, are bought neither of the Governour or Conquerour, of Creditor or Parent; but of a treacherous Friend, a perfidious Husband, or an odious Man-stealer. These are far from conferring any Right, unless what can arise from the most unjust and inhuman Acts in the world. What's now become of all their boasted Right of absolute Dominion? It is fled. Where all our Obligations to perpetual Servitude? They are vanish'd. However, we may perhaps owe them something; and it were but just, if so, they should be paid. Let us therefore, if from the account I have already given we can, make an Estimate of the Ballance.—Supposing then one half of us were justly sold at first by those that had a Right to all our Services, if that may be suppos'd: Suppose likewise that our Masters knew it too, and who the very Persons were: They then would have at most a Right to the Labour of such Persons during Life; and of the rest, till they had earn'd and clear'd so much as was given to the Captain who brought 'em hither. But since it is impossible for them to know on whom to place their several Demands; and since they bought us all at random, without regard to Right or Wrong: let us for once suppose favourably for them, who never favour'd us; let us suppose our Masters innocent of all the Wrongs we first sustain'd. Suppose us Men, Women, and Children come to their Shoar from some far-off unknown Land, under the Power of a strange Captain of a Ship, who pretends he has a Right to sell us. He offers to deliver us, Great and Small, into their hands at 20 *l.* a-piece. They pay the Mony. We are deliver'd up. What are we now in debt? 'Tis plain, I think, that since they neither know nor did regard his Title, they can at best have one but till they're reimburs'd the Cost and Charge which they've been at. 'Tis sure we had a plain and natural Right to Life and Liberty; which to take away upon a weak, presumptive, or a may-be Title, were to make us of less value than Beasts and Things Inanimate: a Property in which, by Reason's Law, is never gain'd against a true and just Owner upon slight Presumptions, whatever may be done by Laws of particular Societys, to which each one agrees. But were it otherwise in mere Possessions, yet Life and Liberty are hardly things of so low rate, that they're to pass as lightly from the Owner, to whom God gave the sole and certain Property, as Beasts, or Birds, or Things Inanimate, which bounteous Nature laid in common, and wherein strictly no Man has more Right than what is necessary for him and his Dependants.

Let any Man but make the Case his own, and he'l soon see the Hardship. Would not any one think himself greatly injur'd, if another should make him his perpetual Slave, only because he gave 20 *l.* for him, to one who had him in his power? Methinks the very naming it is enough to shock a Man; and he should need no further Argument to convince him of the Injustice of the thing. But Men are hardly brought to see what makes against their Interest. Taking the matter now to be as last stated—Suppose Twenty of us bought at once; the Mony paid would be 400 *l.* suppose six of the Twenty Children; suppose also one of us to die each year; reckon the Labour of each of those of sufficient Age at 10 *l.* a year, which is really less than it may be well accounted, seeing a great part of our poor Sustenance is owing to our own Hands and Industry, which we are forc'd to employ in planting Herbs and Roots, whilst we should rest from our more toilsom Labour. By this Computation we should have paid all our joint Debt in three years time. Yet would our Lords but use us as Men, we should not stick to a nice Computation, but frankly serve them three or four years more, before we claim'd our Freedom. Many of us here present have serv'd twice, some seven times the space our cruel Lords can justly claim. Of our hard Labour, let our weary'd Limbs, their well-planted Fields and full Coffers all bear witness. Of their hard and cruel Usage let our torn Backs testify. Of their bloody Inhumanity, let the Corps of our dear Countryman before us, weltring in its Goar; let it, I say, for ever witness against the cruel Authors of our Woe: who not content to make us Slaves, Slaves for Life, do use us worse than Dogs, and deny us the Compassion they would shew a Horse. 'Tis true, they willingly will teach and make us Christians; while they themselves want to be taught, both They and We are Men. In this however we are somewhat better used than are our wretched Friends in *English* Isles; where their hard Masters forbear to do good, lest that oblige them to do more. Ridiculous Superstition! that will not allow their Servants to be Christians, lest they be forc'd to allow them to be Men. This is to found Dominion upon the Gospel of that Divine Teacher Jesus, who told them plain as Words could make it, his Kingdom was not of this World. And as if none were intitled to the common Privileges of Nature, except they please to allow 'em them by Washing or Baptizing, they carefully forbid our Brethren that. What I pray is this, but to make sport with the Creation, and to monopolize the Blessings of our common Mother Earth? Our hardy Tutors know things better. They teach us what themselves seem hardly to believe; and by giving us hopes of another better World, endeavour to make us content that they alone shou'd enjoy this: teach us to do Good for Evil; and when we have done no fault, to turn our Cheeks to the Smiter, and our Backs to the Scourger; to submit not only to froward and unjust, but even to merciless and cruel Masters; remembring us that their Gospel says, *Thro many Sufferings and Tribulations we must enter into the Heavenly Country;* that Country where our dear, our patient, our murder'd Brother's gone. But why shou'd we complain of Death, whose Life's so miserable to us? To kill us, seems the greatest kindness that our bloody Lords can do. We have lost our native Country, our Friends, our Liberty; we are made Slaves to haughty cruel Men; we are fed and work'd hard; their Will's our Law; which when we do transgress, we suffer all the wanton Cruelty they can devise: No Prayers or Tears can touch their harden'd Hearts; relentless as Rocks, they know no Pity. What now remains in Life to be desir'd? 'Tis better far to die, than, being Men, be forc'd to live like Beasts: Beasts! and of those the most unhappy too. Still, tho our Hardships are as great as the Injustice of our Oppressors; tho our Sufferings are as many as the hated Days we live; tho all their Pleas of Right are false or short: methinks I cou'd forgive them all; did they not pretend Necessity for their inhuman Acts. They tell, it seems, the *European*

World; we're of such base, such brutal Natures, that nought will govern us, but downright Force and Fear; That like the Horse we must be broke and rid with Whip and Spur; but with far closer Reins. Abominable Forgery? Hated imposture! What, are we not Men? Have we not the common Facultys and Passions with others? Why else has Nature given us human Shape and Speech? Whence is't that some of these wise rational Masters of ours give us sometimes Charge, not only of their Works and Cash, but of their Persons too; and make us judg when they're debauch'd enough in Wine, and when it's time to lug them home upon our servile Backs? Whence is it that some of us, without the Help of Books or Letters, are found able to deliver a Message, or do Business better, even by their own Confession, than they who intrust us with it? But were it a wonder, that while they use us so like Beasts, we shou'd not act as Men? If they give us no Motives to Industry and Obedience, but a base servile Fear, is it at all strange, when that's remov'd, the hated Service straight shou'd cease? It wou'd be strange indeed, shou'd it be otherwise. Cou'd they be brought to deal with us as Men, they soon wou'd see, we may be wrought upon by gentler Methods far than Blows and Scourges. But while they use us thus, how can they e're expect we shou'd not hate them? how can they hope our Services shou'd once proceed from Hearts they never touch'd, unless with Detestation? Let them make tryal of their own Countrymen, and see what will be the difference 'twixt them and us. As much Slaves as they are already, this likely will be all the odds, they'l hate them more, and bear their Usage worse than we. To finish and compleat our Miserys, these Lords of ours, not content that we are Slaves, Slaves basely us'd for Life, they make our innocent Babes their Property, as if they sprung from Brutes. If their Right to us be so uncertain or so small, as I have shew'd it is; with what Pretence, with what Face can they enslave our guiltless Children? who have committed nothing to deserve the loss of Liberty in a base servile tedious Life, a Life beneath the State of Brutes. Supposing we were justly theirs for Life, which they can never shew; yet still, the most they can demand from Innocents is some small time of Labour, for the little Sustenance which they receiv'd by means of these our Lords. But not content with this, they carry on the wrong, and make them Slaves for Life as they made us; and claim our Childrens Children, and so on, to all Posterity. Thus, our Lords who call themselves White-men and Christians, led by their Avarice and Luxury, commit the blackest Crimes without a Blush, and wickedly subvert the Laws of Nature, and the Order of Creation. Let us, my dearest Countrymen and Fellow-sufferers! Let us in this our great Distress and Misery, look up to the great Author of Nature, whose Works and Image are so basely us'd; and earnestly implore his mighty Aid: Let us beseech him, for sure he hears the Crys and Groans of his oppressed Creatures, either to soften those Adamantine Hearts, which cut us in pieces; or to put it into the Minds of some great, some God-like Men, to come to our Deliverance, that we may sing our Maker's Praise, and with Assurance say, There is a God who governs the Earth, and restrains the Pride and Cruelty of wicked Men.

FINIS.

• 12 •

Anonymous, Truth Brought to Light (London, 1713)

THE ASSASSINATION of Governor Daniel Parke by disgruntled settlers in the colony of Antigua in early December 1710 was one of the most striking examples of the weakness of metropolitan authority in colonial British America. A Virginian, Parke had been a colonel who served under Marlborough and had brought the news of the victory of Blenheim to Queen Anne, who in 1706 rewarded him by appointing him governor over the four Leeward Island colonies of Antigua, Montserrat, Nevis, and St. Christopher. The Leewards had long been an area of contest between France and Britain, and the Queen charged him, as a war-time governor, to put the islands in a state of effective defense. Almost from the beginning, Parke came into conflict with local assemblies, especially the one in Antigua, and his whole tenure was stormy. In particular, Parke seems to have resented the Antiguan Assembly's efforts to use his need for defense appropriations to extract concessions concerning their legislative rights, while Antiguan leaders complained about his increasing high-handedness, peculation, and lechery, the last even with the wives of some of his principal opponents. Following a confrontation during which Parke used troops to disperse the Assembly with bayonets, the assemblymen organized a military force from among the settler population and stormed the governor and his forces, killing Parke and forty-four of the seventy troops that stood with him.

In the aftermath of this battle, some of the officeholders, mostly his appointees, fled to England. To combat the many charges circulating in the metropolis about Parke's behavior, they published this pamphlet, the writer of which is not specified, in his defense in London in 1713. It consists mostly of testimonials from persons sympathetic to Parke, the unidentified author organizing the materials to show that Parke, far from being guilty of any "Male-Administration in Government," had been the victim of "a subtil[e] Combination of some particular, disaffected, and disguested Persons" intent on thwarting Parke's efforts to carry out the commands of "Her Majesty and Her Government" in Antigua. While settlers occasionally managed to get unpopular or arbitrary governors removed, this Parke episode is the only case in colonial British America in which they actually killed a governor. Although metropolitan officials sent a commission to investigate the affair, no person was ever punished for Parke's murder, a fact that further underlines the weakness of metropolitan authority in the face of settler resistance in the colonies. (J.P.G.)

Truth brought to Light;

OR,

Murder will out;

Being a short, but True, Account of the most horrid, barbarous, and bloody MURTHER and REBELLION committed at *Antego* in the *West-Indies,* against Her Majesty and Her Government.

NUMB. Chap. XXXV. v. 31. *Ye shall take no satisfaction for the life of a murderer, which is guilty of death: but he shall be surely put to death.*

v. 33. *So ye shall not pollute the land wherein ye are: for blood it defileth the land: and the land cannot be cleansed of the blood that is shed therein, but by the blood of him that shed it*

Truth brought to Light

The World (by false Suggestion, and indirect Means of the Persons who were chief Actors in this Wickedness) being wholly ignorant of the Truth of this horrid Murder and Rebellion; What follows are only Abstracts of the several Depositions of Persons now in *England, &c.* who were Eye-Witnesses of, and Joint-Sufferers in, the whole Fact, and who are now most of 'em in *London,* ready to justify this Truth.

Matters previous to the Murder of Col. Parke.

Thomas Cooke, Private Centinel in Capt. *Joseph Rookby*'s Company in Col. *Jones*'s Regiment, deposes,

> That calling at *Jacob Morgan*'s House, sometime in *Decemb.* 1709, where there was some Company at Dinner, he ask'd them for something to drink, and they gave him both Victuals and Drink; after which, one of the Gentlemen propos'd to the Deponent, to shoot General *Parke,* and on that Condition, offer'd him a Pistole, which he refus'd, saying, *That altho' he was in great want, he would not earn Money after that manner.*

Some time before, the said General *Parke,* as he was riding on the High-Road through *John Otto Byar*'s Estate, he was shot, out of a Thicket, through his Arm; and (as the said *Otto*'s Son, *Bastian,* since the Death of the said Col. *Parke,* confess'd) it was done by one of his, the said *Bastian*'s, Negroes, by his Command.

It also appears by the Deposition of Col. *George Gamble,* one of the Council of that Island, taken in *June* 1710. that he happening into Company with some of the Malecontents, one of them, *viz.* ☛ *Giles Watkins,* told the said Deponent, in a Discourse relating to General *Parke,* That they had done his Business for him, and would be soon remov'd; the said Deponent answering, That he hoped there were no such corrupt Practices in the Court of *England,* as to condemn a chief Governour unheard; the said *Watkins* reply'd, They would condemn him first, and try him afterwards; and, That they had rais'd a considerable Sum of Money for that purpose; and, if that would not do, no Sum should be wanting; and, That their Agent, ☛ *William Nevin,* would see it effectually dispos'd of to that End; and if nothing else would do, Money should: To which the said Deponent answer'd, That he did not doubt but their Proceedings against the General would appear in the end to be the Effect of Malice and private Pique; That such Attempts were an Argument of a bad Cause; and that Justice would take place.

And by Major *Samuel Wickham*'s Deposition, who was one of the Assembly, taken before the General in Council, in *August* 1708. That in *July* before, at *Jacob Morgan*'s House, he ask'd Mr. *Edward Perrie* (Commissioner of the Customs of 4 and Half *per Cent.*) why he was not lett into the Secret of the Articles they had been forming against the General, as well as Others, he being a Member of the House of which said Articles they had been discoursing? To which the said *Perrie* answer'd, That he should see them, provided he would give his Oath not to divulge them; And the said *Wickham* reply'd, That his scrupling to shew them was base, and unfair, and ask'd the Reason of it: Whereupon, the said *Perrie* told the said *Wickham*, The Design was to prevent the General from having Notice of them, and thereby hinder him from making a Defence.

An Abstract of several Depositions relating to the Barbarous Murther of the late Daniel Parke, Esq; Chief Governour of the Leeward-Islands in Antego, the 7th of December 1710. viz.

Mr. *Michael Ayon*, now in *London*, late Provost-Marshal-General of all the *Leeward-Islands*, deposes,

> That *Tuesday, December* the 5th, 1710. the Assembly of that Island met at St. *John*'s, where they warmly insisted on Appointing their Clerk, as they did before, on Having the Negative Voice lodg'd in their Speaker; but the General refusing to give up the Queen's Prerogative, he the said *Michael Ayon*, Captain *Richard Worthington, George French*, and *Richard Oglethorp*, Gent. now in *London*, with several Others, depose, That the said Assembly forced into the Court-House, (where the General was, with the Council) attended with an unruly Mob, where they insulted him to his Face, by telling him, *He was no General*; and threatening to take him Prisoner at once; but the Officer of the Guard appearing with a few Men, to hinder

> the General from being ill-us'd, the said Assembly withdrew, crying out one and all, *No General;* some of them declaring, *They would give him such a Pill on* Thursday (*viz.* the Day they murther'd him) *that he should not easily digest; and, That they would, by that Day, muster up as many Forces as should drive him* (meaning the General) *and his Granadeers, to the Devil.*

Doctor *Gousse Bonnine, George French,* and *Richard Oglethorp,* (now in *London*) depose,

> That one *John Booth* (*Thomas Kerby's* chief Clerk) told them, *That Two Nights, before the Murther of Col.* Parke, *successively, he had sat up in the said* Kerby's *House drawing of Deeds and Conveyances of several of the chief Actors Estates in that Murther;* and, *That* Henry Symes, (Register of the said Island) *was there, in order to witness and record them,* as the Laws of them Islands, in such Case directs; Which, no doubt on't, was done with that Expedition, at that Juncture, in order to defeat the Forfeitures their intended horrid Villainy would subject them to.

Michael Ayon, Richard Worthington, Doctor *Gousse Bonnine, George French, Richard Oglethorp,* and Others, depose,

> That they have been credibly inform'd, That on *Wednesday, December* the 6th, 1710. the said Assembly sent Three or Four Persons all about the Country, to summon and warn the Inhabitants, in Col. *Edward Byam,* and the said Assembly's Name, to be and appear in Arms in the Town of St. *John's,* the Day following, in order to take General *Parke,* who, they alledg'd, had betray'd the Island, and sold it to the *French;* with other most false, scandalous, and aggravating Reflections, to inrage the People, and encourage them to Rebellion; the said

Michael Ayon, Richard Worthington, Gousse Bonnine, George French, and *Richard Oglethorp,* together with *Daniel Rosengrave,* Gent. and *Charles Bowes,* Serjeant of Grenadier in Colonel *Alexander's* Regiment, and Others, depose,

> That on *Thursday, December* the 7th, 1710, by 7 in the Morning, came to Town a Body of Men arm'd, to the Number of about Fifty Persons, who paraded in the Market-Place, and caus'd a Drum to be beat to Arms;

and the said Deponents *Ayon* and *Oglethorp* separately depose,

> That the General being inform'd thereof, sent them down to read and nail up a Proclamation, setting forth, That whereas he had been inform'd, that the Inhabitants were summon'd to take him Prisoner, it was His Command, that

all Persons who appear'd in Arms, above the Number of Ten, should disperse, otherwise they should be prosecuted as Rebels, *&c.* On which, Mr. ☛ *Samuel Watkins,* and some others of the Assembly, bid the said Deponent carry back the said Proclamation, and tell the General, *To wipe his Backside with it;* adding, *That they had a good mind to take the said* Ayon *Prisoner;* but he made his Escape from them, and told the General what had pass'd.

And all the said Deponents say,

That in a little Time afterwards they marched out, with Drum beating, to a Pasture adjoining the said Town of St. *John's,* where the Party encreased to the Number of about Five Hundred Men, with many of their own Slaves, armed by them, and then marched back again in very regular Order, with Drum beating, into Town, and paraded in the aforesaid Market-Place, where *John Booth, Thomas Kerby's* chief Clerk, by Orders of the said *Kerby* (as the said *Booth* himself since declared) read a Proclamation (given him by the said Party) Three Times, whereby they villainously insinuated to the unthinking Mob, *That as General* Parke *had betray'd the Island to the* French, *they required all manner of Persons to repair to them, and be aiding and assisting to them in taking General* Parke *dead or alive, or else their Estates should be forfeited, and themselves banish'd off the Island, and render'd incapable of ever returning, or inheriting any Estates on the said Island;* or to that effect. After which, they sent Colonel *George Gamble* and Captain *Nathaniel Crump* (Speaker of the said Assembly) to the General, to acquaint him of the iminent Danger he was in, and the Grievances the People pretended to have layn under: To which he return'd such satisfactory and condescending Answers (among others, *That they might sit where they would in the Island, and make what Laws they should think proper for the Welfare thereof; and that he would pass them, provided they did not touch the Queen's Prerogative*) that the said *Gamble* and *Crump* offer'd themselves Hostages for his Security, if he would discharge his Soldiers; which he promis'd to do, if their Party would disperse, or send him up Three or Four more of their principal leading Men; which they said they would, and parted seemingly well-satisfy'd, as the General was in reality, for so great an impending Storm's being blown over. But, contrary to his, and all these Deponents Expectations, they heard a March beat in the Market-place, and saw the said Party march, after dividing themselves in Two Divisions, towards the General's House, by Two different Ways, the One headed by *Piggott,* and the Other by *Paynter;* the former marching towards an Eminence (on which the General had before posted a Serjeant and Six Men) they, on the said *Piggott*'s Approach, laid down their Arms, and ran in to him, and ☛ *Thomas Kerby* advanced some small Distance before the rest, and fired the first Shot against the General, the rest following his Example. But the General did not permit any body on his part to fire, till one of the Soldiers on his Guard was wounded; then they all fired by Command, which they continued doing, till most of them were either kill'd or wounded; when the Rebels perceiving the fire on the Generals side to decrease, the said *Piggott,* with about Forty more, came down, and rushed into the General's House, impudently commanding him to surrender; at which, the General order'd him to be gone, and he refusing, they discharged their Pistols at one another, and the said *Piggot* dropt dead on the Spot: The General was shot in a little while after through the fleshy part of his Thigh, which the Deponent, Dr. *Bonnine* believes not to have been the Occasion of his Death. After which, the whole Party surrounded the House, and kept a continual firing into it, upon all that was left with the General. One *Archibald Cochran,* shot the Deponent *Ayon* through the Body, after a promise of Quarter, and the delivery of his Sword: The Deponent *Bonnine*'s Son-in-Law, Capt. *Beaulieu,* was shot in the Beginning of the Action, of which he dy'd in some short time. Ensign *Lyndon,* and a great many of the Soldiers, were shot dead, and others desperately wounded. The Deponent *French,* although he was desperately wounded in two Places, and lying in his gore at their coming into the House, yet they were so barbarous as to shoot him again in that Condition: What remain'd for 'em to do, was only to pillage and rob the House, which they did effectually, not having left, in half an Hour's time, the least thing of any Value in it.

The said Deponents likewise say,

That ☛ *Daniel Mckenny,* and ☛ *Samuel Watkins,* were Principal Contrivers, Advisers, and Actors of that most bloody and barbarous Massacre, yet none has yet been made an Example of for the same.

Margaret Bryan, of the Island of *Antegoa,* Spinster, deposes,

That she was with General *Parke* the Minute he expired, at one *Wright*'s House, whither he was taken in, out of the open Street, and heard him complain of nothing but his Back, which she felt, and says, that to the best of her Knowledge, 'twas broke.

Lucia French, Margaret Mac-Mahon, and *Mary Harven,* all of that Island, depose,

That going up to the General's House after the firing was over, they saw him strip'd almost of all his Cloaths, and drag'd by one Leg and one Arm (he being yet alive) out of his House, down a few Steps of Stone Stairs which were at the Entrance of his House, and that his Head trailed from one Step to another, till they left him at last exposed to the scorching Sun in the open Street.

Elizabeth Sweegle, of the said Island, Spinster, deposes,

That after the General was wounded, he call'd for some Drink, and she offering him some Water in a Callubash, ☛ *Samuel Watkins* kicked it out of her Hands, and swore, if she offer'd to help him (the said General) he would sheath his Sword in her Gutts, she likewise deposes, That she afterwards saw ☛ Mr. *Andrew Murray,* and ☛ Mr. *Franck Carlisle,* kick and misuse the General, after he was drag'd out of his House, saying, *God damn you for a Dog, if you are going, take this along with you.*

Charles Bowes, Serjeant of Granadiers in Colonel *Alexander's* Regiment, and *Alice Lawrence,* of the Island of *Antego,* Widow, depose,

That they saw ☛ *Thomas Kirby* fire the first Shot against the General.

George French, Lucia French, and *Margaret Mac-Mahon,* depose,

That ☛ *Thomas Kirby* presented a Pistol at the Deponent *George French,* when they helped to carry him out of the General's House wounded, and horridly curs'd him, so that they have no Reason to doubt but he wou'd have shot the said *French,* had not a Gentleman that stood by, interposed in his Favour.

Richard Worthington, deposes,

That when the House was surrounded by the Rebels, ☛ *Thomas Kirby* came arm'd among the rest, and made a Pass with his Sword at the Deponent, which he put by.

Michael Ayan, Richard Worthington, Gousse Bennine, George French, Richard Oglethorp, Daniel Rosengrave, and *Charles Bowes,* depose,

That ☛ *Thomas Kirby* was so far from doing any Acts of Humanity that Day, as he sets forth in a Petition lately presented on his behalf, to Her Majesty, that he was very active to do all the Mischief and Acts of Barbarity he could think of; and they further say, that so many Persons were concern'd with him in the same Action in *Antego,* and that he carries such a Sway, and has so great an Interest in them, that 'tis next to an Impossibility he shou'd meet with a fair impartial Tryal; and that it wou'd be very dangerous for any body to appear against him there.

Michael Ayan, Richard Oglethorp, Charles Bowes, and *Gousse Bonnine,* depose,

That they saw Henry Smith (a Person sent over a Prisoner by Governor *Douglas,* and now out upon Bail) arm'd among the Rebels that assassinated Colonel *Parke* the 7th of *December,* 1710. and several times afterwards heard him applaud the Action, and say, *That if it were to be done again, he would go Ten Miles on his Head to effect it.*

George French, deposes,

That the said ☛ *Smith* told him, after the Murder of Col. *Parke, That were it not for him, and others, there wou'd be nothing done that Day,* (meaning the 7th of *December,* 1710.) *far that the Cowardly Dogs of Planters would run away, and had not Courage to do the Business.*

Elinor Martin, of *Antegoa,* deposeth,

That she several times heard the said ☛ *Smith* declare, *That as he was in the Action of the 7th of* December, 1710. *He did not doubt of having Thanks for it; and were the same to be done again, he would go Twenty Mile on his Head to do it.*

Richard Oglethorp, late of the Island of *Antego,* Gent. sworn before Judge *Powell,* makes Oath,

That on *Thursday* the Seventh of *December,* 1710. being in the Courthouse in the Town of St. *John's,* where were Capt. *John Piggott,* Capt. *John Otto Byar,* Maj. *John Tomlinson,* and several others, he heard them express the following Words: *Damn the Dog,* (meaning General *Parke*) *he has given away several Estates by his damn'd Courts of* Chancery; *does he want Hostages to give him an Opportunity of giving away the rest;* so cry'd, one and all, *Let's away with the Dog, dead or alive;* and addressing themselves to the Mob, then under Arms at their Command, said, *Now Gentlemen, ye may see he has sold the Island, and wants to get off.*

A very false, scandalous, and improbable Suggestion, that a Gentleman in so great an Authority there, as Chief Governour of all the Islands, and who had a better Estate on that very Island, than any of them who had cast the Reflection upon him, should betray it; but it is so inconsistent, that they never yet so much as attempted to prove it.

The Business of Colonel Parke was so very particular, that an Account of that Affair must be acceptable to the Publick. We have therefore inserted the following Relation.

Antegoa, August 24. 1710.

The Rebels of Antegoa, and their Abettors, having been industrious in traducing the Character of the late *Daniel Parke,* Esq; Her Majesty's Governor of the *Leeward-Islands,* as supposing the more they blacken and asperse his Memory, the less odious their barbarous Assassination of the said Gentleman may appear; wherefore, to set the Matter in a clear Light, by a fair and honest Representation, before the impartial and unprejudic'd Part of Mankind, it is thought necessary in the first Place, to publish the following Letter, sign'd by the Lieutenant-Governor, and Council of *Antegoa,* directed to *Richard Carey,* Esq; then Agent for the said Island, in *London,* which, in Justification of the said General *Parke,* was (pursuant to Her Majesty's Order) sent over attested under the Great Seal of the *Leeward-Islands,* being as follows:

SIR,

We have Reason to think, That by the Opportunity of this Packet, and a Vessel lately sail'd from Montserrat, *you'll have Papers sent you, containing certain Articles against his Excellency, (our preesent General) in order, as you are Agent for this Island, to exhibit them to the Lords Committee of Trade and Plantations, or to lay them before some other Board. Now, that you may not be impos'd on by the crafty Insinuations of some ill-designing Men, (who under the specious Colour and Pretence of acting for the Publick Good, artfully stir up Dissention, to gratify their Private Piques and Malice) we have thought fit to let you know, that if any such Papers come to your Hands, to be laid before the Lords Committee of Trade, or elsewhere, (of which we do desire you'd make early and diligent Enquiry) that the same are not form'd by the Representative Body of this Island, but are Matters concerted by the subtil Combination of some particular, disaffected, and disgusted Persons, (as well some Members of the Assembly, as others) towards his Excellency, who, by under-hand Practices and clandestine Means, have brought over several unwary and unadvis'd Persons, to join with them. One Way taken by those pretended Patriots, is, to let none into the Knowledge of these Secrets, but such as will first swear not to divulge them; alledging, that keeping them Secret, will in a great Measure incapacitate his Excellency from making a timely Defence; and to give Opportunity to the Blackness they cast on him, to gain so deep a Tincture, as afterwards will not easily be wip'd off.*

The Station Her Majesty has plac'd us in, gives us a greater Opportunity of knowing better than other Men, whether his Excellency has been guilty of Male-Administration in Government, or not; and as we have consider'd his Actions, and not found sufficient Ground for Complaint, so we cannot see any just Cause for the present Endeavours of others against him.

Some of those pretended mighty Matters laid to his Excellency's Charge, have been drop'd and whisper'd about; but they are so insignificant and frivolous, it would afford Matter of Redicule, more than any thing else, to mention them, and if private Injuries make up part of the Complaints amongst so small a People as we are, it is scarce possible they would remain a Secret.

We think it therefore, a piece of common Justice to his Excellency's Character (as well as our Duty towards him) to let you be appriz'd of these Proceedings, that you may Oppose and Discourage the same, as much as in you lies; and this we recommend to you, as we are your loving Friends,

John Yeamans,
John Hamilton,
Edward Byam,
Will. Codrington,
Thomas Morriss,
George Gamble,
Lawrence Crabb,
William Byam.

To Richard Carey, *Esq; in* London.

Those that impartially consider the following Loyal ADDRESS of the General Council of the *Leeward-Islands,* to Her Majesty, must be either of Opinion, that the Gentlemen who compos'd that Body were in a Conspiracy with General *Parke,* to betray their Country; or must allow the said General to have behav'd himself as a Faithful Asserter of the Rights of the *British* Crown, and a Sincere Lover of his Country, notwithstanding the many Slanders and Calumnies with which he has been aspers'd by Anti-monarchical and Disaffected People.

To the QUEEN'*s Most Excellent Majesty.*

The Humble ADDRESS of the General Council of the Islands of *St. Christophers, Nevis, Antegoa,* and *Montserrat.*

May it please Your Majesty,

We, Your Majesty's most Dutiful and Loyal Subjects, do, with all dutiful Affection to Your Majesty's Person, and Zeal for Your Service; congratulate the Glories of Your Reign.

We, Madam, have many Reasons to rejoice at our happy Prospect, and to thank You for Your Care of us during so troublesome and expensive a War.

The Provisions sent to Two of the Islands, and recommending them to the Parliament on their Misfortunes, are such Instances of Your Majesty's Piety, Charity, and Care of the most distant Parts of Your Government, that all Ages must celebrate Your Goodness.

And we must further thank Your Majesty for making Colonel Parke *our General, whose Vigilance, Conduct, and Courage, has disappointed the Designs of our Enemies, and prevented their gaining any Advantage over us, since we have been so Happy as to have him our Governor.*

And when Montserrat *was lately attack'd, his Expedition in coming down to their Relief, when staying for the Man of War, might have been too late to have saved them; and his following the Enemy to every Place that was in Danger, till they dispersed themselves, may make them more cautious for the future to attack any of these Islands, now we have a Governor so ready to draw the rest to their Assistance, and personally to head them.*

We therefore pray Your Majesty for his longer Continuance amongst us; but we humbly submit it to Your Majesty's Pleasure, in case Your Majesty shall think it necessary for his Justification, that he personally answer the Complaints against him, wherein he is charged with Crimes we are perfectly ignorant of; tho' in the Station Your Majesty hath been pleased to place us; we should be better acquainted with his Actions, than those who have complain'd against him.

We therefore humbly take Leave to inform Your Majesty, that we know of no Male-Administration or Neglect of Duty our General Colonel Parke *has been guilty of, during the whole time he has govern'd these Islands.*

And we hope, that when he has clear'd himself of what his Enemies have laid to his Charge (which we have no manner of reason to doubt but that he will) he may be restored to this his Government.

And we humbly implore Your Majesty, that he may be continu'd our General.

It only remains for us to wish Your Majesty a continual Series of Prosperity, and a long and happy Reign, for the Good of Your People, to whom Your Life is the greatest of Blessings.

Geo. Liddell,
Geo. Milward,
J. Hamilton,
Wm. Byam,
Hen. Burrell,
Ste. Payne,
J. Bevon,
J. Norwood.

Dated at *St. Christophers, April* 6. 1710.

William Martin, *Clerk of the General Council.*

LONDON, Printed for *John Morphew* near *Stationers-Hall,* 1713.

· 13 ·

Anonymous, Some Instances of the Oppression and Male Administration of Col. Parke (1713)

THIS PAMPHLET, also published in 1713 and probably in London, is an answer to the previous one. In addition to providing specific rebuttals to much of the testimony in the earlier pamphlet, the anonymous author denied "that the Inhabitants of *Antegoa* went into that Insurrection meerly out of a wanton Uneasiness under Authority, without any Provocation," and recounted a number of incidents and behaviors to demonstrate the many ways in which Parke's "Tyranny, Oppression, and Male Administration" had contributed to "the Sufferings of the unhappy Inhabitants of *Antegoa* under his Government" and "to what Heighth the Governour carried his Tyranny and Oppression." Essentially, the author argued that Parke had turned Antigua into a military state, using troops to execute warrants and other civil processes and to seize private goods without due process and dispensing with Antiguan law whenever it pleased him. Quoting Parke as declaring that "there was no Law in *Antegoa* worth a Farthing, that he would have none of them, but would determine every thing according to his own Opinion," the author charged that Parke had "engrossed to himself . . . the whole Judicature of the Island," dispensed with acts at his pleasure, used the provost marshal to pack juries, interfered with elections, and "for several Years depriv'd that Island of the Benefit of Assemblies, by frequent Dissolutions and Adjournments." Notwithstanding all these problems, the author wrote, opposition to Parke only reached a boiling point after he used troops to disperse the Assembly during a meeting and threatened "to clap their Speaker in Irons." At that point, the colony's free inhabitants, "already terrified . . . by the implacable Rage of the Governor, the unbridled Licence and Insolence of his Partisans, the Soldiers," and "the defenceless State of the Colony," armed themselves and assembled in the capital, where they urged the governor to leave the colony. When Parke refused and fortified himself with his troops in Governor's House, the settlers' make-shift force marched on them, and upon receiving fire from the governor's troops, stormed the building. During the ensuing engagement, Parke managed to kill one of his adversaries before he was shot by another. This incident showed how far aggrieved settlers were willing to go in removing a person they considered an arbitrary governor. (J.P.G.)

Some Instances of the Oppression and Male Administration of Col. Parke, late Governor of the Leeward Islands, with an Account of the Rise and Progress of the Insurrection at Antegoa, and Remarks on a Paper intituled, Truth brought to light, or Murder will out.

It is with great Unwillingness that the Persons concerned in publishing of this do rake into the Ashes of one who has been so long in his Grave as Colonel *Parke* has; and they are far from having it in their Thoughts to justify that Insurrection, which has been so deeply repented of and lamented by the Persons concerned in it ever since. But since the above mentioned Paper has been handed about with unusual Industry, and that the Drift of it appears plainly to be to possess the World with an Opinion that the Inhabitants of *Antegoa* went into that Insurrection meerly out of a wanton Uneasiness under Authority, without any Provocation, and to load the Persons concerned in it, especially those who stand most in need of Her Majesty's Mercy, with monstrous Acts of Cruelty and Barbarity; It is hoped the Publishing of this will be thought very excusable, and that it will appear to what Heighth the Governor carried his Tyranny and Oppression from the following Particulars taken out of a great Number, the full History of which would make a large Volume.

That the said Governor soon after his Arrival began frequently to make use of Her Majesty's Troops in executing Warrants and other Civil Process, as in the Cases of *Patrick Cuningham, Darby Donavan,* and many others. Nor did he stop there, but made use of them many other ways, to the great Terror and grievous Oppression of the Inhabitants, which will be made out by the few following Instances.

First, The said Governor himself headed a Party of armed Soldiers, and with them entered the House of *Edward Chester,* where some Gentlemen were innocently merry, guilty of no Crime, sent nine of them to Gaol, two of them particularly, upon their offering to be Bail for those who were first committed, had them convicted of a Riot upon view, by *Michael Ayon* and two Justices, Persons intirely devoted to all his Purposes; tho' some of the Justices did not come to Mr. *Chester*'s House till after several of the Persons were committed to Prison: And in the Record of Conviction they were not charged with any particular Fact which made the Riot; nor indeed could the Justices find any colourable one: That this whole Matter was attended with many other very aggravating Circumstances.

That he entered upon the Free-hold of one *Elizabeth Hastings* with a Party of armed Soldiers; and though the House which he took Possession of in this Manner was of very little Value; yet the Circumstances of this Action were of the most Atrocious Nature; the Soldiers who siezed and maintained the Possession, declaring that they had Orders from him to set Fire to her other Houses, if she opposed them.

That he hired the Soldiers to beat the Gentlemen of the Country, promising them a Pistole for every one of them they should beat; and raising his Reward to five Pistoles, if they would beat some particular Persons whom he named to them, and telling them, that if he had some Companies he knew in *Flanders*, he would drive half the Planters off of the Island; and assuring not only the Soldiers of protecting them from Punishment, but also assuring some of the Officers and other of his Friends of Pardon if they should kill any of the Country Party, and of a very extraordinary Revenge if they should fall in the Quarrel; and this he used to do frequently: Part of this Article is proved by the Affidavit of Major *Buer*, and Part by the Affidavit of Sergeant *Bowes*.

That by this Encouragement many high Outrages were committed on the Persons of some of the most considerable Inhabitants; so many Instances of which can be proved, that it is needless to enumerate Particulars.

That by armed Soldiers he seized the Goods of, or rather plundered the Inhabitants; and this with the following Instance will more fully appear in the Case of Mr. *Edward Chester*.

The last Instance is his making use of armed Soldiers as his Guards, in his lewd Night Adventures; and now it will be proper to begin with Mr. *Chester*'s Case, which is briefly as follows:

Mr. *Chester* for Reasons (which afterwards appeared to the World) begged him not to come to his House; that he thereupon threatened *Chester* with the Stocks, and declared that he would come to his House whither he would or not; and that *Chester* might no longer obstruct his Designs, he attempted to take away his Life by a Prosecution set up on purpose, in which he did in the most scandalous bare-faced Manner endeavour (by his Presence and all manner of Artifice) to influence the Coroner's Inquest to find that one *Sawyer* died by a Blow given him by the said *Chester,* and brow-beat his Witnesses, and put Words into the Mouths of the Witnesses against him: but this Design miscarrying, he exprest the utmost Resentment against all Persons who would not co-operate with him in the Design, and particularly against the Justices who bailed *Chester,* tho' it was after the Coroner's Inquest had found that *Sawyer* died a natural Death; and afterwards declared that he did all this only to humble *Chester:* That all his Behaviour was looked upon with the utmost Indignation and Astonishment by almost the whole Inhabitants of that Island, who were no Strangers to the Governor's Motives. That the next Persecution of Mr. *Chester* was by making frequent and groundless Seizures of his Goods, and by this Means got into his Possession a considerable Part of Mr. *Chester*'s Estate. That all this while he frequented Mr. *Chester*'s House at unseasonable Times, and in different Disguises, till at length Mr. *Chester* by perfect Accident found him shulking behind the Door of a Room adjoining to Mrs. *Chester*'s Bed-chamber; that he no sooner found himself discovered but he drew his Sword upon Mr. *Chester,* who was undrest to his Shirt, pursued him out of his House, bid him fetch his Sword, and that he would fight him. At the same time whistled, and there came up two Soldiers with their Muskets shoulder'd, and then he told Mr. *Chester* that he never went unprovided, threaten'd to ruin him, if he would not take in his Wife again, whom he had turned out of doors upon this Occasion. That accordingly he came some time thereafter to Mr. *Chester*'s House with a Party of armed Soldiers, planted them at the Doors, and had a Quantity of Coco seized belonging to *Chester,* of the Value of eight hundred Pounds, which was carried from thence to the Governor's House by the Soldiers. That when the same was by order of the Court of Admiralty to have been restored to Mr. *Chester,* upon his giving Security to abide the Determination of the Queen and Council; and that when Mr. *Chester* had given the Security, and demanded the Coco of the Governor, he refused to deliver it, declaring he would apply the same to the separate Maintenance of Mrs. *Chester,* who never pretended to sue or apply for any such thing.

That another flaming Instance of his employing his Power to bear down and discourage People from any Opposition to him in his lustful Attempts, was in the Case of Mrs. *Dusaussay,* whom he attempted to ravish, and who disclosed the same to her Husband, which produc'd a warm Expostulation between him and Colonel *Parke,* who thereupon had him turn'd out of his Implopyment in the Custom-house, and otherwise so cruelly harass'd and persecuted by Justices of the Peace, Creatures of the said Governor, who refus'd to admit Mrs. *Dusaussay* to make Oath before them of the Violence offer'd to her by the Governor. That he was drove for Shelter to the Woods and Mountains, and at last off of the Island, where he dy'd, leaving his Wife and three small Children in a very miserable Condition, to whom the Governor afterwards caused great Offers to be made to be silent in this Matter.

That he engrossed to himself in Chancery the whole Judicature of the Island, declaring that there was no need of a Chief Justice, that there was no Law in *Antegoa* worth a Farthing, that he would have regard to none of them, but would determine every thing according to his own Opinion, which was always apparently swayed by Corruption or Resentment; that by his arbitrary and illegal Proceedings in this Court all property became very precarious.

That he made as free with the Legislature as the Judicature of the Island, by altering the Writs for Elections of Assembly, Men both in Form and Substance, to exclude particular Persons, and assum'd to himself the Determination of Elections; so that by this Method, the Assembly must have been (in effect) chosen by him; but this not succeeding to his Wish, he for several Years depriv'd that Island of the Benefit of Assemblies, by frequent Dissolutions and Adjournments; and declar'd, that whenever they should meet, he would throw such Rubs in their way that they should do no Business: And when it is consider'd how necessary the Meeting of Assemblies is for the Security of that Colony, and Preservation of the Credit thereof, this Part of that Article will not (it's hoped) be thought a trifling Matter; but this cannot be wonder'd at from a Governor, who took upon him in express Terms, in an Order to the Collector of the Powder-Duty, to dispense with an Act or Statute of that Island in full Force.

That (to have the Persons as well as the Estates of the Inhabitants in his Power) he declared he would have no Provost Marshal, but such as would return such Jurors as he should direct, that accordingly he afterwards appointed one *Michael Ayon* Provost Marshal, who was so proper a Person for his Purpose, that he declar'd he would shoot any Man in the Island through the Head, upon the Governor's verbal Order.

That by his disarming, and suffering to go to ruin the Platforms, and other the most useful Fortifications of the Island, the same was reduced to a very defenceless Condition. That when the Island was in great Danger of being attacked by the Enemy, he drew the Forces to the Town of Saint *John's*, a Place not tenable, nor to be made so, by which Disposition the Landing must have been yielded to the Enemy, contrary to common Sense and all former Experience, by which they had found the great Advantage in disputing the Enemies Landing, and also contrary to the unanimous Opinion of the Council of Officers, so that whether this was a real or affected Ignorance in Military Matters, it concern'd the Inhabitants but very little, since this Conduct must have been fatal to the Island, if the Enemy had made any Attempt upon it.

That great Quantities of Provisions were sent by Flags of Truce, and otherwise to the Enemy, and the Presumptions were very strong, that the same was done by his Connivance, nay the Affidavits of *Jedediah Hutchison*, Esq; late Chief Justice of Saint *Christophers;* and *Peter Heyfield* of the same Island, Chyrurgeon, go a great way in proving that he was concern'd in that Trade; however that Matter was, no Care was taken to prevent it, tho' it carry'd such ruinous Consequences in it to Her Majesty's Colonies; and tho' he was so frequently address'd upon that Head by the Assembly of *Antegoa*. Nor did he stop there, but gave the Command of Flags of Truce to Persons of the most desperate Fortunes, and suspected Characters; and particularly to one *John Bermingham*, against whom he had given Information to the Assembly, that he offer'd his Service to the Enemy to plunder *Antegoa*, and assur'd them that he would have him prosecuted for it. This very much alarm'd the Inhabitants to see such a Person trusted in this manner. Nor did their Fears prove groundless, the said *Bermingham* having since that gone over to the Enemy and plunder'd *Berbuda*, one of the Leeward Islands; and after that, spirited the Enemy up to an Expedition to *Antegoa*, in which he was their chief Pilot, which might have prov'd very fatal to the said Colony, if their Fleet of small Vessels had not been met with by the *New Castle* Man of War in their Passage thither, and dispers'd.

And since his Conduct to the last Minute of his Life, kept pace so well with his Declarations, it will not be improper to close this part relating to his Oppression and Male Administration, with the following Declarations publickly made by him.

That he declar'd if he knew that any Persons were going home to complain of him, he would clap them in a Dungeon, and there they should perish, and that there was more ways to kill a Dog than one.

That in another publick Conversation (when there happen'd some Discourse about an Affront, said to be offer'd to the Governor of a Neighbouring Colony) he declar'd that if he had been served so, he would have drove the People to Rebellion, seized their Estates, and left them to redress themselves.

That he declared publickly at the Island of Saint *Christophers*, upon the receiving of some displeasing News from *Antegoa*, that if he must lose his Government, he would leave the Island of *Antegoa* in a Flame; this last Declaration is prov'd by the Affidavit of *Jedediah Hutchison*.

That the foregoing Instances are but a very small Sketch of the Tyranny, Oppression, and Male Administration of Colonel *Parkes*, and in Consequence of the Sufferings of the unhappy Inhabitants of *Antegoa* under his Government. And if any further Attempts are made to justify that Governor's Conduct, a full History of it shall be publish'd.

That the Truth of the several Matters herein before-mentioned, was clearly made out by Proofs taken publickly in *Antegoa*, in the Presence of Colonel *Parke*, or at least after three Days notice given to him, to attend according to Her Majesty's Directions contain'd in Her Letter, commanding him to repair to Her Royal Presence, to make his Defence to the Complaints (except the Matters to which the Proofs are subjoin'd) and the Proofs to all of them are ready to be produced, if the Truth of the said Matters is called in question.

That by the Proceedings of the Governor, of which the foregoing are but a small Specimen, that Colony was in the utmost Disorder and Confusion, and the Inhabitants under the most distracting Fears, by repeated Advices from *Martinico*, the Arrival of a considerable Force, and daily Expectation of a greater, and the Enemies calling in of their Privateers, which gave but too just Grounds to fear *Antegoa* would be attack'd; and the Fate of *Nevis* and St. *Christophers* a few Years before had sunk so deep in the Minds of the People of *Antegoa*, that their Danger from the Enemy was by much their most anxious Concern.

That (after a long Intermission of Assemblies) the Governor was prevail'd with by the Council to call an Assembly, which no sooner met, but the Governor rais'd such Difficulties, and tenaciously insisted upon them (notwithstanding) the Interposition of the Council, and Submissions of the Assembly, that no Measures could be taken for the Security of the Island. That the Assembly (finding this, and that he had tore their Messages sent to him to remove these Difficulties) resolved to wait upon him in a Body, to add the greater Weight to their Address, which they accordingly did (having first asked leave.) That the Speaker only enter'd the Room where he sat in Council, and tender'd him their Address in a very respectful manner, which he refus'd, clapped his Hand several times to his Sword, charg'd the Assembly with a Riot, and threaten'd to clap their Speaker in Irons; that the Council upon this begg'd him not to esteem the Assemblies waiting upon him with their humble Address a Riot, and pray'd him to suffer it to be read, which he passionately refus'd, commanded the Assembly instantly to withdraw, and accordingly they did in a great Consternation. That immediately after the Assembly had enter'd the Court-house, where the Council-Chamber is, they were follow'd by a Party of arm'd Soldiers, with an Officer at their Head. That their Behaviour made several Members of the Assembly ask some of them if they intended to fire upon the Assembly, that they answer'd, they only wanted Orders so to do. That till the Assembly and their Speaker had been threaten'd and us'd in the foregoing manner by the Governor, he had neither been insulted by Word or Action. That on the contrary they assur'd him they would overcome all Difficulties, that something might be done for the common Security; but after that Usage (it is very probable) that some Members of the Assembly, and others who heard and saw what pass'd, might be transported to very violent Expressions. That this soon reach'd the Ears of the Inhabitants already terrified, on all sides, by the implacable Rage of the Governor, the unbridled Licence and Insolence of his Partisans, and the Soldiers, the defenceless State of the Colony, the great Preparations of the Enemy, and (from his past Conduct, and the present Situation of Affairs) having nothing but Ruin and Destruction in view, if they should be attacked whilst he was at their Head, they flocked to the Town of *Saint John*'s with their Arms, the next Day of the Meeting of the Assembly, which was two Days thereafter. That the Lieutenant Governor, and such of the Council as were then in Town, hereupon addressed him to visit some other Island of his Government, that they in conjunction with the Assembly might provide for their Security, by preparing some wholesome Laws to be laid before him, for his Approbation or Disallowance, and sent the same to him by Col. *George Gamble*, one of their Members, and an intimate Friend of the Governor's. That this having no effect upon him, the Inhabitants then in Arms sent a Message to him by the said Col. *Gamble* and the Speaker of the Assembly, desiring him to dismiss his Troops, and to go to some other Island of his Government, and thereupon assured him that they did not design to hurt his Person. That he gave a most exasperating Answer, telling them he despised their Proposals, that he had Men enough to drive all the Men in the Island before him. That he had loaden his Cannon with Cross-bar, and a hundred Small Shot each: That he expected no Quarter, and would give none: That he had ordered the Town to be set on fire upon their Approach. That Col. *Gamble* and the Speaker begged him to discharge his Troops, reserving his usual Guard, and offered themselves as Hostages, that the Inhabitants should do so likewise. That he thereupon demanded five more to be added to the Speaker, and named such Persons as he knew would not trust themselves in his hands. That *Gamble* and *Crump* upon that told him, that they had no Commission to agree to a particular Nomination. That by this Answer, and the Information they had of his promising the Plunder of the Town and Plantations of the Islanders that should be killed, to the Soldiers, the enraged Multitude became incapable of hearkening any longer to Reason, and marched up in two Bodies to the Governor's House. That the Governor's Party fired first upon the Inhabitants, that after that there was a sharp Fire kept up on both sides for some little time, and several on both sides killed and wounded. At length the Inhabitants advanced upon the Governor's Party, and Captain *Piggot* (who headed the Party of the Inhabitants that were engaged) got up to the Governor's before any other Person, and immediately begged the Governor to surrender himself, assuring him that no Hurt should be done to his Person. That the Governor thereupon fired his Pistol upon him, and one of the Governor's Party at the same time shot him through the Back, of which he instantly died: So that whilst he was endeavouring to save the Governor's Life (which might have been in great danger from the enraged Multitude) he lost his own; and it is commonly believed by the hands of *Michael Ayon*. That presently thereafter the Governor received a Wound in the Thigh, of which he died in about two Hours after. That very soon thereafter the whole Multitude came up to, and great Numbers of them got into the Governor's House, and some Persons were wounded, and other great Disorders committed by them in their first Fury, as always does happen upon such dismal Occasions.

That the first Part of this Account will appear pretty well justified by an Address to Her Majesty from the Lieutenant Governor and Council, who have never shown any Partiality to the Persons concerned in this Insurrection. That what passed betwixt the Governor and the Persons who carry'd the Message to him from the Inhabitants in Arms, is proved by the joint Affidavits of those two Persons. That the Promises made by him to the Soldiers, is proved by the Affidavits of several of them. That the Governor's Party fired first, is proved by the Affidavit of *George Dewit*, a Person of unquestionable Credit, who was no ways concerned in it, and saw the whole distinctly from his own House.

Remarks upon a Paper entituled, Truth brought to Light, or Murder will out.

The first Remark upon the Matters previous to the Murder of Col. *Parke*, is upon the Affidavit of *Thomas Cook*, the Improbability of which is so great, that a Company of Gentlemen, or any of them, should make such a Proposal to a Soldier, who was an utter Stranger to them, to murder his General, that it will sufficiently damn this Story with all thinking People.

The next is upon Col. *Parke*'s being wounded in the Arm, said to be done by the Command of *Bastian Otto:* It is not very likely that Mr. *Otto* should since confess it to be done by his Command; but (let that Matter be as it will) the Inhabitants of *Antegoa* did in general detest and abhor it, and so it cannot affect them.

As to the other two Matters (tho' they might be easily answered) yet they are not material enough to swell this Paper with an Answer to them.

Remarks on that part of the Paper called, An Abstract of Depositions relating to the Murder of Daniel Parke, Esq;

The first Remark is, that the Depositions therein mentioned have been all made in so clandestine a manner, that it has been impossible for the Persons concerned to get at the Knowledge of them, and so cannot be prepared to detect the many Falsities therein contained, tho' several of these Deponents continued in *Antegoa* a long time after the Arrival of the present Governor, before whom they might have made what Depositions they pleased, and the Persons concerned might have had a fair Opportunity of disproving the same, and taking other Measures for their Defence.

The next Remark upon this Paper shall be to the credit of the Persons whose Depositions it is said to be an Abstract of, and First, It is to be observed that these Persons in general have every way discovered a very great Resentment and Rancour in this Affair, and an uncommon Zeal in Pursuit of the Blood of the Persons particularly charged in their Depositions. As to *Michael Ayon,* It is humbly offered to the Consideration of the Reader, that he was carryed or went out of *England* in a manner not very creditable, came to *Antegoa* a Common Soldier, and continued there in very Poor Circumstances till Col. *Parke* found him out to be such a Person as would be proper for, and thoroughly applicable to his Purposes; and accordingly got a Deputation for him to be Provost-Marshal of *Antegoa;* and in some time thereafter made him Provost-Marshal General of the *Leeward Islands,* though that Office was then vested in *John Perrie* by Her Majesty's Letters Patents, and afterwards made him his Private Secretary, and gave him an Ensign's Commission in Col. *Jones* his Regiment; and how far he had given himself up to execute all Col. *Parke*'s Commands, sufficiently is shown by his Declaration that he would shoot any Man in the Island through the Head, upon Col. *Parke*'s Verbal Order. And that will further be made out by the many highly Illegal and Arbitrary things done by him as Provost-Marshal by the Governor's Command, and the great Enormities he has been guilty of by the Governor's Encouragement; and when all this is considered, and how beneficial all these Imployments and his absolute Resignation to Col. *Parke's* Will was, It is humbly hoped his Testimony will have no great Credit.

As to *Richard Oglethrop,* it is to be remarked, that he acted under the said *Ayon* as Under-Marshal, at mean Wages, which had for some time been his only means of Subsistence, and that he and *George French* have always been esteemed Persons of so little Reputation, that their Evidence would be least credited where they are best known, and of such desperate Fortunes that they were glad of this Opportunity to get off of *Antegoa* from their Creditors, and so avoid a Gaol, which must otherwise unavoidably have been their Fate. That they and *Gousse Bonnin* by their extream Poverty are at present drudging for their daily Bread from the Prosecutors of this Affair;

and what may be expected from Persons under such a slavish Dependance, is too obvious to want any further Explanation.

That *Lucia French, Margaret Mac Mahon, Elizabeth Sweegle, Elinor Martin,* and *Alice Laurence,* are all of them Persons noted for their lewd profligate Lives, and infamous Characters. *Lucia French* having been publickly whipt for her enormous Crimes. *Elizabeth Sweegle* having not only been an abandoned Strumpet, and particularly to Col. *Parke,* but having also frankly declared that she would leave not only Father and Mother, but also her Saviour to follow Col. *Parke;* and *Elinor Martin* having been a known Assistant to him in his Lewdness, and, as was commonly reported in *Antegoa,* in his debauching her own Daughter.

That these Matters are not only Notorious in *Antegoa,* where these Persons live, or have lived; but could have been proved by several Masters of Ships, and others who are some time since gone to *Antegoa,* had the said Abstract of Depositions been Published before their Departure.

That *Daniel Rosengrave* did not only publickly, by his Declarations and otherwise, manifest his implacable Malice against, and insatiable Thirst after the Blood of the Persons accused in his Deposition, and had no other bread for the Support of his Life, but from the Prosecutors, but was likewise entertained by them with great Hopes of some Post of Preferment by their Means.

That Serj. *Bowes* was one of the most noted Instruments of Col. *Parke*'s Oppression, and now it must be submitted to the Candid judicious Reader, what Credit is to be given to the Depositions of such Persons, taken in such a manner, that the Persons thereby accused have no Opportunity to provide for their Defence against them.

And now it will be proper to make some few Remarks upon the Depositions themselves, as they stand abstracted in that Paper, especially where the Falsities and Misrepresentations therein contained are not sufficiently detected by the foregoing Account of the Rise and Progress of that Insurrection, which is proved as above, and will upon the Strictest Examinations be found very agreeable to Truth.

The first Matter mentioned to be sworn to by *Michael Ayon* is a sufficient Specimen of the Sincerity to be expected from him in the rest of his Depositions, and that is, that the Assembly of *Antegoa* insisted to have the Negative Voice lodged in their Speaker, tho' they only insisted upon having the Bills past by the Chief Governor, Council and Assembly, signed (as they ever had been) by the Chief Governor first, and afterwards by their Speaker, and always disclaimed any Pretensions to the Negative Voice in their Speaker, nor was that ever claimed directly or indirectly by any Assembly of *Antegoa,* tho' the Bills had always been signed by the Chief Governor first, and afterwards by the Speaker, as will appear by the Minutes of the Assembly relating to that Matter.

That the Matters contained in the Second and Third Paragraph are either not material enough to be answered or remarked upon in this, or are mentioned to be upon hear-say Evidence only.

That the next Remark shall be upon that part of the fourth Paragraph that charges *Thomas Kirby* to have advanced some Paces before the rest, and to have fired the first Shot against the General, and that the rest followed his Example; and affirms that the General would not suffer any on his part to fire, till one of the Soldiers was wounded. That the General's Party fired first, is already proved; and it is to be observed, that after that the Inhabitants did not march in any Order, but every one advanced as fast as he could; and it could not then be hoped that the Inhabitants would not return the Fire upon the General's Party: So that it does not seem to be material who fired first, since every one fired as soon as he thought it would be to any purpose; and indeed there was so great Firing upon both sides immediately after the first Fire from the General's Party, that it was very hardly observable who fired first. And it is further to be observed upon this matter, that a great many Deponents Names are placed at the Front of this Paragraph, as if they had all sworn to every Matter contained in it, when there is great reason to suspect it would appear otherwise by the Depositions; and this Suspicion is the more reasonable, since in another Paragraph Serj. *Bowes* and *Alice Lawrence*'s Depositions are brought to prove Mr. *Kerby*'s firing first, tho' Serj. *Bowes* is one of the Deponents to all the Matters contained in this Paragraph; nor is this candid Practice confin'd to this Paragraph only, as must appear to every observing Reader. It is further to be remarked, that in the Close of this Paragraph the Deponents are made to swear, that *Daniel Mac Kinnen* and *Samuel Watkins* were the principal Contrivers and Advisers of that bloody and barbarous Massacre, though (from the Address and Message which was sent to the Governor) it is plain that great Endeavours were used by the Inhabitants to prevent the bringing Matters to such Extremities, as must end in Blood; and the Deponents above all Men (being Col. *Parke*'s Creatures) could never be made Privy to the Contrivance of this

Matter (if there was any); and it is left to the Reader's Judgment where such Deponents can be presumed to stop in their Depositions.

The Deposition of *Margaret Bryan* is sufficiently disparaged by the Affidavit of *Sarah Colongs,* who washed the Governor's Back, and shrouded him, and declares that she saw no Wound or Bruise about his Back, or in any part of his Body or Limbs, save that in his Thigh; and that he was very uneasy, and tumbled himself to and fro after Doctor *Bonnin* dressed that Wound, which he could not have done, had his Back been broke.

That the Depositions of *Lucia French, Margaret Mac Mahon,* and *Mary Harvey,* declaring they saw the Governor stripped of almost all his Clothes, and dragged by one Leg and one Arm down some steps of Stone Stairs; that his Head trailed from one Step to another, till they left him exposed to the scorching Sun in the open Street, is sufficiently confuted by the Answer of Doctor *Gousse Bonnine,* upon Oath to the Interrogatories exhibited to him at *Antegoa* in Council, who was the Chyrurgion that attended the Governor, and declares that he came out of the House at the same time that the Governor was carried out, and that he neither saw nor knew that any Person had beat, wounded, bruised or dragged him. That he went to the House to which the Governor was carryed, and tarried with him till his Death. It is further to be observed upon this Head that had the Governor (who preserved his Speech almost to the last) after he was brought to that House, been either dragged or otherwise ill used after he received his Wound in the Thigh, he would certainly have discovered to the said *Bonnine,* who was not only his Chyrurgion, but had likewise been with him all the Time of the Engagement, and Mr. *Bonnine* will hardly be suspected of concealing such a Matter, if it had been told him, and this will in a great measure discredit what is said to be sworn to by *Elizabeth Sweegle* in the next Paragraph, whose infamous Character and monstruous Declaration mentioned in the Remarks upon the Credit of the Deponents, will fully prevent her being credited in what she swears.

The next Deposition to be taken notice of is that said to be made by *George French, Lucia French,* and *Margaret Mac Mahon,* that Mr. *Kirby* presented a Pistol at *George French's* Head; when he was carryed off wounded, that they had no reason to doubt but he would have shot *French* had not a Gentleman who stood by interposed in his Favour. As to this whole matter it is to be remarked that the Deponents designedly conceal the Name of the Gentleman who interposed in favour of *George French,* for had they named him, the monstruous Villainous Falsity of this Deposition would have been easily exposed.

The last Answer to, or Remark upon any of the Depositions mentioned in that Paper, shall be to the Deposition of seven Persons affirming that *Thomas Kirby* was so far from doing any Acts of Humanity that Day, as he sets forth in a Petition to Her Majesty, that he was very active to do all the Mischief and Acts of Barbarity he could think of; and it is hoped that it will be thought very natural to observe upon these Depositions (if any such have been made) that they are of such a nature, as must blast the Credit of the Deponents with every fair Reader; for it is not, nor can it be pretended by any of them, that they saw every thing which Mr. *Kirby* did that Day; or had him all the time of that Action in their Eye; and therefore they cannot assert of their own Knowledge, that Mr. *Kirby* did all the Mischief he could; and if what one of the seven Deponents (*George French*) swears before, were true, That Mr. *Kirby* presented a Pistol to his Head, and would have shot him, if a Gentleman had not interposed in his favour, it would satisfy every impartial Reader, that *Kirby* did not do all the Mischief he could, since he was so easily diverted from this. But Mr. *Kirby* was so far from this Temper, that it's proved by the Affidavit of one of the Persons who carried off the General, that Mr. *Kirby* beg'd and pray'd every Person present to take all imaginable care that the General should not be abused by the Croud, and that the Plate in his House should be preserved. That he likewise desired Doctor *Bonnine* to go and dress the said Governor; nor did he stop there, but hindred some Persons (whose particular Friends were killed) from shooting and otherwise ill using the Governor; all which he could clearly prove, were he in *Antegoa*, as well as his Care of *Michael Ayon*, another of the seven Deponents, not only in protecting him from the Rage of some particular Persons highly incensed against him, but also in putting him into a Chair, and sending him to his own Lodgings by one *Philip Trant* and a Negro Man that attended the said *Kirby*. And now it is to be hoped, that what has been already said to the Credit of the Deponents, and to the Depositions, will fully excuse the Publishers of this Paper from taking any notice of the other Depositions therein mentioned, since they are made by Persons who have discovered themselves sufficiently by the foregoing Depositions. Especially since it is high time to close this Paper already (to the Regret of the Publishers) much too bulky, with some Remarks upon the Letter from the Council of *Antegoa* to Mr. *Richard Cary*, and the Address of the General Council of the *Leeward Islands* to Her Majesty, both recited in the Paper to which this is an Answer.

As to the Letter, it is to be observed, that whatever Opinion the Council of *Antegoa* was of at the time of signing that Letter, several of them did soon thereafter very much change their Opinions of him, and acquainted him with their Reasons, which they publickly declared to him in the Presence of a great Croud of People, when the Complaints were under Examination at *Antegoa*, and made then several Affidavits against him. But whatever was the Opinion of the Council of *Antegoa*, or the General Council at *St. Christophers*, the Facts will speak for themselves.

And it is further to be observed, that the Members of the General Council of the *Leeward Islands* are named by the Governor, so that whatever Address is obtained from them, is not much to be regarded; and it is a strong Presumption of his Guilt, to resort to so wretched a Defence.

· 14 ·

Samuel Mulford, Samuel Mulford's Speech to the Assembly at New-York [New York, 1714]

❧

As the proprietor of New York from the time of its capture from the Dutch in 1664, the Duke of York, later James II, managed to thwart powerful settler demands for the establishment in the colony of the kind of permanent representative government that every other English colony enjoyed. Only after the king was overthrown during the Glorious Revolution, and New York changed from a proprietary to a royal colony, did it obtain a secure elected assembly. By the time Robert Hunter (1666–1734) came to the governorship of the colony in 1710, however, the Assembly was firmly in control of the appropriation and disbursement of public revenues in New York and was claiming the same sort of parliamentary status within the colony that its counterparts had long enjoyed elsewhere. Charged by English authorities with trying to lessen the Assembly's authority by persuading it to grant a permanent revenue to cover public expenses, including the governor's salary, Hunter soon found himself at loggerheads with the Assembly which, wholly unintimidated by threats of intervention by the English Parliament, categorically refused to vote a permanent revenue. The resulting financial stalemate left Hunter having to scramble to find funds for various public expenses. After running up a considerable deficit during his first four years in office, he began to search for other means than legislative appropriation to pay his own and the colony's bills, establishing a chancery court to collect quit rents more effectively and using customs officers to collect admiralty and whale fees aggressively.

In April 1714, Long Island resident Samuel Mulford, representative of Suffolk County and an immigrant from Connecticut, vigorously attacked these measures in a speech in the Assembly, which he soon thereafter published and which is reprinted below. Complaining about ship seizures for trifling offenses and Hunter's appointing officers and running up public debts without the consent of the legislature, Mulford made an impassioned case that permitting Hunter "to make as many Debts in the Government as he pleaseth" and to have "the whole Disposing of all the Publick Monies" in his hands would soon "bring us and Posterity to be Tenants at Will" and thereby "alter the Constitution of *English* Government, & cause" the Queen's "Subjects in this Colony to be under Arbitrary Government; their Persons and Estates, at the Pleasure of the Governour" and without "due Course of Law." Calling upon his fellow legislators to make sure that the government was "carried on . . . according to the Laws and Constitutions of *English* Government," he urged the Assembly to continue neither to yield to Hunter's demands for payment of the debts he had created nor to let him have full control over the disbursement of appropriated funds. When Mulford published his speech, Hunter retaliated by having him prosecuted for libel, but the jury refused to convict. (J.P.G.)

Samuel Mulford's Speech to the Assembly at New-York, April the Second, 1714.

Gentlemen;

The ill Measures that have been taken, and the Foundation laid within this Colony, which may bring the Subjects within the same to be Tenants at Will, both Persons and Estates, causeth me to make this Speech to this House; Requesting them to Consider well what they do: and not Sell a Birth-right Privilege for Fear, Favour, Affection or Lucre of Gain; but prove true to the Trust reposed in them: not to make ill Presidents and Laws, pernicious to the Publick: But to endeavour the Government may be carried on, for Her Majesties Benefit, and the Good of the Subjects; according to the Laws and Constitutions of *English* Government.

It is not unnecessary to mention the ill Circumstances the Colony was under in the time when a Duty was settled on the Importation of Goods, for the Support of Government: there was not any Port or Officers appointed, where to make Entry of their Vessels, and get Clearing when Outward Bound, except at *New-York;* where there was so many Officers and Subtil Fellows to Inspect into every nice Point in the Law, and if they were not fulfilled and observed in every particular, their Vessels were Seised: So that not any man was fit for Master of a Vessel to go to *New-York,* except he were a Lawyer; and then they should not escape, except it was by Favour. As I was informed, several were made Sufferers, as followeth; One Vessel coming from the *West Indies,* had some Barrels of Pomento on Board, in which, one Barrel had some Prohibited Goods in it, unknown to the Master: A Sailor makes Information, the Vessel was Seised; altho' the Master proffer'd to make Oath he knew not any thing of it, yet the Vessel and Cargo was Condemned. A Coaster coming to *New-York,* made Entry at the Office, amongst other Goods Twelve Bridles; but afterwards there was but Eleven of them, for which his Vessel was Seised: but he was favoured so much, that for the Sum of *Twenty* or *Thirty Pounds,* he got his Sloop Clear. Another Coaster coming to *New-York;* it seems a Woman sent a Hat by the Master, a Present to a Boy Related to her, Living in *New-York;* the Sloop was Seised about bringing of that Hat: But (as I was informed) was Favoured, that for the value of about *Twenty Pounds* got Clear. These and several other, such like Measures being taken, much discouraged men to come to *New-York*. But in this time, we of the County of *Suffolk*, Namely *Southold, South Hampton* and *East Hampton*, were the greatest Sufferers; we not having an Office to Enter and Clear at: we having some small Coasting Vessels, not suffered to Load and Unload, except they went to *New-York* to Enter and Clear. And Three Sloops, Namely *Benjamin Horton, James Petty* and *Joseph Petty* Masters, coming from *Boston* to *New-York*, there made Entry of their Vessels and Cargo, was detained Thirteen Days before they could procure a Clearing to go home to *Southold*. Such hard Measures discouraged Men to go to *New-York*. And part of the Money granted Their Majesties for Support of Government, was improved to hire Men & Vessels to come down under a pretence of hindering *Indian*-Trade with *Boston*; and to Search our Houses. They Seised *Edward Petty*'s Sloop, that had not been out of the Countrey in about Four Months before (lay at the Oyster Pond all Winter) in *March* fitted to Load for *New-York*, was Seised, carried to *New-York*, there Condemned, because he presumed to take Mr. *Nathaniel Silvester*'s Family and Houshold Goods on Board his Sloop, and carry them to *Rhoad-Island* the Fall before; and so the Poor Man was destroyed, because he did not go 120 Miles for a Permit, to carry him and his 60 Miles. Another Sloop, Namely *John Paine* Master, coming from *Boston* with a Clearing for *New-Haven*, being near Plumgut, the Officer went on Board him, Seised his Sloop, carried her to *New-York*, where she was Condemned because he had a Pillow of Six Pounds of Cotton Wool for his Bolster in his Cabbin, which he did not make it appear he had given Bond for. Another Sloop, *James Rogers* Master, (which he upon Terms had of Capt. *Cyprian Southack*) coming from *Boston* to *Shelter-Island*, was Boarded by the Officer from *New-York*, Seised, Carried away and Condemned, for having no Register. [It seems Capt. *Southack* had a Register when [he] went in her himself and when he put a Master in and went not himself, that Register would pass; but when *Rogers* hath it at *New-York*, it is called no Register.] Another small Sloop, Built up *Connecticut*-River, belonging to *John Davis* of *East Hampton*, took in the River a Load of Boards, went to *Rhoad-Island*, there took in Two Barrels of Molasses, and a Remnant in a Hogshead, went to the Custom-House for a Clearing to go to *New-York*, spake to the Officer to do it Authentick; *Davis* depending it was so, never looked into it until the Officer came on Board him, in or near Plumgut, demanding his Clearing, and read Two Barrels of Sugar and a Remnant in a Hogshead; the Master made answer, Not so; it is Molasses; there was never any Sugar on Board: It seems the Officer of *Rhoad-Island* mistook, and put in Sugar when it was Molasses; and sent under his Hand to *New-York* that it was his mistake; but all would not do, the Vessel was Condemned. So that almost all the Vessels belonging to our Towns were either Seised or Drove out of the Colony! There came a Boat from *Fairfield*, which a Young Man hired to bring him over to be Married; to carry his Wife and Portion home: the Boat was Seised, carried to *New-York* there lies and rots, as I am informed: The Young Man went up the Island, so got home with his Wife; and was compelled to Pay the Owner of the Boat *Thirty Pounds* for it. Our Vessels being thus carried and drove away, we had not Vessels to carry the Growth of the Countrey to a Market; nor bring us such Goods as we wanted: And if any come from *New-York* with Vessel and Goods, and the People would deal with them, the Trader would set the Price on his Goods, and also on what the People had of the Growth of the Countrey: And if the People would have sent their Effects to *New-York*, to have got Money to have Paid their Taxes, or Bought Goods, they were denied to have Fraight carried to *New-York*, or Goods brought from thence in their Vessels: So that they were Compelled to take what they were proffered or keep their Goods by them. *Southold* People being much Oppressed, as they informed me: Wheat then being at *Boston Five Shillings* and *Six-pence* per Bushel, and at *New-York* but *Three Shillings* and *Four-pence*; they had not liberty to carry or send it to *Boston*: Nor any Vessel suffer'd to come at them from thence: and not any coming to them from *New-York*, their Wheat and Grain lay by them, until the Vermin Eat and Spoil'd it; and they were much Impoverished thereby. So that by these and several other severe Measures being taken, whereby several were Destroyed, and much Impoverishing others: to the great Grievance of Their Majesties Leige People; Discouragement to the Inhabitants to Manure their Land, and causing several to Sell their Land, Move out of the Government; because they could not see how they should Live within the same. For where Trade is so Clogg'd, Navigation Discourag'd, Strangers Deter'd to come, causeth Goods Imported to be Scarce and Dear, and the Growth of the Countrey Low; which was the Misery of many in this Colony. Whereby in all probability, the Countrey was twice so much dampnified in settling that Duty, as it would be in a Land-Tax; besides the Flood of Debts which are endeavoured to be put on the Countrey, the greatest part of them created by settling that Duty, running in that Channel. And notwithstanding all the hardship those were under, whereby several Persons was Compelled to Sell part of their Necessary Food, to get Money to Pay their Taxes; the Money that did arise thereby, to the Sum of *Five Thousand Pounds per Annum*, and also several *Hundred Pounds* of the Countreys Money were imbezel'd, so that it was not applied to the Uses it was Granted for; and now endeavoured to be turned upon the Countrey; as if they were their Debts. This Duty was Granted to Their Majesties, for Support of Government, put into Their Majesties Officers Hands, to be issued out by Warrant under the Governour's Hand, by and with the Consent of the Council; it was not put into the Treasurer's Hands: if it had, the one half of it might have prevented any Crying Debts of the Government or Countrey. No doubt but Their Majesties did depend on the Fidelity of their Officers, not to imbezel the Monies: But it was otherwise; it was miserably imbezel'd: Part applied to disturb their Majesties Leige People. So that when there was Sufficient put into their Majesties Officers hands, for the Support of Government, and the same is imbezel'd, it cannot in Justice be a Debt of the Countrey; neither are they liable to make it good. If it had been in a Countrey Treasurer's Hands, appointed by the Countrey, and he had imbezel'd the Money, in such case the Countrey might be answerable for the same. So that in this case concerning these Debts before us, there is not any of them the Countreys Debts, but such as are made so by this House: And now to make such the Countreys Debts which they never created, but have already allowed sufficient to have made Satisfaction for the same, is great Injustice, and a matter of ill Consequence: For if the Governour for the time being may put in whom, and so many Officers as he will; to allow them what Salary he pleaseth; to make so many Debts in the Colony as he will: and the Commissioners at *Albany* to make what Debts they please (as many of these are such) and all these must be the Countreys Debts, then the Assembly may do for Assessors; lay Taxes on the Countrey, and shall not judge for themselves what part of their Estates they must part with for the Support of Government, but leave it to the Governour's good Nature, to let them have such part of their Estates to live upon as he pleaseth. And if I am not mistaken, this is the Foundation laid to bring us to this Condition; and if this House will Build on the Foundation laid, it will certainly do to bring us to be no more Free men, but Tenants at Will, both Persons and Estates: And making those the Debts of the Countrey, which was never created by them, is a large step to bring it to pass. Besides the Injustice to make them so, it is an encouragement to have more Debts made of the same Nature; and likewise makes a President for time to come; so becomes a matter of ill Consequence to swallow up all the Money that shall arise by the Excise: And not passing Bills to put Money into the Treasurer's Hands, so that there shall be little or no Money there for any Uses. But to settle a Duty upon importing of Goods, and let it pass in the same Channel it did formerly, which was so Pernicious to the Prosperity of this Colony. And I Know not how it will be better now than it was formerly: We have not any assurance of it; but leave it to his Excellency's Good Nature, the event thereof may better inform you, It is good to hope for the best; and that there will be no more Crying Debts: but there is but small reason for it; For if 5000 *Pounds per Annum* would not prevent them, I know not how 2800 should do it. By what hath been said, is sufficient to Convince any impartial Man, that the Subjects within this Colony have been lamentably Oppressed, if not Destroyed: Which caused the Assembly to Address Her Majesty that we might have a Treasurer; the Return to our House was by My Lord *Cornbury*, viz.

> I have received Letters from the Right Honourable the Lords Commissioners for Trade and Plantations, containing Her Most Sacred Majesties Commands to me, to permit the General Assembly of this Province to Name their own Treasurer, when they Raise Extraordinary Supplies for Particular Uses; and which are no part of Her Majesties standing and constant Revenue; but the Treasurer so Nominated must be Accountable to the Governour, Council and Assembly: Warrants may be issued by the Colonels, Captains, or other Persons, as the Act shall be directed.

By this we appointed our Treasurer; and several Years he received the Publick Monies (not having to do with Her Majesties standing and constant Revenue) being issued out by an Act, of Governour Council and Assembly, to the great Satisfaction of the Countrey. But I fear it is working about so, that our Treasurer shall be but as a Cypher; and we shall lose the Benefit that we might have had by him, as we had for some Years when the Money was in his hands: For I perceive the Countrey shall not employ or hire a Servant to do any Business for them, but he must be the Queens Officer, and so brought about to be Appointed and Commissioned by the Governour; and have a Salary from him: Neither shall the Bill pass for the Treasurer to Pay the Officers of the Assembly, and the Printer for Printing the Minutes of the House and Acts passed into Law (altho' Passed by the Council without any amendments, yet Rejected by his Excellency) to the great Damage of those Officers, and keep the Subjects in Ignorance, whom should be Subject to Law, and shall be Ignorant what they be. But these are Measures that the greater Advantage may be taken against them, and shall know what Law is, when they are Prosecuted for Transgressing the same. So that by such Methods as have been lately taken, would make a Man think, as if it were purposed that the Countrey should not have any Officers, nor to do with any Money, but what the Governour and Council pleaseth. It is true, it is worded in Her Majesties Instructions, viz. *That you shall not suffer the Publick Monies to be issued out, but by Warrant under your Hand, by and with the Consent of the Council.* I am of Opinion, that it cannot be understood that Her Majesty put those words into the Instructions, purposely to Empower his Excellency to make as many Debts in the Government as he pleaseth; and to have the whole Disposing of all the Publick Monies, with the Advice and Consent of the Council: Which in effect is to say, his Excellency hath the whole Disposing of the same at his Will. For if he may put in Office, whom and as many as he will; and allow them what Salary he pleaseth, and make so many Debts as he see cause in such case, what Member of the Council will gainsay his Paying such Debts as he pleaseth? So that in Reason the Sense must be taken, that it should be so issued that it might not be imbezel'd; but applied to the Uses it was granted for: and not for the Governour to appropriate it at his Pleasure, taking to himself an inherent Right to dispose of the Publick Money, altho' it be never so Pernicious to the Publick. I will not believe that Her Majesty ever intended those words should be Construed to alter *English* Government; nor to deprive the Subject of Property and Liberty. For by Her Command to my Lord *Cornbury,* that the Treasurer should issue it out as the Act directs; which was done by Act of Governour, Council and Assembly: And I am apt to be of Opinion, that it is the most Just way it can be issued; and nothing against the intent of Her Majesties Instructions, as is pretended. I look on such Pretences, only to divert it from coming into the Treasurer's hands; that so it may run in the old Channel that hath been so Pernicious to the Publick; and deprive the Countrey of having any thing to do about the issuing it: But it shall go according to Pleasure. The Injury that the Publick sustained (as before mentioned) was the Occasion of my being against settling it: Not as some pretend, because I was a Merchant. I defy that man that shall make it appear, that I prefer my own Interest to do the Publick an Injury. But I am apt to think, Those that make that pretence are just on the contrary; and care not how they Injure the Publick for their own Interest. They are very like to be the Libellers, that Charge those that speak Truth, and would prevent the Subjects of this Colony to be Tenants at Will, Persons and Estates, with flying in Her Majesties Face, and Charging Her with Tyrany: As tho' speaking Truth, and mentioning matter of Fact was a Crime. It was rather a Crime in the Libellers, to perswade the People that Her Majesty would alter the Constitution of *English* Government, & cause Her Subjects in this Colony to be under Arbitrary Government; their Persons and Estates, at the Pleasure of the Governour for the time being; and so give the Subject an ill Opinion of Her Majesty. I know that within the Realm of *England,* for any man by Speaking, Writing or Printing, to declare any thing that should give the People an ill Opinion of Their Majesties, is Treason by Act of Parliament: But here they do their Pleasure. And I am of the Opinion, that there is some amongst us that would have made Notable Counsellors in King *James* the Second's time: And I wish his Excellency had not any ill Counsellors now, that Bills do not pass now of the same Nature, as they did since he came to the Government.

We have an Undoubted Right and Property by the Law of God and Nature, settled upon the Subject by Act of Parliament; which is not to be taken from them by the Supream Power, without due Course of Law. The End of Law is to Secure our Persons and Estates; the End of Government to put the same in Execution, to that purpose that Justice be done: According to the Words in his Excellency's Instruction, viz. *You shall carry on the Government for Our Benefit, and Good of Our Subjects; according to the Laws and Customs of the Colony.* Now Gentlemen, I am not of the Opinion, that it is for the Good of the Subject, that the Governour should have liberty to make so many Debts in the Government as he pleaseth; and all the Publick Money run that Channel, that he should have the sole disposing of the same to what Uses he pleaseth, without the Consent of them that granted the same for Particular Uses. There hath been Money given to some Officers within this Colony, that instead of doing good, have improved all their Wit and Cunning to destroy, molest and disturb Her Majesties Subjects.

Seeing we have the Priviledge to be an Assembly, granted by Her Majesty, let us not Betray the Trust reposed in us: But Assist in having the Government carried on for Her Majesties Benefit, and the Good of the Subject; and Oppose all Measures taken to bring us and Posterity to be Tenants at Will, left by degrees we are brought to it. Be not drove by Threats, nor drawn by Flattering: But discharge a good Conscience towards GOD and Men. Although a Complaint went Home against us, and Threatned that if we would not settle a Revenue, the Parliament would do it for us; and many Libels to Scandalize, Vilify and Reproach us: and Scandalous Reports raised, as if we had not done our Duty; and would not do any thing for Support of Government, but would let it Starve. Which drew several to Consent to what they did not Well Understand, or else I am much mistaken; for I hope better of them, than to do an Injury to the Publick (tho' some for their own Interest might do it.) If we must be Enslaved, it were better to have it Forc'd upon us, then for us to bring it upon our Selves. And what Justice have any Person or People, when Judgment is given against them before they are called to Answer for themselves: but shall not be suffered to speak. And for those Libellers, they may Write what they please, when Ashamed to set their Names to what they Assert: So I pass them to be such Spirit as would be Troublers of Her Majesties good Subjects. And for those that Report we would Starve the Government, is but a False Narration to make Clamour, and spread a False Report: For how is the Government Starved? When we have helped the Governour to 3110 *Pounds*, for *Three Years* towards his Salary (besides what he hath had in the *Jerseys*.) Which is more than the *Three Governours* of *Boston, Connecticut* and *Rhode-Island* have had for all Three of their Salaries, for the same time. And the other Officers of the Government might have had their Salaries, if his Excellency would have Pleased to Assented to the Bills for that purpose. And seeing we have a Right to Sit here a General Assembly, let us think what Governour *Dungan* use to say; viz. *I cannot do you any Harm, if you can keep your own Dogs from Biting you*. It will be Well if there be not any such amongst us; I hope there is not so many that shall make us Tenants at Will; and make a Man Ashamed to have his Name mentioned to be in such an Assembly. I can but Do or Suffer: but am in hopes, you will Consider well what you do, for the Time Present and to Come.

Much more might have been said, but this may be Sufficient to put you in mind of the *Ill Measures* that was taken, and the *Ill Consequences thereof*; and if it may be Prevented for the future. Although We are Compared to a *Pevish Child*, that Cried for Salt Beef for its own Hurt; yet I hope, you will have the Sense of the *Burn't Child*, which Dreads the Fire: and not be like Persons *Non Compos Mentus*, to Wilfully Run into the same.

S. Mulford.

· 15 ·

[Robert Hunter], *Androboros:* A Biographical Farce in Three Acts [New York, 1714]

THE INTENSE legislative resistance that Robert Hunter encountered during the early years of his governorship in New York, and his loss of metropolitan support with the fall of the Whig ministry in England, eventually forced him, in 1713–15, to negotiate a deal with the New York legislature, whereby he abandoned his quest for a permanent revenue and instead agreed to a five-year revenue bill allowing the Assembly to continue to appoint the treasurer in charge of collecting and disbursing its appropriations. This compromise, and Hunter's success in getting his supporters into the Assembly, led to an abatement of conflict, and for the remainder of his decade-long term he found his administration much more agreeable. As a consequence of his early difficulties, however, he developed a profound contempt for his opponents in the legislature and for such metropolitans as hoped to succeed him, including his immediate predecessor, Edward Hyde, 3rd Earl of Clarendon, and Francis Nicholson, whom the Tory administration in London had named "governor of governors" for the American plantations. A friend of contemporary satirists Joseph Addison, Richard Steele, and Jonathan Swift, Hunter turned to that literary genre, writing, in 1714, *Androborus,* the first play published in colonial English America. Androborus was Nicholson, and both Hunter's foes and his friends were easily identified by those familiar with New York's existing political situation. Through his scathing indictment of their follies, ignorance, and parochialism, Hunter subjected his adversaries to a level of ridicule that may well have turned the political tide against them and ensured his political ascendancy for the remainder of his tenure. Certainly, it was the most ambitious example of political satire produced anywhere in colonial British America before 1770. (J.P.G.)

ANDROBOROS

A

B{i}ographical Farce
In Three Acts, *VIZ*.
The SENATE,
The CONSISTORY,

AND

The APOTHEOSIS.

By Governour {Robert} Hunter.

Printed at Monoropolis *since* 1st August, 1714.

Drammatis Personae.

Androboros,	*Coxcomb,*
Keeper,	*Mulligrub,*
Deputy,	*Cobus,*
Speaker,	*Solemn,*
Æsop,	*Door-Keeper,*
Doodlesack,	*Fizle,*
Tom of Bedlam,	*Flip,*
Babilard,	*Messenger.*

SCENE
Long Gallary in Moor-Fields.

The Dedication To Don. Com. Fiz.

Right Dreadful SIR!

Cerdo Gloucestriensis, an Author of the last Century, of great Sagacity, observ'd well, That *Runto Polimunto Plumpismenoi Raperpandico*—What d'ye stare at? This is good *Greek* for ought you know, and contains a Mystery, which shall continue so, unless you Reveal it; and so no more of that. The following *Elionophysalo Fizlical Farce* having fallen into my Hands by a most surprizing Accident, it seemeth meet unto me that it should, with all due Reverence Kiss yours. Here it lies at your Feet, take it up. Now read the first Act,—Have ye done? What's the matter Man? Have ye got the Gripes? A Plague on your Sower Faces. Bring him a Dram. What have you to do, had you to do, or ought you to have to do with the *Senate?* You smell a Rat, you say. Be it so. But compose your self, and now Read the Second Act,—How d'ye like it, ha? *O Hooo, T'churrrrrrrrrtch,* I can say that as Loud as you can do; and if you'll but leave out these Damnable *R*'s and *T*'s which make it so hard in Pronounciation, and harder in Digestion, I like it better than you do. You don't believe me! and I don't believe in you; and this is a perilous Article in a Mans Belief too; For one who dy'd a very good *Christian,* was sentenc'd by your Sanctity to be bury'd a *Pagan,* only because he seem'd to believe that you were some-what Thick of believing; yet you are a Christian, a very good Christian,

So was your Leader, Major Weere,
Burnt for Bu——ry, God be here.

He had a good Gift of the Gob too: You were bred up in the same Accademy, the same Principles, and the same way of Worship: All the Difference between you lies in this nice point, He Worship't the Dev'l instead of God, and you worship God as if he were the Dev'l. Come to't again, first take two Turns cross the Room, Crossways, I say, Wipe the Sweat from your Brows, and sit down. Now read the Third Act, I'll sing the while,

It is an Old Maxim, et c'est Escrit,
Au trou de mon cul, look there you'll sie't,
When the Head is Be——ck't the Body's Beshit,
Which no Body dare Deny, Deny,
Which no Body dare Deny.

Read on, and be hang'd, don't mind me, Man, I sing for my own Diversion.

But 'tis strange how Notions are chang'd of late,
For 'tis a New Maxim, but odd one, That
Ce que pend a nos culs doit nous garnir latete,
That I flatly and boldly Deny, Deny,
That I flatly and boldly Deny.

What is the Matter now? Is he Dead? or is't a Qualm? Holo, a Hay! Who waits there? some burn't Feathers, *Sal Armoniack?* No, No, Let him smell to the Skirt of his own Garment. So, he Recovers. Poor *Fiz!* who could have thought that you were so quick of Smelling! Come, Man, take Courage; What have You or I to do with it? Let the Gall'd Horse wince, our Withers are unwrung. But tell me, will you be quiet for the Future? You shall be paid for't, nay, you have been paid for't; and it is hard that Men must be Brib'd for Not doing what they ought Not to do. I remember an Odd Fellow upon *Pont Neuf* who got his Livelihood by as Odd a Stratagem; He procur'd himself a Portable Forge and Bellows, which he carried under his Cloak, and having heated a small Iron red hot, he would lug it out and present it to the Gentlemen who pass'd that way, with this Complement, *Good Sir! Pray Sir! give me leave to run my hot Iron into your Arse.* When the Gentleman started at the Extravagance and Danger of the Motion, he continued, *Nay, Sir, if you don't like it, pay me but a Sol Marquee for the heating of my Iron, and there is no harm done.* Now had he insisted upon the Performance of the Operation aforesaid, after payment for the necessary Apparatus, he deserv'd to have his Bones broke; but he was most commonly satisfied, and all the Consequence was a fit of Laughter.

Now, I know that it is not an easie matter for you to get rid of your Forge and Bellows, but can't you blow your Bellows and heat your Iron at home, and quit that unaccountable Rage of Running it into your honest quiet Neighbours Arses, who pay you amply, and meerly for Forbearance? But I have done. Peace be with ye, I mean such a one as he made who made you a COM——

And it was a most Masterly stroke of Art
To give Fizle Room to Act his part;
For a Fizle Restrain'd will bounce like a F——t,
Which no Body can Deny, Deny,
Which no Body can Deny.

But when it Escapes from Canonical Hose
And fly's in your Face, as it's odds it does,
That a Man should be hang'd for stopping his Nose,
That I flatly and boldly Deny, Deny;
That I flatly and boldly Deny.

Long Kept under Hatches, 'twill force a Vent
In the Shape of a Turd, with its Size and Scent,
And perhaps in its way may beshit a Vestment,
Which no body can Deny, Deny,
Which no body can Deny.

But however 'tis Dignify'd or Disguis'd,
That it should be for that the higher Priz'd,
And either Don Commis'd or Canoniz'd,
That I flatly and boldly Deny, Deny,
That I flatly and boldly Deny.

B'uey Fizle.

Androboros.

Scene First, Act First.

Keeper, Deputy and *Tom.*

Deputy. I hope, sir, it is not your intention that this same *Senate,* as they call it, should sit.

Keeper. What harm is there in't, if it does?

Deputy. No great harm, only 'twill {House} their Frenzy; They are big with Expectation of some mighty Deliverance, towards which is to be brought about by means of *Androboros;* I think they call him so; Whether there is or ever was such a Person, I know not: but all their hopes are placed in him.

Tom. Sir, it is *Old Nick-nack,* who has Paganiz'd himself with that Name, which interpreted, signifies a *Man-Eater.* He is now very far gone indeed, He talks of nothing but Battles and Seiges, tho' he never saw one, and Conquests over Nations, and Alliances with Princes who never had a being; and this Senate is mainly intended for his Reception, I hope you will not forbid its Meeting, if you do, I shall loose an Employment, having had the Honor to be appointed Clerk of the Senate this Morning, after the Choice of the Speaker; so I beg you'll not Rob me of that Honor, and your self of some Diversion, and I shall take care that their Session shall be harmless.

Keeper. I wish you Joy with all my heart; But Prethee, *Tom,* What Chance or evil Fate conducted thee to this same Doleful Mansion? I am surpriz'd to find thee in such Company.

Tom. No Chance, I assure you. *Sir,* but free Choice. I found in my reading, That Man was composed of three parts, *Body, Soul* and *Spirit,* and that the two first were entirely ingross'd by two Societys, so I Resolv'd to Exercize my poor Talent upon the Infirmitys of the last, not with any hopes or intention to Cure them, but as others do, meerly to raise my self a Maintenance out of them, here under your Honors happy Auspeces. But, Lo, here they come, Retire to a Corner. If I am seen in your Company, my Project is spoyl'd.

Act First, Scene Second.

Enter *Doodlesack, Babilard. Solemn, Æsop, &c.*

Speaker. Gentlemen, The Honor you have done me, how little soever I may deserve it, lays me under an Obligation to Exert my self to the utmost for the int'rest of this House. I humbly propose, That in the first place we concert and agree upon some necessary Rules for preventing Confusion.

Deputy aside. Well spoke, Mr. Speaker, Tho' 'tis something strange that he who has ever affirm'd, That Laws and Liberty were things Incompatible, should now propose to proceed by Rules.

Mulligr. I desire to be heard before you proceed to Rules, or any thing else; I have a Speech ready.

Doodlesack. Laet onse hearken to Mr. Speaker, and begin with some Rules.

Mullig. I'll have my Speech first.

Coxcomb. D——n your Speech, Let's proceed to Rules.

Babilard. If Rules be necessary to the Speech, let us have the Speech first, but if the Speech be necessary to the Rules, let us have the Rules.

Cox. I'm for neither Speech nor Rules, let us fall upon buss'ness.

Speaker. Gentlemen, The Question is not, as I take it, which you'll be pleas'd to have, but which shall have the Preference; for you may have both in their Turns.

All Confusedly. Speech, Rules; Rules, Speech, *&c.*

Mulligrub. My Speech has carry'd it. Hum, Ha, Ough, Ough, Ough, Ough, *&c.*

Cox. Rot ye, it was not your Cough that Carry'd it; Let off your speech.

Æsop. Mr. Speaker, I do not find that this matter is, as yet, determin'd to the full satisfaction of this House, for which Cause I beg leave to offer an Expedient, which will end the Debate, that is, That we may have both at a time; whilst *Mr. Mulligrub* is Exonerating himself, we may imploy our selves in adjusting and forming the necessary Rules.

All. Agreed.

Speaker. Mr. *Mulligrub,* You may proceed.

Mull. Gentlemen, The ill Measures that have been taken, and the Foundation that hath been laid within this Tenement, to make the Tenants thereof, Tenants therein, is the Cause which causeth me to make this Speech. Our Grievances being innumerable, I shall Enumerate them. The first I shall mention, is this, That tho' the Tenement be large, the Mansions many, and the Inhabitants Numerous, There is but One Kitchin, and one Cellar, by which means we are kept from Eating and drinking What we please, When we please, and as Much as we please, which is our Birth-Right Priviledge by the Laws of God and Nature, settled upon us by Act of Parliament; for which cause I humbly *{illegible half line}* House, Whether it may not be more Convenient that each Mansion have its proper Kitchin and Cellar under the special Direction of the respective Tenants?

To clear up the Necessity of this Method, I'll tell you what happ'ned to me t'other day; One of the Servants of this House, who brought me a

Mess of Water Gruel, being my special Friend, and knowing how eagerly my Stomach stood towards what was forbidden me by the Physitians, conveys a Hand of Pork into the Porrige, but being discover'd he was punisht, tho' he offer'd to take his Corporal Oath, That the Hand of Pork was a bunch of Radishes. But of all others, we of the East End of the Tenement suffer most, for by reason of our distance from the Kitchin, our Porrige is cold before it comes to our Hands. To Remedy this, we fell upon a private Intercourse with the *Bethlemites* on the other side of *Moorfields,* who by virtue of their Charter run at large, by which we broke the Laws pretty Comfortably for a season; but these same subtle Fellows of the Kitchin found it out, and put a stop to't, to the Great Prejudice of the Freedom of the Subject, and the direct Discouragement of our indirect Commerce. I Remember we once Address'd our Superiors, That we might have a Servant of our own, independent of this Plaguey *Keeper;* They were Graciously pleas'd to allow us such a one, with this Restriction only, That the Servant aforesaid might have the Custody of our Straw and Water, but by no means of our Meat and Drink; notwithstanding this, the Keeper will not permit him to take the care and Custody of our Victuals and Drink. What! does he think us *Non Corpus Mentlus,*[1] that we do not know the meaning of plain words! But *I* shall Conclude at this time, with this Exhortation, That since it appears plainly, that we of this Tenement, who are Tenants thereof, are in danger of Being, by the Foundations laid, made Tenants therein, let us not lie Crying thereat, but be Valiant Therefore, and Vindicate our Rights There-from, Our Birth-Right Parliamentary Rights, settled upon us by the Ten Commandments.

Speaker. Gentlemen, Mr. *Mulligrub* has given you time to Concert the Rules of the House, would you have them read by the Clerk, in the Order they have been given to him by the several Members?

All. Ay, Ay.

Tom Reads. Mr. *Speaker* Proposes, That to prevent Confusion, not above Three or Four at most be permitted to speak at Once, except in a Grand Committee, where there is no occasion of Hearers.

Mr. *Coxcomb* humbly proposes, That no Body be allow'd to speak but himself, because for want of the Attentive Faculty, he is like to have no share in the Hearing, and so ought to have Compensation in Speaking.

1. ["Not sound of mind." Malapropism for "non compos mentis."—Tr.]

Doodlesack has given his in a Forreign Tongue, which when interpreted stands thus, That He having but a small share of Elocution, but a very lively and strong imagination, may have leave, as occasion shall Offer, to Express his Thoughts by Staring, Grinning and Grimacing, of which he has so Exquisite a Talent, that those who cannot be said to understand any thing else, perfectly understand him in that Method of Utterance.

Bibilardus Represents. That he is quite Dum-founded by the late fall of Stocks, so in Order to the opening his Mouth, he proposes a Law for raising Int'rest to *Twelve per Cent.*

Æsop has given his Rule in Rhime, as follows,

The Rule that I would advise,
Is, Be quiet, and eat your Bread,
If 'tis good; To be Merry and Wise,
'Tis the Dev'l to be Sullen and Mad.

Coxcomb. Damn all Rules, Let us proceed to buss'ness.

Cobus. Laet onze erst come to some Revoluties.

Coxcom. Resolutions! Ay, begin with that, I like that Motion well enough; it is the shortest way.

Speaker. Let one at a time Propose, and the rest Agree or Dissent, as they think fit.

Coxcom. Resolv'd That neither this House, or they whom we Represent are bound by any Laws, Rules or Customs, any Law, Rule or Custom to the Contrary Notwithstanding.

All. Agreed.

Mulligr. That this House disclaims all Powers, Preheminencies or Authoritys, except it's own.

All. Agreed.

Babilard. That this House has an Inherent and Undoubted Right to the Undoubted Property of those we Represent.

Coxcomb. That this House is the only Undoubted Supreme Inferior and Infimus Court of this Tenement, and that all others are a Nusance.

All. Agreed.

Solemn. Mr. Speaker, being Resolv'd to enter my Dissent to these several Resolves, I shall first give my Reasons for so doing. I believe it is needless to put you in mind of our Origine, from whence we sprang, and how we came hither. It is well known that we were of that Number of Publick Spirited Persons, distinguish't from our Neighbours by an inward Light or Faculty, call it what you Please. The *Romans* call it *Æstrum,*[2] the *French, Verve,* our Northern Nation has indeed given it a Courser Name, which gave us a strong Disposition toward Reformations, Remonstrations, Resolutions, and other Acts of Zeal; in the eager pursuit of which we were apt to throw our selves, sometimes our Neighbours, into the Fire or Water. The Wisdom of the Times thought fit to Erect this Tenement for our Intertainment, where the Exercize of the Faculty aforesaid might be less Dangerous or hurtful to our selves, or others. Here we are Maintain'd at their Charge with Food and Rayment suitable to our Condition, and the Fabrick kept in Repair at the no small Annual Expences of our Landlords. And what Returns do we make? Have not many of us from our private Cells thrown our Filth and Ordere in their Faces? And now in a Collective Body we are about to throw more Filthy Resolves at them.

All. To the Barr, to the Barr.

All. No, With-draw, With-draw.

Solemn. I desire to be heard.

All. With-draw.

Speaker. Sir, It is pleasure of this House that you With-draw, in order to your being heard. [*Exit Solemn.*

Gentlemen, your have heard this mans Insolence. What shall be done with him?

Coxcomb. Hang'd, Drawn and Quarter'd.

Æsop. Ay, but what is his Crime?

Coxcom. For affronting the Majesty of this House.

Æsop. In what? What has he done or said?

Cobus. Dat weet ick niet, but I agree with *Coxcombs* Propositie.

Speaker. I am for Inflicting no Punishment but what is in our power, that is, to Expell him the House.

All. Expell, Expell.

Æsop. Hold a little. I suppose you intend to punish him, and not your selves; I'll tell you a Story.

All. Expell, Expell, *&c.*

2. ["Fervor." Should be "aestum."—Tr.]

Æsop. I beg your patience, 'tis but a short one; it is a Tale of a Pack of Hounds of my Acquantance,

Fowler, the stanchest Hound o'th' breed,
Had got th' ill Will of all the rest;
Not for his Tongue, his Nose or Speed,
Tho' these were all by far the best;
Malice and Envy know no bounds
And Currs have ever bark'd at Hounds.

But that which most provok'd their Spite
Was this, that when they run a Foil
Or Counter, *Fowler* led them right,
Which cost him many a bitter broil,
Snubbing the Rash and Rioters
And lugging laizy Ones by th' Ears.

So at a General Council held
For Grievances, or what you will,
Poor trusty *Fowler* was Expell'd,
That free-born Dogs might range their fill.
And so they did; but mark what came on't,
Hence-forth they made but sorry Game on't.

The giddy Pack, their Guide b'ing gone,
Run Riot, and the Hunts-Man swore,
Strap't some, and some he whipt; but one
He hang'd, a Noisy babling Curr.
In short, the Pack was spoyl'd; Pray then,
Shall *Fowler* be Expell'd agen?

Coxcomb. A Pox on your Tale, let us proceed to the Vote.
Speaker. What is then your pleasure with relation to the Member who is to be Expell'd?
All. Expell'd, Expell'd.
Speaker. Call him to the Bar.

Enter Solemn.

Sir, for *Reasons* best known to our selves, you are Expell'd.
Solemn. Sir, you do me too much honor. [*Exit.*

Enter Messenger.

Messenger. Mr. *Speaker,* The Lord *Androboros* with Two Men in Black desires Admittance.

Speaker. Is it your pleasure he be admitted?

Omnes. Ay, Ay.

Speaker. Let the Clerk go to him with the Compliments of the House, and Conduct him in. [*Tom* a going.

Keeper. St. St. St. *Tom,* a Word with you. Pray who are these same men in Black, who accompany the General?

Tom. Two other special Friends of yours, *viz. Fizle* and *Flip;* The first was heretofore a *Muggletonian* of the other side of *Moorefields,* but having no Butter to his Bread there, he Chang'd their Service for that of this House; He sometime fancy'd himself to be the Pope, but his Brother not relishing that as Derogatory to his Pretentions, he is now Contended to be Patriarch of the Western Empire, of which *Androboros* is to be Sultan; The other, for a wonderful Energy in the two most Unruly Members of the Body, has been follow'd of late by the Women and Boys, but a late sinistrous Accident has Crack't his Voice, and—that now he is but little regarded. But I must be gone. [*Ex. Tom.*

Keeper. The Rogue is a good Painter.

Deputy. He draws from the Life, I assure you.

Act First, Scene Third.

Enter *Androboros* and *Tom, Flip* and *Fizle.*

Androb. Most venerable Gentlemen, Upon my Rounds of Inspection, Prospection and Retrospection, I have understood with Pleasure, that you have sequester'd from your House that wandring Plague, that Kibes in the Heels, and Piles in the posteriors of Mankind.

Æsop. Pardon me, Sir, your Name has not been mention'd here, that I know of.

Androb. I mean *Solemn,* which Act I approve and Commend. It is with no less satisfaction that I now acquaint you, That upon the Earnest Application and most humble Suit of the High and Potent *Towrowmowyoughtough.* Emperor of many Nations, and my good Allies, the Kings of *Agnisagkimaghswoughsayk, Savanaghtipheugh,* and *Bowwougewouffe,* I have undertaken an Expedition against the *Mulo Machians,* your Inveterate Foes. Your

Concurrence to enable me to carry it on with Success, is what I demand and expect; and for your Incouragement, I do Swear by this sacred Image, not to pare these Nails, wash this blew Visage, or put off this speckled *Shirt,* Until I have made that Haughly Monarch Confess himself, in all his Projects for Universal Dominion, my Inferior; and My Delamya, fairer then the fairest Princess of his Blood or Empire. So leaving this weighty Affair to your wise Counsels, We bid you heartily Farewell. [*Exit Strutting.*

Speaker. You have heard what this Man has propos'd. What do you Resolve?

Coxcom. Let us Resolve to Support, Maintain and Defend the undoubted Title of the Great *Androboros* to the Powers and Authoritys he has Graciously Assum'd over this and all other the like Tenements, against all Wardens, Directors, Keepers, and their Abettors.

All. Agreed.

Doodlesack. Laet onze Dissolve, That a Summ not Exceeding Negen Skillingen and Elleve Pence be rais'd for the Expeditie.

All. Agreed.

Speaker. Ay, and 'tis more then 'tis worth.

Babilard. Let us Resolve, That He has behav'd Himself on the said Expedition with Courage, Conduct and Prudence.

Speaker. What! before 'tis over!

Æsop. By all means, lest when it is over you should have less reason for this Resolve. But if after all, we must go to War, I would be glad to be better satisfy'd with the Choice of a Leader; For as to this Mans Prowess, we have nothing but his own Word for't.

Coxcomb. The Choice is a good Choice, and he that doubts it, is a Son— So for that, amongst other weighty Reasons, I second Mr. *Babilards* Motion.

Doodlesack. Ick ock, because it may cast some Reflectie upon our Keeper.

Æsop. Before you proceed any further, I'll beg leave to tell you another Tale, it is but a short one, and if it fails to Instruct, it may divert.

The *Bees* so fam'd for Feats of War,
And Arts of Peace, were once, of Sense
As void as other Insects are,
'Till time and late Experience,
The only Schoolmaster of Fools,
Taught them the use of Laws and Rules.

In that wild state they were Assail'd
By th' Wasps. oft routed and Opprest;
Not that their Hearts or Hands had fail'd,
But that their Head was none o'th' best,
The *Drone* being, by the Commons Voice,
Chose for the Greatness of his Noise.

Thus ill they sped in every Battle;
For tho' the Chief was in Request
At home, for's Fools Coat and his Rattle,
Abroad he was the Common Jest.
The Wasps in all Ingagements, held—
His Folly more then half the Field.

Grown Wiser by repeated Woes,
The Bees thought fit to change their Chief,
It was a *Humble* Bee they Chose,
Whose Conduct brought them quick Relief;
And ever since that Race has led 'em,
The *Drones* are Drums, as Nature made 'em.

But go on with your Resolves; you have mine.

Speaker. I like the last Choice of the Bees, for my part; for by the Law no man can be allow'd to be an Evidence for himself, especially when he happens to be a single one.

Doodlesack. Wishy Washy's; I agree to Mr. *Babilards* Propositie, for the Reasons given, with this addition, That our Keeper is een Skellum.

Coxcomb. And ought to be dismiss't from having any further Authority over us.

Act First, Scene Fourth.

Enter *Keeper* and *Deputy.*

Keeper. To your kennels, ye Hounds.— [*Exit Omnes.*

Deputy. Now, *Sir,* I hope you are satisfied, and for the future you'll keep 'em to their Cells.

Keeper. No, let them enjoy their former Liberty, perhaps they'll stand Corrected.

Deputy. I much doubt it; but I shall Obey.

Keeper. Now, Mr. *Tom.* If I may be so bold, Favour me with a sight of the Minutes of your House.

Tom. With all my heart, here they are.

Keeper. What's here! A *Castle,* a *Wind-Mill,* and *Sheperd* with a *Ram* at his back?

Tom. Ay, *Sir,* a sort of Ægyptian short Hand, containing the substance of their Resolves. The *Castle Renvers'd* and in the Air, denotes the independency of our House; the *Wind-Mill* without Sails, an Expedition without Means or Leader; and the *Ram* butting the *Shepherd on the Breech,* or in other words, dismissing him from having any further Authority over him.—

Keeper. That wants no Explanation. You'll Watch them, *Tom,* and serve them in the same Capacity, if they meet again.

Tom. To the best of my Skill.

Keeper. Let's to Dinner. [*Exeunt.*

Finis Actus Primi.

Act Second, Scene First.

Enter *Babilard, Fizle, Flip, Coxcomb.*

Babilard. You see what our wise Resolves have brought upon us, we shall never do his buss'ness in this way, Muzled as we are; I wish my Advice had been follow'd.

Fizle. Pray what was that?

Babilard. I was for proceeding in the way of secret Representations and Remonstrances against him, which My Lord *Oinobaros,* his declar'd Enemy, might have long e'er this improv'd to his Ruin.

Fizle. That was my own Method, but that which discourages me is, that at Parting my Lord assur'd me, That he would return in six Moneths, and Confirm me in my *Patriarchat;* instead of that, he has himself taken up with the Wardenship of a Spunging-house.

Coxcomb. No, that Method will never do. Have not I, and my Friends transmitted to Mr. *Wry Rump* a Ream of Complaints, as big as the Bunch on his back, which were Referr'd to the Consideration of the Casually sitting Members of the little House, and he was dismiss'd with a Kick o' h' Breech. We must Accuse him of something more Flagrant; Triffles won't do.

Fizle. Why, Then I have another Device for you. You see he can Dissolve our Senate with a Crack of his Whip, so there is nothing to be done that way. Let us incorporate our selves into a *Consistory;* That I believe He dare not touch, without being Reputed an Enemy to the Consistory; and if he does, we may hunt him down full Cry at present.

Flip. That I should like well enough, but I'm afraid the Cunning Rogue won't meddle with us, as such.

Fizle. We'd say, and swear, That he did, and that's all one. I have a Plot in my head, which I hope will do the buss'ness; in the mean time, go you and acquaint the Rest, that they meet us here in full Consistory Immediately. [*Exit Babilard,* and *Coxcom.*

Flip. Pray, Brother, Instruct me in your Contrivance, I may help you out with my Advice.

Fizle. It is briefly this. This same Rogue was ever an Enemy to the short Coats and Scanty Skirts of the Laity, and Consequently to the long Robes and Pudding Sleeves of the others; I'll instantly have my long Coat Beskirted and Besh——, and give out, That it is He, or some of his People, who has don't. If any should be so Heterodox as to doubt the truth on't, I have some ready to swear to the Size and Colour of the T——.

Flip. I like this well; about it streight, I'll attend them here, Open the Consistory in your Name, and Prepare 'em for what is to ensue. [*Exit Fizle.*

Flip. This same *Fizle* is a Notable Fellow for the head of a Consistory, if he had but a Competent Doze of Brains; but These are so shallow that a Louse may suck 'em up without surfeiting, which renders that noble Portion of *Malice,* with which he is Liberally endow'd of little use to the Publick.

Act Second, Scene Second.

Enter *Mulligrub, Doodlesack, Babilard, Coxcomb, Tom, Æsop,* &c.

Flip. In the absence of My Brother *Fizle* whose occasions have call'd him away for a little time, I am to acquaint you, That he has of his own free Will, meer Motion and by virtue of the Plenitude of his Patriarchal Authority, chosen and elected you for his Consistory-men and Counsellors in all Cases and Causes Visible and Invisable.

Coxcom. We are highly honor'd by his Choice, and Promise an Implicit Obedience to his pleasure. [Enter *Fizle.*

Fizle. O Horror! O Abomination! was ever the like seen, heard or read of!

Flip. What's the Matter?

Fizle. As I went to Robe my self for the more decent Attendance on this Consistory I found my Robes in this Pickle! That Vestment, so Reverenc'd by the Antient and Modern World, beskirted and Bedaub'd with what I must not name!

Æsop. Who has done this?

Fizle. Who has done it! Who but the known Enemies to Consistorys and Long Skirts?

Æsop. But methinks your Discretion should have directed you to our Keeper with this Complaint.

Fizle. Our Keeper! One of my Brethren told him of it but now, and he coldly Reply'd, if Mr. *Fizle* from the Redundancy of His Zeal has beshit himself, the Abundance of his Wisdom, methinks, should prevail with him to keep the Secret, and make himself Clean.

Mulligr. A plain Proof the Keeper is the Man.

Coxcomb. Ay, Ay, There Needs No Other Proof; it must be the Keeper.

Fizle. I own, I thought so from the beginning; but what course shall we steer for Redress?

Flip. If I may be thought worthy to advise in a matter of this Moment, we shall immediately Address My Lord *Oinobaros* on this head, he being a Devotee to Long Robes of both Gendres, must highly Resent this Affront, and with the Assistance of *Androboros,* no less an Enemy to the Keeper, may Manage it to his Ruin and our Satisfaction.

Babil. Let Mr. *Fizle* draw up an Address, and we'll all sign it.

Fizle. Gentlemen, If such is your pleasure, I'll retire with the Clerk, prepare one, and submit it to your Approbation.

All. Pray go about it [*Exit Fizle* and *Tom.*

Æsop. I Resent this Affront to the Long Robe as much as any Man, but methinks you proceed too hastily, and upon too slender Grounds against your Keeper. We all know the Malice of Mr. *Fizle's* heart, and that it has Increas'd in proportion to the Keepers good Nature. Had he been oftner Check'd, he had been less Troublesome to himself and us. Let us not provoke our Keeper; for my part, I think he is a good one.

Coxcom. What! is he not an Enemy to the Consistory?

Æsop. No, he is an Enemy to their Folly, and can well distinguish between the Function and the Person who abuses it. Pray give me leave to divert you, 'till *Fizle* returns, with another Tale; It is harmless, and I hope will give no Offence.

In the beginning God made Men,
And all was well, but in the End
Men made their Gods, and Fondly pay'd 'em.
The Worship due to him that made 'em,
And all was wrong; for they Increas'd,
And Multiply'd like Man and Beast.

But none were bold in Reverence
So much as *Phoebus,* God of sense
And Non-sense, Patron, as occasion
Did serve, of Arts and Inspiration.
Once on a day as he was led
About to give a Cast of's Trade,

Whether to Dance, or Sing, or Fiddle,
Or as some say, to read a Riddle,
I know not; but what-e'er it was,
His Vehicle was but an Ass,
And he none of the wisest neither;
For when the Crowd had got together

To pay due Homage to their God,
Strowing with Flow'rs the Path he rode,
And singing Paans, the vain Beast
Believ'd all this, to him Address't:
He Pranc'd, and Flung, and Frisk'd about,
Scatt'ring much Dirt among the Rout,

And bray'd as if h'had got a Pack
Of Dev'ls, and not a God on's back.
The Crowd essay'd by gentle ways,
To Curb his Pride, and smooth his Pace;
But all was talking to the Wind;
For Zeal is deaf, when-e'er 'tis blind.

Finding all other Methods fail,
They seiz'd him by the Ears and Tail,
And took the Idol from his back,

With many a lusty Bang and Thwack.
They let him know, that *Phoebus* was
The God, and he was but an Ass.

How d'ye like it? It is an old Tale, but a true *Eccum Ipsum;* let him speak for himself.

Act Second, Scene Third.

Enter *Fizle* and *Tom*.

Fizle. Gentlemen, I have finish'd the Address Is it your pleasure that the Clerk read it?

All. Ay, Ay.

Tom. reads. To the most Potent Lord *Oinobaros*, Court of *Kynommaria*, Baron of *Elaphokardia*. The General Consistory of *New Bedlam* most Humbly Represent, That we your Excellencies ever *Besotted Subjects,*

Fizle. Devoted Subjects.

Tom. Under a deep sense of the manifold *Bastings* we Enjoy'd.

Fizle. *Blessings*, you Ouph you.

Tom. Blessings we Enjoy'd under your *Wild Administration*.

Fizle. Mild Administration.

Tom. Mild Administration, find ourselves at this time under a *Nonsensical Inclination*.

Fizle. What's that? Let me see't, *Non-sensical Inclination!* It can't be so, It is *Indispensible Obligation*.

Tom. Ay, it should be so.

Fizle. Write it down so then.

Tom. 'Tis done. Finding our selves under an *Incomprehensible Obstination*.

Flip. 'Owns'! That's worse than t'other.

Tom. Cry Mercy, That is a blunder, *Indispensible Obligation* to have Recourse to your Excellencies known *Condemnable Opposition* to our Consistory, and all Things Sacred.

Fizle. I think the Dev'l is in the Fellow. It is *Commendable Disposition*.

Tom. You use so many Long Words, that a Clerk who is not a Scholar may easily mistake one for another. Towards our Consistory, and all things Sacred, Take leave humbly to Represent, That on the *Ev'ning which succeeded the following Day*.

Fizle. Thou Eternal Dunce! *The Ev'ning which preceded All-hallowday*.

Tom. Which preceded *All-hallowday* some open or secret Enemies to this Consistory broke into our *Cupboard.*

Fizle. Ward-Robe.

Tom. Wardrobe, taking from thence some Lumber appertaining to the *Chief of our Rogues,* I mean, some Robes appertaining to the Chief of our Number, which they Inhumanely Tore to pieces and Bedaub'd with *Odour.*

Mulligrub. Hold! I make Exception to that, for there are sweet Odours as well as sower.

Flip. 'Slid; 'tis *Ordure,* (and not *Odour*) which is but another Name for a T—d.

Mulligr. Write it down so then, for a T— is a T— all the world over.

Æsop. And the more you stir it, the more 'twill stink. But go on.

Tom. Now Tho' we *cannot Possibly Prove,* yet we *Affirm Possitively,* That it is our Keeper.

Æsop. How's that?

Fizle. He reads wrong; it is, *Tho' we cannot Possitively Prove, yet we Affirm,* That *possibly it may be our Keeper.* Go on.

Tom. Our Keeper, or some of his People, who is guilty of this *Facetious Fact.*

Fizle. Flagitious Fact.

Tom. Flagitious Fact. We further beg leave to Represent. That this Morning in a Collective Body, by a great *Brutality of Noises.*

Fizle. Plurality of Voices.

Tom. We had declar'd him a *Raskal,* but he had the Impudence to send us packing to our Cells, though we had several *Merduous Matters* under the *Infection of our Hose.*

Mulligrub. Hold! I do not well understand that, Read it again.

Fizle. He cant read his own Hand; it is *Several Arduous Matters under the Inspection of our House.* Go on.

Tom. Wherefore it is our humble and earnest Supplication, That we may be once more put under your *Wild Distraction.*

Fizle. Mild Direction.

Tom. Or that of the *Excrement Androboros.*

Fizle. Excellent *Androboros.*

Tom. That so we may give a *Loose to Our Knavery.*

Fizle. I'm afraid, Sirrah, you are a Knave; Get loose from our Slavery.

Tom. I'm afraid, Sirrah, you are a Knave; Get loose from our Slavery, and fix a *stolid Security for our Nasty Foundations.*

Fizle. Is the Dev'l in thee! A solid Foundation for our lasting Security.

Tom. A solid Foundation for our lasting Security. And your Petitioners, *like Asses as they are, in a durty Pound,* shall never cease to *Bray.*

Fizle. (Raskall it should be) like as they are in *Duty Bound, shall never cease to pray.* (I could swear he reads thus on purpose.)

Æsop. And not be For-sworn. But have you done?

Tom. Yes, an't please your Honors.

Fizle. Gentlemen, do you approve of this Draught?

Æsop. I like it as the Clerk read it.

Mulligrub. I approve of all, except the *Ordure;* I'll have it a T—.

Coxcom. You'll have it a T—, A T— in your Teeth; it shall stand as it is *Ordure.*

Mulligrub. T—d.

Doodlesack. Ick been on the Cant van de T—d.

Babilard. Let us Compromise the Matter, and make it *Turdure.*

All. Ay. agreed.

Æsop. Gentlemen, you have agreed to the Draught of an Address; but what is to be done with it?

Coxcom. Transmitted to *Oinobaros.*

Æsop. For what purpose?

Coxcomb. To ged Rid of our Keeper, and get *Oinobaros* in his room.

Æsop. If you should, my mind Forbodes you would repent the Change.

Coxcomb. Why?

Æsop. Why! why because a man who could never yet Govern himself, will make but a sorry Governour for others.

Coxcomb. Have a care what you say; That is *Scandalum Magnatum.*[3]

Doodlesack. Pray, *Mr. Tom.* Wat is dat Lating? Ick forestaet niet.

Tom. He say my Lord is in a very great Post, call'd, *The Scandalum Magnatum.*

Doodlesack. Is it given him lately.

Tom. No, he has it by inheritance.

Æsop. Be advis'd by me; Lay your Address aside, and keep as you are; As for your Keeper, none of you can say that he has done you any harm; and for my part I am convinc'd, that he has done us much good. I must beg leave to tell you a Story.

3. "Slander of great men."

Coxcomb. Hang you and your Storys; we shan't mind 'em.

Æsop. You may give it the same fair play you did to *Mulligrub's* Speech; hear it, tho' you do not mind it. I pray your patience.

The Frogs, a Factious fickle Race,
With little Maners, and less Grace,
Croak'd for a King so loud,
That all the Host of Heav'n sate mute
Nodding to *Jove* to grant their suit,
And give 'em what they wou'd.

A King they had, of such a size
Who's Entry too, made such a Noise,
That Ev'ry Neut and Frog
Affrighted, run to hide their heads;
Some in the Pool, some 'mongst the Reeds,
Like fools, 'Twas but a Log.

At last, one bolder than the rest,
Approach'd, and the new Prince Address't,
No hurt from thence sustain'd,
He mock'd his former Fears, and swore
'Twas the best stick of Wood that o'er
The Marshes ever Reign'd.

Then all the Croaking Crew drew near,
And in his shade from th' angry Air
Were shelter'd safe, and eas'd,
Nay more then that, they'd frisk and play
Upon his back a live long day,
He Undisturb'd and pleas'd.

The Pertest Frog of all the Pack,
A Toad, some say, his hue was Black;
'Tis true; but that's no matter,
Upon the passive Monarch's head,
At times would Noxious Venom shed,
And both his sides bespatter.

'Twas That same Frog, the Legends tell,
Burst when he only meant to swell,
Soon after these Events.

Be that as 'twill, 'twas He that drew
That giddy Senseless Crowd to new
Sedition and Complaints.

Give us a bustling King, *Dread Sir!*
They cry'd, a King that makes a stir;
This is not to be mov'd.
Jove heard and gave 'm one, who's care
Was, that they should Obey and Fear,
No matter how they Lov'd.

It was a Stork, who's Law-less Rage
Spar'd neither Sex, Degree nor Age,
That came within his reach.
And that was great, for whilst his Claws
Ransack't the Deep, his Vulturs Jaws
Could wander oe'r the Beach.

Then they Implor'd the God to send
From heav'n a Plague, from Hell a Fiend,
Or any but this Curse.
Peace, cry'd the Monarch of the Gods,
Ye Worms; Keep him you have, 'tis odds
The Next may prove a Worse.

Now If you please, you may put the Question about your Address. I take it to be Log or Stork.

Enter Door-Keeper.

Door-keeper. Here's a Courier from *Androboros,* just return'd from the Expedition, who desires Admittance.

Æsop. It is the most Expeditious Expedition I ever heard of; let us adjourn the Address, and receive the General's Message.

Fizle. Let him come in.

Enter Messenger.

Messenger. The Renown'd *Androboros* with a tender of his hearty Zeal and Affection sends this to the *Consistory,* the Senate being Discontinued.

[*Delivers a Letter.*

Fizle Reads.

RIGHT FRIGHTFUL AND FORMIDABLE. We Greet you Well, And by this Acquaint you, That for many Weighty Considerations Us thereunto moving, We have thought fit to adjourn the Intended Expedition to a more proper season, because we have, upon due and Mature Examination been fully convinc'd, that the Mulomachians, our Reputed Enemies, are in very deed our good and faithful Friends and Allies, who, to remove all Doubts and Scruples, have freely offer'd to Consolidate Consistories with us, as also to divide with us the Commerce of the World, generously resigning and yeilding to us that of the two Poles, reserving to themselves only what may lie between 'em. They have likewise Condescended that we shall keep some Forts and Holds, which by the Fortune of the War they could not take from us, and have promis'd and engag'd to Raze and Demolish some Places in their Possession to our prejudice, so soon as more Convenient are built in their room and place. You are further to understand, to your Great satisfaction, that this is a Treaty Litteral and Spiritual, so that having two Handles it may be Executed with the greater Facility, or if need be, the One may Execute the other, and so it may Execute it self. Now these Concessions (tho' it be well known that I hate Boasting) having been obtain'd, in a great measure by the Terror of my Name and Arms, I expect your Thanks. And so we bid you heartily *Farewell.*

Androboros

Æsop. Buzzzzz, Hummmmm, Buzzzzz—

Fizle. What Return shall we give to this Civil and Obliging Message?

Æsop. Return him his Letter.

Coxcomb. No, let us vote him Thanks, a Statue and a Triumph!

Enter Keeper.

Keeper. Be no surpriz'd, I have heard what you are about, and Cordially joyn with you in what you propose, in honour of the Valiant *Androboros,* Having received instructions from my Superiors to use that mighty Man according to his Deserts.

Æsop. What! Is our Keeper Mad too?

Keeper. In the Mean time, all Retire to your respective Apartments, until due Disposition be made for his Reception.

Exit, manent[4] *Fizle* and *Æsop.*

4. ["They remain."]

Act Second, Scene Fourth.

{*Fiz.*} What a man! I'th Dumps, because our Keeper let fall a word or two about Orders to use a certain great Man according to his deserts!

Æsop. I hope he has receiv'd the same Orders relating to you.

Fizle. There is more in this than you Imagine; I ever believ'd, that it would come to this at last.

Æsop. Why? What's the matter?

Fizle. The Keeper undoubtedly has receiv'd Orders to resign to *Androboros.*

Æsop. What then?

Fizle. What then! I'll tell you what then; Then My Brethren and I shall have our due, and you with yours be proud to lick the Dust off our Feet.

Æsop. Ha'nt ye your Allowence?

Fizle. What of that? That's no more then the Law gives us.

Æsop. And you would have more. Law or Custom makes an Inch to an Ell very fair allowance; you, it seems, want an Ell to an inch. I wish your Stint might be some how ascertain'd; but that, I doubt, cannot easily be compass'd. And whosoever, by giving hopes to find an end of your Craving will find himself deceiv'd, I'll tell you a Tale to this *{line missing},*

The Rats, a Tribe much better fed
Then taught, that mortally abhor'd
To work, lov'd ease and eating, fled
For shelter to a *Saxon* Lord,
Who's Barns and Paunch were ever full,
And nothing Empty but his Skull.

Here did they Revel at their ease,
Far from the watchful Pusses Eye;
For he had banish't all that Race
For th' Love they bore to liberty
And Cleanliness, Things to his Nature
As opposite as Fire to Water.

His steward put him oft in mind,
That all his plenty only serv'd
To Fatten Vermin, whilst the Hind

That Labour'd, and his Servants starv'd;
And what was worse, th' Infirm and Poor
Unfed, Unpity'd, ply'd his Door.

To this, the Churle reply'd at length,
And they may all starve on for me,
The Rats eat not above a Tenth,
These would Consume me one in Three,
They are the Rats that would destroy me;
The others cannot much annoy me.

The pamper'd Tribe familiar grown
By this Indulgence, Lodg'd themselves
No more as heretofore they'ad done,
In holes and Corners, and on Shelves,
But in his Robes, and in the upshot,
They ate his very Heart and Guts out.

God beyt't ye. [*Exit Æsop.*

Fizle. Rats! a Dog! I'll Rat ye, ye Whorson Tale-Teller, you Vermin! a Son of a Whore— [*Exit Fizle.*

Act Third, Scene First.

Enter *Keeper, Deputy, Tom* and Servant.

Deputy. With all due Submission. Sir, give me leave to ask you what you mean by the splendid Reception you have promis'd to give to that Odd Man?

Keeper. Very Little besides Diversion. My Superiors, as I am inform'd, have Cloath'd him with Sham-Powers meerly to get rid of his Noise and Trouble; and since these must fall to my share, I'll humour him to keep him quiet.

Deputy. That is not to be hop'd for whilst he lives.

Tom. Persuade him that he is dead then.

Keeper and *Deputy.* Ha, Ha, Ha,

Tom. It is far from Impossible, however Extravagant you may think the Overture. If you'll be rul'd by me, I'll answer for the Success of what I propose, under any Penalties you please. I'm sure he has had the Art to Dream himself into Notions every whit as Absurd. His Imagination is very ductile when 'tis heated, and by a Long Practice upon't, he has made it as susceptible of Impressions from Without, as it has been of these from Within. Do you but when he appears, behave your selves as if he were Invisible, and take no maner of Notice of what he shall say or do, and I'll answer for the rest. Here he comes, mind him not.

Enter *Androboros*.

Tom. I was not present, *Sir*, when he Expir'd, but arriv'd a few Minutes after.

Keeper, So suddenly too! I wish he may not have had foul play.

Androb. Your Servant, Gentlemen, I hope I do not Interrupt you; pray, who is it you speak of?

Tom. No, Sir, he dy'd of an uncommon Disease, The Physitians call it, a *Tympany in the Imagination*, occasion'd by a collection of much indigested Matter there, which for want of due Excretion, made a breach in the Pericrane, at which that great Soul took its flight.

Keeper. Had he made his Will?

Androboros. Pray, Gentlemen, who is it that's Dead?

Tom. I have not heard of any.

Androb. Cry mercy, I thought—

Tom. Only about the time he Expir'd, he Cry'd, I leave This World, this Worthless World to My *Delamya, O Delamya!*

Androb. You Impudent Dog you, dare but to Profane that sacred Name with thy base breath, and I'll crush thee to Nothing.

Tom. Hark, did not you hear an odd Noise?

Deputy. Something like the Humming of a Bee.

Tom. Me thinks it sounded rather like the Breath of the Bung of an Empty Barrel.

Androb. You Sawcy Knave. Take that. [*Strikes him a Box o' th' Ear*]

Tom. It was nothing but a Flea in my Ear. [*Scratching his Ear.*]

And, so, (as I was saying,) with that Name in his Mouth he Expir'd.

Androb. Gentlemen. I am not to be made a May-Game; your betters shall be acquainted with your Conduct. [*Exit.*

Keeper. Run *Tom*. and allay or baulk his Fury. [*Exit Tom.*

What d'ye think of *Tom's* Project, is it Not an Odd One?

Deputy. I hardly believe He'll succeed, but if he does, what then!

Keeper. Then We shall live at ease, he'll dream no more, when he thinks that he's dead. It is amazing that this Mans Visions, like Yawning, should be catching. The Inhabitants of this Tenement are not the only Dupes of his *Quixotism*.

Deputy. That Indeed is matter of Wonder; and if the Countenance given to Folly be not all Grimace, The World is as Mad as he.

Enter *Tom*.

Tom. I have Instructed the Porter, and the other Servants, and have proclaim'd to all, the General remains *Incognito*, until he makes his Publick Entry, and that no notice is to be taken of him, more than if he were Absent, under the Pain of his highest Displeasure.

Keeper. So far all goes well, But you must Intrust *Solemn* and *Æsop* with your Plot.

Tom. I have already. The first is to be my Conjurer.

Keeper. Conjurer!

Tom. Yes, my Conjurer; To him alone, and that too but some times, he shall be visible, to all besides, a shadow, an Empty Name. Here they come.

Enter *Solemn* and *Æsop*.

Keeper. Gentlemen, you have your Q.

Solemn. Do you but keep your Countenance, leave the rest to us.

[*Chairs and a Table, they sit down*.

Enter *Androboros*.

Androb. Sure all the World is Mad, or have a mind to make me so; I try'd to get out, but the Porter lean't his Staff against my Nose, and belch't full in my Chops; a Culverine could not have done more suddain Execution than that Erruption of Barm and Tobacco Smoak.

Solemn. When is he to be Interr'd?

Tom. This Ev'ning, but is to lie in State here till then.

Androboros, I made a Shift to recover my self, and attempted the back passage; but in the Door of the Kitchin I was saluted with a Pale of cold Water, which had like to have been succeeded by a Shovel of burning Coals, but that I made a speedy Retreat. Something's the matter, what e'er it is; I'll listen here and find it out.

Keeper. But why so suddainly? 'Tis strange so Great a Man should be bury'd with so little Ceremony.

Androb. Bury'd, said he!

Tom. It is done by the advice of Physitians, who have declar'd that his Disease was such as makes a man stink vilely after he is dead.

Keeper. The fair *Delamya!* how does she bear the Loss?

Tom. She's Inconsolable, ready to burst her sides.

Keeper. How! *Tom?* Yes, Sir, Excess of Joy makes some People Weep; Excess of Grief makes her Laugh Inordinately, and Cry out Incessantly, *Are these our promised Joys, O Androboros! One Grave shall hold us.* And then she laughs again.

Androb. Androboros, it seems then I'm dead; 'tis odd that I should not know it. I'll try that. [*Takes a Chair.*

Keeper. Poor Lady, she lov'd him well, I doubt she'll be as good as her Word.

Æsop. Who set this Empty Chair by me?

Solemn. Save me, ye Kinder Powers, and guard my Senses!

Keeper. What's the matter Man? What d'ye see?

Tom. It is but a Raving fit, the Effect of deep study: he is often taken so.

Solemn. No, my sense is temperate as yours. Look there, There ☛

Æsop. There is a Chair, What then? [*Shoving it with his Foot.*

Solemn. Have ye no Eyes? Can't you see?

Keeper. For my part I see nothing but what I use to see.

Solemn. Why there, in that Chair sits the Venerable Form of the deceas'd *Androboros,* in nothing differing from that Awful Figure he once made, but that you regard it not.

Keeper. Sure he Raves.

Æsop. That Chair. Why there's nothing in that Chair. There it lies.

[*Strikes down* Androboros, *Chair and all.*

Solemn. O! Offer it no Violence.

Androb. You Old Dog, I'll be Reveng'd. [*Goes off.*

Solemn. See how it Stalks off! With what Majestick Air, and how Stern a Brow! It Resents the Indignity offer'd. Ha, Ha, Ha.

All. Ha, Ha, Ha, Ha.

Tom. Now we have him; it begins to work, if I do not mistake his Looks.

Deputy. I had much ado to contain my self.

Keeper. What's next to be done?

Tom. Trust that to me; but be sure not to mind him, ev'n tho' he should be Outragious. To *Solemn* only he must be visible for some time. Have you got your Conjuring Tackle ready?

Solemn. I have. That will serve the turn. O here he comes again in very pensive Mood and doleful Dumps. All walk off, as if you saw him not; I'll remain alone. [*Exeunt* Keeper, Deputy, Tom *and* Æsop, *passing by* Androboros *without taking Notice of him.*

Act Third, Scene Second.

Solemn *at the Table with Books and Implements.*

Enter *Androboros.*

Androb. 'Tis strange, Wondrous strange, I should take the whole to be a Trick, were it not that my best, my firmest Friends, who never could be Induc'd to practice upon me in this gross manner, behave themselves to my Face as if they saw me not. Whilst I sate at that Table, That only Raskal, *Solemn* saw me, and started and star'd as if he had seen a Ghost; The rest saw nothing. They were talking of my Disease, Death, Burial and latter Will, as of things certain, and of publick knowledge. I think I'm pretty sure that I am Alive, tho' it seems, I am singular in that belief. I See, I Feel, I Hear as I us'd to do, ev'n now I hear my own Voice as plain as can be; I have Thought and Reflection as usual. But, Alas! departed Spirits if they think at all, must think that they do think, that is, that they are not dead,—It may be so.—Ev'n that very Knave who but now could see me, sits musing by himself as if I were not here. I Remember it was the Common Opinion that a Ghost that walks, could be seen but by One of a Company. But why should he be blind now? [*Walks nearer.*

Solemn. It must Portend some suddain Change i' th' State; For Ghosts of Note never walk but upon these solemn Errands.

Androb. He does not see me yet; I remember I was on th' other side when he saw me last. [*Goes to the other side.*

Solemn. If the poor Spirit is permitted once more to haunt these Walls, I'll question it, if my Courage fail me not; he may, perhaps, have something of Moment in Commission.

Androb. If you can't see me, can't you hear me, you old Dev'l you? [*Bawling.*

Solemn. How painful, yet unprofitable are all the deeper ways of Art? The Vulgar undisturb'd, Frequent the silent Shades, and quietly enjoy the pleasure of soft Recess or Balmy Slumbers, whilst I whom Science has rais'd so far above them, have not a peaceful hour. If at any time I would see into Futurity, I must take my *Talisman,* and then all Ghosts or Spectres which chance at that time to crowd the Ambient Air, become visible to me, and to me alone. Not dreaming of any search into the Intellectual World; but by meer Chance, I grasp'd my Talisman thus, when streight—

[*Takes a Tobacco-stopper out of his Pocket. Starts up Wildly.*

Angels and all the Ministers of Grace, Defend me. Be thou a Spirit of Health, or Goblin Damn'd! Bring with thee Airs from Heav'n, or Blasts from Hell, Thou Com'st in such a Questionable Shape, I'll speak to Thee. Thanks Good Hamlet for this again. I'll [*Softly.*
call thee General. Valiant *Androboros,* O speak.

Androb. I tell you, ye Old Fool—

Solemn. O speak, if ought of dire Import.

Androb. Why, I'll tell you, Sirrah—

Solemn. To this our state disturbs thy sacred Shade, impart, O speak.

Androb. Let me speak then, and be hang'd—

Solemn. For sure no common Cause could raise thee from thy silent Herse.

Androb. 'Owns! Can your Talisman make you See, and not make you Hear, You Old Conj'ring *Dog,* you?

Solemn. Its Lips Tremble, as if it would Speak, but this is not the time. Up, Up, my *Talisman,* and give thy Master and the Perturbed Spirit Quiet for a Season.— [*Puts Up his Tobacco-stopper.*
Now all is well again.— [*Sits Down.*
Sure something is Amiss, what-e'er it is.

Androb. Now he has lost Sight of Me again. Take out your what d'ye-call't once more, and may be I may tell you all.

Solemn. If I should impart this Odd Event to others, they'll not Credit it, and to show him in his Aerial Form, I dare not.

Androb. Can you show me to other Folks? I'm glad of that. You shall—

Solemn. Lest the Odious Name of Conjurer should be fixt upon me, and I (such is the prevailing Ignorance and Envy of the Age) instead of being Reverenc'd for my Science be hang'd for a Wizzard.

Androb. Look ye, I'll answer for you.

Solemn. Some other time I'll venture further, Mean while 'tis fit that I retire and ruminate upon this odd Phoenomenon, and find out by my *Talismanick Art* some means to unsear its Lips. [*Exit.*

Androb. Unsear your Ears, ye Old Buzzard, I can speak, but you, it seems, can't hear. He's gone, a Pestilence go with him. I can't tell what to think of it; Am I bew'itch't, or am I really Dead, as they say? It cannot be. Why, is not that a Hand as plain as a Pike Staff? Is not this a Nose? Don't I feel? Yes surely, to my Cost; for my back Akes still with the bruise I got when that Villain *Æsop* Over-set my Chair—yet I remember to have heard the learned say, that it is the Soul alone that Feels, the Body is but a Senseless Mass. If I did not think, I should not feel; then Perhaps I only think I feel. Think! I know not what to think, or whether I think at all, if I am Alive or Dead, or whether I ever was alive or no. Sure all this cannot be a Dream; I wish it were, and that I were fairly awake. O here come my good Friends, *Fizle* and *Flip.* Now I shall know.

Enter *Fizle* and *Flip*

Fizle. You must take no Notice of him at all, before he makes his Publick Entry; He'll have it so, and you know his Humor. Poor *Tom* has been Whipt almost to Death by his Orders, for barely Saluting him.

Flip. That is a little Whimsical, by the by; me thinks he might be visible to his Friends.

Androb. What's that? Pray Gentlemen, let me ask you one Question, because I hear, That there is some Doubt my Visibility; D'ye see me? Am I Alive or Dead? What d'ye Think?

Fizle. I told you so, this he does to try our Obedience. Answer him Not.

Androb. Will neither of you Answer me?

Fizle. At six a Clock I'll meet you here again. Adue.

[*Exeunt severally, without Noticing him.*

Androb. They're Gone, and saw me not! Nay, then 'tis too True. I am Dead, as sure as I'm Alive; Dead, Dead as a Herring, and something worse too; for I am Condemn'd to Converse with no Body, but Old *Solemn,* who ever was a Hell upon Earth to me. Would I could change that Doom for any other. Could I but have the Company of my Fellow Ghosts, I should be in some measure Happy, but that is not my Lot, it seems. If the Old Conjurer can but unsear Lips, as he calls it, or uncork his own Ears, as I take it, I might perhaps prevail with him to Conjure me a little better Conversation than his own. It is Tormenting, that I must be oblig'd to him: but there is no Remedy; I'll Wheadle him with a Story of the other World, of which I know as little as he does; That may work upon him.

Enter Tom, *with a Broom Sweeping the Gallary.*

Tom. What a Clutter is here about the Earthing an Old Stinking Corps; Would he had Lain in State in some other place; but rest his Soul, such was his Will.

[*Sings.*

Whenas Old Nick-Nack *Rul'd this Land,*
A Doughty Blade he Wore.
Four Dozen dragons Hides he Tann'd.
Of Gyants eke Four Score.

Androb. I wonder if the Ghosts of other Men hear all the Vile Things that are said and Sung of them after their Death? [Tom *sweeps the Dust on him.*

Tom.

But now he's Dead, and laid in Clay.—

This Dust is most Abominably Salt, I must qualify't a little.

[*Drinks, and spurts it upon him.*

What a Plaguy Earthy Taste this same small Beer has got, all of a suddain.

[*Sings*

But now he's Dead and laid in Clay,—

Androb. That's a Lye, for I a'n't Bury'd yet, by his own Confession.

Tom.

Alack, and Wo therefore,
The Gyants they may go to play,
The Dragons sleep and snore.

What a Carrion stink here is; the more I sweep the more it stinks.

Androb. Solemn can see me, but can't hear me; This Fellow can neither see me nor hear me; but he can smell me; I'll try if he can feel me.

Tom.

The Dragons sleep and snore.—

The stink Comes that way. [*Buts him on the Breast with the Broom.*
I'll Perfume the Air a little. [*Besprinkles him with the Bottle.*

Androb. Hold, Sirrah, hold. Well, if I were alive they durst not have us'd me thus; This Usage convinces me more than anything else. [*Exit.*

Tom. He has it, he has it; I doubt it will be a hard matter to perswade him to Life again.

Act Third, Scene Third.

Enter *Fizle* and *Flip.*

Fizle. We see, *Tom,* you are very busy. But if it be no Interruption, pray give us leave to ask you, In what manner the General is to make his Entry?

Tom. You have it.

Fizle. Nay, Answer us Directly.

Tom. I do, you have Leave.

Flip. Well then, In what manner is the General to make his Entry?

Tom. Ask him.

Fizle. Thank you for that; Ask him, and have our Curiosity answer'd as yours was. But we know that it depends in a great measure on the Keeper, and you of late are more in his Confidence than we.

Tom. If it depends upon the Keeper, He'll make his Entry by way of Exit? If upon himself, it is Problematical, and admits of several Solutions.

Flip. As how?

Tom. Either, *Hurry-Durry, Hum-Drum,* or *Blud and 'Owns.* Rest you Merry, Gentlemen. [*Exit.*

Fizle. We shall learn nothing from this Fellow; but so far we know, that the Keeper must assist at it; And from a broad by hints we have understood, that if he is destroy'd any how, so the General be not seen in't, He'll take that Trust upon himself; Then all will be Well. Now if we can but Contrive to have the Chair over Loaded, plac'd Upon the Hatch over the Vault, and the Hatch Unbolted, or so weakly Barr'd, that its weight may sink him Down, we shall get Rid of him, and it will appear to the world to be the meer Effect of Chance.

Tom. Peeping. Are you there with your Bears? I shall be up with you. I'll go find out *Solemn,* and try to build on this Foundation of their own Laying. [*Exit.*

Flip. This is Admirable, and cannot fail; Let's loose no time, but go about it streight; I'll get into the Vault, and Prepare the Bolt; do you take care to place the Chair. Here comes old *Solemn;* no more words, but *Mumm.* [*Exeunt.*

Enter *Solemn,* and *Tom.*

Solemn. Are you sure that you heard distinctly? The Excess of the Villany makes it incredible!

Tom. Am I sure that I live? But if you doubt it, the very Tampering with the Chair will Convince you.

Solemn. Away then, acquaint the Keeper, and *Æsop,* leave the rest to me. One thing you must take care be Punctually Observ'd that is, That *Androboros* Friends be planted next to the Chair, by way of Precedency. Quick, Quick, be gone.

Tom. I fly. [*Exit.*

Solemn. When Malice becomes a Moral Virtue, that Couple must be sainted; if the Long Robes were made use of only to Cover the Personal Defects and Blemishes of those who wear 'em, much might be said in their Defence; but when they are worn or lent to Cover Daggers, and Poyson prepar'd for the Innocent, is there a Mortal so devoid of Humanity as to appear on their side? If, as the Philosophers speak, the Corruption of the best Things produces the Worst, the Abuse of Things Sacred must be Dev'lish. O! you are come in good time.

Enter *Æsop.*

Pray get all in order for this same Entry; Neglect not that part of the Ranking of them, which I, *by Tom,* recommended to you. I'll Equip the General, and dispose him for his Triumph: In the mean while do you Intertain 'em with a Tale, or how you please, until he comes.

Æsop. Dispatch then, for they grow Impatient. [*Exit Æsop.*

Enter *Androboros.*

Androb. I hope he has by this time found a way to unsear my Lips or his own Ears, no matter which.

Solemn. Here he comes pat. *Nick-Nack,* How dos't do? I'm glad to see thee Awake with all my heart.

Androb. Is the Dev'l in the Fellow? He can see me now without the help of his Gymcrack; not to mention your odd Familiarity. What d'ye mean by Awake? When was I asleep?

Solemn. Asleep! You have been so Time out of mind. You have been Walking asleep, Talking asleep, and Fighting asleep, I know not how long.

Androb. I'm glad it's no Worse; I Thought I was Dead, at least every body else seem'd to think so.

Solemn. Dead! No, No, No; it is all a Jest.

Androb. Why, you old Raskal, you, Did you not but now start at the sight of me, as if you had seen a Ghost?

Solemn. True, yet you are not actually Dead, but Invisible to all the World besides, and must continue so, so long as I shall think fitting.

Androb. aside. I ever thought this Fellow had the black Art. [*to him*] I wish thou would'st change that Curse for any other. Canst thou not make thy self invisible to me, as thou hast done me to other Folks? So far I own I would be oblig'd to thee, and thank thee.

Solemn. If that will oblige you, 'tis done, Look but into this Tellescope, and in that instant I shall become invisible to you.

[*Looks into a hollow Cane;* Solemn *from the other End blows Snuff into his Eyes.*

It is done?

Androb. Villian, Dog, Raskal, I'm blind; Where are ye, ye Villian, Murderer?

Solemn. Here, This way, This way; You must see with your Ears, until I shall think fit to Unsear your Eyes, General; That is the bargain, if I remember right.

[*Exit* Solemn, Androb. *Groping his way after him.*

Act Third, Scene Fourth.

Curtain drawn, Discovers Keeper, Deputy, Tom, Æsop, Fizle, Flip, Coxcomb, Babilard, Mullegrub, *&c.*

Keeper. Let the black Gentlemen be Rank'd as they desire; I'll do all I can to please 'em.

Æsop. With all my Heart, Only I thought it bad Heraldry that these who are supported by the Chair, should support it.

Keeper. Another time you shall have your way; I'll have it so now; let the Rest observe their distance. [*Here they are rank't,* Fizle *and* Flip *next to the Chair.*

Æsop. I'll keep as distant as I can, that I may be at Ease; *Fizle's* Phiz always gives me the Chollick. I know not why he should be suffer'd to walk at Large, to the Detriment of his Majestys Leige People, whilst so many of his Species up and down the World are Insty'd, Inkennel'd, Impounded or Incloyster'd. Did you ever hear how that came about? I'll tell you, if you please.

Keeper. Come on.

Æsop. And First of the First,

Nature, which nothing leaves to Chance,
Had dealt to Creatures of each Kind,
Provision for their Sustenance,
To some her Bounty had Assign'd
The Herb o'th' Fields, whilst others had
The Spoils of Trees, but All were Fed.

The Grunting Kind obtain'd the last,
A happy Lot; for every Wood
Afforded store of Nuts and Mast,
And *Joves* own Tree did Show'r down Food
Enough for all, could all his Store
Have kept that Herd from Craving more.

But they with Sloath and Plenty Cloy'd,
Wax'd Wanton, and with Tusks Profane,
First, all the sacred Trees Destroy'd,
Which fed 'em; Next invade the Plain,
Where harmless Flocks did graze, and Spoil
With Rav'nous Snouts the fertile Soil.

Jove hears the loud Complaints and Cry's
Of Suff'ring Flocks, and streight Ordains,
That hence-forth Hogs be pen't in Sty's.
And fed with Wash, and Husks, and Grains;
Where ever since th' Unhallow'd Race
Wallows in Fat and Filthyness.

Secondly, Beloved—

Keeper. No, No, We have enough of the first. [*Noise within.* What Noise is that?

Androb. within. I'll have the Villian Hang'd; Dog, Raskal, Rogue, Scoundrel.

Æsop. By my Life, it is the General making his Entry; It seems he has got no Herald for this Triumph, that he thus Proclaims his own Titles.

[Enter *Solemn,* Androboros *following him.*

Solemn. Make way there, Make way; Room, Room for the General; This way,— This way—

[Solemn *Steps aside,* Androboros *Runs blindly upon the Chair,* Fizle *and* Flip *Endeavouring to Stop him, Sink with Him.*

Fizle and *Flip.* Hold. Hold; Help! Help! Help!

Keeper. What's the meaning of this?

Solemn. 'Tis but a Trap of their Own laid for you, Sir, in which They Themselves are Caught.

Coxcomb. Let's be gone! There is no Safety here.

[*Coxcomb, Babilard, Mulligrub Sneaking off.*

Solemn. What! You are a making your Retreat; you need not fear, you are a sort of Vermin not worth the Bait; The others have their Deserts.

In former Ages virtuous Deeds
Rais'd Mortals to the blest Abodes,
But Hero's of the Modern Breed
And Saints go downward to the Gods.

[Exeunt.

Curtain Falls.

FINIS.

· 16 ·

[James Spence and Roderick MacKenzie], The Groans of Jamaica (London, 1714)

THIS PAMPHLET, which created a great stir in London, provides a detailed account of a situation with an inexperienced governor, in this case, Lord Archibald Hamilton, governor of Jamaica from 1711 to 1716, and uninformed provincial judges, which resulted in the engrossment of power by manipulative subordinate officers who enjoyed the ear of the governor. The body of the pamphlet, which may have been the work of the Reverend James Spence, an Anglican minister in Jamaica, consists of a long and detailed account of the many ways in which three men—Richard Rigby, who was secretary and provost marshal; William Brodrick, who was attorney general; and Dr. John Stewart—imposed upon Hamilton and in the process subverted both the governor's instructions from the Crown and provincial laws, enriching themselves through extortion, illegal escheat-brokering, and many other flagrant acts of oppression and obtaining a virtual monopoly of power within the colony. When the Jamaica Assembly, led by Speaker Peter Beckford, endeavored to pass legislation to curb the power of this triumvirate, Hamilton simply vetoed their measures. When Beckford and other island leaders tried to send agents to London to complain about Hamilton's arbitrary government and the illegal machinations of Rigby and his associates, Hamilton refused to let the agents leave the island. The pamphlet appealed to London authorities to free Jamaica from this oppression by "divesting our tyrannizing Triumvirate of all their Power and Places."

The preface to the pamphlet, perhaps written by Roderick MacKenzie, who had gone to Jamaica as Hamilton's secretary but had lost his office after the governor fell under the influence of the triumvirate, is notable for succinctly identifying two of the principal problems that were responsible for colonial discontent with British imperial governance during the quarter century after the Glorious Revolution. The first was the indeterminate nature of the imperial constitution. How, he asked, "should it come to pass, that in all the Revolutions of State, and Changes of the Ministry, which have happened here [in England], these Sixty Years past, and upwards, ever since the happy Restoration of King *Charles* IId. so great an Accession to the Power, Riches and Glory of this Kingdom, as are undoubtedly the several Colonies which compose the *British* Empire in *America,* should . . . lye still so much neglected: under such a precarious Government and grievous Administration, as they have, for the most part, labour'd under, both before and after the late signal Revolution: tho' of late years (as far as I can learn) still worse?" The second problem the author raised was the wide scope of nominal authority that the metropolis granted to colonial governors. Given the fact that Englishmen had "found it necessary to tie up even the best of our Princes, as well as the bad, by good and wholesome Laws," why, he asked, should "a Governor of any Colony of Her Majesty's Free-born Subjects, in the *West-Indies,* so far distant from the Seat of Redress, either by Appeals, or otherwise, . . . be vested with a Power to govern, in a more absolute and unlimited manner there, than even the Queen herself can, according to Law, or ever did attempt to exercise in *Great Britain?*" (J.P.G.)

THE
Groans of *JAMAICA*,
Express'd in a
LETTER
FROM A
GENTLEMAN Residing there,
TO HIS
FRIEND in *LONDON*;

CONTAINING

A clear Detection, and most convincing Narrative

OF

Some of the crying Grievances, and fraudulent Oppressions, which gave the first Rise to the present growing Discontents, Divisions, and Animosities, among the Inhabitants of that Island:

AS ALSO

Particular Characters of the chief Authors and Promoters of these Distractions.

Prov. 27. 5. *Open rebuke is better than secret Love.*

Chap. 28. 4. *They that forsake the Law, praise the Wicked;*
But they that keep the Law contend with them.

Chap. 22. 10. *Cast out the Scorner, and Contention shall go out;*
Yea, Strife and Reproach shall cease.

LONDON: Printed in the Year, 1714.

The Publisher's Preface to the Reader.

Happening to cast my eyes, some Time since, on a late Collection of Familiar Letters, written by some Gentlemen in *Jamaica,* to their several Friends in *London,* touching the then *present State and Administration of the Government of that Island,* and printed *Anno* 1713. and judging that the Bulk thereof may have deterred several Persons, to whose Hands the same may have come, from giving themselves the Trouble of reading and deliberately considering the whole Contents of that Collection; I cull'd out, from among all the other Letters, that one whereof the following is a true Copy; as comprehending, in my Opinion, much more variety of useful Matter, than any one of all the rest. And hoping that such Persons as now have, or hereafter may have it in their Power, to enquire into, and redress all, or any of the Grievances therein set forth, may not grudge the Time they'll bestow on reading the following Sheets, I thought it might possibly be of some use to the Publick, to have it reprinted apart, in the manner you now see the same.

The Author (whoever he be) seems to have been not only at abundance of pains, in procuring particular Information, and making himself fully Master of the several Matters of Fact mention'd in this Letter, but has also so very clearly recited them, and express'd his own Thoughts and Animadversions thereon, and supported the same with such circumstantiated Evidence, and undoubted Authorities, that I reckon it next to an impossibility, for any intelligent and unbyass'd Person to read the whole deliberately; once all over, without being throughly convinced of the manifest and clear Truth thereof; and consequently of the many gross Abuses imposed on the Queen and Her Ministry here, as well as on Her Majesty's Subjects of *Jamaica,* by a Triumvirate of vile, profane, mercenary, and ignominious Upstarts, with the implicite Concurrence and Suffrage of a certain Tool, they have got into their Hands.

Some Readers may possibly object, That the Stile of the following Letter is too serious and prolix; that the making use of such scriptural Texts, and Latin Quotations, as are, here and there, interspersed in it, favours too much of Pedantry; and that, in some Places, the thread of the Narrative seems to be interrupted, with needless Digressions.

The Truth is, I had once some Thoughts of having made an Abridgment of this Letter, so as to have reduced the chief Heads thereof, into a much narrower Compass: But then I considered that such an Abridgement would have quite alter'd the Quality thereof, and be much the same as fathering another Man's Child: Moreover, I considered that no such clear view can be given, to Persons here, of Affairs transacted at so great a distance, as when they are illustrated with all the material Circumstances attending them: And then, as the subject Matter is, of it self, very grievous and afflicting, in many respects; so 'tis no wonder if the Consideration thereof may have put the Writer in a more serious Mood than ordinary, at the Time: Nay, who knows but that possibly he may also have been a Sharer in some of those Afflictions, occasion'd by the fraudulent and perjurious Practices complain'd of, in this Letter: And if so, he must, of course, have been still the more affected therewith: And therefore, in expostulating about the base and horrid unworthiness of some of the Facts therein mentioned, he could not, in a more pathetick and forcible manner, have inculcated a true and feeling Sense thereof, into the mind of his Correspondent, than by appealing to the sacred Oracles, and some approved moral Authors, for a Judgment in such Cases: And such a scriptural strain seems still the more natural, and less liable to Exception, if what I have heard whispered be true; that a certain Clergyman of that Island (who, by the Duty of his Function, may probably have thought himself obliged to *Rebuke, Reprove, and Exhort, in Season and out of Season*) wrote it; tho, as he is now stated, he may not think it convenient to have his Name publickly known, at least while he remains there; because indeed the doing any good Office of that nature, upon the Point of Opinion, Intelligence, Brains, or Conscience, where such a Wolfish Humor prevails, as now reigns in *Jamaica*, is commonly considered as a sort of *Scandalum Magnatûm*;[1] and therefore too frequently exposeth one to the Envy, Hatred, Malice and Revenge of such potent Calumniators, as may likewise be his Judges, even in their own Cause.

Then, as to such Digressions as are to be met with, in the following Letter, tho' they may, at first view, seem to be somewhat Foreign to the chief Design, and subject-Matter thereof; yet, upon a more serious Review, they'll appear to be strong supplemental Arguments, for supporting the verity of

1. ["Slander of great men."]

such general Characters as are given of the several Persons therein named: And as to the supposed Charge of Pedantry, I take it for granted, that none but those who do not understand Latin, will find much fault with using apposite Latin Phrases, on proper Occasions: and even such Persons will, upon perusal, find, if they slip over all the Latin Phrases us'd here, the Sense and Coherence will still remain clear enough, without them.

I must own, it has, oftner than once, been the Subject of my Admiration, as well as Contemplation, how it should come to pass, that in all the Revolutions of State, and Changes of the Ministry, which have happened here, these Sixty Years past, and upwards, ever since the happy Restoration of King *Charles* IId. so great an Accession to the Power, Riches and Glory of this Kingdom, as are undoubtedly the several Colonies which compose the *British* Empire in *America,* should (even in the most noted Periods of that Time, for either Peace or War) lye still so much neglected, under such a precarious Government and greivous Administration, as they have, for the most part, labour'd under, both before and since the late signal Revolution: tho' of late Years (as far as I can learn) still worse and worse.

'Tis true, the present Ministry have had their Heads so much imployed about the weightiest Affairs of State, at home, and in settling the general Peace of *Europe;* that it may, very justly, be supposed, they have not had Time enough, as yet, to look so far Abroad, as to have taken immediate Cognizance of the several Constitutions, present Circumstances, and particular Grievances of the *British* West India Plantations. But, 'tis hoped that, in due Time, these may likewise fall under their serious Consideration.

I know some designing and wicked People have been, and still are, at no small Pains to inculcate into the Minds of all Persons in Authority, whom they have the Opportunity of conversing or corresponding with, very mean Notions and Sentiments of the Births, Education, Manners, Principles, and other Qualities of the Inhabitants of those Plantations; and, under such disadvantagious Characters, their several Oppressors have, from Time to Time, endeavour'd to misrepresent them here, as a turbulent, factious, and uneasie People, never to be pleased, under any Government whatsoever.

To which it may very justly be replied, That, upon an impartial Examination and Tryal, it would manifestly appear, that all the Contentions and Animosities, which, at any time, happen between the Governour and Inhabitants of any of the *West-India* Plantations, have (generally speaking, and particularly as to *Jamaica*) had their first Rise, from some grievous and intolerable Acts of Oppression, in the Administration: And therefore 'tis not to be much wonder'd at, if such should produce some Repinings, Heart-burnings and Discontents, among a People otherways very peaceably disposed; when the wisest of Men found from his own Experience, and left it to us, as a certain Aphorism, recorded in Scripture, that *Oppression maketh even a wise Man mad.*

It cannot be denied, but that, in peopling those Plantations, many Persons of obscure Births and very indifferent Characters went, or were, from time to time, sent and transported thither, as Occasion required: But 'tis as true, that some thousands of Persons of very creditable Families, good Education, and loyal Principles, went thither likewise; some through the Narrowness of their Circumstances; some to avoid the Miseries of the Civil War at home; and others to improve such paternal or acquired Fortunes and Estates, as they thought convenient to carry along with them, at the time.

The present Inhabitants are generally Her Majesty's natural born Subjects, Natives either of *England, Scotland,* or *Ireland,* or born of such, in the Plantations: Many of them are Gentlemen of very liberal Education, some even at Universities: And such having, by their own, or their Forefathers Industry, acquired the Property and Possession of very considerable Plantations and Estates, and being desirous and willing to enjoy the same comfortably, and to live peaceably, as good and dutiful Subjects, cannot but grudge extremely to find, that (as particularly in *Jamaica*) profound Ignorance, accompanied with vast Impudence in some, a stupid, blind, indolent and implicite Acquiescence in others, and a crafty, active, knavish Genius, blended with Lewdness, Atheism and Irreligion in a third sort; and all varnished over, with a servile, fawning seeming Obsequiousness, should be the Chief, if not the only, recommending Qualities, to entitle even the worst of Men, tho' sprung up as suddenly, in one Night's time, as Mushrooms out of a Dunghill, to a Go——r's Favour; while, at the same time, Men of Virtue, Merit and Capacity, are not only discouraged, insulted, and oppressed, but also revil'd, belied and ridicul'd, to an intolerable Degree, with Buffoonry, Impudence and Nonsense; to the great Encouragement of Vice and Immorality, in those Parts.

Could we reasonably suppose, and be assured of a constant Succession of wise, judicious, just, good and pious Princes on the Throne, like Her present Majesty; and of such like Governors, in all Provinces and far distant Plantations, and that these again would, in their Choice of all subordinate Judges, Magistrates and other Officers, regulate themselves by the most apparent Proofs of the Vertue, Merit and Capacity of the several Candidates, for Offices of Trust and Profit: I believe all good Men would join with me in Opinion, That, of all the several Forms of Government on Earth, an unlimited absolute Government would undoubtedly be the best, on many Accounts; but the Experience the World has had of the lamentable Weakness of some Princes and Rulers, of all Degrees; and of the extravagant Passions and insatiable Avarice, Ambition, Lust, and Revenge of some others; has so fully demonstrated the Vanity and Folly of such a fruitless and chimerical Supposition, that the Wisdom of our Ancestors found it necessary to tie up even the best of our Princes, as well as the bad, by good and wholesome Laws.

The Consideration whereof makes it still so much more the Subject of my Wonder; that a Governor of any Colony of Her Majesty's Free-born Subjects, in the *West-Indies*, so far distant from the Seat of Redress, either by Appeals, or otherwise, should be vested with a Power to govern, in a more absolute and unlimited manner there, than even the Queen her self can, according to Law, or ever did attempt to exercise in *Great Britain*.

The Governor of *Jamaica* (*e.g.*) is not only CAPTAIN GENERAL, and Commander in Chief of that Island, and other the Territories thereunto belonging, and likewise CHANCELLOR, and Vice-Admiral thereof; but has also the sole Power of nominating, appointing, continuing, turning out, and putting in again, at Pleasure, as often and whensoever he will, all and every one of the Judges of all the other Courts of Judicature, throughout the said Island; and likewise the Power of calling, continuing, adjourning, proroguing, dissolving, and issuing new Writs, for succeeding Assemblies; at Pleasure, without any manner of Limitation, as to time or otherways: by Means whereof, the Free-holders have been frequently plagued, harrassed and disappointed, in their own private Affairs, by Elections and long Sessions, to little good Purpose, at times very unseasonable for the Planting-Interest; and as frequently prorogued or dissolved again, whenever they could not be prevail'd upon, to comply implicitely with the arbitrary Dictates, and injurious Measures of some few designing Persons, whose constant Plot is to enrich themselves, by enslaving the Inhabitants.

The Governor is likewise, in effect (tho' not nominally) BISHOP of *Jamaica*: For, he's vested with the sole Power of nominating, appointing, and collating Ministers in all and every one of the Parishes of that Island; (which are 17 in Number) has also the granting of all Letters of Administration, all

Probates of Wills and Testaments, all Licences for Marriages, and Licences for permitting School-Masters to teach; the naming and appointing Guardians for absent Orphans: And, in short, is sole Judge of all Matters relating to the Consistorial or Ecclesiastick Law there:

Now, how such an universal Knowledge, Experience and Judgment, both of Men and Things, as seems necessary to accomplish any Man, for the Discharge of so universal and unlimited a Trust, in so many different Capacities as aforesaid, should (without immediate Inspiration) be acquired, by a Person who was never, any way, noted for the Brightness of his natural Parts, and who had not the Advantage of any other Education, but what he had between the Stem and Stern of a Ship, ever since he was sent a young Youth to Sea, in or about the Year 1687. is (I must own) above my Comprehension. And yet (which adds still to the Miseries of that Island) all the Commissions, Commands, Orders, Injunctions, Directions, Judgments, and Decrees of this same Despotick Go——r, (or rather of his Triumvirate Tutors) are incomparably less liable to be reversed, than the Decrees of the most knowing as well as the most learned and judicious Lord High Chancellor of *Great Britain.*

For. 1*st.* There can be no Appeal from the said Go——r's Judgment, unless the *Subjectum Controversiae*[2] be of the Value of 500 *l.* at the least. 2*dly.* None can come off that Island, on any pretence whatsoever, without the Governor's express Leave in writing, under his Hand; which is sometimes not to be obtain'd, but by giving very extravagant Bail, far beyond the Value of the Subject-Matter in Debate; and frequently not, at all, on any account. And, 3*dly,* Even when an Appeal reacheth hither, it cannot be try'd any where, but before the Queen in Council: And the said Governor happening to be born of a great Family, (tho' he be the very Refuse and worthless Dregs thereof) his noble Relations, Allies, and their Friends here, may possibly, be so far prepossessed, by a natural Byass (how imperceptible soever to themselves) in his Favour, and for supporting whatever is said to be for his Power, Interest and Credit (tho', much more properly, for that of his scandalous Tutors) that 'tis ten to one, but a poor Appellant, after all his Trouble, Pains and Expence, may come off, with the weeping

2. ["Subject of controversy."]

Cross, at last; and have to say with the disappointed Alchymist, *Jamque oleam & operam perdidi.*[3]

The melancholly Consideration of all which, as well as of the large Joint-Stock-Purse, raised from the Produce of Prize-Goods, Escheated Estates, and other Spoils of the Oppressed, which that nimble, crafty, and Jesuitical V——n (Mr. *R——by*) has ready at Command (as being absolute Plenipotentiary here, for the Go——r and his scandalous Faction) and likewise of the amazing Reception, Countenance and Protection he has likewise hitherto met with, makes many injur'd and oppress'd Persons in *Jamaica*, who otherwise would be Appellants, sit down tamely, and bear with their Miseries, as well as they can, for the time; rather than attempt swimming against the Stream, while they see the Torrent of their Despotick Go——r's Fury, as well as that of his Tutors and Tools, run with so impetuous and irresistible a Force, as at present; notwithstanding the manifest Bent of the Generality of the Inhabitants Inclinations against them:

But since the said Governor has, by his suffering himself to be (as he has been, all along, and still is) implicitely govern'd, by the arbitrary Directions of the aforesaid Triumvirate, in all the Branches of his extensive Administration; and consequently subjected himself to the Odium of being censured for all their Mal-Practices, under the Umbrage of his Authority; and has hitherto, by the Interest of his Relations and Friends here, screen'd the said Triumvirate from Prosecutions, which otherwise would probably have fallen very heavy upon them; it may seem somewhat strange that a Person ever noted for a wretched, needy and avaricious Temper, should be so far hood-wink'd, as (among many other over-look'd Advantages) to dispense with all manner of Fees, and Perquisites whatsoever, arising by Vertue of his *Episcopal Power* above-mention'd, (which, by the by, are not inconsiderable) these three Years, last past, in favour of his pious and Orthodox Suffragan, Mr. *R——by*, (*vide Pag.* 13, 14, 15, 16.) And which makes such a Piece of Delusion so much still the more ridiculous, the said *Ri——d R——by* has banter'd the Gov——r into an implicite Belief, that he (the said *R——by*) holds the same, not by his Excellency's Favour, but *de Jure*[4] as Deputy-Secretary of the Island: And his trusty Sub-Deputy (Doctor *St——rt*, another of the aforesaid Triumvirate) *de facto* receives the same

3. [Literally, "And now I have lost both the precious stone and the art," that is, I have lost the magic.—Tr.]

4. ["By law, legally."]

now for him in his Absence. But the Reader will readily discover the Reason thereof, and of many much grosser Abuses, by reading the following Letter.

A Letter, containing an Account of the most general Grievances of Jamaica, arising from the Multiplication of Offices in the Person of R. R——by Esq; some of the many fraudulent Practices by which he and his Accomplices do aggrandize their own Fortunes, under the false Pretence of increasing the Queen's Revenue, by escheating many Freeholders Estates, &c. as also some short Hints touching the Characters, Designs and Principles of the said R. R——by and others.

Jamaica, 6 *Octob.* 1712.

SIR,

There having been an Embargo on all Ships here, since the Day of *August,* till *Monday* last; and no Ship arriving here, from *Britain* or *Ireland,* these two Months past, we are impatient to know what should be the Cause thereof, especially since our last Advices put us in hopes of the speedy Conclusion of a *General Peace:* Tho, at the same time, we have been plagued and harass'd here, with *Martial Law,* more than during the Heat of the War; and that too, immediately upon the back of a most terrible and destructive Hurricane; which made the Consequences of *Martial Law* so much the more insupportably grievous, to all the Inhabitants of this Island: But since I reckon that most of the Letters which go by this Conveyance will, of course, be cramm'd with dismal Accounts of the aforesaid Hurricane, *&c.* I think it needless to trouble you, or my self, with any particular Detail of the Effects thereof, at this time.

In my Letter of the 18*th* of *July,* by the *Bignal*-Galley (to which I refer) I gave you some cursory View of the Constitution of our Government here;

and withal some general Characters of the constituent Members of a certain Triumvirate, by whose Contrivance and Influence, the same is, upon every different Occasion, modell'd and metamorphosed so as to suit with their several Purposes, from time to time.

You may remember, it was a current Story here, some Years ago, that when one of the Inhabitants of *Montserrat* happen'd to be condoled here, upon account of the Losses they had sustain'd there, some time before, by a Hurricane; he said, this Island was much more to be pitied than they, since we had got a worse and more lasting Plague amongst us, *(viz. B——k)* whom they had banish'd from *Montserrat,* under a severe Penalty, *never to return thither again;* even tho' he has still, to this hour (as I am credibly informed) a Legal Title to a Plantation there, which he craftily obtained, by treacherously supplanting his Client.

Had it been possible for that Person to have had as lively a Conception, and previous View of Mr. *R——by*'s Contrivances and Actions here, these several Years past, as he had of *Br——k*'s, he would have thought this Island most lamentably plagu'd with a witness, to see them the two chief constituent Members of the *Triumvirate* aforesaid, and acting here in concert. Nor indeed can I foresee when an End may be put to the many afflicting Grievances under which this poor discouraged Island doth now labour, until some Men of Eminence in the Government at home, be fully appriz'd, and take Cognizance of the said *R——by*'s Character and Conduct, in a very special manner: For which end, I adventure to send you now an introductory Account of some part thereof; by which it may appear, that a Person of such Jesuitical Principles and Practices as *R——by* is singularly noted for, is too hard a Match for the Simplicity and plain Dealing of the Generality of our Planters here.

The said Mr. *R——by* having had some Years Schooling on the Foundation of *Eaton* College (as one of his Cotemporaries, a Planter of this Island, informed me) he served some time thereafter in the Quality of Clerk to an Attorney in the *Temple,* (as one of his Father's Apprentices, now likewise a Planter in this Island, told me:) But having, it seems, more aspiring Thoughts, and being of a Family that pretended to some Merit at the Court of *St. Germains,* he took a Trip thither, and remain'd some Years abroad; where (as I am likewise inform'd) he had the chief part of his Education with the Jesuits, both in *France* and *Italy*. However, finding the *Jacobite* Interest decline apace, and being disappointed of what he proposed to himself and sollicited for at *St. Germains,* (as a Gentleman, who was then intimate with him in *France,* likewise inform'd me) he return'd for *England.* But his extreme Modesty not allowing him to put in for any publick Business in *England,* where his Character, and that of his Family, were pretty well known, he transacted, in the Year 1705. with Mr. *Edward Hyde,* the then Provost-Marshal of this Island, for resigning in his Favour, and procuring him (the said *R——by*) a new Grant or Patent for that Office, in consideration of a certain Sum of Money, to be paid at such Times, and in such Manner, and Proportions, as was then agreed upon: And the said Mr. *Hyde* acting only by a Deputy, and knowing (it seems) but very little of the Nature or Value of that Place, was (as I am likewise credibly informed) sufficiently imposed upon, in making that Bargain.

However, Mr. *R——by* arriving here, soon after, with the Character and Authority of Provost-Marshal General of this Island, and giving himself the Air of being a strict Assertor of the Court-Principles then, and still, most in fashion here, did, by his natural Cunning, with the help of his acquired Parts, so transform himself into several Shapes, as Occasion offer'd, and adapt his Measures to such various Purposes as he had in view, that he thereby rendred himself so very acceptable to the then Governor, that, in a short time thereafter, he became the chief Favourite.

At the Governor's Request, Colonel *B——r* (a Gentleman of loyal and worthy Principles, and having a very opulent Fortune here) was prevail'd upon to be Security (for Form's sake, as it were) in a Bond of 4000 *l.* for the said Mr. *R——by*'s faithful Discharge of his Office, as Provost-Marshal; tho' an absolute Stranger to him, at the time: But happening to go, both of them in Company, to the *Bath,* up to Windward, and remaining some time there, drinking the Waters, the said *R——by* did so perpetually teaze that Gentleman with repeated Lectures out of his beloved *Vade mecum*[5] (*Machiavel*'s Works) and, with all the force of his Rhetorick, did so endeavour to inculcate the like political Principles in him, that, ever thereafter, Colonel *B——r* look'd upon him (the said *R——by*) as the most dangerous and ensnaring Person, and of the most loose and pernicious Principles, of all the Men that ever he knew, in this Island: And being, therefore, resolved not to have any farther Dealing or Familiarity with him, gave him Warning to find other Security, for that he was determin'd not to continue bound any longer for him.

The said Mr. *R——by,* upon the Death, or other Removal of the then Clerk of the Council, and Deputy-Secretary of this Island, was, by the

5. [Literally, "Go with me," i.e., ready reference.—Tr.]

then Governor's Favour, in or about the Month of *October*, 1706. appointed to succeed in the Execution of these Offices; and, by Virtue of the same Interest, obtain'd, in or about the Year 1707. from Mr. *Baber*, the Patentee, a Deputation for executing the several Offices and Places of Secretary of this Island, Clerk of the Enrolments, and Commissary-General of Stores, Provisions, *&c.* for the small yearly Consideration of 250 *l.* as I am informed.

And it happening so, that, though many Complaints were exhibited to the Governor, Council and Assembly, against the said Mr. *R——by*, for alledg'd Male-administrations committed, and arbitrary extravagant Fees exacted by him or his Deputies, in or about the Execution of the said several and respective Offices; yet, by his great Power and Interest with the then Governor, the same were always slighted, shuffled, or put off, from time to time, till the said Governor and Council were, by repeated Complaints and Importunities, (as I am credibly informed) prevailed upon, at last, to make an Order, or Rule of Council, That he (the said Mr. *R——by*) or any other succeding Clerk of the Council, should not, as such, demand or receive, from any Tradesman or others, any Gratuity, Fee, or Reward whatsoever; but that, in consideration thereof, such Clerk should be allowed 10 *s.* and no more, out of the Publick Revenue, for every Order of the Governor and Council; touching the Payment of Money, *&c.* or in Words to that effect: Whereupon Mr. *R——by* took occasion, some time thereafter, to compliment Governor *Handasyd*, by resigning the said Office of Clerk of the Council, in favour of Mr. *Silvester Stuckley*, his Excellency's Secretary at the time.

And as a farther Confirmation of the Truth of the aforesaid Charge against Mr. *R——by*, the Assembly of this Island, convened at *St. Jago de la Vega*, on the 17*th* of *April*, 1711. did, upon examining the Truth of the several Matters of Fact, mentioned in the Petitions, or Complaints, then exhibited against him, Vote and Resolve, *nemine contradicente*,[6] *That He (the said Mr.* R——by, *was guilty of having demanded several arbitrary and exorbitant Fees*, &c. And thereupon ordered, That a Bill for regulating Fees (which was in a former Session passed by the Governor, Council, and Assembly, on the like account, tho' refused at home) should be then again brought in, with such proper Amendments, as were directed by Her Majesty in Council: and in pursuance thereof, the said Governor, Council and Assembly, passed *an Act for regulating Fees* accordingly.

6. ["With no one dissenting, unanimously."]

Here I must not omit informing you, That, some time after passing the aforesaid unanimous Resolve of the Assembly, Mr. *R——by* did, by his dextrous Management, obtain a subsequent Vote, *That he had executed the Office of Secretary of this Island to the Satisfaction of the House;* or in Words to that effect; which happen'd thus: While this Matter was depending before the Assembly, he affected a political Sickness, and gave out, in a seeming private manner, that he intended to quit the Island, for the Recovery of his Health, *&c.* and made Offers of resigning some one or other of the Offices then executed by him, to each of several Persons, who, by their respective Relations had Interest with, and Influence on some Members of the Assembly; and having, by means of such Assurance, as he gave the Candidates for these Offices respectively, taken off the Edge of their Friends in the Assembly, who promised to favour him, and use their Interest with other Members likewise, on the aforesaid account, the said last Vote was carried in his favour, in manner above recited: And tho' several pretended Bargains for resigning the aforesaid Offices, to several Persons, were carried on so far, that some of the Parties sent Credit, and others actually remitted Money to *England,* for that effect; yet the real Ends for which the aforesaid pretended Resignments were first offered, being fully answered, none of the said Bargains were ever fulfilled or comply'd with by Mr. *R——by,* to this hour.

However, without any regard to these pretended Bargains, the same Governor, Council and Assembly were so fully convinced of Mr. *R——by's* over-dextrous Management (not to give it a harder Name) in the Execution of the several Offices abovementioned, and of the dangerous Consequences that did and might attend the executing them, by one and the same Person, that, *for prevention thereof, for the future,* they made an Act in the Month of *June,* 1711. *That from and after the first Day of* May, 1712. *no Secretary, or Deputy Secretary, for the time being, in this Island, should be capable to hold, use, exercise, or enjoy the Office or Place of Provost-Marshal, or Deputy Provost-Marshal of this Island, or, by any Ways or Means, to execute or officiate in that Office, or any other Office of Profit in this Island: And that no Provost-Marshal or Deputy Provost-Marshal of this Island, should be capable to hold, use, exercise, or enjoy the Office or Place of Secretary, or Deputy-Secretary of this Island, or by any Ways or Means to execute or officiate in that Office, or any other Office of Profit in this Island: But that the same and all other Offices of Profit in this Island, should be, for ever thereafter, distinct and separate, so as that no two or more Offices of Profit in this Island should, upon any Pretence whatsoever, be in the Hands of any one Person; or any one Person receive the Profits of two or more of the said Offices,* &c.

But the Assembly had at the same time such a dutiful Regard to the Queen's Prerogative in granting Patents, to whom Her Majesty should think fit, that they added a special Clause to the said Act; reserving the same; to the end it might not meet with any Obstruction in obtaining the Royal Assent at home.

Mr. *R——by* carried his Resentment so far against Mr. *Beckford* the then Speaker, and other leading Members of that Assembly, that he, and some few others in his Interest, prevail'd with the then Governor (upon a sham Pretence) to dissolve 'em, in or about the Month of *June,* 1711. (which was but two Months from the time of their first Convention) and to issue out new Writs for another Assembly to be conven'd at *St. Jago de la Vega,* on *Monday* the 23*d* of *July* following: In the Interval of which time, his Excellency, the Lord *Archibald Hamilton,* our present Governor, arriving here, the said new Assembly met accordingly, on the aforesaid 23*d* Day of *July;* have been continued, by several Prorogations, ever since; and are, in all Appearance, likely to be continued the standing Assembly of this Island, as long as the said Mr. *R——by* and Mr. *Br——ck,* our present Attorney-General, are supported in the unlimited Influence which they now have on the Administration of all publick Affairs here; for many of the Members of the present Assembly having, very unexpectedly, and in a most surprizing manner, been chosen, with much more sinister Art than ever was practis'd in, or about any former Elections in this Island; and being, by reason of their narrow Circumstances, and the assumed Privileges they enjoy, of being protected against their lawful Creditors, implicitly devoted to the arbitrary Dictates of Messieurs *R——by* and *B——ck,* in all Matters that can come before them; it is not to be supposed, that such thorough-pac'd Tools will be readily parted with, as long as they can be kept together.

Now, considering that Mr. *R——by,* as Provost Marshal-General, is, by his Deputies, Marshals, and Deputy-Marshals, the Executioner of the Law, both in Civil and Criminal Cases; and is (by Deputation from Mr. *Baber* the Patentee) Secretary of the Island, Commissary General, and Clerk of the Enrolments, for Registring all Deeds and Conveyances, all Bills of Sale, Letters Patents, and other Acts and Matters usually enrolled here; and has likewise, (even to the manifest Prejudice of the Governor himself) the Benefit of all Fees and Perquisites of and for all Probates of Wills and Testaments, the granting of all Letters of Administration, and all Licenses for Marriage, *&c.*

It was no small surprize to most of the intelligent and thinking Men of this Island, to see him, (the said *R——by*) advanc'd yet farther, to be one of the Council-Board, by Virtue of a Privy-Seal, which the present Governor was prevailed upon, by the Perswasions of Sir *C——t W——y*, and Messieurs *K——t* and *T——n*, to bring over along with him, for that end: And indeed the Concern of the Inhabitants for his aforesaid Promotion, seems to be too well grounded, because (as being a Member of the Council, in conjunction with his aforesaid Offices) he acts now in a Legislative, Judicial, and Executive Capacity; and by means of that accumulated Power, together with his manifest Influence on the Governor, in all respects whatsoever, seems to be uncontrolably skreen'd and protected from all manner of Complaints that dare now be exhibited against himself, or his Deputies; and has too great an Opportunity of justifying any Male-administrations that can happen in the Execution of all and singular the Offices and Matters respectively before-mention'd.

Many of the original Deeds and Securities of several Persons Estates in this Island having been, through Course of Time, and the Influence of this Climate, worn and defac'd, and many others quite lost, by the terrible and never to be forgotten Earthquake, which happen'd here in the Year 1692. the great Fire that destroyed all *Port Royal* a second time, in the Year 1702. and, probably too, by the late dreadful Hurricane, which happen'd in *August* last; nothing can possibly be of greater Importance, for the Security of the Freeholders of this Island, touching the quiet and peaceable Possessions of their Estates, than that the publick Records and Enrolments of all Patents, Deeds and Conveyances, be taken Care of, so that as it may not be in the Power of any Person, entrusted with the Custody thereof, to withdraw, conceal, destroy, or otherwise embezzle, any of the aforesaid Records; Yet (to the great Surprize, Disquiet, and irreparable Loss of many Freeholders here, who purchased their Estates for valuable Considerations) a Discovery has been made, within these few Years past, that the publick Records and Enrolments of all Deeds and Conveyances, made here in the Years 1671 and 1672. are lost or withdrawn, (no body can tell which way:) And Mr. *R——by* and his Accomplices having the Opportunity of searching and making Enquiries into such Defects, as may possibly seem to be in the Connexion of several Freeholders Rights to the Possession and Enjoyment of their respective Estates, purchased as aforesaid. Many more sinister Uses have been made, in Mr. *R——by*'s time, of the casual losing of real Deeds, Conveyances and Records, in manner above-mention'd, under the Pretence of escheating such

Estates to the Queen, than ever were made in 40 Years before; which made the Governor, Council and Assembly, in or about the Month of *July*, 1711. pass another Act, intituled, *An Act for the further quieting Mens Possessions, and preventing vexatious Suits at Law,* &c. to prevent the trumping up, for the future (under the false colour of serving the Interest of the Crown) several pretended Grounds for Escheating many honest and laborious Planters Estates, and, at the same time, clandestinely securing Grants thereof to themselves or their Friends, sometimes under borrowed Names, for trifling and very small Considerations to the Crown, bearing no manner of Proportion to the true Value thereof.

And that it may manifestly appear how very grosly both the Crown and the Subject have, of late Years, been, and still are imposed upon, by such sinister and unjustifiable Practices: You are, in the first place, to know, That as there have been but very few (if any) Estates in this Island escheated as aforesaid, before Mr. *R——by*'s time; so upon complaint made, several Years ago, by Col. *R——d Ll——d*, Mr. *Wh——ch*, and others, then at *London*, touching some Abuses of that kind, and particularly in relation to a certain Number of Negro-slaves pretended to have been escheated to the Queen, and of which Mr. *R——by* had obtain'd a Grant in his own Favour, from the late Governor *Handasyd;* her Majesty, for preventing the like Abuses, for the future, was graciously pleased to order, that Restitution should be made of these Negroes, to the rightful Owner, and to give successive Orders and Instructions, ever since, both to the late and present Governor of this Island, *not to dispose of any Fine, Forfeiture or Escheat, of above the Value of Ten Pounds, to any Person whatsoever, without first acquainting her Majesty therewith.*

Yet, to frustrate Her Majesty's most Gracious Intentions, by such her Royal Instructions, all Writs of Escheat being directed to the Provost-Marshal and his Deputies, Care is always taken to empannel such packt Juries as will, either through Ignorance or Design, or both, (tho' upon Oath) make their Return of any Estate, under Inquisition at the Time, to be of as little value as, under any colourable Pretence whatever, they possibly can; and that too, for three several Reasons: 1. To the end that the estimated Value return'd by the Jury may not exceed the Sum limited by Her Majesty's aforesaid Instructions, and so fall within the Governor's Gift, without being obliged to make any Application to Her Majesty, the Lord High Treasurer, the Secretary of State, or the Lords Commissioners for Trade and Plantations, pursuant to Her Majesty's aforesaid Instructions touching the same.

2. Because by how much the less any escheatable Estate is valued by such Jury for the Queen, so much the more room will there be left for the Escheat-Patentee's giving a good round Composition to the Governor, Provost-Marshal, Attorney-General, *&c.*

3. To the end that, in case an Heir happen to appear, and put in his Claim to any Estate escheated as aforesaid, before the Expiration of the three Years allowed and limited by an Act of this Island, the Escheat-Patentee may not be liable to account for the real Value, or Produce of such Estate, during the Time of its continuance in his Possession; but only according to the sham Estimate thereof, return'd by the Jury.

Thus, for Example, *Nathaniel Herring,* Esq; a Member both of the last and present Assembly, having bought a Plantation of about 540 Acres of Land, in the Parish of *Westmorland,* (where great part of his paternal Estate lies) and being one of those Gentlemen who had, all along, too discerning a Sense of the crafty Designs of our Triumvirate, to suffer themselves to have been prevail'd upon, by any artful Insinuations, or circular Contrivances whatsoever, to prostitute their Reason, and the common Interest of the Island so far, as to give the Suffrage of their Votes implicitly, either in Elections or Assemblies, to the fraudulent Proposals, or magisterial Dictates of the said Triumvirate (as too many poor-spirited truckling Fools, and others worse than Fools, have done.) And our vigilant Triumvirate never slipping any Opportunity by which they may exert their Power over, and execute their Revenge upon all Men of stanch and honourable Principles, as occasion may offer; Mr. *Herring* had Notice given him that they were fully determin'd to pick a Hole in his Pocket, by trumping up some Pretence or other for escheating the Plantation which he had then lately bought, as aforesaid, under the Colour of some seeming Defect which they had discover'd in the Connexion of the Conveyances thereof to him. Whereupon, considering that the Judges of the Grand-Court, who were to judge thereof, were absolutely at the Beck and Disposal of the Governor and his Governors, (the Triumvirate aforesaid) That the Appealing from that Court to the Governor and Council of this Island, (as they are now stated) would have been much the same as leaping out of the Frying-pan into the Fire; And that Appealing again from these to the Queen and Council at home, would not only have been attended with great Difficulties and

Expences, and might have had a very uncertain Event; but that likewise in any Event whatsoever, the whole Subject-Matter was not of a Value sufficient to have answer'd all that Hazard, Labour, Costs and Loss of Time; Mr. *Herring* was advis'd (as the safest Course, for making the best of a bad Market) to take the start of the Triumvirate's Tools, by informing against himself; that is, by taking out a Writ of Escheat, on the aforesaid pretended Ground; to the end that, as being the Informer, and at the Charge of suing the said Writ, in the Queen's Name; Custom would, in a great measure, entitle him to have had the Refusal of the Gift thereof from the Governor, upon the Terms and Conditions usual in such Cases. Upon the whole Matter, the Provost-Marshal impanel'd such a Jury, as, upon Inquisition, returned the Value of the said Plantation to be to the Queen no more than *l.* 1 : 2 : 6. And yet, besides all manner of Fees to the Provost-Marshal, Attorney-General, Grand-Court, Clerk of the Patents, *&c.* Mr. *Herring* was, by private Composition with the aforesaid Triumvirate, screwed up, and forced to give a Premium of *l.* 300 to the present Governor, for an Escheat-Patent of the said Plantation, though previously bought by him, as aforesaid.

Nor did they think it enough to pinch him in that manner; but when, at last he agreed to their own Terms, and offer'd, in payment of the said *l.* 300, to give the Governor accepted Bills, under the Hands of his Factors, (two sufficient Merchants at *Kingston*) for the like Value; the Triumvirate would not allow his Excellency to accept thereof: Mr. *Herring* then offer'd (in regard he was necessarily pre-engaged to go 30 or 40 Leagues to leeward, by a Sloop that was ready to sail thither from *Port-Royal,* very early next Morning) to give an obligatory Note under the Hand of his Brother-in-law, *Peter Beckford,* Esq; (who is, you know, a Gentleman of as considerable an Estate and good Credit as any Man in this Island) for the Payment of the said *l.* 300 in 24 Hours time; that is, as soon as the Money could be conveniently brought from *Kingston:* Yet the said Triumvirate still disswaded his Excellency from accepting any Bill or Note whatsoever, in payment of the said *l.* 300, but only ready Money; alledging, at the same time, that the said Mess. *Beckford* and *Herring* must have had some Design of tricking his Excellency, by their urging him to accept of any Note or Bill in Payment of the Premium above-mention'd: Whereupon Mr. *Herring* (to save his then intended Passage by the said Sloop) was forc'd to go immediately to *Kingston,* for the said *l.* 300, which, upon his Return, he paid in Specie, about 9 or 10 a-Clock that same Night, at Doctor *Stewart*'s House; where his Excellency boarded at the time.

And yet, after all, (by the Suggestions and Instigations of this same Triumvirate, *R——by, Br——k,* and *St——t*) their hopeful Pupil, our wise, judicious, learned, pious, great, magnanimous, and generous Governor, (able to defend us both by Sea and Land*) has, several times since, upbraided not only Mr. *Herring,* but likewise Mr. *Beckford,* with alledged Ingratitude, for voting and acting, upon several Occasions, against what he was pleased to call his Interest, after he had condescended to take the above-said Premium of *l.* 300, for what, he said, he was inform'd since, was worth *l.* 500.

By all which you may plainly see after what manner Men of Probity and Integrity, and who have a due Regard to the Interest of their Fellow-Subjects, whom they represent in the Assembly, are, and still must expect to be treated, while the Administration of the Government here is continued in the Hands of these rapacious and devouring Cormorants.

But, to the end this may not seem to be the only Instance of such Proceedings, I'll furnish you with some few others, of many more, that may (if needful) be given of our Triumvirate's over dextrous Management in relation to Escheats; without regard to either the Degree, Quality, Character or Circumstances of the Person aggrieved, or to be aggrieved thereby; provided They may, by any ways or means whatsoever, obtain their Ends: For indeed, all is good Fish to them, that once happens to come into their Net.

Thus, altho' *Nicholas Blake,* of the Parish of St *Elizabeth,* a Quaker, did obtain, from the late Governor *Handasyd,* a Patent under the Broad Seal of this Island, for a Plantation, to him and his Heirs for ever, consisting of two Parcels of Land, which contain, by Survey, about 1100 Acres, in the said Parish, bearing Date the 19*th* of *January,* 1710–11. (whether as having been then escheated to the Queen, or not, I cannot positively charge my Memory, at present: However, I dare venture to say, that Patent was not obtain'd *per formam Pauperis*[7]) yet, be all that as it will, most certain it is that, upon the said Governor *Handasyd*'s Removal and Departure for *England,* our nimble Triumvirate quickly transferring their mercenary Idol-worship from the

* *A Phrase us'd by Mr.* R——y *in a fulsom Panegyrick on the Governor.*

7. [Literally, "In the manner of a pauper," that is, permission given to a poor person to sue without liability for costs.—Tr.]

late to the present Object thereof, fell upon Ways and Means to perswade the said *Nicholas Blake,* that, by reason of some pretended Defect in the above-recited Patent, *&c.* the Lands therein mention'd were still escheatable to the Queen; and that the only Remedy he had left him, for maintaining the Possession, and obtaining the indisputable Right thereof, was (for the preventing any other Informer, as in the aforesaid Case of Mr. *Herring*) to inform, and take out a Writ of Escheat against himself, *&c.* And that, upon his Surrender of the afore-recited Patent, and giving some reasonable Consideration for a new Patent of Escheat, in ample Manner and Form, for the aforesaid Lands and Appurtenances, the same might be unquestionably secur'd to him and his Heirs forever: Whereupon he being prevail'd with to proceed accordingly, the Provost-Marshal Impanel'd such a Jury, as, upon Inquisition, return'd the total Value of both the said Parcels of Land to be, to the Queen, no more than 2 *l.* 2 *s* 6 *d.* And yet, besides all manner of Fees and extraordinary Considerations to the Provost-Marshal and his Deputies, to the Attorney General, the Grand Court, Clerk of the Patents, *&c.* the said *Nicholas Blake* was, by private Composition with the aforesaid Triumvirate and their Pupil, prevail'd with (I will not say forced) to surrender and deliver up the said Patent, which he had so very lately obtain'd from the late Governor *Handasyd,* and to give a Premium of 300 *l.* to the Lord *Ar——d Ha——on,* our present Governor, for a new Patent of the same Lands, granted *de novo,* in *March* last, to him the said *Nicholas Blake,* and his Heirs for ever.

I will not say that any compulsory Arts were made use of, for making *Nicholas Blake* come into the Measures and Agreement aforesaid; for, it may be said, *Volenti non fit Injuria:*[8] But I assure you, he himself complain'd to me, and others too, that it cost him several Journeys from Leeward, besides the Trouble of bringing his Friend *Isaac Gale,* oftner than once, from *Kingston* to *Spanish Town,* to sollicite on his behalf, and to beat down the demanded Premium of 500 *l.* for the said last Patent, before the said Escheat Brokers condescended at last to accept of 300 *l.* for the Governor's Share; and farther too, that a positive Step was put to his obtaining what's commonly granted, of course, to all Persons requiring the same, on the ordinary Conditions (*viz.* an Order for surveying and measuring out some Wast-Land) until first he'd take out the said last Patent, and give up the former, *&c.* which when

8. ["Injury does not happen to one willing."]

done, he then got the said Order to the Surveyor of course. Now whether such Practice will answer the Triumvirate's pretended Zeal of serving Her Majesty's Interest, and encreasing the Revenue of the Crown, I leave it to you, or any other indifferent Person to judge.

It were an endless Labour to enumerate all the particular Circumstances of such Cases; and therefore I shall, for the future, give you only some farther Instances of the scandalous Difference which these Escheat-Jobbers make between the pretended and real Value of such Estates as fall by (hook or by crook) under their Management.

A small Plantation containing, by Survey, about 52 Acres of Land, in the Parish of St. *Elizabeth,* was upon Inquisition, by a Jury, valued to the Queen at no more than 2 *s.* 2 *d.* ½. And yet, in consideration of an Escheat-Patent for the same, Mr. *John Foster* (the Son-in-law, if I mistake not, of the aforemention'd *Nicholas Blake*) paid, as a private Premium, 50 *l.* to the present Governor, beside all ordinary Fees and extraordinary Charges, *&c.* as in the former Cases above-recited.

In like manner, five several Parcels of Land, containing, by Survey, about 200 Acres, situated in the Parish of *Westmorland,* were, upon Inquisition, by a Jury, valued to the Queen only at 8 Shillings and 4 Pence: And yet (beside all Fees, and other extraordinary Charges, as in the preceding Cases) *William Dorrel* of the said Parish of *Westmorland,* in consideration of an Escheat-Patent of the Premisses to him and his Heirs, paid (as I am credibly informed) a Premium, in large Cattle, to the Value of 2 or 300 *l.* to the present Governor; and was, by Agreement, oblig'd to fatten them all at his own Charge, before Delivery.

Here I cannot forbear observing, even with Horror and Indignation, that Persons intrusted with the most important Part of the Administration of the Government of so considerable a Colony as this Island of *Jamaica,* having had tolerable good Education, and professing themselves to be Christians, should yet nevertheless (instead of answering these honourable, just and worthy Ends of Government, for which they were commission'd by Her Majesty) be so depraved in their Nature, so openly profane in their Conversation, and so flagrantly wicked in their Practices, as not only to make the chief Principles of the Christian Religion (not exempting the Sacred Text it self) too frequently the Subject of their licentious Witticisms and Ridicule, but likewise gratify their most scandalously avaricious Appetites, at the rate of looking out for, picking, culling, seducing and imploying Dozens, at a time, of such abandon'd, servile Wretches, as, without any regard to the sacred Nature of an Oath, make no scruple, for certain valuable Considerations (such perhaps as the cramming their nasty Guts full with Meat and Drink, *&c.*) to return, upon Oath, That an Estate demonstratively worth several Hundreds of Pounds, is worth only some few Shillings and Pence. For my part, I must own, it is as yet a Moot Case with me, which of the two, whether such wretched Jurors, or these crafty and designing Knaves who delude and imploy them, are the most criminal, *in foro Conscientiae,*[9] for the manifest Perjuries that necessarily attend such flagitious and most unaccountable Practices.

Yet we have, indeed, a sort of Protestant-Jesuits among us here (at least such as call themselves Protestants, whatever Education they may have had, or Profession they were of, when in *France, Italy,* or *Ireland*) who by fallacious and metaphysical Distinctions, especially in Cases touching the Escheating of Estates, the Pleading in, and judging of Causes, the framing and interpreting of Laws, the consulting, advising and intermediating with the Governor and others in Authority or Power, about Decrees, Judgments, Letters of Administration, Probates of Wills, and Testaments, Favours, Rewards or Punishments, for or against Favourites or Adversaries, *&c.* can as nicely split a Hair, and as nimbly trump up equivocal and elusory Solutions, for tender and scrupulous Consciences, as any *Sorbon, St. Omers,* or *Salamanca* Casuist Doctor of them all.

This brings into my Mind a very diverting Scene, that happen'd here last Winter: *Don Gulielmo Morseo,* Captain General and Governor in chief of the *Spanish* Coast of *St. Domingo,* having been in his Passage to the *Havana,* surprized by one of our Privateer Sloops, stript of a considerable Sum of Money, and other valuable Goods, and brought a Prisoner into this Island; he was, upon the account of his Character, treated as a Prisoner of War, at large, entertain'd very civilly by our Governor, the Triumvirate, the Gentlemen of the Council and others; and frequently invited to dine at our Governor's Table (or rather indeed that of *Stewart* and *Rigby;* the Governor then lodging and dieting with them.) This *Don Gulielmo,* tho' a most bigotted Papist, being nevertheless a declared and irreconcileable Enemy to the Jesuits, and declaiming frequently, with bitter Invectives, against their whole Order, Principles and Morals, as destructive to human

9. ["In the court of conscience."]

Society, and most injurious to him in particular; Mr. *R——by*, on the other hand, (whether only for the sake of Argument, for exercising his Wit, and shewing the Exquisiteness of his Parts, or upon what other Account I shall not say) as frequently contradicted the *Don;* alledging that many of these Maxims and Positions exploded and decry'd by him, were necessary for the Safety and Support of Government, *&c.* Whereupon, after several repeated Conversations and Disputes on these Political Topicks, at different Times, the *Don* at last, with a very serious Air, openly at Dinner, (your Friend Mr. *March* and several others being present) advised our Governor to beware of Mr. *Rigby*, as a dangerous Man (calling him, at the same time, to his Face, *Jesuita Romano, Jesuita Italiano*) for that none but a Jesuit, or a Disciple of that Order, would so zealously maintain their Politicks and Principles. This the *Don* repeated afterwards, in several publick Companies, both in the Tavern and Coffee-house. But, from that Day forward, the poor *Don* was never invited to dine with our Governor; and Mr. *R——by* never ceased till he prevailed with the Governor and Council, to send the said *Don Gulielmo Morfeo*, by one of the Queen's Ships then ready to sail, for *England;* and (as I am inform'd) with as ignominious and opprobrious a Character of him to the Secretary of State, as Mr. *R——by*'s Malice and Resentment could invent.

Nor will this seem, at all, very strange to you, when I assure you farther, That, in the open Coffee-house, in Presence, and to the Hearing of several Officers, and other Gentlemen of undoubted Veracity, this same celebrated Wit and Politician of ours (Mr. *Rigby*) has, with seeming great Alacrity, and all the Marks of an inward Satisfaction and Pleasure, openly read and lectur'd upon several Chapters of Mr. *Whiston*'s late flaming Book, renewing the *Arian* Heresy: From which (without any great Breach of the Rules of common Charity) one might very naturally be apt to conclude, that a Person taking Pleasure in propagating so heretical and dangerous a Doctrine, in such manner as aforesaid, has given too much ground to suspect, that, if he is not already fully confirmed in that Heresy, he is at least pretty far advanced in becoming one of the Disciples of the heterodox Author above-named.

And to remove the Suspicion of my being thought too much prejudic'd on this Head, I must crave leave to acquaint you further, that, on St. *Stephen*'s Day, immediately after Dinner, a certain Gentleman, who, among his many other admirable Qualities, is singularly noted for his consummated

Skill in modern Politicks, was pleas'd, with a peculiar Gaiety of Humour, to entertain our Governor, and some other Gentlemen, then present, (particularly Mr. *Taber,* the Rector of St. *Katharine's* Parish) with a summary and witty Account (as some others beside himself seem'd then to think) of his own Faith, in Words to the following Effect, *viz.* That whatever Divines and Philosophers were pleased to profess, all Men, (excepting Fools and Madmen) made their Interest the chief Object of their Desires, and squared their Actions accordingly, when-ever they weigh'd things deliberately. That, for his own part, tho' (as he said) he had read *Machiavel's* Works several times over, he always found something new therein; worthy of Observation; and own'd withall, that he never found any thing therein, but what he thought might more easily be defended and justified, than many things in the Bible: That, as to the Pentateuch, or five Books of *Moses,* he must beg the Doctor's Pardon, (meaning Mr. *Taber*) if he could not screw up his Belief to such a high Pin, as to think them altogether Canonical, or (to speak more properly as he said) authentick: That as for *Moses* himself, he consider'd him as little better than such another Prophet as *Mahomet:* That by his greater Skill in Magick, and Dexterity in Legerdemain Tricks, he had fallen upon the Knack of making his Serpent eat up the other Magicians Serpents: but that his not having been a better Man than he should have been, was too manifest, even from the Story (allowing it to have been true) which he wrote of himself, of his having murder'd the honest *Ægyptian* in the Highway; and that his having been conscious of the Heinousness of his Guilt, appear'd undeniably from his having hid the dead Body in the Sand, and then made his Escape, and fled away into the Land of *Midian:* That if *Moses* were to have been tried for that Murder, at our Grand Court here in *Jamaica,* he (our said Politician) would not run the Hazard of standing in his stead, for a good round Sum, *&c.*

But, as I would willingly, as far as in me lieth, do Justice to any Person, who, by the Sacredness of his Function, is set apart for the Service of the Altar, I must not omit acquainting you, that (how obsequious soever Mr. *Taber* is alledged to be, upon other Occasions, to too many of our Court-Fashions, and to the Rules of what is commonly, (tho' most absurdly) call'd Good-fellowship) yet he then very discreetly (as I am well assured) took up our Political Dictator, and confuted his distorted Gloss on that Text in the 2d Chapter of the Book of *Exodus,* from the 7th Chapter of the Acts of the holy Apostles, where that Action and Proof of *Moses's* Zeal, for the Safety and Deliverance of his oppressed Brethren, is fully resumed and explain'd. And Mr. *Taber* had, at the same time, the Modesty to own and declare, that the aforesaid Text of the New Testament might probably have escap'd his Memory, and our Dictator might, with some seeming Victory, have triumph'd, at that Instant, if he (the said Mr. *Taber*) had not casually, that very Morning, read the said whole Chapter, because the Epistle for the Day (according to the Service of our Church) is taken out of it.

It would be an endless Piece of Drudgery, to give you a full Recital of the many profane Witticisms with which this Dictator has occasionally diverted himself and some others of his Brethren in Iniquity, about several Fragments of the Sacred Oracles, and the Order of Priesthood in general; for which Reason I'll trouble you now only with one Instance more of this polite and singularly well accomplish'd Gentleman's Regard to Christianity, by the Concern which he shew'd for the most solemn Act of Devotion, as well as the most sacred Ordinance in the whole System of the Christian Religion, *viz.* the Holy Sacrament of the Lord's Supper.

Our present Governor having, in compliance with the Sacramental Test, appointed by Act of Parliament, resolved to receive the holy Communion, on the *5th* of *August*, 1711. as being the first Sunday of the Month, immediately after his having enter'd upon the Administration of the Government here; and none of the Gentlemen of the Council or Assembly happening to have then receiv'd the Communion, with his Excellency, except only Doctor *S——t* and Mr. *R——by;* our polite and nicely well-bred Gentlemen (upon his Return from Church, after Divine Service) was pleas'd to say, That out of Respect to a Person of the Governor's Birth and Quality, and especially at his first Appearance among us as Governor, all the Gentlemen of the Council and Assembly then in Town, ought, in good Manners, to have taken the Sacrament that Day, whatever they'd do, at any other time; and that he thought the Governor should look upon their Neglect in not having taken it then, as a Mark of Disrespect to himself: As if that most sacred institution were to be consider'd and gone about, as a Matter of no greater Weight or Importance than as a Point of meet Ceremony and Complement: But that indeed he, and some few others of his Brethren-Communicants thought no better of it, was too scandalously manifest from the Grossness of their ludibrious and sensual Preparations the Night before, and a Repetition of the same vile (if not worse) libidinous Exercises, the very next Night after receiving it. The whole was such an astonishing mixt Scene of a seemingly

Christian Devotion, impious Profanation, and Heathenish Lasciviousness, as I must own I could not readily have believed practicable, even by the most abandon'd Wretches passing under the Denomination of Christians, had I not then had more than ordinary Proof thereof: And to mend the Matter, after having shot for some time thus at random, one of these worthy Communicants has since, in a most solemn and avowed, tho' licentious Manner, changed Colours. Nor do some People scruple to fore-tell, from several probable Prognosticks, already come to pass, that, as a Proof of his future Constancy, and for the Honour of his Family, he may possibly in time, be prevail'd upon to celebrate a certain Popish Sacrament, from which many thousands, in the Case of *Actaeon* or *Socrates,* would as gladly be absolved.

But here, (to give the Devil his Due, as the Proverbial Saying is) I must do our *Corpus Juris,*[10] Mr. *Br——k,* the Justice to acquaint you, that tho' he be pretty much taken Notice of, for having so many different Lodgings at once, and keeping such a numerous Seraglio of Black Cattle, (a Name ironically given sometimes here, to Negro Wenches) and was, upon our present Governor's Arrival preferred to the Office and Place of her Majesty's Attorney General in this Island, whereby it was thought he would have been oblig'd, of course, to have taken the Sacramental Test; yet so far was this consciencious Gentleman from joining with his Brethren of the Triumvirate, in profaning the Sacrament of the Lord's Supper, by becoming an unworthy Receiver thereof, that he chose rather not to take it at all: And to the end he might not seem singular in that particular, he farther (as the incontrolable Oracle of our Law, a true Son of the Church, and nice Casuist in Divinity) did endeavour to perswade some other publick Officers, particularly Mr. *F———s M——g,* that there was no occasion for their taking the Sacrament on that Account, nor for troubling their Heads about it; for that the Laws of *England* did not reach this Place, except in some special Cases.

So that, to conclude this seeming Digression, I must take the Liberty to assure you, that the many pernicious Consequences which the loose and vicious Examples of some Persons at the Helm of our Government here, produce in the Lives, Morals and Principles, of too many of the Populace, afford no small Matter of serious Reflection; and are so much the rather to be regretted and reformed, because there seems to be such a Measure of Tractability, and Pliableness of Disposition in the Natures of the Generality

10. ["Body of law."]

of the Inhabitants, as renders them very susceptible either of good or bad Impressions, suitable to such Examples as are laid before them, by their Superiors; according to that of the Poet;

Regis ad Exemplum totus componitur orbis.[11]

which makes it still the greater Pity, that these few Persons who have the chief Influence on the Administration of all our publick Affairs, and some of those also who are appointed to be our Spiritual Guides here, are not Men of such solid and well-grounded Principles, or exemplary Lives, as were to be wish'd for; for it is not to be expected, that pure and wholesom Streams can run out of impure and poison'd Fountains. And tho' it be undoubtedly much easier, and attended with far less Pain of Body, as well as with less Care, Anxiety and Perturbation of Mind, TO BE VIRTUOUS THAN TO BE VICIOUS; yet it is generally allow'd, that the Corruption of our Natures has, for the most part, such a predominant Byass on our Inclinations, that we are more prone to imitate vicious than virtuous Examples; and are so much the more so, when such Examples seem to carry along with them the Authority and Sanction of Men in Power; as the same is elegantly express'd by *Juvenal*, in his 14th Satyr:

Sit Natura jubet; velocius & citius nos
Corrumpunt Vitiorum Exempla Domestica, Magnis
Quum subeunt animo Auctoribus. ———[12]

And the same Author, a little after, subjoins the Reason,

———*Quoniam dociles imitandis*
Turpibus ac Pravis omnes sumus. ———[13]

Having thus occasionally given you a transient View of the Complexion and Sentiments of our Modern Politicians here, touching revealed Religion, and some of their religious Exercises; I return now to pursue more closely that which I first proposed should be the chief Subject-matter of this Letter.

11. ["The entire world is arranged by the example of the ruler."]

12. ["Thus nature commands; swifter and quicker does the example of vices at home corrupt us since they enter our mind with great authority."]

13. ["We are all so pliable in imitating scandal and depravity."]

I have already, by several demonstrative Proofs, and undeniable Instances of Points of Fact, shewed you (*Vide Pag.* 6. *& sequentes*) that, under the Colour and false Pretence of serving the Queen's Interest, and encreasing the publick Revenues of the Crown, the Male-Practices of Mr. *R——by*, his Confederates, Abettors, and Tools, have been so grosly fraudulent and oppressive, to the manifest Prejudice of both the Queen and the Subject, that, in the Escheating of Estates (whether justly Escheatable or not) as aforesaid, the private Composition given to the Governor (beside what these Escheat-Brokers have got to themselves) has, oftner than once, amounted to near about 300 times as much as the pretended trifling Value brought of such Escheated Estate to the Queen's Account.

And lest these our Politicians should still nevertheless pretend, that if, upon legal Inquisition, the Jurors may have, thro' Ignorance or otherwise, given ground to suspect them guilty of Perjury, in their having valued Estates, escheatable to the Queen, at such unaccountable Under-rates, as left Room for the Escheat-Patentees to have made some Presents to the Governor, what was that to them, (the said *R——by, &c.* pretty innocent Lambs?) I'll give you now some Instances of the like male-Practices in the Escheating and Undervaluing other Estates, upon account whereof the Governor had no Share of the Profits, but meerly the Satisfaction of gratifying his Favourites, and so has let these (*per vices*)[14] have the whole Benefit of such Escheats as were granted to themselves, whether in their own, or in borrow'd Names; as for example:

Upon some pretended Defect in the Right and Title of one ——— *Jenkins*, an old blind Man, to a small Estate honestly purchas'd by him, and then in his Possession, and upon which he and his Family lived very comfortably, near *Dry-River* in the Parish of *Clarendon;* Dr. *John Stuart* took out a Writ of Escheat against him; the Jury, upon Inquisition, valued that Estate to the Queen, if I remember right, at no more than 12 Shillings and 6 Pence: The Doctor obtain'd a Patent thereof *gratis* to himself, and the honest blind Man was sent a begging, to live upon the Charity of well-disposed Persons. However this Proceeding against the blind Object, who was not able to help himself, rais'd such a general Clamour among all Degrees of People in the Island, that I am told, (how truly I cannot say) our pious and worthy State-Doctor was, through a strange Fit of Compassion and Charity, (Qualities not very

14. ["By turns."]

legible in his Complexion or other Actions) prevail'd with thereafter, to give some small Pittance towards keeping this poor blind Man from starving.

It would be somewhat too presumptuous in me, to assign the Causes either of God's Mercies or Judgments; and therefore I'll not adventure so far as to suggest, that it is as a just Judgment on a certain *Scotch-Irish,* or *Irish-Scotch* Mongrel Doctor (born at or near *Colrain* in *Ireland,* and bred sometime in the West of *Scotland*) for the Perverseness of his Ways, the Viciousness of his Morals, or the Wickedness of such flagrant Practices as are above narrated, he is, in congruity with the well-known Stupidity of his intellectual Faculties, very near being likewise affected with a bodily Blindness: But as it is generally allow'd, that, by the constant Gloominess of his Countenance, the Downwardness of his Looks, his grunting when he eats, *&c.* and the Coarseness of his Manners, in all respects whatsoever, he very much resembles a pretty neat cleanly Creature, (vulgarly called a Hog) I'll take the Liberty to put you in mind of an antient Observation and Tradition, handed down to us by one of the Poets:

Distortum vultum sequitur Distortio morum.[15]

And *Seneca,* in his *Hercules Oeteus,* observeth, that, *Licet ipse neget, vultus loquitur quodcunque negat.*[16] Yea, *Ovid,* after he had in his own Person, and that of many others, multiplied his Observations on the Frailties of Human Nature, not to call them worse, has the following Exclamation in the 2*d* Book of his *Metamorphoses:*

Heu! quam difficile est Crimen non prodere vultu![17]

So that if this busy, officious, and impudent, tho' ignorant Tool, had not been casually join'd in a Party, with some more subtle and cunning Sophisters, he'd soon crumble away into his original, a most abject and despicable Nothing.

Another Instance of one of these Favourite's obtaining the Grant of an escheated Estate to himself, by Patent, under the Broad Seal of this Island, without any manner of Equivalent for the same, to the Governor, you have already set forth in the Person of that polite Gentleman, Mr: *R——by* (*Vide*

15. ["A distorted expression follows the distortion of morals."]

16. ["It is permitted that he himself should deny it, but his face proclaims whatever he denies."]

17. ["Alas how difficult it is not to make known a crime by the facial expression."]

Pag. 7th.) and the better to palliate and carry on his Project by Surprize, the Negroes, for which he obtain'd that Patent, in his own Favour, were, (as I am inform'd) cried out at the Grand Court, and escheated in the Name (if I remember right) of one ——— *Delamain;* tho, at that time, in the Possession of Mr. *James Whitchurch,* then in *England.*

By the like Trick (frequently used too on other Occasions here) of crying out, at the Grand-Court, in the Name of a Person dead many Years since, a Freehold of about 1000 Acres of very good Land, which old Captain *Jones,* then at *London,* has in the Parish of St. *Katherine,* he had very near been nickt out of it; the same had instantly been affirmed by the Court to have been devolved on, and vested in the Crown, upon the account of Quit-Rents; and a new Grant thereof executed in favour of one of our Triumvirate's Tools, to whom the same was previously promised; if a Gentleman then by accident in Court, had not, meerly by the Description and Bounding of the Land, discover'd it to be Captain *Jones's*; and so prevented that designed Fraud.

Then, as to Mr. *Brodrick,* he, honest Gentleman! would not (no, not for the World) take the Benefit of an Escheat to himself: But, to oblige so near and useful a Relation, as his Reverend and Worthy Mother-in-law, Mrs. *Olivia Reid,* he carried on an Escheat for her behoof thus: A Plantation consisting of 900 Acres of Land, by Survey, with the Appurtenances, situated in the Parish of *Westmorland,* late the Estate of Doctor *Hume,* a *Scotchman,* who died in this Island, without any Heirs that we hear of; was, upon Inquisition, valued, by the Jury, to be worth to the Queen no more than 1 *l.* 17 *s.* 6 *d.* (To shew their pretended Exactness there must be always some odd Pence.) What the real Value thereof may be, I have not as yet learn'd; but I am morally assured, by very good Hands, the Governor had no manner of Fee or Equivalent for the Escheat-Patent which he gave of that Estate; unless it be true (as some People do say) that Mrs. *Olivia* had sometime before presented him with a white Cow with Calf: however, be that as it will, I am inform'd there is one remarkable Circumstance that happen'd in the passing that Patent, which I must not omit letting you know, *viz.* After his Excellency had sign'd a Warrant, in common Form, directed to Mr. *Brodrick,* as Attorney-General, and to Mr. *Melling,* as Clerk of the Patents, for preparing a Patent to the said Mrs. *Olivia Reid,* and her Heirs for ever, of the 900 Acres of Land, and Appurtenances aforesaid; Mr. *Br——ck,* upon second Consideration, for Reasons best known to himself, dash'd *Olivia*

Reid's Name out of the said sign'd Warrant, and, instead thereof, interlin'd the Name of *John Graves* (as may be seen by the said Warrant still extant in Mr. *Melling's* Office) and the Patent for the Premisses was accordingly pass'd and executed in the Name of *John Graves*. Now, whether the said Escheat-Patent be really, and *bona fide*, for the proper Use and Behoof of honest Mr. *Brodrick*, or Mrs. *Olivia Reid*, or of the said *John Graves*, or in trust for both, or either of the former two, is to me as yet a Problem.

I find likewise that two small Plantations, containing jointly about 500 Acres of escheated Land, with their Appurtenances, situated, lying and being, in the Parishes of *Clarendon* and *Vere*, respectively valued, by the Jurors, upon Inquisition, to the Queen, the one at 19 Shillings and 7 Pence half-penny, and the other at 8 *l.* 16 *s.* 3 *d.* have been, in *August*, 1711. granted by two several Patents, under the Broad Seal of this Island, to Mr. *Br——k's* Country-man and humble Servant, *John Stafford*, of the Parish of *Vere*, Shop-keeper: That another small Plantation, containing about 20 Acres of escheated Land, with the Appurtenances, in the Parish of St. *Catherine*, valued to the Queen at 5 *l.* was by an Escheat-Patent, granted, in *July* last, to *Richard Stoddard*, Esq; one of the Learned Judges of our Grand Court, and his Heirs: And that 30 Feet square of escheated Foot-Land, with the Appurtenances thereunto belonging, (late the Estate of *Mary Gibson*, Widow) situated lying and being in the Town of *Port Royal*, was valued to the Queen at 9 *l.* and, by an Escheat-Patent, granted in *January* last, to *Robert Snead* of *Port Royal* aforesaid, Turner. But what particular Premiums or Brokerage (beside avowed Fees) may have been given to the G——r and the said Escheat-Brokers (*R——by, St——t, Br——ck*) in consideration of the said Escheat-Patents, with many others of the same nature, I must own he is wiser than I who can tell: For, as none are let into that Secret, but only themselves and their Customers, these Escheat-Patentees; so, few of these do ever disclose what such Patents truly cost them; except when the Parties chiefly aggrieved by that Practice, are forced to save their Bacon, as much as they can, by becoming thus, a second time, Purchasers of their own Estates, as in the Case of *Herring, Blake*, &c-formerly mention'd. (*Vide Page* 8, & *sequentes.*)

Yet, in the general, as it is demonstratively apparent, by what I have already written, that all these escheated Estates (whether justly escheatable or not) are, with a knavish Design, most scandalously and perfidiously undervalued to the Queen, and that the Pretence of encreasing the publick Revenue, by this Escheating Trade, is but a meer Pretence indeed; so, on the other hand, I assure you, it is (with abundance of Murmuring, Heartburning, and Bitterness, and not without some Astonishment too) taken notice of, and daily reflected upon, That Three Persons so lately come hither in such indifferent Circumstances; *R——by* then a Shop-keeper's 2*d* Son, and (as I am credibly informed by Mr. *P——* and others) in disgrace with his Father, remarkable by his old Green Silk Stockins, having neither Money nor Letters of Credit, and indebted for the stipulated Price of purchasing his Patent, and even for the Money that defray'd the Charges of his Voyage, till Colonel *Lowe* generously lent him 50 *l. S——t,* without having so much as tolerably good Cloathing, or whole Shoes to his Feet, and determin'd, thro' Despair (as he told C——l *B——r* and others) to have gone and disposed of himself among the *Spaniards,* till *H——d* took pity of him; and *B——k* worse than nothing, by several thousands of Pounds, Bankrupt in Reputation as well as Credit, almost disown'd (as I have been told) even by his own Family, and not having a whole Shirt to his Back, as indeed he has but very rarely a clean one as yet: It is (I say) remarkably wonder'd at, that such as these should so suddenly, not only jump into Chariots, driving all things *Jehu*-like, before them; but that Two of them at least, should be likewise in a condition to be daily laying out almost incredible large Sums of Money at Interest, upon Mortgages, and making Remittances into *Europe,* to secure their Retreat thither, whenever they come to find this Island's just Indignation and Resentment grow too hot for them. And, to deal ingenuously with you, their Insolence and Tyranny are now become so insupportably great, that they have more than sufficiently verified that old Observation and Maxim,

Asperius nihil est humili cum surgit in altum.

Which I may adventure to translate into a well-known *English* Proverb, thus: *Set a beggar on Horseback, and he'll ride to the Devil.*

I should be far from thinking it a just Reproach to, or derogatory Reflection on these, or any other Gentlemen, that they were once poor; provided they had not taken any sinister, fraudulent, oppressive, or other over-hasty Measures to become rich. But since the wisest of Men, *Solomon,* in the height of all his Glory, has throughout the whole Book of his excellent *Proverbs,* given us many notable Reflections on, and serious Cautions against all violent and hasty Courses to become rich, as well as against the wicked Enticers of others to follow such Courses, I'll take the Liberty to put you in mind of some of them, on this occasion. *Prov.* i. 15. *My Son, walk not thou in the way with them, refrain thy Foot from their Path.* And after having subjoin'd many particular Reasons for that Advice, both in that and other subsequent Chapters, gives then this very express and comprehensive one, Chap. xxviii. 20. *He that maketh haste to be rich, shall not be innocent.* And to convince us, that it is not a very difficult matter, even for Men of very ordinary Talents, to get Riches, especially if they will be so brutish as to lay aside the Principles and Rules of Equity and Justice, to obtain them; the same Wise Man tells us, *Prov.* xx. 21. *An Inheritance may be gotten hastily, at the beginning; but the End thereof shall not be blessed.* And to mortify the excessive Pride, Vanity and Folly of such as are too apt to value themselves, upon the account of their Riches, (which way soever obtain'd) or who arrogantly attribute their being successful in these, or any other worldly Acquisitions whatsoever, to the Excellency of their own conceited Parts, or extraordinary Skill, or personal Merit, he assures us farther, Eccles. ix. 11. *That the Race is not to the Swift, nor the Battle to the Strong, neither yet Bread to the Wise, nor yet Riches to Men of Understanding, nor yet Favour to Men of Skill; but Time and Chance hapneth to them all.* And as a Curse entail'd on such as set their Hearts on purchasing Riches at any rate, he tells us likewise, *Eccles.* v. 10. *He that loveth Silver shall not be satisfied with Silver, nor he that loveth Abundance with Increase.* And to their farther Mortification, *Prov.* xi. 4. that *Riches profit not in the Day of Wrath,* &c.

Yet nevertheless, as an insatiable thirsting after more and more still, *in indefinitum,*[18] is one of the many Curses ever attending Wealth wickedly obtain'd; our Triumvirate have their Inventions always upon the stretch, and their Tools constantly imploy'd, in getting, increasing and multiplying Riches, by many more various and oppressive Ways, Means and Methods, than you can possibly imagine, at so great a distance; a particular Narrative whereof would fill several Volumes: And therefore (beside some few occasional Excursions, or rather Moral Reflections interspersed here and there) I'll confine my self, in this Letter, to the Discussion of what I apprehend may more immediately relate to the first Grounds and Occasion of the three several Acts of the Governor, Council and Assembly aforemention'd; particularly the Escheating Trade.

18. ["Into infinity." Faux Latin.—Tr.]

Our Triumvirate being puff'd up with their almost incredible Success in all their Attempts for gratifying (if possible) their Avarice and Ambition, were not (it seems) as yet contented with their having, by the aforesaid artful Perjuries and other Contrivances, eluded, as much as in them lay, the gracious Intention of her Majesty's above-recited Instruction *(Not to dispose of any Escheat of above the Value of* 10 l. *Vide Pag. 7th.)* but took it likewise for granted, they had got such an absolute Ascendant over his Excellency, in all respects whatsoever, that they might prevail with him, one way or other, to have jumpt over the aforesaid Instruction, for good and all: Because many Estates brought under the Denomination of Escheats (how justly I will not say) are so very notoriously known to be of such considerable real Value, that to have had them respectively valued by Juries, within the Limitation of 10 *l.* each, at most, could not, under the colour of any Sham-Rule whatsoever, be easily projected. For, even by the lowest Rules of Computation, or rather Appreciation, commonly used by our ordinary Escheat-Juries here in *Jamaica,* some of these are valued to the Queen at 20 *l.* some at 30 *l.* some 40 *l.* some 50 *l.* some 100 *l.* some 200 *l.* and some much more. From all which Premisses you may modestly conclude, that the real Value of these Estates so escheated, and not as yet absolutely disposed of, will amount to some small matter more than the Value return'd by the Juries.

However, I am now to give you an Instance of our Triumvirate's Resolution to have made his Excellency break through Her Majesty's aforesaid Instructions intirely; if an Accident had not baulk'd their Design, at that time.

The Estate of *Mary Swintee,* of the Parish of *Port Royal,* deceased, being upon a Writ of Escheat and Inquisition thereon taken in *August,* 1711. by a Jury, valued at 100 *l.* and adjudged by the Grand Court, held in *November* last, to be vested in Her Majesty; our Triumvirate, some time thereafter, represented to the Governor the great Worth and Merit of the Naval Officer here, *William Norris,* Esq; (one of their Favourites and thorough pac'd Tools in the Assembly, the Admiralty-Court, and the Magistracy of *Port Royal*) and therefore intreated his Excellency would be pleased to grant him an Escheat-Patent of the Premisses, which his Excellency promised he would; but upon what Conditions I have not heard.

His Excellency having accordingly given Orders to his then Secretary, Mr. *Mackenzie,* to have drawn a Warrant to the Attorney-General and Clerk of the Patents, to have prepared an Escheat-Patent of the Premisses, to the said *William Norris* and his Heirs; the Note by which the said Warrant was to have been drawn, being very general, except as to the Butting and Bounding, and no mention being made therein (as usual in such Cases) of the Value returned by the Jury, *&c.* he went to the Clerk of the Grand Court's Office, where he found what he wanted.

Mr. *Mackenzie* thereupon deserted making out the said Warrant, till the Triumvirate and Mr. *Norris* complained severally to his Excellency; who thereupon reprimanded him, and gave him fresh Orders to dispatch it, as before: But he being determin'd in his own Mind, neither to write nor countersign a Warrant that would have been a manifest Violation of Her Majesty's particular Instruction above recited, dictated the said Warrant to his Clerk, inserting the Jury's Valuation of the said Estate, and then carried it, with some other Papers, to be sign'd by the Governor, who happening to be, at that time, alone, sign'd them all immediately, in course, as they were laid before him: Whereupon Mr. *Mackenzie* took that Opportunity (he very seldom having any such, as I have been frequently told) to say, He thought himself in Duty bound to expostulate a little with his Excellency, touching the Contents of the aforesaid Warrant; that as he apprehended it to be a manifest Infraction of the aforesaid Article of Her Majesty's Instructions to his Excellency (especially should a Patent pass thereon) he humbly desired to be excused, if he could not perswade himself to countersign it; lest peradventure he might afterwards happen to be blam'd for the Faults of some other People, who (he said, he was afraid) would very little regard who should be blam'd for their Advice, in that, or any thing else, provided they might, in the mean time, compass their own Ends; and that therefore he hoped his Excellency would, upon more mature Deliberation, resolve not to be prevail'd upon, by the artful Perswasions or deluding Practices of any Person or Persons whatsoever, to give away, or dispose of, any Escheat valued above 10 *l.* (and much less this one valued at 100 *l.*) without a special Allowance from Her Majesty, for so doing, *&c.* at which his Excellency colour'd extremely, without speaking one Word; read the said Warrant softly to himself; and then (after pawsing, sometime, thereon) tore away his Subscription from it.

I had this Account lately from Mr. *Mackenzie*'s own Mouth; and to confirm the Truth thereof, he let me see that very Warrant it self, which was on the 4*th* Day of *March* last, sign'd and cancell'd by his Excellency as aforesaid, whereby I observed that some Fragments of several Letters of his Excellency's Subscription were still visibly remaining. But what pass'd thereafter between his Excellency, the Triumvirate, and Mr. *Norris*, touching the Premisses, Mr. *Mackenzie* could not inform me: However, before that Month was at an end, he was made sensible with a witness, that his Conduct in relation to the aforesaid Escheat, was added to the Black List of his other unpardonable Crimes against the Triumvirate; as Mr. *Norris* was to the Number of his avowed Enemies.

I will not anticipate the Vindication of all or any Part of Mr. *Mackenzie*'s Behaviour and Conduct, since he came hither; he being, in every respect, very capable of doing it himself, and designing home very speedily, by the *Defiance* Man of War, if the Triumvirate suffer our Governor to sign his Ticket of Leave: Yet, nevertheless, I cannot forbear taking notice in the general, of the great Discouragements and most unjust Oppressions he has labour'd under, ever since he came hither, and particularly of his having been most arbitrarily imprison'd, for 28 Days time, upon a very false Accusation; and that tho', in compliance with the utmost Extremity required by the Laws and Customs of this Island, for obtaining Leave to go off, he gave in *August* last, 1000 *l.* Security into the Secretary's Office, for answering any Debts that he might be supposed to have contracted here (which I have good ground to believe are none at all) yet (notwithstanding thereof, and the many Sollicitations and Importunities of several Gentlemen on his account) the Governor has not, to this Hour, sign'd his Ticket; nor is there any Appearance of his Willingness to sign it at all; tho' it be no more than what, by the Laws, he is obliged to do, of course. But, be that as it will, I believe Admiral *Walker*, Commadore *Littleton*, Captain *St. Lo*, and indeed all the Sea-Officers here, are so much Mr. *Mackenzie*'s Friends, and so sensible of the base and oppressive Usage he has had from the Governor and his Triumvirate, in all respects whatever, that (under the Rose) he reckons upon having his Passage howsoever, on board the said Man of War, without any regard to his not having the Governor's Ticket; he having already done all that was incumbent on him to have done for obtaining it. And really the extraordinary Earnestness which the Triumvirate do shew for his being still detain'd here, *nolens volens*,[19] by hook or by crook, and their making ridiculous and notoriously false Resolves of Council, to be transmitted home, by way of anticipation, to his Prejudice, seems to me, and to all unbiass'd

19. ["Willing or not."]

Persons here, to flow and proceed from a checking Consciousness of their own Demerits, and a Terror of his exposing them, in his just Resentment, whenever he gets safe again, out of their Clutches, into the Land of Liberty.

And, by the by, to make good the old *Latin* Proverb, *Solatium miseris multos habere pares,*[20] I cannot but think it, in some sense, a Comfort to Mr. *Mackenzie,* (such as it is) That he is not the only one of all the Gentlemen who accompanied our present Governor, the Lord *Archibald Hamilton,* hither, that has been disappointed of his Excellency's promis'd Favour and Justice: For all and every one of them (whether Volunteers, Expectants, or actually Fee'd Servants) whom the Triumvirate, upon enquiring into their several Characters, Capacities and Circumstances, suspected of Understanding, Integrity and Courage enough to have, in their respective Spheres, detected, opposed and frustrated their (the said Triumvirate's) then intended Practices, were, in less than 14 Days time, after his Excellency's Arrival here, not only remov'd (and in some measure banish'd) from about his Person and Confidence; but likewise treated with Insolence and Contempt, and several of them used as if they were little better than mere scoundrel good-for-nothing Fellows.

The Gentlemen who have been thus disappointed are particularly, Mr. *David St. Clair,* a younger Son of my Lord *St. Clair* of *Scotland;* Mr. *Robert Paterson,* the younger Brother of Sir *Hugh Paterson,* Baronet, and very nearly related to the Governor; Mr. *Richard Dereham,* Brother of Sir *Thomas Dereham,* Baronet, (all three Volunteers severally recommended to the Governor's Favour and Patronage, by his Grace the Duke of *Hamilton,* and other Persons of Quality) Mr. *Robert Dowglas,* recommended to his Excellency by his Grace the Duke of *Roxburgh;* Mr. ——— *Elliot,* a young Gentleman, Heir to an Estate, recommended by Sir *Gilbert Elliot* of *Stobs,* Baronet, and Mr. *Baillie,* one of the Lords Commissioners for Trade; *Patrick St. Clair,* Doctor of Physick, and younger Son of Sir *Robert St. Clair,* Baronet; who, tho' he came over in the Quality of the Governor's Physician, with large Assurances of his Excellency's Favour, was, under the colour of a friendly, tho peremptory Advice, commanded by the Governor, to go and live at *Port Royal,* a small Island, about 14 Miles distant from *Spanish Town,* the Seat of the Government, left (as there was indeed just ground to suspect) his Practice should much interfere with that of Doctor *John St——t,* one of our

20. ["Solace to unhappy men is to have many equals."]

beloved Triumvirate: And when, upon the Invitation of several Gentlemen of considerable Interest and Estates, Doctor *St. Clair* return'd again to *Spanish Town,* in about three Months time thereafter, and went to wait upon the Governor, to acquaint him thereof; his Excellency, in a very angry manner, disapprov'd of the Doctor's Return, and has not condescended so much as to speak to, or return him a Hat, ever since.

Lieutenant *John Mebeux,* who came hither a Volunteer with our present Governor, as being specially recommended to his Favour, both by the Duke and Dutchess of *Ormond* severally, is unprovided for, to this Hour; tho' his Excellency has, in the mean time, preferred several others, who never saw a Shot fired against an Enemy, to Commissions in *Handasyde*'s Regiment.

Mr. *Patrick Hamilton,* late Sheriff of the City of *Cork* in *Ireland,* a very modest Gentleman of good Education, honourable and worthy Principles, of Experience in Trade, and of as fair a general Character for Probity, Honesty and Capacity (by a very solemn Certificate, sign'd by the whole Corporation, and under the common Seal of that City, in a Silver Box, with a suitable Inscription) as any Man that ever lived in it, happening to have had great Misfortunes, by Losses at Sea and otherways, during this War, came hither in the Quality of the Governor's Steward; and tho' he was earnestly recommended by the Duke of *Hamilton,* Sir *Alexander Cairns* and others, yet was suddenly dismiss'd quite out of his Excellency's Service; as were likewise Mr. *John Dupray,* a Confectioner, and ——— *Gundimore,* a very good Cook, tho' both were upon stated Wages: But what Wages Mr. *Hamilton* was to have had, I forgot to enquire. This Account I had severally from the respective Persons above-named, and confirm'd by other Hands.

Upon the aforesaid Dismission, the said *Gundimore*'s Wife fell sick, and broke her Heart, and died; and he himself, for want of a Ticket, signed by the Governor and Mr. *Rigby,* in common Form (which was positively refused, unless he could give 1000 *l.* Security; and how could he, poor Man?) was forced to use Means to get off the Island, and return to *England,* by Stealth, about 13 Months since.

John Dupray fell desperately sick, upon his Disappointment; and was at the Point of Death, till his Country-man, Mr. *Lewis Galdy,* an eminent Merchant in *Port-Royal,* thro' Charity and Compassion, supplied him with all Necessaries; and, after Recovery, trusted him with a small Stock, to set up Shop with.

Mr. *Patrick Hamilton* lingred out some time, but could never digest the Shock which his aforesaid unexpected Dismission gave him; was struck into a kind of Despair, tho' he endeavour'd to conceal it; yet the Sense he had of his own Circumstances overcame his Spirits, at last; so fell sick and died.

Joseph Marshal, the Governor's *Valet d'Chambre,* being then likewise predetermin'd to have been dismiss'd; his Wife (who was of a passionate Temper) cry'd out, and roar'd against the Go——r, fell sick, and soon died: And then, upon farther Consideration, for fear of disobliging the Earl of *Orkney* (whom, as I am told, the said *Marshal* had formerly served) he the said *Marshal* has been hitherto continued in the same Station; but upon such a precarious footing, and so frequently hated, that, I am told, he has lately apply'd to Mr. *T——ll,* &c. for other Service.

Thomas MacMullen, who came hither, upon settled Wages, in the Quality of his Excellency's Groom, tho' he serv'd his time to a Barber, happening to marry a Barber's Widow, and praying to be discharged; was dismiss'd, upon Condition to quit his preceding Wages, which he accordingly did.

Mr. *Robert Paterson* return'd home in *December* last.

Mr. *Robert Dowglass* return'd home in *April* last.

Mr. *Gilbert Elliot,* by waiting for the Governor's Ticket (which was refused, till he'd find 1000 *l.* Security) miss'd his Passage, which he took on board the ——— Galley of *Bristol,* in *October* last; fell thereupon sick, and soon after died.

Mr. *Richard Dereham* (after having spent the small Stock of Money he brought along with him, and after having apply'd several times to the Governor and his Secretary, by Letters and otherwise, to put his Excellency in mind of him) was forced at last, through mere Necessity, to enter into very mean Service, somewhere up in the Mountains.

Then, as to Mr. *Mackenzie,* 'tis more than probable, he also had been dismiss'd with the rest, soon after his Arrival here, as an useless Charge, and, in every respect, uncapable of informing or advising his Excellency, touching any thing relating to the Administration of the Government of this Island; because (as if the Change of Climates had deprived Men of the former Exercise of their rational Faculties) he was never here before; in case the Governor himself had not then (as I am credibly informed) acknowledged he was under such particular Engagements to him, that he could not well turn him off, so suddenly, without some Pretence or other against him: Whereupon the Triumvirate's Project ever after, was to manage Matters so, that he should, under the Mask of a pretended Friendship, be kept constantly employ'd in Affairs, which could yield him little or no Credit, Reputation or Profit; and yet might afford them (according to their distorted Insinuations) some seeming Pretence of whispering into the Governor's Ear, such Suggestions and indirect Reproaches, as might tend to lessen his Excellency's Opinion of the Usefulness of the said *Mackenzie*'s Service; that he the said *Mackenzie* should never be allowed to be in Company with the Governor, on any Occasion, but when some or all of themselves were constantly present; and then, by degrees, to pick *German* Quarrels with him, and put his Excellency upon extorting and exacting at last such extravagant arbitrary Shares of his ordinary Fees from him, as no Gentleman, having any competent Measure of Spirit and Capacity, could ever bear with; especially considering the Governor's Express and repeated Engagements to the contrary, both by Word and Writing (as Mr. *Mackenzie* assures me) before he was prevail'd upon to accompany his Excellency hither: And, in Confirmation of what goes before, Mr. *Mackenzie* saith likewise, that since his Arrival here, he never was, to this Hour, allowed to lie one Night in the same House with his Excellency; nor to accompany him, on any one Progress into the Country; nor to ride any of his Horses, nor to use his Chariot or Chaise, on any Occasion whatsoever; tho' too notoriously common to others of much meaner Characters, particularly to a certain Cook-Maid, who pretended to command the same at Pleasure, and also to her chief Gossip, a certain Tavern-keeper, who (tho' never married) has had several Bastard Children to as many different Fathers.

But really one of the most singular and shocking Instances of a vitiated and depraved Nature, as well as a perverse and inhuman Inclination, towards poor Mr. *Mackenzie* (who, on many Considerations, might very reasonably have expected some other sort of Treatment) was this: That when, upon the Death of his Son (a very comely and ingenious Youth) on the *6th* Day of *November* last, at Night, my Lord St. *Clair*'s Son above-named, went very obligingly (at Mr. *Mackenzie*'s Request, and in his Name) the next Morning, to acquaint our Governor thereof; to make an Apology for Mr. *Mackenzie*'s necessary Absence that Day; and to invite his Excellency to the Funeral; his Excellency, instead of condescending to do the poor afflicted Gentleman the Courtesy and Honour of coming, in the Cool of the Evening, so far as 200 Paces, to the said Funeral (from which Mr. *Rigby*, he being then with his Excellency, openly disswaded him) was moreover so void of the Bowels of Christian Charity and Compassion, on that Occasion, that (soon after Mr. St. *Clair*'s Return) two successive Messages were sent, by a Footman, to Mr. *Mackenzie,* requiring his immediate Attendance on the Governor; with peremptory Orders to bring along with him all the Commissions for Colonel *Lowe*'s Militia-Regiment of Foot (which were mostly, if not all, of the said deceased Youth's hand-writing) with soft Sealing-wax, cut Papers for the Seals, *&c.* This was such a surprizing and pinching Dilemma to the said *Mackenzie,* at such a Juncture, that, by Means thereof, he must unavoidably have subjected himself either to the seeming, tho' unjust Censure of contemning and not obeying his Excellency's Commands, if he went not instantly to wait on him; or to the Obloquy and more just Reproach of being thought very unnatural, in case he had then gone, to have busied himself about the finishing Commissions that he knew required no manner of haste, (and which, by the by, were not deliver'd out, in a Month's time, after they were finish'd) when he should have been imploy'd in doing the last Christian as well as Parental Duty to his Son; which not only the Ties of Nature, but even common Decency requir'd at his Hands, and could in no Respect have admitted of any Delay, in this so warm a Climate: Whereupon (to prevent the sinister Design which he suspected, of misconstruing any verbal Answer he could have given, on that Occasion) he sent his Excellency a grave Apologetick Answer in writing; a Copy whereof I have seen. Yet nevertheless when, on the next subsequent Day, after the Funeral (which was, in every Respect, very decently performed; all the Gentlemen of the Council and Assembly, then in Town, except the Governor and Mr. *Rigby,* having been present at it, beside many others) Mr. *Mackenzie* went, in suitable Mourning, to wait on his Excellency (with whom Mr. *Rigby* was, at that time, likewise) neither the one, nor the other, thought fit to take the least notice, directly, or indirectly, of the Occasion of his the said *Mackenzie*'s being then in such Mourning, any more than if they had never heard any thing of the Matter: But, with a very supercilious Air, order'd him to finish the aforesaid Commissions forthwith.

I must own the whole Course of their Behaviour on this Occasion, seem'd to me to have carried along with it, such an unparallel'd Indication of propense Malice, and most barbarous Inhumanity, as even the bloodiest Warriours and Conquerors that ever lived, would so far have scorn'd to have been guilty of, that they seldom or never refused to their vanquish'd Foes, a Cessation of Arms, when demanded, for burying of their Dead. Good God!

That Persons professing themselves Christians, should thus deliberately shew so little Regard to the unavoidable Concern, which common Decency, as well as Nature, requires from a Parent, on so surprizing an Occasion! Whereas the much more religious and compassionate Heathen could so feelingly exclaim against any such supposed Inhumanity, thus:

Quis Matrem nisi mentu inops, in funere nati,
Flere vetat? ———

Who, but a Tyrant-Monster, would forbid
A Parent's Mourning, o'er a Son, when Dead?
Or on his Hearse some parting Tears to shed?

The Consideration of such base and unexpected vile Usage, as poor *Mackenzie* then met with; the Sense he had of his other grievous Disappointments, in the general; together with the sudden Death of his Son, who was not above three Days sick; and his want of sleep, on that Occasion; made such a deep Impression on his Spirits, as threw him into a dangerous Fever, which had very near cost him his Life. And yet, ALL THAT was but a Prologue to the uninterrupted Series and Concatenation of the many studied Arts of arbitrary Violence and unaccountable Oppressions, under which he has, with incredible Patience and Fortitude, labour'd ever since.

I had almost forgot to acquaint you, that as there is seldom or never any General without an Exception, so among those that accompanied his Excellency hither, there happen'd to be one, and but one, Babe of Grace (Mr. *William Cockburn,* the younger Son of one of the Judges in *Scotland*) who having managed Matters so, that he dared not adventure to shew his Head any longer in *England, Scotland, Holland, Hamburgh,* &c, for fear of being clapt close into *Lymbo,* made his Escape hither, as being one of the last Resorts of Persons so slated. Our Triumvirate soon understood what Use to make of such a Tool, whenever Occasion offer'd; and, without doubt, ply'd him accordingly: For tho' he gave himself the Air of joining with others, in condemning and crying out exceedingly against their Conduct and Influence, during the first 8 or 9 Months, after his Arrival here; yet he no sooner had a View of succeeding to Mr. *Mackenzie,* as Secretary to his Excellency, and Clerk of the Council, than he changed his Note, and render'd himself meritorious with the said Triumvirate, and their Pupil, by giving himself openly the Lye, as to his formerly profess'd Sentiments concerning them, and by informing falsly, and even perjuriously, against some of those, to whose Friendship he was most obliged, while he remain'd here in a State of Peregrination, before his Advancement to Mr. *Mackenzie*'s Office.

Mr. St. *Clair* intends to go for *England*, by the *Defiance* Man of War; and is able to give a more particular Account of his own and Mr. *Mackenzie*'s Treatment, since they came hither.

To all discerning and unbyass'd Persons here, it looks like Infatuation, that a Gentleman born of a noble Family, and vested with the Deputation of a sovereign Power, should so far depretiate his own Quality, and prostitute the Dignity and Credit of that Commission which he has the Honour to bear, as, on the one hand, to admit such a notorious Composition of Ignorance and Impudence, as that grunting Mongrel Animal, our Hog-Do——r (tho' a busy officious Tool) to be, on all Occasions whatsoever, whether publick or private, one of his Ex——cy's most familiar and favourite Companions; especially when here are Gentlemen of liberal Education, opulent Fortunes, and honourable Principles, among whom he might easily have made a much better Choice; and, on the other hand, suffer himself to have been so very insensibly at first sight, and ever since implicitly captivated, ensnar'd, and deluded, by the fawning and sycophantick Addresses, the smooth artificial Smiles, the fulsom designing Flatteries, the close and parasitical Attendance, the servile and indefatigable seeming Obsequiousness, the frothy, obscene and prophane Witticisms, the many false Insinuations, and malicious Suggestions, the artful, crafty, and most injurious Contrivances, and with the fallacious, equivocal, gawdy, and affected Oratory of so over fashionable a Demi-Foreigner, and so grosly dis-ingenuous a Sophister, as our *Machiavel Junior,* (the said Mr. *R——by*) whose Character may bear at least some faint Resemblance to that which was given of *Cinna,* one of the *Roman* Consuls, *That he had a Head to contrive, a Tongue to perswade, and a Heart to perpetrate* (and, for ought I know, a Hand also to execute) *any Mischief whatsoever, to gratifie an insatiable Avarice, Ambition, Lust, or Revenge.*

And then, as to our *Corpus Juris, Brodrick,* (the Third Member of our governing Triumvirate) the odiousness of his scandalous Character is so very well known in *England, Ireland, Montserrat,* and this unhappy Island, that I need not trouble you now with any Description of those heterogeneous Parts which compose the same.

Yet still, whenever it happens so, that, thro' the want of either sufficient Penetration and Judgment to discern, Capacity to answer and resell, or Courage to slight the plausibility of such sophistical Arguments, as are advanced under the false Colour (tho' specious Pretences) of serving their Interest, aggrandizing their Powers and Fortunes, and of administring to their Pleasures; Persons in highest Authority suffer themselves to be thus surpriz'd, into a more than ordinary Familiarity with designing Sycophants, they seldom or never escape being sooth'd into an easie and agreeable, tho' fatal Belief, That all the charming Adulations, and fulsom Encomiums of these crafty Parasites are a Tribute really due to some singular (how imperceptible soever) Merit in themselves; according to that of *Juvenal:*

——— *Nihil est quod credere de se*
Non possit, cum laudatur Diis aqua Potestas.[21]

And being thus, by the pleasing Enchantment and Delusion of that false Musick, once plunged into such a deep Lethargy, as shuts up all the Avenues to their Reason; few ever recover such a true Sense and Taste of Persons and Things again, as to take warning from that notable Confession and Admonition of *Ovid,* in the 3d Book of his Elegies:

Desine Blanditias, & verba potentia quondam
Perdere; non ego sum Stultus ut ante fui.

Which I have adventur'd to render into *English,* thus:

Forbear your Fawning; Flatter me no more;
I am not now the Fool I was before.

And, among the many wise Observations of *Solomon,* on the innumerable Mischiefs wrought by Lying and Flattery, he gives the following express Caution, against a dissembling Flatterer, *Prov.* 26. 25. *When he speaketh fair, believe him not; for there are seven Abominations in his Heart.* And, *Ver.* 28. *A lying Tongue hateth those that are afflicted by it, and a flattering Mouth worketh Ruin.* And, without doubt, God comprehended such as these in that Curse which he denounc'd by the Mouth of the Prophet *Isaiah,* ch. 5. 20. *Wo unto them that call Evil Good, and Good Evil; that put Darkness for Light, and Light*

21. ["There is nothing which he is not able to believe about himself, since the power of water is praised by the gods."]

for Darkness; that put Bitter for Sweet, and Sweet for Bitter. And, a little after, *ver.* 23. *Who justifieth the Wicked for Reward, and take away the Righteousness of the Righteous from him.*

It was the saying of a late ingenious Author, That the Inhabitants of a City or Province, whose Governor is himself govern'd by others, must of all People be the most miserable: Alluding, no doubt, in some respect, to that of the Wiseman, *Eccl.* 10. 16. *Wo to thee, O Land, when thy King is a Child,* (that is, a Person not capable of discerning or distinguishing Good from Evil; Right from Wrong, Truth from Falshood, Vice from Virtue, or how to decree Justice and Judgment, *&c.*) And in Confirmation thereof, God complaining of the general defection and perverseness of his People, threatens to punish them by the Mouth of his Prophet *Isaiah,* ch. 3, 4, 5. *And I will give them Children to be their Princes, and Babes shall rule over them. And the People shall be oppressed, every one by another, and every one by his Neighbour: The Child shall behave himself proudly against the Ancient, and the base against the honourable.* And then, *ver.* 12. *As for my People, Children are their Oppressors, and Women rule over them.* Now if the Governor of a Province or Colony, happen to be a Person not endowed with such Qualifications as are necessary for good Government, but must himself be implicitely directed by others; then how much more miserable must the Case of that Province or Colony be, when these others are no way accountable for such Governor's Male-Administration; and when that Province happens to be so far distant from the Imperial Seat and Fountain of Government, that the Remedy of going thither to sue for Redress, may probably prove worse (if worse can be) than the Disease it self.

I shall ever pay a due regard to the Memory of that gallant and worthy Gentleman, Major General *Selwyn,* who, upon his first Arrival here, *Anno* 1701. in the Quality of Captain General, and Governor of this Island, being continually teazed with the officious Advices, Whisperings, and Insinuations of Two very crafty and designing Persons, (Colonel *H——ry L——we,* and Colonel *R——d Ll——d*) touching the Constitution of the Island, the Characters, Humours, and Inclinations of certain particular Persons, *&c.* with the view of screwing themselves into his Favour, so as to become his chief Confidents and Tutors; heard them out, very patiently, for several Days; and then, at last, express'd himself to them in Words to the following Effect: *Gentlemen, I have given you a full hearing; I thank you for your Advice; I'll observe so much of it as I think convenient; I can easily see what you drive* *at; but I would have you take notice, that I came not hither with a slabbering Bibb, and leading Strings: Yet, Gentlemen, if you please to compromise the Matter, You* (Mr. L——we) *shall govern for one Month, and you* (Mr. Ll——d) *shall govern another Month; but, depend upon it, I shall govern, my self, all the Time after, during my stay here.* This was so obvious a Rebuke for their petulant officiousness, that neither they, nor any other, pretended to direct him ever after; except, when he thought fit to ask their Opinions or Advice in Matters under deliberation at the Time. He was a Gentleman of a very goodly Presence, of bright natural Parts, and very good acquired Endowments; an excellent Soldier; impartial in the Administration of Justice; frugal without Parsimony, and generous without Prodigality. In short, God did not think us worthy of being long blessed with such a Governor; for he died before the end of that Year.

After so long a Digression, it is high Time now to return to the Discussion of what I first proposed should be the chief subject Matter of this Letter.

I have already given you several Instances of the vile Practices of our Escheat-brokers, in the escheating of Estates, whether really escheatable or not: And have still, in store, many more Instances of such to give; but will confine my self, at this Time, to only one Instance more, which, for the singularity of some Circumstances attending it, deserves your special Consideration.

By an Act of the Governor, Council, and Assembly of this Island, and confirmed in Council at *Whitehall,* by King *Charles* IId. Intituled, *An Act for encouraging the settling of this Island,* It was Enacted, *That any Alien then settled, or that thereafter should settle in this Island, and take the Oath of Allegiance, should, to all Intents and Purposes, be fully and compleatly Naturalized; paying only* 5 l. 10 *s. for a proper Instrument purporting the same, under the Broad Seal of this Island.*

Upon the Encouragement of the aforesaid Act, an indefinite Number of *Jews,* and some other Foreigners of different Nations, and Religions, came and settled here; purchas'd Freeholds, *&c.* and amongst the rest, one *William Kupius,* a Native of *Holland,* settled, and was Naturalized here; and purchased a considerable Plantation, with a suitable Number of Negroes, in the Parish of *Clarendon;* married the Daughter of Colonel *Bernard Andreas,* in the Neighbourhood; and had by her, one Son, and one Daughter.

Upon the Death of the said *William Kupius,* some Years since, and of his said only Son some Time after; the aforesaid Plantation, Negroes, and other Appurtenances, fell of course to his then only surviving Child, *Anna-Williamina-Bernarda Kupius,* an Infant.

The said Infant being under the Guardianship of the said Colonel *Andreas,* her Grand-father; and her Mother (the Daughter of the said Colonel *Andreas,* and Widow of the said *William Kupius,*) happening to intermarry with Mr. *Anthony Swimmer,* the said Colonel *Andreas* (as Guardian aforesaid) did let the said Infant's Estate (*viz.* the said Plantation and Negroes) in Farm, to the said *Anthony Swimmer,* at 300 *l.* yearly Rent, during the time of her (the said Infant's) Minority. But, both the said Grandfather, and Mother of the said Infant, happening to die soon after; she, the said Infant, was then left under the Guardianship, and to the sole Care of her Step-Grand-Mother, or Grand-Mother in Law, the Widow and Executrix of the said Colonel *Andreas.*

By this time, our Escheat-Brokers began to prick up their Ears and had not even Discretion enough to conceal their Wishes and Hopes, that the said Infant *Anna-Williamina-Bernarda Kupius* (who was then aged about 8 or 9 Years) might likewise go soon the way of all Flesh: Because in such Case, these voracious Vultures did not doubt of getting their Talons fasten'd upon her aforesaid Estate, for want of Heirs.

Now comes on the Mystery of Iniquity:

The said Infant happening to be somewhat troubled with a little Tumour or Swelling in her Groin, one Mr. *Newsam,* a neighbouring Chyrurgeon, was thereupon consulted, and took her in hand, to cure her: But before he had time to take proper and necessary Measures for that End, her said Grand-Mother-in-Law was, by the Mediation and Letters of Advice (as I am credibly inform'd) of a certain useful Matron (one of *Æsculapius*'s Setters) prevail'd upon to bring the said Child forthwith up from the *Leeward* to *Spanish* Town, to be put under the immediate Care of Dr. *John Stewart,* as the only Doctor in the Island, who could infallibly cure her, of all Distempers whatsoever, if curable, *&c.*

Sooth'd thus with the pleasing Allurements aforesaid, the honest well meaning Grand-Mother (Mrs. *Andreas*) settled and left her Grand-Daughter (the Infant above-named) at Mr. *Merick*'s House in *Spanish-*Town, where she remain'd about a Year, under our infallible Doctor's (I had almost said, Butcher's) Hands.

He began his tender Experiments, by making a large Incision, which (after some few Dressings, *Secundum Artem*[22]) he said, was a *Fistula:* This was succeeded by several other large Incisions, round the said Infant's Thigh, very near, if not quite into the Bone; and to give some seeming Colour (as was then generally thought) to such an extraordinary and violent Piece of Practice, he call'd a certain Under-Practitioner to his Assistance, for Dressing, in his own Absence, those Wounds or *Fistula's*, which he himself had, with so much Tenderness, thus made. In short, after he had kept the aforesaid Infant (who was not then above 9 Years of Age) in a continued Torment, with repeated Incisions, Issues, Applications, Counter-applications, and the D——l and the Doctor knows what besides, for about the Space of one whole Year, and was, from time to time, very liberally paid by the Grand-Mother, Mrs. *Andreas;* he told her at last, *That the said Infant was incurable; that he had done all he could to her; and that he would not give himself any farther Trouble about her;* or to that Purpose: Whereupon, Mrs. *Andreas* took the said Infant home to *Leeward,* and sent for one Dr. *Page,* under whose Care (notwithstanding the unaccountable Butchery aforesaid) the Child recovered apace, for 4 or 5 Months together, and was likely to have done very well; 'till in his Absence, she contracted a Cold, which threw her into a violent Flux and Fever, of which she dy'd before he could reach her.

It is needless here to trouble you with a Recital of the many Reflections past upon Dr. *Stewart*'s Method of Practice above-mention'd; and how He and some other certain Doctors had very high Words upon it, at *Sarah Turner*'s Tavern, in *Spanish* Town.

But, by the bye, I must own, I am the less scrupulous in believing him very capable of committing such a design'd piece of barbarous Inhumanity (if prompted thereto either by Malice, Revenge, or the view of private Interest) when I consider after what Manner he has treated several others; and particularly for Instance, Mr. *Mackenzie,* (the Governor's late Secretary aforesaid) soon after his Arrival here; which was thus,

Mr. *Mackenzie* happening, one Day after Dinner, to say (in discoursing transiently on general Heads) That the Musketo-Flies had been very busie about his Legs, the Night before; and that, between sleeping and waking, he had ruffled a little of the Skin of his left Leg, somewhat above the Anclebone; Dr. *Stewart* would needs thereupon come officiously next Morning

22. ["In accord with the practice of his skill."]

(as he did without Invitation) to see Mr. *Mackenzie*'s Leg, under the pretence of Friendship, and to bring with him (as he said) a little Ointment, to draw a new Skin upon it; but instead thereof, bringing a Stiletto ready drawn (that is, a Lancet hid in the Palm of his Hand) and taking hold of *Mackenzie*'s Leg, then turning his back round, and placing himself in such manner as rendred it impossible for his Patient to see what the Doctor was going about to do to his Leg; and *Mackenzie* supposing that the badness of the Doctor's Sight made him probably chuse that Posture, to bring the Object the nearer to his purblind Eye; the Doctor all of a sudden, without the other's previous Knowledge, or Consent in the least, and holding still *Mackenzie*'s Leg fast lock'd under his Arm, made 5 or 6 slight Incisions cross one another, about the Ancle-bone, at which he being very much surprized, cry'd out in a great Passion to the Doctor, what, in the Name of G——d, he meant by so doing? To which the Doctor answered very gravely, *It was only to make the Blood start, for preventing the Stagnation thereof;* tho' there was not the least shadow of any ground imaginable for supposing, and much less dreading any such Thing. Then the Doctor calling forward his *Myrmidon,* who was ready at hand, with a large Gallipot, full of some sulphureous, liquid stuff, bathed *Mackenzie*'s Leg with the same, which made it instantly smart so extremely, that to alleviate the Pain thereof, and to cool the fiery Heat which the said bathing had occasion'd, the Doctor then bedawb'd and plaister'd it, all over, with a thick Ointment which his *Myrmidon* had ready in another Gallipot for the purpose; and so wrapp'd the Ancle quite round with a Plaister and linnen Bandage, and charg'd the said *Mackenzie* not to untie it, before next Morning, upon any account whatsoever, and leaving the said Gallipots with him, told him his Ancle (tho' it should smart a little) must be bath'd and drest once more therewith, in manner aforesaid; and that thereafter he would apply something, which, he doubted not, would in a short time, perfectly heal it.

After Dr. *Stewart*'s Departure, Mr. *Mackenzie* became, by Degrees, so very sensible of a continued growing Heat, and extraordinary gnawing Pain, in and about his Ancle, that he could hardly contain himself from pulling off the Plaister and Bandage; but, with much ado, he kept it on, according to the Doctor's Direction, till next Morning; at which time Dr. *Blair* happening to make him a friendly Visit, from *Kingston,* was surpriz'd to see him confin'd to his Chamber, with a sore Leg; and enquiring into the Cause thereof, and being informed of all that Dr. *Stewart* had done to it, soon discover'd (after undressing it) that the Practice was in every Step thereof, the Effect of premeditated Malice and Villany; and that nothing but a very strong Corrosive could have made such a Cavity in one Night's time, as appear'd then in Mr. *Mackenzie*'s Leg; and therefore in Colonel *Blair*'s Presence, avowedly discharged Mr. *Mackenzie* (as his Friend) from making any farther Use of these Applications prescribed by Dr. *Stewart;* from which time forward Mr. *Mackenzie* never, to this Hour, could, with any Patience, hear of taking any of Dr. *Stewart*'s Prescriptions, in any Case whatsoever; nor, indeed, any other Person that has a just Notion of the Man, or a due Regard to his own Safety.

Yea, our very Females (many of whom were formerly this our *Æsculapius*'s Partizans and Setters) are of late become so sensible of the Grossness and Falsity of those innumerable Stories which he had, from time to time, imposed upon their Credulity; of his sticking at nothing to compass his Ends; and of the Danger of trusting him, in any respect whatever; that the Generality of them (especially these of the better sort) have already quite dropt him, in so much that, at this time, he has not (as I am credibly informed) three Patients in all this Island; and therefore gives himself the Air of saying now, that since he has got an Estate to live on, at his Ease, he'll not give himself the Trouble of practising Physick any longer.

But, as to the Point in hand, the said Infant, *Anna-Williamina-Bernarda Kupius,* happening to die as aforesaid, in *January* last, at Mrs. *Andreas*'s House; and Mrs. *Andreas* having thereupon sent an Express to Dr. *Stewart* (as being one of the Favourite-Triumvirate) with an Account thereof, and desiring his Mediation and Assistance, for obtaining her a Grant of the Escheat of her said Grandchild's Estate, if escheatable; the Doctor (as I am informed) return'd for Answer, that she was too late, *&c.*

Several Gentlemen in the Parishes of *Clarendon, Vere,* and St. *Elizabeth,* were likewise desirous to become Purchasers of the said Estate, if escheatable; and signify'd their Willingness to have given, some four, some 5000 *l.* and upwards for the Grant thereof; beside ——— *&c.* But the common Report goes, that Mr. *Pennent,* one of the Assistant-Judges of the Grand Court, sent some *Spanish* Arguments *per* Express, to secure the Governor's and our Triumvirate's Favour, for letting him have the Refusal of the aforesaid Estate, at the Current Value in such Cases.

Whatever may be in that, I know not: But certain it is, that Mr. *Pennent* play'd his Cards so well, with these Escheat-Brokers (the Triumvirate above-named, of whom Mr. *R——by* is the Chief) that no other Pretender is now admitted into Play; tho' 'tis more than probable, that some other Person, no way concern'd with these Brokers, might readily give better Conditions to the Governor, if he were not in a State of Pupillarity, under the absolute Direction and Management of these Escheat-Leaches.

Mr. *Pennent* having taken out a Writ of Escheat in common Form, directed to the Provost-Marshal; Care was taken to summon such a Jury of 12 honest Men of the Neighbourhood, upon the Inquisition, as return'd, upon Oath, the Value of the said *Kupius*'s Estate, at no more than 1456 *l.* to the Queen; tho' it be well known, that Mr. *Swymmer* pays 300 *l.* a Year for the same: And as it cannot be reasonably supposed, that the Deceased Colonel *Andreas,* late Guardian to the said Deceased Infant, would have been too precise and severe in letting a Lease of his said Pupil's Estate, to his own Son-in-Law (the said Mr. *Swymmer*) at too high a Rent; it is generally said, that Mr. *Swymmer* has made another good Estate out of the said *Kupius*'s Estate, in the Compass of some few Years last past; and farther, the said *Kupius*'s Estate produces (as I am informed) about 120 Hogsheads of very good Sugar a Year: which being modestly computed at 20 *l. per* Hogshead, makes 2400*l.* a Year. Out of which the ordinary Charges being deducted, it must be allowed that the Remainder will much exceed the 300 *l.* yearly Rent payable for the same, as aforesaid. But beside the Plantation, Sugar-work and Houses, *&c.* belonging to it, there are (as I am informed) about 120 Negroes upon it; which Negroes being moderately valued at 25 *l. per* Head, will instantly yield 3000 *l.* What the remaining Personal Estate, beside the running yearly Rent, may amount to, I cannot tell: But, by what is already said, you may easily perceive there is some small Matter of Difference between the real Value of the said *Kupius*'s Estate to the Possessor or Purchaser, and the sworn estimated Value thereof to the Queen; a Difference (tho' not proportionably quite so very ridiculous as some of the other Instances of less Value already mentioned, which are as 300 to 1) yet so grosly wide and scandalously shameful, that 'tis hard to tell where such perjurious and fraudulent Practices may end; if some timely stop be not put to this growing and horrid Evil.

The only Obstacle in our Triumvirate's way, at present, is, Her Majesty's aforesaid Instruction, *Limiting the Governor from disposing of any Fine, Forfeiture, or Escheat, above the Value of* 10 l. *without special Leave,* &c. This sticks so close in their Stomachs, that, sometimes, they cannot forbear even openly cursing the Commissioners of Trade, who prepared the Draught of that Instruction, as being a great Hindrance (they say) to the Dispatch of Business, *&c.* And the aforesaid Limitation disturbs their righteous Spirits, still the more; because it gives all real or pretended Heirs the longer time, for putting in their Claims to any escheated Estates, after the Escheat-Patents are past; which, if not done within the Space of three Years, their Pretensions are ever after foreclosed.

However, as our Triumvirate take all Occasions to magnify and extol our Governor's great Power and Interest at home; they assure their Escheat-Clients, that his Excellency makes not the least Doubt of prevailing with Her Majesty, to revoke the aforesaid Limitation; and give him a Discretionary Power, in relation to all Escheats whatsoever; or at least to give him the Grant or Disposal of such particular Escheats as he'll think fit to ask.

Now whether the said *Kupius*'s Estate be justly escheatable, for want of Heirs, is, with many People, still a Question, because they seem to be pretty well assured, that the said *William Kupius* deceased (Father of the aforesaid Infant likewise deceased) had several Brothers, Sisters, and other near Relations; lately (and for ought they know, still) living in *Holland.* So that if such nearest Relations or Heirs be duly and timely apprized of the common Practice of this Island, with respect to the Right of Naturalization, they may easily obtain the Benefit of being naturalized, either here, or in *England;* and so have a clear Right to the said Estate of Course; in case they make their Claim within the Space of three Years, as above.

If it should be pretended that the afore-recited Act of this Island, for naturalizing Foreigners, is expired; I humbly apprehend that to be a Mistake: For tho' King *Charles* II. confirmed it, among several other Laws, for no longer time, than 21 Years, from the 1st of *November,* 1683; yet that Act being in its own Nature perpetual, *for encouraging the Settling of this Island,* it remains still in Force here; till the same be especially declared void, and disallow'd of by the Queen.

Yea, moreover, as all former Governors, since the Commencement of the said Act did; so the present Governor continues, to this Hour, as Occasion offers, to grant Patents of Naturalization, to all such Foreigners as come and settle in this Island, if they require the same, pursuant to the aforesaid Act. And, as a farther corroborating Evidence thereof, when some naturalized *Jews* died lately here, without naturalized Heirs, the Wives, or other nearest Relations of such deceased *Jews,* having made Interest by some of the

Triumvirate, obtain'd, first of all, Patents of Naturalization, founded upon the aforesaid Act (to qualify them for obtaining Letters of Administration, *&c.*) and then got Letters of Administration, of Course: So that what is Sauce for a Goose is Sauce for a Gander, for, *Majus & Minus non differuns specie.*[23]

But if it should still nevertheless be determin'd, that the aforesaid Act is void, even since the Expiration of the 21 Years above-mention'd, then all the Patents of Naturalization granted, since that time, both by the late and present Governor, would likewise be void of course; as having been unwarrantably granted: And so there would be more fine Work for our Escheat Hunters, contrary to all publick Faith, and the Design of peopling this Island.

So that if any such Heir to the said Infant *Kupius* appear, in due time, and Care be taken to apprize the Queen fully of his Case, it is probable (considering the inhuman Cruelty of those previous Steps taken to make the aforesaid Estate escheatable, and then the perjurious and fraudulent Measures taken after, to conceal the real Value thereof, from the Queen and her Ministry, when escheated, as aforesaid) Her Majesty may, from an equitable Regard to such Heir's natural Right, by Proximity of Blood, from the general Indulgence intended to all Foreigners whatsoever (even *Jews*) by the Laws and Customs of this Island, and from the singular Goodness of Her own Royal Disposition, be induced to dispense with the strictness of any accidental Right arising to the Crown, merely from the want of a bare formality; that is, such Heir's not being Naturalized in the strictest Form, before, perhaps, he could be apprized of his having a natural Right to any such Estate.

Upon the whole Matter, I am fully perswaded, that the most effectual Remedy, for preventing, and frustrating for the future, the many wicked Designs, crafty Contrivances, manifest Perjuries, and grievous Oppressions, now practised, and artfully carried on, under the false Colour and Pretence of serving the Queen's Interest, by the escheating of Estates, in manner above narrated, would be, to obtain a special Order and Instruction from Her Majesty, to the Governor of this Island, for the Time being, That all Estates in this Island, escheated or to be escheated to the Queen,

23. [Literally, "Greater and lesser not differing in appearance." Translated loosely in the text.—Tr.]

and not already granted, by Escheat-Patents, to particular Persons, shall (upon Notice given to the Inhabitants, by Proclamation, or otherwise) be exposed to Sale, by publick Outcry, In St. *Jago de la Vega*, commonly called *Spanish* Town, during the Sessions of the Grand Court; and then and there, be Sold to the highest Bidder, complying with the ordinary Conditions of Sale, without respect of Persons; and that all Sums of Money arising from such Sales, be paid into the Hands of her Majesty's Receiver General, for the Time being; and be appropriated to the Support of the Government of this Her Majesty's Island, and the contingent Charges thereof; and not (as at present, and for some Years past) be sunk into the private Pockets of such as make it their Business to abuse the Queen, and oppress Her Majesty's Subjects, by their vile, corrupt, and perjurious Practices above mention'd.

Should such an Instruction be obtained, it would, at once cure us of all our Grievances touching Escheats; for it would, for the future, prevent our Triumvirat's making (as, to the great Reproach of the Inhabitants, they have hitherto made) a May-game of too many neighbouring Planters, by stirring them up one against the other, and involving them in vexatious Suits at Law, with the mean and precarious Views of getting cheap Bargains of each others Estates, if, by hook or by crook escheatable; it would leave no room for the Provost-Marshal's packing of scandalous Juries of perjured Wretches, upon Inquisitions, to return upon their Oaths, sham Estimates of such escheatable Estates as fall under their Cognizance, by which they frequently make the pretended Value not to exceed the One, two, or three hundredth Part of the real Value thereof; it would make all Freeholders equally zealous that all Estates truly Escheatable should be escheated, and disposed of to the best Advantage, for the publick Use of the Government; because by such means there would be the less occasion to raise Taxes on their own Estates, for the contingent Charges of the Government; and be likewise a means to keep up the Value of their Plantations, so as not to be depreciated, by reason of the present easie Purchase of escheated Estates.

But while a Triumvirate of such crafty, designing; and industrious Jugglers, as are before described, are (with the help of such a Machine as they have got into their Hands, and the assistance of some other servile and mercenary Associates) still kept at the Helm here, and have Credit enough to be believed at home, to the prejudice of honest Men, who may not have the Opportunity or Advantage of so direct, easie, and free a Correspondence,

I am afraid that the obtaining such an Instruction as is above humbly proposed, is a Thing more to be wish'd, than hop'd for, very suddenly.

And really, the same Consideration (I must own) makes me farther afraid, That even (the three first above recited Acts of this Island, which were made and calculated to abridge, in some measure, the exorbitant Power of the said Triumvirate, (*viz. An Act to prevent any one Person from holding Two, or more Offices of Profit in this Island: An Act for regulating Fees,* &c. And *an Act for the further quieting Men's Possessions, and preventing vexatious Suits at Law*) may not probably obtain the Royal Confirmation, so readily as were to be wish'd: Because by several Letters from *London,* we have Advice, long since, that Mr. *Rigby* (who by his Office, as Deputy-Secretary, is the only Person obliged to make authentick Copies of all Acts of this Island, and is paid for the same, and for these Three in particular) took care to contrive Matters so as the first two of them (made and sent home in *June* 1711, to be confirmed) wanted the necessary Solemnity of having the Broad Seal of this Island affixed to them; for the want whereof, these Acts are still laid aside, till other Office-Copies be sent home in due Form, under the aforesaid Seal, if not already sent.

Yet, in the mean Time, He (the said *Rigby*) took occasion to employ his own and his Friends utmost Art and Industry, to prepossess some in Authority at home (particularly Sir *Edward Northey,* the present Attorney General) with Prejudices against the said Acts, tho' more immediately against that one, touching the Multiplication of Offices in his own Person (vide Pag. 4.) and the better to obtain his End, by grosly misrepresenting both Persons and Things, and by not Stating the Case fairly, (a Trick he the said *R——by* seldom or never fails being guilty of, in any Case whatever) and by falsly suggesting that the aforesaid Act in Relation to Offices was calculated against the Royal Prerogative; he has already, by way of Anticipation, obtain'd the Opinion of the said Attorney-General, *That the Two Offices, of Provost-Marshal, and Secretary of this Island, are not incompatible, to be held and executed by one and the same Person,* &c. As if that were the Point in Debate. No, That was never, in the least, once deny'd or contraverted, by any of the Promoters of the said Act. But these Two Offices having never been executed by one and the same Person, before Mr. *Rigby*'s Time; the Assembly had not occasion till then, to discover the great Inconveniences thereof. And Mr. *Rigby* having, by many fraudulent, over-dextrous, and oppressive Practices, made it manifest to them, and to all the Inhabitants in general, that it then was (and still might be) highly inconvenient, and of pernicious Consequence to have these Offices (which in many Cases ought to be Checks upon one another) executed by one Person, especially a Person having otherwise such an accumulated and over grown Power, and dangerous Influence on the Administration of the Government here, as the said *Rigby* then had, and still has, yet more and more.

And the Truth is, the Assembly wanted neither sufficient Ground nor Inclination to have declared him (the said *Rigby*) incapable of enjoying or executing any publick Office whatever in this Island, ever after; could they have expected the Governor's concurrence: But knowing the transcendent Power which He (the said *Rigby*) had got over the then, as well as the present Governor, they thought it adviseable to soften their Resentment, and be contented with obtaining some part of their Design, by the general Words of the said Act; rather than lose the whole, by bearing too hard on him, in express Terms at once.

Many Things not directly incompatible in the Eye of the Law, or in the strict Sense thereof, may yet nevertheless (as in the present Case) be very highly inconvenient, and Injurious in their own Nature; for *summum Jus, summa Injuria,*[24] 's an old and true Maxim: And tho', from a dutiful Regard to the Queen's Majesty, the Promoters of the said Act did specially reserve the Royal Prerogative therein, yet they do still humbly hope that Her Gracious Majesty will never be induced to exert Her Prerogative in the utmost lawful Extent thereof, to the manifest Prejudice of Thousands of Her Subjects here, and who Trade hither: for the sake of a single Person so notoriously obnoxious as Mr. *Rigby* is.

As to the other Act sent home likewise in *June* 1711, without the Seal of the Island, *viz. The Act for regulatng Exorbitant Fees,* &c. All I can say to it as yet, is, That, under the plausible Pretence of securing the Estates and Interests of such Orphans and Creditors as happen to be in *England,* from Time to Time, the same nimble Gentleman above-named has projected, and, in the last Session of this present worthy Assembly, carry'd on, and obtained the passing of an Act that entitles him to demand legally now, from all Administrators and Executors whatever, many of those Fees which he formerly exacted Arbitrarily, and which (I am informed) were partly the occasion of making the aforesaid Law, for regulating Fees, *&c.*

24. ["The greatest power, the greatest injury."]

Then as to the abovemention'd Act pass'd in the first Session of this Assembly, in *July* 1711, entituled, *An Act for the further quieting Men's Possessions, and preventing vexatious Suits at Law.* Tho' Mr. *Rigby* appear'd, at first, most violently against the passing thereof; yet finding all the Gentlemen, both of the Council and Assembly, who have any considerable Freeholds in this Island, as well as the other Freeholders in general, very much bent on having it pass; and finding likewise, that upon examining and comparing the Draught thereof, it agreed verbatim with the Amendments made (as I am informed) by the late Attorney-General (Sir *James Monntague*) and approved of, by Her Majesty in Council, to an Act of a former Assembly, bearing the same Title with this Act, and sent home to have been confirmed at that Time; he (the said *Rigby*) thought fit to acquiesce and agree to this Act at last; and that he may be the less suspected of acting another Part, behind the Curtain (which he seldom fails of doing on any such occasion) gives himself an Air of seeming now very zealous for its obtaining the Royal Assent: But, as we have too much Experience of this Polite Gentleman's *Machiavelian* Sincerity, to think that his Words should agree with his Designs, in a Case wherein he thinks his private Interest concern'd; I have good ground to believe and affirm to you, for a Truth, that (according to his usual under-hand Practices) he has already set all the Engines he can at work, and will leave no probable Means unessay'd, to prevent (if possible) or at least, obstruct and retard the Confirmation of the aforesaid Act, at home.

I must own, had Sir *James Mountague* (who is said to have made the aforesaid Amendments) been continued Her Majesty's Attorney General to this Time, I should incline to believe it more than probable, that he would have thought himself obliged in Honour, to have favour'd the passing of the aforesaid Act, as it now stands; That is, He would have given his Opinion frankly and readily for its obtaining the Royal Sanction; as being according to his own Amendments.

But I am afraid, that on the other hand (according to the proverbial Saying, *new Lords new Laws*) the present Attorney General (to whose Hands the aforesaid Act must come of course) will not think himself any way tyed up, by his Predecessor's Opinion; but do therein according to the apparent Weight of such new Arguments, as in the present Juncture of Affairs, may possibly be offer'd for, or against the reasonableness or unreasonableness of the aforesaid Act, as it was last pass'd here, and transmitted home. For which Reason, I wish the Gentlemen of this Island now residing in *England*, may take some care to apprize him fully of the real Grounds and Necessity of having such an Act; and give him to understand farther, that, if it should happen to meet with the misfortune of being return'd hither again, with any new Amendments whatever; other succeeding Attorney Generals may, in like manner, make farther Amendments to it, still *in indefinitum;* and that, by means thereof, an Act so absolutely necessary for the Peace, Quiet, and Welfare of this Island, may perhaps be lost, for good and all.

I once proposed to my self to have made an end here: But being now informed that the Ships are not to sail as yet; I take occasion to acquaint you farther, that tho' this Island were fully redress'd in Relation to the Escheats and other Grievances aforemention'd (which I humbly apprehend can never be) without stripping and divesting our tyrannizing Triumvirate of all their Power and Places here, at once, yet these are not the one hundredth Part of the many fraudulent and arbitrary Practices, by which the said Triumvirate, with the assistance of their servile Associates and Abettors, do daily abuse the Queen's gracious Goodness, and oppress Her Majesty's Subjects here: For, as in several Cases, They make a handle of the Queen's pretended Interest to rob and defraud the People; so, in several of the very same Cases; these Jugglers make frequently a handle of the People's pretended Interest, to defraud Her Majesty of Her Just and Legal Right: As, for Example:

When, pursuant to the Act of Parliament of the 6th Year of the Queen's Reign, entituled, *An Act for the Encouragement of the Trade to* America, and pursuant to the Orders and Instructions of the Commissioners of Her Majesty's Customs thereupon, the Collector here (*Peter Beckford,* then Junior, Esq;) was demanding, and had received some of the Duties payable by the said Act, for all Prize-Goods, in manner therein required; our projecting Politicians procured the then Governor's Order in Council (*non obstante*[25] the express Words of the aforesaid Act of Parliament, for present Payment)

> *That the said Collector should take Security of all Prizes brought in, or to be brought in, That they would answer all such Duties as should be due by Law, when thereunto legally required: And that a Copy thereof should be given to the said Collector, &c.*

Had I not been very well assured that the aforesaid Order was drawn, written and sign'd by that Polite, Ingenious, and most dextrous Gentleman,

25. ["Not withstanding."]

Mr. *Rigby* (as he was then Clerk of the Council here) I might possibly have inconsiderately adventured to comment a little on the artful loosness of the Draught, and seeming Design thereof; but his own subsequent Conduct, ever since, in relation to the Subject matter of that Order, has sav'd me that trouble, and sufficiently explain'd the honesty of his Meaning, and sincerity of his Intention by it.

Tho' the said Collector (Mr. *Beckford*) has had the Advantage of a generous and liberal Education, at the University and Inns of Court; is unquestionably well affected to the present Constitution, both in Church and State; and is (as you very well know) not only a Native of this Island, but Proprietor of one of the most considerable Estates, if not the greatest in it (which must be allowed to be some Security for the sincerity of his Inclinations to promote its Interest) and tho' his endeavouring, on all occasions (especially when he was Speaker of some former Assemblies) to have stemm'd, as much as in him lay, the then growing Tide of the apparent Designs of our projecting and indefatigable Triumvirate, was a sufficient manifestation of his Zeal for the Peace, Quiet, Welfare and Prosperity of the Planters in general: Yet when, in the discharge of his Duty to the Queen, he endeavour'd, pursuant to the Act of Parliament and Instructions aforesaid, to have collected the Duties, legally due and payable to Her Majesty, on all Prize-Goods then brought in hither, our projecting Politicians (whose Business, for the most Part, is to fish in troubled Waters) soon found out a Way, by traducing the said Collector, as an alledged Enemy to the common Interest of this Island, and by suggesting other ridiculous Prejudices against the Nature of his Office, to raise a *Posse* of poor deluded mobbish Privateers, to threaten, insult, and bully him, or at least his Deputy, from putting the said Law duly in Execution: Which tumultuary Proceeding, together with the Governor's Order aforesaid, compell'd the said Collector to sit down contented with getting only Bonds, for the payment of those Duties, from the several Agents of the Captors of the said respective Prizes; with such Securities as they could, or thought fit to give for the same.

Here it is to be observed, that, by a general Combination between the aforesaid Agents and Bond-Projectors, whenever they were to give Bonds for the aforesaid Prize-Duties, they always pretended to be in such extreme hurry, in fitting out the said Captors again to Sea, or the like, that they could not possibly spare Time then, to settle and adjust the exact and particular Sums which the aforesaid Prize-Duties amounted to, and for which they were to give Bonds: But, in a Braggadochio-manner, to prevent the least suspicion of any sinister Design in them (honest Gentlemen!) would needs force upon the Collector or his Deputy, Bonds containing Penalties amounting to perhaps Five, Ten, or Fifteen Times as much as was, or could have been reasonably demanded of them: So that upon adjusting and comparing the Sums really due for the aforesaid Prize Duties, and unsatisfied, the first of *June* 1711, (since which Time the Prize Duties ceased) with the Penalties of the Bonds granted for the same; the Penalties amounted to 51830 *l.* whereas the Duties or real Sums for which these Bonds were granted, amounted only to 9043 *l.*

Now to unriddle the mysterious Iniquity of this Janus-like Bond-Project, it will be necessary to shew you, how our Politicians have made it cut, like a two edged Sword, both forward and backward, and effectually to answer, ever since, all the various sinister Ends proposed by it.

Whenever any of the said Captors demanded a fair Distribution to be made of the Produce of the several Prizes wherein they were concern'd, so as they might receive their respective Shares thereof, their Agents had always one general Answer ready coin'd, and in Store for them, *viz.*

> That, in regard the said Collector had compelled them (as they alledged) to give Bonds and Security to the Queen, for the full Value (if not more than the Value) of what the said Prizes might amount to; it could not be reasonably expected, they should part with any of the aforesaid Price Goods, or the Produce thereof, while those heavy Bonds lay over their Heads, and while they were at a continued Expence, upon account of Law Charges, and for soliciting to get the said Bonds remitted, and made void by Act of Parliament, *&c.* or to such Effect.

Then, *vice versa,* under the plausible Colour of a most tender and compassionate regard to the pretended Case of the said Captors, our Triumvirate Projectors procur'd Addresses from the Governor, Council, and Assembly, by means whereof, together with the joint Endeavours of their Associates and Abettors, a Parliamentary Injunction was obtain'd, to put a stop to all Proceedings on the aforesaid Bonds, till the end of the next ensuing Session of Parliament.

So that, by thus artfully magnifying the Queen's Claim against the Captors, on the one Hand, and by setting up the Captor's pretended Interest, against the Queen's Right, with the other Hand, these Rooks (the aforesaid

Agents and their juggling Triumvirate, Confederates and Abettors) have, all this Time, kept the above mentioned Sum of 54830 *l.* among them; or, at least, the Produce of all the aforesaid Prize Goods; which, instead of being less, may (for ought I know, and more probably too) have amounted to more than the double of that Sum, all which is laid out (as I am credibly informed) partly on Mortgages, at 10 *l. per Cent.* (the common Interest here) and partly on Trade, *&c.* from the consideration whereof, you may easily perceive, That *'tis no wonder if a Hook thus doubly baited should catch Fish;* or that a Number of Persons thus combining together, and laying aside all Principles of Humanity and Justice, for compassing their worldly Ends, should soon obtain a more than ordinary Portion of the *Mammon of Unrighteousness.*

Many of the aforesaid poor Captors being, in the mean Time, dead, or removed into other Parts, and such of them as remain still living here, being thus quite tired out, and brought into Despair of ever recovering their Rights, have, at last, thro' the mere necessity of their Circumstances, compounded their several and respective shares of the aforesaid Prizes, with their said Agents, and some few others concerned with them, for little or nothing.

Whereupon a grievous Complaint was, on the 11th of *October,* 1711. made to our then sitting Assembly (the same that is still continued by several Prorogations) and the Consideration thereof was, with a very formal Air, referred to a Committee: But Mr. *Brodrick* (one of the said Triumvirate) being Speaker, and the Majority of the Members being Tools to him and his Associates, the Subject matter of the aforesaid Complaint was slurr'd over in silence, without ever taking any the least further Cognizance thereof, to this Hour.

From all which, you may reasonably conclude, that tho' the Parliament should now be induced to remit the said Bonds, it is not probable that the poor Captors can ever reap any Benefit thereby; unless the Parliament should, in their great Wisdom, Compassion and Justice, think fit, at the same Time, to interpose their Authority so far, as to take care that a special Commission be sent to dis-interested Persons here, for enquiring into the great Abuses aforesaid, and for re-inflating such of the said Captors as are living, (and the Executors and Administrators of such of them as are dead) in *statu quo;* without any regard to the aforesaid Compositions; and allowing them Interest likewise for the Time that their Money is detain'd by the said Agents: Which would be a very considerable Relief to the poor Captors; and the Queen's just Right, as to the aforesaid Duties, may nevertheless be still reserv'd. Thus would these Rooks be caught in the Net which they spread for the Feet of others.

——— *Neque enim Lex justior ulla est,*
Quam Necis Artifices arte perire suo.[26]

But that which I am further surprized at, touching this Affair, is to have it positively affirmed, from several Hands, that, for inducing the Commissioners of Her Majesty's Customs, to make a favourable Report to the Honourable House of Commons, for remitting the aforesaid Bonds, *&c.* our late Governor *Handasyde*, Colonel *Richard Lloyd*, Mr. *Charles Kent*, Mr. *Richard Thompson*, Mr. *Edward James*, and Mr. *James Knight*, late Inhabitants of this Island, should deliberately adventure upon exposing themselves so far, as to give in such a formal Certificate under their Hands, to the said Commissioners, relating to the aforesaid Bonds, and to the Case and Circumstances of the respective Persons thereby bound, as they could not (or, at least refused to) make Oath, to the Truth thereof, when thereunto required by the said Commissioners, pursuant to the Directions of the Act of Parliament, enjoining that all Examinations and Proofs in that Matter, should be taken upon Oath.

Had these Gentlemen been ever, any way, noted as scrupulous Nonjurors, on all former Occasions, or been professed Quakers at the time, there might be some charitable Room left for extenuating the Imputation of that gross Disingenuity, which such a Proceeding seems to have fixed upon them: But since neither the one, nor the other, can be pretended, it is plain, they gave in that Certificate, with a premeditated Design, to have thereby imposed on the said Commissioners, in the first Place, and then on the Parliament, of course; without ever supposing that they would be put to the Test of swearing to the Truth of what they had then certified as aforesaid.

'Tis true, the Law does not take hold of Persons, for barely saying or certifying a Falshood under their Hands, as it does for Perjury: But, in my humble Opinion, they are equally punishable, *in foro Conscientiae;* when

26. ["Nor indeed is any law more just than that the contrivers of murder perish by their own craft."]

done knowingly, *& animo injuriandi.*[27] Yet, we too frequently, see, that, tho' to avoid a temporal Punishment, some People will not so readily venture upon doing the one, they'll not always scruple much to do the other, when they think it may serve a particular Turn, for advancing their own or their Friend's Interest.

From my having thus expatiated so fully on the subject Matter of Escheats, Prize-Duties, Multiplication of Offices in one Man's Power, *&c.* you may possibly imagine, that the most considerable Grievances of this Island, and the Oppressions we lie under, are generally comprehended under these few Heads. No! I assure you, not the one hundredth Part of them: For, were I to launch out into that boundless Ocean of Corruption; the Proceedings in our chief Courts of Judicature (*viz.* the High Court of Chancery, the Grand Court, the Court of Admiralty, and the Council, which together with our Governor makes, you know, a Court of Appeals here.) I could easily give you such flaming Instances of arbitrary, illegal, violent, unjust, oppressive and most scandalously corrupt Practices (and that chiefly too by the notorious Influence of our dearly beloved Triumvirate) in the Distribution of what is here called Justice, that any serious, intelligent, and indifferent Observer (if such a one could be here found) would be apt to conclude that, in this Climate, Virtue was to pass for Vice, and Vice for Virtue; and that Right and Wrong had made a mutual Exchange of their respective Qualities and Properties.

To go to Law here, is, in effect, the same as to try who has the heaviest Purse, and who can part with his Money most freely: For most commonly, if the Cause be pretty considerable, 'tis ten to one, but that he who sees best, may come best speed, according to that of *Solomon,* Prov. 19. 4. *Wealth maketh many Friends,* and ver. 6. *Every Man is a Friend to him that giveth Gifts.* And Chap. 17. 23. *A wicked Man taketh a Gift out of the Bosom* (that is, secretly) *to pervert the Ways of Judgment,* never regarding what goes before; *ver.* 15. *He that justifieth the Wicked, and he that condemneth the Just, even they both are Abomination to the Lord.*

But our Judges have this to plead, in their own Justification, That it is not to be expected they should judge and determine Law-Suits, according to the common Rules of Law and Equity, since none of them was ever bred to the Knowledge of the Laws. As for Example: Tho' Chancery-Suits are

27. ["For injuring the soul."]

very frequent, and industriously swell'd up, to a prodigious Bulk here, of late Years; yet, this Island never having had any other Chancellor, than the Governor, for the time being; and our late Governor's Education having been generally confin'd to the Exercise of Pike and Musket; it need not be much wonder'd at, if he understood (without Inspiration) little more of the Office of a Lord Chancellor, and the deciding of abtruse and knotty Law-Cases, than he did of what he commonly (by Mistake) call'd the Creed of St. *Ignatius;* meaning that of St. *Athanasius:* To which, he said, he could not be easily reconciled.

And our present Chancellor (that is, our Governor) having been always bred at Sea, from a Youth upward, even before the Revolution; and never employ'd or conversant in any other Business, before he came hither; I cannot well apprehend how the bare Pre-eminence of a superior Birth, should entitle him to a more inspired Knowledge of the Laws, than the former.

Our present Chief-Justice, and chief Judge of the Grand-Court, (that is, the Courts of Queen's Bench, Common Pleas, and Exchequer, all in one) was likewise bred at Sea, from a Boy upward, and happening to get the Command of a Frigat, had the good or bad Luck (I can't tell which) to lose her, on a Rock, in sight of *Port Royal,* without any Stress of Weather: So, not thinking it convenient to return home, settled here, and became first a Planter, and then a Judge.

The next in course, is honest Judge *Careless:* He was a Soldier in one of the Regiments of Foot-Guards, at *White-hall;* and his Captain, willing to save himself the Trouble of paying his Company's weekly Subsistence-Money, entrusted this same *W——m C——less* to do it for him: But Mr. *C——less* aiming (it seems) at greater Matters, than carrying a Musket, borrow'd one Week's Subsistance of the Company, drew his own Pass, and made the best of his way hither, *Insalutato Hospite.*[28] Some say he sold himself to the Master of the Ship in which he was transported, to be a Servant for a certain Term of Years; but under Redemption. However, be that as it will, he married a Planter's Widow, and is now the first of the Six Assistant-Judges of the Grand Court. But nevertheless he still retains so much of his former Integrity, that if a Colt or Steer happen to straggle out

28. [Literally, "With the guest not having paid his respects," that is, without saying goodbye.—Tr.]

of a Neighbouring Penn, he very charitably receives it into his own; and to prevent its straggling farther, claps on his own Mark upon it.

All the other Assistant-Judges are likewise Planters of indifferent Estates, and have no Salaries. So that, upon the whole Matter, while the absolute Power of nominating, appointing, continuing, discontinuing and changing, these Judges, at Pleasure, remains in the Gov——r for the time being, and while a Triumvirate of such Persons as *R——by, Br——ck,* and *St——t,* or any two, or one of them, stand instead of an Oracle to such a Gov——r, touching all Matters relating both to Law and Gospel (as they do now, and have done for some Years past) I dare venture to assure you, that very few (if any) will be made or continued Judges, merely from the Consideration of the Brightness of their Qualifications, or Integrity of their Characters, in other Respects; and consequently that none but their own Creatures, Dependents and Associates can well reckon upon being tolerably secure, either as to the Liberty of their Persons, or Property of their Estates, under such a precarious and corrupt Administration, as we now labour under.

I shall now conclude this long Letter with the Recital of a Story, which I cannot forbear mentioning to you, because of the Shrewdness of the Allusion.

News arriving here, some time since, from *Barbadoes,* that heavy Com-plants were sent home, against Mr. *Lo——r,* the present Governor of that Island, for some alledg'd arbitrary Proceedings in the Administration of his Government there; and that, as to Mr. *Do——s,* the Governor of the Windward Islands, he was (as they phras'd it) playing the De——l upon two Sticks; fining, imprisoning, compounding, *&c.* at Pleasure; especially in *Antegoae,* under the Colour of enquiring into the Manner and Occasion of the murdering his Predecessor, Colonel *Parks;* insomuch that some reported he had made 20, some 40 or 50 (God knows how many) Thousands of Pounds, since he came thither; and that there was a grievous Complaint sent home against him, *&c.* Which piece of News (whether true in Fact or not, I know not) being publickly told or repeated at our Governor's Table; Mr. *R——by* (our Prolocutor as well as Dictator General) without taking any further notice of the aforesaid News, was pleas'd, after some few affected Smiles and Grins, to entertain his Excellency, and some few others, then present, with the following Story, *viz.*

That a certain *Vice-Roy* of *Mexico* understanding that the chief Inhabitants had sent home very grievous and heavy Complaints against him,

> to old *Spain*, upon account of vast Sums of Money, which they alledged he had exacted from them, in a very arbitrary and oppressive manner, during the time of his Government, *&c.* he wrote to his most intimate Friend at *Madrid*, for Advice how he should behave, on that Occasion, and whether he might venture to go to Court, *&c.* That thereupon his Friend sent him Word, if the Complaint was true, and that he had got all the Treasure they said he had got, he might freely come to Court, with great Safety; but that otherways he must expect to be ruin'd and undone: or in Words to that Purpose.

I must acknowledge, that as Mr. *R——by* is a Person of indefatigable Industry, so he has a very singular Faculty of inculcating his own seeming Sentiments, both of Men and things, into the Minds of such weak People as are not upon their Guard, against the Subtilty of his Attempts, and who cannot so readily penetrate into the Perniciousness of his double Designs: He has likewise a more than ordinary Talent in bringing his Votaries to be upon a Level with himself, as to the Loosness both of his Principles and Practices: Yet nevertheless still hope that he, and such as he, may, in due time, find there is a Difference to be met with, between a *Spanish* and a truly uncorrupted *British* Ministry; especially in a Case that concerns the Liberty and Property of *British* Subjects. However, the Slyness of his Insinuation, in telling this Story immediately upon the Back of the aforesaid News, brings into my Mind that Observation of *Solomon*, Prov. 18. 16. *A Man's Gift maketh Room for him, and bringeth him before great Men.*

I am, SIR,
Your most humble Servant,

FINIS

· 17 ·

[William Gordon], A Representation of the Miserable State of Barbadoes (London, 1719)

ROBERT LOWTHER, governor of Barbados from 1711 to 1717, was only one of a number of royal and proprietary governors who during the late seventeenth and early eighteenth centuries offended colonial leaders so deeply that they petitioned London authorities to recall them. The core of this selection is a pamphlet by William Gordon, an Anglican clergyman in Barbados, in which the author lays out the case against Lowther in some detail. Noting that Lowther had sacrificed all vestiges of just governance to "his Grand End of making a great Estate at once," Gordon cataloged the many ways that Lowther "with great *Arbitrariness* and *Corruption*" had turned his administration into a shocking abuse of power, extorting annual contributions from the chief officeholders, perverting the administration of justice by putting it up for sale, suspending barristers who opposed him in court, turning his political foes out of civil and military office and even out of their estates, showing total contempt for Barbadian law, engrossing the illegal trade with French colonies to himself, illegally seizing ships on trumped-up charges, manipulating elections to get a majority of his supporters in the legislature so he could thereby gain control over and for several years divert to "his own Use" all public monies, and otherwise making the "Liberties and Properties" of Barbados "the Instruments and Handles to divest them thereof."

Gordon used Lowther's long record of being "thus Despotick in his Government" into a lament at the lack of metropolitan oversight over Crown governors. "It is not possible for Persons in *England* to form any just Idea of the vast Influence a *Barbadoes* Governor, that will act contrary to his Instructions, has over the Liberties, Properties, and Estate of (almost) every Man under his Government," Gordon complained, asking for his recall.

Preceding the pamphlet is a long preface prepared and signed by seven prominent Barbadians who were in England in early 1719 and dismissing a Barbadian grand jury address in support of Lowther that had appeared in the London press. Following the pamphlet are some of the principal documents relating to the case. In response to this effort metropolitan authorities undertook a careful examination which led to Lowther's dismissal in 1720. (J.P.G.)

A

REPRESENTATION

OF THE

Miserable State

OF

BARBADOES,

Under the Arbitrary and Corrupt Administration of his Excellency, ROBERT LOWTHER, Esq; the present Governor.

Humbly offer'd to the Consideration of His Most SACRED MAJESTY, and the Right Honourable the Lords of His Majesty's most Honourable Privy-Council.

WITH A PREFACE, containing REMARKS on an ADDRESS, printed in the *Postman,* and in the *Whitehall Evening-Post* of *May* 14. 1719.

LONDON: Printed for BERNARD LINTOT, between the *Temple-Gates.*

The Preface.

We should not have publish'd this Representation, *till after the several Facts therein alledged had been fully proved before His Majesty; much less should we have stoop'd so very low, as to have taken notice of a* Barbadoes Grand Jury's Address; *if many Persons of Consideration, who are Strangers to the Methods of Procuring such Addresses, had not been imposed upon, by the Ostentatious Manner of Dispersing This over the whole Kingdom, in the Publick Prints, as the Act of a Grand Inquest for the Body of the Island; and at the same Time artfully Suppressing the Names of the Sixteen Mean Illiterate Addressers.*

Before therefore any Remarks are made on the Address *it self, 'twill not be improper to give some Account of the Nature of the Court, and of the Grand Jury and their Addresses.*

The Court of Grand Sessions has been for about Twenty Years last past, by the Laws of the Island, appointed to be held every Second Tuesday *in* June *and* December. *The Governor, in Council, appoints a Chief Judge for the Time, and nominates Persons to return Six Freeholders out of every Parish, (whereof there are Eleven) to serve as Jurors; out of whom the Judge chuses Seventeen to be a Grand Jury: And great Precaution is used in the Choice of them, that no Refractory Person, who will be so Unreasonable, as to desire to know, whether what he is directed to say, be True or False, be of the Number.*

The Business of this Grand Jury, besides Finding of Bills, is to Sign Four Addresses; One to the King, One to the Governor, One to the Judge, and One to the Speaker of the Assembly.

These Addresses are generally drawn by some Lawyer, or Favourite, and very often by the Governors themselves; and always brought to the Grand Jury, ready for Signing.

The Address to the King, is, "To Thank Him for their Incomparable Governor, *under whose* Wise and Just Administration, *they are perfectly Happy; To pray for his Continuance; And to assure His Majesty, That none but Seditious, Turbulent Spirits, find Fault with his Conduct."*

The Address to the Governor, is "a Fulsome Panegyrick on his Matchless Good Qualities; a long Detail of the Blessings they enjoy under his Government, and a severe Censure of whatsoever Thing or Person is obnoxious to him."

The Address to the Judge, is "an Admiration of his wonderful Qualifications, and wise Conduct, whereby he has raised himself to the Great Posts of Honour and Trust in the Island, and discharged them all, especially that of Judge, with Universal Applause."

Thus far all is well; till at last comes the Address, or rather, The Presentments to the Speaker, stuffed with so many sorrowful Complaints of "Grievances, Hardships, and Wants which the Island labours under," that one might justly conclude them the most miserable People in the World.

In this Ridiculous and Inconsistent Manner, has this Farce been acted at every Grand Sessions for above Twenty Years; and Every Governor, *or* President, *who has had the Command of the Island in that Time, has of Course had all the* Fine Things *said to him, that his own Inclinations, or the Imagination of his Sycophants could invent. Let the Sentiments of the People be what they will about the Governor, 'tis become a Duty Incumbent upon the* Grand Jury, *to Address, Commend, or Censure, just as they are directed; which it would now be as Rude and Unreasonable in them to Refuse, as to come into his Presence, without giving him the Civility of their Hats.*

Indeed, about Fourteen Years ago, an Attempt was made (tho' in vain) to rescue the Grand Juries *from this Blind Obsequiousness, and Deserved Contempt, by having them named, or made choice of by* the whole Court, *and not by* the Judge *alone: But that was too Inconsistent with the Governor's Interest, and therefore miscarried.*

This Impartial and Fair Account of Addresses *in general, is sufficient to wipe off the ill Impressions this particular one may have made: And we should not say any more of it, if there were not couched in it Two very Unworthy and Malicious Reflections; one on* the Right Reverend the Lord Bishop of *London, and the other on* the Honourable Society for Propagation of the Gospel in Foreign Parts.

We have been credibly inform'd, that Mr. Waterman, *a Lawyer, by whom a great Part of the* Address *was penn'd, has thought himself bound, in Vindication of his Honour, to declare, That those Two Clauses were sent from* Pilgrim; *and that he was not at Liberty to Alter One Letter in either of them.*

As to the Clause about Ecclesiastical Jurisdiction; *since that Jurisdiction is at his Majesty's Disposal, we have Reason to believe, that whatever His Wisdom shall see fit to alter therein, will give entire Satisfaction to all Persons, who are any wise concerned with it; Though we cannot but look upon it as an Amazing Piece of Assurance, to find, that a Falshood can be so Boldly and Roundly averr'd, which is capable of a Confutation not only from the Attestation of many Gentlemen now in* England, *but also from the very Laws and Records of the*

Island: For the Ecclesiastical Authority is neither Inconsistent with the Constitution, nor feared and detested by the People; nor was it ever so much as found fault with before; for now about Thirty Years that it has been establish'd There.

It is, and has been establish'd by the uninterrupted Authority of Five Successive Kings *and* Queens, *under the same* Seal Manual, *and in the same Individual* Order of Instructions, *That the Courts of* Chancery, Errors, *and* Exchequer, *are establish'd: Which* Instructions *are allowed to be Laws, where the Laws of* Great Britain *and* Barbadoes *are silent, and are with* the Patent, the very Foundation of the Constitution, and *Magna Charta* of the Island. *Nay, so far is this Jurisdiction from being Inconsistent with the Constitution of* Barbadoes, *that if the Laws of that Island (instead of the Laws of* Jamaica) *had been thought worthy to have been consulted for its Authority, there would have been found among them a Law confirmed by* the Crown; *which gives all the Acts of Parliament relating to the Discipline of* the Church of *England, the same Force in* Barbadoes *as Here.*

Neither is this Jurisdiction Fear'd or Detested. We do indeed believe, that there are some that fear it, and particularly the Governor's Lady's Two Sisters; *who both of them live Publickly, Avowedly and Impunely, as Wives to one* Richard Wiltshire, *to whom they are both married, and by whom they have Issue: And which makes the Crime still more Flagrant, One of them was married to, and had Lawful Issue now living by,* John Wiltshire, *the Elder Brother of the said* Richard; *and the Issue of both the Brothers by one Sister, and of both the Sisters by one Brother, live promiscuously in the same House, and eat at the same Table, with the said* Richard and his Two Wives, *without either Shame or Concern. Whether the Disturbing the Repose of these the Governor's* Brother and Sisters in Law, *be not the true Cause of the Fears and Detestations, is humbly submitted?*

The other Reflection in this Address, *is couched in such Ambiguous Terms, that tho' the Scope of it be levell'd at One of* THE WISEST AND GREATEST BODIES IN THE KINGDOM, *yet the Pretended* Abuses and Misapplications, *which Mr.* Lowther *is therein said to have discover'd, not being particularized, and never having been mention'd or communicated to the* Society, *either by the* Addressors, *the* Governor, *or any Person whatsoever; 'tis impossible to say any thing further to this Clause, than barely to remark, That if Mr.* Lowther *has made any Discoveries of* Abuses and Misapplications, *he ought first to have acquainted the* Society *with them, before he had sent a vaunting Account of them all over the Kingdom, in the Publick Prints. But this is not the first Instance of Mr.* Lowther's Mal-Treatment *of that* Right Reverend and

Honourable Body; *who, notwithstanding all their Moderation, and Desire of Peace, have been once already forced to complain to His most Sacred Majesty, against his Arbitrary and Injurious Treatment of them. And as they have now appointed a considerable Number of their own Body, to enquire into the Meaning and Grounds of that Clause; it would very ill become us, to Anticipate or say imperfectly, what they will see fit to offer on that Head.*

They have many more, and far greater Lets and Hindrances, to Encounter with and Surmount, in their unwearied Endeavours to pursue their GLORIOUS *Designs of Converting* Infidels, *than this Pitiful Mean Piece of Malice: And we don't doubt, but their Wisdom and Zeal, which have been so often Conspicuous on other Occasions, will, on this, effectually* put to silence the Ignorance of foolish Men.

As to the Representation; *The Reader is desired to observe, That it does not contain One Tenth Part of the Particular Facts, which are ready to be proved against Mr.* Lowther; *of which we shall give a* Specimen, *in the Annexed* Order *of the* Lords of His Majesty's most Honourable Privy Council; *and are ready to give many more, if Mr.* Lowther's *Agents force us to it; as they have done to this, by their Publication of a Ridiculous Address. The* Representation *was sent from* Barbadoes, *with a Letter to Sir* Robert Davers, *Sir* Charles Cox, &c. *Sign'd by a great many Gentlemen, who (with their Families) are a Majority of the Island; and a Copy of it deliver'd to his Grace the Lord President, and another to the Right Honourable Mr. Secretary* Craggs, *with the following Letter.*

LONDON, *Feb.* 3. 1718–9.

My LORD,

Herewith We humbly presume to send Your Lordships a Copy of a Representation, which has been delivered to Us, with a Letter, sign'd by a great many of the most considerable Gentlemen and Merchants in *Barbadoes,* whose Names Prudence obliges us to conceal, whilst Mr. *Lowther* continues Governor, because we would not expose them to the Resentments of One who has it so much in his Power to injure those who complain of his Male-Administration.

We are fully persuaded of Your Lordships tender Regard for so considerable a Colony; and do therefore with the greatest Chearfulness submit the Enclos'd to Your Lordships Consideration; and are, my Lords,

Your Lordships
Most Obedient

Humble Servants,

Robt. Davers,
Charles Cox,
Abel Alleyne,
Wm. Walker,
Jno Walter,
Thos. Pindar,
Jno. Alleyne,
Edwd. Morgan,

The Right Honourable the Lord President.

A Representation of the Miserable State of Barbadoes, under the Arbitrary and Corrupt Administration of his Excellency Robert Lowther, Esq; the present Governor. Humbly offer'd to the Consideration of his most Sacred Majesty, and the Right Honourable the Lords of His most Honourable Privy-Council.

When Mr. *Lowther* came to his Government of *Barbadoes* in *June* 1711. he found the Factions and Parties, which had formerly disturbed the Peace of that Island, almost extinguished. There had not been, for above a Twelvemonth before, any Struggle made for being Civil and Military Officers, or chosen Assembly-Men; but on the contrary, a general Inclination to Reconciliation and Agreement. And, that the Governor might not think it his Interest to stir up any new Animosities to get Money; the then Assembly, to keep him in good Humour, gave him larger Sums of Money, than had ever been given to any Governor before. But Publick Presents, how large soever, did not prove sufficient to satisfy his Expectations; and therefore other Ways were fallen upon, to compass his Grand End of making a great Estate at once, particularly the following.

1. Causeless Seizures of Rich Vessels.

2. Extorting large Pensions from the Secretary, Provost, Marshal, Register in *Chancery,* and other Patent Officers.

3. Selling, delaying, and preventing Justice, in Causes that came before him in *Chancery* and Error.

4. Buying the Publick Debts for half the Value, which he could immediately turn into Cash, and get 50 *per Cent.* by them, in case the Assembly would, by an Act of the Island, vest him with a Power to prefer the Publick Orders for all Debts (He call'd) Emergencies, to others, tho' of a Prior Date.

In Pursuance of this Scheme, he order'd the Ship *Oxford,* of *Bristol,* to be seiz'd; and when all the Custom-House Officers refus'd seizing her (well knowing that she was not liable to Seizure) he got a Purser of a Man of War to make the Seizure; and prosecuted the Cause with such Violence, that *Richard Carter,* Esq; a Barrister at Law, was by him arbitrarily suspended from practising as a Barrister, or exercising his Profession, only for being of Council for the Ship *Oxford.*

He suspended Mr. *Skeen* the Secretary, because he refus'd to allow him a Pension of 400 *l. per Ann.* out of the Fees of his Office. He kept a Cause of *Haggot* against *King* hanging up in *Chancery* all the Time he was Governor; and tho' it was every *Chancery* Court-Day put down on the List for Hearing, yet he always pass'd it by uncall'd; only because Mr. *Haggot* would not consent to the Marriage of a young Lady, under his Guardianship, to a Person to whom Mr. *Lowther* own'd he had sold her for 1500 *l.* And in order to accomplish his Bargain, he was about taking her from Mr. *Haggot,* when she was married; and he actually did despoil him of the Guardianship of her Sister; declaring, that *no Parent had a Right to appoint a Guardian to his Child.*

In the Cause *Bentley* against *Downs.* Whilst *Downs* was his Creature, he never would hear it: But when *Downs*'s Party was turn'd out by him, the Cause was hurried on, Courts held out of Course, contrary to all the Rules and Practices either before or since, and a Decree pass'd in a few Weeks.

In the Cause *Burke* against *Bullard,* 'twas said he received Bribes on both Sides; but it is certain *Bullard,* against whom the Cause was given, obliged Mr. *Lowther,* when he was recall'd, to refund by the Hands of his Confident Mr. *Slingsby* 100 Guineas, because they had not kept their Words with him in giving the Cause for him.

To get the Publick Orders preferr'd or postpon'd as he pleas'd, was to be done only by an Act of the Island: Because by the former Laws, all Orders for Publick Debts, were payable, according to the Priority of their Dates and Numbers. This Point the Assembly refus'd to give up, because they saw the bad Influence it would have upon the Publick Credit: And he thereupon seem'd to recede from his Demand, till he had privately and underhand spirited another Party to act in Concert with him; and then he dissolv'd the Assembly, turn'd all of them out of their Offices Civil and Military, and preferr'd his new Party, of whom a Majority were elected Assembly-Men. But, contrary to his Expectations, the New Assembly prov'd as unmoveable as the Old; and no Sollicitations could induce them to give up the Grand Point of sinking the Publick Credit, by calling such Debts as the Governor pleas'd Emergencies; and thereby vesting him with a Power to prefer or postpone the Payment of them. This Inflexibility of theirs provok'd him not a little: He upbraided them with Obstinacy, and told two of them, whom he believ'd to have the most Influence: —

> *You know, Gentlemen, this Ministry are not my Friends, or you dare not refuse me this. By God, if I had a Ministry that were my Friends, I would make you be glad to eat Grass with your Cattle.*

At last, when neither Flatteries nor Threats would prevail, he made Court to the Party he had turn'd out; who (for the sake of being *Colonels, Judges,* and *Justices of the Peace,* and having all the *Places,* and *Offices*) promis'd to gratify him. Whereupon he turn'd out all his new Officers; restored those he had formerly turn'd out; dissolv'd the Assembly again, and call'd a new one; and all in the Space of a few Weeks: And with great *Arbitrariness* and *Corruption,* got first an Equality, and then a small Majority of the new Assembly, who gave him a Power of disposing of the Treasury as he pleas'd.

For such his Arbitrary Conduct, he was, upon Application to her late Majesty Queen *Anne,* recall'd by an *Order* under *her Sign Manual;* which commanded him upon Receipt thereof, to deliver up the Seals, Commission, Instructions, and other Ensigns of Government, to Mr. President *Sharp.* Which Order he disobey'd, and held the Government, and did all Judicial Acts of Government which any Governor can do, for many Weeks afterwards. Soon after his Return to *Great-Britain,* her Majesty died, and the Complaints dropt; and before the Gentlemen of the Island could inform His present Majesty of his Conduct, and lay their Grievances before him, Mr. *Lowther,* upon Pretence that he was recall'd out of Pique by the late Ministry (tho' he had continued the usual Term of Three Years) yet got himself nominated again for the Government; and return'd to it in *May* 1715. Immediately upon his Arrival, he dissolv'd the Assembly, and turn'd out most of the Officers Civil and Military, and did not leave so much as a

Captain of Militia, or a *Justice of Peace* in Place, who was not entirely at his Devotion. At the same time it was industriously spread all over the Island, that *whoever would venture to oppose his Measures, must expect to be represented to his Majesty, as a Person disaffected to the present Establishment.*

The Gentlemen he turn'd out, tho' most of them were, and always have been, remarkably zealous and steady in their Affections to the *Illustrious House of* HANOVER; yet considering what a distracted Condition *Britain* was then in; and that it was probable and natural for His Majesty and his Ministers to give Credit (at least) for some Time, to the Representation of a Governor whom they believ'd sincerely in their Interest; considering also, that it would be extremely difficult, as well as very expensive, at so great a Distance, and under such Disadvantages, for Strangers to set Matters in a true Light; being also too well acquainted with Mr. *Lowther*'s Resolute, Revengeful and Malicious Temper, did (upon the whole) judge it most for the Interest of their Country not to disoblige him by Opposition, but to live quietly at home, without expecting or desiring any Publick Post; or concerning themselves with any Publick Affairs; or so much as censuring or blaming any Part of his Conduct. And accordingly, when he *dissolv'd the Assembly,* and call'd a new one, there was not so much as one Cross Vote in the whole Island; and he was suffer'd to nominate every *Member,* who were accordingly elected, *Nemine Contradicente.*[1]

This Generous Regard to the Tranquility and Good of the Island, miss'd of its desir'd Effect. Mr. *Lowther* was pleas'd to term it Cowardice; and said, that it proceeded from their knowing he stood so well with *the Ministry.* And accordingly, without any Regard to the Blind Obedience paid him by every Body; and notwithstanding he got what Sums of Money he pleas'd to ask for, from the Publick, yet he went on to Satiate his Revenge in Crushing and Oppressing all those, whom he suspected to have had any Hand in contributing to his former Removal; and soon made even Gentlemen of Sense and Interest to dread and fear him.

An Instance of which, out of many, we have in *Richard Carter,* His Majesty's *Attorney-General* in that Island.

That Gentleman (as had been observ'd) had been silenced by him in his former Government, and suspended from practising as a Barrister at Law, only because he would not support him in the Causeless and Arbitrary

1. ["With no one dissenting," that is, unanimously.—Tr.]

Seizure of the *Oxford;* whereby he was forc'd to come for *England* for an Order to be restor'd; which he obtain'd; and by the Advice of his Counsel, sued Mr. *Lowther* in Damages, and recover'd 2000 *l.* and yet to avoid his Frowns, was glad to make Mr. *Lowther* a Present of the 2000 *l.* notwithstanding he had good Friends in *Britain* to support him, and is a Person of known Affection to the present Government.

It is not possible for Persons in *England* to form any just Idea of the vast Influence a *Barbadoes* Governor, that will act contrary to his Instructions, has over the Liberties, Properties, and Estates of (almost) every Man under his Government: For he is, in effect, sole Judge in all Causes in Law and Equity, as having the Nomination of the Judges, and turning 'em out at Pleasure, without any Reason.

The *Militia* too (which upon very good Grounds is so constituted, as to be a Sort of *Standing Army,* being the only Defence in Time of War) has a great Influence over People's *Liberties.* With the Assistance of these, He chuses the *Assembly:* Who, by being of his Making, are consequently the more Obsequious to him.

Mr. *Lowther* (who seems as much influenc'd by his Avarice as his Revenge) being thus Despotick in his Government, was not satisfied with Twice as much Money as ever any Governor got from the Country; but swallow'd up all the Taxes, as fast as they were rais'd. Even the Funds, which raise the immediate Subsistance-Money of the Poor *Matrosses, Soldiers and Gunners,* (who watch and guard the Artillery, Forts and Magazines of the Islands) have been wholly diverted into his Coffers; and the poor People driven to sell their Orders for their Annual Allowance, at 50 *per Cent.* Discount. There has not been One Publick Debt paid since he has been Governor, tho' many of 'em be Nine Years standing: And yet, when Mr. *Walker* was about Ten Months *Treasurer* in his Absence, the same Taxes paid above 8000 *l.* Debts, and all the Annual accruing Charges; and paid the Soldiers, Matrosses and Gunners, or at least rais'd Money for the doing it. For Mr. *Lowther* (upon discovering that Mr. *Walker,* the Treasurer, had 2300 *l.* ready Cash, to pay the Matrosses and Gunners, as soon as Mr. *Lowther* should Sign their Order for their last Half Year's Subsistance Money) press'd Mr. *Walker* to pay it to himself; and upon Mr. *Walker*'s Refusal, because it was by an express Law appropriated to another Use; he got Mr. *Walker* turn'd out from being Treasurer, and Mr. *Sutton* put in; and in the mean Time refus'd to Sign the poor People's Orders, till Mr. *Sutton* receiv'd, and paid the

Money to him; whereby the poor People were driven to sell their Orders to some rich Person, for a trifling Value.

If any Person, who has any Debt due from the Publick, asks for Payment at the Treasurer's Office, they are laugh'd at for Fools; and ask'd, *Don't you know that all the Money goes one Way?* Indeed, after Three Years Receiving all the Publick Money for his own Use, he has at last rais'd a Tax to pay Debts; some Part of which, we hope, will be applied to that Use.

The *Publick Justice* is also set to Sale, and the Administration thereof so perverted and interrupted, that 'tis in vain for any one (who has a Demand either in Law or Equity, that will admit of the least Contest) to commence a Process, unless Mr. *Lowther* be retain'd.

Some Persons have been divested of their Rights, to the Value of several Thousand Pounds; and when they have pray'd for Liberty to Appeal to His Majesty in Council, (which cannot be but by *the Seal* of the Island) Leave has been deny'd them.

Others have been turn'd out of their *Plantations,* without due Course of Law. Others have been refus'd to be admitted Parties, to defend fraudulent Causes and Suits brought against their own Estates.

Some have had Causes on the List in *Chancery* (where Mr. *Lowther* presides) ready for Hearing, without being call'd or gone upon for several Years; whilst others have commenc'd Original Causes, and had 'em hurry'd on and determin'd in less than Three Weeks, contrary to the Laws, and establish'd Rules of the Court.

Such is Mr. *Lowther's* Interest in all the Courts of Judicature, that every body applies to him, who wants Favour. And tho' Bribery, which is transacted with so much Privacy and Secrecy, is of all Crimes the most difficult to be proved; yet if a Thousand concurring and convincing Circumstances, as well as plain Proofs of some Bribes, be of any weight, it will appear, that he has got a great deal of Money by that *vile* Method.

His Management of the *Militia* is as unjustifiable, as his Distribution of Justice. He took the Bridge Regiment (which is the largest, and in the Limits of which, all the Merchants and Traders of the Island reside) into his own Hands, and calls himself the Colonel of it: And to make the Merchants the more dependant upon him, he calls the Regiment in Arms twice as often as the Law requires, (contrary to an express Law); and upon the Non-Appearance of any Person, he causes Executions to issue, and sends out his *Marshals* to levy Fines. And when any Person remonstrates to him, That the

Calling of 'em in Arms, and Levying such Fines, is directly contrary to Law; He answers, "Damn your Laws: Don't tell Me of the Laws. I will do it; and let Me see who dares dispute it?"

Mr. *Lowther* has such Influence on Trade, that the Merchants, to keep in Favour with him, (besides many Presents) are forced to sit down under these Oppressions, and pay these illegal and arbitrary Fines for themselves and Servants.

In *October* last, Mr. *Lowther,* taking Advantage of an Order of His Majesty, not to supply the Rebels at *Martineque;* obliged the Assembly to pass a Law, whereby every Person was restrain'd from going, without his License, to *Dominico, Tobago,* St. *Vincent's, Desiado,* or St. *Lucia,* (all of 'em *English* Islands) between which and *Barbadoes,* there were above Thirty Sail of Vessels, employ'd in bringing Mastick, Fustick, Greenheart, and other Dying and Hard Wood, and Turtle.

That Law occasion'd a great Consternation among the poorer Sort of Traders; there being above a Hundred Families supported only by the Wood and Turtle Trade: And when they came to petition for Licenses, very few were granted; and those upon such Terms, that the Poor could not go to the Price of them.

The Prejudice done to the Island of *Great Britain,* is also so very flagrant and notorious by that Law, which was only for a Year, that 'tis hoped (notwithstanding the great Advantage Mr. *Lowther* makes of it, by Selling Licenses) he will not venture to continue it for a longer Time.

By that Law, Mr. *Lowther* has engross'd all the *French* illegal Trade to himself; and he is so jealous of Rivals therein, that he will not let Persons, who have their Negroes stollen, or run away to the *French* Islands, go down with his Letter to bring them back: A Thing like to prove of fatal Consequence to the Colony.

Mr. *Lowther* has persecuted, in a violent and implacable manner, the Persons and Relations of all those, whom he suspected to have been concern'd in Solliciting, or Procuring the Order to recal him from his former Government; and is still persecuting them, even to Ruin. Mr. *Cox,* Colonel *Peers,* Major *Hannis*'s Children, Colonel *Sandeford,* Mr. *Gillegan,* Mr. *Gordon,* and Mr. *Walter,* of the Kingdom of *England,* are all of 'em many Thousand Pounds the worse for his Oppressions, and Arbitrary Behaviour towards them. Even Mr. *Forbes,* the present Deputy Provost-Marshal, has many illegal Hardships and Violences done him in his Office; because he will not pay his Excellency an Annuity out of his Fees; and because he will not take Directions from him what Writs to serve, and what to delay, he threatens to suspend him.

So many Ways has Mr. *Lowther* of oppressing the People, to enrich himself, that even Strangers, who are forced into the Island by Stress of Weather, are constrain'd to give him one half of their Cargo to save the other. Witness the Ship St. *Lewis* of *Lisbon*.

Even under the specious Pretence of settling the Publick Accounts, he has, for private Gratuities, discharg'd those who were real Debtors to the Country, for nothing; and extorted vast Sums of Money from others, who owed nothing (as he himself had acknowledged, after he had promis'd to discharge them in any manner they should desire) because their Presents were not large enough.

The Instances of Mr. *Lowther's Tyranny, Oppression, Injustice,* and *Arbitrary Conduct,* are too numerous to be particulariz'd.

The *Publick Credit* is lost. The *Publick Debts* are unpaid. The poor Soldiers, Matrosses and Gunners, are robb'd of their Subsistance Money, and are forc'd to take half; and yet the Publick pays the whole.

Justice is denied, delay'd, and perverted; and the Laws, which should protect the People in their Liberties and Properties, are made the Instruments and Handles to divest them thereof, and are broken and despised.

Trade is put under many illegal Hardships; and violent Persecutions carried on without Mercy or Remorse. And to crown all, and in order to prevent Complaints, an infamous Scandal is thrown on His Majesty's Ministry, THAT THEY ARE HIS FRIENDS, AND WILL SUPPORT HIM. And the Committee of Correspondence (who send all Advices to the Agents) are his own Creatures; who act entirely by his Direction, not only without the Approbation, but even without the Privity of the Council and Assembly: Before whom, they have not thought fit to lay any one Letter, that they have sent to, or received from their Agents in *London*.

The Gentlemen of *Barbadoes* have not in this, exaggerated one Crime of Mr. *Lowther's*.

If it should be thought strange, that no Complaints have been lodged before this Time, the Gentlemen will frankly own the Reasons of their Silence, which follow.

1. When Mr. *Crow* govern'd *Barbadoes* in the same Arbitrary and Corrupt Manner, tho' not to so great a Degree of Violence, *Her Majesty* called him

home; having declared the Complaints against him to be fully proved. And yet upon his coming home, soon after the Change of *the Ministry*, he, by representing, that he had fallen a Sacrifice to my Lord *Sunderland*'s Resentment, found Means to get himself acquitted by the then New Ministry, upon Pretence that the Complaints were not fully proved.

2. When Mr. *Lowther* was called Home, just before the *Queen*'s Death, he, by pretending that he was made a Sacrifice to the former Ministry, and for want of a true Representation on behalf of the Inhabitants of the Island to His Majesty, was reinstated in his Government.

3. Another Reason that induc'd the Gentlemen to Silence, was, because there is not in the whole Island, a Justice of Peace who will, or dares take a Deposition that in the least reflects on Mr. *Lowther*.

4. A Fourth Reason of Silence was, that considering it is not usual for any Governor to hold that Post above Three or Four Years at most; and Mr. *Lowther* having enjoy'd it Seven, they were in hopes, he would have been recall'd of Course; and so determin'd to delay representing their Grievances, till they should have a Liberty of getting proper Proofs. Nor would this Representation have, as yet, seen the Light; but that it is given out in *Barbadoes*, to prevent and discourage Complaints, that Mr. *Lowther* has renew'd his Government for Three Years longer; and therefore we have taken the Liberty to send this impartial Account of some of our Grievances. To prove these Allegations in *England*, (tho' much easier than in *Barbadoes*) would be a Work of great Fatigue and Expence, tho' it be notoriously true, yet the Gentlemen are willing to undertake it, if thereunto required. However, they hope, it will be thought sufficient, if they fix upon some material Articles of Complaint, which they will prove, and make out, and prosecute Mr. *Lowther* upon; either before *his Majesty in Council*, or in *Westminster-Hall*, or *where* His Majesty shall direct; whenever Mr. *Lowther* shall be recall'd to answer them; but hope they shall not before. For the Gentlemen are too well acquainted with the Terror and Dread which every one under Mr. *Lowther*'s Government stands in, not to know their Evidences dare not appear whilst he is Governor. And therefore, by prosecuting of him before he is recall'd, they would only enable him, by the Influences of his Power and the Publick Money (which he has the uncontroulable Disposal of) to get himself acquitted of these Crimes; which, upon a fair Enquiry, they know they shall make fully appear against him; and which they are determin'd to prosecute him upon whenever he shall be out of his Government.

Articles of Complaint, against his Excellency Robert Lowther, *Esq; Governor of* Barbadoes.

1. That the said *Robert Lowther* has stopt, or endeavour'd to stop, all the Avenues to Justice against him; by Turning out all Justices of Peace whom he suspected would take any *Affidavit* against him; by declaring, That *the Ministry had promis'd to support him;* And that whoever went to oppose his Measures, should be represented as *disaffected:* And by taking to himself (exclusive of the *Council and Assembly*) the sole Direction of *the Committee of Correspondence* with the *Agents of the Island.*

2. That the said Governor being *Chancellor, Ordinary,* and *Chief Judge* of the *Errors* from the Inferior Courts, does delay, pervert, and obstruct the Administration of Publick Justice, and deny Appeals from Arbitrary and Illegal Decisions, to His most *Sacred Majesty;* contrary to his *Instructions,* and the *Constitution* of the Island.

3. That the said Governor did carry on an Illegal Commerce, and stop others from their Legal Trade, contrary to several Acts of Parliament; whereby he has not only forfeited his Government, but is by the said Acts render'd INCAPABLE of Holding any Government under His *Majesty.*

4. That the said Governor has diverted the Publick Money, rais'd and appropriated for the Payment of the Publick Debts; by drawing Orders payable to himself on the Treasury of the Island; and receiving, and converting to his own Use, 18000 *l.* contrary to his Instructions, and to the great Oppression of the Creditors of the Publick; whereof 2300 *l.* was rais'd in Mr. *Walker's* Treasurership, and was only applicable to the Payment of the Gunners and Matrosses; who were thereby drove to sell their Orders to a great Undervalue, by reason the said Governor converted that Sum to his own Use.

5. That the said Governor frequently calls the said Inhabitants into Arms, and levies Fines for their Non-Appearance; contrary to an express *Law* of the Island.

6. The Complainants humbly crave Leave to prove, That the said Governor is guilty of all, or many other of the *Facts,* mention'd in the foregoing *Representation.*

Barbadoes, July 15. 1718.

At the Council Chamber, Whitehall. *The Twelfth Day of* March, 1718.
By the Right Honourable the Lords of the Committee for hearing Appeals, Complaints, *&c.* from the Plantations.

His Majesty having been pleased by his Order in Council of the 6*th of* January *last, to refer to this Committee the humble Petition of* Francis Lansa, *Part Owner of the Cargo of the Ship* St. Louis *of* Lisbon, *belonging to the said Port, in behalf of himself; and the rest of the Owners of the said Cargo; Complaining of Mr.* Lowther, *Governor of* Barbadoes, *and his Secretary; and also of Mr.* Lassels, *Collector of His Majesty's Customs there, for Extorting from* John Demoracin, *the Master of the said Ship, the Value of Two Thousand Pounds in Gold and Sugars, before the said Ship was permitted to sail from thence, she having sprung a Leak, and put into the said Island only to refit, as by Affidavits of the said Master appears. Their Lordships this Day taking the same into Consideration; and thinking it proper, before the Hearing of the said Petition of Complaint, that a Copy thereof should be transmitted to the said Governor* & alias *for their Answer: Are thereupon pleased to Order, That a Copy of the said Petition of Complaint, which is hereunto annexed, be transmitted unto the said Governor, Secretary, and Collector of the Customs, who are hereby required to return an Answer thereunto, together with such Depositions, or other Proofs, as they shall think necessary to support the same: And that free Liberty be given to the Complainant, or his Attorneys, or any other Persons concern'd, to make Affidavits before any Judge or Magistrate in the said Island, of what they know touching the said Matters. And that such Judge or Magistrate do summon before them such Persons as the Complainant, or his said Attorneys shall name, which the said Governor is to signify to such Judge or Magistrate as soon as may be. And that the Complainant, or his Attorney, is to deliver unto the said Governor,* &c. *Authentick Copies of such Affidavits as they shall make in this Matter. As also, that the said Governor,* &c. *do deliver unto the said Complainant, or his Attorneys, Copies of their Answer, and of such Depositions as they shall think necessary for their Defence, within the Space of One Month after the Receipt of this Order. As also, that within Twenty Days after receiving each others Proofs, the said Governor,* &c. *do in like manner exchange with the said Complainants the Replies that shall be made by Affidavits, or otherwise, before they be transmitted to their Lordships. And that the whole Matter be returned to this Board under the Seal of the said Island, within the Space of Six Months from the Date hereof. And His Majesty's said Governor of* Barbadoes, *the said Secretary, Collector, and all others whom it may concern, are to take Notice hereof, and Govern themselves accordingly.*

EDWARD SOUTHWELL.

To the KING's Most Excellent Majesty.

The humble Petition of Francis Lansa, *Part Owner of the Cargo of the Ship St.* Louis *of* Lisbon, *belonging to the said Port, in behalf of himself, and the rest of the Owners of the said Cargo.*

SHEWETH,

That the said Ship, in her Passage from *Brazil* to *Lisbon,* having sprung several Leaks dangerous to the said Ship and Sailors Lives, was obliged to bear away for your Majesty's Island of *Barbadoes;* where she arrived on the 7th Day of *May,* 1715; and where Monsieur *Jean de Morassin,* Master of the said Ship, after making out his deplorable Condition, easily obtained from the Honourable *William Sharpe,* Esq; then President and Commander in Chief, an Order, or License, in Writing, to land her Cargo into Her Majesty's Store-House, to enable him to refit the said Ship.

That on the 13th of the said Month, and before the Master could land any of his Cargo, his Excellency *Robert Lowther,* Esq; having arrived to be your Majesty's Governor, sent for the said Master, took the said License from him, and tore the same to pieces; and threaten'd to seize your Petitioner's Ship and Cargo.

That to prevent the said Seizure, and to procure License for Landing, and afterwards Exporting your Petitioner's said Cargo, the said Captain was constrained to give the said Governor Thirty Eight Ounces of Gold Dust, Twenty *Moydores* to his Secretary, and Twenty six Chests of the finest Sugar, between him the said Governor and *Henry Lassells,* Esq; Collector of your Majesty's Customs there.

That being thus stript of the Gold, with which he should have supported his Seamen, he was forc'd to sell another considerable Part of his Cargo at an Under-Rate. Besides which, there was unjustly taken from him, in your Majesty's Warehouse, under Pretence of Shifting the Sugars from Chests to Hogsheads, a very great Quantity thereof in all, to the manifest Injury of your Petitioner, and the rest of the Owners, the Sum of Two Thousand Pounds; as by the said Master's *Affidavit,* hereunto annex'd, will appear, in the manifest Breach of the Hospitable Laws of Nations in Amity with each other.

Wherefore your Petitioner humbly prays, Your Majesty will be graciously pleased to Order the said Governor, and the said Henry Lassells, *to make a Restitution of the said Gold and Sugar, in such manner as Your Majesty in Great Wisdom shall think fit: And your Petitioner shall ever pray, &c.*

John Demoracin, of the Kingdom of *Portugal,* late Master of the Ship St. *Lewis,* belonging to *Lisbon,* maketh Oath, and sayeth; That in the Year 1715, this Deponent's Ship, in her Passage from *Brazil* to *Lisbon,* sprung several dangerous Leaks, which obliged this Deponent to put into the Island of *Barbadoes,* on or about the 18th Day of *May* (*N.S.*) in the same Year. That on his Arrival in the said Island of *Barbadoes,* he applied himself to the Honourable *William Sharpe,* Esq; then President and Commander in Chief of the said Island; and upon representing his distressed Condition, readily procured the said President's License, to land the Cargo of the said Ship into the King's Warehouse, until he should stop his Leaks, refit his Ship, and proceed on his said intended Voyage. And this Deponent further saith, That on the 24th Day of the said Month of *May,* his Excellency *Robert Lowther,* Esq; (who in that Interval) arrived in the Quality of Governor of the said Island of *Barbadoes,* sent *Henry Lassels,* Esq, Collector of His Majesty's Customs, for this Deponent, before he had unladed any of his Cargo: And the said Governor did then take from this Deponent the said President's License, and tore it in pieces; and threaten'd to seize this Deponent's said Ship and Cargo. And thereupon the said *Henry Lassells* told this Deponent, That he must make the Governor a Present, or else he would have no Leave to refit his Ship. Then this Deponent asked the said *Lassells,* what Present? To which the said *Lassels* reply'd, That this Deponent could not give him less than Seven or Eight Pounds of Gold Dust. Then this Deponent told the said *Lassells,* that he had not so much; but that he this Deponent would give him a Pound. And the said *Lassells* told this Deponent, that it was not enough; and would not do. And upon this Deponent's Exclaiming against the said Extortion, the said *Lassells* told this Deponent, That the King gave him the Government on purpose to get Money. And this Deponent further saith, That he this Deponent having no Prospect of obtaining Leave to unlade his said Ship, and refit her, did at last consent, and agreed to give him the said Governor Forty Ounces of Gold Dust: But as this Deponent was weighing the same to the said *Lassells,* he this Deponent put only the Weights of Thirty Eight Ounces into the Scales; so that only Thirty Eight Ounces of Gold Dust was weighed, and put into a white Tin Canister: And this Deponent did go with the said *Lassells* to the said Governor; and in the Presence of the said *Lassells,* did deliver the said Governor the said Canister, with the said Thirty Eight Ounces of Gold Dust, which the said Governor took, and put into his Gown Sleeve: And then laying his Hand on this Deponent's Shoulder, in a friendly manner address'd himself to the said *Lassells,* saying, That this Deponent was an honest Man, and should have Leave to do what he desired. And this Deponent further saith, That afterwards this Deponent had several Papers and Petitions drawn, as the said *Lassels* did advise; and deliver'd his Cargo into the King's Storehouse, under the Care of the said *Lassells.* And this Deponent, upon Surveying the said Ship, and finding her incapable of going to Sea again, applied for Leave to hire another Vessel to carry her Cargo to *Lisbon;* but before this Deponent could obtain the same, this Deponent was constrained by the said *Henry Lassells* to give, by way of Present, unto the said *Henry Lassells,* for his own and the Governor's Use, Twenty five Chests of the finest of his Sugar; and also Twenty *Moydores* to Mr. *Isaac Lenoir,* the Governor's Secretary, and one Chest of Sugar to the said *Lassell*'s Book-keeper. All which said Presents were extorted from this Deponent, who did not make them voluntarily, but out of Necessity, and by that Means to preserve the Remainder of his Cargo. And this Deponent further saith, that after he had obtained License to hire a Ship to carry the said Cargo to *Lisbon,* the said *Henry Lassels* obliged this Deponent to consent to the shifting of a great Part of the said Cargo from Chests to Hogsheads. And that this Deponent received from the said *Henry Lassels* Fifty two Hogsheads and one Teirce of Sugar, for One hundred thirty two Chests, notwithstanding that the Difference between the Weight of a Hogshead and a Chest is very inconsiderable. And the said *Henry Lassells* having received from the said Governor all the Papers necessary for this Deponent's Protection and Justification, did refuse to deliver the same to this Deponent (who could not go to *Portugal* without them) until he had extorted from this Deponent a Receipt for all the said Cargo, and forced this Deponent to sign a Paper or Papers, purporting a General Release on all Accounts, notwithstanding that this Deponent never had any Dealings or Accounts with the said *Henry Lassells.* And this Deponent further saith, that for want of the said Gold Dust to support his Charges and pay his Sailors, he was obliged to sell another Quantity of his Cargo at an under Rate, and to great Loss, which otherwise he had been under no Necessity of doing. And this Deponent further saith, that the Value of the said Gold and Sugar extorted from him under the Pretence of Presents, and of the

Sugar wanting and taken away, under Colour of shifting it, was about Two Thousand Pounds *Sterling,* or upwards.

JEAN DEMORACIN.

Jur. 24. *die Nov.* 1718.
Cor. me in Canc.[2] *Magro.*
W. FELLOWS. *True Copy.*

March 20. 1718–9.

Jean Moracin *being this Day sworn before the Lords of His Majesty's most Honourable Privy Council, did affirm the Contents of the said* Affidavit *to be true, and to be sign'd by him.*

EDWARD SOUTHWELL.

FINIS.

2. ["Sworn on the 24th of November before me in Chancery." Probably Magro is a town or county or last name.—Tr.]

· 18 ·

Elisha Cooke, Mr. Cooke's Just and Seasonable Vindication (Boston, 1720)

ELISHA COOKE, JR. was the son of a prominent Massachusetts politician of the same name who had opposed the new charter the colony received in 1691, and the grandson of a Governor of the colony. Like his father, Cooke was a prominent leader of the anti-prerogative forces in the Massachusetts assembly. He was also a clerk of the Supreme Court and a judge in Suffolk County.

Cooke's *Just and Seasonable Vindication* was written in response to Governor Shute's refusal to allow Cooke to serve as Speaker of the House in 1720, a prerogative that the Crown in England had last used in the 1690s. When the assembly refused to choose an alternate Speaker, Shute dissolved it and called an election. But the new assembly continued to insist on its right to select the Speaker. Shute and Cooke also clashed over whether the woods in Maine (where Cooke owned land) were reserved for the use of the Royal Navy as the surveyor-general, John Bridger, claimed, or whether Cooke and other landholders could harvest the timber for profit.

Cooke held that the right of the House to choose its own Speakers was justified by "Perpetual Usage" as well as by a 1692 Act of the Massachusetts assembly which stated that the representatives in the colony's general court should be the sole judges of the election of their own members. Cooke also maintained that the colony's charter did not give the governor a veto power over the election of the Speaker, because it did not involve the lawmaking power of the General Court. And he warned his readers that should the governor get the power to veto the House's choice of a Speaker, nothing would stop him from interfering in their choice of other officers. For the House to acquiesce in this matter would, Cooke contended, give "a Deadly wound to the Constitution," and deprive "the People whom they Represented of their proper Rights." Cooke also refused to allow the governor to waive the veto in his case as he was concerned that it would set a bad precedent. Rather, fundamental principles needed to be defended forcefully as the "happiness or infelicity of a People" depends on "the enjoyment . . . of Liberties." However, Cooke insisted that he was not an opponent of prerogative powers, arguing that when "rightly used" they are for "the good & benefit of the people," just as "the Liberties and Properties of the People are for the Support of the Crown."

Two years of constitutional conflict ensued, with the House refusing to provide money for colonial defense, and voting to reduce Shute's salary. In 1723, Cooke went to England to defend the colony's case before the Board of Trade. He eventually had to accept an explanatory charter which affirmed the governor's right to overrule the assembly in its choice of a Speaker, stated that the Crown controlled the timber in Maine, and limited the House's power to adjourn itself. Fearing the loss of the charter, the assembly accepted these changes reluctantly. However, this did not end the constitutional conflict between governor and assembly in Massachusetts, with the two clashing over whether the governor should be granted a permanent salary for the next two decades. (C.B.Y.)

Mr. *Cooke's* Just and Seasonable

VINDICATION:

Respecting some Affairs transacted in the late General Assembly at *Boston*, 1720.

Mr. Cooke's Just and Seasonable Vindication, &c.

An Account of the sudden and unheard of Dissolution of the General Assembly, on the Thirtieth of *May* last past; with the Reasons given for it in his Excellency the Governours Speech, being put into the Gazette, and other Publick News Letter, the Sixth of *June* following, hath without doubt made subject Matter for much Talk and Debate through Town and Country: Which necessarily lays me under an indispensible Duty to Vindicate my Proceedings, during that short Sessions; lest by Silence I might seem to own the things I am charged with.

The Honourable *House of Representatives*, at the Opening of the Sessions on the 25th of *May*, making Choice of me, tho' much inferiour to many, their Speaker, appoints a Committee to Report the same to his Excellency.

Who Returned that his Excellency said it was very well.

Notwithstanding which in the Afternoon, Mr. Secretary *Willard* brought a Message from the Board. That his Excellency the Governour is now in Council, and expects there to receive the Message of the House, respecting their Choice of a *Speaker*. The House Ordered a Message to be sent up to the Governour; That the House sent a Committee in the Forenoon to his Excellcy's House; That the House had Chosen *Elisha Cooke* Esq; their *Speaker*.

Who Returned Answer that his Excellency said it was very well.

The Members having attended the Orders of the House Returned Answer, that his Excellency said he Expected that Message now he is in the Chair, and that he had neither received such a Message, nor given such an Answer.

And then a Message was Sent to the Board, that the House are ready to proceed to the Choice of Councellours, and desire them to Join in the Choice. Who Returned that his Excellency said no such Election should be made till he is acquainted who is Chosen *Speaker* of the House.

Upon which a Message was Sent to the Governour then in the Chair, by the same Committee that waited on him in the Forenoon at his House, *viz.* Major *Chandler*, Colonel *Dudley* and Mr. *Coffin*, that the House had Elected *Elisha Cooke* Esq. their *Speaker*. Who Returned that his Exellency said, that the Gentleman Chosen *Speaker* had formerly affronted him as the Kings Governour, and that therefore he did Negative the Choice, according to the

Power given in the *Royal Charter* of this Province: and desiered the House to proceed to Elect another *Speaker.*

But in a very short space of time, a Message was Sent up to the Governour that the House had Elected a *Speaker* according to the Ancient and Undoubted Rights and Usage of that House, and therefore Insisted upon there Choice. And at the same time to the Board, that the House desiered they would Join with them in the Election of Councellours, who Returned that his Excellency had Negatived the Choice and he was no *Speaker.* And soon after Mr. Secretary *Willard,* brought down a Message that his Excellency Ordered him to acquaint the House, that he was Informed, that Governour *Dudley,* did in his Government disallow a *Speaker* Chosen by the House, and that his Proceedings were Approved by the Commissioners of *Trade* and Plantations, and that he was thereupon directed from the said Lords Comissioners, to acquaint the Council, that it would not be tho't fit that Her Majesty's Right of having a Negative upon the Choice of a Speaker be given up, and which was reserved to Her Majesty, as well by the *Charter,* as the Constitution of *England.*

The Board acquainted the House, they are ready to Join with them in the Choice of Counsellours, they forthwith proceeded to bring in their Votes, appointed a Committee to carry them up, and Report the several Elections that should be made; which they performed: And on the next Morning, *May* 26. the House appointed a Committee to wait on his Excellency, with a List of Councellours newly Chosen for his Approbation. Signed, *Elisha Cooke,* Speaker.

And the House being Informed, his Excellency had Adjourned the Council, till *Saturday,* Ten a Clock inquired of the Committee, whether they had attended that Service, who Reported, that both in the Forenoon and Afternoon, as soon as they understood his Excellency was in the Chair, they were going up to wait on him with the List, but perceived he was withdrawn. And then the House Adjourned to the same hour.

And on *Saturday* Morning, the aforesaid List, was Returned by Mr. Secretary, with the Governours Approbation, and Non-acceptance, under his Hand writing, a little below the Paper, Signed by me as aforesaid, without any Reservation, Challenge or Exception, respecting the Speaker. Whereupon the House went on with the Business that lay upon their Table; then the Secretary brought down a Message, that his Excellency expected

Mr. Speaker, and the House to attend him forthwith in the Council-Chamber, who went up, and then the Governour advised them to make choice of another Speaker, for Reasons therein Offered. They Returned to their own Chamber, & after Debate, the Question being put, *Whether the House upon the Reasons assigned by his Excellency, would proceed to the Choice of a new Speaker?* It passed in the Negative, *Nemine Contradicente.*[1] And quickly after, the House sent a Message, to acquaint his Excellency, that the House had passed the said Vote, which was sent up by a Committee of Nine Members. And the House Adjourned to *Monday* following, 4 a Clock Afternoon, (having first passed upon some County Treasurers Accompts).

It could therefore be no little surprize, that after the Governour had signified his Pleasure on the Choice of Counsellours, without any Exception, Challenge or Reservation as aforesaid, he should send in for the House, and enter upon the Chusing a new Speaker, and further observe to them the Person Chosen, had Invaded the King his Master's Rights, in the Woods, in the *Province of Main,* tho' Confirmed to him by an Act of the *British* Parliament; and that he had Received Thanks from the Board of Trade, for removing him out of the Council. One would have thought that Matter had once and again been fully heard, argued and debated in the General Court; There being a large Committee of Both Houses, who made their Report, which was Read & Accepted in the *House of Representatives,* who had before them the several Memorials, Evidences, Receipts of Monies paid Mr. *Bridger,* and all things relating to that Affair, were well inabled to make a true & impartial Representation thereof; and after Mature Consideration had, Reported that Mr. *Bridger* had not made out his Alligations against me; But that the said *Bridger* had obstructed the Inhabitants of this Province, in their Just Rights and Priviledges, by his Arbitrary and Unwarrantable demanding Money of them for liberty to improve their Rights in Logging: Which is a sufficient Vindcaition for me; notwithstanding the Removal from the Council before spoke of.

And I have little or no reason to question, but that if the Honourable the Lords of Trade and Plantations, had been furnished with the Papers the General Court had: And verily the Honour and Justice of the House of *Representatives,* that had given me Thanks, respecting that Matter. The Report of the Committee, and several Votes since of the House.

1. ["With no one dissenting," unanimously.]

Considering also that I was then a Member of His Majesties Council, and not seeking any Advantage to my self, but endeavouring to bode off a very grievous and dangerous Insult and Violation upon the Liberties and Properties of the Country, by one under colour of Authority, from his Majesty to inrich himself I suppose only, such circumstances attending that affair, made it justly Reasonable for all the Papers to be transmitted to them, they would have been of a different Opinion, and not displeased at what I had done; for it had been then clearly demonstrated to them, that the Surveyor, was by me thereby prevented from making shameful havock of Trees fit for Masting His Majesty's Royal Navy, by Selling Liberty to Persons for filthy Lucre, to go any where in the Woods, Cut, Fell and Carry off such, and so many Trees as their private Occasions called for. Which practice if continued, had soon wasted the most valuable Pine Trees, to the unspeakable prejudice of the King his Master, whose Bread he then eat. So that I humbly presume, without the least vanity or arrogancy to my self, I may truly affirm, that I was not only Instrumental in Securing His Majesty's Loyal and Dutyful Subjects in their just Rights, but also prevented great Stroy and Wast of the Woods: and preserved them for His Majesty when his occasions call for them.

If Mr. *Surveyor* now he is in the Province of *New-Hampshire,* and his leisure will permit him, would in the mean time take some care they are not sent to *Spain.*

Furthermore, Mr. Agent *Dummer* would never undertake to prove before the Board of Trade, that the Lands, with all the Woods in the *Province of Main,* are the Property and Legal Purchase of *that* Province. And that if the King has, or had a Right to reserve such and such Trees; yet in fact, no such reservation has been made with respect to those Lands, because they did belong to a private Subject; which is a Case specially excepted in the Charter; and whatever Estate he had in it, the Province as now having purchased his whole Right and Title: Were he in the least apprehensive, that he should be accounted an Enemy to the King for thus arguing, and that the Agent hath gone this length is evident by his Letter, he defends my Innocence, in which he writes, the Honour & Justice of the Assembly is concerned. By which it may fairly be deduced, that whatever the former Sentiments of that Board, touching *that* Matter have been, they have other Views of it now.

And as to the Ill Treatment his Excellency mentions, he received from me: Whatever of this nature happened it was personal, and the several

Gentlemen of the Town, that I had the favour to converse with, who having heard and understood the Truth and Circumstances of that matter, have of their own accord at divers times said that in their Oppinion, I had done every thing that could be expected, to remove all misunderstandings that his Excellency entertained against Me on that Score, and for some time past I did suppose, that the Governour had laid aside all these Resentments, because in the Month of *December* last, I Received a joynt Commission with other Gentlemen, under the Seal of the Province and the Governours Signing, to Treat with the Commissioners of *New-Hampshire,* & Issue a Controversie relating to the Bounds of the Two Provinces, which Settlement if Accomplished, had not only a Relation to, but very much effected His Majesty's Woods in the Province of *New-Hampshire,* and I being one intrusted by that Commission, was then thought a proper Person, and his Excellency confide in My Prudence, with the other Gentlmen in that affair, tho' it so necessarily concerned his Majesty's Woods.

During the Debates & Controversie between the Governour and the House, touching their Right of Chusing a Speaker, and his Power of Negativing. It was intimated to me, if I would wait upon his Excellency, and say to him, I was sorry for the Misunderstandings *that* had happened between us; and pray, that *what* had passed *might* be forgot, and endeavour always to discharge my Duty to the Governour, as well as my Country, or Write to a Third Person to that purpose, to be Communicated to him; all things would be accommodated, the Governour allow me to continue *Speaker,* and the Publick Affairs of the Province go on, but otherwise his Excellency would further insist on the Negative he had passed on me; & having according to my weak Capacity, weighed & considered the Circumstances then attending me, and Station I stood in, could not perswade my self, that I could with safety comply with these Conditions; And I do solemnly avow, that no perverse temper, or any private View or sinister end, forbid me closing therewith: But a just fear for, and tender Regard to the Rights and Liberties of this People was the sole occasion of my Non-compliance.

It being my firm belief, that the House of Representatives have an Indubitable Fundamental Right to Chuse their *Speaker,* & the Governour no Negative Voice in that Election, which to Me is made Unquestionable, not only by the best of Evidence, *Perpetual Usage,* but also by an Act of the Great & General Court or Assembly of this Province, Held at *Boston June* 8th. 1692. And Continued by Adjornment to the 12th of *October* following; The first General Court Held after the Arrival of the present Charter. And the aforesaid Law having Passed the Royal Assent is a good Law to Us. In which Law among other things, it is Enacted, that the *Representatives in any Great and General Court, shall be the Sole Judges of the Elections and Qualifications of their own Members, and may from time to time, Settle, Order and Purge their House, and make such necessary Orders, for the due Regulation thereof as they shall see Occasion.*

Now if the Representatives at any time Assembled, are of Opinion that it will be for the Settling, or better Regulating the House to have a *Speaker,* are they not Invested with Power sufficient by that Law to Appoint One. This none will oppose, but the main Objection Remains,

Why may not the Governour have a Negative Voice in that Election? The best Reason I am capable of Assigning at present is; That in my Humble Opinion the Charter has not given it him, and the aforesaid Law Vesting that Election Solely in the House restrains him.

Let Us a little Examine the Charter, which is the only Rule to direct us in the right Path. That Declares and Enacts, *That in the Framing and Passing all Orders, Laws, Statutes* and *Ordinances, and in all Elections and Acts of Government, to be Made, Passed* or *Done, by the General Court or Assembly, or in Council; The Governour for the time being shall have a Negative Voice.*

Now the Election of a *Speaker,* is not an Election Made and Passed by the General Court, or an Act of Government, the Council never Voting, or intermedling in that Choice. It is no Election passed in Council, therefore the Governour {has} no Negative Voice. These two being the only Instances, wherein the Charter mentions the Governour's Negative: and this falls under neither of them, exceptions or Reservations. And the Governour can claim no more than the King has Reserved. And should any Doubt arise hereupon, all Grants, and Pattents are Construed in favour of the Grantees. Whoever argues for the Governour's having a Negative over the *Speaker,* must at the same time allow he may Negative the Clerk, Monitors, Messenger of the House, or any other Officer whatsoever, that they shall think meet to appoint.

Grant this, & it will necessarily follow, that the Governour has a much more stronger right to Negative the appointment of Committees, Allowances of Money, all Votes or Bills of that House, that in their ordinary and usual course heretofore, had the Concurrence of the Board before they can be of force, even before ever they come to the Council for their Consideration.

And if the Governour can have a Negative on things transacted in the House, before they have had the Concurrence of the Board, that part of the Legislature would be in a great measure useless; which cannot be the intent or design of the Charter. *Uno Absurdo dato Mille sequntur.*[2]

And seeing there was an Essay to break in upon so valuable a Right of that House, I may Venture to say the Matter in Debate then before them was of as great Concern and Importance, to the Representative Body of this People, as any heretofore before that order of Men; had they *then* given up the Cause, Ages to come would justly said, they had given a Deadly wound to the Constitution and well being of that House, and deprived the People whom they Represented of their proper Rights, which would have been a Reproach to them when in their Graves; But like those worthy Patriots of their Country, that went before them in the like Case, properly Opposed and Repelled all Attempts of that Nature; so have they, and in so doing behaved themselves as became true and Faithfull Assertors of the Peoples Liberties, and in No wise Infringed the Prerogative of the Crown. And could they *then* sound out the Person that stood between the Governour and them, to advise him in that Article, he deservedly ought to have been distinguished.

And now after the Governour had given out to be in his Power to Negative the *Speaker*, and as far as he could put that power in force, and advance his Arguments as far as they would bear, to induce the House into the same Sentiments with himself, advising and directing them to Chuse another *Speaker;* the House notwithstanding, even to a man firmly adhere to their first Vote of their undoubted Right of Chusing Exclusive of the Governour's Power of Negativing. Had I then, who was but a Servant of theirs, especially without their privity and consent, taken up with those Overtures; would they not very justly faulted me for betraying them, and basely given away as much as I could the Rights of that House, because whatever Concessions I had come into, they must have been made as terms, & certainly had been taken, and understood by all, that it was for no other end or purpose, but that the Governour might continue me in that place the House had put me in; for had I said or done any thing at that juncture, it must come from me in order to take off the Negative, which had been a demonstration beyond all contradiction, that either I supposed it in the power of

2. ["From one absurdity a thousand follow."]

the Governour to effect what he had been aiming at, or arose from a jealous fear, that the House would not abide by themselves. The first of which I have plainly given my tho'ts of; and had I harboured so mean & dishonourable an opinion of the House. So well knowing their steady Carriage and Conduct, it would have been very Criminal in me; how therefore could I expect to escape the displeasure of the House, and whole Country, and ever after Ranked among those despicable Wretches that would Sacrifice their Country to serve themselves. Which if I know my self, neither frowns or favours shall wittingly oblige me to do. This Matter being rightly stated will easily be understood.

The Governour Assumes a Power, enforces it as far as the Matter will bear, perceiving the Assembly are not willing to Submit to it, is content upon certain Conditions to Wave the Matter, Terms are Agreed on, a final Issue put to the Controversie. Will not this afford all succeeding Governours a good handle to do the like, and produce this very Instance as a Precedent for them to Negative a *Speaker*, and no easie thing for the Assembly to withstand it. Precedents are of great force. Few Men at first see the danger of little Changes in Fundamentals, every design therefore of alteration ought to be most Warily observed and timously Prevented, for its the Interest of the People, that Fundementals should be duly Guarded, for whose benefit they were at first laid.

The happiness or infelicity of a People, intirely depending upon the enjoyment or deprivation of Liberties; Its therefore highly prudent for them to inform themselves of their just Rights, that from a due sence of their inestimable Value, they may be encouraged to assert them against the Attempts of any in time to come.

One Material thing I cannot well omit, because since the rising of the Court, I have been told of it by several, as what I could not easily Answer. On the Morning of the Day the Governour dissolved the Court, a Gentleman of the Assembly at my House, in the hearing of others of the Representatives, gave me good Assurance that the Governour, Provided I would pomise to be Dutifull and Loyal to the King and seek my Countrey's good, he would pass it by, or take off the Negative he put on Me, and the affairs of the Court go on as if nothing of that nature had been, affirming that this he took from the Governours Mouth.

This being nothing but what every Loyal Subject, and true Lover of his Country's Weal, is or ought to be in the Daily practice of, should I therefore make the least Scruple or Hesitation, and not chearfully shew forth a forwardness to comport therewith, who would not be, apt to Cry out & say, my preverse Temper and Obstinate Humour carried Me beyond all bounds of Moderation.

But parhaps every one at first sight may'nt see through this. Why should I be singled out of the whole Assembly, I freely confess my Powers are Weak, but in Loyalty to the King, and Faithfulness to the Intrest of My Country, I desire to go behind no Man.

When the Gentlemen appointed by the Governour, to Administer the Oaths to the Members Elected, see that they Made and Subscribed the Declaration, Took & Subscribed the Oath of Abjuration; did any one of them, or the Assembly, discover any Reluctancy in Me or the least shew of Unwillingness thereof, have I ever been taxed for deserting my Country, or any time backward, when in my power to promote the Good of it. If so, some shew or pretence, should I have this Test enjoyned me.

No the Matter don't pinch there neither, but lies in this Narrow. The Governour has been pleased to say, that I had Invaded the King's Rights, receives a Memorial of Mr. *Bridger,* in which he attempted to prove it, and dresses me up as an Enemy to King GEORGE; and the Governour did not see meet to let me know any thing of it. He three days after he had dismissed me the Council, nor gave me an opportunity to disprove the falsities in that Memorial, which had been no hard task, and clear up my Innocency, which obliged me to apply to the General Court for Relief; and in process of time, in a legal due course, I was fully acquitted from these false Imputations, which perhaps was not well accepted by some. The Governour being apprised, that my Conduct respecting that Business was so publickly Vindicated by an Assembly at one time; at another, having the Honour to be thanked by the House therefor at another Sessions.

Mr. Agent *Dummer* directed by the Assembly to attend the Board of Trade, and disclose that Matter to them, that they might perceive that for want of the whole Papers, they were brought in to make such a Representation as they did, being capable of judging *Ex parte tantum.*[3] And these Votes and Orders, differing so vastly from his Excellency; should he by any act of Mine, lessen the force of them; doubtless it would be a satisfaction to him. And had I been alured to promise, that now I would be Faithful and

3. ["From one side only."]

Loyal to the KING. What Improvement might not been made of it, had I by my own Act now at once undone all that the Assembly had done in my behalf. Would it not been Argued against me. What better or other proof is requisite to prove fact, than what comes from a man's own mouth. If Mr. *Cooke* was not conscious to himself, that heretofore he had been Undutiful and Disloyal. What reason had he to promise that he would (as by the timing of it had followed) *de futuro*[4] ingage to be Loyal and Dutiful, would this been the genuine and common Construction put upon it; and all the Evidences and Demonstrations imaginable, to evince the contrary of none effect. What would the Consequence be, not only the Governour's getting of the Assembly, his Negative Power in the Choice of a *Speaker*, which of it self was sufficient to restrain me from any such needless promise at such a time; but I had also Exposed my self, being so well assured of my Innocency, and good design in the Management of that Affair. As well as greatly endangered the former Assembly's Supporting me, to be accounted not much more looked upon with an Evil Eye.

Therefore its best that the labouring Oar still lie upon some Body, and I hope my Conduct will be such that they may strive in vain, to prove in any Article I have been willingly injurious to His Majesty's Intrest; And if time shall discover that I have not of late begrudged some Cost and Pains to detect in order to put an End to a much greater Mischief and Injury done to His Majesty, in a Neighbouring Province, than the dispoiling Him of His Woods there, will it be Misrepresented by Mr. *Surveyor.*

If any one thinks I take the least Pleasure or Satisfaction in putting this forth at such a Critacal Juncture as it is now with Us, they are not a little Mistaken, this Method is no ways agreeable to Me, but very perplexing even to think of undertaking this My so Reasonable Vindication; Nothing save the Duty to My Country, & the Grand Law of self preservation, should have perswaded Me. And I now do ardently desire that when the next Assembly come together, there may be a good Understanding and Harmony betwixt them, every Man of one Heart and one Mind, Studying to advance those great Ends they are sent for, and that none in the least Measure will aspire, to lessen the Prerogative of the Crown, nor willingly come into or depart from any thing that then, or hereafter may be made Use of for the lessening or abridging the Peoples Rights and Properties, because the Kings

4. ["In the future."]

Prorogative when rghtly used, is for the good & benefit of the People, and the Liberties and Properties of the People are for the Support of the Crown, and the Kings Prerogative when not abused.

The Kings Prerogative and the Subjects Liberty, being both determined by Law.

This being now the Sixth time the Town of *Boston,* have seen good to Command Me to Represent them in so many several General Courts, I must freely own their Maintaining and keeping up their good Opinion and kindness for Me, is a favour Accompanied with all the Obliging Circumstances imaginable, and is an Earnest of their approving my former Service. And that which adds weight to their kind Regards to Me, is that notwithstanding the endeavours of some few to traduce Me, they have not been prevailed upon to lessen or alter their former Sentiments of Me, but rather Confirm them to Me; and their bestowing upon Me so singular an Honour at this time, I unfeignedly and sincerely wish, may lay Me under Stricter Ties, and yet stronger Obligations at all times, to Exert My self in my low Sphere, to promote and advance the Honour and Service of King GEORGE, So Glorious a Prince as our Nation, and We in these Provinces, are by the favourable Smiles of Heaven blessed with. To whom as in Duty Bound, as I always have, so hope ever shall bear true Faith and firm Allegiance, Intirely seek the Good and Wellfare of my Dear Native Country, ever Rejecting and Contemning all Private View and Interests, more especialy when in Competition with the Publick Good, & in every State and Condition, Study to Abase and Behave my Self to the Powers that are Ordained over Us, as becomes every Good *English Man* to do. And this I Willingly and Heartily, Profess and Declare in the Fear of GOD, to be My Resolution and fixed Principle.

Boston in *New-England. June 15th* 1720.

Elisha Cooke.

· 19 ·

Anonymous, A True State of the Case between the Inhabitants of South Carolina, and the Lords Proprietors of That Province [London, 1720]

BEFORE THE establishment of Georgia in the 1730s, Proprietary South Carolina was England's southern-most North American colony, bordering on territory claimed by Spanish Florida and deeply involved in trade with the powerful southeastern Indian confederations. In 1715, the unanticipated Yamasee War, the largest rising of indigenous peoples against the colony up to that time, produced devastating effects that underlined for South Carolina settlers the proprietary regime's total inability to defend them and inaugurated a movement to transfer jurisdiction of the colony to the Crown. Fueled by the proprietors' subsequent veto of several laws that the South Carolina legislature considered essential to preserve the public credit and "the Liberties and Properties of his Majesty's Subjects" in the colony, this movement resulted in the peaceful overthrow of the proprietary regime in 1719. Controlling the legislature and representing a widespread consensus that included all but a few prominent proprietary officials, the leaders of this uprising drew up the selection below. Depicting South Carolina settlers as "an abandoned People," they used this document to present a long history of proprietary neglect and maladministration, charging the proprietors with having violated the terms of their charter by ignoring its guarantee of the settlers' "right to all the Libertys of *Englishmen* born in *England*," assuming a "despotic Authority, exceeding the Royal Power in *Great Britain*" in abrogating beneficial laws, and otherwise "trampling upon the

Rights and Libertis of His Majesty's Subjects" in the colony. They expressed the fear that "this hopeful Province will be lost to the *British* Empire and called upon the Crown to take South Carolina under its protection. Metropolitan authorities took the first step in this direction in 1721 when they organized a royal government for South Carolina. (J.P.G.)

A True State of the Case between the Inhabitants of South Carolina, and the Lords Proprietors of that Province; containing an Account of the Grievances under which they labour.

That his late Majesty King *Charles* the Second, by his Charter dated the 24th of *March,* in the 15th Year of his Reign, granted unto the Lords Proprietors, and to their Heirs and Assigns, the Province of *Carolina,* with Privileges and Jurisdictions requisite for the Government and Safety thereof, and made them absolute Lords and Proprietors of the same; who having besought leave of his Majesty, by their Industry and Charge, to transport and make a Colony of his Majesty's Subjects into the said Country (at that time inhabited only by People who had no Knowledge of God) being thereunto excited with a Zeal for the Propagation of the Christian Faith, and Enlargement of his Majesty's Dominions; as is amply set forth in the said Charter.

Notwithstanding which, the Lords Proprietors have not to this Day been at any Charge, or used any Endeavours to propagate the Gospel amongst the said barbarous People; neither have they been industrious at their Charge to transport and make a Colony of his Majesty's Subjects in the said Province; but have hindred the peopling the same by violating their Covenants made with them, who by their Promises were invited to be at the charge of transporting themselves thither.

And tho one principal Design of his said Majesty, in granting the said Charter, was for the good Government and Safety of his Subjects in the said Province; yet the Lords Proprietors have so abused the Trust and Confidence thereby reposed in them, by their confused Administration over his present Majesty's Subjects there, that they are neither safe in their Liberties or Properties, the Government being abandoned to evil Ministers, and the Inhabitants exposed to the Ravages of most barbarous Enemies.

That the Lords Proprietors were by their Charter impower'd to build and found Churches, Chappels, and Oratories within the Bounds of the said Province, and to cause them to be consecrated according to the

Ecclesiastical Laws of *England*, with full Privileges, Prerogatives, and Franchises necessary for the same; yet they have not to this Day erected any Church, Chappel, or Oratory, for Divine Worship, nor any School for the Education of Youth in the Principles of the Christian Religion; nor ever reserved any Places for the same in any Parts where they have sold Lands; nor procured the Consecration according to the Ecclesiastical Laws of *England*, of any of those built by the Inhabitants.

That the Lords Proprietors are by the said Charter impower'd to confer Titles of Honour upon such of the Inhabitants there, as were capable of the same, and who for their Deserts might expect the same; but instead thereof, they sent over Blank Patents to their Governour and Receiver General, for creating Landgraves and Cassiques, in order to have them sold at a certain Price: So that the Persons intitled by their Deserts to any Marks of Honour, thought this Procedure so mean, that it was beneath them to accept thereof.

That the Lords Proprietors are by the said Charter impower'd to erect within the said Province, such Forts, Castles, Cities, Towns, Boroughs, Villages, and other Fortifications, and the same to furnish with Ordnance and other Habiliments of War, for the Safety and Welfare of the said Province; but the Lords Proprietors have never set apart any of their Lands for erecting Towns, Villages, or Fortifications, nor contributed one Penny towards the raising any Forts, or other Fortifications, which the Inhabitants, almost to their Ruin, have been obliged to build; otherwise, by the Incapacity of the Lords Proprietors to assist them, that Part of his Majesty's Dominions had been lost to his Empire.

That the Lords Proprietors, contrary to express Powers in their Charter, not to make any Laws in the said Province, but what were consonant to Reason, and as near as might be agreeable to the Laws of *England*, and so not to extend to the binding, charging, or taking away of the Right of any Person or Persons in their Goods or Chattels; yet they did in the Year 1704, under their Hands and Seals, ratify two Acts of Assembly of that Province; one entituled, An Act for establishing religious Worship in that Province, according to the Church of *England*, and for erecting of Churches for the publick Worship of God, and also for the Maintenance of Ministers, and building Houses for them, wherein they established a Commission for displacing of Rectors or Ministers there: and the other entituled, An Act for the more effectual Preservation of the Government of that Province, by requiring all that should be chosen Members of the Commons-House of

Assembly, and sit there, to take the Oaths, and subscribe the Declaration appointed by that Act, and to conform to the religious Worship of that Province: by which Act a great part of the Inhabitants were excluded from being Members of the Assembly. And tho it was represented to the Proprietors, that corrupt Practices were used by their Government to have those Acts passed; that it was contrary to the Rights and Liberties of his Majesty's Subjects; yet they refused any Redress, until Application was made to the House of Lords of *England*, who after weighing the Nature of the said Acts, addressed her late Majesty Queen *Anne*, setting forth, that the first Act was not warranted by the Lords Proprietors Charter, being not consonant to Reason, but repugnant to the Laws of *England*, and destructive to the Constitution of the Church of *England;* and that the latter was founded upon Falsity in Fact, repugnant to the Laws of *England*, contrary to their Charter, an Incouragement to Atheism and Irreligion, destructive to Trade, and tending to depopulate and ruin the Province: and besought her Majesty to deliver the said Province from the arbitrary Oppression under which it lay, and to order the Authors thereof to be prosecuted: Which Matter being referred to the Lords Commissioners of Trade, they, *May* 24. 1706. represented to her Majesty, That the making such Laws was an Abuse of the Powers granted the Lords Proprietors by their Charter, and a Forfeiture of such Power; and humbly offer'd to her Majesty, that she would be pleased to give directions for re-assuming the same into her Majesty's Hands. Which Representation her Majesty approved the 10th of *June*, and declared the Laws mentioned therein should be made void by the Powers that made them: and order'd, that for the more effectual proceeding against the said Charter, Mr. Attorney and Mr. Sollicitor General should inform themselves concerning what might be most necessary to effect the same.

That by the said Charter, his then Majesty saved the Faith, Allegiance, and sovereign Dominion due to him, his Heirs and Successors, for the said Province, and the Right and Interest of the *English* Subjects in the same, and declares them Liege People of the Crown of *England*, and to have right to all the Libertys of *Englishmen* born in *England;* yet the Lords Proprietors have assumed a despotic Authority, exceeding the Royal Power in *Great Britain*, in repealing and abrogating, by themselves alone, several beneficial Laws, after most solemn Ratification of the same by their Deputies, with the Consent of the Representatives of the Freemen met in Assembly; and thereby trampling upon the Rights and Liberties of his Majesty's Subjects.

And this sometimes is done by two or three of the Proprietors, who have Proxies from the absent ones, or from the Guardians of those under Age, tho the same Proprietors, or Guardians, give Proxies to their Representatives in this Province, who on their behalfs ratify the said Laws, contrary to any Power in their Charter, endangering the Safety of his Majesty's Subjects there, and the Derogation of the usual Method theretofore practised in the like Cases; tho their Deputies and Freemen there never denied to repeal any Laws when recommended by the Proprietors. This, with the Uncertainty of the Administration of the Government, by reason of several Alterations from time to time in the same, hath put us under unspeakable Hardships, destroying all publick Credit, so necessary here to defend us against our Enemies, and defeating Measures taken for the Preservation and good Government of the Province.

That the Exercise of their Government is injurious to his Majesty's Subjects; for that they whose Powers and Prerogatives are united in them all, not to be disjointed, take upon them to send a Governour, as the *Palatine's* Deputy, and each other Proprietor a Deputy, which vote as a Council of the Province; a Body which in all other his Majesty's Colonies is formed to be a Barrier between the Governour and People. But here they are wholly dependent upon their Constituents, and think themselves obliged to carry every thing in favour of the Proprietors, and obliged by an Oath to do nothing repugnant to their Interests, without any regard to the publick Good of the Colony. And when any of their Deputies vote against them, or their Governours private Interest, they are turned out. These Deputies have power to reject any Law; but if it passes them, the Governour pretends another Negative upon them; and sometimes a Negative hath been appointed upon the Governour: And the Lords Proprietors assume a Power of repealing those Acts ratified by their Governour and Deputies. So that the Lords Proprietors, who by their Charter ought to have but one, assume three and four Negatives upon the Laws agreed to by the Assembly; and having no Council between them and the People, they suffer no Law to pass, or any longer to be in force, than suits with their private Views, to the loss of publick Credit, and destruction of the Liberties and Properties of his Majesty's Subjects.

That they are impower'd by their Charter to erect Cities, Boroughs, Towns or Villages, by granting Charters of Incorporation to any Body of People; yet they have neglected so to do; neither have they settled any County Jurisdiction, Court Baron or Court Leet, for the Conservation of the Peace of this Colony, but have abandoned all to Disorder and Confusion, under the Management of one Person, who solely holds all Courts of King's-Bench, Common-Pleas and Exchequer, Assize, County Courts, and Sessions, in *Charles-Town,* the only Place of Judicature in the whole Province; who makes what Lawyers, and takes what Fees he pleases, summoning all Parties to attend his Courts: No Appeals but from himself to himself, nor any Method of Appeals settled to his Majesty and Council, as in other Colonies: No Process issues in his Majesty's Name, all the Officers taking what Fees they please: he adjourning Courts, and putting off Tryals, to multiply his Perquisites, which are arbitrary; daily exacting new Fees; undertaking himself to draw Writings, and after judging of the Validity of them; sending for the Lawyers, and giving secret Advice to them and their Clients: and insists that no Authority there can call him to account, or remove him, nor the Proprietors themselves, unless proved guilty of Misdemeanours before them in *London,* he having Words in his Commission to that purpose: But the Lords Proprietors have had no regard to the publick or private Persons injured by him, and would not be induced to remove him.

That when in 1715 the *Yamasee Indians* had, at the Instigation of the *Spaniards* at *St. Augustine,* cruelly massacred his Majesty's Subjects in those Frontiers, and committed most barbarous Depredations in the very Heart of the Settlement, upon being repulsed, the *Spanish* Garison protected them, and bought their Plunder, and furnished them with Arms (tho then at peace with *Spain*) to renew their Depredations; which being represented to the Proprietors, they never regarded the Lives and Estates of his Majesty's Subjects. And it was also represented to them, that the said Garison protected Rebels, Felons, Debtors and Negroes that fled thither; which forced us to guard that Frontier in time of Peace; but to no purpose, the Lords Proprietors never giving any Answer to the same.

That notwithstanding the great Expence of the War with the *Yamasee Indians,* which not only preserved the Proprietors Lands not yet settled, but also such Lands as they have appropriated to their own use, they have contributed to no part of the Charge thereof (except about 150 small Arms) and upon Application made to them, declared their Incapacity to assist us.

That when a bloody *Indian* War broke out at *North Carolina,* it was insinuated to the Assembly by the Lords Proprietors Deputies, that if they would raise Money, and send Assistance thither, they should be reimbursed out of the Quit-Rents; yet notwithstanding thereby that Province was saved to the Lords Proprietors, they never to this Day refunded one Penny of all that Expence.

That in 1718 one *Thatch*, a notorious Pirate, took several Ships trading to this Province, and several of our Inhabitants Prisoners, and went directly to *North Carolina*, where, under pretence of accepting his Majesty's Pardon, by the Connivance of the Proprietors Governors, in the face of that Government, he committed several Acts of Piracy; and several Parcels of Piratical Goods were found in their Governours and Secretary's Custody; so that *North Carolina* became a Nest of Pirates: Of this his Majesty's Governour of *Virginia* complain'd to the Lords Proprietors, but they took no notice of the same.

That as soon as we had driven the *Yamasees* from our Lands, near *Port Royal*, to strengthen that Frontier, and to encourage new Comers, *viz.* in *February* 1716, two Acts were passed for dividing those Lands amongst such of his Majesty's Protestant Subjects as should come and settle the same, (exclusive of such as had Lands already in that Province) Abstracts of which being sent to *Great Britain* and *Ireland*, about 500 of his Majesty's Subjects transported themselves to take the Benefit of the same. But all this was interrupted, by the Proprietors repealing these Acts in *July* 1718. under pretence that the Lands being their own, they would dispose of them as they thought fit; and made a Distribution of the said Lands, far short of that made by the said Acts, which the new Comers were forced to comply with, and began their Surveys. And then to the utter Ruin of the new Comers, and in Breach of their publick Faith, the Proprietors in *April* 1719, ordered all those Lands to be surveyed for their own Use. And tho they had paid their Purchase-Money to the Proprietors Receiver for those Lands, yet are not only refused the having their Titles confirmed, but the said Receiver refuses to return their Money. Hereby the old Setlers in that Frontier, missing the Reinforcement of the new Comers, again deserted their Settlements, and left them open to the Enemy; and the new Comers are reduced to that Want and Poverty, that most of them are daily perishing, having spent all their Substance, and those that have any thing left, removing off the Province.

That notwithstanding many Addresses to the Lords Proprietors, to take some Measures to prevent the *French* incroaching on this part of his Majesty's Dominions, and especially at the beginning of the Treaty of *Utrecht*, they not only abandoned all by an unaccountable Neglect, but *May* 1715, the *French* took possession of *Mobile*, (which belonged to the Government) and built a Fort there, and are since further incroaching, by making Forts at the Mouths of the Rivers belonging to this Province, and arising near our Settlements. So that having made themselves Masters of *Pausacolo,* a *Spanish* Port, they surround this Settlement from the Mountains to the Sea, whereby all the Nations of *Indians* towards those Points, lately under our Government, are now subjected to the *French.*

So that by the late *Indian* War, our subduing the Pirates, a Defensive War against the *Spaniards,* the Demolition of our principal Fortifications by Storms, and the Expences to repair the same, the vast Presents we are obliged to make the *Indians,* to keep up a Party amongst them from depending intirely upon the *French,* and the weak and unsteady Government of the Proprietors, who rather oppose than contribute to the strengthning of us, whereby we have lost all Credit, no body venturing to trust any publick Funds contrived for our Support, we are reduced to the last Extremity in Debt, without prospect of extricating our selves, all our Funds anticipated for several Years to come, our Expences increasing, without any View of answering them; which makes our Enemies look on us as an abandoned People, void of Royal Protection. So that without the Assistance and Government of his Majesty, this hopeful Province will be lost to the *British* Empire, to the endangering *Virginia,* and other his Majesty's Dominions, and the irreparable Loss of the Beneficial Trade of the same.

· 20 ·

Jeremiah Dummer, A Defence of the New-England Charters (Boston, 1721)

Jeremiah Dummer (1681–1739) was the longtime agent for the colony of Massachusetts and Connecticut in London. A graduate of Harvard, Dummer also studied at the universities of Leyden and Utrecht, becoming, in 1703, the first American to receive a doctorate in philosophy. In addition to his labors as a colonial agent, Dummer was instrumental in creating the library of the new college of Yale in Connecticut.

Dummer wrote *A Defence of the New England Charters* in response to a series of attempts by the Board of Trade, dating from the early 1700s, to dissolve the charters of the proprietary and corporate colonies in America. By making them all royal colonies, the Board, with Parliament's help, sought to centralize the empire, fearing that the excessive autonomy of the chartered colonies undermined imperial defense and commerce. In responding to the Board of Trade's initiatives at length, Dummer laid out one of the most sophisticated accounts of the rights of the American colonists in the eighteenth century. For Dummer, the sanctity of the charters rested on the fact that the privileges they contained were the benefits the colonists received in return for risking their lives in settling the colonies, a risk which, Dummer reiterates throughout the pamphlet, benefited England as much as it did the settlers. As he put it, the colonists had been granted the privileges contained in the charters "on this express Condition, of settling Colonies for the Benefit of the Crown." Since this was done "at a vast Expence, and through incredible Difficulties," . . . "to strip the Country of their Charters after the Service has been so successfully perform'd, is abhorrent from all

Reason, Equity and Justice." Dummer further argued that the Crown had no right to interfere with colonial property rights by removing the charters since the colonists and not the Crown owned the soil of the Americas. The colonists had purchased it from the natives, and had then proceeded to labor on it, creating value where none had existed before. Although the Board of Trade's attempt to resume the charters came to naught, Dummer's pamphlet provides an important window into the colonial understanding of law, liberty, and rights in the early eighteenth century. (C.B.Y.)

A DEFENCE
OF THE
NEW-ENGLAND
CHARTERS.

By JER. DUMMER.

Pulchrum est Patriae benefacere, etiam benedicere haud absurdum est.[1]

SALLUST.

LONDON: Printed by W. WILKINS, Reprinted at *BOSTON:* in *N.E.* by S. KNEELAND, for S. GERRISS and D. HENCHMAN, and Sold at their Shops.

MDCCXXI.

1. ["It is noble to do good deeds for one's native country; it is also not absurd to praise it."]

To the Right Honourable the Lord Carteret, One of His Majesty's Principal Secretaries of State.

My Lord,

Having lately had the Honour of presenting the Humble Address of the Province of the *Massachusets Bay* to His Majesty for the Continuance of their Charter Privileges, which they apprehend in some Danger; It seem'd agreeable at the same Time, to explain the Right which the Charter Governments have to those Privileges. Nor could an Argument of this Nature be so properly address'd to any other Person as Your Lordship who, in Your high Station, have all His Majesty's Colonies and Plantations within Your Province, and under Your immediate Care.

My Lord, the Colonies I plead for, ask only Justice; yet if their Circumstances should require the Royal Grace, they humbly hope they have some Claim to it from their firm and exemplary Loyalty. For it may be said to their Honour, that it is not known there is a single Person in all the Charter Governments, whatever there may be in the rest, who is not zealously devoted to His present Majesty, and to the Succession in His Illustrious Family.

It would be, my Lord, a rash and ill-judg'd Attempt in me, to enter here into Your Lordship's Character, as the manner of Dedicators is; I shall not therefore presume to mention those great Abilities which have distinguish'd Your Lordship in foreign Courts as well as our own; but only beg leave to express my Thanks for that amiable Goodness, so conspicuous in Your Lordship, which softens the Brow of the Minister, and makes our Access easy, when publick Business calls us to attend Your Lordship.

May You long continue an Ornament and Support to His Majesty's Councils.

I am, *With profound Esteem and Respect,*

My Lord, *Your* Lordship's *most Obedient and Devoted Servant,*

Jer. Dummer.

A Defence of the New-England Charters.

The general Name of *New-England,* includes in its common Acceptation the Province of the *Massachusets-Bay,* the Colony of *Connecticut,* the Government of *Rhode-Island,* with *Providence* Plantations, and the Province of *New-Hampshire.* The Three former are Charter Governments: The last, *viz. New-Hampshire,* never had any peculiar Privileges, but is under the immediate and absolute Direction of the Crown. The *Massachusets,* as it is the first of all the Colonies in Extent of Territory and Number of Inhabitants, was the first incorporated, having obtain'd their Charter from King *Charles* the First, in the Fourth Year of his Reign. The Colony of *Connecticut* receiv'd theirs from King *Charles* the Second in 1662, and the Fourteenth Year of his Reign. The Government of *Rhode-Island* had theirs in the Year following. These Charters agreed in all the main Points, confirming to the Patentees their Title to the Soil, and giving them ample Privileges for the well ordering and governing the respective Plantations: They had Power to make a Common Seal; to plead and be impleaded; to call General Assemblies; to make Laws, so as they were not repugnant to the Laws of *England;* to assess the Freemen; to constitute all Civil Officers; to array the Inhabitants in warlike Posture, and use the Martial Law, when Occasion requir'd. And it was provided further, That in case any Doubts should arise, the Charters should have the most favourable Construction for the Benefit of the several Corporations.

Invited and encourag'd by these Advantages, a considerable Number of Persons dissenting from the *Discipline* of the Establish'd Church, tho' agreeing with it in *Doctrine,* remov'd into those remote Regions, upon no other View than to enjoy the Liberty of their Consciences without Hazard to themselves, or Offence to others. Thus the Colonies went on increasing and flourishing, in spite of all Difficulties, till the Year 1684, when the City of *London* lost its Charter, and most of the other Corporations in *England,* influenced by Fear or Flattery, complimented King *Charles* with a Surrender of theirs. In this general Ruin of Charters at Home, it could not be expected that those in *America* should escape. It was then that a *Quo Warranto*[2] was

2. [Literally, "By what right," that is, a writ directing a person to show "by what right" he exercises powers of office.—Tr.]

issu'd against the Governour and Company of the *Massachusets Bay,* and soon after a Judgment was given against them in *Westminster-Hall.* At the same Time Sir *Edmund Andross,* then the King's Governour of *New England,* did by Order from Court repair to *Hartford,* the Capital of *Connecticut,* with arm'd Attendants, and forcibly seiz'd their Charter for the King. *Rhode-Island,* finding there was no Remedy to be had, made a Vertue of Necessity, and peaceably resign'd theirs. But as soon as the News arriv'd of the happy Revolution in *England,* these Two last mention'd Governments re-assum'd their Charters, and put themselves under the old Form of Administration, in which they have continu'd ever since. The Government of the *Massachusets,* cautious of offending their Superiours at Home, and considering there was a Judgment against them in the Court of *Chancery,* tho' most unfairly and illegally obtain'd, did not think it adviseable to make this Step; but sent Agents to Court to supplicate, in a humble Manner the Restoration of their Charter. To what Mismanagement, or other Cause it was owing, that they did not obtain it, and that this Loyal Corporation was the only one either in *Old* or *New-England,* that did not recover its lost Liberty under our late Glorious Deliverer King *William,* 'tis now too late, and therefore to no Purpose, to enquire. A new Charter was order'd, which the Province now has, and is not much more than the Shadow of the old One. For by these new Letters Patents, the Appointment of a Governour, Lieutenant-Governour, Secretary, and all the Officers of the Admiralty, is vested in the Crown. The Power of the Militia is wholly in the Hands of His Majesty's Governour, as Captain-General. All Judges, Justices, and Sheriffs, to whom the Execution of the Laws is intrusted, are nominated by the Governour, with the Advice of His Majesty's Council. The Governour has a Negative upon the Choice of Councillors, which is both *peremptory* and *unlimited:* He is neither oblig'd to render a Reason, nor restrain'd to any Number. All Laws enacted by the General Assembly are to be sent Home for the Royal Approbation or Disallowance. There is, besides, one very comprehensive Article inserted in this Charter, that no Laws, Ordinances, Elections, or Acts of Government whatsoever, shall be of any Validity, without the Consent of the King's Governour signify'd in Writing.

By these Reservations, the Prerogative of the Crown, and the Dependance of the Province thereon are in the most effectual Manner secur'd, if there had been any Danger before, as I hope in the Sequel of this Discourse, to demonstrate there was not. And yet it happens unaccountably that this

Charter of King *William*, so limited and restrained, is as obnoxious as either of the other which have their full and entire Force. Accordingly when about Six Years since a Bill was brought into the House of Commons, and twice read, for regulating the Charter and Proprietary Governments, This was one among the rest, and the first nam'd in the Bill. And tho' the Honourable House thought fit, upon hearing the Petitions presented to them on that Occasion, to drop their Proceedings, there is Reason to believe they may at another time resume them. It is in this View, that I have put together my Thoughts on the Subject, which for Methods sake I have dispos'd under the following Heads.

1*st*, I shall endeavour to show, that the Charter Governments have a good and undoubted Right to their respective Charters.

2*dly*, That they have not forfeited them by any Misgovernment or Male-Administration.

3*dly*, That if they had, it would not be the Interest of the Crown to accept the Forfeitures. And,

4*thly*, I shall make some Observations upon the extraordinary Method of Proceeding against the Charters by a Bill in Parliament.

1st. Proposition, *That the Charter Governments have a good and undoubted Right to their respective Charters*

As to the first Point there can be no Difficulty. The Charters were Granted by the Crown, and the King is acknowledg'd to be the Head and Fountain of all Corporations and Franchises. For tho' my Lord *Coke* takes notice, That a Body Politick may be establish'd by Prescription, yet such Prescription is only valid upon a Presumption that there was an Ancient Grant of the Crown, which by the Injury of Time was afterwards lost. I need not insist upon what no Body controverts; but it is material to observe, that the *American* Charters are of a higher Nature, and stand on a better Foot, than the Corporations in *England*. For these latter were granted upon Improvements already made, and therefore were Acts of meer Grace and Favour in the Crown; whereas the former were given as Praemiums for Services to be perform'd, and therefore are to be consider'd as Grants upon a *valuable Consideration;* which adds Weight and Strength to the Title.

To increase the Nation's Commerce and enlarge her Dominions, must be allow'd a Work of no little Merit, if we consider the Hardships to which the Adventurers were exposed; or the Expence in making their Settlements; or lastly, the great Advantages thence accruing to the Crown and Nation. It would be an endless Task to recount all the Disappointments, and Disasters that befel the first Planters in these Enterprizes. I shall therefore only say in General, that after many Dangers in their Voyages over the *Atlantick*, which was not such an easy Navigation a Hundred Years ago as it is now, they arriv'd at an Inhospitable Shore and a waste Wilderness, where there were few of the Necessaries, and not one Accommodation of Life; where the Climate was so extreme, the Summer Heats so scorching, and the Winters so long and so cold, that the Countrey seem'd scarcely habitable; and to sum up their Misfortunes, they found themselves inevitably engag'd in a War with the Natives. So that by Fatigue and Famine, by the Extremity of the Seasons, and by a War with the Savages, the first Planters soon found their Graves, leaving the young Settlements to be perfected by their Survivors.

To omit all this, I shall only be particular in the Expence, which was above 200,000 *l.* in setling the single Province of the *Massachusets Bay.* The Account stands thus: The Freight of the Passengers cost 95000 *l.* The Transportation of their first Stock of Cattle came to 12000 *l.* The Provisions laid in for Subsistance, till by Tillage more could be rais'd, cost 45000 *l.* The Materials for Building their first little Cottages came to 18000 *l.* Their Arms and Ammunition cost 22000*l.* These several Articles amount to 192000 *l.* not taking into the Account the very great Sums which were expended in Things of private Use, that People could not be without, who were going to possess an uninhabited Land. I must add, that 192 Ships were employ'd in making this great Plantation, and Twelve Years were spent before it was brought to any tolerable Degree of Perfection.

As great, however, as this Expence was, I believe it will appear that the Settlement of *New-England* was not more chargeable to the Adventurers, than it has bin in its Consequence profitable to *Great Britain.* There is no sort of *British* Manufacture, but what the Subjects there demand in a greater or less Proportion, as they have Ability to pay for it; every Thing for the Use Convenience, Ornament, and (I say it with regret) for the Luxury and Pride of Life. Some of the oldest and most experienc'd Traders to those Parts have by Computation made these Exports arise to the Value of 300000 *l. per Annum.* The Imports from thence are equally beneficial to the Kingdom.

They brought home Bullion as long as they had any left; and now they are so exhausted they can no longer send it directly, they continue to remit it by the Way of *Spain, Portugal* and the *Streights;* It is there they sell their Fish, and the Produce of it comes hither in Gold and Silver, or Bills of Exchange, which is the same thing.

Other and better Returns than Money it self they make in Masts, the fairest and largest in the whole World, besides Pitch, Tarr, Turpentine, Rosin, Plank, Knees for Ships, and other Species of Timber for various Uses. These, especially Pitch and Tar, were formerly purchas'd of the *Swede* with Crown Pieces at intollerable Prices; but since the Encourgement given for their Importation from *New-England,* they have fallen to half the Value. It is to be farther consider'd, that what we take of these Commodities from our own Plantations, is brought Home in our own Ships, and paid for with our Manufactures.

New England also imports Logwood for the dying our Woollen Goods in Quantites sufficient for our own Use, and a Surplus with which we furnish *Holland, Hambro',* and other Markets in *Europe.* It is wholly owing to the Industry of the People of *New-England,* that this useful Commodity is reduc'd from 30 and 40 *l. per* Ton, which we us'd to pay for it to the *Spaniard,* to 12 *l. per* Ton, which is the present Price, and out of this 12 *l.* there is 4 *l.* 5 *s.* 0 *d.* paid to the Crown for Custom.

Other Articles might be mention'd, as Whale-Oil and Finns, which are yearly imported from *New-England* in no contemptible Quantities. They are useful in several Manufactures; and if not had from thence must have been purchas'd of the *Dutch* with ready Money and at excessive Prices.

'Tis true, *New England,* makes no Sugar, but it assists the Islands that do; without which Assistance they could not make it, at least not cheap enough, and in sufficient Quantities to answer the Markets in *Europe.* For if the Sugar Islands were oblig'd to sow Wheat, and plant as much *Indian* Corn as they wanted, they must needs plant the fewer Canes, and by consequence make the less Sugar. From thence they are also supply'd with Horses for their Mills, Timber for their Sugar Works, Staves for their Cask, and what is more considerable, with Barrel Pork, Mackrel, and refuse Cod-Fish for their Negroes, without which their Labour would yield nothing to their Owners. For were they to feed their Slaves with Beef and other Provisions from *Britain* and *Ireland,* the Expence of a Plantation would devour the whole Produce of it. There are now such great Quantities of Sugar made in the *French* and *Dutch* Plantations, and so much imported from *Brasil* by the *Portuguese,* that our Sugar Islands need all Advantages to make this Commodity cheap and in Plenty, that we may be able to out-do, or at least equal our Neighbours in the foreign Markets.

It may be added, that *New-England* is a good Nursery of Seamen for the Navy. I believe I may affirm, that there was hardly a Ship, during the last War, in the Royal Navy without some of *their* Sailors on Board, which so distress'd the *New England* Merchants, that they were oblig'd to man their Ships with *Indians* and Negroes.

What I have said amounts to this: THAT *New-England* receiv'd her Charters on this express Condition, of settling Colonies for the Benefit of the Crown:

That she was at a vast Expence, and through incredible Difficulties accomplish'd the Work even beyond what was ever hop'd or expected.

And then the Conclusion, that I would draw from these Premises is this, THAT to strip the Country of their Charters after the Service has been so successfully perform'd, is abhorrent from all Reason, Equity and Justice.

But it is urg'd, *That the Crown does not take back the Soil; though it does the Charters;* which indeed is saying very little or nothing. The Crown, strictly speaking, neither did nor could grant the Soil, having no Right in it self. Queen *Elisabeth* gave out the first Patent to Sir *Walter Rawleigh* in 1584; and if she had any Right, what was it and whence deriv'd? It was not a *Right of Inheritance,* because those Countries did not descend to her from her Ancestors. Not of *Conquest,* because she neither conquer'd, nor attempted to conquer them. Besides, it would be pretty hard to conceive how a Conquest, where there was no preceeding Injury or Provocation, could create a Right. Nor did it arise by *Purchase,* there being no Money or other valuable Consideration paid. Nor could she claim by the *prior Discovery or Preoccupancy,* as the Civilians speak, because that gives a Right only to *derelict Lands,* which these were not, being full of Inhabitants, who undoubtedly had as good a Title to their own Country, as the *Europeans* have to theirs. And sure no Body will say in plain Terms, that we have any Claim upon the Foot that we were *Christians,* and they *Heathen;* which yet I know some Persons of no obscure Fame have tacitly suggested. *Rome* it self, as imperious as she is, never carry'd her Pretences to this Height: For though some of her Doctors have taught, absurdly enough, that *Dominion* is founded in Grace, none of 'em ever said that *Property* was. There remains then no other Right than what is deriv'd from the native Lords of the Soil, and that is what the honest *New-England* Planters rely on, having purchas'd it with their Money. The *Indian Title* therefore, as it is decry'd and undervalu'd here, seems the only fair and just one; and neither Queen *Elisabeth* by *her* Patents, or King *James* by *his* afterwards, could give any more than a bare *Right of Preemption.*

And yet admitting that the Crown granted the Soil, to how little must the Value of such Grants amount, all Circumstances consider'd? The Patentees were not only oblig'd to travel a Thousand Leagues beyond Sea, but to purchase their Grants over again of the Natives, before they could be put into Possession. The Land it self was of a rough savage Nature, incumber'd with unprofitable Woods, and of no Use till by vast Labour and Expence subdu'd and cultivated. For to speak the Truth, those Parts were but *bare Creation* to the first Planters, and their Labour *like the Beginning the World.*

So that which Way soever we take it, I think it's plain, if the Crown resumes the Charters, it will take away the Whole it gave, and deprive the Patentees of the only Recompence they were to have for all their Toils and Fatigues, which they thought to have conveyed safe to their Posterity. Could they have imagin'd this, could they have foreseen that their Privileges were such *transitory things,* as to last no longer than their Work should be done, and their settlements compleated, they had never engag'd in so hazardous and difficult an Enterprize. They would never have parted from their Native Land being neither Criminals nor Necessitous; and those Countries which have since added so much to the Wealth and Greatness of the Crown, might have been a barren Wilderness to this Day; or what is worse, and more probable, might have bin fill'd with *French* Colonies, whereby *France* would have reign'd sole Mistress of *North America.*

I believe it will be generally allow'd, that my Argument is thus far right, if I can make good my second Proposition,

VIZ.

2d Proposition. *That these Governments have by no Misbehaviour forfeited their Charters.*

That these Governments have by no Misbehaviour forfeited back their Charters to the Crown.

Some of the ablest Common Lawyers that *England* could ever boast of, have maintain'd that a Corporation, being an *Ens Rationis,*[3] is in it's Nature indissolvable, and that therefore no Abuse of it's Franchises can effect it in point of Forfeiture, or determine its Being. If this Argument should be thought too subtle and metaphysical, I hope however it will be allow'd an Extreme on the other side, that a Corporation should be threaten'd for *every* Offence to be seiz'd into the King's Hands. The Subjects Abroad claim the Privilege of *Magna Charta,* which says that no Man shall be fin'd above the Nature of his Offence, and whatever his Miscarriage be, a *Salvo Contenemento suo*[4] is to be observ'd by the Judge. If therefore they have committed Faults, let them be *chastiz'd,* not *destroy'd;* let not their Corporations be dissolv'd for any other Crime than a Failure of their Allegiance. But I need not go into this or any other nice Point of Law, it being sufficient to show that the Charter Governments are clear of the several Facts which have been objected against them, and assign'd as matter of Forfeiture. In the Bill that was brought into the House of Commons, there were two Allegations against the Charter and Proprietary Governments, which I shall first answer, and then go on to consider such other Complaints as I have met with from Time to Time against these Governments.

The 1st Charge against the Charter Governments, that they have neglected the Defence of the Inhabitants; answered.

The first Charge in the Bill against the Charter Governments is, that *they have neglected the Defence of the Inhabitants.* This I must own, if true, and such Neglect was voluntary, while they had the Means and Power of Defence in their Hands, was a high and treasonable Breach of their Trust, and would be the strongest Argument that could be brought for a Resumption of the Charters. But now, if I shall prove that these Governments, especially the *Massachusets* and *Connecticut,* have in all past Times defended the Inhabitants both by Sea and Land, as well against the *French* as *Indian* Enemy: If I shall prove that they have all the late War protected one of the *King's Provinces* lying on their Confines, which would otherwise inevitably have bin lost; and that *another* of those Provinces took no Part in the War,

3. ["A product of reason."]
4. ["With his own necessary means of support intact."]

but maintain'd a shameful Neutrality with the Enemy, whereby the whole Weight of the War fell on the *Massachusets;* If I shall prove that they have frequently carry'd offensive Arms into the *French* Territories, and made one important Conquest, since annex'd to the *British* Crown; and that all this was done at their own vast Expence; then, I hope, *New-England* will stand fairly acquitted of this suppos'd Crime of *Neglecting to defend the Inhabitants,* and be allow'd not only irreprehensible in this respect, but to have highly merited of the Crown and Nation.

These Facts are so certain and so well known, that I'm perswaded this had never bin assign'd as a Reason for dissolving the Charters, but with a special View to *Carolina,* which, when this Bill was brought into the House, was reduc'd to extremity by a War with the *Spanish Indians;* and being neither able to defend themselves, nor obtain Succours from their Lords Proprietors, address'd the Crown to take them under its Protection. It was therefore natural enough to mention this in the Bill; though with humble Submission, it being the single Case of one Proprietary Colony, it should in all Reason have bin restrain'd to that, and not extended to the Charter Provinces, which are neither alike constituted, nor were in the same Distress. For *New-England,* as I shall presently show, has defended it self from the first Beginning to this Day without being burdensome to the Crown, though not without great Struggles and Difficulties.

'Tis true, they did not commence Hostilities, nor even take up Arms of Defence, till they found by Experience that no other Means would prevail. The first Planters, far from using the barbarous Methods practis'd by the *Spaniards* on the *Southern* Continent, which have made them detestable to the whole Christian World, sought to gain the Natives by strict Justice in their Dealings with them, as well as by all the Endearments of Kindness and Humanity. To lay an early Foundation for a firm and lasting Friendship, they assur'd the *Americans,* that they did not come among them as Invaders but Purchasers, and therefore call'd an Assembly of them together, to enquire who had the Right to dispose of their Lands; and being told it was their *Sachems* or Princes they thereupon agreed with them for what Districts they bought, publickly and in open Market. If they did not pay a great Price for their Purchases yet they paid as much as they were worth. For it must be consider'd, that Land was of little Use to the Natives, and therefore but of little Value. They liv'd chiefly on Fish and Fowl, and Hunting, because they would not be at the Pains to clear and break up the Ground. And as for their Meadows and Marshes, they were of no Use at all, for want of neat Cattle to feed them, of which there were none in those Parts of the World.

The *English* had no sooner made some necessary Provision for themselves, than they apply'd their Cares for the Benefit of the *Indians*, by endeavouring to bring them from their wild manner of Life to the civil and polite Customs of *Europe*. For this purpose, they mark'd out Land to build *Indian* Towns, supply'd them with all proper Utensils for Building, prescrib'd to them forms of Government, and above all, omitted no Pains to bring them acquainted with the Gospel. After some Time, when it was found necessary, the Colony made a Law to forbid any Person's purchasing Land of the *Indians* without the Approbation of the General Court, to prevent their being over-reach'd or ill us'd in their private Bargains: and some Land, lying very convenient for them, was by another Law made inalienable, and never to be purchased out of their Hands, than which nothing could more demonstrate the Colony's Care and Concern for the Natives.

I thought my self oblig'd to make this Preface to the main Argument, that I might wipe off an unworthy Aspersion that has been cast on the first Setlers of *New-England*, that they never treated the Savages well, but encroach'd on their Land by Degrees, till they fraudulently and forcibly turn'd them out of all. It was far otherwise, as I have shown; yet nothing could oblige the *Indians* to Peace and Friendship. They were alarm'd with the strong Jealousies of the growing Power of the *English*, and therefore began a War with a Resolution to extirpate them, before they had too well establish'd themselves. Yet as terrible as this Prospect was to Two or Three young Colonies, who had work enough to defend themselves against Famine, which in a cold barren Country surrounded with Enemies star'd them in the Face, they nevertheless made no Application to the Crown for Assistance, but drew up Articles of Confederacy among themselves, by the Name of the *United Colonies of* New-England, for their mutual Defence. This done, they took the Number of all the Males in the several Plantations, and raising a Poll Tax according to each Person's respective Ability; they with one Consent laid aside their Ploughshares and Pruning Hooks for the Sword and the Spear, and under the Command of Major-Generals, whom they chose after the manner then in *England*, march'd directly to the Enemy's Head-Quarters, and strongest Fortifications, from whence they drove them with great Precipitation. Nor did they stop there, but pursu'd them through all their Recesses, 'till they oblig'd them to enter into a Solemn Treaty of Peace. Such however was the perfidious Nature of the *American* Savages, that they soon renew'd the Hostilities, tho' to their own fatal Cost. For if the *English* experienc'd a Variety of Fortune, as could not but be expected in the Vicissitudes of War, yet they were for the most part victorious, and in the Course of some Years, after many terrible Slaughters of the Enemy, subdu'd and utterly extirpated Seven or Eight fierce and populous Nations.

I am sensible some have endeavour'd to depreciate these Conquests, as gain'd over a rude barbarous People unexercis'd to Arms; which if granted, still it can't be said, that *the Defence of the Inhabitants was neglected;* and therefore the Charter Governments can fall under no Censure, if they should be thought to have merited no Praise. But if it be consider'd, that the *New-England* Forces contended with Enemies bloody in their Nature and superiour in Number; that they attack'd them in deep Morasses, defended with Fortifications sufficiently strong, tho' not regular; and that the Assailants were not provided with Canon, nor could approach by Trenches, but advanc'd on level Ground: And if to this be added the vast Fatigues of their Campaigns, where Officers and Soldiers lay on the Snow without any Shelter over their Heads in the most rigorous Winters; I say, if a just Consideration be had of these Things, Envy it self must acknowledge that their Enterprizes were hardy, and their Successes glorious. And tho' the brave Commanders who led on these Troops, and most of them died in the Bed of Honour, must not shine in the *British* Annals, yet their Memory ought to be sacred in their own Country, and there at least be transmitted to the latest Posterity.

The inland Parts being now at rest, the War was remov'd to the Frontiers, which were cruelly harrass'd by other *Indian Tribes,* animated and assisted by the *French* of *Canada,* who have given the *Massachusets* but few Intervals of Peace, and those very short ones from that Time to this Day. All this while THAT Government was never wanting to protect the King's Subjects within their Jurisdiction, even in the remotest Parts of it. They kept Troops on foot, no less than Six or Seven Hundred at a Time, to cover the Barrier Line, and built Forts wherever they were necessary; one of them nam'd *William-Henry,* but commonly call'd *Pemaquid* Fort, because built on a River of that Name, was in the Heart of the Enemy's Country, and deserves a particular Description. It was built of Stone in a quadrangular Figure, 737 Foot in Circumference, without the outer Wall, and 108 Foot square within the inner ones. It had 28 Ports, and 18 Guns mounted, 6 being 18 Pounders. The Wall on the South Line fronting to the Sea was

22 Foot high, and above 6 Foot thick at the Ports, which were 8 Foot from the Ground. The round Tower at the West End of this Line was 29 Foot high: The Wall on the East Line was 12 Foot high, on the North 10, and on the West 18. It stood 20 Rod from High-Water Mark, and was garrison'd with 60 and sometimes 100 Men. The Expence in building and maintaining this Garrison was considerable, yet the Province chearfully submitted to it; nor did they decline rebuilding it, after it was surpriz'd and demolish'd by the *French,* for any other reason, but that it was found by Experience, the Enemy could come many Miles wide of it, and attack their Frontiers. They therefore built Forts at *Saco* and *Casco,* and other Places most expos'd which answer'd the same End.

By this Care the Power of the Enemy was very much broke, and the King's Province of *New-Hampshire* from whence the Royal Navy is annually supply'd with Masts, has been preserv'd, which otherwise must have unavoidably been lost, being unable to help it self, and receiving no Succours from Home. *New-York,* another of the King's Provinces, has always kept it self in a State of Neutrality, contributing nothing to the common Safety, whilst the *Canada Indians,* join'd by Parties of the *French,* us'd to make their *Route* by their Borders without molesting them, and fall upon the Out Towns of the *Massachusets.* This Behaviour was the more unpardonable in that Government, because they have 400 regular Troops maintain'd among them at the King's Charge, and have the five Nations of the *Iroquoise* on their Confines, who are entirely dependent on them, and might easily, had they bin engag'd in the common Cause, at all Times have intercepted the Enemy in their Marches, and thereby have prevented the Depredations committed on his Majesty's Subjects. Solemn and repeated Applications were made to the Government of *New-York,* by the Governours of the *Massachusets, Connecticut,* and *Rhode-Island,* in joint Letters on this Subject, but in vain. The Answer was they could not think it proper to engage their *Indians* in an actual War, lest they should endanger their own Frontiers, and bring upon themselves an Expence which they were in no Condition to provide for. And thus the poor Charter Colonies were left to bear the whole Burden, and do all the Work themselves.

The Province of the *Massachusets Bay* has been equally sollicitous to protect their Inhabitants by Sea, against any Foreign Invasion. For this End they have kept their Militia well train'd and disciplin'd and by an Act of the Assembly oblig'd all Persons, under proper Penalties, to be well provided with Ammunition and Arms, that they might be ready in case of a sudden Descent from Abroad. *Boston,* which is their Capital Town, and principal Sea-port, is fortify'd with Two Batteries to the Sea, one at each End of the Town; and about a League from it, at the Entrance of the Harbour, there is a strong beautiful Castle, which is by far the finest Piece of military Architecture in the *British America.* It was built by Colonel *Romer,* a famous *German* Engineer, at the Countries Expence, and is call'd *Castle William.* It is a *Quarre* surrounded with a cover'd Way, and join'd with two Lines of Communication from the main Battery, as also a Line of Communication from the main Gate to a Redoubt, which is to prevent the Landing. It is well situated near the Channel, to hinder Ships from coming up to the Town, which must all come within Pistol shot of this Battery. It is mounted with 100 Pieces of Cannon, several of which are plac'd on a Platform, near High-water Mark, so as to rake a Ship fore and aft, before she can bring her Broadsides to bear against the Castle, and some of these Cannon carry 42 Pounders. In Peace there is an independent Company of 50 or 100 Men, I'm not certain which, that constantly are on Duty; but in time of War 500 able Men are exempted from all other military Duty, to attend the Service of the Castle at an Hours Warning, upon any Signal given of the Approach of an Enemy. To prevent the Castle's being surpriz'd, there's a Light-House built on a Rock appearing above Water two Leagues from the Town, which makes a Signal to the Castle of the Appearance of any Ships and their Number. The Castle again warns the Town, and if there be 5 Ships or more in time of War, an Alarm is given to all the adjacent Countries by firing a Beacon. The Province has also a Galley or Frigate well man'd in time of War, to guard the Coast from Privateers, and to convoy their Home Trade. In short, nothing that could be done for Defence of the Subject by Sea or Land, has bin left undone. It is really astonishing to consider, and difficult to believe, that these little Governments should be able by their own Strength, and at their own Charge, to perform such great Things.

And yet this is not all that must be said in their Defence. For as I have before observ'd, they have discover'd a noble Zeal to enlarge the *British* Empire, by undertaking several chargeable Expeditions against the strongest *French* Settlements in *America.* In the Year 1690 they made an Armament against *Port Royal,* which was a Nest of Privateers, and a *Dunkirk* to the *American* Trade; besides that it was the Head Quarter, from whence Parties of *French* and *Indians* issued out, and fell upon the Eastern Parts of *New-England*. They made themselves Masters of the Place with all the Country of *Accadie*, and Sir *William Phipps* who commanded in chief, administer'd to the Inhabitants an Oath of Allegiance to the Crown of *England*; in which State that Country remain'd till the Peace of *Ryswick*, when it was deliver'd up to the *French*. The great Service done the Crown by this Acquisition, is now too well known to need being particularly mention'd.

The *New-Englanders* being willing to pursue this good Success, made an Attempt against *Canada* the same Year, with a Fleet of 32 Sail of Vessels, besides Tenders, having on Board 2000 Men, whilst at the same time a little Army of 1000 *English* and 1500 *Indians* were to march by Land and attack *Mont-Real*. 'Tis true, they fatally miscarry'd, (and who can answer for the Fortune of War?) But this ought not to lessen the Merit of an Enterprize, which they so well intended, and by which they so greatly suffer'd. It cost 150,000 *l*. in Money, and what was infinitely more valuable, the Lives of 1000 Men. Nor were these Vagrants, such as are pickt up here in the Streets, and disorderly Houses, and thence press'd into the War, but Heads of Families, Artificers, and robust young Men, such as no Country can spare, and least of all New Settlements, where Labour is the dearest Thing in the World, because nothing so much wanted as Hands. They did not indeed fall by the Sword of the Enemy, if that could alleviate their Misfortune, but by a Camp Fever, by Famine, and various Disasters in their return Home, occasion'd chiefly by the early Approach of a severe Winter which made it impracticable for Provisions to follow them.

Great was the Distress to which these poor Colonies were reduc'd by this expensive and improsperous Expedition; yet by the wise Conduct of the Governments, and the Industry of the People, they so well recover'd themselves in less than 20 Years, as to resolve upon making another Visit to their *French* Neighbours, whom they saw daily growing in Power, and threatning in time to destroy all the *English* Settlements. But not thinking themselves strong enough to deal with *Quebeck*, they were content to make only an Attempt on *Port Royal*, which was done accordingly, tho' not with the former Success, the *French* Fort being now strong and regular, and well provided for a Defence or Siege.

Not discourag'd by this Repetition of Misfortunes, when the late Queen signify'd to these Governments, her Royal Intention to reduce *Canada*, and requir'd them to provide their Quota of Troops; it can't be imagin'd with what Alacrity they came into it, and made in all Respects ample Provision for it. And tho' the Court altering their Measures did not see meet at that time to proceed in the Design, yet the Colonies were put to near the same Charge as if they had.

The next Year they rais'd a Body of Troops again, which commanded by Colonel *Nicholson,* with 500 Auxiliaries from hence, made another Descent upon *Port Royal* and reduc'd it. For which Service they were promis'd by her then Majesty considerable Advantages in respect of Trade and the Fishery, to which it's hop'd a just regard will be had, when *Nova Scotia* is brought under a Civil Establishment.

One may imagine now that these Colonies were quite out of Breath, and needed a little Rest. Yet presently after, when the great unfortunate Expedition was set on Foot against *Canada* under the Command of General *Hill* and Admiral *Walker,* they furnish'd more than the Quota assign'd 'em, and provided all Necessaries for the *British* Troops in so short a Time, that if they had not been animated by an extraordinary Zeal, would not have been possible. And notwithstanding some People found it necessary to blame *New-England,* the better to excuse themselves, yet it has been acknowledg'd to me by *English* Gentlemen, who were then on the Spot, and well experienc'd in these Affairs; that such a Fleet and Army wanting the Necessaries they did, could not have been dispatch'd on so short Warning from any Port in *England.*

My Answer to this Article of Accusation would be imperfect, if I did not still further observe, that these Governments have assisted and reliev'd the most distant of His Majesty's Islands, and the remotest Settlements on the Continent, when in Distress, upon no other Inducement, than that of being their Fellow Subjects. I'll give Two or Three Examples.

When in the Year 1703, or about that Time, *Jamaica* was in Fear of an Invasion, and desir'd some Help from the Government of the *Massachusets;* They, notwithstanding the length of the Voyage, which is often 8 or 9 Weeks, sent them two Companies of Foot, commanded by Colonel *Walton,* and Captain *Larimore,* both very gallant Officers. The Companies arriv'd safe, and serv'd there two Years, sometimes on Shore, and at other Times as Marines on Board the Man of War, then in the Service of the Island; and I believe very few of these Soldiers ever returned to their Native Country.

In 1705, when *Nevis* was plunder'd and ruin'd by *Ibberville, New-England* charitably, and of their own accord rais'd 2000 *l.* for their Relief; which they sent in two Vessels, each having 1000 *l.* on Board in Flower and Salt

Provisions for their Subsistance, and in Materials for Rebuilding their Houses and Mills. This they did generously, neither desiring nor receiving any Returns, when that Island came into more prosperous Circumstances.

And now lately, when *Carolina* was ingag'd in a War with the *Spanish Indians* and wanted Arms and Ammunition, they were supply'd with both from *Boston.*

Upon the whole, what a vast Fund of Merit have the Charter Governments rais'd to themselves from a long Series of Faithful and Heroick Services! And how strangely out of Countenance must this Objection look, *that they have neglected the Defence of the Inhabitants!* I have only to wish, that His Majesty and His Ministry had leisure from the important Affairs of the Nation, and of *Europe,* to consider their Merit, and then I assure my self, instead of depriving them of their present Privileges, they would continue them forever; and, if there were room for it, add as many more.

The 2d Charge in the Bill against the Charter Governments, that they have exercis'd arbitrary Power, answer'd.

The other Charge in the Bill is, *That they have exercis'd arbitrary Power.* If this be aim'd at the Proprietary Governments, which however I don't accuse, I have nothing to say, but am sure that the Charter Governments stand clear of it. The Thing speaks loudly for it self. For in the Governments, where there are Charters, and those Charters entire, all Officers Civil and Military are elected by the People, and that anually; than which Constitution nothing under Heaven can be a stronger Barrier against arbitrary Rule. For should it be allow'd, that the People, *corrupted* or *deceiv'd,* might instead of wise Magistrates chuse Tyrants and Oppressors to Lord over them one Year; yet it can't be imagin'd, that after they have felt the Smart of it, they will do so the next. Nor can there be a greater Obligation on the Rulers themselves to administer Justice than that their Election depends on it the next Year. Hence the frequent Choice of Magistrates has bin ever a main Pillar, upon which all who have aim'd at Freedom in their Schemes of Government, have depended.

As the Reason is incontestible, so the Fact is apparent, that these Governments, far from retrenching the Liberty of the Subject, have improv'd it in some important Articles, which the Circumstances of Things in *Great Britain* perhaps don't require, or won't easily admit.

To instance in a few; There has bin from the beginning an Office erected by Law in every Country, where all Conveyances of Land are enter'd at large, after the Grantors have first acknowledg'd them before a Justice of Peace; by which means much Fraud is prevented, no Person being able to sell his Estate twice, or take up more Money upon it than it's worth. Provision has likewise been made for the Security of the Life and Property of the Subject in the Matter of Juries, who are not return'd by the Sherriff of the County, but are chosen by the Inhabitants of the Town a convenient Time before the sitting of the Courts. And this Election is under the most exact Regulation, in Order to prevent Corruption, so far as Humane Prudence can do it. It must be noted, that Sherriffs in the Plantations are comparatively but little Officers, and therefore not to be trusted as here, where they are Men of ample Fortunes. And yet even here such flagrant Corruptions have been found in returning Juries by Sherriffs, that the House of Commons thought it necessary in their last Session to amend the Law in this Point, and pass'd a Bill for choosing them by Ballot.

Redress in their Courts of Law is *easy, quick* and *cheap*. All Processes are in *English*, and no special Pleadings or Demurrers are admitted, but the general Issue is always given, and special Matters brought in Evidence; which saves Time and Expence; and in this Case a Man is not liable to lose his Estate for a Defect in Form, nor is the Merit of the Cause made to depend on the Niceties of Clerkship. By a Law of the Country no Writ may be abated for a circumstantial Error, such as a slight Mis-nomer or any Informality. And by another Law, it is enacted, that every Attorney taking out a Writ from the Clerk's Office, shall indorse his Sirname upon it, and be liable to pay to the adverse Party his Costs and Charges in Case of Non-Prosecution or Discontinuance, or that the Plaintiff be Non-suit, or Judgment pass against him. And it is provided in the same Act, That if the Plaintiff shall suffer a Nonsuit by the Attorney's mis-laying the Action, he shall be oblig'd to draw a new Writ without a Fee, in case the Party shall see fit to revive the Suit. I can't but think that every body, except Gentlemen of the long Robe and the Attornies, will think this a wholesome Law, and well calculated for the Benefit of the Subject. For the quicker Dispatch of Causes, Declarations are made Parts of the Writ, in which the Case is fully and particularly set forth. If it be matter of Account, the Account is annex'd to the Writ, and Copies of both left with the Defendant; which being done Fourteen Days before the Sitting of the Court, he is oblig'd to plead directly, and the Issue is then try'd. Whereas by the Practice of the Court of *King's-Bench,* Three or Four Months Time is often lost after the Writ is serv'd, before the Cause can be brought to Issue.

Nor are the People of *New-England* oppress'd with the infinite Delays and Expence that attend the Proceedings in *Chancery,* where both Parties are often ruin'd by the Charge and Length of the Suit. But as in all other Countries, *England* only excepted, *Jus & Æquum*[5] are held the same, and never divided; so it is there: A Power of *Chancery* being vested in the Judges of the Courts of Common Law as to some particular Cases, and they make equitable Constructions in Others. I must add, that the Fees of Officers of all sorts are setled by Acts of Assembly at moderate Prices, for the Ease of the Subject.

It were easy to mention other Articles, but that I perswade my self it is needless. The Charter Governments are celebrated for their excellent Laws and mild Administration; for the Security of Liberty and Property; for the Encouragement of Vertue, and Suppression of Vice; for the promoting Letters, by erecting Free-Schools and Colleges; and in one Word, for every Thing that can make a People happy and prosperous. To these Arts it is owing, that *New-England,* though she has attain'd but little more than the Age of a Man, with all the Disadvantages under which she labours in respect to her Trade and Climate, and almost a perpetual *Indian* War, has hitherto flourish'd far above any other of the Plantations.

This being the Case of the Charter Governments, let us turn the Tables, and see how it far'd with them when in an *evil Reign* they lost their Charters. Then the Governour of *New-England* with Four or Five Strangers of his Council, Men of desperate Fortunes, and bad if any Principles, made what Laws, and levy'd what Taxes they pleas'd on the People. They without an Assembly, rais'd a Penny in the Pound on all the Estates in the Country, and another Penny on all imported Goods, besides Twenty Pence *per* Head as Poll Money, and an immoderate Excise on Wine, Rum, and other Liquors. Several worthy Persons, having in an humble Address represented this Proceeding as a Grievance, were committed to the common Gaol for a High Misdemanour; deny'd the Benefit of the *Habeas Corpus*[6] Act; try'd out of their own County; fin'd exorbitantly, and oblig'd to pay 160 *l.* for

5. ["Law and equity."]

6. [Literally, "You have a body." A writ directing the sheriff that "you have a body" for confinement and are required to produce a charge in court to justify imprisonment.—Tr.]

Fees, when the Prosecution would hardly have cost them so many Shillings in *Great Britain*. And to compleat the Oppression, when they upon their Tryal claim'd the Privileges of *Englishmen*, they were scoffingly told, *Those Things would not follow them to the Ends of the Earth*. Unnatural Insult; must the brave Adventurer, who with the Hazard of his Life and Fortune, seeks out new Climates to inrich his Mother Country, be deny'd those common Rights, which his Countrymen enjoy at Home in Ease and Indolence? Is he to be made miserable, and a Slave by his own Acquisitions? Is the Labourer alone unworthy of his Hire, and shall they *only* reap, who have neither sow'd nor planted? Monstrous Absurdity! Horrid inverted Order!

These Proceedings, however Arbitrary and Oppressive, were but the Prelude: The Catastophe was, if possible, yet more dismal. Having invaded their Liberties, by an easy Transition the next Attack was directly on their Properties. Their Title to their Lands was absolutely deny'd by the Governour and his Creatures upon two pretences: One, that their Conveyances were not according to the Law of *England*; the Other, that if they might be thought to have had something like a Title formerly, yet it now ceas'd by the Revocation of their Charters. So that they who had fairly purchas'd their Lands, and held them in quiet Possession for above Fifty Years, were now oblig'd to accept new Deeds from the Governour and pay for them a third Part of their Value, in order to ascertain their Titles or otherwise they would be seized for the Crown.

It would be an Injury to Vertue, if I did not in this Place pay distinguish'd Honour to the Memory of an honest and worthy Patriot, Col. *Shrimpton* long since deceas'd, who being rich in Lands, was courted to receive new Patents *gratis*, that others might be drawn in by the Authority of his Example; but when he was appriz'd of their Design, he chose rather to have his Lands seiz'd (and they were seiz'd) than by such a base Complyance betray his Countrymen into the Snares prepar'd for them. I should not have thus far entred into the Detail of Things so long past, but to show from Experience, as well as from the Reason and Nature of the Thing, that Charters are not the *Causes* of Arbitrary Government, but indeed *strong Works* rais'd against it, which once thrown down, Oppression rushes in like a Tide, and bears down every thing before it.

Having thus answer'd the Allegations of the Bill, in a Manner which I hope may be satisfactory, I am next to consider such Arguments as I have met with in Conversation from Persons in the Ministry and others.

The Third Objection, that the Acts of Trade are disregarded, answer'd.

What I have heard most insisted on is,

That the Acts of Trade and Navigation, made on purpose to render the Plantations beneficial to Great-Britain, *are disregarded in the Charter Governments; and that this Evil cannot be effectually cur'd, but by a Resumption of the Charters.*

To which I answer very particularly and distinctly,

1*st.* The Complaints on this Head are for the most Part of an old Date, and when the Bill against the Charters was depending in the House of Commons, were produc'd from the Files of the Plantation Board, whither they had bin transmitted in former Reigns, when Custom-house Officers in the Plantations were such great Rarities, that One Collector serv'd Four entire Provinces. And can it be thought strange that Merchants, whose Business is Gain, should have sometimes for Lucre transgress'd the Acts of Trade, when there were no Officers to see them duly observ'd? The Case is vastly different now. Officers of the Revenue are multiply'd, and are extremely rigorous, so that instead of *their* Complaints of unfair Traders, the Merchants on the other hand greatly complain of the Oppression of the Officers. I've seen an Account of such intollerable Hardships impos'd on fair well-meaning Traders, under Colour of Law, that one would hardly give Credit to the least of the Articles, if the Whole had not bin deliver'd publickly in an Assembly of one of the Provinces by a worthy Member, and afterwards printed with his name to it. The Author I refer to, after a Recital of the several Facts, in which he is very full as to every Circumstance, draws up this melancholly Conclusion, That the Custom-House Officers had by their violent Practices either seiz'd or driven away all the Vessels belonging to that Part of the Country, so that they had no Sloops left to carry their Produce to Market in the adjacent Colonies.

2*dly.* If there be some *late* Complaints, perhaps upon Examination, they will appear to be ill grounded. I can speak this knowingly with respect to a Complaint, transmitted not long since by the Surveyor General of *North America* and the Collector of *New London,* against His Majesty's Colony of *Connecticut.* These Gentlemen, one or both of them, drew up a Charge against that innocent and loyal Colony in very severe Terms, as *setting the Laws of Trade and Navigation at the utmost Defiance.* Whereas in Truth and in Fact, the Instances they produc'd of such Defiance were clear Proofs of that Colony's Inclination to support the Laws of Trade and their own Traffick; and on the contrary, what the Custom-House Officers insisted on was manifestly subversive of both, and could serve no End in the World but enhancing the Collectors Fees. The Case is this. There are on the Coast of His Majesty's Colony of *Connecticut* Eight convenient Ports or Harbours for Shipping. The Government there did from the Beginning place a Naval Officer in each of them, to see that the several Acts of Trade were duly observ'd. After the Act of the 7th and 8th of King *William*, the Collector of the Colony appointed a Deputy in each of these Ports, who requir'd all Masters of Vessels, Outward and Inward-bound, to Enter and Clear with him as well as with the Naval Officer, whether they had any Goods on Board paying a Duty to the Crown or not; which they submitted to, tho' not oblig'd by Law, as Sir *William Thompson* the late Sollicitor General has upon a full and impartial State of the Case given his Opinion. The present Collector thinking it best to receive all the Fees himself, refuses to make any Deputations, or allow the Power of the Naval Officers to be sufficient in his Absence, but commands all Masters of Vessels whatsoever to repair to the Port of his Residence, and there to Enter and Clear with him: By which Regulation Seven of the Eight Ports are left open for illegal Traders, to the great Detriment of the Crown; whilst with equal Injury to the Subject, Sloops sailing from one Town to another, or perhaps to a neighbouring Province with no better a Cargo than a few Deals and Turnips, shall be oblig'd to go sometimes 120 Miles out of their Way, which often happens to be further than the Port of Delivery, to find the Collector. The Agent for the Colony has fully represented this Hardship to the Commissioners of the Customs, and shown the Injury that will be done to the King as well as the Subject by this Establishment; but all in vain, there is no Redress; and what puts one out of all Patience, this very Case is cited as one Allegation among others to support the General Charge against the Charter Governments that they carry on an illegal Commerce.

3dly. If it were true that some Persons did now and then concern themselves in an illegal Trade, can it be thought just or reasonable that the whole Community should suffer for their private fault? No Body will say that the Acts of Trade are perfectly observ'd in the Provinces immediately under the Crown, or in *Great-Britain* it self. I believe there is no Corporation in the Kingdom, being a Sea-Port, wherein there are not at some Time or other contraband Goods imported, or other Goods clandestinely run, to the prejudice of the King's Duties. In this Port of *London* great Abuses are daily committed in spight of the utmost Vigilance to prevent them. The Fraud of relanding Callicoes after a pretended Exportation, only to receive the Drawback, is a most flagrant Instance, if One either considers the Perjuries that attend it, or the immense Sums that are thereby rob'd from the Publick, or the vast Injuries that are done by it to the honest Linnen-Draper. And yet, whoever us'd this, or any other Cheat of the like Kind, as an Argument to disfranchise this Ancient Corporation? The Rule of Law is, *Noxa Caput sequitur;*[7] and it is agreeable to Natural Justice that every Man should suffer for his own Transgression. On the other part, if a Corporate Body were to forfeit their Privileges for every private Person's Offence, they would be of no Value. A Charter so limited could not stand a Week, nor would be worth the Expence of the Great Seal.

4*thly*. I Might still make a further Remark. If the Grievances complain'd of were not antiquated Stories, but subsisting at this Time; if they were fairly represented; and lastly, if it were equitable that the Crimes of Persons in a private Capacity should be expiated by the Publick, yet no Conclusion could be drawn from these Premises prejudicial to the Charters, because the dissolving them would be no Remedy in any sort. The Reason is plain, that putting this Case, not only the Inspection of Trade, but the Prosecution, Tryal, and Punishment of every Offender would rest in the same Hands, and be carry'd on in the same Manner as before. All the Officers of the Revenue are *in the present State of Things* appointed by the Crown; all Breaches of the Acts of Trade, saving a single one excepted by Act of Parliament, are cognizable only in the Court of Admiralty, where the Judge and every inferiour Officer are created either by Commissions under the Broad Seal, or by Warrants from the Lord High Admiral. The Laws of the Country are not pleadded in that Court, but Acts of Parliament, and when they are silent, the Civil and Maritime Laws take place. The Forms of Proceeding, were *they* of any Consequence are regulated after the Manner practis'd in *Doctors Commons*. If then his Majesty should resume the Charters, nothing more could be done to preserve the Acts of Trade than is at present, and therefore how plausible soever this Pretext may appear at first sight, it's plain upon a nearer View that there is no Weight in it.

7. ["The liability follows the person responsible."]

I am appriz'd that the Judge of the Vice-Admiralty in *New-England* has often complain'd home of the frequent Prohibitions serv'd on him from the Courts of Judicature there, which he says, *Weaken and in a manner suppress the Authority of that Court, and all the good Ends for which it was constituted.* But neither does this Matter in the least relate to the Charters, though there were Reason for the Complaint, as on the other hand, I shall immediately show there is none. The Right of the Courts of Common Law within the province of the *Massachusets,* to restrain the Excesses of the Admiralty Jurisdiction, are not deriv'd from their Charter, but from subsequent Laws of the Province, confirm'd afterwards by the Crown; which Power therefore, whether the Charters stand or fall, will remain unhurt, and still the same. But the Matter of this Complaint is wholly groundless, which I must particularly show, because a Handle has bin taken from it to hurt *New-England* in its Charters. I therefore take leave to say, That the superiour Court of Judicature for the Province of the *Massachuset's* Bay has a legal Power to issue Prohibitions to the Court of Vice-Admiralty: That it is very fitting and necessary such a Power should be lodg'd in that Court: And, lastly, that the particular Cases wherein the Judges of that superiour Court have hitherto exercis'd this Power, were apparently without and beyond the Admiralty Jurisdiction.

To begin with the Power it self: 'Tis founded on An Act of the Assembly pass'd in the 11th Year of King *William,* and by him confirm'd, entitl'd, *An Act for establishing a superiour Court of Judicature, Court of Assizes and General Gaol Delivery.* The Act after a Recital of several Powers vested in the Court, has this general Clause: *And the said Court is hereby vested with the same Power as fully and amply to all Intents and Purposes whatsoever as the Courts of* King's Bench, Common-Pleas *and* Exchequer *within His Majesty's Kingdom of* England *have or ought to have.* By Consequence then, if the Court of *King's Bench* has a Power to restrain the Court of *Admiralty* in *England,* this Court of Judicature must have the same in *New-England.*

The Reasons for such a Restraining Power are as strong in *New-England* as in *Great-Britain.* It has bin ever boasted as the peculiar Privilege of an *Englishman,* & the grand Security of his Property to be try'd by his Country and the Laws of the Land; whereas this Admiralty Method of Tryal deprives him of both, as it puts his Estate in the Disposal of a single Person, and makes the Civil Law the Rule of Judgment; which though it may not perhaps properly be call'd Foreign, being the Law of Nations, yet 'tis what he has not consented to himself, or his Representative for him. A Jurisdiction therefore so founded ought not to extend beyond what Necessity requires, that is, to nothing but what is really transacted on the High Seas, which not being *infra Corpus Comitatus,*[8] is not triable at Common Law. If some Bounds are not set to the Jurisdiction of the Admiralty, beyond which it shall not pass, it may in Time, like the Element to which it ought to be confin'd, grow outrageous & overflow the Banks of all the other Courts of Justice. This Danger is still greater in the Plantations, where neither the Judge nor any of the Inferior Officers of the Admiralty have Salaries, or perhaps other Dependance than upon what they get by their Fees, and therefore must be strongly tempted to receive all Business that comes before them, however improper for their Cognizance.

In vain do the Advocates for the Admiralty urge on this Occasion that an Appeal lies home, and therefore if a Cause try'd there be found to be *Coram non Judice,*[9] Justice will be done to the injur'd Party on the Appeal. For if this Argument has any Force, it would take place in *England,* because an Appeal lies here from the Sentences of the Admiralty to the Court of Delegates, and yet that is not thought a sufficient Reason to prevent the Court of *King's-Bench* from granting Prohibitions when they think them necessary. Besides it is to be remark'd, that the Appeal does not lie to the *King* and Council as it does from other Courts, but to the Judge of the Admiralty, and therefore one may imagine that the Appellant will have but a *cold Cause* of it; for I believe it has bin rarely found that any Court was forward to limit its own Power.

If then the Court of Judicature in *New-England* has a right in general to award Prohibitions against the Court of Vice-Admiralty, there will, I believe be no Dispute as to the particular Instances wherein they have exercis'd this Power. Hitherto there have bin but Three; nor did the Judges come into these, but upon solemn Argument first had before them by the ablest Lawyers on the Spot. Not that I suppose there was any real Difficulty, but it being a Case *prima Impressionis*[10] in that Country, 'twas thought proper to proceed so deliberately.

8. ["Within the territorial body of the county."]

9. [Literally, "Before an improper judge," i.e., a void judgment.—Tr.]

10. [Literally, "The first of the impression," i.e., without precedent.—Tr.]

One Prohibition was granted on a Libel fil'd upon the Wool Act of the 10th and 11th of *William* III. which provides, That all Offences therein mention'd shall be try'd in some *Court of Record,* which 'tis certain the Court of Admiralty is not. Another was issu'd to stop Proceedings in a Cause which had bin try'd before at Common Law, and receiv'd the Judgment of the Court. If the Court of Vice-Admiralty should assume such a Prerogative as this, instead of being confin'd to Maritime Affairs, it would be the Supreme Court in all Causes, and the *Dernier Resort* of Justice. The Third Prohibition was upon a Charter Party made and executed upon the Land with a Penalty under Hand & Seal, which nevertheless was libell'd in the Court of Admiralty, and the Judge would very gravely have heard and determin'd it, on a Colour of it's having relation to a Voyage, or at least to something which was to be perform'd on the Seas. Altho' this is so far from being a good Reason, that there are many Cases in the Books, where a Cause has bin *wholly Maritime,* and even the Contract made upon the High Seas, yet because it was reduc'd to Writing afterwards and Seal'd on the Shore, it has bin adjudg'd to be without the Admiralty Jurisdiction. My Lord *Coke* is so clear and full upon this Subject, and the Limits of the Admiralty Jurisdiction are so exactly describ'd in the several Acts of Parliament made for this End, to say nothing of the Cases in the Books, where great Damages are given for infringing the Rights of the Common Law, that I shall refer to them* and pursue this Argument no further.

The 4th Objection *That they have made Laws repugnant to the Laws of* Great Britain, *answer'd.*

Another Thing alledg'd against the *American* Charters is, *That their Governments have made Laws repugnant to the Laws of* Great-Britain *contrary to the Powers given them, and thereby have incurr'd a Forfeitur of the Charters.*

* Vid. *My Lord* Coke's *Fourth* Institutes, *as also the several Statutes of* 13 R. 2. Cap. 5. 15 R. 2. Cap. 3. *By the Statute of the 2d.* H. 4. Cap. 11. *in Case a matter Tryable at Common Law be brought into the Court of Admiralty, the Party griev'd shall recover double Damages. See the Statute of* 27 Eliz. Cap. 11. *as also the Cases in the Books, particularly that of Sir* Josiah Child *and* Sands *in* Salk. 31, 2. *where an Action was brought on the Statutes of* 13 R. 2. 15 R. 2. *and* 2. H. 4. *for arresting a Ship by Admiralty Process, the Matter not being within the Connusance of that Court, and tho' there was no Suit, nor any Plantiff or Defendant, yet it was held to be a Prosecution, & double Damages were recover'd, Error was afterwards bro't, and the Judgment affirm'd.*

If the *Massachuset* Charter were singly in Question, this Allegation would have no place, because no Act pass'd by that Assembly has the Force of a Law till the King's Governour has assented to it, and then it comes home for his Majesty's Approbation, who if he pleases, annuls it. There is therefore no Danger of their making Laws repugnant to the Laws of *Great-Britain;* or if they should, there being a Remedy always at hand, if it be not made use of, the Fault will lie some where else, and can't affect the Province.

But let us examine a little, whether any of the other Governments acting under Charters may deserve this Censure; in order to which, we must consider what this Phrase [REPUGNANT TO THE LAWS OF ENGLAND] imports. I believe it will be easily allow'd, that a Law may be *various* from the Laws of *England,* and yet not *repugnant* to them; or otherwise these Governments must make no Laws at all, which no Body will say, who knows that a Right of Legislature is the most essential Part of their Charters, and what indeed the Reason and Nature of the Thing make absolutely necessary. Every Country has Circumstances peculiar to it self in Respect of its Soil, Situation, Inhabitants, and Commerce, to all which convenient Laws must with the nicest Care and Judgment be adapted; whereas the Laws of *England* are calculated for their own Meridian, and are many of them no ways suitable to the Plantations, and others not possible to be executed there.

This Point, however clear and evident, has not bin always rightly understood. There was a pretty extraordinary Instance of it a few Years since, with respect to a Law in force in *Carolina* for choosing Jury-men by Ballot. This was part of their Original Body of Laws fram'd by the famous Earl of *Shaftsbury,* and what they had found by Experience a great Preservative to their Liberties and Properties. Yet I don't know how it happen'd, the Lord Palatine and other Lords Proprietors of that Province, imagining this Law to be repugnant to the Laws of *Great-Britain,* and that they should thereby incur a Forfeiture of their Charter, directed their Landgraves to get it repeal'd. The People in that Government, unwilling to part with what they so much esteem'd, sent over two Deputies express to set the Matter in a fair Light before their Lordships. When they arriv'd, I accompany'd them at their Desire to the Board, where after some short Debates, we satisfy'd their Lordships that their Charter could be in no Danger on this Account, and that one Law might be various from another without being repugnant to it.

Having premis'd this Distinction, I answer the Question in direct Terms, That *then a Law in the Plantations may be said to be repugnant to a Law made in* Great-Britain, *when it flatly contradicts it, so far as the Law made here mentions and relates to the Plantation. Contraria sunt ad idem:*[11] And therefore one Thing cannot be said to be contrary to another, that does not immediately relate to it, and diametrically oppose it. For the Purpose, if a Law pass'd here has its Force restrain'd to *England, Wales,* and the Town of *Berwick* on the *Tweed,* no Law in the Plantations can properly be said to repugn it; because whatever Diversity there may be between them, yet one having no manner of Relation to the other, they are not repugnant. I believe I am Right in my Logick, but am sure I am as to the legal Acceptation of the Phrase, because what I advance is founded on the Words of an Act of Parliament. It is the 7*th* and 8*th* of King *William,* which (Cap. 22. Sect 9*th.*) Enacts, *That all Laws, By-Laws, Usages or Customs at this Time, or which hereafter shall be in Practice, or endeavoured or pretended to be in Force or Practice in any of the Plantations, which are in any wise repugnant to the before-mention'd Laws or any of them,* So Far As They Do Relate To The Said Plantations Or Any Of Them, *or which are any ways repugnant to this present Act, or to any other Law hereafter to be made in this Kingdom,* So Far As Such Law Shall Relate To And Mention The Said Plantations, *are illegal, null, and void, to all Intents and Purposes whatsoever.* If then we'll take the Sense of the Phrase from an Act of Parliament, (and where can we have a better Expositor?) no Man will pretend that there ever was a Law made in the Plantations repugnant to the Laws of *Great-Britain.* And yet I am apt to think that if an Assembly should do a Thing so illegal, they ought to be punish'd for it themselves, and not their Constituents. They were chosen and delegated by the People to frame Laws according to the Powers given them by their respective Charters, which if they exceed, why should a whole Country suffer for their Offence? This would be to punish the Innocent for the Guilty, and is not agreeable to the Law in other Cases, where if the Trustee does any Act that is illegal and beyond his Trust, the *Cestuy q. Trust* is not oblig'd by it, nor to be hurt for it.

If the Words will receive any other Construction than what the Act of Parliament has put upon them, I think it must be suppos'd to be this; that the Patentees should not under colour of their particular Charters presume

11. ["They are opposites on the same basis."]

to make any Laws inconsistent with the great Charter and other Laws of *England* by which the Lives, Liberties and Properties of *Englishmen* are secur'd. It seems reasonable enough to think that the Crown might intend by this Injunction to provide for all it's Subjects, that they might not be oppress'd by arbitrary Power; but in whatever distant Part of the World they were settled, being still Subjects, they should have the Usage of *Englishmen*, be protected by the same mild Laws, & enjoy the same happy Government, as if they continued within the Realm. Consider the Expression in this Light, and the Colonies (which I am defending) are still safe, having in no respect impair'd, but many Ways improv'd the Liberty of the Subject, as I have before shown under another Head. If hereafter so unaccountable a Thing should happen, that those Privileges which were design'd as Fences against Oppression and Despotick Power prove the means to introduce both, and the Body of the People should petition to be reliev'd from the Yoke of their Charters, for my part, I'll be no longer an Advocate for them. Only in the mean Time, I heartily wish they may not be disturb'd, but rest in Peace till then.

A 5th Objection, that the Charter Colonies will grow great and formidable, answer'd.

There is one Thing more I have heard often urg'd against the Charter Colonies, and indeed 'tis what one meets with from People of all Conditions and Qualities, tho' with due respect to their better Judgments, I can see neither Reason nor Colour for it. 'Tis said, *that their encreasing Numbers and Wealth join'd to their great Distance from* Britain *will give them an Opportunity in the Course of some Years to throw off their Dependance on the Nation, and declare themselves a free State, if not curb'd in Time by being made entirely subject to the Crown.* Whereas in Truth there's no Body tho' but little acquainted with these or any of the *Northern* Plantations, who does not know and confess, that their Poverty and the declining State of their Trade is so great at present, that there's far more Danger of their sinking, without some extraordinary Support from the Crown, than of their ever revolting from it. So that I may say without being ludicrous, that it would not be more absurd to place two of His Majesty's Beef-Eaters to watch an Infant in the Cradle that it don't rise and cut its Father's Throat, than to guard these weak Infant Colonies to prevent their shaking off the *British* Yoke. Besides, they are so distinct from one another in their Forms of Government, in their Religious Rites, in their Emulation of Trade, and consequently in their Affections, that they can never be suppos'd to unite in so dangerous an Enterprize. It is for this Reason I have often wondered to hear some Great Men profess their Belief of the Feasibleness of it, and the Probability of i'ts some Time or other actually coming to pass, who yet with the same Breath advise that all the Governments on the Continent be form'd into one, by being brought under one Vice-Roy, and into one Assembly. For surely if we in earnest believ'd that there was or would be hereafter a Disposition in the Provinces to Rebel and declare themselves Independent, it would be good Policy to keep them disunited; because if it were possible they could contrive so wild and rash an Undertaking, yet they would not be hardy enough to put it in Execution, unless they could first strengthen themselves by a Confederacy of all the Parts.

But to return from this short Digression: Our Neighbours of *Holland,* who are allow'd to be a wise State, did not entertain these Jealousies of their Subjects in *India,* when they were a young & growing Plantation, nor do they even now when they are a potent flourishing People. Had they done so, and in consequence of it restrain'd and check'd them, *Holland* would not at this Day have drawn such immense Riches from that Part of the World, and furnish'd all *Europe* with *Indian* Commodities. And yet what Reason can be assign'd for the Jealousies we entertain of our Colonies, which the *Dutch* have not, and far stronger with respect to their *Batavian* Subjects? If the Distance be urg'd as an Argument, every body knows that *New-England* is but a thousand Leagues from the *British* Shore, but the *Dutch* must run eight Times that Ground from *Amsterdam* before they arrive at *Batavia.* Or if the Number and Power of the Inhabitants should give any Umbrage, this is an Article which with respect to *Batavia* won't admit of the most distant Comparison. The General of that Place maintains a Port superiour to many Sovereign Princes in *Europe,* and has all the Kings in *Java* in a manner Tributary to him. He has 3000 standing European Troops, not reckoning the Natives & all the *Dutch* Inhabitants live in that flowing Wealth and Plenty which makes *Batavia* look like the Capital of a Great & Mighty Empire. But do the States of *Holland* look on this their prosperous Condition with envious or jealous Eyes? Just the reverse; they do every thing in their Power still to promote and advance it, well knowing their foreign Plantations can't thrive, but they must receive the Benefit of it themselves, and therefore justly esteem the Wealth of their Subjects Abroad as their own Riches. Why then should not *Great-Britain* form the same Judgment, and proceed by the like Measures in regard to her *American* Dominions, from whence she receives the greatest Advantages? It were no difficult Task to prove that *London* has risen out of the Plantations, and not out of *England*. 'Tis to them we owe our vast Fleets of Merchant Ships, and consequently the Increase of our Seamen, and Improvement of our Navigation. 'Tis their Tobacco, Sugar, Fish, Oil, Logwood and other Commodities, which have enabled us to support our Trade in *Europe*, to bring the Ballance of some Countries in our Favour, which would otherwise be against us, and to make the Figure we do at present, and have done for near a Century past, in all Parts of the commercial World.

The Mother Kingdom must therefore needs rejoyce in the Prosperity of every one of her Colonies, because it is her own Prosperity. The Fable of the Belly and Members illustrates this Argument. It would be unreasonable for the Belly to grudge the Labour of digesting the Food and dispersing the Blood and Juices to the extream Parts, seeing they return purify'd and exalted in the Circulation. There's a close Analogy between the Natural Body and the Body Politick; as in the one, a Finger can't ake, but the Whole feels it, so in the other the remotest Plantation can't decay, but the Nation must suffer with it.

If it be said that the Charter Colonies are not so valuable as some of the rest, I answer, that the Inhabitants have the more need of their Charters to make them amends; for People must have some Incouragement to sit down on a cold and barren Soil. Yet I have shown before that they are many ways of great Use and Advantage to the Crown; to which I add, that they will be more so than ever in a few Years, to strengthen the *British* Empire in *America* against the formidable Settlement of *Loisiana*, which for some Years past has bin carry'd on by the *French* with great Expence, and with the utmost Vigour and Application. This Country was given by the late *French* King to the *Sieur Croizat*, but is now (as every Body knows) in the famous *Missisippi* Company, who have a Fund of a Hundred Millions of Livres for this very Purpose, and are daily sending over a vast Number of People for Tillage, as well as all sorts of Artificers, with proper Materials for making a Settlement. It is situate on the great River of *Missisippi*, and by help of the superiour Lakes and Rivers, on some of which the *French* have already erected Fortresses, a Communication may be made between *New-France* and the Gulph of *Mexico,* which indeed was the very Scheme of the *French* Court in projecting this Enterprize, as is expresly declar'd in the Preamble to *Croizat*'s Patent. 'Tis easy then to see that the *French* will be hereby enabled to draw a Line, and in Time have a Chain of Towns on the Back of all our Colonies from the Borders of *Cape-Breton* to the westermost Part of *Carolina.* And what *Briton* can consider this without being in Pain for the Fate of our Provinces in future Times? Especially since we know that the *Illinois* and other Warlike *Indian* Nations lye near the *French,* and for many Reasons, which it would be too much a Digression to recount here, are devoted to their Interest, and by consequence ready at all Times to joyn their Forces in any Attempt against us.

This being the Case, I think with humble Submission, it is very preposterous to amuse our selves with vain, imaginary Prospects of what is scarce possible to come to pass, & neglect doing what is absolutely necessary; I mean, the enlarging and supporting our Provinces, that they may be able to defend themselves against being one Day totally extirpated by a Foreign Power. And then I have only to suggest an old approv'd Maxim, *That every Thing is best preserv'd by the same Principles by which it was at first form'd,* and consequently the best Method of encouraging the Charter Colonies is, to preserve their Privileges inviolate, without which they had never bin setled.

The 3d Proposition, *That it is not the Interest of the Crown to resume the Charters so forfeited.*

Another Proposition I advanced was, That if these Governments should be adjudg'd to have forfeited their Charters back to the Crown, yet it is not the true Interest of the Crown to resume them.

It is a generally receiv'd Opinion, that the People in the Plantations have an Interest distinct from that of the Crown; when it is supposed at the same time, that the Interest of the Governours, they being the King's Representatives, is one with the Crown; and from these Premises it is concluded, that there can't be too much Power given to the Governours or too little to the People. Whereas with humble Submission, I conceive this to be a very wrong Judgment, and that the Reverse of it is true. The only Interest of the People is to thrive and flourish in their Trade, which is the true Interest of the Crown and Nation, because they reap the Profit of it. When on the other Hand, the View that Governours generally have is private Gain, which being too often acquir'd by discouraging and oppressing Trade, is not only an Interest distinct from that of the Crown, but extreamly prejudicial to it. The Trade of a young Plantation is like a tender Plant, & should be cherish'd with the fondest Care; but if instead of that, it meets with the rough Hand of Oppression, it will soon die. The proper Nursery for this Plant is a free Government, where the Laws are sacred, Property secure, & Justice not only impartially, but expeditiously distributed. For to what purpose shall the Merchant expose his Estate to the Dangers of the Sea, the Enemy, and many more Accidents, if after all he can't save it at Home from Rapine and Violence?

As this is evident, so is it that whatever injures the Trade of the Plantations, must in Proportion affect *Great-Britain*, the Source and Center of their Commerce; from whence they have their Manufactures, whether they make their Returns, and where all their Superlucration is lodg'd. The Blow then may strike the Colonies first, but it comes Home at last, and falls heaviest on our selves.

That Governours are apt to abuse their Power and grow rich by Oppression, Experience shows us. We have seen not many Years since, some Governours seiz'd by their Injur'd People, and sent Prisoners to *Whitehall*, there to answer for their Offences. Others have fallen Victims on the Spot, not to the Fury of a Faction or a Rabble, but to the Resentment of the whole Body of the People, rising as one Man to revenge their Wrongs. Others after being recall'd, have been prosecuted at the *King's-Bench Bar*, pursuant to an Act of Parliament made in the Reign of the late King *William*, whereby it is provided, That Governours shall be impleadable at Home for any Injuries done in their Governments Abroad. We have had more than one flagrant Instance of this very lately, where Governours have bin convicted and censur'd not so properly for oppressing, as for a direct plundering their People, and such other Acts of Mis-rule and lawless Power, as one would not have thought it possible they should have committed if Experience had not shown it to be more than possible.

I don't however intend by what is here said, to reproach our own Nation, as if we were greater Sinners than others, or to reflect on the present Times, as if they were worse than the former. I know that the same Abuses have bin practis'd in every Age as well as this, & in Foreign Colonies as well as our own. The ancient *Romans* were as brave & as vertuous a People as any in the World, and yet their Proconsuls or Governours were very guilty in this respect. Their Corruption was so notorious as to be distinguish'd by the Name of *Crimen Repetundarum*,[12] a Phrase not us'd in any other meaning, and deriv'd from the Obligation which the *Roman* Senate laid on their Governours to make Restitution.

Nor have the modern Governours in the *French* & *Spanish* Plantations bin less Criminal. It's a famous Story of a Great Minister at the Court of *Madrid*, who writ to his Friend the Vice-Roy of *Peru*, that great Complaints were made against him for having extorted immense Sums of Money from the People in his Government; *Which*, says he, *I wish may be true, or else you are undone*. It seems the same Thing that wounded him, was necessary to heal him; and what put him out of Favour, was the only Thing could restore him,

Indeed it can hardly be expected but these Corruptions must happen, when one considers that few Gentlemen will cross the Seas for a Government, whose Circumstances are not a little streight at Home, & that they know by how slight & uncertain a Tenure they hold their Commissions; from whence they wisely conclude, that no Time is to be lost. And then for the Account to be rendred at Home, that is not thought of at so great a Distance, for *Procul a Jove, procul a Fulmine*.[13]

To enlarge then the Power of Governours, is to give them greater Power to oppress; and to vacate the Charters is to enlarge their Power, the Government in that Case of Course devolving upon them; as we see in those Plantations which never had any Charters, but are immediately dependent on the Crown. There they have, in a manner, the intire Legislative & Executive Powers, or at least so great an Influence on the constituent Parts of the Former, as leaves them little more than Nominal Sharers, serving rather as Screens to the Governour than a Defence to the People. The Militia is absolutely vested in the Governours, which influences all Elections of Representatives: They appoint Judges, Justices, Sheriffs and other Civil Officers with the Consent, it's said indeed, of the Council; but that such Consent voluntary or involuntary will ever be refus'd, seems too much to be expected, if we consider that altho' the Governours do not indeed appoint the Council, yet they recommend proper Persons to the King; and it may be supposed, that a Gentleman who is intrusted with the chief Command of a Province, and is

12. [Literally, "The crime of money that must be returned," i.e., bribery or extortion.—Tr.]
13. ["Far away from Jupiter, far away from the thunderbolt."]

actually on the Spot, will be thought the best Judge who are fit to serve, and therefore his Recommendations will almost always prevail. Besides, if there be a Turn to serve, or an Emergency real or imaginary, & any of the Members should be so refractory as not to give into his Measures with an implicit Faith, the Governour can suspend as many of them as he pleases; and when he has reduc'd the Board under a Number limited in his Instructions, he can then fill it up to that Number *instanter,*[14] with whom he pleases; and who will they be, may we presume, but such as are passively obedient to his Will? And too many such there are to be found in all Colonies so constituted, who are content to be *sadled* themselves, provided they may *ride* others under the *chief Rider.* I must farther observe, that where there are no Charters, there are Courts of Equity establish'd, in which the Governour is always Chancellor, and for the most part Chief Justice, and Ordinary at the same time; which puts the Estates, Lives and Liberties of the Inhabitants, saving the Liberty of Appeal at Home, intirely in his Disposal; and even an Appeal in all Cases under a considerable Sum, in all Cases; of the ordinary Jurisdiction, and in all Cases Capital, is either disallow'd by his Instructions, or wholly in the Governour's Breast to allow or not.

The Sum of my Argument is, That the Benefit which *Great-Britain* receives from the Plantations, arises from their Commerce: That oppression is the most opposite Thing in the World to Commerce, and the most destructive Enemy it can have: That Governours have in all Times, and in all Countries, bin too much inclin'd to oppress: And consequently it cannot be the Interest of the Nation to increase their Power, and lessen the Liberties of the People. I am so sanguine in this Opinion, that I really think it would be for the Service of the Crown & Nation to incorporate those Governments which have no Charter rather than Disfranchize those that have.

The 4*th* Proposition, *That it seems inconsistent with Justice to Disfranchize the Charter Colonies by an Act of Parliament.*

The last Thing I propos'd to consider was, how far it may be consistent with Justice, to deprive the Colonies of their Charters, without giving them a fair Tryal or any previous Notice.

14. ["Without delay."]

It is certain, that Bills of Attainder, such as this would be, have bin seldom us'd in *England*, and then only upon the most extraordinary Occasions: As when flagrant Crimes have been committed of a new and unusual Nature, against which the Law had made no Provision; or when the Witnesses have avoided, and perhaps by the Contrivance of the party; or lastly, which is the most common Case, when the attainted person having himself absconded, and fled from Justice, has thereby made such an extrajudicial Proceeding Justifiable. It is also as certain that neither of these Things can be pleaded in the present Case, which I need not be particular in showing, because not suggested, nor is there the least Colour for such Suggestion. And yet I pretend to know the People in the Charter Governments so well, and to be so thoroughly acquainted with their meek Principles of Obedience, that I dare affirm if such an Act should pass, however rigorous and severe they might think it within themselves, they would not let fall an indecent Word of their Superiours, but would receive the News with the lowest Submission: So great is their Loyalty to the King, and so profound their Regard for the Resolutions of a *British* Parliament, the wisest and most august Assembly in the World. However, seeing there is no such Act already pass'd, and 'tis to be hop'd from the Honour & Justice of Parliaments, never will, it can't be thought a Crime modestly to state the Hardship of the Case: I don't mean with respect to the Merits of it, which have bin already consider'd, but as to the *Manner of Proceeding by Bill in Parliament*. It is a most sacred and unalterable Rule of Justice, and has ever bin so esteem'd by all the civiliz'd Nations of the World, that no Person be depriv'd of Life, Liberty or Estate, or any thing he possesses, till he has had Time and Opportunity to make his Defence. And if the Matter in Judgment be of great Value, dearly paid for, and long enjoy'd, it adds much to the Weight of the Argument, and aggravates the Injury in depriving the Possessors unheard. Now this is the Case of the Charter Governments. How great the Purchase Consideration was, has been before said; but how valuable the Charters themselves are can never be said, Liberty being inestimable. And for the Time they have enjoy'd them, were they not on Record, it would be what the Civilians call *Immemorial*, one of them being above Fourscore Years standing. It seems therefore a Severity without a Precedent, that a People who have the Misfortune of being a Thousand Leagues distant from their Sovereign, a Misfortune great enough in it self, should UNSUMMON'D, UNHEARD, IN ONE DAY be depriv'd of all their valuable Privileges, which they and their Fathers have enjoy'd for near a Hundred Years. It's true, the Legislative Power is absolute and unaccountable, and King, Lords and Commons may do what they please; but the Question here is not about *Power,* but *Right: And shall not the Supream Judicature of all the Nation do right?* One may say, that what the Parliament can't do justly, they can't do at all. *In maximis minima est licentia.*[15] The higher the Power is, the greater Caution is to be us'd in the Execution of it, because the Sufferer is helpless & without Resort.

When in an Arbitrary Reign, the Charter of *New-England* was vacated, a *Quo Warranto* first gave the Colony Notice to prepare for their Trial. Altho' this was a Prosecution at Law, and the High Court of Parliament is not strictly confin'd to the Forms of the Courts below, yet it is not doubted but the great Fountain of Law & Justice will have some regard, if not to all the Rules made for inferiour Judicatures, yet to such as are Essential to Justice. And so in other Cases it has. For the Purpose: If a Bill be brought into the House of Commons that touches any Man's Property in *Ireland,* it must lie 30 Days, that the Party may have Notice and not suffer unheard. Why then should not a reasonable Time be allow'd to the Subjects in *America,* in Proportion to their more distant Situation; seeing they are no less the Subjects of the Crown, than the Inhabitants of *Ireland;* and Liberty is at least as valuable as Property; and surely the concern of whole Provinces challenges as much regard as the Interest of a single Person. If it should be said, as I confess a great Minister once said to me, That *the Regulation of Charters must be look'd on as Part of the publick Oeconomy, and not as the Affair of any particular Person or Province;* I humbly apprehend, with the utmost Deference to that great Person, that this does not reach the present Case. It's indeed very reasonable that all publick Affairs be subject to the Determination of the publick Wisdom, and there's no Occasion to notify any Body, because every Body is suppos'd to be present in the Representative Body of the Whole; but here the Provinces to be censur'd & depriv'd have no Representative in Parliament, and consequently must be consider'd as absent Persons suffering unheard.

I know of but one thing more that can be said to palliate a Proceeding against the Charters in this way, which is, *That the Provinces always have their respective Agents at Court, who may be heard by Petition before the Bill passes into an Act.* To which I answer, first, that sometimes they have

15. ["In the greatest power is the least license."]

Agents here, and at other Times they have not. Next, that a Bill may pass into an Act without the Knowlege of the Agents, they having no Citation. This had once like to have bin the Case, when a Bill of this Nature was formerly brought into the House of Commons; and certainly had prov'd so, if the Agent for *New-England* had at that nice Juncture bin indisposed in his Health, or but a Day's Journey out of Town, or if he had not bin more than ordinarily active & diligent when he was in Town. And, lastly, I must oberve that Agents are only instructed in Things that fall within the ordinary Course of Business, & when any thing of a new & extraordinary Nature is brought on the Carpet, they have a general Instruction to pray for Time in order to notify their Principals, & receive their special Commands. Besides, it's well known that the Right Honourable the Lords Commissioners for Trade and Plantations were, at the Time before mentioned, prepared to urge many Complaints both New & Old; to which Facts it had bin impossible for any Agent to answer *ore tenus,*[16] without being ever appriz'd of them. To conclude, what *those Governments* desire of their Superiours at home is, that they may not be judg'd and condemn'd unheard. And I cannot but flatter my self they will obtain it, whether I consider the Reasonableness of the Demand it self, or the celebrated Justice & Lenity of His Majesty's Government, or the Importance of the Thing in Question to the Provinces concern'd. I mention this last particular, being sure they would reckon the loss of their Privileges a greater Calamity, than if their Houses were all in Flames at once. Nor can they be justly blam'd, the one being a reparable Evil, but the other irreparable Burnt Houses may rise again out of their Ashes, and even more Beautiful than before, but 'tis to be fear'd that Liberty *once lost, is lost for ever.*

Thus I have ventur'd into the World my Thoughts on the *New-England* Charters; happy! if my imperfect Essay may provoke some learned Pen to do full Justice to the Subject, which yet in the great Scarcity of Friends that these Governments have, seems too much to be expected. In the mean Time, being my self a Native of one of them, I could not forbear showing my Good-will; for how little soever one is able to write, yet when the Liberties of one's Country are threatned, it's still more difficult to be silent. The Dumb Son of *Croesus,* when he saw an Attempt made on his Father's Life, broke into sudden Speech by a strong Effort of Nature. It's a fine Passage in

16. [Literally, "As far as the mouth," i.e., orally, without written statement.—Tr.]

Sallust, which I've plac'd in the Title Page of this little Work, *Pulchrum est Patriae benefacere, etiam benedicere haud absurdum est.* Every Man would be ambitious to do his Country each of these Services, and if I have not been Fortunate enough to attain to *Either* of 'em, THIS shall be my Satisfaction, that I have always aim'd and endeavour'd at *Both.*

FINIS.

· 21 ·

[Samuel Cranston and] R. Ward, A Vindication of the Governour and Government of His Majesty's Colony of Rhode-Island (Newport, 1721)

CLASHES BETWEEN metropolitan customs officials and colonial shippers were ubiquitous throughout southern New England from the last quarter of the seventeenth century on, and this *Vindication* provides an excellent example of the literature that could be produced out of these conflicts. It refers to an altercation between John Menzies, judge of the vice-admiralty court, and the local political establishment in Rhode Island, a charter colony that elected its own governor and was free from many of the metropolitan oversights to which royal colonies were subjected, over Menzies's attempt to seize for the Crown the cargo of a ship which he judged to have violated English navigation laws. When Menzies placed an advertisement in the *Boston Gazette* charging Governor Samuel Cranston and his Council with illegally setting aside his judgment in this case and Governor Samuel Shute of Massachusetts prevented them from answering Menzies in the same publication, Cranston and his colleagues published this pamphlet in their defense.

Following his first election in the late 1690s, Cranston had been annually elected governor for the next twenty-nine years, and under his direction the Rhode Island legislature had inserted restraints on English control of its water traffic into the statutes it passed to require enforcement of the English navigation acts, thereby ensuring that port administration in the colony would be largely administered by local officers and that revenues derived from that enforcement would go to the colony rather than to metropolitan officials. As Cranston and his councillors made clear to Menzies, who had suggested that Shute was the Vice Admiral for Rhode Island as well as Massachusetts, Rhode Island had never acknowledged that anyone except its own governor could act as vice admiral in that colony, and they expected vice admiralty judges to keep within "Bounds and Limits" that "did not Intrench upon the Liberty and Property of this His Majesty's Colony." Charging that Menzies had acted without ever having applied "to the Government for their Advice, Approbation or Concurrence," they declared that he had both "Illegally and Unwarantably intruded upon the Government, and Erroniously Represented them" in his Boston advertisement. Whatever mandates Menzies had received from London, Cranston and his colleagues thus implied, did not exempt them from the requirements set down in provincial laws. Although Connecticut, also a charter colony, was the only other English American colony that enjoyed such sweeping protections, this case shows how colonials sought to use provincial law to protect themselves from what they regarded as unwarranted intrusions into their concerns and unwonted violations of their interests. (J.P.G.)

A

VINDICATION

OF THE

Governour and Government Of His Majesty's Colony of *Rhode-Island,* &c.

From the unjust Aspersions and Calumnies of *John Menzies,* Judge of His Majesty's Court of *Vice-Admiralty* in the same: Relating to the Proceedings of said Government, in the Affair of several Slaves, and other Goods Imported into said Colony, from a Ship lately lying at *Tarpawlin-Cove,* &c.

A Vindication, &c.

Whereas *John Menzies* Esq; Judge of His Majesty's Court of Vice-Admiralty in this Colony, having by way of ADVERTISEMENT, in the *Boston* Gazettes, and News-Papers, Falsely, and Opprobriously charged the GOVERNOUR and COUNCIL of this His Majesty's Colony of *Rhode-Island* and *Providence* Plantations, with Proceeding Illegally, and Unwarrantably in setting aside the said Judge's Decree on several Slaves, *&c.* as Unjust; thereby endeavouring to Scandalize and Reproach the said GOVERNOUR and GOVERNMENT, to Cover his own Arbitrary and Lawless Decrees: And His Excellency SAMUEL SHUTE Esq; Governour of the Province of the *Massachusets-Bay*, not suffering this Government to indicate themselves by way of ADVERTISEMENT in the *Boston* Prints; Therefore are Obliged to Publish a true State of the Case, for their own Justification, and for the better Information of those who have Read Judge *Menzies*'s Advertisements, and have been abused thereby.

Upon the twenty fourth or twenty fifth of *April* last, Capt. *Benjamin Norton* of *Newport*, arrived at *Tarpawlin-Cove*, in a Ship of about two hundred and fifty Tons, Loaden with White Sugar, Cocoa, and Negroes; the which Ship, (by the Testimony of the Sailors that did belong to her) was a *Dutch Guinea* Trader, that lay at Anchor at the Island of *Dominico*, one of the *French* Carribbee Islands, and was there disposing of their Cargo of Slaves among the *French* of *Martinico*, in Exchange for *Sugar, Cocoa*, &c.

When one *Roberts* a Pirate took her at said Island, and after about two Months Possession of her, (at the Island of *Hispaniola*) gave the said Ship and Cargo to the abovesaid *Benjamin Norton*, who was then their Prisoner and had been taken by them some time before they took the aforesaid Ship.

And this Government being inform'd of said *Norton*'s Arrival at *Tarpawlin-Cove* with said Ship, and that he had broke Bulk, and put on Board several Sloops and Boats, several Negroes, and great quantities of Sugar and Cocoa; and also that several of said Slaves, and some of the said Sugar and Cocoa was Imported into this Colony, out of the said Ship, in a small Sloop belonging to *Newport*; His Honour the Governour immediately issued forth a PROCLAMATION, Requiring all Persons within this Colony, that had Received any of the said Negroes, Cocoa or Sugar, or was knowing to the same; should forthwith Discover and Deliver the same into the Hands of the Authority of this Government; And that on the Contrary, he or they so Concealing the same, should be Prosecuted as Accessories of PIRACY: Which PROCLAMATION was Published in every Town in the Colony, and a Warrant granted forth to the Sheriff, to Search for the same. WHEREUPON, Nineteen Negroes, Twenty Bags of Cocoa, and Seven Hogsheads of Sugar were deliver'd up to the Government, and by them Secured, until the Council and Assembly should give further Order for the same.

On the twenty seventh of *May*, during the Recess of the General Assembly, between their *May* Sessions, and Adjournment in *June*, Judge *Menzies* (without the Knowledge of this Government) opens his Court of Vice-Admiralty, and Decrees, That the twenty Bags of Cocoa, and seven Hogsheads of Sugar, were Forfeited to the KING, the GOVERNOUR and the Informer: But before any Copies were given of that Decree, the said Judge made another Decree, of the same Date, different from the Former, and orders the same to be Sold by Publick VENDUE, and the Price to be Lodged in the Collector's Hands, for the space of three Months; and if no Claimer in that time, then to be Forfeited. (As was ordered in his first Decree that was stifled) The Negroes likewise were ordered to be Sold, and the Price to be Lodged with the Collector; and if no Claimer within the time of three Months as aforesaid, then to be Forfeited to the Vice-Admiral, or as His Majesty should Determine; or to the King, the Governour, and the Collector: But before the time appointed for the Sale, the Judge makes two other Decrees of the same Date, (out of Court, and never Published) much different to the two former; wherein he orders the Price of the Cocoa and Sugar, to be Lodged twelve Months and a Day in the Collector's Hands, without any Claimer appear to Avouch the same, or to the Vice-Admiral, or others Authorized by His Majesty, or to the Informer, as in Case of Seizures. And failing of any such Claimers within the twelve Months, then the same was declared Lawful Seizure, and to belong to the King, the Governour and Collector. The Price of the Negroes was to be Lodged in Mr. *Augustus Lucas* his Hands, until the Judge should otherwise Determine: The which was to be conveyed out of the Colony, as the said *Lucas* did Declare some time after.

On the thirteenth of *June*, the Assembly Met according to Adjournment, and they being Inform'd of the Judge's indirect Proceedings, Recommended the Matter to the Governour and Council; desiring them to take the same into their Consideration, and to take such proper Measures as would be for the Profit of the Owners of said Goods, and the Credit of the Government.

The Governour and Council taking the Premises into their serious Consideration, and upon due Debate of the Matter, it was Voted, That whereas the Honourable *John Menzies*, Judge of the Court of Vice-Admiralty in this Colony, had without their Knowledge, Advice or Concurrence, Ordered, and Decreed, that the Disposition of the aforesaid Negroes, Cocoa and

Sugar as he thought fit, and to Convey the Price of the same out of the Colony, was a Contempt of the Government.

And the Governour and Council was at the same time informed, that in some of His Majesty's Governments in the *West India* Islands, Piratical Goods, *&c.* had in the like Nature (though not with the like Contempt) been Condemn'd and Disposed of by the Admiralty Courts, whereby the said Governments have, and are Exposed to Satisfy and make good the same.

It was therefore Resolved by the Governour and Council, That as Judge *Menzies* had acted in the aforesaid Premises without their Knowledge, Advice or Approbation, so they would have no Reference to what he had done; but to prevent his further Proceeding in the like Nature, gave Orders to the Sheriff, not to Deliver the Negroes, Cocoa and Sugar, without their Directions: And on the fifteenth of *June*, the Governour and Council Ordered, That the aforesaid Nineteen Negroes, Twenty Bags of Cocoa, and Seven Hogsheads of Sugar, being *bona peritura*,[1] should be Sold at Publick Vendue, on the twenty third of *June;* and that the Governour, Deputy Governour, and Collector of His Majesty's Customs, should Order the Conditions of Sale, and Receive the Price, to be Secured for One Year and a Day for the Claimers: And if none Appeared in that Time, till His Majesty's Pleasure should be known thereon.

On the twenty second of *June*, about Ten of the Clock before Noon, the aforesaid Judge *Menzies*, Mr. *Augustus Lucas*, Deputy Judge, and Mr. ——— *Boydell.* Register of said Court, came to the Governour's House, and soon after them, the Deputy Governour and three Assistants. (After the usual Complements) Judge *Menzies* said, That the Governour and Council had interrupted him in the Execution of his Office; and demanded the Delivery of the aforesaid Negroes, *&c.* and that he might Proceed according to his Decrees without Interruption: And then produced his Commission, and Read a Paragraph thereof Relating to Pirates, Amplifying upon the same; and one other Paragraph, wherein the Government was to give him Assistance in the Execution of his Office: After which Mr. *Boydell*, having a Paper in his Hand, Read it; wherein the Judge Required sundry Things, much as he had done by Word of Mouth, Upon which, the Governour Requested a Copy of what was Read, that he might be capable to Answer it: Judge *Menzies* Replied, That we had heard it, and that was sufficient.

The Governour told the Judge, That his Proceeding was without the Knowledge or Approbation of the Government; and that he design'd (as

1. ["Perishable goods."]

they were informed) to carry the Price, or Produce of the Negroes, *&c.* out of the Colony; and that the Government deemed themselves Responsible for the same: For which Reasons, they had taken Methods to Secure themselves, and Read a Copy of the Council's Order to the Judge. After which, the Judge requested the Governour to give him that Copy which had been Read: The Governour told him, it was a Copy he kept for his own Service; and that if he pleased, he might have a Copy from the General Recorder.

Then the Judge said, That the Price of the Negroes, *&c.* in case of no Owners, belong'd to the Vice-Admiral, and that he design'd to secure it for him. The Governour then asked the Judge, Who he deemed to be Vice-Admiral of this Colony? Who reply'd, His Excellency Colonel SHUTE. The Governour told the said Judge, that Matter had often been Debated, and particularly in Col. *Dudley*'s Administration, but it was never granted by this Government. Then the Judge Reply'd, For which Reason it was incerted in his Commission, and he deem'd himself to be Vice-Admiral here. The Governour told him, Tho' our Charter did not expresly say any thing about the Vice-Admiralty, notwithstanding he presumed there was the like Authority given, and that the Power of Vice-Admiral was vested in him, during his present Capacity, throughout the Jurisdiction of this Colony. The Deputy Governour told the Judge, that by our Charter, all Fines and Forfeitures were given to the Colony; and Read that Paragraph to the Judge, the which caused some needless Discourse, foreign to the Matter then before us; but it was not insisted upon, nor once mentioned, that the Price of the Negroes, *&c.* or any other Fines or Forfeitures belong'd to the Governour as Vice-Admiral. This is the Truth and the Substance of what pass'd at the Governour's House. About two of the Clock in the Afternoon, the Marshal of said Court delivered to the Governour from said Judge, a Paper wherein (after setting forth how he had Read his Commission under the *Great Seal* before the Governour, *&c.*) the said Judge Desires and Requires the Governour in his Majesty's Name, to deliver up the Negroes, *&c.* and that he might not be interrupted in the Sale thereof; and that the Court-House and Town School-House be ordain'd for the holding his Court, and that he might have Access therein at all seasonable Hours.

About four of the Clock *Post Meridiem* the same Day, the Governour return'd Answer to the Judge, That as he had done, so he should upon all Occasions, give all due Aid and Assistance, as well as Encouragement to him in the due Execution of his Office, according to his Commission, so far as he kept within the Bounds and Limits of the same, and did not Intrench upon the Liberty and Property of this His Majesty's Colony: And for what he Required in the several Paragraphs, he had no Authority as Governour to make any Answer to the same, until he had advised with the Council and Assembly, and received their Instructions thereon. That as to the Court-House and Town School-House, he had not the Disposing of either; but that as he had not met with any Obstruction therein, so he presumed he would meet with no other Treatment for the Future: PROVIDED he did not meddle nor set up any Court there that should any ways Intrench upon the Acts and Orders of the General Assembly, or General Council; in which Cases, he was advised to Obstruct his Accession into either of said Houses.

Judge *Menzies* made no further Application for the said Houses, but opens his Court at a Publick House; and on the same Day, passes a Fourth Decree about the Cocoa and Sugar, and at the same time Decrees the Surveyor and Searcher to pay a Fine of *Ten Pounds*, for not giving him a sample of the Cocoa and Sugar, which was in the Possession of the Sheriff.

On the twenty third of said *June*, early in the Morning, a Citation came out against the Deputy Governour and Collector, citing them to appear before him to answer for some Contempt (as he said) by them committed against his Court, upon the Penalty of *Fifty Pounds* each. The Governour being inform'd thereof, advised with such of his Council as was near at Hand, and it was thought Advisable to grant forth a Prohibition, to prohibit the said Judge from proceeding in Opposition to, and Contempt of the Governour and Council's Acts and Orders. A Prohibition was thereupon drawn up, and Read in the Presence of the Judge and his Officers, (by the Sheriff) before the Judge opened his Court that Day. Notwithstanding the said Prohibition, the Judge opened his Court and in Contempt of said Prohibition, Decreed that the Deputy Governour and Collector should each of them pay a Fine of *Fifty Pounds* for their Contempt, as is set forth in said Decree: And upon passing said Decrees, he immediately mounted his Horse, and Rode the *Back Way* out of Town in a *Violent Rain, {inked out}*—At two of the Clock in the Afternoon of said Day, the Negroes, Cocoa and Sugar, were Exposed to Sale at Publick Vendue, pursuant to the Council's Order; and in a few Hours was all Sold at a good Price, and is Secured according to the Governour and Council's Order.

After the Judge's Departure, the Governour was informed, That the Deputy Register was seen to cut a Leaf out of the Register Book. The Governour upon the said Information, sent for the said Deputy Register, and upon his Examination, he readily confessed that he had cut a Leaf out of said Book by the Judge's Order. The Governour then demanded of the said Deputy Register, the Copies of all the said Judge's Decrees about the Negroes, Cocoa and Sugar; and in two or three Days after, the said Deputy Register delivered several Copies to the Governour; who upon Examination, and Perusal thereof, found that the first and second Decrees were missing, with the first Conditions of Sale. The Governour then Demanded Copies of them also; to which the Deputy Register answered, That he had given his Honour Copies of all the Decrees that he had Registred in his Office, and that he could give no other. The Governour then told the Register, that the Collector had Copies of the second Decrees Attested by him. (The first as the Governour was informed, was stifled before any Copies were given out) The Deputy Register made answer, He might make the best of them he could, for they were not Registred in his Book; so that the Governour could not obtain the said Copies any other ways than from the Collector's Copies; by which it may justly be presumed, that the Judge's first and second Decrees were cut out of the Register Book; for he that will cut out one Leaf, will not scruple to cut out more to serve the like Turn.

This is a true and exact NARRATIVE of the Governour and Council's Proceedings, relating to Judge *Menzies*, about the Negroes, Cocoa and Sugar, which the said Judge has so Unfairly and Erroniously set forth by way of *Advertisement* in the *Boston News-Papers;* to the which in the next place is answered.

1st. Judge *Menzies* in his said *Advertisements,* Charges the Governour and Council, That they Illegally and Unwarrantably Obstructed his Sale of the aforesaid nineteen Negroes, Cocoa and Sugar, expresly contrary to His Majesty's Commission, *&c.*

Answer. The Governour and Council were at great Trouble, Charge and Expence, in Recovering and Securing the said Negroes, *&c.* for the Lawful Owners, or in Default thereof, as His Majesty should Dispose of the same; and that Judge *Menzies* was never possess'd of the said Negroes, *&c.* nor did he ever apply himself to the Government for their Advice, Approbation or Concurrence therein; but on the contrary, in an Arbitrary and Contemptuous manner, Condemns the same, in such manner as his several Decrees set forth; thereby to Defraud the Owners, and impose upon the Government, (by Clandestinely conveying the Price out of the Colony) who deemed themselves Responsible for the same, in case of any Imbezelments, which they had just Grounds to suspect was design'd; so that we presume it will appear, that Judge *Menzies* has illegally and Unwarrantably intruded upon the Government, and Erroniously Represented them.

2dly. Judge *Menzies* in his *Advertisement,* charges the Governour and Council with refusing him a Copy of their Act, when demanded by him, on Pretence that the Ordering and Disposing of such things did belong to them by their Charter; and that the Governour as Vice-Admiral, has a Right to the Value thereof, *&c.*

Answ. The Governour Affirms to the Contrary, that the Judge was not denied a Copy; but that he told the Judge in his own House, that he might have a Copy out of the Recorder's Office: But the Deputy, as he has inform'd since, did say, That if the Judge would not give a Copy of his Demands (by Words) in Writing, that he ought not to have a Copy of the Council's Act. However, if that had been Concurr'd with by the Governour and Council, (as it was not) it would not have amounted to a Denial, as the Judge unfairly Affirms: Neither was there any Pretence made by the Governour and Council, that the Ordering and Disposing of such, belonged to them by their Charter; or that the Governour had a Right to the same as Vice-Admiral: Neither was any such thing insisted on, any other ways than Transiently by the Deputy Governour as is aforesaid.

3dly. The Judge Affirms in his *Advertisement,* That *John Wanton* and *Nathaniel Kay* Esqrs; had ordered two Parts of the Produce of said Negroes, *&c.* to be Lodged in their own Hands, and the third to be given to the Governour.

Answ. The Council requested the Governour to Receive the whole Price and Secure it, as was ordered; but the Governour Refusing, without some other was joined with him, the Council therefore to gratify the Governour, added the Deputy Governour and Collector with him; so that his asserting that *Wanton* and *Kay* gave the Governour one third part, is False and Scandalous.

4thly. The Judge says this Day and the Day preceeding, (but does not say in what Month or Year) the Doors of the Court-House were shut, and the Judge of the Admiralty (it would have been Decent to have said Vice-Admiralty) denied Access thereunto, unless he would comply with their Acts of Council.

Answ. This Article is very unfairly and unhandsomely Represented; for the Judge had no positive Denial of Access into the Court-House, but as the Governour intimated to the Judge, as I afore Rehearsed, (*viz.*) That if he the said Judge held any Court in said House, any ways to Meddle or Intrench upon the Acts or Orders of the General Assembly, or General Council, in that case he was advised to deny him access. Besides, the Court-House Doors were shut every Day, but in the times of the Sitting of the Courts, or some Publick Meetings; so that it is no ways strange to have the Door shut two Days together.

Wo unto them that Decree unrighteous Decrees, and write Grievousness which they have Prescribed.

Sign'd by Order of the Governour and Council.

R. Ward, Secretary.

· 22 ·

David Lloyd, A Vindication of the Legislative Power (1725)

David Lloyd (1656?–1731) was a leading politician in colonial Pennsylvania. Born in Wales, he met William Penn while studying law in England in the early 1680s. Penn asked him to provide legal assistance to the fledgling colony, and then appointed him Attorney General of Pennsylvania in 1686. In 1693, Lloyd was elected to the colonial assembly where he took the lead in opposing Pennsylvania's involvement in the empire's war against the French. As Attorney General, he opposed the Vice Admiralty courts, comparing them to Charles I's hated ship money. For his opposition to royal authority, Penn stripped Lloyd of all offices. From his seat in the assembly, Lloyd then pushed a politically weakened Penn into agreeing to the Charter of Privileges in 1701, which made Pennsylvania a unicameral polity, and led to a long dispute between Lloyd and Penn's Secretary, James Logan.

In the 1720s, another constitutional dispute broke out, this time between Governor Keith and James Logan, over the latter's opposition to a paper money bill which the governor saw as a remedy for a severe economic downturn, and which Lloyd had pushed through the assembly in 1723. On a visit to England in 1724, Logan received instructions from the Penn family commanding Keith to veto any further paper money bills, and not to approve any more laws without the consent of the council. When Keith criticized these instructions, Logan responded with a *Memorial* in which he defended the right of the Penn family to bind the colony's governor, and argued that the colony needed a council with legislative authority.

Unsatisfied with Keith's reply to Logan, Lloyd penned the *Vindication,* arguing that the Charter granted to Penn by Charles II was "the Fundamental Constitution" of the colony, and that it gave the proprietor the power to appoint a deputy to govern the colony, but not the power to limit his authority in any way by instructions, a point Lloyd buttressed with references to English case law. Lloyd also contended that the charter gave the "whole Legislative Authority" in Pennsylvania to the "Governour and the Representatives of the People," which meant that there was no legal basis for Logan's claim that the governor's council needed to approve all laws. Lloyd also argued that because the legislative power of the freemen of the province stemmed from the royal charter, it was not subject to alteration by the proprietor or his heirs. What's more, these rights were granted by the King to the original settlers in return for expanding his empire. To Logan's claim that the council should function as an upper house because it was made up of men of wealth who have an interest in the colony, Lloyd replied that "a mean Man of small Interest . . . may do more good to the State than a Richer or more Learned Man." Lloyd also accused Logan of collecting excessive rents on behalf of the proprietor; and of ignoring the colony's unique form of unicameral government in favor of the English model of King, Lords, and Commons.

Despite the assembly sending an address to the Penn family defending Keith in 1725, the governor was dismissed by the Penn family the next year, and the Privy Council vetoed the colony's paper money acts. (C.B.Y.)

A Vindication of the Legislative Power, Submitted to the Representatives of all the Free-men of the Province of Pennsylvania, now sitting in Assembly.

May it please this Honourable House,

Having perused *James Logan*'s Memorial and other Papers lately published by your Authority, I find the Governour hath vindicated the Powers of our Legislature and the method you are now in, with such convincing Arguments, urged with so much clearness and good reasoning, that it seems needless to say any more; yet, I hope, it will be no offence to offer some legal Authorities to prove what has been so Excellently advanced in favour of the Rights and Liberties of the Subject, as well as the regular Powers and Franchises of Government in the Points now under Consideration.

It is Evident to me, that the Royal Charter granted to our late Proprietary *William Penn,* under the great Seal of *England,* may safely be deemed the Fundamental Constitution of our Legislative Authority, by which Charter the late King *CHARLES* the second, in a very gracious and bountiful Manner, was pleased to signify his Royal Will and Pleasure in these Words, *to wit,*

> *That we,* reposing special Trust and Confidence in the Fidelity, Wisdom, Justice and provident Circumspection of the said *William Penn,* for Us, Our Heirs and Successors, *Do Grant* free, full and absolute Power by Virtue of these presents, to him and his Heirs, to his and their Deputies and Lieutenants, for the good and happy Government of the said Country, to Ordain, Make and Enact, and, under his and their Seals, to publish any Laws whatsoever, for the raising of Money for the Publick uses of the said Province, or for any other End, appertaining either unto the publick State, Peace or Safety of the said Country, or unto the private Utility of particular Persons, according unto their best Discretion, *By and with* the Advice, Assent and Approbation of the Free-men of the said Country, or the greater part of them, or of their Delegates or Deputies, *Whom,* for the Enacting of the said Laws, when and as often as need shall require,

> We will, That the said *William Penn* and his Heirs shall Assemble in such sort and form as to him and them shall seem best.

By Virtue of this Clause the Proprietor had Power to make Deputies and Lieutenants, in which Case (as it is in all other Cases where a Deputy may be appointed) the Law says, he has full Power to do any act or thing which his Principal may do: And that is so essentially incident to a Deputy, that a Man cannot be a Deputy to do any single act or thing, nor can a Deputy have less Power than his Principal, and if his Principal make him *Covenant, That he will not do any particular thing which the Principal may do,* the Covenant is void and repugnant; as if the Under-Sheriff Covenant, that he will not Execute any process for more than *Twenty Pounds* without special Warrant from the High-Sheriff; this is void, because the Under-Sheriff is his Deputy, and the Power of the Deputy cannot be restrained to be less than that of his Principal, save only that he cannot make a Deputy, because it implies an Assignment of his whole Power, all which was adjudged by the Court of King's Bench, the 13 *William* 3. in the Case of *Parker* and *Kett,* where the Debate arose concerning the Steward of a Mannor-Court.

The Case of the Under-Sheriff here cited by *Holt,* is reported by the late Lord Chief Justice *Hobart* thus, *viz.* If a Sheriff will make an Under-Sheriff, *Provided* that he shall not serve Executions above 20 *l.* without his special Warrant, this *Proviso* will be void: For, tho' he may chuse whether he makes an Under-Sheriff at all, or may make him at his will, and so remove wholly, yet he cannot leave him an Under-Sheriff, and yet abridge his Power, *no more than the King may in Case of the Sheriff himself:* But it was said, that the Case here was not so, that the restraint of Executions above 20 *l.* grew not on the part of the Sheriff, but on the part of the Under-Sheriff by his Covenant, which might stand for good, notwithstanding the repugnancy to his Office; but the Covenant here was holden void, as being against *Law* and *Justice.* For since by being made Under-Sheriff, he is liable by Law to Execute all Process he could, no more than the Sheriff himself, Covenant not to Execute Process without another's special Warrant, for that is to *deny or delay justice.*

This last Case was that which Governed the opinion of the Council (when Judge *Mompesson* assisted) to declare that part of Col. *Evans's* Commission void, which reserved to the Proprietor the final Assent to all such Bills as he passed into Laws in this Province. Therefore, I admire how

James Logan (being not only present at those Debates, but either drew up or copy'd and signed that solemn Resolution of the Council, and knows how it was approved of by the Assembly at the same time) can so strenuously insist upon the Restriction now in Debate, which is as much against Law and Justice as the Instances in the above quoted Cases could be.

The next thing observable in the above recited Clause of the Royal Charter, is the Right and Power of Legislation, granted to the Proprietor and his Heirs and to his and their Deputies and Lieutenants, by and with the Assent of the Free-men of this Province; which being expressed as amply as any Liberty or Privilege of that kind can be granted, I am induced to conclude, that, by Virtue of this Grant, there was such a Right originally vested and become inherent in every Free-man of this Province as wanted not the help of any Grant or Charter from the Proprietary to confirm it.

But the Proprietor, pursuant to the said recited Clause, made Charters which prescribed the form of Assembling the Free-men to act in Legislation after the Modes mentioned in the Memorial; and it may be the People were regardless of a new Charter after the Resignation of the first, not out of any liking they had to be convened by Writs, but as the Right of Meeting together to make Laws was virtually in them by the said Royal Grant, so the form of their Elections and Assembling might be settled by Law, which was effected afterwards by an Act to Ascertain the number of Members of Assembly and to regulate Elections, which passed in the fourth Year of Queen *Anne*'s Reign, and settled yearly Elections of Representatives in Assembly without Writs, and appointed the Time when and by whom those Elections should be made, as also the Time of the Assembly's Meeting, and how they should qualify themselves to act, choose their Speaker, and be Judges of the Qualifications and Elections of their own Members, sit upon their own Adjournments, appoint Committees, prepare Bills in order to pass into Laws, *Impeach Criminals* and redress Grievances *&c.*

By this Law and last Charter (wherein the Proprietary, according to his Right made one side of the agreement, which he could not alter or avoid without the Concurrence of the parties concerned on the other side) it is evident, That the whole Legislative Authority here is lodged in the Governour and Representatives of the People; and I have met none so senceless as to say, that the Governour is thereby concluded or having a Council to advise and assist in Legislation and other matter relating to the State, and I have known divers of the Members of that Board very serviceable in that Station, and, I doubt not, may be so still, therefore I desire they may not withdraw from their Service nor insist upon a Negative to the Acts of those that Represent them, which, by a reasonable Construction of the said Law and Charter, is lodged with the Governour, and is so vested in him by his Commission stamped with the Royal Allowance and Authority of the King's Letters Patent, That the Proprietary could by no Instruction or other Act whatsoever, without the Governour's Consent, divest him of his Right to Govern, unless by resuming the Government or Deputing another in his stead. And if the Governour has given any Bond or Covenant to observe Instructions that abridge or restrain the Authority granted him by Commission to Exercise the Powers of Government in this Province, the same is void, as appears by the above cited Resolutions, from whence it may be observed how careful the Law is to keep Powers entire, as the best means to preserve good Order in States and Governments, where no such absurdity can be admitted, as to allow the Persons Represented to controul the Acts of their Representatives, especially in those Matters which the other Branch of the Legislature may think to be reasonably Proposed.

And altho' the Law declares, that Bonds and Covenants (given to Guard the Principal, when he would diminish or abridge the Power of his Deputy) are Repugnant to his Office, and therefore void and against Law, having a tendency to deny or delay Justice (as in our Case) yet, if the Governour came under any Security to observe the Directions of the King's Grant, which forbids to depart from the Faith and Allegeance due to the King, or to maintain Correspondence with his Enemies, or to commit Hostility against such as are in League with him, or Transgress against the Laws of Trade and Navigation, or for discharging of his Trust and Duty in the Administration of the Government according to the purport of the said Royal Grant and the Laws and Constitutions of this Province; I conceive that in those Cases such Security is binding upon the Governour and will be most effectual and available in Law, unless some illegal or repugnant Condition be annexed thereunto.

As to the Power of making Ordinances with the assistance of other Persons than the People's Delegates, it appears by the Patent, that those Ordinances cannot be Extended, in any sort, to bind change or take away the Right or Interest of any Person or Persons for or in their Life, Members, Free-hold, Goods or Chattels, nor are they directed to be made except sudden Accidents happen, whereto it may be necessary to apply

Remedy, before the Free-holders or their Delegates can be assembled to make Laws,—Besides our Law-makers (who ought to have Notice of such Occasions) may be convened as soon as the Magistrates and Officers of the respective Counties, who are to assist in making Ordinances: But if the Ordinance-makers should happen to get the start, yet when the Delegates of the People come together and acquaint the Governour of their readiness to assist him in the publick Service of the Government, and to answer the Exigences thereof, I think the Power of making Ordinances should then be waved, and the Legislative Authority applyed to, because their Acts are deemed more Extensive and Binding, as appears by the express Words of the said Patent.

But if the Governour could be prevailed with not to Summon the Assembly upon such Emergency, or when Assembled would not Concurr with them in what may be for the Publick Good, as the Case was, when former Governours, being under an ill direction, withstood the Representatives proposals and cordial Advice, and (contrary to Law and Charter) set up Ordinances instead of Laws, to the great dissatisfaction of the Assembly then attending who declared themselves ready and willing to Concurr in a regular Establishment, according to the Laws and Practice of *England*, instead of what was Imposed by Ordinance, which highly concerned the Lives, Liberties and Estates of the Subjects; There are divers Worthy Members of this House have been well acquainted with these Proceedings, and if it were not so, yet the Journal of that Time will manifest what I hint.

It may do well for the Secretary to Consider, with what views he acted his part in that Tragedy; and whether it was not designed to render the People's Power in Legislation useless whereby this Country, from a State of Freedom, should be changed into an Arbitrary Government, subjected to the Power of one Person, as the Secretary in another case materially observes. I am apt to think by what I gather from this Memorial and some more of these Printed Papers, that the ready way to bring us under this Change must be by enjoyning a Negative upon the Governour and Assembly, and checking the Freedom of Communication between them by Speeches and Messages, and then get a new Council, (for the present Members of that Honourable Board will not give in to this Arbitrary Scheme) who must be such as will assent to all the Secretary proposes, and when a Council Board is thus furnished, any Body (without much Penetration) may guess who that *one person* must be.

It is further to be observed, that altho' the main scope of the Memorial is against the plain Rules of Law and Justice, yet the Author would seem to applaud *English* Government, by King, Lords and Commons, supposing that to be the Plan by which the Governments of the King's Plantations are Modeled, and from thence, or from the conceit he has of his own Scheme, he takes Occasion to undervalue the Frame of our present Government, which the late Proprietary, with the Advice and Approbation of the People's Delegates in a most Solemn Manner settled, and of good Purpose and full intent Lodged the Powers of Legislation in the Governour and Representatives of all the Free-men of this Province in General Assembly; and not only so, but he vents his most abusive Reflections upon former Assemblies, and like an evil Minister and ungrateful Servant would insinuate, that the Proprietor's Intention did not Correspond with the express Words and real Design of his Charter of Privilege, and brings this for Instance, "That the Proprietor never intended to bind himself, nor ever in Fact did bind himself up from a Right to lay his Deputy under Restrictions in Legislation;" I think this point is so fully cleared by the foregoing Authorities of Law, that it may satisfy the Secretary himself of the Falshood of his Position; for if it were true (as I believe it is not) that the Proprietor, by his Charter Grants, did not intend to be bound by the Rules of Law (which must be the main Support of all his Powers) it would render him Inconsistent with himself, and prove him unworthy of the Trust and Confidence which the King, by His Royal Grant, reposed in his Fidelity, Wisdom, Justice and Provident Circumspection. I find the Council is taken Notice of in the Charter of Privileges to some purposes, but not to share in the Legislative Power, yet I know none would be against their Advice and Sentiments upon Bills brought up to the Governour, for that they are Men embark'd in the same Interest with the People, and for the most part aim at the publick Good, but not for the Reason given by the Secretary, *to wit,* That they "have as large an Interest in the Colony, as the like number of any others." It is probable he may see a Service in the Comparison, which I cannot penetrate, but, according to my Experience, a mean Man of small Interest, devoted to the faithful discharge of his Trust and Duty to the Government, may do more good to the State, than a Richer or more Learned Man, who by his ill Temper and aspiring Mind becomes an opposer of the Constitution by which he should act.

However since an Interest in the Colony is pointed out as a Qualification to act for the good of the Publick, it may be supposed, that the Members of

Assembly will think it as reasonable, that the Governour may be referred to the Approbation of their House, consisting of some Ancient Settlers, who have a good Competency, and others, who are descended from such as brought considerable Estates into the Province, and went through great Difficulties in the first Settlement of this Wilderness, to the hazard of their Lives and Estates, amongst the Indian Natives, and spent their Strength and Substance in Emproving the Country, and by their indefatigable Industry upon the Land, which, you know, would have been of little worth to the Proprietary or any Body else, if Divine Providence had not Blessed the Labours of the first Settlers and succeeding Inhabitants, who made this City and Province of Value to the Proprietary and his Family, and afforded a Competency to themselves, who in the Enjoyment thereof, with the aditional favours of Peace and Plenty under a mild Administration, have great reason to lay the good of the Publick and it's true Interest as close to Heart as any others.

And if we Consider this and much more that may be truly said in favour of first Adventurers and Settlers of this Province, and observe what regard the King had to them in His Royal Charter, and how they are made Sharers with the Proprietary in the greatest Rights, Liberties and Privileges thereby Granted, without the least Encroachment upon his Precedency, I think it will clearly appear that the second Paragraph in the Memorial would have been expressed with more Decency and Truth, if the Author had directly allowed the King to be the first Founder of this Province, and rend[e]red the Privileges granted, immediately to flow from him (the Fountain of Justice) as well to the People as the Proprietary, for it is evident, that the King was very well apprized, and so was the Draughts-Man of the Excellent Charter, That this part of the *English* Empire could not be Enlarged, nor the true Design of the *Grant* answered, without due Encouragement to the Adventurers, which was never urged or wittingly insisted on in Diminution of any Rights, Royalties or Powers of any kind really and truly belonging to or reserved by the Proprietor: Therefore under these and the like Considerations, "the Wisdom of this House (as the learned Author observes to another purpose) will never suffer Notions infused into the Populace, by designing Men, nor any of those Notions have Truth, Justice, and clear Right on their Side."

I cannot leave this Subject without observing, that the first Purchasers bought their Lands dear, and came under perpetual Quit-Rents, which far exceeded what the Proprietors of the adjacent Provinces required of their Tenants: But when they came up to be handled in Secretary Logan's Office, they were told they must pay Half a Crown or a Crown *English* Money for every City Lot forever which the Proprietary had freely given to his Purchasers, expecting, as was thought, but *Twelve Pence* Sterling *per Annum,* for every Hundred Acres of their Lands; and when they came for their Patents there was a Reservation of three full and clear fifths parts of all Royal Mines, free from all Deductions and Reprisals for Digging and Refining the same; Whereas the Royal Charter had reserved but one fifth part of such Mines, clear of Charges. You may find by your Journal divers other Instances of the Secretary's Abuses and ill Treatment of the People, to which, for brevity sake, I refer.

But in the Nineteenth Paragraph of his Memorial he reflects, pretending that the Lieutenant Governour was referred to the Proprietary's Quit-Rents for his Support. And in the Twenty ninth Paragraph he says, the Proprietor in his Absence never received *one Penny* to himself or his Family from the Government, tho' others had large Sums. Now if this has any meaning it must be concluded, That Colonel *Evans* was deny'd Support and our present Governour has had large Sums from the Government, if so, then it plainly shews the difference between acting as a free agent in affirmance of our Constitution by Law and Charter, and submitting to an ill Management Distructive to the whole.

I have by the foregoing paragraphs, as briefly as I could, considered the real State of our Case, with respect to the Powers of the Kings Letters Patent, with the Law and Charter of the Province, and humbly offer to this Honourable House my real Sentiments upon the whole relying upon the Cases I cited, all which I freely submit to better Judgments. There is something in the latter part of the Memorial that shews an Inclination in the Author, That the Case may be fairly and impartially Stated from all the Grants that can be pleaded, and be referred to some of the King's learned Council in Law: For my part I wish that were done, and indeed if those that formed the late Instructions had done so, it would have saved a great deal of Trouble which they unhappily Occasioned, besides the ill Blood it brought amongst many of the Inhabitants.

There are some other things which I could not avoid taking Notice of, as the Memorialist's apparent design against the Constitution of this Government, and disregard to the just Merit of the first Adventurers, who embarked on the Administration of the Government and first Settlement of this Country at their own Charge, as also the Taunts and Neglect of all Duty towards the present Inhabitants, which seem to be diffused all over his *{illegible}*, and so are the Imputations that he unfairly throws at former Assemblies, which, with the Enormities there offered to our Governour by an affrontive Treatment, I leave to the Censure of this Honourable House, where such matters are properly Cognizable. And so I conclude,

Your Real Friend,
DAVID LLOYD

Philadelphia, the 19th of the Month called March, 1725

· 23 ·

James Logan, The Antidote (1725)

JAMES LOGAN (1674–1751) was William Penn's secretary in Pennsylvania, a member of the provincial council, and a noted scholar. He resisted the rising power of the provincial assembly under David Lloyd, fought to have the council serve as an upper house, and vigorously asserted the proprietorial rights of the Penn family to land in the province. His opposition to the assembly earned him the enmity of Lloyd who tried to have him impeached in 1707.

In the early 1720s, Logan and Lloyd clashed again over whether the Penn family could instruct the colony's governor, William Keith, to oppose the assembly's plans to issue paper money, despite Keith's approval of the policy. The family also ordered Keith to treat the colony's council as a legislative body, and not pass any laws without the support of a majority of the councilors. When Keith criticized these instructions in a speech to the assembly, Logan replied with a *Memorial*, to which Keith responded. When Lloyd weighed in on Keith's side (see Selection 22), Logan published *The Antidote* in which he contended that Lloyd's claim that principals (like the Penn family) could never bind deputies (like Governor Keith) was based on an erroneous reading of English case law.

Rather, in areas where the principal has some legal discretion, he can, Logan maintained, bind his deputy; and this was the case with the colony's proprietor who, according to the royal charter, is "to apply Justice, Wisdom, and provident Circumspection" in governing Pennsylvania. To Lloyd's claim that the colonial council was a merely advisory body, Logan replied that the council in Maryland sat as an upper house, and that it was also a proprietary colony whose charter had "exactly the same" wording about the legislative power of the people as Pennsylvania's. What was more, such a council would provide the colony with a further check on arbitrary power. As for Lloyd's argument that the settlers in Pennsylvania had risked their lives to expand the king's empire and thus should not have to pay perpetual quit rents to the proprietor, Logan said that he had "not heard of One English Life lost, by any Act of Hostility" in the founding of the colony, adding that the rents in the colony were lower than those levied elsewhere in America. In any case, the original settlers had agreed to pay these rents in return for a better life across the ocean.

Although Lloyd replied to Logan's *Antidote* in another pamphlet, the dispute over paper money ended the following year (1726) when the Penn family removed Keith as governor, and the Privy Council vetoed the paper money acts that Lloyd and Keith had championed. (C.B.Y.)

The Antidote.

In some Remarks on a Paper of David Lloyd's, called A Vindication of the Legislative Power. Submitted to the Representatives of all the Freemen of Pennsylvania.

[*Si mihi pergit quae vult dicere, ea, quae non vult audiet,* Terent.[1]]

An Extraordinary Step in Politicks having been made here last Winter, the Matter was drawn into a Controversy, which notwithstanding the Design in bringing it on the Stage, was managed with an Appearance of Decency towards the late Proprietary and his Family; till our present Chief Justice David Lloyd, finding one Side of Dispute carried an Air of Opposition to that Interest, which he had for many Years past taken too much Pleasure in opposing: He could not, it seems, let slip the agreeable Occasion, without indulging his Inclinations in a Performance, to which, whether he had any justifiable Call, will appear from the following Remarks on it.

The Case itself is this,

The Proprietary, in appointing his Deputies in Government, ever gave them Instructions for their Conduct, which were nearly the same to each successively, since his last Return to England; and from our present Governour a Bond was taken for the Observance of those to Him, of which the Principal were these, To suppress Vice, and discourage Faction: To be advised by the Council in all Things of Moment: Not to intermeddle in Affairs of the Proprietary's Lands: To preserve a good Understanding with our Neighbors and Indians: To guard the Religious Rights of the People, and above all, to Maintain Liberty of Conscience: And some of these, especially in relation to the Concurrence of the Council, from an Occasion given, were lately prefs'd further, in certain private Instructions, which by the Governour's communicating them to the Assembly, have been published to the World. This Piece of Conduct produced from me a Memorial to the

1. ["If he continues to say to me those things which he wishes, he will hear those things which he does not wish to hear."]

Assembly; and this Memorial an Answer to it from the Governour. David Lloyd was so highly pleased with the Performance in this latter, that, to express his Satisfaction and perhaps in Return to the Complement pass'd upon him, when on Occasion of these Debates, he was term'd our Oracle of the Law, he thought fit to step out as a Champion for the Cause, and from the Treasures of his Profession, to undertake by Legal Authorities, as he calls them, to make it appear, that It was not in the Proprietarys Power to lay his Deputy under any Restriction: That the Governour cannot be bound by any Instructions, save what relate to his Allegiance, the Acts of Trade, and the Constitution: (So that even in Affairs of the Proprietary's Lands and Rents, he is free to assent to what Acts he pleases) and that the Obligation taken by the Proprietary, for his Securety, is against Law, and utterly void. And then he advances to treat the Proprietary himself so injuriously, and load him with such Reflections, that it may justly raise our Astonishment, how a Person cloth'd with a Profession, which ought to imply that lovely Spirit of Meekness and Charity, which makes the true Characteristic of the Christian Religion, should for so long a Tract of Time, foster the contrary Spirit of Revenge, and breath it out against the injured Object of his Resentments, not only during Life, but now for seven Years after his Decease. A Persecution unknown even to ancient Pagans, whose Sayings on this Head ought to load some Christians with Confusion.

To that Performance, tho' in Appearance principally pointed against me, as well as to others of the same kind, I resolved to be silent; having been long satisfied on my own Account that Time seldom fails to do Justice to Truth in such Cases, and that while my Benefactors own me Grateful; while my Employers after Twenty-Five Years Experience acknowledge me Faithful; while my Creditors confess my Justice, and all Attempts against my Reputation, in Point of Honesty, return only on my Acusers Heads, it is not worth my Time, to be at any Pains in my own Vindication, to those who advise with their Consciences, in forming their Judgments; and the Sentiments of others, I shall ever disregard. But having been lately assured in the County of Chester, that the Author has endeavour'd there to recommend himself as a Patriot, by that Paper and to diffuse the Venom of it amongst the People, I think it my Duty to give it a proper Antidote, by shewing, that his Law is misapplied, his Reasoning false, his Reflections on the Proprietary, unmerited and unjust, and that the whole Performance, instead of being a Service to the Publick, is truly a Dishonour to the Government.

To begin with his Legal Authorities, offered, as is pretended, in Favour of the Rights and Liberties of the Subject, and the Regular Power and Franchises of Government, yet wholly confined within the narrow Limits of this single Point, That a Deputy cannot be restrained by his Principal; he produces only two reported Cases; the first, in their natural Order and in Time, is from Hobart, page 12. where Sir. D. Norton High Sherif, appointing one Chamberlain his Deputy, took a Bond with Security, to indemnify his Principal from Escapes, &c. with this farther Condition, that the Deputy should not execute any Extent, &c. for above the Value of Twenty Pound without Notice first given to the High Sherif, and a Special Warrant obtained of him for the same.

The Sherif sued the Bond on an Escape, and had Judgment by the whole Court, on that very Bond, which therefore with D. L.'s Leave, was not declared void but that Part of the Condition by which the Deputy was restrained from executing Writs, &c. above a certain Value, was declared so, for these plain Reasons, as they naturally arise from the Report, viz. That a Sherif, being in relation to the Service of Writs, &c. only a Ministerial Officer, he must execute all the Legal Writs, that are brought to him, in which the King himself cannot abridge his Power: That having appointed a Deputy, that Deputy is under the same Obligations, and cannot be restrained by the High Sherif, any more than the High Sherif can be restrained by the King. And that this is highly reasonable, as well as 'tis Law, is what every rational Man must allow, for otherwise had the Sherif any such Power, he surely might deny or delay Justice.

This is an approv'd Case, and is universally allow'd, but what Relation it bears to the Matter in Question, is submitted to the Judgment of every impartial Man to determine. The other is an extraordinary One; and that it may be the better understood (if that be possible.) I shall here give it at large, in the Words of the Book, as it stands in Page 95. Of Salkeld's Reports, published in 1717. viz "Charles Kett being seized in Fee of a Copyhold, demised it to his Wife for Life, Remainder to Charles his Son in Tail, and if he died without Issue, under Age Remainder to Elizabeth his Wife in Fee. M. Keck the Master in Chancery was Steward of this Mannor by Patent, ad exercendum per se vel deputatum.[2] M. Keck appointed one Clerk to be his Deputy, who acted as such many Years, and was sent for by Chas.

2. ["For the purpose of carrying out the duty by himself or by a deputy."]

Kett, to take a surrender of the Lands. Clerk went not himself but by a Writing under his Hand and Seal, appointed A. and B. to be his Deputies joyntly and severally, only to take this Surrender, which was done by A. accordingly, and afterward presented and Elizabeth Kett the Defendent admitted thereupon by Clerk." Here the Point in Question, as far as it can be collected from the Report, which is exceeding imperfect, was, Whether A. Deputy to the Deputy Steward, had good Authority to take the Surrender? The Court judged he had, and in delivering their Opinion, Chief Justice Holt is said to have express'd himself in the Terms transcribed by D. L. in eight or Ten Lines of his Paper, in which these three Things are very surprizingly asserted, viz I That a Deputy has full Power to do any Act or Thing, which his Principal may do. II. That a Man cannot be a Deputy to do any single Act or Thing. III. That a Deputy cannot make a Deputy. Now unless, whatever is delivered to us, by the Name of Law, is to be implicitly believed, as a Matter of Faith, without the Use or Exercise of our Understandings, we may without Breach of Modesty, say, that all these Assertions are irreconcileable to the known Law of the Land, or to the Case itself, in the express Words of it. For to the Ist, 'tis well known, (and Judge Hobart, in the first Case, gives some Instances of it) that there are divers Things, which a Sherif (the Officer mentioned in both Cases) can and must do in his own Person, which his Deputy cannot do. 'Tis therefore not true, that a Deputy has full Power to do any Act or Thing, which his Principal may do, as this Book expressly has it. To the II.d, in the Case before us, "A and B are appointed by Clerk to be his Deputies jointly and Severally, only to take this Surrender, which was done by A. accordingly." And this by the Judgment of the Court was allowed to be good: Therefore, either this Judgment was wrong, or otherwise it is not true, That a Man cannot be a Deputy to do any single Act or Thing only. Besides, that Deputies may be appointed for one single Act or Thing, as well as Attornies are appointed to receive one particular Debt, to confess one Judgment, &c. is so clear, and well known, that it needs no Words to confirm it: And this very Case in the subsequent Reasoning, implies it. To the III.d, in the same Case, "Clerk Deputy to Keck appointed A. and B. his Deputies, and the Appointment was judged good: Therefore, either this Judgment was wrong in this also, or else it is not true, That a Deputy cannot make a Deputy. I can also shew him an indisputed Authority where it is said. That the Deputy of the Deputy is the Deputy of the first Officer, Altho' there be twenty, the one under the other, &c. But the

Law is not my Business, and I choose to argue only from D. L.'s own Quotations. He has therefore been extreamly unfortunate, in this printed Essay of his Skill, after a Practice of above Forty Years, in producing an Authority, in order to prove a certain Bond void, from a Case, in which Judgment was given for the Plaintiff, on the Bond there sued by him. And yet much more so, in bringing in for his main Support, another Case which, could his Eagerness for the Cause have allow'd him Time to consider it, he might easily have perceived is inconsistent (as the Words stand there fairly printed) with it self, with the Law, and with common Sense and Reason.

But it may be charged as a Presumption in one, who makes no Pretence to Skill in the Law, to question so great an Authority as Sir John Holts, deliver'd in a Book (in Appearance) so pompously recommended by the late Lord Chancellor and 12 Judges; And I should freely acknowledge it a Piece of Arrogance, if such a Person as I, should oppose the real Judgment of that great Man, tho' I find his opinion after learned Arguments, and long Discourses used on the Bench to support it, has sometimes been over-ruled by the other Judges; as in the Case of Lane v. Cotton, &c. in the same Book, Pag. 17. But the Opinion, as 'tis printed in the Case before us, is so exceedingly inconsistent, that I take it to be incumbent on us, in respect to that great Name, now to allow it to be His. Serjeant Salkeld, from the Character given of him in the Front of the Book, was undoubtedly an able Lawyer, but the Work itself is posthumous and published (in Confidence, it may be presumed, that the Elogium of the Man, might pass for one to the Book it self) without any Manner of Account, in what Condition these Reports were left by the Serjeant at his Death, by whom they were digested, or whether ever they were revised; all which is generally expected in posthumous Pieces, to prevent the World's being imposed on by Booksellers, or others, who resolve at any Rate to make a Penny by their Publications and most commonly by ostentatious Proposals for Subscriptions. But however this be, 'tis evident not only from this Case, but several others, that the Book wanted the last Hand or the Author. Now is this singular, for divers printed Cases have been afterwards adjudged not to be Law, and as Chief Justice Holt himself frequently observed of some others, that they were misreported in the Books. He could not but have pass'd the same Censure, and probably with more Resentment had He lived to see this published, as from Him with such Imperfections.

But as 'tis no uncommon Thing for Lawyers to be at a Plunge, not only with Book-Cases, but even with Statutes; The Rule then is to expound the

Law by the Reason of it, and this in our Case (if I mistake not) will render the Matter plain, viz. In all Cases, where the Principal has it not in his Choice, whether he will do an Act or forbear it, as a Sherif in the Execution of Writs, these his Deputy is equally obliged, and his Principal cannot restrain him; nor is there one intelligible Case in the Books (if I am rightly informed) that will carry this Point any further. But where the Principal is not obliged by the Course of the Law, to do any Act, or to do it in one Manner more than in another, but is to apply Justice, Wisdom, and provident Circumspection (The Words in the Royal Charter introductory to the Grant of Powers) in deliberating whether, or in what Manner, it is to be done; there I presume no Man of Skill and Integrity will pretend, that a Deputy, to such a Principal, may not be restrained by Instructions. Deputies are of various Kinds, and the Nature of their Office or Trust gives the Rules for them. Those for a Deputy Sherif are no more to be applied to a Lord Deputy of Ireland; than the Law of a Constable, to the Office of an Admiral. It springs from a Narrowness of Conceptions, peculiar to some Men, to argue from a Word or Name, without Regard to the Nature of the Thing in Question: And it would be equally absurd to apply the Rules for one Kind of Deputy (excepting that great one of Fidelity) to all others, because the Word every where consists of the same six Letters, as to argue from the Books, that because a Serjeant in Westminster, must appear at the Bar, in a white Coif, therefore Serjeants with Maces or Halberts, must present themselves in the same whimsical Dress, in their respective Duties and Stations. But from what honest Principal D. L. should on the late Occasion, think it incumbent on him, by his Judgment in the Case, to set the Governour at large from any Obligations, when he cannot but know the Law is, That for a Deputy, Respondeat Superior (the Principal must answer) or how he can answer in his Station, for giving any Judgment on a Bond, that is not yet before him, (which is just of a Piece with acting the Barrister on the Bench) I shall leave it to himself to account for to such as believe his Character gives them a Right to demand an honest Reason for the several Parts of his Conduct.

And having thus far done with his Law, to bring the Matter to a short Issue, I here engage to deposite two English Counsels Fees, against one from him, if he will venture on the Decision of the Learned there, that I have here interpreted the Law about Deputies right and that he has officiously mistook in his Judgment, for which Reason, among divers others, I presume, it will never in these Cases, be referr'd to.

In closing his Authorities, he says "It was the Case in Hobart which [in the Year 1704.] govern'd the Opinion of the Council (when Judge Mompelson assisted) to declare that Part of Colonel Evans's Commission void, which reserved to the Proprietor the final Assent to all such Bills as he passed into Laws, and therefore admires that I, who was not only present at those Debates, but either drew up or copied and signed that solemn Resolution, can so strenuously insist upon the Restriction now in Debate, &c." and on the other Hand, I cannot but admire, that he should either furnish the Governour with this, or produce it himself, as if it were at all to the Purpose, or that because he cited it to R. M. he could imagine the Council wanted a Law-Case to inform them, of what from the King's and Proprietor's Charters, before them, was so plain, that it could not possibly want such Explication.

But pray, what is that Opinion to the Point in Hand? The whole is printed in the Paper called, The Governour's Defence, &c. and is only this, that the saving there mention'd, was void in it self; but did not vacate the rest of the Commission; and that the Laws pass'd by Governour Evans, under the Great Seal, could not be annull'd by the Proprietary, without the Assembly. Now I would ask, by what Kind of Reasoning it will follow, that because, a Law, when pass'd under the Seal, cannot be annul'd by the Proprietary, but is binding upon Him, therefore (tho' all our Laws derive their Force from His Authority) He has no Right to direct in the passing of them, when the very Reason here given, shews the Necessity there is for his Caution. Which is much the same, as if it should be argued, that because Lands sold and convey'd by an Attorney, fully impower'd, are no longer the Constituent's, but the Purchaser's, therefore a Constituent has no Right to limit his Attorney: or because a Marriage consummated, cannot be annulled by Parents, therefore Parents have no Right to restrain there Children in Marriage: A kind of Reasoning that I confess, is well adapted to the Law we have had, and therefore I am pleased to see them come so naturally together.

I must here also mention another old Nostrum of D. L.'s, which he has laboured to inculcate, and of late with some Success, viz That because the Proprietary cannot make a Law without the Consent of the People (a Restriction which the happy English Constitution indispensibly requires) therefore no others can be concerned in Legislation, but the Proprietary himself or his Deputy, and the Representatives of the People; which has of late been largely insisted on, and to support the Opinion, the Words of the Royal Charter have been prolixly quoted: Upon which I shall here discharge, what I have been told, was incumbent on me, viz. To shew by what authority I look upon me, to expound those solemn Evidences for our Constitution in a quite different Sense (as 'tis said) from all others who have yet consider'd them, by frankly declaring that I never expounded these Words of the Charter in a Sense differing from any Man I ever knew, or heard of. D. L. and those who borrowed of him only excepted, That the Language in granting the Powers of Legislation, in the Royal Charter for this Province is exactly the same with that for other Proprietary Governments. That Maryland is the ancientest Government of that Kind now existing, that I know, as we are the latest; and that in Charter for that Province, the Words by which the Assent of the People in Legislation is required, are so exactly the same with those in the Charter for this Province, as the Copies lately printed here will fully show, that they have both been undoubtedly from the same Draught. And to close the whole, That, in Maryland, (as well as all the English Colonies, this only excepted) they have, and ever had a Legislative Council, upon the foundation of the same Words, and no other, which from our Charter are advanced to prove, it is not in our Power to have One. I am therefore not the only Person, who has expounded these Words in that Sense, because in our Great Grandfather's Days they were in the same manner expounded, and thro' several Generations, have continued the same to this Day. I would not however be thought desirous to renew that Argument, which by this Time is brought before its proper Judges; but I take this Occasion, as a very fit one to discharge so incumbent a Duty, which, I hope, will be receiv'd, as fully satisfactory, by those who imposed it.

What next ensues, is an Instance for such mean spirited Envy and Prejudice, that it would extort one's Pity; for speaking of our Constitution of Assemblies, tho' he well knows, that by the Royal Charter, their Manner of convening and whole Establishment, entirely on the Proprietary, yet lest any Honour should redound, or Gratitude be thought due to Him, he turns off the whole (in his 7th Paragraph) to an Act of Assembly passed in the 4th of Queen Anne, and from that Act declares the Privileges of our Assemblies, as if from thence they were deduced to us; When we must either suppose him exceeding ignorant in his Station, or else allow him to know, that from the Act he mentions, there is not one single Privilege derived; and that in these Points, It only repeats the Exact Words of the Proprietor's Charter, without the least Addition, Explanation, or Variation whatsoever, and if he knew this, what an Excess of Biass must it require, to translate that to another Merit, which was purely the Proprietary's gratuitous Grant in his Charter? Tho' had the whole been founded on such an Act, it would have argued the same Goodness in the Proprietary, exerted either by himself, or by that Deputy who pass'd the Act viz, Colonel Evans, whom he elsewhere treats so injuriously, tho' he pass'd not only That, but near as many others in Number, with One Assembly, and many of them very valuable, as have been enacted in this Province, in the Ten Years last expired. From the same Spirit, is also that trifling Cavil in his 16th Paragraph, at my terming the Proprietary the Founder of this Colony; a Title the Governour freely allow'd, in repeating it with a kind of Applause. But D. L. must omit no Occasion, it seems, of shewing that in these Cases, he cannot change. In the next Paragraph to this, viz the 17th, without any Manner of Occasion given, but from the Overflowings of his Heart, he pushes out his Reflections in a Torrent: The first of which is this, The first Purchasers (says he) bought their Lands dear, and came under perpetual Quit-Rents, which far exceeded what the Proprietors of the adjacent Provinces required of their Tenants. And if this were true, as 'tis, egregiously false, Pray what was that to D. L. who neither was one, nor was then perhaps in a Condition to be one of these Purchasers? The first adventures into America run extream Hazards, and paid dear for their Settlements with their Blood; those of the Virginia and Maryland having sometimes lost Hundreds, in a Battle with the Indians. But for some Years before the Grant of this Province, then almost surrounded with English Colonies, I have not heard of One English Life lost, by any Act of Hostility: Which therefore might justly make some Disparity in the Consideration, to be paid for Lands here; and yet we shall find this Difference lies just on the other side. In Maryland the first Quit-Rents were two Shillings Sterling in Gold or silver, for one Hundred Acres. Afterwards they were raised to Four Shillings: And if there has been a Relaxation, it was for the valuable Consideration, first of Two, and now of Three Shillings, paid to their Proprietary in Britain, for every Hogshead of Tobacco shipt in the Country for that Kingdom, which amounts to much more, than all the Quit-Rents ever did: Besides that they now also pay Purchase Money. In Virginia and New York, the Quit-Rent to the King, is Two shillings and six pence per Hundred Acres; and the Charges of the Grant (especially in the latter) equal a Purchase. In North and South Carolina, (Proprietary Settlements) they are a penny per Acre: In Jersey the whole Country being entirely sold off to certain Purchasers, they could reserve no Quit-Rents to themselves, but for the Lands granted, before the sale, to others, about Four Shillings per Hundred is required.

These are the terms in the Neighbouring Colonies; when in this Province, the Conditions were only Forty Shillings per Hundred Acres, and the Quit-Rent but one Shilling, which is so far from being the highest, as D. L. falsely affirms, that it is evidently the lowest that has been set in any of the Colonies round us. These, I say, were the Terms of the first Proprietor's Grants to the Purchasers: And when they were published, it was undoubtedly surprizing to see what Numbers, with Gladness accepted them in order to quit their native Soil, their Friends and Relations, and to trust themselves with their Families, on the boisterous Waters, to which most of them had been utter Strangers. No less than 32 Ships (as had been affirmed) came in the first two Years, freighted with Passengers and their Goods, to seat themselves in a Wilderness, under the Government and Conduct of that great and good Man, who maugre All that D. L. can offer to the contrary, will still be justly stiled the Founder, as he was the Father of this Colony. Then, delivered from the Severities of that Reign against Dissenters, and arrived in a Land, that upon reasonable Endeavours, yielded the agreeable Prospect of Plenty; Love united their Hearts dilated with Joy, and thro' a Desire, at least, to presage the best, viz the Continuance of it, the Capitol Town, as I have elsewhere observed, had the Name given it of Brotherly Love: then, Freedom to the people, with the full Enjoyment of the Faces and Company of their Friends, without Restraint, was sufficient Happiness. The Proprietor, with the vast inward Satisfaction, of having contributed to the Ease of such Numbers, saw himself surrounded, with grateful Hearts, and cheerful Countenances, the Acknowledgments they joyfully returned, for the Paternal Affection and Tenderness extended to them, by their Proprietor, Governour, and Friend, united in one Person. They were then, as the Israelites, after they had seen their wonderful Deliverance thro' the Red Sea, before any Corah or Dathan appeared, and so for some Time continued: But as those chosen People had some such amongst them, as charged their mighty Leaders with taking too much upon them, so Here, Instruments started up.—But I must end this Digression which I hope will be excused, as the natural Result of an honest Indignation, at the Vileness, and such Falshood and Malice, thrown out, without any Provocation, against the Deceased, whose Memory, the Europeans here (after the Example of the poor Native Indians) unless abandon'd to the foulest Ingratitude must forever Revere.

He goes on in the next Sentence to say, But when they came to be handled in Secretary Logan's Office they were told they must pay Half a Crown, or a Crown English Money, for every City-Lot for ever, which the Proprietor had freely given to his Purchasers, expecting, as was thought, but Twelve Pence Sterling per Annum, for every Hundred Acres of their Land. And here again, is an exact Match to the Preceding. The Proprietor granted Lands to the first Purchasers, by Deeds of Lease and Release, referring for the manner of Location, to certain Concessions, by which concessions it was agreed, that there should be laid out in the City Liberties, two Acres for each Hundred of the first Five Hundred Thousand Acres purchased. But of other Lots in the City, there was not the least Mention: For this the Proprietor most judiciously reserved to himself, that not only those Purchasers (tho' they had vastly the Preference) but all others who might incline to build in, and improve the Town might be accommodated. On laying out the City in 1682. the Rent was fully settled between the Proprietary and the Purchasers at Five Shillings for one Lot of 102 Foot in Breadth, the whole Length between the Front and Second-Street, and the same for 132 Foot in the High-Street, Two Shillings for 51 Foot on the West-Side of the Second-Street, and part of Chestnut-Street, and One Shilling for about 50 Foot in all the other Streets, then designed in the City Plot: But for these last, such as were no Purchasers (commonly called Renters) paid about 5.s. more or less. Now, where or how D. L. might then be passing his Time, is out of my Reach to guess; but sure I am, that I was scarce well out of Coats, when these Rents were not only settled, but most of the valuable Lots were confirmed on those Terms by Patent, under the Proprietor's own Hand, of which D. L. who had been a Conveyancer here, for at least twice Seven Years, and Deputy Recorder for many Years, before the Proprietary's last Arrival, could not possibly be ignorant. And when Eighteen Years after that Agreement, I came into the Office, I strictly pursued the same, to the best of my Knowledge in the few Lots, that then wanted Confirmation; or if I ever miss'd it, 'twas by Misinformation only. This Assertion therefore, that Half a Crown or a Crown Yearly was demanded from every City-Lot is so notoriously false, and the intended Insinuation against the Proprietary, so dishonourable that I shall say no more of it, than to leave those who can approve of such Publications, to make it up with their own Consciences; for the Author (I much doubt) is in these Cases past Reproof. No Man being more sensible than himself how trifling these Reservations are, when compared with the Value of the Lots; seeing he received from me, One Hundred and Seventy Five Pounds for one vacant Lot, for which the Proprietary had no other Consideration (besides his Benevolence to the first Purchasers) than two Shillings Sterling Yearly.

He still proceeds in the same Paragraph, to say, And when they came for their Patents, there was a Reservation of three full and clear fifth Parts of all Royal Mines, free from all Deductions and Reprisals for digging and refining the same. whereas the Royal Charter had reserved but one Fifth, &c. Sure D. L. would not have it thought, the Proprietor accepted of this Province from the King, in Trust only for others, without any Interest to himself: If not, why might he not reserve his own? Those Mines never pass in a Grant; but where they are expressly named. But they were named in none of the English Deeds, I ever saw; therefore what Part of them, the Proprietor was afterwards pleased to grant, appears to have been a Favour, and as such claims an Acknowledgment instead of a Reflection. And now having in this Paragraph, thrown plentifully about him, to give it the better Countenance, as if leveled at mę only; he winds it up with referring to the Journals of the House for divers other Instances of my Abuses and ill Treatment of the People; that is, such other Instances as the preceding: for I challenge the World to produce either from those Journals, or otherwise, one Instance of my having knowingly wrong'd any Man, either in my Publick or Private Capacity, since I first knew the Difference between Wrong and Right: And in this I cannot but think myself fortunate, that tho' I entred young into very great Trusts, which the Proprietary (neither by my Seeking, nor with the Approvation of my own Judgment) was pleased to repose in me, yet when my Fidelity to my Master turned his Enemies upon me, and my Reputation and Conduct was racked, as on the Tenters, and pryed and searched into, with the most rigid Scrutiny that ill nature could apply, all my Crimes were made up of such Articles as those now brought by D. L. in that invidious Paragraph, on the Stage.

In his next he says, I reflect, pretending the Lieutenant Governour was referr'd to the Proprietary's Quit-Rents for his Support. And surely I may well pretend it, when I can shew it under his own Hand. But on that just and plain Observation, in my Memorial viz, that "If Lieutenant Governours are not liable to any Restrictions," seeing the Proprietary in his absence, never received one Penny to himself, or his Family from the Government, tho' others have had large Sums; "it would be much more eligible and safe for the Proprietary, when He could not personally reside in the Province, to divest himself of the Government, and resign to the King, under whom He might be sure of such Orders, which must then be necessarily obey'd (tho' his own might not) as would effectually secure him against all Infractions on his Proprietary Rights." D. L. with a singular Turn is pleased to say, Now if this has any Meaning, it must be concluded that Colonel Evans, [Here he knows the Person, it seems, who was referr'd to the Quit-Rents, tho' just now it was called a Pretence] was deny'd Support, and our present Governour has had large Sums from this Government: If so, then it plainly shews the Difference between acting as a free Agent in Affirmance of our Constitution by Law and Charter, and submitting to an ill Management destructive to the whole. At which I cannot say, I am surprized, because I am not now to admire at any Perversion or Degree of Disingenuity, from that Quarter in this Cause; of which whether this be an Instance or not, others will judge. But I must hereupon take the Freedom of giving him a Caution; viz That if he resolve to Rake into those unhappy Times, to which he too justly applies the Word Tragedy it may tempt me, who have it in my Power, from good Originals, his own Draughts, Letters, &c. to entertain the World with what would much better be for ever sunk in Oblivion, viz: The History of his Conduct in this Province from the Year 1700. when he first let in his mighty Resentments, on being removed by Order of the Lord Justices in 1699. from all Offices of Trust and Power, to the Year 1710. when the Country, quite tired with his Impositions, served him on their Part, as the Regal Authority had done before. But as I have the highest Aversion to such fruitless Contention; and as it would engage me to revive the Memory also of his nearest Associates, now deceased, whose Names and Characters ought rather to lie buried in Silence with them in their Graves; nothing less than Necessity shall oblige me to so disagreeable a Task. I must however tell D. L. that when he presided not in the Assembly, Colonel Evans was provided for not only by a large Sum given at once, but by a further Appropriation for three Years, which tho' somewhat scanty, yet continued during his Time in the Administration. But upon the Occasion here given, and the Notice he has, elsewhere in his Paper taken of Ordinances, I am obliged with more Plainness to tell him, and inform the World, that the Point in Difference between that Gentleman and the Assemblies, wherein D. L. truly presided, which made the most Noise, was the Establishment of Courts, that had faln in 1706. by the Repeal of a former Act for appointing them. The Governour applied to the Assembly to restore them by a Law; and a Matter of this Importance, all rational Men expected, might without Delay or Difficulty be dispatched. But all those Expectations proved vain. D. L. Talents that Way were relied on, and for a Proof of them after a Months Adjournment, he produced a vast Bill of about 20 Sheets, crowded with Matters, so far from being essential to the Constitution of Courts, that some of them were never before, nor have never since, in these Parts, to the best of my Knowledge, been either proposed or heard of; yet by the Influence and Management of the Draughtsman, they were so strenously insisted on, under the Name of Privileges, (of which the Licensing of Publick Houses solely by the Justices was one) that unless the Governour would give into them, the Country must still languish, under an entire Stop to the Administration of Justice, of which they had been deprived, for about twelve Months before. The Governour hereupon, after many fruitless Endeavours, for a Law, had Resort to the only proper Expedient in his Power, which was to restore them by an Ordinance, the sole Method that had been allow'd by the Crown, in some of our Neighbouring Governments. And the more effectually to prevent exceptions, this was drawn, as near as could be, in the express Terms of D. L.'s Bill, in all the Parts essential to the Constitution of our Courts; as their Number, their Nature, their Terms or Times of Sitting, with what else was truly necessary for a regular and uniform Establishment of them, throughout the Province. Yet such was D. L.'s Opposition at that Time that this necessary Provision for procuring to the People their primary and greatest of all Rights in Government, was so highly Remonstrated, and declaimed against, as illegal, because not founded on an Act of Assembly; and so wildly were the Inhabitants arroused, that I have seen some who had been summoned to serve on a Grand-Jury, in a Court of Quarter-Sessions, openly in the Face of the Court deny its Jurisdiction; which whenever the Tragedy of that Time, mentioned by D. L. comes to be wrote, I suppose, may properly be allowed to make one fine Scene of it. Yet on the other Hand, when in the Year 1719. On the Repeal of another Act of the same Kind, our present Governour in affirmance of our Constitution as the Words are, or to prevent any Stop or Failure in the Administration of Justice, thought fit to continue the Courts, without waiting or applying for either Law or Ordinance; we then saw the Quondam great Patriot for these

Privileges, as now Older and Wiser, very quietly submitting, and without any other Appointment than a Commission and a Salary, (which doubtless carries much Strength both in Law and Reason with it) acting in the highest Station of our Courts, condemning Criminals, &c, without Hesitation, all which, I here say, was acted well, and shews, that on proper Considerations, advanced Years may enable a Man to reform his Judgment in one Case tho' they may not on the old Core, till all contending Passions are laid equally quiet in the Dust. Yet in this Case, the least that could be expected (one would think.) from such a Patriot, in that Station, after such mighty Clamours in the Days of Tragedy, might have been to move for a Law at least: But for two Years and a half (the salary coming duly in) there was, as far as I have heard, a perfect Silence in the Matter till the late Attorney-General considering the Weakness of that Foundation for our Courts, thought it necessary to move for one, and without any Delay obtained it. And so much for the Comparison. Thus having, if I mistake not, made good what I proposed, which was to shew the Weakness both of D. L.'s Law and Reasoning, and that his Reflections on the deceas'd Proprietary were unmerited and unjust; to the Breast of every considerate honest Man, I shall now leave it to be judged, how far consistent his Performance is with the Honour of this Government, either in Respect to our deceased Founder, his Family now living, or to any other Person acting under their Authority. He has called it, I hear, his Legacy, that when dead, he may yet speak; and no Man, I believe, will envy him the Reputation, of having his Memory and Sentiments, in that manner, perpetuated. I have been told also, that he pretends, he was called by the Assembly to the Work: But that nowhere appears, nor is it to be credited: He had only Leave to print it, as they ordered divers other Things to be published, not because they approved of them, but for another obvious Reason. I ought next to proceed to his Treatment of my self: But his Reflections are so unbecoming a Man of Spirit, and are so silly with their Spite, that I cannot think it worth either my own or my Reader's Time to consider them: His whole 12th Paragraph, closing with a Sting in its Tail at some One Person, is such a trifling Composition of Jargon; that the civillest Thing can be said of it, is to allow it no meaning at all; for granting it any, it must be only this, that in all Governments, where the Council has a Negative, that is in all the other English Governments in America, there is more Danger of Arbitrary Power in one Person, from Two Checks, than there can be from One; which is too irreverent toward an English

Constitution, and too outrageous an Attack upon common Sense, to imagine it could be intended by him. But as he seems willing to trace a Great Example, that had been set before him, in charging me with affecting Power, and is pleased to distinguish me from the other Members of the Council-Board; I must here in my own Vindication, once more challenge all Mankind, to produce one single Instance, where I have ever arrogated, courted or coveted Power, in any publick Affair whatsoever: Or that during the 23 Years, that I have been of that Board I ever made one Motion there, against the true Interest of the Country, for which I freely appeal to all the other Members of it, now living. My own Conscience bears me witness (and the angriest of my Enemies cannot prove the contrary, but) that I have been equally Faithful to the Proprietary, and Just to the Inhabitants, yet Envy against the One (with some Political Views elsewhere) has laboured to incense the Others against me. I have (also) been surprizingly charged with falsifying the Council's Minutes: But the Event of that Inquiry, before its proper Judges, fully shews that Innocence is not rashly to be attack'd, and possibly may prove, that Weapons form'd against it may happen to return where they were never expected, or intended.

I shall now come to his latest Clause, where for a finishing Stroke he tries to put the Bear-Skin on me, as if I were to be run down immediately in a common Hunt: But I cannot have so mean an Opinion as he seems to entertain of the Judgment of the People. 'Tis true, they have sometimes been misled: Men may be stagger'd by new Pretences, and false Colourings may impose on their Understandings for a Time: But Rectitude is the natural Disposition of the Soul, and when forced from it by Arts or Illusions, yet (like the Needle panting after its Pole) being left to it-self, it will shew, that Truth and Justice, are the real and adequate Objects, of its Esteem, its Love, and Desire. I am not therefore apprehensive of much Danger from temporary Mistakes. I have been charged with Disrespect to some former Assemblies, and I acknowledge I have blamed them: Both Kings and Parliaments have err'd and Mankind have openly censured the one or the other (and some both) for certain Proceedings in England, towards the middle of the last Century: Yet this no ways derogates from either Regal or Parliamentary Authority the Powers of both being justly accounted as sacred, within their respective Limits. No Parliament, 'tis probable, was ever conven'd more regularly than that I have hinted, of Nov 1640. Yet all Men condemn their excessive Abuse of Power: No Assembly, perhaps was more duly elected, according to our Constitution, than that of 1709. yet the Country, at their next Choice, shew'd so entire a Dislike of their Proceedings against the Proprietary, that (as I was informed then in Britain) they were all turn'd out to a Man. I may therefore be allow'd to be still of the same Opinion with the Country, who never shew'd themselves more unanimous, than they did generally on that Occasion. Nor is it more a Crime to persist in it, than to be faithful to my Trust, the true Source of my Troubles here. But if, because I have opposed the unjust Attacks made upon the Proprietary, any can be so wild, as to imagine me disaffected to the true Interest and Privileges of the People, they must, when they consider my Circumstances in the Place, with my Family, either conceive me exceedingly blind to what regards my self, or acknowledge the gross Absurdity of supposing, that to strengthen an Interest, to which my Posterity can have no nearer Relation, than all the rest of the Province, I should favour the least Appearance of Oppression or Arbitrary Power, (were it true that Attempts of that kind had ever been made here) or deprive my Children of the least Advantage, they might in common with their Neighbours justly claim. No sensible Man who believes me Master of any competent Degree of Reason, can imagine this. On the contrary, I can truly affirm, my Views and Aims (however calumniated) have constantly been the same, viz Universally to promote Justice, the only Foundation, on which any Establishment can become truly great, safe and honourable. And as I have already, in this Paper, taken Notice of that amiable Disposition to Love and Union, which with an honest Simplicity, and an open Integrity, shed a beautiful Lustre on the first Adventurers with the Proprietary into this Province; and which seem to have drawn down such a Blessing on their Endeavours, that the Settlement soon became the Wonder, at least, if not the Envy of the Colonies round us; so, nothing in relation to the Publick, has been more earnestly my Desire than that our Conduct might still continue a just claim to the same Esteem and Reputation. But alas! the Pale has been broke into. George Keith, the Grand Apollyon of this Country's Peace, gave the first fatal Blow. Hence the Minds of Numbers were tainted and soured, not only one against another, but against the Proprietary himself, who could not but condemn the Proceedings of that turbulent conceited Man, and from hence more easily succeeded those unnatural Disputes I have mentioned, joyned with Revenge, which cost the Country vast Sums, besides the Confusion, without the least Benefit to the People; had even all that was contended for, been gain'd. These 'twas thought, in 1710, were happily ended; and may the Spirit be for ever crushed, and never suffer'd to raise its monstrous Head again. Let the Proprietary, who is still our Governour in chief (and may he ever be encouraged to continue so) have his Own, as well as the People Theirs, with proper Securities from the Person He intrusts and not be placed in a worse Condition, by weak Pretences from the Law, or otherwise, than any private Man would be content with, in the minutest of his own Affairs, where he confides in another: Let us with an unshaken Regard to Right, study and promote the Credit and Honour, the true Interest and Peace of the Publick; ever guarding, as we would against Fire to our Houses, or Leaks at Sea, against that Grand Reproach, that Destructive Bane, to Families, Communities, and Countries, Intestine Divisions. We are bless'd with mighty Privileges, not only those of an English Subject, to their utmost Extent, and those other plain Ones, granted by the Proprietary's Charter; but these also, which can never be too highly valued, an Exemption from Racking Rents for Lands, oppressive Taxes, Tythes, and Military Appointments. Let us therefore be grateful and quiet, without hazarding any of those we really enjoy, by endeavouring, to be better than very well; which has ever been attended with Danger. Nor led by Sounds only, make our selves the Property of designing Men, who to compass their own Ends, amuse with the Charm of misunderstood Words, and empty deluding Prospects. Let us cheerfully support and obey the Regular Powers of Government, and as far as possible, preserve our publick Credit. These Things (if I mistake not) will truly redound to our Honour; and my hearty and constant Endeavours for these will be found the only Crimes, for which I can be charged, in Relation to this Province.

Philadelphia, 25. Sept. 1725.

J. LOGAN.

Advertisement.

These are to certify all whom it may concern, that those ingenious Persons, who have heretofore, either in Print or Manuscript, treated any Thing I have wrote, with Scoffs, Invectives, Trifling Cavils, Drollery, Scurrility, &c, may freely go on in their Way; for I shall ever think such Performances, in what relates to myself, below my Notice. Nor shall I have more Regard to any Reply that may be offered to this Paper, unless the Law produced in it, be Standard, The Arguments carry some Reason, and the Assertions some Truth in them, and be to the Purpose: But I shall by my Silence, shew a just Contempt of every Thing relating to the Publick, that is not solid, or becomes not a serious, honest Man.

J. L.

· 24 ·

John Bulkley, "Preface" in Roger Wolcott, Poetical Meditations (New London, 1725)

JOHN BULKLEY, surgeon, clergyman, and supporter of Andros. Like his father before him, Bulkley attended Harvard. In 1703, he was ordained in the new frontier town of Colchester. Although he complained about what he called "his long confinement in the wilderness," he had access to his family's extensive library, and he read widely in the law as well as in medicine. Despite his isolation, he was involved in several important public controversies. He supported the Yale tutors who were dismissed for their belief in Episcopal ordination; yet he was also a staunch defender of orthodox Calvinism against the new sects. His theological writings also demonstrated an engagement with rationalism. His 1713 election sermon, *The Necessity of Religion in Societies*, stressed "the reasonableness of religion." In an ordination sermon delivered a year before his death (*The Usefulness of Reveal'd Religion, to Preserve and Improve that which is Natural*), he once again sought to show the compatibility of reason and revelation, arguing that most of the doctrines of faith were "no other than what nature teaches." In a testimony to the esteem with which he was regarded by his peers, Charles Chauncy reckoned that Bulkley was among "the three first for extent and strength of genius and powers that New England has yet produced." The others were Jeremiah Dummer and Thomas Walter. Bulkley died in 1731.

The origins of Bulkley's preface lay in his friendship with a young poet, Roger Wolcott, later the governor of Connecticut. Bulkley encouraged the youth in his literary endeavors, arranging for the publication of Wolcott's *Poetical Meditations,* a verse account of the Pequot War and of the origins of the colony of Connecticut. This subject matter—in particular the quest of John Winthrop Jr. to obtain a charter for the colony—led Bulkley to write a preface related to the ongoing dispute between the colony of Connecticut and the Mohegan Indian tribe over ownership of the tribe's traditional hunting grounds. The colony claimed that the tribe had in fact ceded the land to the colony as a result of several treaties and subsequent deeds. The tribe, with the help of a prominent Connecticut family, argued before a series of royal commissions that they retained the title to the land. Bulkley, drawing heavily on Locke's theory of the origin of property rights in labor, argued that the Mohegans, because they had not labored on the land, did not in fact have any title to it. In using Locke in this way, Bulkley offered a powerful natural law account of the right of English colonists to land in the New World, an account which, moreover, did not rely on purchase or treaty or, indeed, on any form of Crown grant. Bulkley's use of Lockean natural law theory was one of the earliest in New England. (C.B.Y.)

POETICAL Meditations,

BEING THE

IMPROVEMENT

OF SOME

Vacant Hours,

By ROGER WOLCOTT, *Esq;*

WITH A

PREFACE

By the REVEREND

Mr. Bulkley of Colchester.

NEW LONDON:

Printed and Sold by L. Green, 1725.

The Preface.

§ 1. The buisy and restless Soul of Man which in all Ages has been Fruitful in *Many Inventions,* as it has been greatly Disserviceable to the Good and Comfort of Humane Life by the Discovery of things Prejudicial to it; so at the same time may we not say, has made some Compensation by the Invention of others of a Proportionable Advantage and Benefit. It were easy by a detail of some of the many Useful Arts found out by Man to give Evidence of this, but it must Suffice at Present, to Instance in one only, *viz.* That *Art of Writing, or Expressing* all Sounds, and Consequently the Conceptions of our Minds, by a *Few Letters Variously Disposed or Plac'd,* the Commodity or Profit of which to Mankin'd is so Various & Extensive as not to be easily accounted for. This Art is stiled by One* *Adamirandarum Omnium inventionum humanarum Signaculum. i.e.* The Wonder or Master-piece of all Humane Inventions: And how deservedly is it so, whether we Speak with Reference to the *Strangeness* or the *Benefit* of it? How Strange is it that by the Various Disposition of so *Few Letters* as Our *Alphabet* contains, *all Sounds* should be express'd, and thereby all the conceptions or Ideas of our Minds! And as for the *Commodity* of it; not to mention others, from hence it comes to pass that we are Furnish'd with so much Useful History, which bringing into our View both Persons and Things most distant from us in time and place, does greatly delight and entertain us, and at the same time Instruct or Teach and Furnish us with a main part of our most useful Knowledge.

§ 2. In the Early Ages of the World, before this most certain way of Communicating the Knowlege of things was found out; other *Mediums* were made use of for that end, the Principal of which seems to have been Representative *Symbols* or *Hieroglyphicks,* which way or Method of Communication every one knows still Obtains among many *Unletter'd Nations* in the World. But this as its very uncertain on the Account of that great Variety of *Interpretations* such Symbols are liable to, and as the Misconstruction of them, its reasonable to think, has been none of the least Prolifick Fountains of the *Heathen Mythology,* by which the Antient & True Tradition of the First Ages of the World has been so much Corrupted and Alter'd, so is now out of use with such Nations, as among whom the *Use of Letters* has been Introduced. I said above that to this we are Debtors for the useful History we are Furnish'd with: and I must observe on this Occasion that there are two ways in which those who have Oblig'd us with it, according to their different Genius and

* Gallileo

Humours, have Improv'd this Noble Invention in Composing the Historys they have put into our Hands; that some therein have Confin'd themselves to *Poetical Numbers* and *Measures,* others not so restricting themselves, have Written in *Prose,* which last in latter Ages has been the more common way. That a considerable part, especially of our more *Ancient History,* is delivered to us in the former of these ways, is known to most that are not Strangers to Books, a considerable part of the Writings both of the *Latin* and *Greek* Poets what are they but *Poemata Historica?*[1] Among the former, *Ovid* assures us his Book *METAMORPHOSEON,* in part, at least is no other when in the beginning of it he Invokes the Gods in these Words, *viz.*

> ——— *Dij Coeptis* (———)
> *Adspirate meis, Primaque ab Origine Mundi*
> *Ad mea Perpetuum deducite Tempora carmen,*

In English thus rendred by one,

> ye Gods Vouchsafe (———)
> To further this mine Enterprise;
> and from the World begun,
> Grant that my Verse may to my time
> his Course directly run.

And whoever has read it with understanding can't but see its so.

§ 3. I cannot forbear Observing here with what Pleasure I have taken notice of the great *Harmony* or Agreement there is in the Account he there gives of the most *Antient Things* with that of the *Sacred History:* And that we have in that Composure of his a Lively Specimen of the Truth of what the Learned Observe concerning the *Writings* of the *Heathen,* viz. That they frequently give in Testimony to the Truth of the *Sacred History,* particularly in its Account of the Eldest Times. With what Accuracy has he given us the History of the creation? It looks rather like the Narrative of a Learned *Jew* or *Christian* than an *Heathen;* for besides the Philosophy of it, it so well Harmonises with that of *Moses,* that one would be Tempted to think that either he had Convers'd with his Writings, or had the Knowlege of it convey'd to him by some Secret *Cabbala,* as its Affirm'd by some of *Pythagoras* and *Plato;* or which is more probable that the general Tradition of it Preserv'd in the World, tho' in many Places it was grosly disguis'd and corrupted, yet in others retain'd much of its Primitive Purity, for not so much

1. ["Poems about history."]

as mentioning the Absurd Hypothesis of the *Aristotelian* & *Epicurean Philosophers* concerning the Origine of the World, like the *Inspired Historian,* he Ascribes it to the *Divine Efficiency.* Having spoken of the *Chaos* (differing from him in Words, not in sense) wherein the contrary, jarring Principles of all Bodies lay without Form or Order, He thus goes on—

Hanc Deus & Melior litem Natura diremit,
Nam Caelo terras, & terris abscidit Undas,
Et liquidum spisso secrevit ab Aere Caelum,
Quae postquam evolvit, Caecoque exemit Acervo,
Dissociata locis concordi pace ligavit.

Thus rendred by the forementioned Author,

This Strife did God & Nature break & set in Order streight
The Earth from Heaven, the Sea from Earth, He parted orderly
And from the thick & foggy Air, He took the lightsom Sky
Which when He once unfolded had, & sever'd from the Blind,
And clodded heap: He setting each from other did them bind
In endless Friendship to Agree.

And further, Having shewed what places the several parts of matter in that *Confus'd Mass,* on their Separation took, according to their respective Gravitations, as also how the terrene and more gross parts of it were formed into a *Globe,* furnished with *Bays, Fountains, Pools, Lakes, Rivers, Valleys, Mountains,* and various sorts of *Living Creatures;* as if the Inspired History had been before him.

He goes on;

Sanctius his animal, mentisque capacius altae.
Deerat adhuc, & quod dominari in caetera posset
Natus homo est: Sive hunc divino semine fecit,
Ille Opifex rerum, Mundi melioris Origo:
Sive recens tellus, seductaque nuter ab alto
Æthere, cognati retinebat semina caeli:
Quam Satus Japeto mistam fluvialibus undis
Tinxit in effigiem moderantum cuncta deorum.

Thus rendred

Howbeit yet of all this while, the Creature wanting was,
Far more Divine, of nobler Mind, which should the res'due pass
In depth of Knowlege, Reason, Wit and high Capacity
And which of all the residue should Lord and Ruler be.

Then either he that made the World, & things in Order set
Of Heavenly Seed engendred Man; or else the Earth as yet
Young, Lusty, Fresh & in Her Flowers, & parted from the Sky
But late before, the Seed thereof as yet held Inwardly.
The which *Prometheus* tempering *strait with water of the Spring*
Did make in likeness to the Gods that Govern every thing.

The like Agreement with the Sacred History, I might remark in the Account he gives us of the State of *Innocence* stil'd by him the Golden Age, the *Flood,* &c How well does his Character of the former agree with that Idea of it Divine Revelation has Imprinted on our Minds? And the latter he Ascribes to a Concurrence & Co-operation of the same causes in Nature that *Moses* does. Its true he Writes in the Strain and Manner of others of his Tribe, who are wont generally to mingle a great deal of *Mythology* with the Truth; yet notwithstanding how easy is it for every Intelligent Reader to trace in him the Footsteps of the Sacred History, particularly in its accounts of the most Early Times?

§ 4. And may we not with equal Truth say the same of *Virgils* Æneids? which seem to be no other than a *Mythological* History of the Affairs of *Æneas,* or the Various Occurrences of his Life; to which *Homer* his *Iliads* with others from the *Greeks* might be added. Its Observed by some Learned Men, that this was the most Antient way of Writing, and that *Prose* is only an Imitation of *Poetry,* and that the *Grecians* in particular at their first delivery from *Barbarism,* had all their Phylosophy and Instruction from the poets, such as *Orpheus, Hesiod, Parmenides, Xenophanes,* &c.—which seems to have Occasion'd those Lines of *Horace, Cap. de Arte Poetic*

——— *Fuit haec sapientia quondam*
Publica privatis Sacernere, sacra Profanis:
Concubitu Prohibere Vago; dare jura Mavitis:
Oppida moliri: leges incidere ligno.
Sic honor & nomen Divinis Vatibus atque
Carminibus venit.

The sum of which is this, *viz.*

That in Old Time *Poets* were the Lights and Instructors of the World, and gave Laws to Men for their Conduct in their several Relations and Affairs of Life.

And Finally, To this seems to agree that of *Cato* in his Distichs,

Si Deus est Animus nobis ut carmina dicunt,
If God a Spirit be as Poets Teach, *&c.*

§ 5. I have premis'd this in way of *Apology* for the manner in which this *Worthy Person* has given us the *Ensuing History,* in Composing which he has Diverted some of his *Leisure Hours.* And from hence tis evident he has for a Precedent some of the most *Antient History,* and has trod in the steps of many of the most Eminent *Sages* and earliest *Writers* History gives us any Knowlege of, who have taken that same way to raise up Monuments to, and eternize the Names and Actions of their Admired *Heroes.*

§ 6. Its undoubtedly true that as the Minds of Men have a very different *Cast, Disposition* or *Genius* leading to & accomplishing for very differing Improvements, so generally speaking, those are the most Accomplished to make a Judgment on any Performance that have by Nature a Genius Leading to and Accomplishing for the same: And it being so, and withal there being none among the *whole number of Mortals* less furnish'd for a Performance of this Nature *than my self,* I may well be excus'd in Omitting the part of a *Censor* or *Judge* upon it, further than to say that the Intelligent Reader will herein discern an uncommon *Vigour* of *Mind,* considerable *Reading,* and see reason to say, that herein we have a *Specimen* what good parts cultivated with a laudable Ambition to Improve in Knowlege will do, tho' not Assisted with those Advantages of *Education* which some are favoured withal.

§ 7. Some there are that have remark't, That the *Accomplish'd Poet* and the *Great Man* are things seldom meeting together *in one Person,* Or that its rare those Powers of Mind that *make* the one, are found *United* with those that Constitute the other. And perhaps it may be a Truth which for the main holds true. For whereas what is properly call'd *Wit,* (which is no other than a ready Assemblage of Ideas, or a putting those together with quickness & variety wherein there can be found any *Congruity* or *Resemblance;* or to speak more plain, an aptness at Metaphor and Allusion) is what, as I take it, makes the *Accomplish'd Poet;* exactness of Judgment, or Clearness of reason (which we commonly and truly say makes *the Great Man*) on the other hand lies in an Ability of Mind nicely to distinguish its Ideas the one from the other, where there is but the least difference thereby avoiding being misled by Similitude, and by Affinity to take one thing from another. And the process of the Mind in these two things being so *contrary* the one to the other, tis not strange if they are Powers not ever *United* in the same Subject, yet this notwithstanding, all must say, this is not a Remark that universally and without exception will hold true; but that how contrary and inconsistent soever the process of the mind in the exercise of these two Powers may seem to be, yet there are *Instances* wherein they are United in a Wonderful Measure: And many Men in whom we find a great deal of *Pleasantry* or *Wit*, are notwithstanding very *Judicious* and *Rational*. And tho' Modesty forbids me to say this of the *Author*, yet this I shall venture to say, *viz*. That whatever may be said in Commendation of this Performance by the Accomplished for a Judgment upon it; yet that there will not that Honour be done him thereby, as I conceive may with a great deal of Truth and Justice otherwise.

But however it be as to that, and whatever the Sentiments of the Judicious in affairs of this Nature, may be of this Composure, yet I presume all will approve of the design of it, which (as to the main of it at least,) being no other than to pay a just debt to the Memory & procure due Regards to the Family of one, who not only being view'd in his own *Personal Accomplishments* was a Person of distinguishing Worth, but many ways Highly *Deserv'd of the Publick*, every one must Confess is Laudable, it being very Consonant to the Natural Notice of what is Good and Excellent Engraven on the Minds of all Men, as appears by the Honours done, even by *Unletter'd Nations to their admir'd Heroes*. Be sure every one not Insensible of *our Valuable Enjoyments* so far forth continu'd & secur'd to us under the *Present Constitution* Obtain'd by the *Agency and Influence of this Noble Person* whose Name and Praise are here Celebrated, as they will say he was a *Publick Benefactor*, highly Deserv'd of us all, and tho' Dead justly Challenges a *better Regard to his Surviving Posterity* than by some at least, has been pay'd to them, and that his *Name* is not to be mention'd without a Blessing on his Memory, so that this is but a just *Tribute* to it.

§ 8. For my own part whatever Opinion some may have of me as to my Principles in *Politicks*, and tho' perhaps our Present *Frame or Model of Government* is not the best that might be, but capable of a change in some points to the better, yet can freely confess that I look upon it as an *Indulgence* & *Favour of Heaven*, a just ground of *Gratitude*; & that as its a *Constitution* capable of rendring us a People *more Happy than we are*, so that the Infelicities we Labour under in the Present Day, which truly are not few or small, are rather owing to the *want of a due Use*, or rather an *Abuse* of it, than *the Constitution it self*.

§ 9. I am no Admirer of those *Despotick Forms of Government* which as they Obtain in some places, so are not without their Advocates in others, where the Blessings they enjoy under the good & gentle Administrations of *better Forms* might convince them of their Folly and Teach them better. I firmly Believe that *the Law of Nature* knows no difference or Subordination among Men besides those of *Children to their Parents* and *Wives to their Husbands,* and that these Relations only excepted, all Men are otherwise *Equal, Free* & *Independent* & remain so till by *Contracts,* Provisions and Laws of their own they divest themselves of those *Prerogatives:* Nor is it I conceive in the Power of any Person or Persons to transfer or vest that Despotick Arbitrary Power in any other Person or Persons, which some in Authority Exercise over the Lives and Fortunes of their Subjects: for no Person can Transfer to another more Power than he has in himself, and such an ARBITRARY Power over himself or any other to Destroy his own or the Life and Property of another, is what none on Earth can lay Claim to. Worthy to be Inserted here are the Words of that Great Man Mr. *Lock,* who well understood the true Origine of all Lawful Authority, and what Powers over themselves or others, Persons by the Law of Nature & Antecedent to their Entring into Society are Vested with;

> *This* i.e. *Arbitrary, Despotick Power,* says he, *is a Power which neither Nature gives (for it has made no such Distinction between one man and another) nor Compact can convey: For man not having such an Arbitrary Power over his own Life, cannot give to another such a Power over it, but its the effect of Forfeiture only, which the Aggressor makes of his own life when he puts himself into a state of War with another.* ———

And a little after,

> *And thus,* says he, *Captives taken in a Just and Lawful War, and such only, are subject to a despotick power which as it arises not from compact, so neither is it capable of any, but is the state of War continued.*

Thus that man of deep Tho'ts Pag. 320, 321. And tis not to be doubted but that whatever some men (may I not say foolishly eno') have advanced for the support of the Absolute power of *Supreme Rulers* (taking their Notions of Civil Power probably from some mistaken texts of Scripture, & general Speculations founded on some Equivocal terms, such as *King, Sovereign, Supream, &c* Yet the true Measures of all lawful Authority, be it *Supream or Subordinate,* are to be taken from the nature of that *Compact* or Contract that is the true Origine of it, & Vests it in those that wear it: Nor is this Doctrine I think in the least Inconsistent with that that asserts the *Jus Divinium*[2] of

2. ["Divine right."]

Civil Power; or that the *Powers that be are Ordained of God,* & therefore Challenges *Obedience to them* not *for Wrath meerly,* but *for Conscience sake.*

§ 10. I presume there are not many in this Popular, *Levelling Day* who will not readily Subscribe this Doctrine, and more than that, who will not say that in Lawful Governments that are founded in Compact, the more general Error is that *too much Power is given up by the Community,* and Vested in *their Rulers;* I am very sure among us at least, there are not many, who (Pardon me if what I say be amiss) generally speaking are a People Trained up, but too much, in *Principles of Rebellion and Opposition to Government;* and who as to *the Constitution* Obtaining among us, as Popular as it is, yet think it *Defective by Error on the other Extream?* Yet all this notwithstanding, certain it is Despotick Forms are not the only that are Prejudicial to the ends of Government, but those Erring on the other Extream are perhaps as Inconsistent with them, and of this, besides their but too often Exemplifying the Condition of *Ephesus* at a certain time when *Paul* was there, *Act.* 19. We need not go far from Home for Evidence. Our *English Constitution* at Home seems to be an Happy mean between these two Extreams, Wisely contriv'd to secure from the ill Consequents of either of them. A *Constitution* it is wherein as one says, Tho' the *Executive Power* be Lodg'd solely in the King, yet the *Legislative* is divided between him and his People, by which as the King has Bounds set to his Prerogative, so the People have their Privileges which Assert their Liberty. Such a *Constitution* it is as allows enough to a King of no Tyrannical Temper, and what is Sufficient to secure the Ends of Government, and enough to the People to Preserve them from Slavery. There is *Monarchy* without *Slavery,* a *Great King,* and yet a *Free People;* such a *Monarchy* as has the main Advantages of an *Aristocracy* in the Lords, and of a *Democracy* in the *Commons,* without the Inconveniences of either. In a Word, a *Model of Government* so Perfect and well Adapted to the Ends of Government does it seem to be, that as the things wherein other Constitutions, (and in particular *Ours* in this Colony) Harmonizes with it, seem to be its great Perfects, and those wherein it differs its great Imperfections, *though by many Cry'd up* for our Glorious Privileges.

§ 11. Perhaps what I have already Written may have given some Exercise to the Patience of the Reader, however having *put Pen to Paper,* I shall Presume to detain him a little longer on a matter which as it has been the Occasion of much Debare and Contention as well as many other Evils among us, so my Tho'ts are here led to it by some Passages in the Eusuing Muse. Tis the matter of *Native Right* as its commonly called, or the *Right the Aborigines of this Country* (all or any of them) had or have *to Lands* in it. An Interest this is which every one knows has not wanted many Advocates among us, especially of late Years, who have endeavour'd to Advance or set it up as our only Valuable Title to whatever Lands are in the Country some perhaps Acting in what they have done with a real Perswasion of this, but far the most no doubt on other Considerations.

§ 12. For my own part, I have ever thought this a *matter more Talk'd of* than *Understood,* and am ready to think of those who are of the abovemention'd Opinion in this matter, that they have Drank in *this Article of their Faith* as perhaps they have many of the rest, without *due Examination* or Search into the matter.

§ 13. I Presume we are generally Agreed there is such a thing as *Native Right,* to speak in the Vulgar Phraise; or a Right which the *Aborigines of any Country* and Consequently of this, (or some of them at least) have or had to Lands in it, I mean to *particular Tracts,* or Parcels of it: I suppose there are few that in this Point bring them down to a Level with the *Bruital Race,* how Barbarous or Uncultivated soever they were: And sure I am that none will Deny it that considers that as there never was any among Mankind, even the most Barbarous but what were Capable of *Impropriating Lands* as well as other things, so that among the *Aborigines of this Country* there was that found that was Sufficient for that end. Yet notwithstanding to Assert *their Right in that Extent* that many do, and suppose it, without excepting any, to extend *to all Lands* in the Country, whether Cultivated by them or not; is what I never could, nor yet can see any Sufficient reason for. And though I know to countenance and give a currency to this Opinion the Authority of those Truly Worthy Men that were the first Settlers of *English Colonys* here, as well as that of the several Governments in the Country from the begining to this Day, is wont frequently to be alledged in Discourse by our *Bigots* to this Principle, who would bear us in Hand they were one and all of the same Perswasion, and accordingly accounted no Lands in the Country their own till Obtain'd of the *Natives* by *Compact* or otherwise, yet for my own part I could never think so Dimunitively of them, or at least many of them as to Believe they Acted on this Principle in the Regard they shewed the *Natives* & their Pretended Claim to the Country, by entring into Treaties with and allowing them Gratuities for the Lands, but rather that they Acted on Prudential Considerations taken from their own & the Natives Circumstances.

§ 14. And as it is an undoubted Truth, that the *Aborigines of this Country,* some or all of them had Right to *Lands* in it, so is it equally certain that of what Extent soever it was it arose from one of these Two Things, *viz.* Either the *Law of Nature,* or *Positive Laws* or Constitutions of their own (Tacit or Express) Regulating or Determining the matter of *Property,* one or other of these must give them what they had. And by Consequence nothing with any certainty can be Determin'd upon the extent of the *Claims or Properties* of any Single Person or Number of them, till first it be determin'd what *their Condition* was, whether they were a People in the *State of Nature,* and so had only what the *Law of Nature* gave them, or had quitted that State, entred into *Communities,* and by *Compact* one with another, and Positive Constitutions of their own (Tacit or Express) had fixed *the Bounds* of each *Community* respectively and Settled or Determin'd the matter of Property in Land within themselves severally: and in case this last be found, *viz.* that they had entred into Communities and Perform'd those Consequent Acts, further it must be Determin'd where the Bounds of *each Community* respectively were, and what Disposition or Settlement *the Laws of each Society* or Community made of the Lands within their Limits severally. These are things which perhaps few of those who have appear'd with such Heat and Zeal for the forementiond Principle, ever thought of, yet I am well assur'd there is no Intelligent Person but will readily grant that till these things are Determin'd nothing with any certainty can be Known or Resolv'd upon the extent of the *Claim or Property* of any among them, whether Single Person or Community.

And because diverse Persons are of Different Sentiments in this matter, *viz.* What the Condition of the Persons I am now speaking of was as to this, at the time of the first Access of the *English* to the Country when such *Large Tracts of Land* are suppos'd by some to be Obtain'd of them; some being of Opinion they were a People in *the State of Nature,* others that they had *quitted that State,* entred into *Communities* and put on some Form of *Civil Policy,* &c—and because as I said nothing can be Determin'd as to the extent of the Right or Property of any of them without a Determination of this matter, Altho' I shall not Presume upon an *Umpirage* of it, yet shall examine each of these *Hypothesis* and on a Supposition of the Truth of both of them severally, shall shew what can be Determin'd upon the extent of the *Rights* or *Properties* of any of them: Which when I have done I am prone to think, that those who with such Confidence, and to the no small Harm and Injury of their Country have Appear'd on the side of the forementioned Extravagant Principle, will see they have not such Evidence of the Truth of it, as perhaps now they think they have.

§ 15. I take it for granted & think it needs no Proof, that as all men are and ever were *Born Free,* Equal and Independent as to *Civil Subjection or Subordination,* so there was a time when the *State of Nature* obtained in the World. As there is a wide difference between *Paternal Authority* or Power and *Civil or Political,* so tho' the first has been from the Beginning and is as old as the Relation between *Father and Son;* yet the other is not so: But as in the beginning of the World men were few in Number, wanted not Room, having the wide World before them, had not the like Temptations to Contention and Strife, nor were exposed & in danger of Enemies, as since so did not presently find a necessity of *entring into Society,* but continued for some time in that Free Equal, Independent State wherein they were Born, having no other Law than that of Nature, & not knowing what *Political Power or Authority was.* And this is what is Intended by the state of Nature. How long it was in the Beginning that men continu'd in this state, before there were any instances of their Embodying into any form of *Civil Policy* is uncertain; Nor is it strange we are left so much in the dark, & History is so silent in this matter, since the time was so long before *the use of Letters* obtained in any parts of the World: yet that such a state as this did precede that of Civil Society as the Sacred History it self seems to intimate to us in those words of Cain (Gen. 4 12. *And it shall come to pass that every one that findeth me shall slay me.* Which seem evidently to imply this state of Nature then obtaining, and that every man then look'd on himself as having in himself right to punish the Transgressions of the Law of Nature) so I presume is not doubted of by many in this day, wherein I suppose it is generally received for good Doctrine, that *Compact is the Origine* of Government, at least as far forth, or wheresoever it was begun in Peace. Yea if we may believe *Josephus Acosta,* and I know no reason why we may not, even these latter Ages of the World have afforded instances of this nature, I mean of persons in the state of nature, or without any form of *Civil Policy* among them. His words are these, viz.

> *There are great & apparent Conjectures that these men, speaking of the Aborigines of* Peru, *for a long time had neither Kings nor Common Wealths, but liv'd in Troops as they do this day in* Florida, *the* Cheriquanaes, *those of* Brasil *& many other Nations, which have no certain Kings, but as Occasion is offered in Peace or War, they chuse their Captains as they Please.* Lib 1. Cap 25:

Nor is it unlikely there may be Multitudes in the World, who even to this day remain in this state as perhaps may appear more probable by and by, when something further has been added Descriptive of it; which that so I may be the better understood in what follows, I shall do in this place.

§ 16. This *State of Nature* then is a state wherein men not having any *Common, Establish'd, Positive Law* (Tacit or Express) or Judicature to appeal to, with Authority to decide Controversies between them, and punish Offenders, Every man is Judge for himself, and Executioner.

> *These* says that Worthy Person* before mentioned, *who are United into one Body, and have a Common, Establish'd Law and Judicature to Appeal to, with Authority to Decide Controversies arising between them and Punish Offenders, are in Civil Society one with another, but those who have no such Common Appeal, I mean on Earth, are still in the State of Nature, each being (where there is no other) Judge for Himself and Executioner.* Treatise of Government, p. 247.

and afterward p. 280. accounting for the Defects of this State, he says,

> 1. *There Wants in it an Establish'd Settled, known Law Receiv'd and Allow'd by common Consent to be the Standard of Right and Wrong, and the common Measure to Decide all Controversies arising between Men. For though the Law of Nature be Plain and Intelligible to all Rational Creatures, yet Men being byas'd by their Interest, as well as Ignorant for want of Study of it, are not apt to allow of it as Law binding to them in the Application of it to their particular Cases.*
>
> 2. *In the State of Nature there wants a Known, Indifferent Judge with Authority to Determine all Differences according to the Establish'd Law, for every one in that State being both Judge and Executioner of the Law of Nature, Men being partial to themselves, Passion and Revenge are very apt to carry them too far, and with too much Heat in their own Cases, as well as Negligence, and Unconcernedness to make them too Remiss in other Mens.*
>
> 3. *In the State of Nature there often wants Power to Back and Support the Sentence when Right; and to give it due Execution, they who by any Injustice Offer'd will seldom fail where they are Able, by Force to make good their Injustice. And such Resistance many times makes the Punishment Dangerous, and Frequently Destructive to those who Attempt it.*

Thus that great Man

* Mr. *Lock.*

In a Word, In this State as Men have no other Law than that of *Nature* or *Reason* to be the Measure or Standard of *Right* and *Wrong*, and are without any *Common Superior on Earth*, with Authority to decide Controversies and a Force or Power to Execute his Sentences, to whom they might Appeal when Disputes arise, so every Man has right in himself both to Judge of *the Transgressions* of that Law, and *Punish them* as far as he is Able. And from this short account of this State 'tis easie to see both what it is, and wherein it differs *from a State of Civil Society*, for whereas in *this State* men have no other Law than that *of Nature*, & every man has in himself right to Judge of & Punish the Transgressions of that Law; in that of *Civil Society* there are other Laws for a Measure or Standard of Right and Wrong, and this Right of Judging and Executing, is given up by every Individual into the hands of the *Community*: For which reason in *this State* all Private Judgment in any matters ceases, and the Community is *Umpire*, and by settled standing Laws made by themselves, indifferent and the same to all Parties, and by men having Authority from the Community to Execute those Laws, decides all Differences that happen between any particular Members, concerning any matter of Right, and punishes all Offences with such Penalties as the Law has Established.

§ 17. Now on the Supposition that *the Aborigines of this Country*, before and at the time of the *First Discovery & Planting of it* by the *English*, were in *this State*, and not to be considered as having put on any Form of *Civil Policy*, let us enquire what can be Determin'd concerning the *Extent of their Rights to Lands in it*: And here it must be consider'd that during the continuance *of this State* with any Persons, though all have a Right or *Claim to the Earth*, as well as all other things made for the Use and Comfort of Man, by Vertue of *the Grant of the most High*, the Great Proprietor of the World, whereby as the *Psalmist* says, *He has Given the Earth to the Children of Men;* Yet as by that they are made but *Commoners* in them, and can Claim only *as such*, so there is I suppose but one way whereby any particular Person can begin a Property in any thing, be it *Land* or *any thing else*, exclusive of the rest of Mankind, and this is by adding to it something which is his own, for Instance his Labour, which is his alone, and no one else has any Right to. Thus in this State the Law of Nature or Reason to which alone Men are Subject, and which gives them what ever they have, this Law I say makes and allows the Land a *Man Tills & Subdues* to be his *Peculiar Property*: by his *Labour*, which is his own, (and no man else has any Right to) bestow'd upon it, he does as it were Inclose it from the Common; and that *Deer,* or *Hare,* or *Fruit* a Man spends his Time and Strength in the Chase and Gathering of, it allows to be his Property: he does thereby take them out of that *Common State* wherein Nature had made them. Worthy to be Inserted here are the Words of that great Man* before mention'd,

> *Thus* says he, *this Law of Reason makes the* Deer *the* Indians *who has Kill'd it, tis allow'd to be his Goods, who has bestow'd his Labour upon it, though before it was the Common Right of every one*—He adds, *And amongst those who are Counted the Civiliz'd Part of Mankind, who have Made and Multiply'd Positive Laws to Determine properly, this Original Law of Nature for the begining of Property in what was before Common still takes place, and by Virtue thereof, what* Fish *any one Catches in the Ocean, (that great and still remaining Common of Mankind) or what* Ambergrease *any one takes up here, is by the Labour that removes it out of the Common State Nature left it in made his Property who takes that Pains about it.* Thus he,—

Indeed after any Portion of the Earth, or any thing else is by this means taken out of the *Common State* it was in before, and a Property is begun in it, this State of Nature seems to Admit of other ways of fixing a Property in the same thing or things by others; Thus in this State, that Land or other thing I began a Property in by my *Labour,* may become the Property of another Man, *by Gift or Purchase* as well as in a State of *Civil Society:* but Labour only seems to be the thing that begins Property, and first takes things out of their Common State. As in the begining before Men entred into Society, this was the begining of it (*Cain* & *Abel* had their Right of Property, the one in *the Lands he Cultivated,* the other in *the Flocks he kept;* from their Labour spent on them) so 'tis ever since where the same *State of Nature Obtains,* nor can it be begun that I can see otherwise.

§ 18. And to this voice of the Law of Nature, *viz.* that *Labour in this State* shall be the beginning of Property, seems well to agree the voice of God Himself in the Gift or Grant he made of the Earth, the Creatures & Productions of it to Mankind, *Gen.* 1. 28.—Where we find that *Cultivating and Subduing the Earth,* and *having Dominion* are joyned together: Thereby assuring us that as in that Gift he then made of it in common to men, he did not design it should serve to their benefit & comfort only by its *Spontaneous*

* Mr. *Lock.*

Productions, but that it was his will that by *Art and Industry* in Subduing and Cultivating of it they should draw still more from it, so that this should be their *Title to it* at least during the continuance of *that State of Nature*, & till by positive Constitutions of their own, the matter of property should be otherwise Determined and Settled.

§ 19. And if this be true, as I think it is, *viz.* That in the beginning of the World before men entred into *Society*, & *so in all Ages and Places since* where *the State of Nature obtains*, and there are no *Positive Constitutions* (Tacit or Express) Regulating the matter of Property, *this is the only Way* of beginning a Property in things, be it *Land* or what else you please, it seems no way Difficult to Determine upon the extent of mens Properties during the continuance of this state of things among them, for this being the Cause and *Original* of all *Property*, must be the *Measure of it* too, whatever ways of fixing a Property in things thus firstly impropriated, may be consequent upon it: As far as *Labour extends*, and things by that are taken out of the common state *Nature* left them in, so far the *Right of Property* must extend and no further, what is beyond this must remain still in the same *Common State* it was made in. And further, at the same time Reason forces us to conclude that as to a Right of *Property in Land particularly*, it can't be of great Extent during mens continuance *in this State*, at least so long as they continue their Simple, Mean, Inartful way of Living, are mainly fed and cloth'd with *Roots, Fish, Fowl, Deer, Skins*, &c. The Spontaneous productions of Nature, & have those provisions of it in such plenty that want does not oblige them to Cultivate or Till the Earth. While things continue thus among them, what Temptation can they have to Impropriate much, especially if at the same time the necessary Utensils, such as *Ploughs, Hoes, Axes*, &c. are wanting, as we all know was the case with *the Aborigines of this Country* before the arrival of the *English* to it.

§ 20. And now from what I have thus said concerning the way of *Original* or *Primary Impropriation* in the state of Nature, it can't be difficult to determine of the Extent of the properties of *the Aborigines of this Country*, or any of them in Land at the time of the Access of the *English* to it, on the Supposition of their being in *this State;* Inasmuch as it assures us their *Labour* or *Improvement* was the measure of it. And to instance in the *Moheags* in particular, or any of them, concerning whose *Pretended Claims* there has been so much Noise and Strife in the Country, which even to this Day is not ended, what has been said assures us that on the Supposition of their being in this state at that time, instead of such *large Territories* they have been ignorantly (as well as knavishly enough no doubt) tho't by some to have, *they had really good Right or Title,* but to here and there a *few spots of it,* viz. only to so much as by the means abovementioned they had separated and inclosed from the rest of the Country. I shall not presume upon an *Umpirage* in this matter, by saying they were doubtless at that time in *the State of nature.* I Remember what the Judicious Mr. *Hooker* in his Learned treatise of *Ecclesiastical Policy, Lib.* 1. *Sect.* 10. Suggests concerning the defects of Polities civil in their beginnings in the more early Ages of the World, and perhaps it is a difficult thing to fix the bounds between the *State of Nature* and that *of Civil Policy,* or say how far the Rights of the Law of Nature must be given up or Retained by persons in order to their belonging to the one or the other: yet thus far I shall venture to say, *viz.* That if what has been said Descriptive of this *State of Nature* be true, as I think it is, and if withal we may make a Judgment of the Customs and Way of Living of the Persons I am now speaking of, at that time, by the Customs & Manners of the more Uncivilizd part of their Survivors at this day, who I imagine may reasonably be thought the Liveliest Images of their *Ancestors,* and most to retain their *Customs;* if we may do so I say, the Probability seems to lie on the Affirmative side, *viz.* That they were with their Brethren in *Peru, Florida, Brasil,* &c. before mention'd from *Acosta,* to be rank't with those in a State of *Nature.*

§ 21. Who that is not a Stranger to them will say the forementioned Essentials of a state of *Civil Policy* are to be found among them? that they have any *Established, Setled, common Law* received and allowed so much as by a Tacit Consent to be the *Standard* of Right and Wrong and the Common Measure to decide Controversies arising among them? And herewith a known, Indifferent Judge with Authority to determine differences according to this Established Received Law? Who knows not that an Attempt to find these things among them is like a search for the Living among the Dead? And that when *Controversies* arise among them, without a reference of the matter to the decision of any *Common Umpire* or Judge every one looks on himself as Vested with the *Rights of the Law of Nature,* and accordingly is *Judge for himself* and *Executioner!* This every one knows is the common, uninterrupted Practice of those of whom I am now speaking of, and what is accounted *Reputable and Laudable* among them in all Disputes where the Contending Parties are capable of it, and in such as issue in the *Death* of either of them, consonant to the same Law the *nearest Relative or Relatives* of the *Slain*, look on themselves as the Persons concerned *to do Justice* on the *Murderer*, and accordingly fail not to watch all opportunities, till at length by Surprize or Violence they compass it, and by the *Gun*, *Hatchet* or *Knife*, end the Controversy.

§ 22. I think I am not *Injurious* in this *Account* of the *Present State* of *things* among those of *Our Natives* as we call them, I am now speaking of, nor can I so much as Suspect a *Censure for it*, since it is no more than what most that are not Strangers to them know. The Tragical end of *Mahomet* Eldest Son, as I take it, to *Owaneco*, with the like Tragical Occasion of it, is yet Fresh in our Memories, and its needless for me to Relate: and who knows not that That was but one Instance of that Justice, which is as Frequent among them as there is the like Occasion? This every one I think must say looks very much like *the State of Nature*, (if the forementioned Account of it be true) and if it be not an Evidence of its Obtaining among a People, is at least an Evidence of such *an Imperfect State of Civil Policy* as borders very near upon it. And if it be so with these now, we have I believe reason to Conclude the Condition of their *Ancestors* Living at the Time of the *Access of the English* to the Country, and before, was not better; for who can think that these *their Present Survivor* are more degenerate and farther removed from a State of *Civil Policy* than they were? For my own part, I have ever tho't on the other hand that even the main *of that Shadow of it* which is now among them is of *later Date*, assumed by them partly from an Humour *of Conformity to us* their New Neighbours, and partly for other *Reasons* and not a continuance of Ancient, Immemorial Customs among them.

§ 23. Nor is it as I conceive any *Conclusive Evidence* of the contrary that they Liv'd in *some sort of Society* or Neighbourhood and had their *Chiefs* or *Superiors* among them, whether they were such as were so *by Nature* and *Age*, or *by Election:* Since *the State of Nature*, tho' it Banish or Implys an Absence of *all Inequality among Men* as to *Civil Authority* or Jurisdiction, yet does not exclude *all Inequallity whatsoever*. The State of *Nature* is a *State of Subjection* to the Dictates and Direction of *the Law of Nature*, which Law is so far from Banishing *all Inequality* or *Subordination* among Men, that *it Ordains it in diverse Instances* of it, particularly in the Relations of *Parents* & *Children*, *Husband* & *Wife*, *Captain* & *Souldiers*, right reason which is this Law says there shall be *Subjection* & *Subordination*. These Inequalities therefore are no ways Inconsistent with this State, nor of themselves Evidences it does not obtain among any. And these I think it *not Improbable*, were the only *Inequalities* or *Subordinations* among the Persons I am now speaking of at this time and perhaps ever before. Their *Chiefs* or *Superiors* seem to have been either such as were so by *Nature* or *Age, Ancient Fathers,* or *Military Heads* chosen by them to lead them out against *their Enemies.* Thus where *Families* among them happened to be *Numerous,* continued *entire together,* and tho't themselves *Sufficient to Subsist by themselves* without Uniting with others, (as was oft the case no doubt, in that Day when there was no want of Land, all the Country, excepting *here and there a Spot,* was an Uncultivated Wilderness, all Provisions of Nature Accommodate to their Plain, Mean, Inartful Way of Living were in great Plenty, and nothing found to give Price to them farther than this did, and Consequently *Temptations and Occasions* of Strife or *Contention* among them were few and rare, during this Day or Time I say) *the Fathers* of such Families *in Succession* seem to have been their only *Superiors* or *Chiefs,* and by the exercise of their *Paternal Authority,* (to which such Families had been Accustomed) maintained *the little Order* was among them: They seem to have been their *Captains* or *Leaders* too when Occasion requir'd, unless by reason of some Defect of *Body* or *Mind* they were Incapable of it. But when the case happened to be otherwise, as no doubt it often did, and *diverse Families* saw a necessity of *Uniting together* for their better Security against *Foreign Force,* their *Superiors* or *Chiefs* were by Election, and seem to have been chosen by them for no other end than to *be Generals of their Armies,* as among their Brethren in *Peru,* &c. before mention'd. Nor do they seem to have had but little, if any *Dominion at Home in times of Peace.* In this Respect they seem (if the Comparison may be allow'd) to be like *the Judges in Israel of Old,* who certainly were little, if any thing, more *than Generals of their Armies.*

§ 24. These I am much inclin'd to think were the *only Superiors* or *Chiefs* they had among them, and which perhaps by an Abuse or Misapplication of the Term, *Sachem* (which probably in its Original sense intends no more than a *Chief Father or Captain*) have in later times gone by the Name of *Kings* or *Civil Heads.* And tho' perhaps some will say this is all but *Conjecture* or *Chimaera,* and as such only to be regarded; yet I must tell them I can't but much incline *to this Opinion,* and think I shall do so till I can see some further evidence of *the Essentials of Kings* in them than ever yet I did, and can believe that there is so much of Spell in that Title or *Epithet* that the bare Application of it to a Person is Sufficient without any thing else, to make him *in fact* so. But whatever may be the Truth as to this, and on which side soever those who are Judicious, & more Learned in these things than I, may resolve the matter, yet supposing what I have Discover'd as my *Prevailing Opinion* in the case, to be Truth and that after all the *Honours done their Chiefs* by the Glorious Titles of *Kings, Emperors, Allies,* &c. they were but *Chief Fathers* or *Captains* and really in *the State of Nature* with the rest of their Brethren, I think its pretty clear *the Properties* of any or all of them in Lands were of no greater extent than has been above expressed, and Consequently *vastly short* of what by many wanting Probity and Sense we have been born in hand they were.

§ 25. I come now to consider the *Second Hypothesis, viz.* That how *Defective* or *Wanting* soever their State might be as to the forementiond requisites *of a State of Civil Society,* and though Judging by what was generally Practiced among them, (every one retaining in his own Hands *the Rights of the Law of Nature*) they seem to have been in that State, Yet that they had *really quitted it,* entred into *Communities,* and by *Compact,* and at least *Tacit Constitutions* of their own, settled the *matter of Property,* both with *their Neighbours* respectively, & *severally among themselves;* and that these forementiond *Customs,* with others of the like Nature arguing *the State of Nature* obtaining among them, were rather from a *Defect* in Establishing proper Methods for the Execution of their Laws, than Evidences that they had none.

§ 26. I have already expressed *my Sentiment* in this matter, which whether it be right or wrong, matters not as to what is now before me, which is to *Consider this Opinion* and see what (upon a Supposition of the truth of it) can be determined upon *the Claims or Pretensions* of any of them to Lands in the Country. And I am pretty well assured this Opinion, (how fond so ever our *Bigots to Native Right* are of it, yet will less serve that Interest, at least *in the Present Day,* than the former; in as much as on a Supposition of it; tho' it must be allow'd they had a *Common Property* considered as *Communities* or *Politick Bodies,* and besides this that some or all the Members of each Community respectively had severally particular Properties of their own Exclusive of the rest of Mankind, yet) all becomes so Perplex'd and in the Dark, and so many Difficulties inextricable, *at least in the Present Day,* unavoidably attend all, that nothing certain can be determin'd upon the Properties of any of them, whether *Communities* or *Particular Persons;* I shall give some Evidence of this, when I have Premised this, *viz.*

§ 27. That allowing it *to be true* that they *had quitted the state of Nature,* and put on *some Form of civil Policy,* yet it does not from thence necessarily follow that Lands were brought under the Regulation *of Compact,* or any *Positive Constitutions of their own,* (tacit or express:) Or that they were held by them any otherwise than as in *the State and by the Law of Nature.* Certain it is there is no necessary Connexion between those things, the *Former* does not infer the *Latter;* A People may put on some Form of *Policy* without any Determination of the matter of *Property in Lands* whether by *Compact* with Neighbouring *Polities* or any *Positive Constitutions* of their own. And for my own part I never yet saw any sufficient Reason to conclude there was any thing of this nature done by them before the Arrival of the *English* here: Nor do I think it will seem probable there was, to any that considers their poor, mean, barbarous *way of Living,* the great Plenty of all the *Provisions of Nature* that requir'd, the very little use they made of *the Earth* further than to walk upon it, together with their want not only of that Communication with other parts of the World, but of any thing among themselves that might give a Value to the Provisions of Nature over and above what their own Necessities did. Their way of Living the *Poet* well describes when accounting for the Golden Age, he tells us of Men then,

Contentique cibis nullo cogente Creatis,
Arbuteos fatus, montanaque fraga legebant;
Cornaque & in duris haerentia mora rubetis,
Et quae deciderant patula Jovis arbore glandes.

And men themselves contented were with plain & simple *Food,*
That on the Earth of natures gift, without their Travel stood,
Did *live by* Respis, Hipps & Haws, by Cornets, Plums & Cherries
By sloes & Apples, Nuts & Pears & loathsom Bramble-berries,
And by the Acorns dropt *on ground from Joves broad tree in field*

Certain 'tis Nature prepared the *main Materials of their Subsistence* without any *Art or Labour* of theirs; they had but little more to do than to *Catch or Gather* what they had provided for them. And during this State of things among any Societies of Men, of what Consideration or Value *can Land be to them,* especially when these spontaneous Provisions of Nature in all Places are in such Abundance that there is *no danger of Want,* and all means of Communication or Trade with other parts of the World, together with *the Use of Money,* among themselves, (which things might impair their Stock of Provisions and give a Value to them over and above what their own Necessities did) are wholly wanting, as we all know was the case with the *Aborigines of the Country?* Surely it could not be of such Value to them as to put them upon a Partage or Impropriation of it farther than was done before by *the Law of Nature.* Let us suppose an *Island* so Separated from the rest of the World as to be under an utter Impossibility of any Commerce with it; wherein there were Inhabitants embodied together in *Civil Societies,* yet Living almost entirely on what *Nature prepared to their Hands,* and so disproportioned in number to the quantity of their Provisions that after their Consumption of what was needful for them, there remained enough for perhaps *Ten times the Number,* and at the same time nothing in the *Island* either because of its *Commonness* or *Perishableness* fit to supply the place of *Money;* what Inducement could such Societies have by *any Compact* either with one another, or among themselves respectively, to fix a *Property in Lands,* beyond what was done in the way before mentioned by *the Law of Nature,* for my own part I can't Excogitate any. And who knows not that this was *the very Case* with the Persons I am speaking of, before the Arrival of the *English* here. For this reason I think it highly *Probable,* yea next to *a Certainty* that such *Lands only* as their Poor way of Living rendred their *Tillage* of necessary (and how small a part was this compared with the rest of the Country?) they put *any Value upon:* the rest they looked upon as of no more Price, nor Advantage to be Impropriated than *the Air they Breathed in:* and therefore (like other things of the like Nature in all Communities) lay Neglected in that *Common State* wherein Nature left it. Nor let this be thought strange, since from *Divine Revelation itself* we have pretty good assurance that it is no more than *was Common* in the more Early Times of the World: There we find that in those Days men did not always immediately upon their *Entring into Society,* set out the Bounds of their *distinct Territories,* and by *Laws* within themselves respectively *Settle the matter of Property;* but suffered a great, may I not say the greatest part of the Land? to lie in *the same Common State* it was in before. Even in *Abraham's* time we find men *wandred up & down* with their *Flocks & Herds* freely and without Molestation, seeking *Pasture* where they liked best; and that *Abraham* himself did this in *a Country* where he was a Stranger, and there were many *Kingdoms* or *Communities of Men,* and they not newly formed neither. Which to me seems a pretty good Evidence that at least a great part, yea Probably the greatest part of *the Land lay in Common,* that the Inhabitants Valued it not, at least so far as to think it worth their while to come to a

Partage of it, and fix their *respective Properties* in it: The reasons of which no doubt were their Rude, Mean, Inartful Way of Living, Feeding and Clothing themselves mainly *with what Nature Prepar'd, in* which Preparations as they were in *great Plenty,* so Probably they had *no Money* or any *Equivalent* of it that might give a Value to any thing above what *their way of Living did.*

§ 28. I make no doubt there are those who will *not Scruple to say* the contrary to this is *Evident in the Aborigines of this Country,* and that in Fact they had *by Compact* and Constitutions Positive (Tacit or Express,) Settled the matter *of Property in Lands, each Society* with *its Neighbours,* and among *themselves severally:* But be it so, I think its Probable, if not more than so, from what I have said, that *they had not,* and though I suppose I know the reasons on which they may so assert, as well as they, yet as I think they will scarcely *weigh in the Ballance* with the Evidence to the contrary given above, so desire to see some further and better reason for it before I believe it. Its very true that when after *the Arrival of the English here,* by *Conversation* and *Commerce* with them they were made Sensible of the Value of the *Money* they brought with them and made tender of for *Land,* they could not then but see that the *Lands* beyond what they Improved, and so held by the *Law of Nature,* might be very Profitable to them, and on this I doubt not they were full enough in their Assertions of this Nature, *viz.* that *by Compact* and *Constitutions of their own* they were entituled to such and such *Limits respectively;* but this I think can carry with it *little Evidence* of the thing to one who knows what *they were,* and withal considers what is universally observable in *their Posterity* at this Day, when such a Temptation is laid before them. To all which I may add what I suppose comes pretty near a Demonstration in the case, *viz.* their *Palpable Contradictions* one of the other in their Pretensions, or the Accounts they gave, on this Occasion, of *their Respective Claims* or Properties, One *Sachem* or *Community* often Claiming *what another did.* This who knows not to be fact as *to Lands in this part of the Country,* where the Claims of *Hiums, Uncass,* and *Sannup* are found to interfere, the Consequence of which has been that *Persons Claiming under them,* have endeavoured each one to set up his Title in Opposition to the other, to the no small Expence of Time and Money, as well as Hurt of the Publick.

§ 29. Now supposing this to be so, 'tis Evident *the Hypothesis or Opinion* of their having quitted *the State of Nature* & put on some *Form of Policy,* meerly, does no Service to the Interest the *Zealous Assertors of it* endeavour to Advance by it, does not extend *Native Right* one Inch farther than the former Opinion did: for the Unavoidable Consequence of it is this, *viz.* that as no *Societies* of them had any *common Right or Property,* as such, so neither any *Particular Member* of those *Societies,* any by virtue of any *Positive Constitutions* or otherwise than by *the Law of Nature:* and that setting aside here and there *a Spot* this or the other Person or Persons Improved and so Impropriated and *Held* by *the Law of Nature,* all the rest of *the Country* Remained in the same *Common State* wherein it was made, as much the Property of *the Kings of the Indies* on the Opposite side of the Globe *as Theirs.* Now, in order to the rendring this Opinion of any Service to the end for which its *so Zealously* Avouch'd and Advanc'd *by Many,* its not enough to assert, yea & make evident too that *Our Aborigines* had quitted *the State of Nature* and put on some *form of Policy,* but further, as I before observed, that they had *by Compact one with another, & Positive Constitutions* (Tacit or Express) Determined and *Settled their Bounds* and the terms of *each Community* respectively, and after this is done it will be of no advantage still to the pretensions of any *Particular Community,* or any *Member* or *Members* of it, till we are assured *what bounds by Compact* with its Neighbours it had, and what Settlement *its Constitutions* made of *the Lands within it:* which I conjecture none can do without *the help of Divination.*

§ 30. Which brings me to what I proposed, which was to shew that on a Supposition of the Truth of this (*viz.* that *Our Aborigines* were to be considered as in *a State of Society Civil,* and had by these consequent Acts Determined and Regulated *the matter of Property*) all their Rights or Properties instantly become so Perplext and in the Dark that nothing can be Known or Determin'd upon them, and consequently *no good Title* possibly founded on them. And in pursuance of this, and at the same time to convince the bold Avouchers of this Opinion, I would Demand of them in a few things;

1. On a Supposition of the truth of this, *Who can account for the true extent of the common Properties of their Respective Communities, or any one of them?* If I have not been Misinformed some pains was formerly taken both in this and some *Neighbouring Governments* for a Resolution in this point: and for that end *Persons were Deputed* to Enquire & Obtain the best light they could of the Natives. What success attended these endeavours in *Other Governments* I know not, but in this I suppose *none at all.* Its true the Gentlemen Deputed by this Government to enquire into the Claim of the *Moheags* made return of something to the Assembly which they call'd an Account or description of their Claim by certain Abutments, and which the Assembly

so far had regard to as, if I mistake not, to allow of its Entry on record. But yet can any of those who would perswade us to think that *Native Right* is our only *Valuable Title,* Acquiesce in this or think it of any value, when at the same time their Neighbours, the *Pequots, Quinebaugs, Nahanticks,* (all of them as worthy of Credit as the *Moheags,*) give another Account, some of them claiming *all the Lands* within those Limits, saving the *Moheags* had *none,* & others of them claiming at least *Large Tracts* within them. I suppose none will deny this to be Fact, or if there be that shall do so, that the Claimers under *Hiums* and *Sannup* will stand by me in it. Now if *Native Right* be our only *Valuable Title* what shall be done in this case to know where or in whom *this Right to these Lands* is? Certain it is if they were *Communities,* or *Bodies Politick* properly so Called, they had *a Federative Power,* and if in the Exercise of it, they made a *Partage of the Lands,* in this part of the Country among them, their Title Respectively was good, & as good in *one Community* as another; and what shall be done in this Case? how shall we be satisfied which of them *speaks Truth,* & consequently where *the Right is* and of whom to be obtained? Nor can it satisfy any but Fools to be able in this case to say they have *Purchased of the Natives.* Nor is there any thing I know of can help in this case but a Supposal of *the Falseness* of all *their Pretensions* to a Partage or Impropriation of the Lands *to any Limits:* and that whatever *Compacts* they made Determining *their Bounds* respectively, they had therein a Sole Reference to the *Hunt* or *Game,* and Designed only an Impropriation of that; at the same time not having the least Regard to the *Lands,* nor caring, excepting as above, *who had it,* it being a thing of *no Price to them.* And this as it is Undoubtedly the Truth of the matter, so reduces the *Right* or *Property* of such *Lands* to *some Certainty,* lets us know *where or in whom it is,* and to whom we must Apply for the fixing a *Property* in them. But supposing this Difficulty attending this Opinion were removed and the common Right *of each Community,* set out by Monuments. Yet

2. *Who could tell us what Disposition or Settlement the Constitutions* (*Tacit or Express,*) *of each Society made of the Lands within their Limits respectively?* The Resolution of this is *as necessary* as the other in Order to a *Determination* upon the extent of the *Properties* of any or all of them. I take it for Granted and think it needs *no Proof,* that as all Men by Vertue of the Grant of the *Most High* before mentioned, are not only *Commoners of the Earth,* but *equally so,* none having *a Right* by that to Claim more or *larger Portions* of it than others, so that when any numbers of them enter *into Society,*

and by *Compact* with Neighbouring Societies Settle *their Limits,* the Lands within such Limits are the common Right *of the Community,* and equally so; and that the several Members *remain Commoners* in an equallity, till *by Constitutions* of their own they make *another Settlement* of them; And because this is supposed (by such as assert the Politick State of the Natives) to have been done by them long before the Arrival of the *English* here, I therefore Demand what Disposition or Settlement did *their Constitutions* make of the Lands within *their respective Limits?* When they came to a Partage or Impropriation, did they Impropriate in *an Equallity,* or if not, what other Settlement did they make of them? Or if this be thought an Unreasonable Demand, because of the generality of it, I Demand *what Settlement* did the Constitutions *of any one Community* (to Instance in the *Moheags* Our Neighbours) make of the Lands within their Limits? To be more particular here,

(1.) *Where or in whom did they place the Lands?* I Observed but now they were Originally or Firstly *in the Community,* and equally so, and must remain so till by Acts of their own they make a Disposition of them *into another Hand or Hands:* and reason will tell every Man it must be so. Now if by *Acts* or *Laws* of their own they Alter'd *the Original or Primary State* of the Lands, I Demand what *was the Alteration?* Where or in whom did they *Place or Settle them?* Did they Settle them in *any One single Person or Relation,* or in a *Certain Number of Men* of any certain Order or Character? On the Supposition of the Truth of the Opinion I am now considering, nothing can be Determin'd of *the Extent,* no nor *the Reallity* neither of the Property of any of them till this be Resolved. I know very well Our *Bigots* say here, that *their Constitutions vested all the Lands* in *their Kings,* or in *the Crown,* (to Use our *English* Phrase,) but besides that that is spoken without *any Proof,* or any *Possibility of it* as I imagine, besides this I say, allowing it be *Truth,* yet it brings not *the State of the Lands* in any *particular Community* to any *Certainty,* nor Resolves us in *whom the Property of all* or any Part of them is till we are also Resolved in the following Particulars also, *viz.*

(1) *What they intend by Sachems or Kings in whom their Constitutions vested the Lands.* Whether such as were so *de jure* or *de facto,*[3] i.e. whether such as were *Rightfully* or by *the Laws & Constitutions* of the *Society* so, or *in Fact* only. And in order to this we must be Resolved of the particular *Form*

3. ["By law or in fact."]

of Policy agreed upon in the several Societies, *viz.* Whether in case it was *Monarchial,* that they were *Hereditary* or *Elective Monarchies,* and not only so, but moreover whether *Uncass, Sasacus, Aramames* or any other *Chief among them,* of whom we would obtain Lands, *be King or Monarch* according to the *Fundamental Laws* or Constitutions of the Society yea or not. For if not (the *Lawful Kings Right of Property* being meerly & altogether from the Concession or Grant *of the Community*) they can't have any pretence to it; nor possibly make out *a Good Title* to any other.

(2.) *We must be resolved how or in what sense they vested the Lands in them:* Whether so as to make them *their Inalienable Right* or Property, as the case seems to be with *Land in some Constitutions;* Or Alienable: And if in this last sense, whether they were *so Absolutely* put into their hands, that they had *Right of Disposal* where & to whom they saw cause, or *in Trust only* for the Use and Benefit of the Societies Respectively? In which sense, as I understand it, all Lands in our *English* Dominions are by *Our Constitution* vested in *the King or Crown;* and Lands in *this Government* are by *the Charter* Vested in *the Corporation,* and for that Reason are Alienable from it, and may become *the Property of others.* If their Constitutions Vested the Lands *in their Kings* in the first sense, by what *Right* or *Authority* did they Alienate or Dispose of them *to others?* All Alienations made by them must be *ipso facto* Void: For if *the Communities* in Vesting the Lands in them gave them *no power of Alienation* they could have none. If it be said they were Vested in them in the second sense, *viz.* With *an Unlimited Power* of making *Alienations* of them to whom they saw cause; I say this is *Incredible;* For if Lands were of such Value with them that they saw it worth their while to bring them under the Regulation of *Positive Constitutions,* its unreasonable to think they should in this sense put them into the Hands of *any Person or Persons* whatever: and by Consequence (supposing *the Hypothesis* I am now examining be true, and that Lands *by their Constitutions* (Tacit or Express) were Vested in *their Kings*) it can't be imagined they had Right or Power to make *a Partage or Division* of their Dominions among *their own Children,* to the Exclusion of the rest of the *Community.* For which reason I have ever tho't *Allawanhoods,* alias *Joshua's Right* nothing worth, even upon *the very Principles* of the Advocates or Assertors of it. And if the last sense be asserted (which indeed carries with it the greatest Probability if any thing of this Nature was done among them) then I Demand again *by what Right or Authority* did they Divide their Dominions among *their Children* (an instance of which was but now given) or make *Conveyances of them to the English?* Such Alienations must be as Void as on the Supposition of the Truth of the first sense.

(3.) *And in case their Constitutions Vested the Lands in their Kings in this last sense,* viz. *In Trust,* &c. *before we can be Resolved of the State of the Lands in any Society, and of the reallity and extent of the* Right *or* Property *of any particular Member or Members of them,* we must be resolved also *whether any Alienations* were made by *their Kings* to *their Subjects,* and what *they were,* together with the Tenures in or by which they were to be holden of *the Grantees.*

§ 31. Its possible in what I have now said, I may not have expressed my self in *the most Proper Terms:* It requires perhaps more Knowlege of *the Law* for a Person to be Able in an Affair of this Nature, to do so, than I may pretend to. However I hope what I have said is *Intelligible,* and being so may Suffice as to what I Scope at in it: which is to shew *what little Service this Hypothesis* concerning *the Aborigines* of this Country does to the Interest many endeavour to Advance and Serve by it: and that a Supposition of its Truth Inevitably Involves *their Rights or Claims* in so many Inextricable Difficulties and renders them all so *Uncertain,* Perplex't and in the Dark that *nothing Certain* can be Known or Determined upon them. And though perhaps some may think what I have here Advanc'd as necessary on *this Hypothesis* to be Resolved, in Order to a Determination upon their Rights, *Absurd,* Yet I can't but think all those that think of things, not with the Multitude, (who generally Speaking have too much *Rubbish in their Brains* to think of any thing with distinctness) but as they are *in themselves,* will say that without a Resolution of them nothing can *be Determined* with any certainty upon this Matter.

To Conclude; The sum of what has been said is this, *viz.* Either they were a People *in the State of Nature* or *they were* not; this I suppose all must allow, there being no *Third State* wherein any Persons either now or at any time heretofore were. If they were *in the State of Nature,* they had then Right *of Property* only in such *Lands as they Impropriated* (and held) by *the Law of Nature,* which as we all know was only here and there *a small spot* in the Country. If it be said *they had Quitted that State* and put on some *form of Policy,* then I say either they had *by Compact and Positive Constitutions* of their own (Tacit or Express) Settled *the matter of Property,* or they had not: If it be said *they had not,* then it follows that *the State of the Lands in the*

Country was not altered *from what it was before;* but they all (excepting only what was *Impropriated* by *the Law of Nature*) remained in *the same Common State* and Equally the Right of every Man, as they *were before,* while *the State of Nature* continued: Nor was the *Prince* or *the Peasant* distinguished as to Right of *Property* in them otherwise than as in *the State of Nature.* For as *Property in Lands* is not included in the notion of a *King,* or the want of it in that of *a Subject;* so the making one Person a *King,* and another *a Subject* simply in it self, will not make a Right of *Property,* and *give it* to the One, or *Banish it* from the Other, without some other *Act or Acts* concurrent with it. If it be said *they had brought the Lands in the Country* under the regulation of *Compact & Constitutions* of their own, then it will follow that they had given *up their Title* by the Law of Nature, that what was before *by the Law of Nature* the Title of any of them *to Lands,* was not, at least, *qua* such, their Title now; but that what *Right or Title* any or all of them had now was by *their Constitutions Positive* the inevitable consequence of which must be that till *those Constitutions* are declared, and we assured what they Determined upon this matter *of Property,* nothing can be known or determined upon *the Rights of any of them,* we can't say where or in whom *Right or Property* was, whether in *the Prince or People,* some or all of them. And this having never been done, 'tis beyond me to see of what Advantage *this Hypothesis* can be to the End for which its so Zealously Asserted by some.

But its time to hasten to an End, and from the whole that has been said, I can't but think the following must be allowed to have *Considerable Evidence* of Truth in them, how contrary soever to *Vulgar Sentiments* in the Present Day, *viz.*

1. *That such Lands only as any of our Aborigines Subdued and Improved, they had a good Right or Title to.* For altho' we are sure they had *the Law of Nature* giving them a *Right of Property* by *their Labour,* in what before lay *in Common* and was Equally the Right of every *Man,* yet we are not sure (nor indeed have we so much Evidence as amounts to a Probability) of their having *any other Law* to Entitle them *to Lands* or any thing else, on any Conditions whatsoever.

2. *That Supposing their Chiefs to be Kings or Civil Heads Properly so called, yet there is more Reason to suspect a Right of Property in them, than in any of their Subjects.* Yea the more reason to suspect it because of *their Dignity.* Nothing ever did or can appear Evidencing so much as *a Probability* of such a Right in them by the Positive Constitutions *of their Communities;* and as

for Acquiring it *by Labour* in Subduing and Cultivating, its reasonable to think *their Exaltation* rendered that too great a Stoop for them.

3. *That supposing the* English *to be the first* (of Civiliz'd Nations) *in the Discovery of the Country, they had* (the Royal Allowance and Favour Concurring) *an Undoubted Right to Enter upon and Impropriate all such parts of it as lay Wast or Unimproved by the Natives and this without any consideration or allowance made to them for it.* Whatever ties *Prudential Considerations* might lay them under to Acknowlege them, and present them with *their Gratuities* under the Notion of their being a Price for Lands; yet all such Lands being like the Ocean it self, *Publici vel Communis juris,*[4] they could be under no Obligation from the Head of Justice. We have as much Assurance of this as we have that Lands were held by *the Natives* only by the *Law of Nature,* and of that I think pretty good Evidence has been given in what has been said on this Argument. And by Consequence it follows also,

4. *That as that Darling Principle of many,* viz. *That Native Right is the only Valuable Title to any Lands in the Country is Absurd and Foolish and may with Reason be look't upon as one of our Vulgar Errors;* So that the *Endeavour of any,* whether in more early or later Times *to Maintain and Propagate it,* (to the Prejudice of *New Settlements,* and not only to the Disturbance of *Honest Men* in their Possessions and Improvements, but *Ejectment out of them,* as well as the Hurt of *the Publick,* as they have been without any Justifying reason, so) *must be look'd upon as very Culpable.* Its well known that not only *in the more Early Days* of the Country, but in later *Times* there have been those, and they not of the *Plebs* only, who with a great deal of Zeal and Application have laid out themselves in this Affair: A Zeal and Application which, without a Crime I think, I may say, would have been more Decorous in them had it been otherwise Employ'd. *Native Right they have told us is our only Title, if we have not this, we have Nothing.* Its not an easy thing to Account for *the Train of Evils* that have ensued hereupon, not only to *Particular Plantations and Persons,* but to *the Publick* in the great Delay and Embarasment of Business in *Our Assembly's,* as well as the *Multiplication of Suits* in the Law beyond Account. But how unjustifyable must these things be when in all, the Persons I am speaking of, have endeavoured to impose upon us but a meer *Chimaera or Fiction?* I can't forbear mentioning here that among other Methods improved by them in the management of their

4. ["Of public or common law."]

Design, One is, They have Endeavoured rather to work *on Our Passions* than *Our Reason,* or to Fright us into a *Belief of this Doctrine* and a Resolution to stand by it, than to gain us over to it by any Evidence of its Truth. For whereas they have been very Sparing *of Demonstration* they have been as liberal in *Assurances* (or rather Asseverations) that 'tis the Only Security of Our Interests against the *Claim of One beyond the Seas;* and that if *Native Right* will not Invalidate the *Duke's Pretensions,* we have nothing else that will. Such *Nonsense* as this were it found only in some of our *Homunculi,*[5] might be *Easily Overlook'd;* but when Men *of Education and Character* shall Talk at this rate its scarcely to *be forgiven.* Nor is this *the worst neither,* but what deserves still a *more severe Censure* is their want *of Truth and Honesty* in all, or that whereas in all they have acted under the *specious umbrage* of serving *the Publick,* tis notorious that *Nothing less than this* has been in design with them; but that on the other hand they have been under the Governing Influence of *those Corrupt Views* which (Supposing or Allowing there were Sufficient Reasons in the Nature of the thing, for what they have done) could do no other *than render them very Guilty* therein. I think I am not too severe *in this Censure,* nor in the least break in upon *Charity by it,* since they themselves have given and daily give that Evidence of its Truth, which (as the Blindest Eye can't see, so) Amounts to a Demonstration in the Case.

FAREWEL.

John Bulkley.
Colchester, *December* 24 1724.

5. ["Little men, weaklings."]

· 25 ·

J. N., The Liberty and Property of British Subjects Asserted (London, 1726)

THE OUTCOME OF THE South Carolina 1719 revolution against the proprietors continued to be uncertain for almost a decade, with the proprietors endeavoring to get the colony back and most of the settlers pressing for a continuance of the royal government that the Crown had instituted in 1721. Published in 1726 in response to still another proprietary initiative, this selection provided a powerful statement of the settler position. It consists of two parts. The body of the pamphlet took the form of a letter to a proprietary supporter in England and is signed by J—— N——. One scholar has identified the author as John Norris, a London merchant and long-term promoter of settlement in and sometime resident of South Carolina. But the title page announced that the author was "an Assembly-Man in Carolina," and no contemporary document identifies Norris as having been a member of that body. Indeed, the unsigned preface, which is as long as the letter and which provided a brief history of the colony and affirmed the ideas expressed in the main text, is more likely to have been the work of Norris.

If the author cannot be identified, however, the point of view expressed effectively laid out the arguments, developed over the previous century, for settler entitlement to traditional British rights with regard to liberty and property. Castigating his English correspondent for labeling the South Carolina revolution as "Rebellion, Theft, Ingratitude, and what not," he charged the proprietors and their supporters with "aiming at the Shadow of Regal Power, without the least Power or Capacity to support it" and utterly failing to live up to the compact represented by their original charter. He denied that settlers had any intention of interfering with the proprietors' title to the land and denounced proprietary efforts to sell the colony to the South Sea Company in 1720 as a blatant attempt to barter "the honest Planters and Merchants of *Carolina*" according "to the Practice[s] of the Coast of *Africa*" for the sale of slaves. "Can we call that Liberty and Property," he asked, "when honest free-born Subjects of *England* were exposed to Sale, and liable to be bought and sold like Negroes?" "Like true *Englishmen*, averse to Tyranny, and not willing to be driven to the Slave-market," South Carolina settlers, acting through their "little Senate" which, however "small and inconsiderable" it might appear from "three thousand Miles distant," was the settlers' chief bulwark against all "Threats" to the "Subversion of our Liberties . . . as *Englishmen*," had "set up a Governor of their own" and thrown themselves upon the mercy of the Crown. By these actions, they thus showed themselves to be both "loyal and affectionate to our King, and zealous for the Liberties of our Country, in Opposition to all Promoters of arbitrary Power." He assured his correspondent that six years later, the settlers remained "unanimous" in their resolve "not to be enslav'd" again by arbitrary and inefficient proprietary government. As the author of the preface added, it would be ungenerous and contrary to the "Spirit" of a nation renowned for liberty to deny it to "our Brethren" in the colonies merely because they were "settled in America." (J.P.G.)

THE

Liberty and *Property* OF BRITISH SUBJECTS ASSERTED: In a LETTER from An ASSEMBLY-MAN in *Carolina,* To his Friend in *LONDON.*

Protect us mighty Providence!
*What wou'd these * * * * * have?*
First they wou'd bribe us without Pence,
Deceive us without common Sense,
And without Power enslave.

Earl of *Dorset.*

LONDON.
Printed for J. ROBERTS in *Warwick-lane,* M.DCC.XXVI.
(*Price 6 d.*)

The Preface.

The following Letter being read one Day over a Bottle, where I happen'd to make one of the Company, seem'd to express such a true Spirit of Liberty and Love to Mankind, that the Question was immediately put, Why should it not be printed? We all agreeing that it could not reasonably give any Offence, and might be entertaining; it fell to my Lot to introduce it to the Publick.

So much by way of Introduction, and now for the Letter it self, which upon second reading gave me such Pleasure, that I dream't all Night of nothing but Liberty and Property; and had as it were a Vision of all the great Assertors of them, from the ancient *Greek* and *Roman Free States,* to the Time of our own glorious Revolution. I heard *Solon* crying: *O my Country! my dear Country!* as when he was about leaving *Athens* upon the Usurpation of *Pisistratus.* I saw the excellent *Socrates* dying a Martyr to Liberty, by the Command of his Scholar *Critias,* and the rest of the thirty Tyrants. I without Difficulty follow'd *Xenophon,* and his ten thousand gallant Countrymen in their March of above 1000 Miles, and that too, in the Face of more than 400,000 *Persians,* who vainly endeavour'd to oppose these Sons of Liberty. I had a lively Representation of the Battles of *Salamis, Platea* and *Marathon,* and many other glorious Struggles for the old *Grecian* Liberty. The *Romans* next appear'd contending for it; from the first *Brutus,* where it took its Rise, I had a View of the *Camilli, Manlii, Fabii,* and the *Scipio's*, to the last *Brutus,* where we may properly say it ended; for unhappy *Germanicus* lived not to make a Stand for Liberty, the Friends of Tyranny taking care to destroy him as soon as they but suspected his generous Principles. Then methought I heard *Tacitus* crying out,* *Plebs sordida Circo & Theatris sueta. Quam inops Italia, Plebs urbana imbellis, nihil in exercitibus validum praeter externum.*[1] Which is as much as to say in plain *English; Those who used to dispose of Kingdoms and Provinces are now busied only in Opera's and Masquerades; and that People who never found any Enterprize above their Spirit to undertake, and Power to accomplish, with their Liberty, have lost their Vigor and Virtue.* It would swell these Sheets too much, was I to relate all the particulars of this Vision; and few or none surely are ignorant of the glorious Struggles that have been made for Liberty in this Nation: In short, the old

* Annal. L. 3.

1. [Literally, "The multitude disgraceful and habituated to the Theater, the very worst of the slaves or those who after they had wasted their property were supported by the shame of Nero." Translated very loosely in text.—Tr.]

Grecian and *Roman* Notions of it are hardly to be found in any other Country, and none have so much Reason to boast its Enjoyment. Tho' some Persons have made it a Pretence for ill Purposes, yet 'tis what all true *Englishmen* must still hope to enjoy, since there is nothing that they are naturally more fond of. This Consideration (one would think) should perswade all disinterested and unprejudiced Persons of the Reasonableness of the following Letter, since 'tis very contradictory both to Virtue and Justice, whilst we are tenacious of Liberty our selves, to see our fellow Subjects deprived of it, without the greatest Concern, and Reluctance. And tho' the Climate of *Carolina* is, we are told, much the same with *Italy*, yet as the Inhabitants are at present entirely Strangers to Popery and Priestcraft, why should they be thought to partake more of the Nature of the base modern *Italians*, than of the illustrious old *Romans?* These generous Patriots of Liberty afford ample Instructions in the Matter we are now speaking of; for, whilst they retain'd their ancient Virtue, they were not content with enjoying Freedom themselves only, but carried it wherever their Eagles flew; their Conquests as well as their Colonies were enfranchised by them; and their being Vanquishers was a Misfortune to none but Tyrants.

What have We been fighting and contending for these 30 Years, but what these industrious Planters and Merchants now desire? And shall we be anxious not only for the Liberty of *England*, but of all *Europe*, and not allow our Brethren a Title to it, because alas! they are settled in *America?* Or do we imagine that the generous Nature and Spirit of *Englishmen* was dampt in their Passage thro' the Ocean? If this be the Case, we need only attend to the short Account that is hereafter given of them to find Reason for more favourable Sentiments.

Carolina is situated between 29 and 36 Degrees of *Northern* Latitude, upon that Circle of the Earth that affords Wine, Oil, Fruit, Grain, Silk, and most other rich Commodities; and is said to have been first discover'd by Sir *Sebastian Cabot*, (a Native of *Bristol* by *Venetian* Parents,) who call'd it *Carolina*, from the Name of his Majesty King *Charles* I. (which is what the *French* likewise arrogate, as done in honour of their *Charles* IX.) but the Truth of this Relation is greatly suspected: However it is certainly the *Northern* Part of that Region, where *John De Lion* a *Spaniard* landed in the Year 1512; and gave the Country the Name of *Florida*, from the perpetual Spring which it seemed to be bless'd with.

Eight Years afterwards, *viz.* A.D. 1520, the *Spaniards* sent *Vaquez de Ayllon* thither, but to little or no Purpose: And, in 1526, *Pamphilio Narvesi*; who, with his Companions, was starved to Death: The Fate of *Ferdinando Soto*, who follow'd him ten Years after, was much the same; for tho' he brought 900 Foot and 500 Horse with him, yet he and most of his Men were destroy'd either by Want or Sickness, or were kill'd by the *Indians;* the Remnant, led by *Lewis Moscos,* escaping with great difficulty. These ill Successes made the *Spaniards* desist from their Attempts in *Carolina.*

The next who came were the *French* under *John Ribaut,* in the Reign of *Charles* IX. being sent by the famous Admiral *Coligny* with two Ships: These were the first of any European Nations who made a Settlement in this Country; but for want of Supplies, *&c.* (the Civil Wars then raging in *France*) they return'd Home again: Two Years after, Peace being made, *Coligny* procured other Ships to be sent to this Country, under the Command of *Lewis Laudoner,* who finding no Mines, and his Provisions being almost spent, resolved to return Home also; but as he was preparing to depart, *John Ribaut* arrived with three Ships more, which procured them a kind Reception from the *Indians,* who promised to conduct them to the *Apalataean* Mountains bordering on *Virginia,* where they expected to discover Mines: And thus the *French* conceiv'd great Hopes of this their Settlement, when the *Spaniards* under the Command of *Peter Melanda,* arriving with a Squadron of Ships and Forces, drove them from their Forts, kill'd *Ribaut* and 600 of his Men, after having promised to give them Quarter, and forced *Laudoner* and his Companions to quit their Settlement and return Home. But not long afterwards *De Gorgues,* a French Gentleman, at his own Expence, fitted out three stout Ships, and with 280 Men sailed to *Carolina,* where he re-took the Fort, and put all the *Spaniards* to the Sword, and destroyed all the rest of the Forts and Garrisons, being assisted by two of the *Indian* Kings, because of the Aversion they had to the *Spaniards.* After this the *French* travel'd towards the Mountains, and are said to have converted several *Indians;* but we have no Account of their making any Settlement here, or of the *Spaniards* endeavouring to recover the Country: So that it probably lay deserted by all *Europeans* from the Year 1567 till 1622, when under the Reign of *Charles* II. several *English* Families, flying from the Massacres of the *Indians* in *Virginia* and *New-England,* were driven on these Coasts, and settled near the Head of the River *May:* As appears from the Relation of Mr. *Brigstock;* who gives us an Account of his being honourably entertain'd here by his Country-men, in the Year 1653.

Thus this Country, being abandon'd both by the *French* and *Spaniards,* was free to any that had a Mind to settle in it. And the Pretence of *Cabot's* Discovery gave the Crown of *England* a Sort of Title, upon which that of the Proprietors is founded. However King *Charles* II. thought fit, from these Pretensions, to make a Grant of this Country by a Patent, bearing Date

March 24th, 1663. and renew'd two Years after to *Edward* Earl of *Clarendon,* then Lord high Chancellor, *George* Duke of *Albemarle, William* Lord *Craven, John* Lord *Berkley, Anthony* Lord *Ashley,* Sir *George Carteret,* Sir *William Berkley,* and Sir *John Coleton;* from whom the present Proprietors claim, either by Inheritance or Purchase.

In persuance of this Grant, Encouragement was given for People to settle in this Province, and when there were so many Inhabitants that a Form of Government was necessary, 120 Articles, call'd *Fundamental Constitutions,* were agreed to, and sign'd by the Proprietors on the 1st of *March,* 1699. which *Constitutions* were drawn up by that famous Politician, the Earl of *Shaftsbury;* and *were* (as it is express'd in the last Article) *to remain the sacred, and unalterable Form of Government of CAROLINA for ever.*

The 1st Article of these Fundamentals, is, that *a* Palatine *shall be chosen from amongst the Proprietors, who shall continue during Life, and be succeeded by the Senior of the other Proprietors.* The Executive Power in most Cases is in the *Palatine* and three other Proprietors, who are authorized to execute the whole Powers of the Charter; and their Deputies in *Carolina* have this by Commission from their Principals, and are call'd the *Palatine*'s Court.

By the *Constitutions* there are to be three Hereditary Noblemen in every County, created by Patent under the Great Seal of the Province; one call'd a *Landgrave,* and two call'd *Cassiques,* who, with the Proprietors or their Deputies, the Governor and Commons, compose the Parliament. The Number of the *Landgraves,* according to the Fundamentals, should be 25, and that of the *Cassiques* 50 to make a Nobility; therefore as there are few or none of either at present, they are not summon'd to make an Upper House, but the *Governor* and the *Deputies* arrogate that Title to themselves only. The *Commons* are chosen by the Freeholders of every County, as the Knights of Shires in *England,* and were at first to sit in an House by themselves, and all have equal Votes, and were to meet once in two Years, or oftner if Occasion required.

The Courts of Justice, besides the *Palatine*'s Court, are that of the Chief Justice, the High Constable, the Chancellor, the Treasurer, the Chamberlain, and the High Steward; besides which, there are the Great Council, and the Hundred Courts. There is likewise a Sheriff, and four Justices of the Peace in every County.

The Laws of *England* are in Force in *Carolina,* but the Proprietors by their Deputies, with the Consent of the *Parliament,* or *Assembly* as tis now call'd, have Power to make *By Laws* for the better Government of the Province; so that no Law can properly be made, or Money rais'd, unless the People by their Representatives consent thereto. One of their Laws is well worth taking Notice of, that is, their Method of choosing *Juries,* which is by making a considerable Number of Paper Billets, on which the Names of the most substantial Freeholders are written. These Billets are put into a Hat, and twenty four are chosen out of them by the first Child that happens to pass by; then out of these twenty four, twelve are chosen at the next Court: An admirable Method to prevent Fraud and Bribery! and it would prevent a great deal of Injustice, were this Method practised for our *Middlesex* Juries.

The Difficulties and Dangers attending the first Settlement of this Colony, being a Discouragement to People from coming to it, the Proprietors enter'd into a joint Stock, and fitted out Ships to transport People and Cattle thither, the Charge of which amounted to 12000 *l.* besides as much more disbursed by single Proprietors, to advance the Colony: For there were several Planters settled in *Carolina,* before the present Lords Proprietors Patent was granted.

Things being thus establish'd according to their Grant, about the Year 1671. Colonel *William Sayle* was made Governor, and *James Carteret* Esq; Sir *John Yeomans* and *John Cook* Esq; Landgraves. But the *Constitutions* being found deficient in several Cases, *Temporary* Laws were added, and the Form of Government settled thus,

A Governor named by the *Palatine.*

A Council consisting of
- 7 Deputies of the Proprietors.
- 7 Gentlemen chosen by the Parliament.
- 7 of the eldest Landgraves and Cassiques.

An Admiral	Surveyor
Chamberlain	Treasurer
Chancellor	High Steward
Chief Justice	High Constable
Secretary	,

Register of Births Burials, and Marriages,
Register of Writings
Marshal of the Admiralty.

All which were nominated by the Proprietors respectively. The *Quorum* of the Council were to be the Governor, and 6 Counsellors, 3 at least being Deputies of the Proprietors; and because there were not Inhabitants enough to make a Parliament, according to the *Constitutions*, it was order'd to consist of the Governor, the Deputies of the Proprietors, and 20 Members chosen by the Freeholders, of whom ten were to be elected by *Berkley* County, and 10 by *Coleton* County; which Number was increased, as more Counties were laid out, and more People came to settle in the Province; so that for many Years there have been sufficient for a regular Parliament or Assembly. To Governor *Sayle* succeeded Sir *John Yeomans*, and to him *Joseph West* Esq; in 1680. He was one of the first Planters, and in 1682 held a Parliament at *Charles Town*, in which several Acts were pass'd and ratify'd by him, and the Proprietors Deputies: He was succeeded by *Joseph Moreton* Esq; 1683, under whom several Acts were likewise pass'd; the Year following, Sir *Rich. Kyrle* of *Ireland* was made Governor, but he dying within the Year, *Joseph West* Esq; was nominated again, in whose Time, the Lord *Cardross*, afterwards Earl of *Buchan*, with ten *Scotch* Families settled in *Carolina*; but his Lordship soon return'd home, and his Followers were dislodged by the *Spaniards*. The next Governor was *James Coleton* Esq; Brother to the Proprietor, who called a Parliament, A.D. 1687.

To Mr *Coleton* succeeded several Gentlemen, but in what Order is not certain; *viz. Smith, Quarry, Southwell, Ludwell*, and lastly *Thomas Smith* Esq; (as tis supposed a second Time) about the Year 1694; at whose Instigation one of the Proprietors, *John Archdale* Esq; was sent over in *August* 1695, to settle the Country and redress Grievances, which he at last with much Difficulty effected.

Mr. *Archdale* returning home, *Joseph Blake* Esq; also a Proprietor, was appointed Governor in his Stead: In whose Time, *Major Daniel* brought new *Constitutions* from *England*, consisting of 41 Articles, call'd the last *Fundamental Constitutions*, and sign'd by *John* Earl of *Bath*, Palatine, and the rest of the Proprietors; but they were never confirmed in Parliament at *Carolina*.

Mr. *Blake* dying about 1700, after some Dispute for the Office between *Joseph Moreton*, as eldest Landgrave, and Col. *James Moor*, the latter was chosen Governor, and as such confirm'd by the Palatine. His Successors were Sir *Nathaniel Johnson*, &c. * * * The Disputes and Transactions, that happen'd under their Administration who succeeded this Governor, are so well known to all that are in any wise concern'd in them, and would be so little entertaining to indifferent Persons, that the Reader will not be displeased at this being passed over; but we must not forget, that upon an

Address from the House of Lords, and a Representation from the Commissioners of Trade, *May* 24, 1706. to her late Majesty, Praying, *That Directions might be given for reassuming the Charter into, her Majesty's Hands by* SCIRE FACIAS,[2] she was pleased to order, *that for the more effectual proceeding against the said Charter by way of* Quo Warranto,[3] *Mr. Attorney and Solicitor General do inform themselves fully concerning what may be most necessary for effecting the same.*

This was the State of *Carolina* at that Time, but it is in so much Confusion at present, that no regular Account can be given of it: However, the very Misfortunes of the Colony serve to shew how valuable it is, since it has in some Measure flourish'd notwithstanding the great Discouragements attending it; which no doubt is owing to the Advantage of the Climate, and very probably to its being at first planted by genteel and noble spirited People, well skill'd in the Art of Traffick.

The present Inhabitants are esteem'd to be 2500 White-men, able to bear Arms, and the Slaves 40000. Their Stock of Cattle is almost incredible, every Planter possessing from one to two thousand Head: and no Wonder, since they live all the Winter without Bother. Their Mutton, Beef and Veal is very good, and their Pork the best in *America*, no Part of which affords such Plenty of naval Stores and other useful Commodities; as is undeniable, since (to say nothing of other Particulars) the Price of Pitch, by what comes from *Carolina*, has been, of late, reduc'd from 40 to 10 Shillings *per* Barrel: Several rich Mines have likewise been discover'd, but neglected for want of Miners; and by Reason of their great Distance from the *English* Settlements: However, none of the Plantations abounded so much in Money as this Colony, till ruin'd by the PAPER PROJECT; and they would soon be again in a flourishing Condition, were their Government settled to the Satisfaction of the People, being in other Respects bless'd with all the Advantages both of Art and Nature.

Charles Town, their Metropolis (if we may so call it) stands on a Point very convenient for Trade, which they carry on considerably both to *Europe* and the *West Indies*. It is situated between two pleasant, navigable Rivers,

2. [Literally, "You cause the party to know." A writ based upon a record directing the sheriff that "you cause the party to know" the charge brought against him and require him to show cause that the record should not be enforced.—Tr.]

3. [Literally, "By what right." A writ directing a person to show "by what right" he exercises certain powers of office.—Tr.]

which bring large Vessels up to the very Town, where there is a handsom Church well endow'd, and a good Harbour five Miles distant from the Inlet; the Streets are regular; the Buildings are of Brick and Wood, very near and commodious; the Town is guarded by a strong Fort and regular Fortifications, and the Militia well disciplin'd, the Horse being Gentlemen all well cloath'd and mounted; and such good Soldiers were they formerly, that they advanced to attack *St. Augustino*, and were able to defend themselves against the *French* under Monsieur *Moville*, before their Spirits were dejected, and their Strength wasted by Oppression and Poverty.

The Country about *Charles Town* is a spacious Plain of 300 Miles Extent, abounding with Woods, and enriched by Rivulets: The Temperature of the Air is much the same with *Lombardy*, and the Soil no less fruitful, producing naturally Vines, Olive and Mulberry-Trees, and immense Quantities of Rice when duly cultivated: And tho' the Grapes (which are very large and the Flesh hard like a Cherry) are not fit for Wine, they might easily have very good, by transplanting such Vines from *France*, or other Countries, as wou'd agree best with the Nature of the Soil and Climate, especially in the more southern Parts, where vast Tracts of Land remain yet uninhabited; besides *Port-Royal*, a most commodious Harbour, where People begin to make Settlements; for the Inhabitants of the Colony are very good Neighbours, the Merchants being very fair and generous Traders, and the Country Gentlemen exceeding hospitable, free and courteous.

Carolina, in short, whether consider'd for Delight or Profit, is a most desirable Country, being capable of producing whatever we can wish for, either as to the Conveniencies or Pleasures of Life: The Air is sweet and wholsome, the Climate moderate, and the Soil extremely fertile: The Fruits come easily to Perfection; the Corn yieldeth manifold Increase; the Cattle multiply exceedingly, and the Inhabitants are vigorous and healthy.

A Letter from an Assembly-Man in Carolina, &c.

SIR,

Your last of the 16th of *November*, 1725, was transmitted me safely, by the Hands of Mr. *J*—— *B*——; in which you charge me with being one of the principal Promoters of the Petition to the Crown of *Great-Britain*, for nominating a Governor, and continuing to protect the loyal Subjects of this Colony; instead of applying to the Lords Proprietors, our Natural Lords, (as you stile them) whose Property you say it is to command us, and who gave us our Land; the former Part of which Assertion shall be spoken to anon; and as for the latter, I beg leave to observe, that the Lands, we possess, were sold, and not given.

The withdrawing our selves from the Subjection of our Lords, you term Rebellion, Theft, Ingratitude, and what not; and as you seem to enter so heartily into these empty Clamours, for that Reason, I thought 'twas proper more largely to communicate the real State of the Affair, as well as the real Sense of the Assembly of *Carolina,* which, however it may be regarded by you in *England,* with us in *Carolina* is our little Senate; and every Scoff which you think fit to throw upon this small and inconsiderable Assembly (being three thousand Miles distant) is no less to us than so many Threats of the entire Subversion of our Liberties which we, as *Englishmen,* cannot in the least relish; but especially when we consider from whence all this had its Rise, namely, from a little whimsical empty Passion and Pride in some Persons pretending the Authority of our Lords Proprietors, and aiming at the Shadow of Regal Power, without the least Power or Capacity to support it. I cannot perswade myself, that our good Lords Proprietors do by any means authorise (but are rather unacquainted with) such wicked Intentions and Proceedings, most of them being Persons of Quality, and some of them having been great Asserters of Liberty themselves; most probably their Agents impose upon them by confounding Property and Power; the former of which consisting in Lands not yet sold, Quit-Rents, Mines, *&c.* the People of the Country desire not to violate; but as to the latter, they are indeed very jealous of them, and so resolve to keep them within the strictest Limits of the Charter, as long as they are able to defend themselves; and let what will happen, they can at worst forsake their Plantations, and retire up farther into the Woods and Hills, and trust to the Mercy of the Indians, rather than be enslaved by the *Switzers,* or any other Mercenaries who shall be sent amongst them, as some Folks threaten.

These Men would cover the Oppression and Plunder of so many hundreds of industrious Planters, under Pretence of Incroachment of Property, which they support by Noise and Clamour, in order to raise such a Mist, as may hinder People from seeing into their real Intentions. Thus do they oppress the industrious Planter and poor Merchant, who bring yearly 6000 *l.*

Sterling into the Customs of *Great Britain;* not to mention that the said Province consumes, of the Produce of *Britain,* above one hundred twenty thousand Pound *per Annum.*

The Gentlemen, who threaten us at this Rate with an additional Force of Foreigners, are either ignorant or forgetful of two Statutes, which are a great Comfort to this Colony: The Words are these, *Or to move or stir up any Foreigner to invade this Realm, or any other his Majesty's Dominions or Countries under his Majesty's Obeysance, all such Persons to be deem'd and adjudged Traitors.* Stat. 13. *Eliz.* c. 1. 13. *Car.* II. c. 1. §. 7.

I must own, Sir, there was a Patent or Charter granted about the Year 1663, by his late Majesty King *Charles* the Second, and renewed two Years after to *Edward* Earl of *Clarendon,* and seven other Patentees;—which we conceive to be no less binding to them than to their *natural* Subjects, as we are call'd. I won't venture to say how far *Compact* is concern'd in all Governments; but certainly it is the sole Foundation of such as owe their Power to Patents only, which is all our natural Lords can pretend to claim by; and how far they have perform'd their Part of the Bargain, will be very visible, from comparing the Threats and Proceedings of some People, who pretend to act by their Authority, with the Conditions of the Charter, which *streightly enjoins,* &c. *That the said Province be of our Allegiance and liege People of us,* &c. *That no Ordinance shall be made, but by and with the Consent of the Freemen of the said Province. That no Taxes shall be laid, nor Property violated, but by and with the Consent of the Free People,* &c. So that their Right is not indefeasible; and doubtless the Patent was granted for the Propagation of the Christian Religion, &c.—according to the Form of other Patents and Grants. But by the By, I have heard some affirm this Patent to be violated by the Proprietors Conformity Bill: However, in both these Charters the Inhabitants of the Colony are treated as Freemen.

I own what is alledged farther, that the Expence of forming this Settlement stood our Lords in near 12000 *l.* though I suppose they are not unmindful that the single Proprietors, whose Heirs are now Members of the Assembly, were at no less Charge. But if our Lords were then so great in Wealth and Power, as to be able to defend the Colony against the *French, Spaniard,* and *Indians;* the Crown then surely needed not to have been petition'd to send a Governor and Forces to defend the Colony, when the *Indians* began the last Massacre; and when the Assembly apply'd to the Proprietors, who could not then defend them: Tho' now that things are quiet, some Folks are very desirous of appointing Governors: So that when there is likely to be any Danger or Expence in defending us, then we are the King's Subjects; but when there is any thing to be got by us, then we belong to our *natural Lords* again.

As a principal Condition of the Charter was to protect the Colony, that must necessarily cease when Protection is withdrawn, either willingly, or for want of Ability: And ceasing to protect, we all know, is generally esteemed no less than a downright Abdication of Power. Besides, 'tis a known Maxim, that *where there is no Peace, there can be no Justice, nor any Justice, if the Government, instituted for the good of a Nation, be turn'd to its Ruin:* And, as it is undoubtedly in the Power of the Sovereign, who grants Patents, to withdraw them on their being abused (which has been done, to the no small Advantage of a neighbouring Colony, and without Detriment to the Proprietary) if his Majesty should think fit to resume his Colony of *Carolina* into his immediate Care, I hope none will presume to question the Procedure, since our most gracious King is undoubtedly Supreme over all Persons, and in all Causes, as well in his Dominions in *America,* as in his Kingdoms of *Great-Britain* and *Ireland:* And, since the People of *Carolina* are no less remarkable for their Duty, Zeal and Affection to his Majesty's Person, Administration and Family, than any other of his Subjects, they have surely no less reason to hope for an equal Share of his Compassion and Tenderness; and how can that be express'd more effectually than by preserving them from Oppression and Tyranny?

And this naturally brings into my mind, that these pretended Friends to the Proprietors, who now scruple to allow the best of Princes the Nomination of a Governor, would nevertheless, in the Year 1720, have sold that, and all other their Rights, to a Set of Jews and Brokers: For in that Year they barter'd, according to the Practice of the Coast of *Africa,* for the Sale of free, and natural Subjects, as you call us; and so the honest Planters and Merchants of *Carolina* were to be sold to their honester Friends the S. Sea Directors.

How far Men of such Principles are to be trusted with the Sovereignty of Colonies, our Superiors I hope will decide: But upon these Proceedings, some of the Inhabitants, like true *Englishmen,* averse to Tyranny, and not willing to be driven to the Slave-market, from that time set up a Governor of their own, till his Majesty's Pleasure, who they knew would protect his Subjects in their just Rights, could be known; and the bold and adventurous

Governor of the Proprietors, (a very proper Person to command a frontier Colony) submitted without Resistance to the Orders of the Assembly for fear of Bloodshed, as you term it: O! compassionate Governor, who scrupled Bloodshed, but would not scruple to have sold us to Directors worse than Executioners. Can we call that Liberty and Property, when honest free-born Subjects of *England* were exposed to Sale, and liable to be bought and sold like Negroes? Who knows what might have been the Consequence of such a Bargain? For 'tis shrewdly suspected, that the *Pretender,* &c. * were greatly concern'd in it. Was there not Reason then, think ye, for obtaining a *Scire Facias,* when we were no longer protected, and were going to be sold? It is true, this *Scire Facias* was not prosecuted when the King appointed a Governor, since that was all the Colony desired by it; and the Proceedings of that Governor shew, that his Majesty is the best Judge who are fittest to govern any part of his Dominions; for Mr. *Nicholson* acted so generously, that instead of two thousand Pounds Salary which was offer'd him, he was contented with one; and, not being afraid of shedding Blood, that of our Enemies I mean, rescued us from the Massacres of the *Indians,* and the Insults of the *French* and *Spaniards.*

You seem to mention in your Letter, that the Agent in *England* did not speak the Sense of our Colony, when he petition'd the King to take the Government into his own Hands: You are quite mistaken; for it was the real Opinion of the Colony, and it will be ratified in a full and free Assembly, whensoever such a one shall be called; tho' if some Folks should influence the Nomination of a Governor, it is not impossible but he may follow the riotous Practices with which Governor *M*—— aw'd the Assembly, and by which some of his Friends have endeavoured to succeed in their own Country to Voices in a more honourable Assembly, but were discourag'd by the Patriots of Liberty in *England,* whom I hope we shall always endeavour to imitate, by shewing ourselves loyal and affectionate to our King, and zealous for the Liberties of our Country, in Opposition to all Promoters of arbitrary Power.

Our Agent, however his Authority may be disputed, has undoubted Instructions from the Colony; who refuse not to acknowledge themselves Tenants, but then they pay their Rent for Protection only, for their Lands were purchased, and by hard Labour cleared from the Woods: And would it not be grievous, should they suffer for their Industry? But the Proprietors, you say, complain of the Non-Payment of Quit-Rent; the People of

Carolina will not differ with their *Lords* upon this Account, tho' they have a very good Pretence for it, at least during the Time of the *Indian* War, of which *Carolina* was the Seat, and the total Expence of which was defray'd by his Majesty and the Assembly only; for when a Country becomes the Seat of War, all Rents cease of Course, according to the general Custom of *Europe*, whatever it may be in *America:* Besides, you may be pleased to consider, that the People of *England* are all Tenants as well as we; and where Lords of Manors have neglected repairing Bridges, *&c.* the Manors-Tenants have ceas'd to pay Quit-Rent; and when Court Leets have not been duly and legally held, the King's Bench has justified the Tenants in refusing the Payment of Rents; and when Lords of Manors have neglected to nominate Constables and other Officers, as their Duty oblig'd them, the Legislature intermeddled, and, for the good of the Commonweal, impower'd the Justices in their Quarter-Sessions to nominate those Officers for them: And how much more necessary is it in our Case? This proves the Duty of Lord and Tenant to be reciprocal; so that the Lords Proprietors ceasing to protect the Colony, and leaving it to the King to protect us; where could the Homage of the Tenants be due, but to his Majesty only? For by the Law of *England*, where the inferior Lord forfeits his Right, it returns to his Superior; and the Manor of *Carolina* (if the Palatinate of our Natural Lords may be call'd so) holds under the Manor of *Greenwich*, as you'll see more fully hereafter.

I believe none of our Assembly will deny that the Proprietors have a Right to the Province, as far as any *Englishman* may be said to have a Right over another that is not his indented Servant; but this will more plainly appear by the Words of the Patent itself, which, as far as they relate to this Argument, are these: *We do, by these Patents,* &c. *make, create and constitute the said Earl of* Clarendon, *&c. Proprietors of the said Province,* &c. *saving always the Faith and Allegiance, and sovereign Dominion due to us, our Heirs and Successors for the same, to be holden,* &c. *as of our Manor of* East Greenwich *in* Kent, *in free and common Soccage, and not in Capite or by Knights Service, yielding or paying yearly to us,* &c. *for the same, the fourth Part of all Goods, Mines,* &c. *which shall from Time to Time happen to be found, over and above the yearly Rent of twenty Marks.* And I will venture to affirm farther, that the Manner, in which some pretending to be their Agents have exercised their Authority, is contrary to the Grant, as well as derogatory to the Right of a free People; and the Abuse of it is no less than the Forfeiture of the

Authority itself; nor does our Assembly conceive, that the great Distance we are at from the Fountain of Justice should deprive us of the Benefit of it.

You say, that your Friends, in refusing some Acts of Assembly, have proceeded by his Majesty's Order, particularly in the Affair of repealing the Paper-Money; I wish, as in this, they proceeded by his Majesty's Order, so in all other Things they had proceeded by the same Orders; then had we not been that wretched People we are, nor groaned under this Load of Paper-Money, which I fear must inevitably be our Ruin.

As to the Proprietors indefeasible Right of Government, of which you speak, I am at a Loss what you mean: We cannot conceive that any Charter will impower them to make Slaves of British Subjects, much less to sell us to the *Swiss Cantons*, which some Folks have insinuated. I am sure, in the Charter, as I have already said, the King does *streightly enjoyn*, &c. *That the said Province be of our Allegiance, and Liege People of us;* and such I presume are not the *Switzers:* You may be pleased to consult, on this Account, the two Statutes before cited of the 10 *Eliz.* and 13 *Car.* II. And by the Act of Settlement, it is farther enacted, That no Foreigner shall be naturaliz'd, nor have Power, Civil or Military, but by Act of Parliament: And such, we conceive, are not the Resolutions of our natural Lords the Proprietors; nor can, what you call the great Expence they were at, which was no less so to the Planters, give their Agents a Right to tyrannize over us; if they grumble at this first Expence, which was in all but 12000 *l.* what will they do at the expending 13000 *l.* yearly, which will be the least Expence of maintaining a Battalion, and that will not be sufficient to defend us.

In tender Consideration of the Estates of our very good Lords the Proprietors, the Assembly wishes they would leave the Expence of protecting us to the King, and not load their Land with Mortgages for our Defence; since the whole Value of their Proprietorships amounts but to 3600 *l.* according to a late publick Valuation, which can never repay the Expence of maintaining the *Swiss* amongst us; especially on the Foot proposed by the *Swiss* Count *de* ———, who insists upon such extravagant and arbitrary Conditions, as in all probability are design'd to enslave us.

But as you write with some vehemence that it is violating Property, to take the Nomination of a Governor from our natural Lords; the Inhabitants of this Colony, poor as they are, would gladly buy out this Property at a greater Rate than its Value, according to a Market-price; two of their Proprietorships being not long since set up at Auction by a Decree of Chancery, and sold but at 400 *l.* each; an excellent Price for the ninth Part of a Kingship! at which Rate we are willing to buy them all out, rather than to put them to the Trouble and Expence of transporting an additional Force of *Swiss,* who may indeed be dangerous Guests, since Care has been taken to leave us nothing to bribe them with but Paper-money, the Value of which they can't read.

I doubt not but the *Swiss* Treaty is one of the Reasons why some Persons are averse to Mr. *Nicolson*'s returning as Governor; since they know he will not suffer any Troops to come among us, but such, whose Fidelity to his most Gracious Majesty King *George,* and Affection to the Protestant Succession he could be assured of; and these *Swiss* may perhaps be *Papists* and *Jacobites.*

But you'll say, that a King's Governor may frighten many of the Merchants from *Carolina;* surely Mr. *Nicolson* is less likely to frighten them than an overgrown blustering *Swiss* with a huge pair of Mustacho's, living upon free Quarters: But according to you, Men who have defended themselves against the *Indians,* and attack'd the *Spaniards,* can have no occasion for beaten mercenary Hectors to defend them; and if these Gentlemen *Switzers* should have belong'd to the *French* the last War in *Flanders,* as some People suggest, they certainly have been beaten, and may be disaffected to the Government, and so help to promote those barbarous and unnatural Designs of which we have already had Experience from some late Proceedings. In my humble Opinion, some People would fain be Kings, but don't know how; would govern without Power, and have all the Advantage of a Patent, but perform nothing stipulated in it; when all things are calm, they would then be at the Helm, but upon the least Ruffle of a Storm, call out to the King for Protection, and put the Expence upon him, whilst they would reap the Profit of selling his Subjects: But rather than we will submit to be sold like Negroes, we would—I say, we will be willing to purchase our Freedom, tho' with the Sale of all our Effects; for 'tis better to starve with Freedom, than live in Bondage.

Upon the whole therefore, you would do well to quit this Shadow of Supreme Power, which you vainly aim at, for the sake of real Property, which then may quietly be enjoyed: For, besides the Resolution of the Colony, not to be enslav'd, (which, I assure you, is unanimous) if your Scheme go on, and a War should break out between *Great Britain* and *Spain,* we are inevitably undone; especially should the *Swiss* be brought amongst us, since they'll readily go over to the best Paymaster; for besides our Poverty, and consequently Inability to defend ourselves, the Mischief on it is, that if the King doth not nominate a Governor, we shall probably lose our best Defence, the Independent Company and the Assistance of the *British* Men of War, whose Officers seldom care to receive Orders from any Governors, but such as are appointed immediately by his Majesty.

But the Misery which threatens *Carolina,* should we lose his Majesty's Protection, and the Proprietors nominate a Governor, is too terrible to every Inhabitant to be thought of, or reason'd cooly upon; for from the time that the King ceaseth to nominate a Governor, he will probably withdraw his Forces both by Sea and Land, and leave us to defend our selves: But alas! What Defence can a Colony make, who are already exhausted, already an hundred and twenty thousand Pounds in Debt? Whose Credit is so broken, that their Bills are at eighty *per Cent.* Discount? What is to be expected, when the White People are averse to Proprietor-Governors, and the Faith of the *Indians,* with whom Peace is but newly made, uncertain; the Fortifications of *Charles-Town* lately demolish'd by a Storm, and this Weakness well known to our implacable Neighbours the *Spaniards,* who want not Baits to allure them to invade the Planters, they possessing above forty thousand Negroes besides Cattle? Doubtless, on the King's withdrawing his Garrison and Men of War, (to two of which we owe our present Safety) they will think us abandon'd by the Crown, and then the Instances of private Lords Proprietors will have but little Weight to prevent their invading us; since 'tis well known, how little they regarded the Remonstrances of his Grace the Duke of *Portland,* concerning the Piracies committed by them on the *Jamaica* Men: For since the Peace, the *Spaniards* have taken from them above forty sail of Ships, besides landing at different times, and carrying off above three hundred Negroes; nor has the Duke, tho' a King's Governor, ever been able to obtain any Satisfaction from them. How much less Reason then have we to expect it, who have none but feeble private Persons to apply to for Relief?

But such Ravages are but small Losses in Comparison of what we have to expect! The *Spaniards* from St. *Augustino,* which is contiguous to our Frontier, and which, in happier Days we besieged, will, through the very Road we made, invade our Country naked of Troops and Men of War: And we, alas! unable to defend our selves, must stay under these sad Circumstances, for Succours from *England,* and those Succours, according to your Scheme, must be *Switzers*. Alas! what a wretched Condition! murder'd by the *Spaniards*, and plunder'd, instead of being protected by our *Swiss*, famous for Ravages, Murthers, and Treachery, and, of late, for Cowardice too, from which Cruelty is inseparable. But I hope we have better things to expect from his Majesty, in whose Mercy and Goodness, next under God, is our Trust.

I beg you'll excuse me, Sir, if Affection for my Country has made me too warm or bitter in my Expressions; make this your own Case, and I am confident you'll not blame our unhappy Colony, nor be averse to pardon,

CAROLINA, *Charles-Town, Jan.* 15. 1725–6.

SIR,
Your very humble Servant,
J—— N——.

· 26 ·

Daniel Dulany, The Right of the Inhabitants of Maryland to the Benefit of the English Laws (1728)

IN THE WAKE of the Glorious Revolution, Lord Baltimore lost his right to govern Maryland following a revolt by a group of Protestant settlers. But in 1715, after converting to Anglicanism, the Baltimore family had its proprietorial rights restored. In the 1720s, an economic downturn led to a dispute between the proprietor and the lower house of the assembly over the appointed council's refusal to assent to an act intended to alleviate the plight of tobacco planters. Angered by this refusal, the lower house responded by passing a series of resolutions in 1722, the intent of which was to weaken the proprietor by claiming the benefit of English common and statute law that would be less susceptible to proprietary veto than an act of the assembly. When Baltimore refused to grant the extension of English law to the colony, Daniel Dulany, a young lawyer from Annapolis who had come to Maryland twenty years before as an indentured servant, led the charge against proprietorial prerogatives.

As the constitutional crisis reached a deadlock in the late 1720s, Dulany put pen to paper and articulated the house's position in a pamphlet entitled *The Right of the Inhabitants of Maryland to the Benefit of the English Laws*. Dulany first denied Baltimore's claim that the colonists were a conquered people and thus not entitled to the benefit of English law and its attendant rights. Rather, he argued that the original colonists in Maryland had risked their lives "to enlarge" the King's "Empire in a remote Part of the World . . .

inhabited by a People, savage, cruel, and inhospitable." In return for taking such risks, the royal charter had guaranteed them all the rights that English subjects at home enjoyed, a point Dulany reinforced by noting that the allegiance subjects owed their monarch was predicated on the protection the Crown afforded their person and property. Dulany also drew on the case law about the extension of English laws outside the realm, concluding that when English settlers went to a place without civilized laws they were entitled to take their own laws with them. In a powerful concluding passage, Dulany drew on Lockean natural rights to argue that, in addition to their rights as British subjects, the first settlers to Maryland had a natural right to construct political authority on their own, consenting to such laws as they saw fit.

In 1732, Lord Baltimore arrived in the province in person, determined to break the constitutional impasse. With the aid of a new and more skillful governor, he was able to assert his powers more effectively, including offering lucrative jobs to many of his opponents in the lower house. Although his actions ended the dispute over the extension of English laws in Maryland, the question of what rights the colonists had would be a source of tension in the empire down to the Revolution. (C.B.Y.)

THE

RIGHT

OF THE

Inhabitants of *MARYLAND,*

TO THE

Benefit of the *ENGLISH* Laws.

Oh Liberty! Oh Servitude! How amiable, how detestable are the different Sounds! Liberty is Salvation in Politics, as Slavery is Reprobation; nor is there any other Distinction, but that of Saint and Devil, between the Champions of the one, and of the other.

Cato.

ANNAPOLIS: Printed by *W. Parks*, MDCCXXVIII.

To all true Patriots, and sincere Lovers of Liberty.

Gentlemen,

The following Sheets are not made publick, because the Author of them is fond of appearing in Print; but because the Representatives, of the People of MARYLAND, whose Request, bears the weight of a Command, with him, desired they should be publish'd. The Design is *honest,* and what every Body ought to wish, had been undertaken by a Person more *equal* to it; that the Right contended for, might have appeared in its *proper* Lustre; and all Objections to it, have been obviated, as I am firmly persuaded they may be. For my *own Part,* I shall think my Time very well spent, if the Objections, with which I expect this *weak* Performance will be encount'red; or a *generous* Concern, to see so *good a Subject,* so weakly managed, excites some able Lover of *Liberty,* to *establish* the *Truths,* which I have faintly *endeavour'd* to *establish.* I heartily wish this may happen, as well as every Thing else, conducive to the *Prosperity* of the Province of MARYLAND; and am, very sincerely,

Gentlemen, Your most Obedient, and Faithful, Humble Servant,

D. DULANY.

The Right of the Inhabitants of Maryland, to the Benefit of the English Laws.

As there has been a pretty warm Contest, concerning *The Right of the Inhabitants of* Maryland, *to the Benefit of the* English *Laws;* as well *Statute* as *Common:* And as the Matter is in Dispute, and it is of the utmost Consequence to be at a Certainty about it; It behoves every Man, that has any Regard to, or Interest in the Country, to use his utmost Endeavour to put it in a true Light: For as *Laws* are absolutely necessary, for the good Government, and Welfare, of Society, so, it is necessary, that People should have some Notion of those *Laws,* which are to be the Rule of their Conduct; and for the Transgression of which, They will be liable to be punished, notwithstanding their Ignorance. If this be necessary? as without Doubt it is; Then it is certainly of the greatest Importance to know, whether a People are to be governed by *Laws,* which their *Mother-Country* has experimentally found, to be beneficial to Society, and adapted to the Genius, and Constitution of their Ancestors; or to compose a new Set of *Laws,* which will be attended with very great Difficulties; and an Expence, vastly disproportionable to the Country, in it's present Circumstances. Or whether, They are to be governed by the Discretion, (as some People softly term the *Caprice,* and *Arbitrary Pleasure,*) of any Set of Men?

This, or the like Enquiry, cannot be of any great Moment, but to those that are FREE: For, such as have the Misfortune to be in a State of Bondage, are in the Condition of *The Ass in the Fable;* sure to be as heavily laden as they can possibly bear, without rendring them useless to their Masters.

But the *People of Maryland* are *Freemen,* and will certainly continue to be such, as long as they enjoy the Benefit of Laws, calculated for the Security of Liberty, and Property, and the Rights of Mankind: But should They be so *infatuated* as to give up, or so *miserable* as to forfeit, (which God forbid!) the Benefit of such Laws; They may then, bid adieu to all the Security They have, of enjoying with any Degree of Certainty, anything, however dear, and valuable.

These Considerations put Me upon enquiring, in the best Manner, my very weak Capacity, and other Disadvantages, would admit of, into the Right, which the People of *Maryland* have, to the Enjoyment of *English Liberties;* and the *Benefit of the English Laws:* Which I take to be, and hope to prove are, convertible Terms. In which Enquiry, I have found very good Reasons, (at least, They seem so to Me,) to convince Me, that said *People* have such *Right.*

To the End, therefore, that I may be undeceived, if I am mistaken; or That I may confirm others, in the Truth, and Reasonableness of what I contend for; as well as the mighty Advantage it is of, to the Inhabitants of this Province, I will endeavour to prove the Right.

I. As the People are *English,* or *British* Subjects, and have always adhered to, and continued in their Allegiance to the Crown.

II. As the Rights of *English,* or *British* Subjects, are granted unto Them, in the *Charter of the Province,* to the Lord Proprietary.

But before I proceed to treat of these several Rights, it will not be amiss, to observe, that the Law of *England* consists of the *Common* and *Statute Law. That the Common Law, takes in the Law of Nature, the Law of Reason, and the revealed Law of God;* which are *equally* binding, *at All Times, in All Places, and to All Persons,* And such Usages, and Customs, as have been experimentally found, to suit the Order, and Engagements of Society; and to contain Nothing inconsistent with *Honesty, Decency, and Good Manners;* and which by Consent, and long Use, have obtained the Force of *Laws.*

The *Statute Law,* consists of such Acts of Parliament, as have been made from Time, to Time, by the whole Legislature; some of which, are declaratory, or alter the Common Law; I mean, such Part of it as consists of Usages, and Customs, that received their Force and Sanction from the Consent of the People; when those Usages, and Customs, have been mistaken, misapplied, or found to be unsuitable to the Order, and Engagements of Society, in order to make the whole Body of the Law, best answer the true End of all Laws, *the Good and Safety of the People.*

Some, have restored the People to the Rights, that were theirs, by the *Common Law,* (which contained nothing inconsistent with *General Liberty and Property,*) and which ill Men, had at Times, invaded, and infringed; and have made *New Barriers,* (if I may so speak,) to prevent future Infringements, of the like Nature; and paved out a certain, determinate Path, for every Subject, suffering Violence, and Oppression, to be remedied; And taken Care to make it the Interest as well as it ever was, and ever must be, the indispensible Duty of the *Magistrate,* to allow the Subject, the Benefit of the Law; by rendering the *Magistrate* himself punishable, if he should neglect, so essential a Part of his Duty.

Some Statutes, are Introductory of new Laws, which may be divided, into such as are by the Words, or Subject Matter of them, of general Use and Extent; such as are more confined; and such, as are made for particular Ends, and Purposes. I shall have Occasion to treat of the first of These, *only.*

This Law, of *England,* is the Subject's Birth-Right, and best Inheritance; and to it, may be justly applied, what the great Oracle of the Law, the Lord *Coke,* saith of the Common Law.

> Of Common Right, that is, by the Common Law; so called, because this Common Law, is the best and most Common Birth-Right, that the Subject hath, for the Safeguard and Defence, not only of his Goods, Lands, and Revenues; but of his Wife, and Children, his Body, Fame, and Life, also.

[1]'Tis this Law, that will effectually secure every Honest Man, who has the Benefit of it, in his Life, the Enjoyment of his Liberty, and the Fruits of his Industry. 'Tis by Virtue of this Law, that a British Subject, may with Courage, and Freedom, tell the most daring, and powerful Oppressor, that He must not injure him, with Impunity. This Law, uprightly and honestly applied, and administred, will secure Men from all Degrees of Oppression, Violence, and Injustice; it tells the Magistrate what he has to do, and leaves him little Room, to gratify his own Passion, and Resentment, at the

[1]. I. Inst. 142.

Expence of his Fellow-Subject. It suits the Degrees of Punishment, to the Nature and Degrees of Offences, with a due Regard to the Circumstances of Aggravation and Extenuation; as well as to the Frailties and Infirmities of Human Nature. 'Twas of this Law, that it was truly said, by an *honest, bold Patriot,* an hundred Years since, in Parliament;

> Our Laws, which are the Rules of *Justice,* are the *Ne plus ultra,*[1] to King, and Subject; and as They are the *Hercules Pillars,* so are they the Pillar to every *Hercules,* to every *Prince, which He must not pass.* [2]

It was upon the Foundation of this Law, that it was resolved in the House of Commons, in *March,* 1628, *Nemine contradicente,*[2]

> I. That no Freeman ought to be detained, or kept in Prison, or otherwise restrained, by command of the King, or of the Privy Council, or any Other, unless some Cause of the Commitment, Detainer, or Restraint, being express'd, for which, by Law, He ought to be committed, detained, or restrained.
>
> II. That the Writ of *Habeas Corpus,*[3] may not be denyed; but ought to be granted to every Man, that is committed, or detained in Prison, or otherwise restrained, though it be by command of the King, the Privy Council, or any other; He praying the same.
>
> III. That if a *Freeman* be committed, or detained in Prison, or otherwise restrained, by the Command of the King, the Privy Council, or any other; no Cause of such Commitment, Detainer, or Restraint being expressed, for which by Law, he ought to be committed, detained, or restrained; and the same be returned, upon a *Habeas Corpus* granted for the said Party; then He ought to be delivered or bailed.
>
> That it is the antient, and indubitable Right of every *Freeman,* that He hath full and absolute Property, in his Goods and Estate; that no Tax, Tallage, Loan, Benevolence, or other like Charge, ought to be commanded, or levied, by the King or any of his Ministers, without common Consent, by *Act* of Parliment.[3]

1. ["Not be not more beyond," i.e., "the limit."—Tr.]

[2]. *Mr. Creswell's Speech, March* 1627: *Rushworth*'s Collections, Vol. 1, p. 506.

2. ["With no one dissenting," i.e., "unanimously."—Tr.]

3. [Literally, "You have the body." A writ directing the sheriff that "you have the body" for confinement and are required to produce a charge in court to justify imprisonment.—Tr.]

[3]. *Rush* I. B. 513.

And this Law is not to be altered, but by the whole Legislature, and we may as reasonably apprehend, that a whole People will be seiz'd with a Delirium, as fear such a Change.

Having given this Short Account of the Law it self, which I hope will not be thought altogether useless, I shall now proceed, in the Method I proposed, of proving the Right, of the Inhabitants of *Maryland,* to the Benefit of *English* Laws.

I. As they are *English,* or *British* Subjects; and have always adhered to, and continued in their Allegiance to the Crown.

The First *Settlers of Maryland,* were a Colony of *English* Subjects, who left their Native Country, with the *Assent and Approbation* of their *Prince;* to enlarge his *Empire* in a *remote* Part of the World, destitute of almost all the *Necessaries of Life,* and inhabited by a People, *savage, cruel* and *inhospitable:* To which Place, they (the *first Settlers,*) *transported themselves,* at a *great Expence;* ran all the Hazards, and underwent all the Fatigues incident to so dangerous and daring an Undertaking; in which Many perished, and Those that survived, suffered All the Extremities of *Hunger, Cold and Diseases. They were not banished* from their *Native Country,* nor did *They abjure it.*

It pleased *God,* in process of Time, that some of those People, their Posterity, and others that followed, met with such Success, as to raise a Subsistence for Themselves; and to become very beneficial to their *Mother-Country,* by greatly increasing its Trade and Wealth; where in, They have been as advantageous to *England,* as any *of Her Sons,* that never went from their own Homes, or under-went any Hardships; allowing for the Disparity of Circumstances. And it cannot be pretended, that ever They adhered to the Enemies of their King or *Mother-Country;* departed from their Allegiance, or swerved from the Duty, of *loyal, and faithful Subjects:* These are Truths, too evident, and too well known to be denied, by any One, that has the least Share of, or Regard to, Truth, or Common Honesty.

This being the Case of the People of *Maryland,* it will not be amiss, to observe the Opinions of the two great Civilians, and Politicians, *Puffendorf,* and *Grotius,* in Relation to Colonies: The first, says,

> That Colonies may be, and often are, settled in different Methods: For, either the Colony continues a Part of the Commonwealth It was sent from; or else, is only to pay dutiful Respect to the Mother-Commonwealth, and to be in Readiness to defend and vindicate its Honour.

[1]*Maryland* is undoubtedly a Part of the *British Dominions*, and its Inhabitants are Subjects of *Great Britain*, and so are They called, in several Acts of Parliament.*

And Grotius saith, "That Such, enjoy the same Rights of Liberty with the Mother City."[2] And again, in another Place, "For they are not sent out, to be Slaves, but to enjoy equal Priviledges, and Freedom." [3]Thus far these great Men.

It is an established Doctrine, that *Allegiance, and Protection,* are *reciprocal;* and that a Continuance in the *One,* entitles the Subject to the Benefits of the *Other:*

> As the Ligatures, or Strings, (says Lord Coke) do knit together the Joints, of all the Parts of the Body, so doth Legiance join together, the Sovereign, and all his Subjects.[4] For as the Subject oweth to the King, his true and faithful Legiance, and Obedience; so the Sovereign is to govern and protect the Subject.[5] Between the Sovereign, and the Subject, there is a double and reciprocal Tie; for as the Subject is bound to obey the King, so is the King bound to protect the Subject.[6] And Subjection draws to it Protection, and Protection Subjection.[7]

Every Subject has a Right to the Enjoyment of his Liberty and Property, according to the established Laws of his Country; when that Right is invaded, Recourse must be had to the Law for a Remedy: And a Man, who hath the Benefit of the Law, is sure to have Reparation for any Injury that has been done Him; and is secure against future Wrongs: But, if he has not the Benefit of the Law, he must not only submit to past Injuries, if done by a Person Superior to him, in Power; but be exposed to future Insults, whenever Power, and Inclination, concur to oppress Him: From whence, it necessarily follows, that the greatest Advantage, which the Subject can possibly derive, from the Royal Protection, is the Benefit of the Laws; that so long as the Subject hath That, he is secure of every Thing which belongs

[1]. Law of Nature and Nations, B. 8. Chap. 11. S. 6.

* 12 Car. 2. Cap. 34. 15 Car. 2. Cap. 7. Sect. 5. 25 Car. 2. 11 and 12 W. 3 Cap. 12.

[2]. *Grotius* of the Rights of War and Peace B. I. Cap. 3. S. 21.

[3]. B. 2 Cap. 19. 8. 10.

[4]. 7 Co. Rep. 4. b.

[5]. ibid. 5. *a. Regere et protegere Subditos suos.*

[6]. *Duplex et reciprocum Ligamen, quia sicut Subditus Regitenetur ad Obedientiam ita Rex Subdito tenetur ad Protectionem.* 4 Co. Rep. 5. a.

[7]. *Protectio trahit Subjectionem, Subjectio Protectionem Ibid.*

to Him; that when He loses It, He loses every Thing; or at best, hath but a very uncertain, and precarious Tenure, in any thing: This Subjection, and this Protection, are not bounded by any Space, less extensive than the *British* Dominions.

This, Reason speaks loudly, and Numbers of Authorities are not wanting to confirm; tho' I intend, to confine my self to One, which is the Case of St. *Paul;** which is so well known, that a particular Recital of the Text is needless; and therefore, I shall only observe, that the Apostle claimed the Benefit of the *Roman Law,* not because, he was born in *Rome,* or *Italy;* or indeed, in *Europe;* for he was born in *Asia:* Nor did he claim the Priviledge of a *Roman,* in *Rome, Italy,* or *Europe;* but in *Judea:* There was no Dispute of his Right, because he was born in a remote Province of the Empire; There was no Pretence, that the Laws which were securitative of the *Roman*'s Rights, were confined within narrower Limits than those of the *Roman* Dominions. Instead of any Pretence of this Kind, the *Roman* Captain, was afraid of being called to an Account, for having violated the *Roman* Law, by inflicting a Punishment, that it did not allow of, on a Person, entituled to the Benefit of that Law; And that, as hath been already observed, in a very remote Corner of the Empire.

The Province of *Maryland,* is as much a Part of the *British* Dominions, as *Tarsus* the City, or *Cilicia* the Country, of St. *Paul*'s Birth, was Part of the *Roman* Empire: And consequently, a Man, born in *Maryland,* hath as good a Right, to demand the Benefit of the Laws of his Mother Country, as the Apostle had, to demand the Privileges of a *Roman.* One would be apt to think, that if there was any Difference, in the two Cases, the *Marylander,* would have much the better of it; for his Ancestors were *English,* and St. *Paul*'s Ancestors were not *Romans.* In a word, the People of *Maryland,* are not out of the Reach of their Prince's Protection, nor so foolish, or wicked, as to disown their Allegiance, to the best, and most gracious of Kings. What the Learned Mr. *Locke,* says of natural Equality, being I conceive, applicable to the present Purpose, I am certain it will be very acceptable;

> *A State of Equality,* (says that great Man) wherein all Power and jurisdiction, is reciprocal; no one having more than another: There being nothing more evident, than that Creatures, of the same Species, and Rank, promiscuously born, to all the same Advantages of Nature, and the Use of the same Faculties, should also be Equal, One, amongst another,

* Acts Chap. 22 v. 25, &c.

> without Subordination, or Subjection; unless, the Lord, and Master of them All, should, by any manifest Declaration of his Will, set One above Another, and confer on Him, by an evident and clear Appointment, an undoubted Right, to Dominion, and Sovereignty.*

Can any Thing be more evident, than that All the Subjects, of the same Prince, living within his Dominions, adhering to their Allegiance, and in a Word, behaving themselves, as dutiful and loyal Subjects ought, and promiscuously born under the same Obligation of Allegiance, Obedience, and Loyalty to their Prince, and to the same Right of Protection, should also be entitled to the same Rights, and Liberties, with the rest of the Subjects, of the same Prince, of their Degree, and Condition? Or can any thing be more clear, than that Subjects, having an equal Right to Priviledges, must also have an equal Right to the Laws, made to create or preserve such Privileges? And without which, they cannot be preserved; unless the supreme Power, by any manifest Declaration, distinguish some Subject from Others, by depriving some, of their Privileges; and continuing them to Others.

If the People of *Maryland* are thus unhappily distinguished, they must submit? But if on the contrary, They have a Right, in common with the rest of their Fellow Subjects, to *English* Liberties, and Privileges? 'Tis absurd to say, They have not a Right to the Means of preserving them.

By what hath been, and will be said; I hope, that the Right of the People of *Maryland*, to the Benefit of the Laws of *England*, is, and will be evidently proved; and that it will be likewise proved, that That Benefit, is of infinite Advantage, to any People, who receive the same, in the full Extent of it. If so, it will necessarily follow, that to deprive the People, of the Advantages, derivative from the Laws of their Mother Country, would be greater Injustice, and Oppression, than they could suffer in any particular, or indeed in many Instances; by so much, as the necessary, and only Means, to secure Men in all their Rights, is of greater Consequence, than any particular Part of their Property.

I have heard of some Men, who have advanced, that the People of *Maryland*, have a Right to *English* Liberties, but not to *English* Laws; and wonder, Why there should be so much to do about those Laws! When we may do as well without, as with them. Such Notions are the Effect of Ignorance, in some, and of something worse in Others: And, (as I hope to prove,) are big with

* *Locke* of Civil Government. Chap. 2. *Sect.* 4.

Absurdity: All the Rights, and Liberties, which the *British* Subject, so justly, values Himself upon; are secured to Him, by the *British Laws:* And when, and as often as those Rights, and Liberties, are invaded, Recourse must be had to the Law, for Reparation: Right, and Remedy, are inseparable; and when the latter ceases, the former is extinguished the same Instant. "A Man, (saith a great Lawyer,) hath no Right to any Thing, for which the Law gives no Remedy."[1]

It was held by as great a Judge, as ever sate in *Westminster Hall,* clearly;

> That a Devisee, might maintain an Action, at Common-Law, against a Tertenant, for a Legacy, deviled out of Land; for, where a Statute, as the Statute of Wills, gives a Right, The Party, by Consequence, shall have *An Action at Common Law,* to recover it.[2] The same Judge, held that it was a vain Thing, to imagine, there *should* be a *Right,* without a *Remedy.*

Want of Right, and Want of Remedy, are *Termini convertibiles.*4[3] And of the same Opinion was a former Judge,[4] And there never was One of a contrary Opinion.

It is very evident to every Man's Reason, without any judicial Decision, or other Authority, That to have a Right to a Thing, without any Means or Remedy to maintain that Right, is of no Service. And it is well known, that in all civil Governments, the only certain, and just Remedy, is the Benefit of the Law. Of this, some that advance the foregoing Notions, are aware; but they very well know, that it ought to be carefully concealed, from Those, that they would impose their destructive Doctrines upon, as *Orthodox.*

Others are so good natured, as to allow the People of *Maryland,* the Benefit of the Common Law; but contend stiffly, that they have no Right to any of the Statutes; and that having the Liberty of supplying that Defect, by making *Acts of Assembly,* to suit all their Purposes; or even, of Re-enacting such of the Statutes themselves, as may be convenient for them, they have no Occasion for the Statutes at All; Whence then, say they, these Apprehensions of wanting Laws? 'Tis only the Statute-Law you have no Right to, nor Occasion for. As to the Power of Legislation, I shall say something hereafter.

[1]. *Vaughan's* Reports 253.
[2]. *Holt* and *F. Salkeld's,* Rep. 415. Vol. I.
4. ["Exchangeable terms."]
[3]. 6 Mo. Rep. 53. the great Case of the Aylesbury Men.
[4]. 6 Co. Rep. 58.

What I contend for, is, that we derive our Right to *British* Liberties, and Privileges, as we are *British* Subjects: That as such, We have a Right to all the Laws, whether Statute, or Common, which secure to the *Subject*, the Right of a Subject, as inseparably incident to those Rights; that the Right to the Liberties, and Privileges; and the Benefit of the Laws, have the same Foundation: And therefore, If we may be deprived of any Part of that Right, without our Consent, or our being convict of any Crime, whereby to forfeit it? We may, by the same Reason, and Authority, be deprived of some other Part; and this, will naturally render the Whole, uncertain; and our Lives, Liberties, and Properties, *Precarious*.

I have no Notion of a Certainty, in any Thing, that I hold by so slender a Tenure, as the Will of another; but think it vain, and arrogant, to call it Mine.

Those, that would vouchsafe Us the Benefit of the Common Law, but would entirely deprive Us of the Benefit of *any of the Statutes*, would leave Us in a *poor Condition*, with Regard to our *Liberties*: For *all the Rights*, which the *English Subject* was entitled to, by the *Common Law*, were at Times, invaded by Men of Power, and Authority; and the very *Invasions* themselves called by the *Iniquity of Men, and Times*, the *Law of the Land*: And *that very Law*, which was calculated, and instituted, for the *Defence*, and *Safeguard*, of *Property*; preverted to the *Destruction* of *Property*. By the Law of Nature, All Men were *equal*; and by *that Law*, the *Law of Reason*, and the *revealed Law of God*, Men are enjoyned, to treat One Another, with *Humanity, Justice*, and *Integrity*.

Yet, such has been, and is, the Depravity of Human Nature; and so little, has the Love of Equity, and Justice, prevailed among Men; that the excellent Rules, which the Laws already mention'd dictate, have not been sufficient to keep them, within *just* Bounds, or to restrain them, from treating one Another, with the *greatest Cruelties* imaginable: Whence, it became *absolutely* necessary, to make some further Provision by *positive Laws;* such as our Statutes, to oblige Men, to comply with, what the Love of Justice would not, but the Fear of Punishment, might induce them to comply with, and to punish the Disobedient, and Refractory. All which have been found by Experience, to be little enough, to keep *Ill Men*, in Order; or secure *Good Men*, from *Violence*, and Oppression. This hath been the Case, in *England* it self; A Nation, that has abounded, with Men of *great* Abilities, *great* Interest, and *opulent* Fortunes; that were *Patrons of Liberty, Lovers of Justice*, and such as preferr'd the *Good of their Country* to *All* their own particular Concerns: And that were therefore, *Checks to Oppressors, and Violators of Laws*, *and the Rights of Mankind:* Yet the Virtue, Resolution, and Endeavours of these Worthies, were not sufficient, to secure themselves, or their Fellow Subjects, in the Enjoyment of their Rights and Liberties; or the Law, from being polluted by Ill Men, in Authority; or turn'd to the Destruction of the Best, for opposing the Ruin of their Country. That this, hath often been the Case in *England,* everybody knows, who is at all acquainted with its History; and I believe it has been so, in all other Nations. Such calamitous Circumstances, were not to be born, by a Free-People, who were possessed of the Means, to provide for their own Safety.

Magna Charta was made, which as all eminent Lawyers agree, is, and indeed, by the Words of it, appears to be, *A Declaration* of the Common-Law:[*] The 29th Chapter is not long, and ought to be read by every Body, and (in my humble Opinion,) taught to Children, with their first Rudiments; the Words of it are,

> No Freeman shall be taken, or imprisoned, or disseised of his Free-hold, or Liberty, or free Customs; or outlawed, or exiled, or any way destroyed: Nor (says the King) will we pass sentence upon him, but by lawful Judgment of his Peers, or by the Law of the Land:—
>
> *To None will we sell; To None will we deny; To None will we defer Justice, or Right.*

If new Rights, or Liberties were granted, they would be particularly granted; and there would be no Occasion to refer to the Laws of the Land.

By another Statute, subsequent to *Magna Charta,* it is provided

> That no Man, of what Estate, or Condition that he be, shall be put out of Land, or Tenement; nor taken, nor imprisoned, nor disinherited, nor put to Death, without being brought in to answer, by *due* Process of Law.[a]

This Statute, directs no new Process of Law; and enacts over again, what seems to have been provided for, by *Magna Charta,* which was in full Force, when this Statute was made.

By another Statute, made but Fifteen Years after the last, and in the same Reign: It was assented to, and accorded for the good Government of the Commons; that no Man, be put to answer without Presentment before

(*). Inst. 81.
(*a*). 28 Edw. 3, cap. 3.

Justices, or Matter of Record, or by due Process, or Writ Original; according to the *old Law of the Land.*[(b)] To recite but a very small part, of all the Statutes, that have been made, to confirm, and establish the Subject's Rights, and Liberties that were his, by the *Common Law,* would be too tedious: I shall therefore, confine my self to a few Instances: In the Preamble, and several Parts of the Body, of the Petition of Right; a great Number of Statutes are mentioned, that confirm'd the Subject's Right, in his *Liberty* and *Property;* which were then in Force, and yet had all been violated:[(c)] Wherefore, it was thought necessary, to declare against the Violation; and establish the antient Rights, in a Parliamentary way, which was accordingly done.

In the Sixteenth Year, of the Reign of King *Charles* I. very great Complaints were made of the Star-Chamber, and Council-Table, That the Judges of the former, had not confined themselves to the Points, limited in the Statute of H. 7. c. I. which impowered the Great Officers of the Crown, and other Great Men, to proceed and punish some particular Offences;

> but had undertaken to punish, where no Law did warrant, and to make Decrees for Things, having no such Authority; and to inflict heavier Punishment than by any Law was warranted: That the Proceedings, Censures, and Decrees, of that Court, had been found by Experience, to be an intolerable Burthen to the Subject, and the Means to introduce an arbitrary Power and Government: That the Council-Table, had of late Times, assumed to it self, a Power to intermeddle in civil Causes, and Matters only of private Interest, between Party and Party, and had *adventured* to determine of the Estates, and Liberties of the Subject, contrary to the *Laws of the Land,* and the *Rights and Priviledges* of the Subject.

The Court of Star-Chamber was entirely dissolved, as were several other Courts; and the following, ample Parliamentary Declaration made:

> Be it enacted and declared by Authority of this present Parliament, that neither his Majesty, nor the Privy Council, *have,* or *ought* to have, any Jurisdiction, Power, or Authority, by *English* Bill, Petition, Articles, Libel, or any other arbitrary way whatsoever, to examine, or draw into Question, determine, or dispose of, the Lands, Tenements, Hereditaments, Goods, or Chattles, *of any of the Subjects of this Kingdom;* but that the

(*b*). 43 Edw. 3. cap. 3.
(*c*). 3 Car. I. c. I.

> same, ought to be tryed, and determined, in the ordinary Courts of Justice, and by the ordinary Course of the Law.*

Great Officers transgressing this Law, are liable to severe Penalties.

The Preamble to the *Habeas Corpus* Act, shews, what Shifts, and Evasions, were used, to elude the Force of the Laws, that were instituted, to secure the Subject's Liberty; the Words are:

> Whereas, great Delays have been used, by Sheriffs, Gaolers, and other Officers; to whose Custody, any of the King's Subjects, have been committed, for criminal, or supposed criminal Matters; in making Returns, of Writs of *Habeas Corpus*, to them directed; by standing out an *Alias, & Pluries Habeas Corpus;*[5] and sometimes more, and by other Shifts, to avoid their yielding Obedience to such Writs; contrary to their Duty, and the known Laws of the Land; whereby many of the King's Subjects, have been, and hereafter may be, long detained in Prison, in such Cases, where by the Law they are bailable; to their great Charges and Vexation.[1]

Therefore, Provision is made, to oblige all Officers to perform their Duty, and to punish such as shall not do so. There is no Part of the Royal *Prerogative,* abridged, or retrenched by these Statutes; no new Liberties, or Priviledges are granted to the Subject. Here are ample, and large Declarations in Parliament, of the Subject's Rights; loud Complaints of the Violation of those Rights; The Rights, themselves, confirmed; and the knavish Chicanes, and crafty Inventions, that were introduced to deprive the Subject of his Rights, are abolished; and more easy, plain, and direct Ways, for the Subject, to come at the Benefit of Laws, established in their Room.

By the first Act for settling the Succession of the Crown, a Parliamentary Declaration, of the Rights, and Liberties of the Subject, was thought necessary; not because the Subject had forfeited his Rights, and Liberties; or demanded new: But because, those that antiently belonged to him, had been invaded, and violated.†

(*). 16 Car. c. 10.

5. [An *alias* writ is issued as a second effort to serve the primary writ, in this case the *habeas corpus,* when that primary writ has had no effect; a *pluries* writ is a third writ issued when the previous writs have been unsuccessful.—Tr.]

[1]. 31 *Car.* 2. C. 2.

† 1 *W. & M.* c. 2.

From what hath been said, it is evident; that the *English* Subject, had very ample Rights, and Privileges, by the Common Law; and it is manifest by the several Statutes already mentioned; and a Multitude of others, as well as the *English* History; that the Common Law, though frequently confirmed in Parliament, was not sufficient, to secure Him from Oppression, and Violence: And there is no other Remedy, when Laws are violated, but to punish the Violators, and establish, and confirm the Laws; which have been frequently done, and sometimes with great Difficulty, and the Expence of a great deal of Blood, and Treasure.

Whoever has read the Parliamentary Proceedings, in the *Last*, as well as Queen *Anne*'s Reign; will find, that when the Safety of the Government, rendered a temporary Suspension of the Execution of the *Habeas Corpus* Act necessary; it was always opposed, when proposed to be of any considerable Duration: And the longest Time of Continuance of any of those Acts, that I ever saw, was not above 18 Months; so careful has the *British Parliament* been, to preserve to a People, justly fond of Liberty, and wisely jealous, of everything, that might be destructive of, or hurtful to It; the Benefit of a Law, that is a great Support and Preservative of Liberty.

This shews, that the *British* Subjects, esteem the several Statutes, that have been made to confirm their Common Law Rights, to be of mighty Consequence, and Advantage to them: And any one, may well imagine, that if any Attempt should be made, to abrogate those *great Defences* and *Bulwarks* of the People's Liberty; every body would be alarmed, and dread the Introduction of the same, or greater Mischiefs, than those, that render'd the making so many confirmatory Acts necessary: And it would be stupid, and irrational, to think the contrary.

If then, the Case was, as hath been already mention'd, in *England?* That, notwithstanding its Common Law, entitles the People, to *ample Liberties and Priviledges;* that there were great Numbers of *brave, honest Patriots,* who understood the Laws of their Country, perfectly well, and who never fail'd to use their utmost efforts, in Opposition to every Violation of that Law; that notwithstanding all they could do, themselves, and others, were insecure in their Lives, Liberties, and Properties; and Things were brought to such Extremities, that it became necessary, to confirm, and strengthen, the antient Rights by the *Legislative Authority:* And that, although That was frequently done, yet Oppressions were frequently renewed, and wicked Men in Power, always found Pretences, to oppress those, that would not abett, or would oppose their Crimes; and they have never wanted Instruments, to execute all their villainous and destructive Schemes.

Let us consider our own Circumstances, and enquire, Whether the Number, Ability, Interest, or Fortune, of our Patriots bear any Proportion, to those that *England* has been blest with, in all Ages? Whether we are greater Lovers of Justice, and Equity, than other People, or have less Occasion for Laws, to restrain those that are unruly amongst us, and to secure and protect those that are peaceable, and innocent, than our Neighbours have? And whether Men of the greatest Authority, and Interest among us, may not have as strong Inclinations for Power, and Dominion, and of Lording it over their Inferiors, as we are told Great Men in other Parts of the World have? By a serious Consideration of these Things, we may be able, to form some Judgment, of the Condition we should be in, if we were to forfeit the Benefit of all the Laws, that have been made; I mean, the Statutes to declare the Subject's Right at the Common Law; and to establish, strengthen, and confirm, that Right. "If Men (says an ingenious Author) will be great Knaves, in spight of Opposition; how much greater would they be, if there were none." *

Some People, will object several Book Cases; wherein the Judges have resolved, that the *English* Laws did not extend to *Ireland;* 'till it was expressly enacted that they should: And, that the *English* Acquisitions in *France,* were never governed but by their own Laws: From whence, the Necessity of enacting the *English Statutes,* in *Maryland,* before it's Inhabitants can have the Benefit of them, is often inferred.

But this Objection, (I conceive) will be of no great Weight; when it is considered, that those Countries, were inhabited, by civilized, sociable People, conversant with Arts, Learning and Commerce; that had Laws, suited, and adapted to the Order, and Engagements of Society; by which, themselves, and others that went to live among them, might be peaceably, and happily governed: The Cause was wanting here, and so must the Effect be; for *Maryland,* before it was settled by the *English,* was, as to Law, and Government, in the same Condition, with an uninhabited Wilderness: "And in Case of *an uninhabited Country,* newly found out, by the *English* Subjects; *All* Laws in Force in *England,* are in Force there." (†)

(*). *Cato's* Letters.
(†). *P. Holt* c. 1. 2 *Salk* 411.

The native *Indians,* were *rude, savage, and ignorant;* destitute of *Letters, Arts, or Commerce; and almost, of the common Notions, of Right, and Wrong*— A People, thus qualified, must make *excellent Preceptors, for Englishman!* and shew, (without Doubt,) *worthy Examples,* for their Imitation!

In the Dispute between the Earl of Darby, and the Sons of a former Earl, about the *Isle of Man,* when it was urged, that the *English* Laws, extended to that Island; it was alledged, and proved, that they were governed by other Laws, which Laws, were shewn in Writing: For which Reason, (I conceive, though the Book is silent in that Particular,) it was adjudged, that the *English Laws* did not reach the *Isle of Man.**

In a Word, it seems clear, that the Reason of the adjudged Cases, turns upon this, that even in the Case of a Conquered Country, the People ought to enjoy their own Laws, until they are actually abrogated, and others instituted in their room, by the Conqueror. This appears plainly in *Calvin's* Case,† where a Distinction is made between the Conquest of a Christian Kingdom, and the Kingdom of an Infidel.

> Upon this Ground, there is a Diversity between a Conquest of a Kingdom of a Christian King, and the Conquest of a Kingdom of an Infidel; for, if a King come to a Christian Kingdom by Conquest, seeing that he hath *Vitae et necis potestatem,*[6] he may at his Pleasure, alter and change the Laws of that Kingdom; but until he doth make an Alteration of those Laws, the antient Laws of that Kingdom remain.

And it appears plainly in History, that some of the wisest, as well as most successful Nations in the World, have been very careful to avoid making such Changes, lest they might beget an irreconcileable Hatred between the Victors and Vanquished; whereas, leaving the latter the Use and Benefit of their own Laws, would make them submit, with the less Reluctance, to the Government of their Conquerors; and there is neither Policy, nor Humanity, in making People desperate.

> Thus did the *Goths,* when they overcame the *Romans;*‡ So had the *Romans* done, when they conquered the *Germans* and *Gauls:* What

(*). 2 *Anderson's* Reports, 116.

(†) Co. *R.* 17 C.

6. ["The power of life and death."]

‡ *Grotius* of the Rights of Peace and War. B. 3. chap. 15.

would our Empire now have been (says *Seneca*) if a wholesome Providence had not intermix'd the Conquered with the Conquerors. Our Founder *Romulus* (says *Claudius,* in *Tacitus*) did so prevail by his Wisdom, that he made of those that were his Enemies, the same Day, his (Subjects and) Citizens; and he tells us, that nothing contributed so much to the Ruin of the *Lacedemonians* and *Athenians,* as their driving away the Conquered as Strangers. Histories give us Examples of the *Sabines, Albans, Latins,* and other *Italian* Nations, till at last *Caesar* led the *Gauls* in Triumph, and then entertain'd them at his Court. *Cerealis,* in *Tacitus,* thus addresses the *Gauls;* You your selves generally command our Legions, you govern these, and the other Provinces; you are denied or debarr'd of nothing: Wherefore love and value that Peace and Life, which the Conquerors, and Conquered enjoy equally. *Polibius* admires the Moderation of *Antigonus,* that when he had *Sparta* in his Power, he left to the Citizens their antient Government and Liberty; which Act acquired him Praise throughout *Greece.*

Thus the *Capadocians* were permitted by the *Romans,* to use what Form of Government they pleased, and many Nations after the War, were left free. *Carthage* was left free, to be govern'd by her own Laws, as the *Rhodians* pleaded to the *Romans* after the 2*d.* Punick War; And *Pompey* (says *Appian*) of the Conquer'd Nations, left some free to their own Laws. Thus the Government continued among the *Jews* in the Sanhedrin, even after the Confiscation of *Archelaus.*

When all Empire is taken away from the Conquer'd, there may be left them their ordinary Laws about their private and publick Affairs, and their own Customs and Magistrates. Thus *Pliny*'s Epistles tell us, that in *Bithynia,* a Proconsular Province, the City of *Apamea* was indulged to govern their State as they pleased themselves. And in another Place the *Bithynians* had their own Magistrates, their own Senate. So in *Poictus* the City of the *Amisni,* by the Favour of *Lucullus,* was allowed its own Laws, The *Goths* left their own Laws to the Conquered *Romans.* We read in *Salust,* the *Romans* chose rather to gain Friends than Slaves, and thought it safer to govern by Love than Fear. *Julius Caesar* told *Ariovistus** that *Fabius Maximus* fairly Conquered the People of *Auvergne* and *Rouerge,* whom he might have reduced into a Province, and made Tributaries to the Empire. But he forgave them and did not doubt, but it might be easily

(*). *Caesar*'s Commentaries.

> prov'd, upon further Search into Antiquity, that the *Romans* had a very good Title to that Country; But since it was the Pleasure of the Senate they should remain a Free People, they were permitted the Use of their own Laws, Government, and Customs.

Critognatus, the *Gaul,* thought he could not use a more favourable or prevailing Argument with his Countrymen, to encourage and unite them against the *Romans,* than to tell them that the *Romans* design'd to possess their Country, and make them perpetual Slaves; and that they never made War upon any other Account. "If you are ignorant (says he) of their Transactions in remoter Countries, cast your Eyes upon the Neighbouring *Gaul,* which is reduced to a Province, deprived of its Laws and Customs; and labours under an Eternal Yoke of Arbitrary Power."

I have heard it asserted, that *Maryland* is a Conquered Country; which, by the By, is false; and that the Conquered, must submit, to whatever Terms, the Victor thinks fit to impose on him: Were the Case really so, The *Indians,* must be the *Vanquish'd,* and the *English* the *Victors;* and consequently, the *Indians,* would be liable to the Miseries, in which a Conquered People are involved: Otherwise, the Conquerors themselves, must be Loosers by their Courage, and Success; which would be but a poor Reward of their Valour; However gross, and absurd, these Notions appear to be, at the very first View, to every Man of Common Sense; yet, have they been insisted on, with great Confidence, by Men, that have had more Knowledge than Honesty.

But suppose even this, to be the Case, that the *English,* by being brave and successful, had forfeited their *Native Rights,* and become *Slaves* by their *Acquisition:* Yet, even that, as the Case stands, would not reduce them to the Condition, wherein some kind People wish to see them; *viz.* Being excluded from any Right to, or Benefit from the *English* Laws. For the Charter of *Maryland,* does not only contain a Grant of the Country, with several Prerogatives to the Lord Proprietary: But also contains a Grant, to the People, of all the *Rights, Privileges, Immunities, Liberties,* and *Franchises,* of *English* Subjects: Which brings me to the second Thing I proposed: *viz. The Right which the People of* Maryland, *have to the Benefit of the* English *Laws,* by the Charter of the Province, to the Lord Proprietary: The Words whereof, pertinent to the present Purpose, are:—

> *And We* also of our *mere special Grace,* injoyn, and constitute, ordain, and command, that the said Province shall be of our Allegiance; and that all,

> and singular, the Subjects, and liege People, of Us, our Heirs, and Successors, transported, or to be transported, into the said Province; and that the Children of them, and such as shall descend from them, there, already born, and hereafter to be born; shall be *Denizens* of Us, our Heirs, and Successors, of our Kingdoms of *England*, and *Ireland;* and be, in *All Things, Held, Treated and Esteemed, as the Liege, Faithful People, of Us, our Heirs, and Successors, born within our Kingdom of* England: And likewise, any Lands, Tenements, Revenues, Services, and other Hereditaments whatsoever, within our Kingdoms of *England*, and other our Dominions, may inherit, or otherwise purchase, receive, take, have, hold, buy, possess; and them may occupy and enjoy, give, sell, alien, and bequeath: As likewise, All *Liberties, Franchises, and Privileges, of this our Kingdom of* England, *freely, quietly, and peaceably, Have, and Possess, Occupy, and Enjoy, as our Liege People, Born, or to be Born, within our said Kingdom of* England; without Let, Molestation, Vexation, Trouble, or Grievance, of Us, our Heirs, and Successors; any Statute, Act, Ordinance, or Provision, to the contrary thereof, notwithstanding.

It would be difficult, to invent stronger, or more comprehensive Terms than these, whereby *All* the Liberties, Franchises, and Privileges, of *English Subjects*, are granted to the *People* of *Maryland:* And this Charter, which I have seen, in the Old Books, of the Council's Proceedings, has been confirmed, by Act of Parliament.

The *English* Subject, as hath been already mentioned, and proved, (as I conceive,) had an undoubted Right to his Liberties, Franchises, and Privileges, by the Common Law: Yet those Liberties, Franchises, and Privileges, were *all* invaded, and violated, and Multitudes of good Men were first deprived of the Benefit of the Law, and then exposed to Rapine, and Oppression: These Oppressions, always produced Murmurings, and Discontents, and sometimes Slaughter and Bloodshed; and last of all, Acts of Parliament, to heal the Breaches, that had been made in the Laws;[1] and to establish and confirm the antient Rights of the Subject. The Acts thus obtained, have always been deemed, as *essential* a Part of the Security, of the Subject to his Rights and Privileges, as the Common Law it self: And, as he was insecure, before they (the Statutes) were made; so would he be rendered, if they were abrogated, or *He* deprived of the Benefit of Them: For

[1]. History of *Magna Charta*, and the Transactions of several Reigns before it, in the Book called *English Liberties*. p. 8, 9, & 10.

the Benefit of the Laws, is so necessary to support the Liberties, which they were instituted to confirm and establish; That the Abrogation of such Laws, would in Effect, be an Abolition of the Liberties themselves.

Here then, by these Words of the Charter, the Liberties, Franchises, and Privileges of an *English* Subject, are granted fully, and amply, to the People of *Maryland;* the Benefit of the Laws, securitative of those Liberties, &c. as inseparably incident to the Liberties themselves, are also granted, by Implication: This is Doctrine, that I am confident, will not be gainsayed by any Lawyer: For these, are established and uncontroverted Maxims: That, when the Law gives a Thing, it gives a Remedy to come at it.[2] Things incident, are adherent to the Superiors, or Principals.[3]

They, that are to have the Conusance of any Thing, are also, to have the Conusance of all Incidents, and Dependants thereon; for an Incident, is a Thing necessarily depending upon another.[4] When the Law gives a Thing, All Things necessary for obtaining it, are included.[5] When a Thing is commanded to be done, every Thing necessary to accomplish it, is also

[2]. *Lou le Ley done chose, la wo done Remedy a vener a seo.* 2 *Roll*'s Reports 17.

[3]. *Wingate*'s Maxims, 127.

> If a Man be seised of Lands in Fee-simple, and having divers Evidences and Charters, (some of them containing a Warranty, and some not,) conveys the Land over to another, without Warranty; upon which he may vouch; the Purchaser shall have all the Charters, and Evidences; as well those containing the Warranty, as the others: For as the Feoffer had conveyed over his Land absolutely, and is not bound to Warrant the Land, so that he might be vouched to Warranty, and to render in Value; And the Feoffee is bound to defend the Land, at his Peril: For this Case, it is reasonable, that the Feoffee should have all the Charters, and Evidences, as incident to the Land; although they be not granted to him, by express Words.

I Co. *R.* I. Lord *Buckhurst's* Case.

> A Grant of Reversion, includes a Grant of the Rent, by Implication, as incident to the Reversion. 1 Inst. 151. a.

[4]. Wingate's Maxims 131. 1 Inst. 56 a *Wood*'s Inst. 263.

> Quando Lex aliquid alicui concedit, concedere videtur etud, sine quo, res ipsa esse non potest. {"When the law concedes something, it appears to concede that without which the matter itself is not able to exist."—Tr.}

[5]. Upon a Writ of Estrepment, directed to the Sheriff, whereby, He is commanded to prevent any Waste being done; It was resolved, that he might resist all those, that would do Waste, and that, if he could not otherwise prevent them, he might imprison them, and make a Warrant to others, so to do: And that if it were necessary, he might take the Power of the County to his aid—5 Co. R. 115.

commanded.[(b)] So when a Power is given, to do any Act, a Power is therein included, of doing every Thing, without which, the Act could not be compleatly done.

I hope, the Passage out of the Charter, the Authorities produced, and the Nature of the Thing; are sufficient, to convince every unprejudiced Person, that if the first Settlers of *Maryland,* had really lost their native Laws, and Rights, and been in the Condition of a Conquer'd Country; that they, by this Charter, are put into the same State, and Condition, that their Fellow-Subjects residing in *England* are in, as to their *Rights* and *Liberties:* And, as it is already (I humbly conceive) proved, that the Benefit of the Statute, as well as the Common-Law, is the *only* Bulwark, and *sure* Defence of the Subject's Life, Liberty, and Property; I would ask this one short Question,—How the People of *Maryland,* can have the Benefit of what is granted them by the Charter, if they are deprived of the Means, *viz.* The Benefit of *All* the Laws that are necessary to secure them, in the Enjoyment of what is granted?

It seems very strange to me, that any One in his Senses, should imagine it out of the Prince's Power to treat his Subjects in this remote Part of his Dominions, with Mercy, Clemency, and Tenderness; or to confer so great a Favour on them, as the Laws of their Mother Country: But that he may treat them with Rigour and Severity: This, as strange as it seems, hath been advanced by an eminent Lawyer, as I am inform'd: And others, of less Knowledge, relying (I suppose) on his Authority, and Judgement, have given into the same wild Sentiments: I shall use no other Arguments to confute such extravagant Notions, so void of Loyalty, and Common Sense, but a Passage out of the celebrated Mr. Waller's speech, in Parliament; wherein, he *elegantly* exposes some Men's Notions of the Law, not unlike those whom I have been speaking of, in relation to the King's Power:

> As if the Law, says he, was in Force for the Destruction of the Subjects, and not for their Preservation; that it should have Power to kill, but not to protect them: A Thing, no less horrid, than if the Sun should burn Us, without lighting Us; or the Earth serve only to bury, and not to feed and nourish Us!

(b). Quia quando Aliquid mandatur. Mandatur & omne per quod pervenitur ad aliud. {"Because when something is commanded, everything is commanded through which it is obtained."—Tr.} 2 Inst. 423.

It may, probably, be supposed, that I give up the first Right, I mentioned; by laying so great a Stress on that which is deriv'd from the Charter:—But I am far from it,—For I should think the Right *good,* had the Charter never been made; as were the Rights of *English* Men, to all the Liberties, confirmed by *Magna Charta,* and other subsequent Statutes, before they were made: And as the Confirmation of the Subject's antient or Common-Law Rights, by several Acts of Parliament, is very beneficial to the Subject; so the Grant, or Confirmation of the same Liberties by the King, to the People of *Maryland,* is also very advantageous. It is no new Thing, even in particular Cases, to have a Grant from the King, to a private Person, of a Thing in which he really had a Right, and the King had none.*

It hath been objected, that truly, We have a Power of Legislation; that if any of the *English* Laws, are suitable to the Circumstances of the Province, we may enact them a-new: And from thence, 'tis inferred, that there is no Reason, to contend so much for the *English* Laws; and, indeed, that we have no Right to them, since we are so amply provided for otherwise. To this I answer,

That the Power of Legislation, granted to the Lord Proprietary, and the People of *Maryland,* was design'd as a Benefit, and not as a Prejudice: For it could hardly be suppos'd that a New Colony, vastly distant from their Mother-Country, exposed to the Insults of a cruel and savage Enemy; and inhabiting a Wilderness, must not be at a Loss, in some particular Cases, to apply the Rules of the Common-Law, or general Statutes; (were they ever so conversant with them,) which happens to be the Case, in Great-Britain, it self, and occasions the making of new Statutes, almost every Session of Parliament; and not to have it in their Power to provide suitably to any Emergency, by Laws of their own, would expose them to many Inconveniences; to prevent which, no better Expedient could be thought of, than to grant Them a Power of Legislature, under proper Restrictions. Thus it is in all

* The Possessions of the Prior of *Shiells,* were seized into the King's Hands, because (as it was alledg'd) he was an *Alien;* Whereupon he sued a Writ of Right to the King; setting forth, that at another Time, he was Prior of *Andover;* and his Possessions were seized into the King's Hands; although he was the King's Subject, born in *Gascoin,* within the King's Allegiance: Upon this, the King, of his *special Grace,* commanded his Escheater to make Restitution; and yet the Judges declared, The King had no Right to seize. So was it done, in the Case of *Reniger* and *Fogasa,* in the Commentaries, p. 20. Only, no mention is made of the King's special Grace.

Corporations; the Members of them, have a Power, with the like Condition, expressed, or implied, that is annext to the Power of Legislation, Granted to his Lordship, the Lord Proprietary, and the *Freemen of Maryland,* to make By-Laws, for the particular Utility of their own Country. And I believe, no Lawyer, or Man of Sense, ever imagined, that such a Grant, divested those that accepted of it, of the Rights they were born to in Common, with their Fellow Subjects.

Besides, if we consider the prudential Part, it is impossible that We can be ignorant, That the enacting so many New Laws, would take up a vast deal of Time, and occasion a greater Expense, then our Circumstances will admit of: And when all is done, they will not be any better than they are now, nor near so good, unless great Care be taken in transcribing them: And I have the Opinion of a very eminent Lawyer, "That it is never prudent, to change a Law, which cannot be better'd in the Subject Matter of the Law." * There is another Circumstance, that (as I humbly conceive) is of great Weight, and deserves the most serious Consideration; which is this: Should We attempt to enact such of the *English* Statutes, as may be supposed to suit the *Condition* of the Country, upon a Supposition, that We have no Right to them, without so doing; and that We should miscarry in that Attempt, which is not impossible, it would be such an Argument against the Right we contend for, as we could not easily get over; besides the Danger of its being made a Handle, to overturn a great deal, that hath been heretofore done, by Virtue of the Statutes.

Thus, I have endeavoured to prove *The Right of the People of* Maryland, *to the Benefit of all the* English *Laws, of every kind,* that have been instituted for the Preservation, and Security of the Subject's Liberty, from Reason, and Authority; and to represent to my Fellow-Subjects, the great Advantage they derive from the Laws of their Mother Country; and how highly they ought to esteem them.

And I beg leave to add, That Men, from a *State of Nature and Equality,* formed themselves into Society, for mutual Defence, and Preservation; and agreed to submit to Laws, that should be the Rule of their Conduct, under certain Regulations. Let us suppose the first Settlers of *Maryland,* to be a Society of People, united and combined together, for mutual Defence and Preservation; and sensible, not only of the Use, but also of the Necessity

* *Vaugh.* C. I.

of Laws, and conscious of their own Incapacity, to make such as might suit their Occasions, and procure their Welfare and Safety: I say, suppose them under these Circumstances, without any Regard to their Rights, as *English*, or *British Subjects*, or by Charter: And that they actually agreed, to make the Laws of their Mother-Country, (of which it is to be presumed, they had a general, or at least, some Notion,) to be the Rule of their Conduct, with such particular Provision, as they should, at Times, find necessary to make, in particular Cases: And that upon long Tryal, and Experience, of those Laws; they became convinced, of the Equality, and Justice of them, and consequently, fond of them: Will any one say, that they are obliged, to change those Laws? Or, to have them upon other Terms, than they have always had them, without their own Consent, or the Interposition, of the supreme Authority, of their Mother Country? It is manifest, by the judicial Proceedings, (which my Lord *Hale* says, make one formal constituent Part of the Laws;*) and the Manner of Transferring Property, in *Maryland*, that the People, since the first Settling of the Provinces, have in all Cases, (some few excepted, which particular Acts of Assembly provided for,) looked upon the Laws of *England*, as well *Statute* as *Common*, to be *their Laws*, and the *Rules of their Conduct*. The Tenure, by which they hold all their Land, is *Free* and Common *Soccage;* which is a *Common-Law* Tenure. A *great Part*, of the most valuable Land in the Province, is intailed, by Virtue of the Statute *de Donis*.[1] A *greater Part*, devised by Virtue of the Statutes of *Wills*.[2] And *not a little*, conveyed by Deeds of Lease, and Release, by Virtue of the Statute, for transferring *Uses* into *Possession*.[3] The Statute of *Frauds and Perjuries*, has always been allowed to affect Devises, not made conformably to it.[4] And as in *England*, *Usages*, and *Customs*, in Process of Time, have obtained the *Force of Laws*, which they always, afterwards, continued to have, 'till they were altered, or abrogated by the Legislative Authority; so those Laws, that have been received in *Maryland*, though the People had no other Right to them, but that *Reception*, and the long-continued Use of them; ought to have the *Force* of *Laws*, until other Provision is made, by the Legislature of the Province.

* *Hale*'s History of the Law.

[1]. 13 *E*. I. c. 1.

[2]. 32 *H*. 8. c. 1. 34, 35 *H*. 8. c. 5.

[3]. *H*. 8. 1. 10.

[4]. 29 *Car*. c. 3.

· 27 ·

"Amicus Reipublicae," Trade and Commerce Inculcated ([Boston], 1731)

THIS SELECTION, published anonymously by an author under the pseudonym Amicus Reipublicae, is one of the more thoughtful and sophisticated examples of colonial writing in the political economy genre. On the most general level, the pamphlet can be read as a celebration of commerce. Declaring "*That Trade or Commerce is principally necessary to a People's flourishing in the World*," he used the examples of ancient Tyrus and modern Holland to show that "a free and liberal *Commerce*" was the principal stimulus to labor and the development of "a habit of Prudence and Industry" necessary for a prosperous society, being at once a provider of goods unavailable locally, "an Engine of State, to draw men in to business, for the advancing and en[n]obling of the Rich, for the support of the Poor, [and] the strengthening and fortifying the State," and the essential ingredient "for increasing the Wealth, Civil Strength, and Temporal Glory of a People."

Yet, the author was hardly an advocate for a pure free market. On the contrary, he saw economic problems as "distempers of the State" to be remedied by active intervention. To counter New England's "languishing" trade and "the Inundation of Miseries flowing in by an ungoverned Commerce," his central concern, he included a lengthy consideration of the benefits of government measures to increase and stabilize the money supply and stimulate its circulation, to establish price regulations to prevent inflation, to concert with other New England colonies in the creation of widely participatory government-sanctioned and regulated companies for trade that would lead the commerce of the entire region into "the best Channels for the publick Good," and to pursue an ambitious and "regularly managed" public works program that would provide employment. (J.P.G.)

Trade and *Commerce*

INCULCATED;

IN A

DISCOURSE,

Shewing the Necessity of a Well-governed *Trade,* in order to a Flourishing Common-Wealth.

With some *Proposals* for the bringing *Gold* & *Silver* into the Country for a Medium of *Trade,* as also for the better Supporting the Credit of the *Paper Currency.*

By *Amicus Reipublicae.*[1]

Printed for the *AUTHOR.* 1731.

1. ["Friend of the republic."]

Trade and Commerce Inculcated, &c.

The Knowledge of the True Interest of ones Country, although the Study of it be most Commendable and Necessary, most Delightful and Natural to the Generous Enlarged Soul; yet perhaps there is no kind of Learning more generally neglected. The many dependent Causes, and seeming Counter-workings of things in relation to the Common Interest, renders the Science very abstruse and intricate, and very difficult to acquire in any measure of Perfection, it being difficult to distinguish the first moving, from dependent causes, or rather the Cause from the Consequence or Effect; and then that Selfish principal that naturally leads the minds of men, very rarely finds opportunity for Studies of a Publick nature, except what may be meerly in subservience to Self-ends, which is not always the best for the Publick good.

Hence proceeds the many different notions in men and the many warm Debates that happen about measures for promoting the publick Interest, every one being jealous for his own Interest, is ready to mistrust, condemn, and oppose all measures proposed for publick Benefit that himself don't understand, or at least fancys not to be consonant with his own particular advantages.

It may be observed, that not only in *New England*, but also in the *English American* Plantations in general, (notwithstanding the multiplying of the Inhabitants and increase of Business in some respects) there is evident declinings in, and many growing inconveniences attending the Business, Trade, and Affairs in general. And altho' many are apt to complain of the disadvantages of the times, and almost all are persuaded that the Current of Affairs runs very much out of order, yet very few agree in Judgment as to what may be the prime or principal causes of these distempers in the State, and much less as to means proper for the removal of the same.

Some are prone to be of opinion that the meer Imprudence of men in their private Capacities must needs be the Cause; others are apt to suppose the defect to be in the publick Administration or Leading of Affairs; some in this respect, and some in that: And while people are thus divided in their opinions, nothing can be agreed upon as proper to prevent the Inundation of Misery flowing in upon us.

Now what I would here attempt, is, to unfold the Causes of these Inconveniences that attend our State, in order step by step as they have slyly & insensibly taken hold upon it; and then to consider of some means proper for the removal of those Inconveniencies, and for the preventing the miseries Impending thereby.

In order to which I shall observe,

That Trade or Commerce is principally necessary to a Peoples flourishing in the World.

Altho' the Wealth and Flourishing of a People depends upon Diligent Labour as the Efficient of its Substance, or as a Cause without which it cannot be; yet Labour will not be improved to any considerable degree of Wealth, without the advantage & encouragement of a profitable *Commerce.* In all Labour there is profit, because none will Labour, but with a foresight of Profit; for Profit is the final Cause of Labour; and as there cannot be much profit by Labour without *Commerce,* so *Commerce* is the Cause of Profit by Labour, and consequently the cause of Labour, that is of the abundant Labour in order to Wealth and Flourishing.

The various constitutions and circumstances not only of Countries but also of particular Persons in the same Country, calls for a mutual communication of Goods or useful Commodities to supply each other with what the one wants and the other has to spare.

No Country has in it every thing that is useful and conducive to the comfortable Subsistance of its Inhabitants, independent of exchange or communication with other Countries; nor will the Accommodations, Faculty or Means of any particular Persons, afford them the same but by *Commerce.* And since each Country has but its peculiar Commodities to be raised in abundance, *Commerce* is necessary to a suitable distribution and digesture of it, holding it in value, and therefore necessary to the encouragement and support of Labour.

Trade or *Commerce,* is an Engine of State, to draw men in to business, for the advancing and enobling of the Rich, for the support of the Poor, for the strengthning and fortifying the State; and when it is wisely conducted and vigorously carried on, it is the King of Business for increasing the Wealth, Civil Strength, and Temporal Glory of a People.

Solomon the wise King of *Israel,* by his policy in *Trade,* advanced the Business & Wealth of his Kingdom filling it with Riches, Strength, Beauty and Magnificence, above all the Kingdoms of the Earth.

Tyrus, the Crowning City, being situate at the entry of the Sea, became the Merchant of the People for many Isles; although seated upon a meer Rock, yet she became Renowned for Temporal Glory & Beauty; many

Kingdoms and Countries occupied in her fairs; the Ships of *Tarshish* did sing of her in her markets, for that she was replenished and made very glorious in the midst of the Seas.

Holland (by relation) was such an obscure spot of Earth, as though GOD had reserved it only for a place to dig Turf in for the accommodating of those Countries wherein he hoards up the miseries of the winter. It naturally affording scarcely any one Commodity of use; yet by *Merchandize* and *Trade* it is now become the Store-house of all those *Merchandizes* that may be collected from the rising to the setting of the Sun, and gives those People a name as large and as high as any Monarch this day on Earth; and this their Glory is owing to their peculiar Policy, good Regulations, Customs, and Restrictions in *Trade;* that being the principal object of their Care and Protection, having little besides to depend upon for their Support; whereas in other Countries, being well accommodated for other business, the *Trade* has been sometimes carelesly neglected and left to private discretion, which has proved the Ruin of all.

It is observable, that such Countries who have had the least dependencies upon other means, have gained such Policy in *Trade,* as to outvie the more Fertile and Productive Countries in Strength, Riches, and Worldly Grandeur.

Hence it is, that *Trade, Merchandize* and *Commerce,* are become the only object and care of the great Princes and Potentates of the Earth, as knowing that the Returns and Effects of *Commerce* is Riches, and the plenty of all things conducing to the benefit of humane life, for the Supporting of their Crowns and Grandeur, and Fortifying their Countries and Kingdoms with Reputation and Strength. *Mol. Praef. De Jure Maritisino.*[2]

It is the Bounty, Pomp, and Grandeur, peculiar to a free and vigorous carrying on in *Trade,* that ordinarily makes good Business for Labouring men.

The proper Fees and Immunities of a free and liberal *Commerce,* are very enriching to the Common-Wealth, naturally providing Stores and Plenty for a commodious and profitable carrying on; when with a dull *Trade* plenty makes little profit, but rather a discouragement in business; but as a People advances in Wealth and Worldly Magnificence, so the demand for all kinds of business will be enlarged. It requires much labour and business to furnish the Rich and Noble with their magnificent Buildings, rich Furniture,

2. ["On the maritime law." The Latin should be "maritimo."—Tr.]

costly Apparel, and sumptuous Fare; also to provide for and replenish the Store-houses of the rich Merchants, and also for the effecting a Produce to exchange for Money to line their Purses, Bags, Coffers, *&c.* in order for an able carrying on, all which must be produced by Labour and good Business. And then,

According to the demand for Labour, so will Labour be undertaken and carried on.

Men are ordinarily allowed to work six Days in a Week for their support; but yet one or two Days in a Week, will serve well for an *Indian,* or one that will live like an *Indian,* or an Hermite. Now if all were disposed to live mean, saving and plain, there would be but a small demand for the produce of those who effect great Stores for the Market, more than to purchase what they have occasion to expend; there would then be more Sellers than Buyers; which would soon discourage the Industry of the Laborious & Prudent.

Sometimes the Charges of Religion, as Tythes, Offerrings, Magnificent Buildings, and costly Preparations, Dedicated to Religious Services, as also a great part of time set apart for Holy Exercises, greatly enlarges and quickens the demand for Labour.

Sometimes the Charges of War, Military Service, Building of Fortifications, and other Warlike Provisions, greatly enlarges and quickens the demand for Labour; as also does any great and notable Works or Undertakings of the Publick Charge. But,

The most wealthy and liberal demand is, when there is valuable Riches, Silver and Gold as well as other precious Substance to be had in exchange for Labour to a plentiful degree, advancing of the Common-wealth, enabling Men to improve and dispense with Labour in an able and forehanded way of living.

Now either of these occasions hinted at, may serve greatly to draw a people out of an Idle habit, encouraging Industry, Virtue, &c. being Profitable to Labouring Men, and a support to Poor Men; but when a People have no Business but only to provide for Common Occasions, or Necessities in a poor declining Reipublick that have no means to Convert their produce into that which shall enable and set them before hand for Business, (tho' this demand is apt to swell into many Extravagancies in an active fruitful Country,) yet this is most oppressive to Poor Men, and ruining to the Common-Wealth, being an Inlet to Idleness and almost every other Ill-habit.

Had *Sodom* and *Gomorrah* been Politick in *Trade* and accustomed to Manners of Civility & Magnificence according as the fertillity of their Soil, would have endured it, they might have been diverted from the Sins of Idleness, fulness of Bread, *&c.*

But what I would have understood, is this, that any People whatsoever considered as a Common-Wealth, have Rich Mines in their Capacity of Labour, and carrying on Business, and with suitable policy in *Trade,* it may be drawn out and refined to a wealthy & flourishing State, altho' of but mean advantages, as to the produce of their Soil; and when quick profit lies ready to embrace the *Business* and *Trade* in general, as it may be undertaken and enlarged, the Business will be undertaken & carried on to very great degrees, and by continuance will do more to reduce a People to a habit of Prudence and Industry than is possible to be effected by Whip, or Hunger or by all the penal Laws that can be Invented for the Suppressing of Idleness, *&c.*

And contrarywise, a People may be possessed of a Fruitful Rich Country, and yet for want of good Regulations, and Policy in *Trade,* the business of the Country (considered in the mean) will be rendered greatly disadvantagious and unprofitable, as to any enlarged undertaking. However some through their better means may enlarge their Business with Profit, yet it must be upon the disadvantage and discouragement of some others, which disposition in a Publick State will inevitably in continuance reduce the most industrious Generation of People to an habit of Idleness, *&c.* And the more fruitful the Country, the more Intolerable the Consequence, as Idleness is the leader of most kinds of Vices.

To shew how this Indisposition may take place in Reipublick, I shall lay down a few Principles or Maxims in *Trade,* which may be serviceable to the Purpose,

And in the first place,

1. To a profitable carrying on of *Trade,* there must be some suitable Specie of Universal Currency to be made use of as *Money* to accommodate, facilitate and even the Exchange.

The benefit of a suitable Current Medium in *Commerce,* is so obvious and well understood, that no Country or People of *Policy* and *Trade* is willing to do without it; and those who esteem it the least, are willing to take it upon occasion. That steady Value which the esteem of Men has put upon *Gold* and *Silver,* but *Silver* especially, it being aptly formed into peices of greater and lesser quantitys, and those of a determinate value convenient for Exchanging, and easy to be known, has rendered it the most agreeable Medium, by which to rate the value of all Merchandize, and to be made use of in purchasing the same. Now whatsoever is thus Useful and Current, is called *Money*, and into such a universal Currency, the overplus of produce may be converted, maintaining the value in greater abundance, than what could be without it; upholding the vend, by a free and profitable Commerce, digesting every thing to the best advantage, enlarging the demand for, and encouraging of, all good Business; and for a Country to be well stockt with Money renders it Able and Powerful: for *Money* is not only a Defence, but, *Money answers all things*.

2. There is a certain proportionate quantity of running Cash, requisite to the carrying on of a current free Trade, and that more or less according to the ability of the People to effect, purchase, improve, dispense with and consume of the produce.

When there is not a sufficiency of money to accommodate the Commerce, the produce or merchandise of the Country will be like stagnate waters & the Commerce may not be carried on with Profit to the commonwealth, but the Trade being incommodious and dull, there will be nothing in demand but to answer necessities, and the vendible species being scarce will domineer over & discourage all other kinds of Merchandize, and the Barter will be so disagreeable and incommodious, that men will rather carry on their dealing by a general Trust and running in Debt, than which there can hardly be a greater Snare to the Common-Wealth: for in this case, every thing must be discouraged to very scarcity to maintain the Currency of it, and the Business and Trade will jumble and run retrograde, and by so much the more as the money falls short of a suitable supply to set people before hand for undertaking and carrying on Business.

But Money being plentiful, it will not only enable them that possess it to undertake and furnish for themselves largely to the encouragement of Labour, but like a princely able Merchant, it will freely & voluntarily collect all kinds of necessary and useful Commodities in store for the Market, maintaining a due decorum in the valuation of every kind of thing, the exchange being managed to the best advantage. Therefore,

3. As the Business and Trade of a Country is or may be enlarged, so there should be Money always ready or impending to be brought in, by Trade to increase, and enlarge the Current stock proportionably thereunto.

For as a Country increases with Inhabitants, Riches and Trade, so there will be more Money requisite to carry on the Trade withal; and if the Trade be regularly managed, it will naturally supply it self with Money. For,

4. The Medium of Trade (or Money) is ordinarily gain'd by, and comes in the ballance of Trade.

When the produce of a Country is so large that the Export exceeds the Import, of Goods brought in from other Places to be consumed in it; the overplus will be coming in Cash to ballance the Trade.

Hence some have urged the necessity of lessening the imports of our Merchandize, by retrenching our expences in Apparel, Tables, *&c.* as a necessary means to turn the ballance of Trade to our advantage in order to accommodate our Commerce with Money, as it were by an immediate and forcible Change in our manners.

But,

5. To hold the Ballance of Trade to the advantage of bringing in Money, it is necessary that money should be maintained in such Credit, that it may be profitably brought in for a Medium of Trade in exchange for the Countries Produce.

The ballance of Trade hangs upon the Credit of Money, and where Money is in best Credit or heaviest in esteem, there turns the ballance of Trade.

When any Country can afford its produce at so cheap a rate that those who improve themselves in Trade can purchase the same with Money, and export it to advantage, their own interests will put them upon bringing Money into such a Country for that end, and so long as the Merchandize or Labour of the Country is held to a suitable valuation, the Money will come in and remain in a sufficient plenty for its ordinary occasions; but so long as the Labour or Merchandize of the Country is rated higher than it is worth in Money, we shall find but few imployed in bringing in the ballance from other places in Money; but it will be the interest of every Merchant to send it out of the Country as fast as it comes to his hand. And let our Export be ever so large our Import will exceed it so long as there is money to ballance the same, which will be so much to the Countries disadvantage and to lessen the Import, would but lessen the demand for the Export.

Thus the Premisses being granted this Conclusion necessarily follows, *viz.*

That the Flourishing of a People or Common Wealth depends upon the maintaining a just Credit upon Money, or holding a suitable low valuation upon Merchandize.

The Truth of this Conclusion may be illustrated under two Propositions.

I. *That the most valuable of Money, as it is used for a Medium of Trade, is not only liable but very apt to sink below its just Credit.*

II. *That the undervaluing of Money or over rating value of Merchandize, is most detrimental and ruinous to the Common Wealth.*

Prop. I. *That the most valuable of Money, as it is used for a Medium of Trade, is liable and very apt to sink below its just Credit.*

This Proposition may be resolved in answer to two Queries that may be raised upon it.

1. *Wherein does the Credit of Money consist?*
2. *When may Money be said to be undervalued or sunk below its just Credit?*

1. *Wherein does the Credit of Money Consist?*

Answ. *The Value or Credit of Money does not consist meerly in the denomination of its Weight, as being rated upon it self, by reckoning so many* Shillings *to an* Ounce, *or the like:* for let there be ever so many *Shillings* reckoned to an *Ounce of Silver,* or *Pounds* to an *Ounce of Gold,* this does not determine the value or credit of *Money.*

But,

The Credit of Money consists in its validity in purchasing the necessaries of livelihood: and therefore when its said that such a certain weight in *Silver,* will purchase such a certain quantity of Labour, or Produce, this determines the Value or Credit of Money: and as the *Labour* or *Merchandize* of the Country is high or low valued, so Money is low or high Credited.

2. *When may Money be said to be under valued, or sunk below its just Credit?*

Answ. *There is a certain just and proportionable value belonging not only to Money, but also to every kind of useful Commodity, and that more or less according to the Labour that is necessary to produce the same.* As suppose one Man imployed to raise Corn while another is imployed to dig and refine Silver; at the end of some certain space of time, the compleat produce of Corn and that of Silver, are the just and natural prices of each other, and each the value or price of so much time as is required to effect or produce the same: and if a days labour be taken up to produce a Bushel of Corn or one quarter of an ounce of good Silver, then the bushel of Corn is worth one quarter of an ounce of Silver, and either of them the just price of a days work. *Ceteris paribus.*[3]

3. ["Other things being equal."]

Or if the Mines should fail or prove so difficult that a days labour will produce but one eighth part of an ounce of Silver, then one eighth of an ounce of Silver, will be worth either the Bushel of Corn or the days work, as well as the quarter was in the case aforesaid.

And so likewise if the Silver be brought in by Trade, what the produce of a days labour will ordinarily exchange for of Silver, allowing reasonable profit to the Trader, so much of Silver is the just and honest price of the produce. Thus Labour is evermore the true and just measure of values, and so the Riches of a Country are to be valued by the quantity of labour it can purchase, and not by the quantity of Money they possess: for a man may be as rich, or live as long with one ounce of Silver in one Country as in another with two ounces of the same, for his support. Therefore not the intrinsick virtue, but the outward esteem bears the Currency and value upon Silver, and the labour or cost of producing, gives the Rule for a just and honest valuation: for in ages past Silver has been more than six times of the value that now it is, viz. in *Great Britain,* good Wheat sold for *four pence per Bushel,* and Labour at no more than *one penny per Day.*

Now when any Country so values their *Labour* or *Merchandize,* that he who undertakes to dig and refine Silver, or to raise a produce in order to gain it by *Trade,* if he may not produce enough in a day by the means to pay himself for his days work, so that he may ordinarily purchase the produce of a days labour in any other specie by his Silver so obtained, then Silver is undervalued. Or if the value of Merchandise or Labour in general, be so high upon Money or Silver, that there becomes a peculiar profit in the export of Silver for foreign *Trade,* above what may be in the export of the Countries Produce, so that the Silver becomes exhausted and very scarce for a Medium of *Trade,* then Silver is undoubtedly under-valued.

But this in general, when Money will not ordinarily answer for it self, in bringing of it in for a Medium of *Trade,* then it is under-valued and sunk below its just Credit.

But some may argue, that the reason why men don't ordinarily *Trade* for Money, but always bring in Goods, is because the Goods are wanted, which gives the profit to the bringing in Goods. Now this can't be the reason, because Money is always, or for the most part, in a more severe demand than *Goods* or *Merchandize;* but the profit peculiar of bringing in Goods, is occasioned by the discount of Money, in the general high valuation of

Merchandize or *Labour;* were it not for the discount or low value of Money at home, the profit would be as well in the export of our produce which is wanted in other places, (or would be with due encouragement upon our own business) as foreign Goods are wanted among us; but when Money is under-valued, there is no advance in the export, for if the Return be in Money, there will be loss in the Voyage.

When *Connecticut* goes to *Boston* with its Produce, there is profit in the Export, because Money is in as good Credit in *Connecticut* as in *Boston,* and the same advantage has *Boston,* with *Connecticut,* in their Goods; but when *New England* Trades with the *West-Indies,* or elsewhere, the advance or profit is in the Import, but none in the Export.

Now there is a natural propensity in all People to raise the value of their Produce or Merchandize, in which men so universally agree, that the value of Merchandize is much more naturally strain'd up above the just value of it, than held down to a just valuation as valued upon Money. And this is occasioned from divers motives. And principally in the first place,

1. *From a Greedy desire of Gain.* It is the principle of some People to strain up & get as much as ever they can for what they have to Sell, without regard to Reason or Justice, and when this Principle comes in vogue, he must suffer wrong that don't stand by it. And then,

2. *From Scarcities of Provisions.* When any kind of necessary Provisions are become scarce, such as are straitned, will give an extravagant price, rather than suffer; and ones necessity being anothers opportunity; the price is raised, and then other things will naturally rise to the fixing a general high price, rather than for that which is raised, to fall: for says one and another, *If I can't have so much for it, I'll not sell it.*

3. *From the Monopolizing Spirit of the Merchant.* It is the Practice of some Merchants to bid high for any Commodities that are in demand, to engross the *Trade,* enlarging their Business, & Custom thereby: and sometimes they will Monopolize such kinds of provisions as are much wanted, and then raise the price at their own discretion, occasioning the prices of things to raise in general.

4. *From the Scarcity of Money.* Money is put into the Ballance in competition with all kinds of *Merchandize,* and so there is an everlasting struggle for the preferrence in value: for in all dealing, *Money* stands a party on one side or the other, even in Barter, each Specie that is laid on the board, magnifies it self against *Money,* to bear up its own value; so that the Credit

of *Money* is bartered in all dealing; and when *Money* is scarce, it can but seldom appear in the defence of its own cause, but is forced to make use of Trust for its Advocate; but Trust being in no great esteem (however necessary) cannot deal with that advantage in the behalf of *Money*, as ready *Money* it self might do; and this gives *Merchandize* a peculiar advantage against it, to bear down its Credit; the scarcer Money is, the less able to maintain its Credit, being imployed chiefly in a necessitous *Trade*, Buying the most dear and scarce Provisions, or in Paying long trusted Debts, which Trust has made to its great disadvantage. Some indeed being straitned for *Money*, may be forced to part with their Estates upon base terms, as things in general run high, yet, there is nothing occasions *Money* to sink in Credit, so much as the scarcity of it; and altho' it be in a severe demand, when scarce, yet this only supports Extortion; for however poor Men get their Money, they are yet forced to lay it out in the most scarce and dear Provisions, or to very little advantage, and thus Money for want of a plentiful substance, becomes soiled and out of Credit, being over-run with Trusting and Bartering and a necessitous *Trade*. It may seem unreasonable to some, that the scarcity of Money should sink the value of it, when the scarcity of other things does but raise their value, but it must be considered, that the nature of Money in its use and improvement, is quite different from that of Merchandize. But more of this as I may find occasion afterwards. And in reflection upon the several Motives as before hinted, I shall make this Observation, *viz*

That from some one or more of these several Motives, the value of *Merchandize* has almost ever a disposition to rise, sinking the Credit of Money; and however the customs and laws of some Countries, may provide well against it, yet it is a disposition natural to all, and if the *Commerce* or *Trade* of the Country be not well protected and guarded against it, it will prove ruinous to the Common-Wealth, this propensity to sink the Credit of Money, has been eminently prevailing in *New England*, as in three particular Instances.

1. This occasioned the odds formerly made between a payment in *Money*, and a payment in *Pay* (as the Countrys produce was then called) which was one third of the value, the Countrys produce was indeed as good as *Money*, at a just value, but being rated one third too high, *Money* was found one third better in foreign dealing, and this occasioned the Merchants to make that odds.

Again,

2. This occasioned the alteration in the weight of Money, adding near one quarter of the value to the same weight; it being easier to perswade People to take a less weight under the same denomination, than to lower the high prices of things. And indeed one half of the weight would have done as well under one half of the denomination, by a suitable low valuation upon *Merchandize*, and as near to any rule of Justice in the valuation of things. However, it is an irregular way of maintaining the Credit of *Money* by such shiftings, tho' no other than what some of the more Arbitrary Powers in *Europe* find occasion to practice, where the subjects have not that politick freedom as some other states are vested with; the power of regulation being lodged more in the head, and not in the States.

But then the last instance to be mentioned under this head, may be,

3. This occasioned the wretched Fall, and still increasing Discount upon *Bills of Credit*, of which I shall have occasion to speak something afterwards.

And so I now pass to the second Proposition, *viz.*

That the undervaluing of Money, or over rating the value of Merchandize, is most ruinous and detrimental to the Common Wealth. As has been already noted; the Ballance of *Trade*, is dependent upon the Credit of *Money*, and the suffering the Credit of *Money* to sink below its just value upon *Merchandize*, looses the advantage of this Ballance; for the turning of the Scale is either to advantage or to disadvantage, and when the advantage of this Ballance is lost, by the turn of the Scale, the impending disadvantages (like the breaking up of a dam) will flow in without measure.

But to consider of the disadvantages or Ill consequences of sinking the Credit of Money in particular, in order to clear up the proposition. I shall observe in the first place, That, *The undervaluing of Money, or over rating the value of Merchandize, forbids the Export of Merchandize to extend the Import.* As before noted, no persons Interest, will bring in *Money* when under valued, but the Interest of every one to send it out as it comes to hand, this subjects the Export to the Import, putting the Business of the Country to a very great disadvantage causing many Obstructions in the same: For, in a Trading Country, *Money* being in Credit increases the demand for Labour for the bringing of it in, which causing Wealth greatly increases the *Business & Trade* of the Country, by Magnificent Buildings, costly Furniture, sumptuous Living, and great Undertakings Publick & Private, so that not only a greater supply of Money may be called in to Accommodate the *Commerce*;

but the Country will be able to purchase and dispense with more in Credit and Grandeur, which must all be erected upon the foot of Labour, and all would be found profitable by the increasing demand for it. On the contrary, Money being discouraged, the demand shrinks, Men become Poor, and behindhand, unable to purchase, and consume; Idleness will prevail, the Business of the Country become starved, and Men hardly able to Live one by another.

Secondly, *The undervaluing of Money, or over rating the value of Merchandize, in a Country, exchanges the peculiar advantages or best means of gaining of Wealth, for the common Labour of other Countries discouraging its own Labour.* When the *Labour* or *Merchandize* is in general, high valued, the Merchant may not make profit by it, but only in the high value of the Return, which must not be in Money, for that is undervalued, but the return must be in the common and cheaper Labour of other Countries; and so let the Advantages of Mines, Fishery, Timber, Tar, Turpentine, or the best means that possibly may be had, be ever so great in themselves, yet there can be no profit by them, except in ballancing the same with foreign Goods or Labour, which serves to lessen the demand for Business at home: for the less of Labour bestowed upon the Commodity, the more profit in the Exportation.

Thirdly, *The undervaluing of Money, or over rating the value of Merchandize, dreins a Country of Money.* It is natural for Money to Center and Circulate where it is in best Credit, every Trader chuses to lay out his Money where he can have the best penny worth; and when Money is in good Credit in a Country, it naturally flows in, and centers there; but when the *Labour* or *Merchandize* of the Country comes to be prized above what it is worth in Money, then the Money becomes *Merchandize,* and the Merchants will gather it together, and send it out of the Country for advantage in foreign *Trade;* and when it is so, the Medium of *Trade* will become very scarce.

The disadvantages that attend the want, or scarcity of Money, are indeed many and great, & the difference between a Country well supplied with Money, and a Country that is destitute, are much the same in proportion as the difference between a Rich and a Poor Man; I don't mean a poor man meerly with respect to the meanness of his possessions, but with respect to his Misery, Entanglements and Thraldom, for these will inevitably abound in an active Trading Country, that has not a suitable stock of Money to set it before-hand in *Trade.*

But there is great difference in mens opinions as to the sufficiency of the Stock, some complaining of scarcity, when others suppose it to be sufficiently plentiful.

Now to decide this Controversy, I would lay down one certain and undeniable Rule to be observed in the case, *viz.* Whenever it is so that men being straitned for Money, will allow exorbitant Interest for the use of Money, giving good security for it, *then* Money is most certainly too scarce for the good of the Common-Wealth.

Although some men through their meer imprudence, may be reduced to great straits for Money, or for such necessary provisions as must be purchased with Money; yet such will never give large Interest when Money is reasonably plentiful, or may be ordinarily had for moderate Interest, with good security, nor can any one extort large Interest for Money when it is reasonably plentiful, any easier than he can extort an immoderate price for any other Commodity when it is plenty.

Some of the necessary Concomitants and proper Consequences which naturally accompany and follow the scarcity of Money, are these, viz. 1. *Obstruction and Discouragement in Business.* 2. *Running in Debt.* 3. *Exorbitant Usury.* 4. *Devastation of Estates.* 5. *Extortion in Dealing.* 6. *Sinking of Credit.* All which with the scarcity of Money, are mutually enforcing causes and consequences of each other.

1. *The want of Money is not only in it self a privation of Wealth, but also an exceeding hindrance & discouragement to all good business.* That general Currency, which is, and may be put upon those species which may be conveniently improved for a Medium of *Trade* as what (in common speaking) we call Money, is the thing which makes way for Wealth, the general Currency, is a Vehicle into which the superfluity of produce may be converted to the maintaining the value, in great abundance; and the great demand there is for a general Currency in a wealthy Trading Country, makes room to increase their Wealth to a great degree, and with an ample supply of Money the Trade and Business shall remain profitable, maintaining all in Credit and value, digesting every thing to the best advantage. And with this encouragement the business of the Country would be followed with a common industry, when otherwise the People might become like the *Cretians,* always liars, evil beasts, and slow-bellies. As a little leaven leaveneth the whole lump, so a little indisposition in a Publick State may be an occasion of wretched Consequences. But howsoever,

No People can be able and before-hand for business or in a way of advancing of the Common-Wealth with only their ordinary provisions, for as Money is the thing that enables and gives life to business, encouraging and making profit in *Commerce,* so without Money a large produce of any kind so as men may have in store to enable to undertake largely in business, would under value it so that it would not answer the cost of producing; unless many others are straitned for want: for who would change a wanted scarce Commodity, for that which is plenty, or that which he does not want, or is not in demand; so I say the business must (in that case) be carried on with the scarce and not with the plenty. But Money when plenty is all things that a man wants, and every one is ready to take it; I say when plenty, because when scarce it is but the vice lord under the most scarce & wanted Provisions to Tyrannize over the plenty; but a plenty of Money makes every thing the more Current though not so very scarce therefore I say when Money is scarce the Country must and will be kept to short allowance and while the market is Glutted and discouragement laid upon the produce, some may be suffering for want, not having acceptable species to purchase withal: so that the business of the Country must needs suffer discouragement, and poverty increase thro' such incommodious means; he that gains must multiply in Bills, Bonds, *&c.* and so be in a way of making purchase upon some declining mans inheritance; but this makes no good business for Labour nor interest to the Publick, but the more labour is discouraged thro' such means the more it will be, for as People become behindhand they become the less able to purchase & dispense with the produce of Labour.

2. *The Scarcity of Money occasions People to run in Debt.*

The direct or immediate exchange of Commodities is seldom agreeable and Commodious for each party in *Commerce,* & he that has to sell, will rather wait a considerable time for his Money, rather than take the trouble of what he don't want; and not only the fore-handed Farmer that wants Money to buy land, but also such as are under engagements for Money & want to redeem their land, these will always stand for Money, & will readily embrace a promise rather than fail, especially with an advance in the price. And when the Country is so declining & Money may not be increased or brought in as the People increase, as their Trade & Business should increase, & as their running into Debt will increase, the generality of men will become involved, disappointed & foiled, & the disadvantages will be such that every one that looks into the management and discipline of the times, may read'em without my trouble of writing. For as these debts which naturally disperse through the *Commerce* of the Country increase, so the necessary produce falls more and more short of ballancing the accounts, and to suppose every Debtor should raise a produce sufficient to answer his debt, it would produce such glut of Provisions, that the Creditors would never take 'em off nor could it possibly be, but instead of this as the Debt increase, the Country becomes less and less able to dispense with and take off the Produce, which scants the demand, lessens the profits, increases and augments the entanglements to the great ruine to the Common-Wealth, Whereas if there were a suitable stock of running Cash to circulate and ballance the Accompts and not to be consumed, this might serve to release one debtor from another and remain circulating over and above to the great advantage of the Common-Wealth.

3. *The Scarcity of Money occasions Interest to be at a very high Rate.*

To what proportion some men will, and do advance for the Interest of Money in cases of necessity, it is a scandal to the Country and its Religion, and Policy, to say; and how this cursed gain is inclined to eat and devour mens Estates that are forced to submit to its Tyranny, the undoing and ruining experience of many in these times may Witness.

When Money is scarce, the allowing of Interest steals into the whole Trade of the Country, first by advance in the price, for a long trust, and then there must be allowance for further forbearance, so the allowing of Interest interposes instead of Moneys circulating, and the Debts remain obstructed, swelling and breaking out in the ruin of many. And when men may have a great and certain profit in letting their Money to use, they will be the less inclined to improve their Money in *Trade,* or in any good undertaking for the Common-Wealth: but the Money must circulate chiefly in cases of necessity, being hired from the Usurer, and naturally gathering to him again, whereby the yearly Interest allowed, may be much more than what there is of Money passing through its repeated going out upon hire as well as by the common allowing Interest for Money where the Principle never was in Money, as in Cases of purchase, without Money to pay, and thus the course of Money is turned to the spoiling of *Trade,* and to the ruin of the Common wealth. And altho' the letting Money to Use is the most Ignoble practice a rich man can follow (except to lock it up in his Chest like a miser) yielding no profit, but by wrong to the Common-wealth, to the hirer, and to the poor in general, undermining and cutting off deeds of Man hood and Charity, yet poor men must esteem it a high favour to hire

Money at 10, 15, or 20 *per Cent,* looking upon the Usurer as the only man to stand him in stead; but certainly if Money could be improved without hire it would afford more profit in business: for an intolerable company of Usurers must be maintained out of the common business of the Country for the meer non-improvement of their Money; It is a mysterious moth to the Common-wealth.

4. *The Scarcity of Money occasions extraordinary shiftings and devastation in Estates.*

When through the Scarcity of Money People are generally become involved, it is morally impossible but that there must be now and then a Farm set off to ballance Accompts; for the Creditors will never take the produce of the Debtors to full ballance, for it is almost impossible for the Creditors who have been and are the most productive party to find occasion for a produce sufficient, but these being under the best advantages can supply the market, upon cheaper terms than the other can, and live by it; and then when men become foiled and boggled and their land begins to shake, the Usurer begins to look out, and having the command of the Money he gathers in a Sum to about one third of the value of the Farm, which he fancies to get, & lets it to the owner, & taking good security for it upon the Farm, he needs to take no further care; or if he sees a man inclining to fall behind-hand, he will readily find him Money upon large Interest, and so the man falls in and becomes a prey to the Usurer before he is aware.

I have known good Estates of land spunged out for little more than half the worth with all the Interest. And thus the estates of many good honest men must fall a sacrifice to the straitness of the times, and men must generally stand upon their guard, or suffer and thus lands become the *Merchandize* & the *Bills* and *Bonds* must be the *Medium;* Estates scarcely remaining with the second generation. Now if the Land-Mongers & Usurers of the times, could bequeath their Faculty with their Estates, to their children, it might answer their highest end and concern; but their Children are commonly as good Game for the Extortioners of the next age as any: for commonly those that begin low get the art of rising as well as any, and them that begin high as well gain the art of falling; so that the best we can do for our Children is to promote the flourishing of the Common-Wealth by encouragement upon business.

5. *The Scarcity of Money occasions Extortion in dealing.*

As has been observed, the want of Money discourages the business of the Country to very short stores, subjecting the Country to extreme scarcities:

for when a People are obliged to run so near the Wind, it is but a small variation to make a glut or a scarcity, and seldom if ever but that there will be both in some particular species; but then the scarce will run exceeding high, and men must buy for necessity with very great disadvantage; for the scarce provisions however dear, must be purchased with Money, and that which is plenty however cheap will hardly fetch Money, and however the prices of things may be raised by trust or bartering, yet the necessitous man must give after the dearest rate in Money, when his own labour or produce will hardly fetch Money one third below the just market price, so that he will rather hire Money of the Usurer than part with his Labour upon base terms; and thus plenty is discouraged by the Tyranny of Scarcity, and in the end banished or bandied from one specie to another, so that men become variable in business, now in this and then in that, being discouraged from one thing to another; the necessitous man being oppressed on both sides; the mean time being obliged both to buy and sell to disadvantage, and the number of such increasing through the many disadvantages attending.

6. *The Scarcity of Money causes the Credit of Money to sink.*

However Money when scarce will play the Tyrant, and domineer over and under value Plenty when lying meerly at its Mercy, yet before plenty will yield to its Tyranny, it will flee the Country, or at least have nothing to do with Money, but rather bear up its Credit in some suitable proportion with Scarcity, by a manly barter of one plentiful specie for another; or it will deal with Money behind its back, or at a distance by the mediation of trust, who being an unfaithful representative of Money suffers his Credit to sink, and Money being forcibly imployed in dealing with Scarcity is strangely run down by it, and when it comes to fulfil the bargains Trust has made in its behalf, it is forced to stand by them be they ever so mean, so that as scarcity runs down the Credit of Money in its own advance, plenty standing at a distance dealing with Barter, and Trust will maintain its Credit & Advance if possible, in some proportionable Degree, so that Money must either sink and die, or flee the Country, it must certainly yield but only as Extortion may take its part, but then Money must be a Slave to Extortion, so that the scarcer Money is, the scarcer it may be both by its sinking the Value, and by sending of it out of the Country, but since Bills have been in Use, the Effect appears only in sinking, and had not Silver-Money been supported by a foreign Credit, it might have sunk in some considerable Measure as the Bills have done; but the foreign Credit, and not the intrinsick Value of

Silver and Gold, has supported their Value among us, so high as that there might be but just a reasonable Profit in sending of it out of the Country; but since Silver being 23 or 24 Shillings per Ounce, and *West India* Goods being plenty has fallen among us here there has been great Quantities of Silver brought into the Country as it were, in Lieu of *West-India* Goods; but as the *West India* Goods have fallen, so the Plenty of Silver not being in Demand as Money has caused it to sink in Value; and then the Notion of Calling in and hoarding up Bills has not only raised their Value, but has cut off almost all Trading for Money, so that what passes is as it were only by Force in paying Debts and the Market of Provisions greatly spoiled, because not Money to purchase, nor will they answer Ingagements for Money because Money is in such severe Demand through the Notion of the Bills and so of Debts in general, their Capacity of being raised equal to Silver Money, and that by Force in a short time; not that the Scarcity of the Bills does in the least incline to raise their Value but only from the Necessity of their being answered in Money upon Penalty of rigid Forfeiture: For according as before observed the meer Scarcity of Money or Bills (when free to pass as Money and not to be hoarded up with a Notion of a speedy Advance by calling in) does not tend to raise their Credit, but rather to sink it, and however the Plenty, Thraldom, and Inability of the present time has glutted the Markets, spoiling the digestive Faculty of our Trade putting great Wrongs and Discouragements upon all commendable Negociations, yet we see that such Species as are so scarce as to command Money, will maintain their Credit against it, and other Species will barter at an equal high Rate, and when Debtors find themselves bitten by the mad Dog, there will scarcely be any more promising Money upon the present Terms of Dealing, but yet we must expect that if the Bills must be called in without suitable Provision against the vile Injustice and Wrongs impending, there will be Multitudes forced to surrender their Estates upon base Terms, and many even undone, which Overture will be abundantly aggravated from the meer Fear or forethought of it: For when once the Rumour is spread, that Bills are like to rise in Value, and the Prices of Provisions and Merchandize to fall, every one will be eager to put off what he has to sell, and more than he can well spare, at any tolerable Rate, for Fear of being forced to a worse Market; so that no more than the meer Perswasion or Belief of it, is enough to make it so; and not only from the Fear of some but also from the Desire of others to take the Advantages of such a Turn; but then to let those pass which are already involved, let Money or Bills be brought to what Degree of Credit soever, in a Way of such Irregularity and Fraud; yet we shall find the general or mean Value of it to sink and decline in the ordinary Course of Trade, and by so much the more as the medium shall be found scarce: For as it has been, so it will probably be again, when the Merchant considers the Disadvantage of Trusting, he will advance the Price of his Merchandize; and not only in Consideration of being out of the Use of his Money, but also because he sees the Prices of Goods rises and Money sinks; and agreeable to these trusting Prices will be the market Prices of Things in general, and the more certainly as the Money is scarcely used in Trade: For when it is so, it must be improved chiefly in purchasing the most scarce and dear Provisions, or in paying old and long trusted Debts; and altho' Money down will command Respect and a due Deference before Trust, yet the Presence of it is so scant that the Prices of Things in general will rise under the Notion of trusting; and altho' scarce Provisions will be current, and answer the greater Part of these Debts, yet as they must be scarce to make them current, so they will be dear to the sinking the Credit of Money whose stead it answers; and thus the Scarcity of Money sinks its Credit, and the faster it sinks the faster it may until by some extraordinary Interposition of Causes (as in the present Juncture) alters the Course of Things.

Here I would a little demonstrate what kind of Credit the Bills have lost as in their Discount upon Money from time to time. In Order to which observe,

1. *The Bills of Credit have all along carried a full and just Credit, and an undoubted Currency according to the market Price of Things.* However for Want of a distinct, foreign and steady Value, they could not become one Quarter, or one third better than Merchandize or Provisions as they have been raised so much and more above their just Value upon Money in the market Prices; whereas Money being maintained in a steady Value, by a steady Value upon Merchandize in foreign Countries, so our Merchandize being raised one third above its just Value, Money became one third better than other Species to improve in foreign Trade.

Therefore,

2. *That Discount that is made upon Bills of Credit additionally from time to time is no other than the cutting off, and taking away the Hold of Extortion, not giving to the Bills that cruel oppressive Value (which some fancy to be intrinsically placed in Silver) which the foreign Credit of Money holds upon Money as*

it is undervalued at Home, when used for a Medium of Trade, by the raising the Value of the Merchandize or Provisions valued thereupon. That Gold and Silver are intrinsically valuable I don't deny; but that the intrinsick Value is the Rule by which the steady Credit of Money is maintained as a Medium of Trade, I absolutely deny: For Men don't look at the intrinsick Worth of Money as they deal, but at the Value of the Commodity that is purchased, how it agrees with the market Price.

When Money was found one third better than the Countries Produce at the high market Price as in foreign Trade; the Extortioners would nevertheless take the full Price in Money, being the Men that so raised Things to such Extremity, and altho' in the Way of ordinary Commerce, this Rigour was taken off by the just Lenity and Interest of the Merchant, in discounting one third of the Value of Merchandize, when paid in Money; yet the Extortioner would take all the Advantages of Scarcity, Necessity, &c. to strain-up the Value of his Produce, taking the full Price in Money, and generally the poor necessitous Man was forced to give it however hardly he came by his Money.

Now the Bills of Credit don't carry this unjust Rigour so long as not especially to be answered in Money but at the market Price, as may be valued from time to time; for when the Extortioner has raised the Price of his Produce, he may expect to give in some suitable Degree as dear for what he has occasion to buy be it Lands or Merchandize, for ought any Discount that will be made in the Behalf of his Money; and in these Respects Bills of Credit are greatly to be applauded for their exact Justice between Man and Man; when as Silver Money being subject to be undervalued is a very Tyrant and common Plague, if recoverable by Law: For it must be brought in and held by Force, remaining extreamly Scarce, through its Propensity to leave the Country being in better Credit abroad, whereby it becomes a Medium of Extortion and Injustice; and it is but an Act of Justice for either Money or Bills to submit to a Discount, as the Price of Provisions or Merchandize is raised; for why should Money be undervalued in dealing, and yet hold a certain intrinsick Worth making an unequal Exchange? But then altho' it be just for Bills to submit to a Discount when Goods are raised in Value, yet thereby they become a deceitful Standard by which to rate and fix the Value of Credit; the Wrongs of this has been greatly complained of and indeed has been intolerable, especially to Salary-Men, Land Lords, Widows and Orphans, or Legatees, as in many Cases; under which Consideration there has usually been Allowances made; but the Usurer especially more than doubling his yearly Interest; and the Creditors in the Advance of their Goods as they trusted them out; so much the more sinking their own Credits by their unreasonable asking for Goods; but then suddenly to regain the Credit of the Bills, and so consequently of all Credits when Men have generally run themselves in Debt at large, as in the Allowance of large Interest making great Purchases, advancing Salaries, Legacies, &c. and all according to the Intention of Money sunk one half or two thirds in its Discount upon Silver, I say then, to make a sudden Retrieve of the Value of Money without some Way to relieve and right the Debtor by a suitable Abatement in the Payment of his Debt according to the true Intention of the Contract, so that the same Labour may pay the Debt as was intended, will (as seems to me) be as grand a Cheat as ever the Country endured: For no Men more likely to gain by this Cheat, than those who gained by the former, for many Men by running in Debt have by this Time ordered their Business so as to become able Creditors, their Estates it may be consisting chiefly in Credits; but a foreseen gradual sinking of Credit can't be a Wrong comparable to the Wrong of an unexpected, sudden Advance by hoarding up for a speedy calling in, for how many ingenious generous spirited Men must be ruined by the Means! The most of the outstanding Bills have been emitted equal to Money, not to Silver at Proclamation rate, but equal to our former sunken Bills, or Silver at 16, 18, or 20 Shillings per Ounce, then what Justice can it be for these to be answered in Silver at 6 or 8 Shillings per Ounce? If I am newly become Possessor of an old sunken Bill, sunken gradually through 500 Men's Hands, or be it a new Bill put out upon the old sunken Tenour, never passing better than Silver at 20 Shillings per Ounce, what Reason can there be that I should have it answered to me in Silver at 8 Shillings per Ounce, the Debtor never having received half that Value for it?

Indeed every Debtor ought to answer his Debt to the same Value as was intended when the Contract was made and therefore those that have taken Bills out of the publick Treasury upon Loan ought to return as good a Value in to the Treasury again even to the same Value in Silver as what the Bills would have purchased when taken out, notwithstanding the Bills sinking in their passing from Man to Man in the mean time, for since it is not possible to right those that have suffered the Wrong (if such there be by the Bills gradual sinking) the King ought to have the Profit; for as the Loss has been a general Loss in the Hands of all Possessors of the Bills from time to time, so the Profit should be a publick Gain, and not to those whose Lot it shall be last to possess the Bills, and perhaps villainously hoarding up for the Purpose, hindring their due Circulation; nor yet to those who have taken the Bills out of the publick Treasury at five per Cent, and let them out at ten per Cent, or if they have improved them in their own private Use, yet they ought to return the same Value in to the publick Treasury as they took out: for doubtless they put them away in the first Place, for that Value in some good Specie as they best liked. They that take out of the Bank ought to be obliged to return a certain Value even the same that they take, either in Silver or some other Currency to the same Value, and if they return the same Bills not to have regard to the Denomination of the Bill, but to the Credit of it, at the Time as it will answer for Silver Money, whether risen or fallen, and yet the Bills must be lawful Money, in all Payments publick or private according to their current Rate as the Law now provides; but only the Loan Office to be made good as aforesaid: for if Traders or Market-men will sink the Bills, and undervalue them in their Commerce, so let it be, the Law is not obliged to make the Bills better than what Traders are pleased to call Pounds, Shillings, and Pence, in their Way of Dealing, and it would be unjust so to do; for if Merchandize and Labour, publick and private, be raised above their Worth in Silver, why should it be answered to that Value, but this ought to be a Rule, that every Debt except passing Bills be answered to what was intended in the Contract, and therefore as Merchandize is raised, so Credits, Salaries, Rents, and yearly Payments should in Honesty be raised, and this would be a Means to prevent the sinking of the Bills.

1. *By diverting the Creditor from raising the Value of what he trusts out, to make up the Damage of his Credits sinking.* For when the Merchant sees that his Credits will sink, he still advances the Value of his Merchandize to make up the Damage which still sinks it so much the more. Now if the yearly Discount upon Bills were computed, and Allowance to be made accordingly, with respect to the Time when the Debt was contracted, this might in some measure divert the raising of Merchandize to make up the Damage as aforesaid.

2. *This would greatly discourage and divert such leading Merchants and Traders who are greatly indebted to the Loan Office, as well as to other Merchants, Usurers &c. from raising the Value of Merchandize and sinking the Credit of Money to lighten and facilitate their Payments.* For it is to be feared that such Men have been very accessary to the sinking of Credit, for indeed

their Interest would lead them much that Way; could I perswade my Creditor to let me have my Bond for one half or two thirds of what I gave it for, it would be considerable Gain to me. But as to the Occasion of the sinking of our Bills of Credit, People are of various Opinions. Some say that the Occasion of their sinking was from some particular Gentlemen of ours, that traded with *New York* Merchants, and refused to accept of our own Bills equal to Money, therefore they have ever since been disposed to sink. Others say the Occasion of their sinking is the Want of a Demand for our Produce at Home, viz. *Great-Britain,* whereby Money being in a peculiar Demand to make Returns is rather advanced above the Bills, being bid up for to the Discredit of the Bills; but it is most certain that neither of these is the Cause or Occasion of the sinking of our Bills, but rather the Consequence of their being sunk: For what Man would be so foolish as to take a *Connecticut* Bill equal to Silver Money, when the Bill might lawfully be answered with Indian Corn at two Shillings and six Pence per Bushel, and Wheat at five Shillings per Bushel, which is not so good as Silver Money by near one half? Or when the market Price of our Provisions and Merchandize, valued either upon Money or Bills is double of their real Worth in Silver? And who would not give Silver its just Preference for making a Return to *Europe,* where Silver is of a much greater Value? Had not our Provisions & Merchandize been over-rated in Value, our Produce would have answered the European Trade sufficiently, and with as much Profit as Silver and Gold; and what that would not answer might have been supplied by our own Manufacture without purchasing more than we can pay, ingaging what we have not, if our European Trade can't be carried on without Silver Returns, what shall we do when the Silver is gone? But the high Valuation of Merchandize not only spoils the Demand for our Produce, but it has dreined us of Money and sunk our Bills of Credit to the exceeding Detriment of the Common-Wealth; the same Cause that reduced us to the Use of Bills of Credit in Lieu of Money, has likewise caused the Bills of Credit to sink from time {to} time; and those are exceedingly mistaken that impute the misfortunes of our Trade to the Use of Paper Money: For our Condition was not good when we first came to the Use of Paper Money; our Paper Money has indeed done us exceeding good Service, and might be yet cultivated to exceeding Advantage; but yet one while to have a tolerable Stock of running Cash, or passing Bills, and another while, when Men and Trade has increased and Money should increase, then to have the Bills a calling in and hoarding up without farther Additions or Stocks to fill up the Vacancy is intolerable irregular State Policy, if not a fraudulent Cheat; but there has never yet (since I can remember) been near a Sufficiency of Currency to accommodate the Commerce, not in the most plentiful Times, and how our Trade can be carried on with a less Supply this Year than it could do with some Years ago, I cannot conceive, unless by some means our Numbers had been diminished, or if we think to force in Silver Money and turn our Credits into Silver, by lessening the Paper Stock, we shall find the Silver come in very slowly rather like a Captive, than a natural Subject taking the first Opportunity to depart, so long as our Commerce remains under the present Regulation.

But this we may take up for a Lamentation, viz. That such kind of Policy smothers the best Principles, obstructs the best Proceedings and Discourages the best Men, advancing Oppression, Extortion and Usury with all close handed ignoble Principles and Practices.

Having rambled over some of the Inconveniencies and ill Consequences of an irregular Trade, I come now to consider of some Measures proper to revive a drooping Common-Wealth, or to prevent the Inundation of Miseries flowing in by an ungoverned Commerce. And how a new English Plantation, or People may best advance themselves in the Interest of the Crown and Government, both of which I shall endeavour to resolve in one, for to me it seems that the best Account such a People may stand in to the Interest of the Crown, must be by strengthening themselves in Trade, encouraging their own Business enabling themselves to take off, improve and dispense with as much of the Effects and Produce, of *Great Britain*, as may be in a Way of Commerce, strengthning and fortifying themselves against the Invasions of the common Enemy, and by their Prudence and good Managements to encourage as many good Subjects as may be to come in and settle among them.

When a People are low and behind hand, and under Incommodious Circumstances they cannot be of that Importance to the Crown, nor of that Account or Advantage to their Correspondents in Trade, as they might be if under a flourishing State, not only because they are unable to exchange for, improve and dispense with the Effects of their Correspondents, but also because their Poverty and Disadvantages discourages the replenishing and strengthening of the Country by the coming in of labouring, and handycrafts Men, Men of Business and Trade from other Countries, besides many other Disadvantages attending, which in new Plantations must needs be great Damage to the Crown, by suffering the Interests of other Princes and States to prevail and gain the Ground, and for a few People to hold and obscure a large fruitful Country by such Incommodities is of no Advantage to themselves nor their Posterity, but rather tends to spoil and corrupt their Manners to the great Detriment of Church and State.

Therefore to consider of some proper measures to cultivate & encourage Trade and Commerce, may well answer the matters proposed.

That a competent Stock of running Cash is highly necessary to the Support of Trade and Commerce is very evident, and it is no less certain that as a Country replenishes with People, and the Business and Trade to be enlarged the current Stock must of Necessity be enlarged, or the Trade must suffer. For the obtaining the medium of Trade, two methods are more commonly in Use in the World.

First, *By trading for Money, viz. Silver & Gold bringing of it in from other Places in Commerce*

Secondly, *By omitting Bills upon the publick Credit to be improved and accepted as Money*

New England has practiced both of these methods and in both has been miserably foiled falling short of maintaining or holding the Substance of the one, or the Credit of the other. The Occasion of which I imagine has been the Want of regular well governed Markets not holding a just Valuation upon Provisions and Merchandize: For, to the bringing in Money by Trade, or to the Support of the Credit of the Bills valued thereupon, it is absolutely necessary that Money should be held in a just Esteem, by a suitable low Valuation upon Merchandize. Now whether to endeavour the Acquisition of a plentiful Stock of Money to carry on our Trade, or to supply the Want thereof with Bills of Credit shall be judged best by our Rulers at Home, I can't determine: For to some it may seem not right for any particular Plantation to raise the Value of Money higher than others do: For their so doing may tend to rob other Plantations of their necessary Medium to the Detriment of their Commerce; but I do believe it is more Criminal, for any of the Plantations to undervalue Money to the Detriment of their own Commerce, I say more Criminal because Self Preservation is first required.

And since it is so that the English Plantations in general, have so far sunk the Credit of Money by their repeated advancing of the Value of their Produce, that in all Parts Money is become intolerable scarce, I can't but think it commendable for any People to be first in the just and most necessary Cause of advancing the Credit of Money, and let others advance as they see Occasion: For as Money becomes scarce so should the Value of it be raised both to encourage the bringing of it in, and for the extending its Validity and Serviceableness in Trade.

Again, Some may fancy that to increase the current Stock with Bills of Credit, must needs put us out of Favour with our Rulers at Home, supposing that we have not Power to maintain the Credit of the Bills, and therefore to increase the Quantity of the Bills must needs increase and aggravate the Wrongs that will be suffered by the increasing Discount upon the Bills.

But it may be considered that altho' our Bills should remain under their present Disadvantage of sinking, yet the Increase of the Stock will not increase or aggravate the Wrongs impending by their sinking, but rather lessen them. For in the first Place,

1. *We must consider that the Wrongs sustained by the increasing Discount upon the Bills is not so much to the Possessor of the Bills, but chiefly to him whose private Credits are valued upon the Bills depending upon the Credit of the Bills for their Value.* The Bills ought to be kept circulating and then the Damage in their sinking would be little or none to the Possessor. But private Credits depending upon the publick Credit for its value, being more than ten-fold of the value of the passing Bills, and to be answered with sunken Bills, or advanced Provisions or Goods, causes the Wrongs suffered by the Bills to be beyond compare with the Wrongs suffered in the Bills.

And if there were but the one tenth Part of the Bills passing that now there is, yet if all the private Credits must bear their Weight upon them as now they do, the Damages of their sinking would not be the less but the more; because the less Currency the more trusting and the worse pay. For in the next place,

2. *We must consider that (as has been already demonstrated) the Scarcity of the Medium or Currency does but hasten the sinking of Credit.* The scarcer the Medium or Money, the greater will be the Weight of Credits depending upon it for Support, and the more obstructed and invalid will these Credits be through bad and difficult Payments, and upon this Consideration the Prices of Goods will rise the faster, and Money being more used in Name, and less in Substance, the more it will cripple under the Weight of Credits depending thereupon for Support; unless the foreign Demand for it (as in the Case of Gold and Silver) causes a Discount upon Merchandize at the

market Price, when good hard pieces are laid upon the Board, but this will not bear in Bills of Credit. So that the Plenitude of Bills is, the support of their Credit and lessening to the Damage of their sinking.

Many are of Opinion that we can't have flourishing Times until Gold and Silver are called in for a Medium of Trade, and the Use of Bills laid aside, laying the Blame of every unlucky Turn to the Bills of Credit, as if they were a Flam put upon the Country to maintain our Trade and Genteelity, beyond our Industry and Ability; and that the only Way to call in Money, must be to lessen our *British* Trade, retrench our Expences, &c. living more upon our own and less upon foreign Labour, condemning our Finery, Prodigality, &c. In answer to which a late judicious Writer having considered of our Case, as being a dependent Government in our civil Relation to the Crown of *England*, also in some Degree a dependent Merchandize upon the same Kingdom, and in no Capacity to be otherwise, until come to a greater Perfection in Manufactures,

> Therefore (saith he) Men may talk of shortening our British Trade, whilst they are weary, upbraiding us with our Finery, &c. which are Themes more proper for the Pulpits, than for Statesmen to talk of, [for what were ingenious Mysteries and Inventions dignified for with Lawrels for working Wood, Iron, Brass, Leather, &c. into fine Coaches and Chariots; and Horses as fine and proud as they suited to them; why were these made, &c. And turning glittering Earth & glutinous Matter of Worms into Embroideries, &c. but to furnish a generous People that would banish Sordidness, & live bright & civil with fine Accomplishments about them.] Therefore I say if we will live upon Ground Nuts and Clams, and cloath our Backs with the Exuviae or Pelts of wild Beasts, we may then lower our Expences apace, and renounce this Branch of our Merchandize; but if we intend to live in any Garb or Port as becomes a People of Religion, Civility, Trade and Industry, then we must still supply our selves from the great Fountain—.

To this I would add that to lessen our Import of *British* Merchandize, or to lessen our Expences in Provisions in Furniture, Apparel, Buildings, &c. would indeed lessen our Business in providing the Ballance, lessening the Demand for our Produce, but it would not perswade one Penny in Money to come in among us, as Money to purchase our produce, so long as our high prices forbids the profit in bringing of it in, unless Men are laid under a Necessity to answer their Obligations or pay their Debts in Money, which would be a main Support to Extortion under our present Regulations, for ready Money would have so little Influence in the Valuation of Things, and Money would be so seldom ingaged that those who would be obliged to bring it in or procure it, must do it to their very great Disadvantage, and the Trade would greatly suffer through the Scarcity of it, and all the Advantage would be to gratify the Humours of miserly Men, that want a peculiar very hard and difficult to be obtained to be a Medium of Extortion and Oppression, to be a plague to poor Men. We are twice better without it than with it, unless we could have it come in freely with profit, and kindly accepted at its just value, which must be by fixing a suitable low value upon all our Merchandize, and not left to the Will of every Cut-Throat, to raise the Price. I can't think our Rulers at Home, would be against our encouraging such Quantities of Money to come in among us as might enable us to carry on our Trade ably and freely, to support our publick Ministry, Civil and Ecclesiastick, to which a good Stock of Currency is absolutely necessary. Or if we may not trade for Money to such a Degree as our Commerce would require, I can't imagine our Rulers at Home would disallow of our emitting such Supplies of publick Credit from time to time, as might set us in a Capacity for a liberal Commerce. Since this is the practice not only of *Great Britain*, but also of many other of the most politick States in *Europe*, where jealous Ignorance, don't forbid good Proceedings for the Common Wealth.

It is undoubtedly for the Interest of his Majesty that every one of his Plantations be provided with a sufficient current Stock to uphold a flourishing Trade, and whether we obtain it in trading for Money, viz. Gold and Silver, or whether by emitting Bills of Credit, yet it seems to me the first good step to be taken in order to either, will be to set a just Value upon all the principal Produce and Merchandize of the Country, that may be conveniently rated by Number, Weight or Measure, which Value is scarcely one quarter of the Denomination of their prices at this Time, being valued upon Bills of Credit, that is their just value in Silver at *Six Shillings and Eight Pence* per Ounce; so then the just Value of our passing Bills is no more than one Quarter of their Denomination in Silver at the rate aforesaid, and so likewise the Bills should be valued, since they are so much fallen, and so let the Credits of the Country be valued, so that the same Bills, or the same Species whatsoever may be of the same Validity and Consequence in Trade, or in paying of Debts, as now they are only that Money might be advanced and encouraged to come in and circulate *five Shillings* in Silver being as good as *twenty Shillings* of our Bills, as they now pass, or of our Credits or Merchandize, only giving to and fixing the value of Money as Gold and Silver, this would not wrong one Man but be a Benefit to many; but then there must be heavy Duties laid upon all Export of such Species as don't submit to the stated market price, and let the Ports of Entry be well guarded, & the Markets be carefully regulated, giving to every thing its just Due, and necessary Encouragement, as may be thought convenient by judicious Men from time to time. And if only the principle Commodities of our own Produce were thus stated, other things would easily and naturally submit to an equal value in the course of Trade, and if once the great Swells of advancing Prices were Abated every ones Interest would lead him to a Conformity to the Market, and then Men would know their Business without huckling and bantering: For such a Limitation would be no more of a Bondage than to oblige a Traveller to go the straitest and best Way to the End of his intended Journey. I should as soon chuse to travel in a strait Lane, as to have all the Woods before me to chuse out a better Way.

Holland is renowned for good Regulation in their Markets, and mercantile Affairs, if we go there with a Cargo to trade, we have no occasion to banter about the Price, only say what we have to sell, and what we want to buy, the price is judiciously set on both sides, you shall have your Lading ready for Return immediately, of that which is choice in its kind, the just decorum in the value of their Merchandize, encourages Stores of all kinds, so that no Business suffers, but then they hold such a value upon their Money, that we shall rather take their Goods than their Money to bring away, for we may have our Choice which we will take at the market Price.

Some may think it a great Wrong to be limited to a low price for their Produce; but what Damage could it be, if they may buy as cheap as they sell: it matters not how small the Weight of the Money is, if the value be but steady and the Credit good.

The several Governments in *New-England* being mutually dependent in Trade, it may seem the more difficult for any one of them to fix upon good Regulations, and where there is several Communities in Government under one in Commerce, it would be best for them to concert their measures with each other, but yet every Government may regulate their own Markets, if they take suitable measures for it. Any one Government might take in and send out their Merchandize under the Regulation proposed, carrying on their Commerce with the other Governments, as *New-England* trades with *New York,* and the same of their Produce might answer their Trade with other Places, nearer or farther off as it would otherwise do; we might improve their Money and they ours as it might seem profitable in Trade, and however other Places value their Merchandize, yet when it comes into our Jurisdiction we may denominate it by what value we please. And although we might not make so much Profit in laying out our Money with them, yet we might make as good Profit in the Exchange of Goods.

Now if by any such Means the Prices of Things might be limited (as the Practices of some Places in the World, as well as Reason it self teaches it might and ought to be) so that Merchandize in general should not be overrated, being valued upon Money we might emit Bills to such a Degree, that Men would not hire Money to give above five per Cent, with undoubted Security, and yet the Bills would hold equal Value to Silver and Gold. But to pretend to make Bills equal to Money, when Money it self is undervalued (as when we reckoned Wheat 5 Shillings, Barley 4 Shillings, and Indian Corn at half a Crown per Bushel) I say then to pretend to make Bills to hold equal value with Money, we had as good value our Bills upon Carbuncles, or any other precious Stones that we know nothing of the Value, as to value them upon Money only as the Denomination of Money is put upon Merchandize in general, the Name it self can't suddenly fall to the Ground, and the meer Name of Money put upon our Merchandize and Credits is all that has supported the Credit of our Bills.

But only let our Produce be justly valued upon Money, and our Bills being put out equal thereunto, would hold equal value with Money, and being of equal value they are preferrable to Money at their current Rate. I say they would hold equal value with Money, because the market Price of things being held to their just value upon Money, the Countries Produce will be as profitable in foreign Dealing as Money, and as the Bills always have been, so they would be then current for any kind of Produce, at the market Price, the Merchants would not then allow the Advance or bid higher upon Money for the Advantage of it in foreign Dealing, it being as good at Home as abroad, or if they should advance upon Money, yet the Prices of things not being suffered to rise, the Bills would hold their value notwithstanding so long as current for Goods at the stated market Price.

That Bills are preferrable to Money at their current Rate appears in three particulars, as has been observed by a credible Author.

1. *In the Ease of compting and carriage, and preventing Damage to the Receiver by Counterfeit, clipped light or base Coin (which is obvious to all).*

2. *In its Safety in travelling, laying up, &c. as visible as the other.*

3. *In the Advantage that is to be made by the Exchange on the Account of such Conveniencies.*

Whereof take two Examples,

1. Examp. *The Bank Bills of* Holland *are ordinarily better by at least three per Cent.*

2. Examp. *Those in* Venice *are better than Money by twenty per Cent; and the odds would have been more but that Laws were made with severe Penalties to prevent their rising higher.* Now the Cause of this Advance upon the Bills was as followeth; The Bills at their first putting out being of equal value with Money, they were preferred because of their Conveniency as aforesaid, so that Men would ordinarily give *ten Shillings* to have *One Hundred Pounds* changed for Bills, which Practice soon advanced the current Rate of Bills to that proportion, & when this was become the current Rate of the Bills, then other *ten Shillings* was allowed for the Exchange of a *Hundred Pounds,* upon Account of the peculiar Conveniency of the Bills as aforesaid, and so *ten Shillings* upon the *Hundred Pounds* would be advanced successively upon the current Rate; the Advance of the current Rate following up the Advance for the special Conveniency of the Bills, until the Bills became *twenty eight Pounds* in *one Hundred* better than Money, and with much Difficulty restrained and reduced to *twenty* per Cent odds, and there fixed.

And if it be demanded, *What induced that State to allow it so high?*

The Answer is easy, viz. The State of *Venice* had made Use of the Moneys deposited for Security, in their publick Occasions, and having promised for Satisfaction of Creditors to raise the like Sum if they should have Occasion for it, they reap this Advantage of the People's high Opinion of the Bills, that they are thereby assured that never will any Creditor come to ask them a 100 l for a Bill or Bills, when he may have 120 l. from another Hand: A notable Way to pay a vast Debt; and all the while (it may be) not one Ducket in the Bank to answer it.

The *Venetians* under divine Providence owe their present good Fortune, Strength and Glory in a peculiar Degree to their Bank Bills. They are a People who have raised themselves from a Company of unfortunate mortals, who to escape the Extremity of their Condition, pursuing them on the

Continent, fell upon the broken Banks or Islets at the upper End of the *Adriatick* Sea, many Ages ago; where they built their Town, now become the famous City of *Venice*. And after some time they projected a Bank of Credit to support them in their Settlements of Trade. And in a peculiar Sense by this means, &c. are become one of the most splendid People on Earth; and are able both by Sea and Land, to vie it with the Great Turk, and now stand on that side of the World, a firm Barrier to Christendom against the haughty Infidel. Their Bills of publick Credit have been exceeding Serviceable in supporting their worldly Affairs, and yet possibly for some scores, if not some hundreds of Years, have not kept one Ducket in their publick Treasury to keep up the Credit of them. The Bank of *Venice* subsisting of two Millions and three hundred Thousand Dukets, which is about the Value of twenty hundred thousand Pounds of our Bills as they now pass, which has been improved in their Commerce for many Ages with as much Advantage as if it had been so much good Silver.

Now if Money were held in such Credit among us, that it would remain circulating for a Medium of Trade as a Colleague with the Bills, by holding a just Valuation upon Merchandize, we should soon find the Bills the most current and acceptable pay, at their full value or Denomination, as now they are and always have been at their current Rate, since their Currency has been experienced. But some are of Opinion that it is not in the power of the civil Authority to command or state the value of Merchandize, so that it shall not rise: And indeed Experience teaches that a bare Law for stating the value is not effectual for the purpose, it has been proved in *New-England;* nor indeed will the setting up of one Post in a Frame, cause it to stand firm without others to support it. Now in Order to hold the value stated, it is necessary,

1. *That the value of the most principal Commodities improved in Commerce, especially for Exportation be stated.*
2. *That the stated Price be rather below than above the real value thereof in Money; otherwise it can't be serviceable in respect to the holding of Money among us.*
3. *That the Export of any Specie be incumbered so long as not submitting to the market Price.*

That not only the Power of giving Law unto, but also the Power of lending in the Affairs of Commerce, should fall into the hands of honest, wise, prudent and publick spirited Men. Therefore

It is very proper that Governours, Magistrates and Rulers, should be not only Men of the greatest Integrity, Policy and Largeness of Heart, but also Men of great Influence in Trade.

Solomon the royal Merchant of *Jerusalem* was an eminent Patron of Trade; his Interest, Wisdom, Policy and exceeding Liberality and largeness of Heart, moved him to undertake notably in Trade, which not only enriched himself, but also his Kingdom in an extraordinary manner, the Benefit thereof extending unto all the correspondent Nations round about; his Interest in Trade was so great that without Question he had the Advantage of governing and leading the Trade of the Kingdom in the best manner, he put such a value upon Money, without Question as would make it profitable bringing of it in, encouraging other Nations to come and lay out their Money with him for his Merchandize.

Had not King *Solomon* studied or projected in matters of Trade, as well as in matters of Justice and Equity, or had he not largely undertaken in Trade and Merchandize, as well as in Husbandry and Farming, his Gold might have remained at *Ophir,* his great Buildings & Merchandizes, with the chief of his Wealth might have remained in it's Chaos. But his great Wisdom could not overlook Trade, nor the proper measures for it's promotion and management, or any of the Requisites thereunto belonging.

Nor is it beneath the Quality of the greatest Princes to promote Trade & Commerce; for why? their Interest and Safety depends upon it; and according to the Saying of Sir *Edward Cook;* Trade and Traffick is the Life of the Common-Wealth.

But forasmuch as it is very rare and not ordinarily to be expected, that the leading Part of Trade, falls into the Hands of such trusty, skilful, unanimous publick spirited Managers, as will without fail accommodate their private Interests to the true Interest of the publick. Therefore the practice of *Great Britain* as well as others of the most politick free States of *Europe* has been found not only necessary but very effectual for the holding of Trade and Commerce under good Regulations; viz. The setting up Companies for Trade.

These Companies being constituted under good Regulations and many Interests united therein of the heads of the Common-Wealth, as well as of Undertakers in every kind of Business and Calling, are able to lead the whole Trade of the Nation, so that no Interloper or private Merchant can monopolize or make head contrary to the publick or common Interest. These Companies will take the value from one Specie and put upon another as they see occasion giving encouragement to what kind of Business they see good, and what they loose in the one hand they gain in the other; and being compounded of good Common-Wealths Men, of every kind as aforesaid, their Influence is very benign both to Planters and Traders (for indeed that which is the best for the one is best for the other, being mutually dependent upon each others Prosperity for their own) and being Men of Generosity and largeness of Heart, they are neither afraid to trust Providence with their Estates in Trade, Sea-faring &c. nor yet their Trustees, or Factors, but engage like Men in earnest to do their Country good; the footing of their Trade being laid by the Generosity of publick spirited Men.

And this is what I take to be the next good Step to be taken in order to upset the declining State of *New-England*. If each Government would constitute and set up a Company for Trade, with suitable Regulations, Priviledges, and Power for ordering the matters of their Trade, it might do much more to enliven, strengthen and encourage the Business of the Country, than what private Trade will ever attain unto. Each Company being made up of interested Men from every part of the respective Governments might uniform and concert their measures and Rules, agreeably to the Times and Places of their Trade, and their Interests being united thereby in every Branch of their Trade, would influence the Commerce of the whole Country, to such a Degree as to lead it in the best Channels for the publick Good, when a private Trade cannot be so well governed being in many separate Interests, and variously disposed, acting under various Principles.

It is not the great Estates of a few Men, that will answer the End or Notion of a publick Trade, but such a Composition would be liable to lean and shift according to the Disposition and Circumstances of the Undertakers. Nor would such a Trade have that Influence nor Assistance in every Part of the Country, nor would the Interest of the Country so readily concert with its Regulations: But the Strength of the publick Trade is to have many Proprietors, some in every part of the Country, Men of Business to assist and accommodate it with the best Means; and a Company so qualified and composed would undoubtedly wax and become great, enduring for many Generations, increasing not only with the Advance of the beginning Stock, but also with the Addition of the Interests of more Proprietors uniting from time to time, and none to be drawn out but by the Advice and Consent of the Majority of the Proprietors; whereas if but few concerned therein, the Death of one, the bad Fortune of another, and the Discouragement or fickle

Mind of another might break up & dissolve the Company. The publick Trade is not so much for the particular Benefit of the Proprietors, but for the Common-Wealth, & therefore he that expects a direct present Benefit to himself in the Trade, and would therefore joyn therein, meerly for Self Interest, has a wrong Notion of it, as well as he that expects to bear sway or have power of voting according to his Interest therein, according to the manner of a private Trade. Indeed such as would contribute largely into the publick Stock, should be first regarded for Betrustments therein, as having approved themselves great Benefactors to the Publick, and Well-wishers to the Cause by their great Liberality in and towards the Affair.

But the publick Trade must not be ruled or swayed to accommodate any particular or private Interest, or lean from the Common-Wealth for its own meer Advance or Gain, as will and may a private Trade, but the publick Trade must stand upright for the Common-Wealth, which can't more likely be than by there being many Proprietors, and each of them to have an equal Vote. And then if Money may not be traded for to a sufficient Plenty for carrying on of the Commerce, or in order to a more speedy bringing of it in, there might be Banks of Credit emitted, and the Bills might be more safely and conveniently committed to the Use and Improvement of such Companies, to be answered by them in Money, by a certain Time, if Occasion be, the Bills being emitted upon the Security of their Estates, and under the Patronage and Inspection of the Government, than in any other Way whatsoever.

To illustrate this, I will borrow a few Arguments from the judicious Writer before-mentioned, which are as followeth.

> As to a private Bank, there be very good Reasons to be given, why a particular Company of Gentlemen should be intrusted with such a grand Affair, for the Service of a Country (*scil.* under the Inspection of the Government &c.) that is to say in our Case, if our Country and Government find their own Bank (as to their Apprehension &c.) is fatigued with some such Incumbrances and Inconsistences as that they neither can nor will dispense with—So that the Country is quite Heart-sick of their own measures; I am very well assured upon very good Argument that a private Bank shall cure them, and do every thing to their Satisfaction.
>
> I shall with convenient Brevity offer a few preliminary Thoughts relating to the present Subject, and then point at Persons proper to be intrusted with the Affair, and the Reasons of it.

1. A few preliminary Thoughts, wherein I shall distinguish between a publick and private Bank, viz.

Imprimis, A publick Bank of Credit is some what precarious, yet it carries a vast Bounty with it, to those Countries who have the Wisdom to give it an honourable Reception; but to others it is but a common Plague. There be two Principles absolutely needful to preserve it in a Country, viz. Prudence and a publick Spirit in Men of Estates; if such Men will but wisely govern their private Interests in Favour of it, they will soon shackle other Men's and bridle their Recusancy, and bring them to Conformity. A wise Government may project, but it is wise and great Men under Government, must cultivate such a Projection for a publick Good—. 1. *As to their Trade.* When Men come to buy a Supply with Bills, they accommodate them at the old Money Price, and take the Bills without higling or making any Distinction &c. 2. *As to their Bonds and Obligations for Specialties.* When the Debtor comes, possibly he inquires Sir! there is a Bond of one thousand Duckats in your hands against me, Will you take Bank Bills? Reply, Bank Bills Man! there is nothing will suit me better than Bank Bills,—I will abate Part of my Interest if you will clear the rest, and the whole Principal by the Bills. I do assure you my good Friend, and you may tell it to your Neighbours, that we in the Merchandize do prefer the Bills, above the Money. (For Reasons &c.)—Now such a prudent Temper circulating and influencing the principal Members of such a grand Community, (or Government) will soon become a Law for all other Men, &c. Thus it has been in *Holland, Venice, New-York* &c.

But on the other hand, Where the Bills have gone up and down and been ridiculed, its owing to head Men, and Men of Fortune, *Aviae Versa;* as in *France, Sweedland* and *South-Carolina* &c. Now it seems to me plain, that if those civil Powers, or States that have stood and lookt on, and seen their noble Projections for the Advance of Trade trampled upon, and could not possibly prevent the Prostitution; if they had (I say) when they discerned things lapsing into such Confusion, resigned the Management of the Bank to principle and suitable Gentlemen, or turned their publick into a private Bank; they might have easily recovered the Glory and sufficiency of their Bank &c. Especially if supporting and reinforcing the Bequestment with due Sanctions. As (1.) *That the Profit shall be fixed in the Trustees* &c. (2.) *That the Government inspect* &c. (3.) *That the Bills shall be held as current and lawful Money in answering all Assessments, and also in discharging all Creditors to the Publick, as their own Bills* &c. And tho' in this Method the sensible Profit seems a Booty to some particular Men; but the general Good by keeping up a valuable Medium for all Business, is as equally Beneficial to all Men in common, as tho' done by the Government; so it will hold in any Example in the World, as I imagine, and so in our own Case, where there is found such Defects as cannot be remedied otherwise &c.

2. *The Persons to be intrusted must be Men of known Integrity, of real Estates, good Influence, and considerable Trade.* A convenient Company of such Men imbodied by a Charter from the Government, &c. may manage a Bank of Credit as matters may be circumstanced better than the publick Government, viz. when things are out of joynt as in *France*, &c. and as some think in our own Case, in some Degree as has been said, &c. I say such Men by their Example and wise Management, can do more to bring things to right and keep them so, than all the Menaces, penal Laws, or Wisdom of a Government.—Now I say it appears to me, that there may be such Gentlemen involved in this Affair, who (can upon the aforesaid Presumptions) do more than the Government, or than any regular Monarch upon Earth. I shall just point at such Men as are proper in this Case, *scil.* Landed Men &c great Merchants, who (though worth many thousands) keep the main of their personal Estates, stirring in a way of Trade, both in their own and other Countries. And also such other Gentlemen of great Estates and of great Wisdom, who though they keep up a very considerable Trade and Merchandize, yet let out Money at Interest; and as their Gain this Way is less, so also is their Risque: There is a sort of wise and very prudent Men, that are a kind of amphibious Beings, who live in both Elements, Land and Water, these are eminently qualified as Members for a private Bank; and also rich Farmers and Mechannicks, Men of Character and Influence (according to their Sphere) in the Places where they live.

Note, These Qualities are pointed at in the Supposition of a Company embodied meerly for the Management of a Bank, to be taken and improved in their private Affairs, severally according to their Securities given, when as in the Supposition of a Company for Trade, and improving a Bank only in their united Interests, under publick Regulations by Officers or Committees appointed (though such noted Men are the best and most suitable yet) those Qualifications are not so necessary to every Member, but the Majority should be of such Men, and farther what Man soever he be that will venture considerably of his Estate, to be improved in such an Affair, though but, by being Surety for such a Value or Part in the Bank so improved, must be look'd upon as a true Friend to the Common-Wealth, for that mean spirited Men will not venture their Estates out of their own private Management; and the greater the Number of such publick spirited Men, the less requisite for each to be vested with large Possessions. But farther he saith,

> The main of these Men must belong to our Metropolis, and other Sea-Ports and Towns of Trade, and others to be dispersed through the Province. A convenient Company of such Persons so qualified and incorporated, I do imagine, shall be capable to carry on a Bank of Credit, with greatest Advantage, with an immense Good and Benefit to the Publick.
>
> And that such a Community are capable of doing great Service in this Affair is obvious from the following Reasons.
>
> 1. *For that this Company of Gentlemen can regulate the Prices of all things yearly, in the common Course of Trade and Commerce.* The wild and insulting Prices of Things have ruined the foreign Banks, &c. and possibly something of this Nature has been a Diminution to our own &c. Now there is a sovereign Remedy provided in this Projection against such an Inconveniency and Mischief, for by the Wisdom, Precautions and Examples of those Men, they will thereby conduct all such Points, as though Controulers and absolute masters of the Market, and yet hurt no Man's Property, or infringe Liberty, and hereby Equity in Commerce will be better upheld, excessive Demands suppressed; the Honour and Credit of the Medium maintained, and the just and reasonable Gains and Profits, of all Men suited and secured; for we must note that they are Men of different Functions, and their own Interests as well as Honour will oblige them always to steer right and do well for other Men; for if they hurt others, they hurt themselves, and no Man need suspect or fear, no not a Knave, much less a wise honest Man under this Head, for that it is a sure Maxim, viz. Self-Interest will neither cheat nor lye; for that is the string in the Nose (through the World which governs the Creature.—Other Reasons I shall omit the Recital of; this being enough to the Purpose.

I am greatly perswaded that the well managing of the Banks in *Europe* with their regular holding of the Credit of Money is greatly owing to the Conduct and Rule of their Companies, as well as to their peculiar good

Laws and Customs in Trade; when as the Kings of *Spain* and *France* are obliged by their prerogative Power (as their Occasions sometimes require) to advance the Credit of their Money with notable leaps, whereby their Money is rendered very unstable in Value: nor could the King of *Sweden* with his big and majestick Looks or imperial Orders rescue his Bank Bills from the Contempt they met with in his common Markets.

Indeed the Nature of the Produce or staple Commodities, manner of Business &c. of some Countries is such that renders the Trade much the easier governed.

As in *New-York,* Wheat being the staple Commodity, and so largely produced, it is very rare that ever they fail of a large Export in that particular, and although if a Scarcity should happen one Year, yet another Year may fully recruit their Stock, whenas the Produce of *New-England,* being more variably advanced, sometimes abounding in this, and sometimes in that, and when Stocks for Pasturage become shortned, it requires some Years to recruit them, by which means the Prices of things becomes wild and advancing, but then *New York* is a more direct Market, being almost the sole Port of Entry, for the whole Community in Trade, and their Markets much better regulated than in *New-England,* which is the Cause of the steady value upon their Bills, and not so much in the meer certainty of the Fund. Wherefore it must needs be highly necessary to the flourishing of the Common-Wealth of *New-England,* to encourage and promote the setting up of Companies for Trade, laying aside all doubtful mistrustful Apprehensions of what may be the Event, but rather expecting the same good Success which has occasioned so many Companies to be set up in *Great Britain,* and that has occasioned the Constitution of one in *Virginia* by a Charter from the Crown, Our Rulers at home greatly regard their Companies, enlarging them with great and peculiar Immunities and Privileges. Then how comes it to pass that we must be so wary as not to venture into such a method? Although we are not so able yet we might do something in proportion to our means; the less able we are, the less Trade will serve, and not only so, but the more need to unite our Strength and Interest in the Promotion of what is so much wanted, viz. a regular leading in Trade. And the Government by giving no greater Power to a Company of Traders, than they have ordinarily to bestow, upon a Body of Proprietors in any other Concerns for a regular Management, would be sufficient to hold them in Form.

But alas! Mistrust some, this is only an Intregue to introduce that forlorn Enemy to the Publick, viz. A Bank of Credit! What to allow a parcel of whimsical Fools to turn their Estates into so fickle a matter as Bills of Credit! Certainly these inadvertent Persons will undo themselves, and then we shall have them come crying to the Government for Relief; an awful Thing! And not only so but there may be many more Snakes in the Grass that we don't see, we have Credits lye at Stake, and to multiply Bills will certainly sink them, i.e. and now if we should emit no more Bills our Credits may for ought we know turn all into Silver Money.

But Gentlemen, You take us wrong, we consider thus in our Schemes, The Affairs of our State are under a miserable Indisposition, our Trade (which is the Nurse of the Common-Wealth) sorely languisheth for Want of a sufficient Medium, and a regular Leading. Our Medium of Trade (for want of a larger footing, and a more direct and forehanded Improvement) sinks and cripples every day, at a great Rate, and so sinks the Common-Wealth; and the faster it sinks the faster it may; and although we have waded thorough a long plunge of Difficulty, maintaining our Commerce in some sort hitherto with the help of Banks, additionally as our Medium has more and more fallen short; yet since the perpetual sinking has put a Damp upon farther proceeding in this method for Relief, & yet the sinking Disposition still remains upon all our Credits, & our Trade still becomes more and more destitute and uncapable of digesting our Produce to Advantage (however dear as well cheap some of our Produce is rendered through Gluts and Scarcities) these things does evidently portend or forebode some notable Overture in our State. For,

To suffer our Banks to dwindle and die, (as they must if something in special be not done to prevent it) waiting for the Bills to recover their Credit, or for Silver to come in Voluntier, or by forcing of it in by Law, without giving of it an honourable Invitation in the Advance of its Credit, more than what meer Obligations will do, the Country can't endure it: What Injustice, Oppression and Misery will break in upon us, and what an overthrow in our State and Affairs will be intolerable to undergo, and a Shame for a politick People to suffer.

We are got very far upon the Shoals, and if we can't alter our Course, nor have no way to help our selves, but by making the best of a common Wreck, our Case is bad, some may make shift in small Floats, but the Body of Wealth must sink, some of the dire Effects we may already see and feel, but they will yet appear much more notorious, as our Banks approach their

Exit. And therefore it is out of good Will and Pity, to our Country, to our selves, and our Brethren, and for the Benefit of the publick, and for the Interest of our Sovereign, his Crown and Government, that we do consult the Promotion and Enlargement of Trade in these measures. And altho' if our honourable Rulers don't see it so necessary or so likely to be beneficial to the publick; yet if they don't see any evident Injury coming thereby to the Publick it may be hoped that to gratify a number of generous well meaning Subjects, they will (as *Saul* to *David* when he would go forth to fight with the Philistine) give some suitable Allowance and Protection, notwithstanding the Disdain of some of our elder Brethren.

For who is this irregular Monster that he should defie or threaten the State or Common-Wealth of *New-England?* Let no Man's heart fail because of him; for your Servants will go and fight with him, only bid us go, cloathing us with your Armour of Protection, allowing us the Power and Priviledges of a Company for a Coat of Mail, and a small Bank of publick Credit, (such as we can give good Security for) for a Sword; and who knows but we may prevail, notwithstanding our Smallness and Youth in matters of Trade. For altho' but few may appear in the forefront of the Battel, yet the Smiles of the Government in their Regards to those will doubtless be an Inducement to a great Body to advance and joyn with them; there is a great Army of Israel ready to pursue the Conquest, when once the Champion of the Philistines is smitten in the Forehead. However some may (for want of good manners and a rational Ingenuity) ridiculize and undervalue the Persons appearing to undertake in the Cause, upbraiding them with their Circumstances, Callings &c. (as *Eliab* did *David*) yet if the Cause be good this Defect may well be made up with the Addition of able, wise and suitable Men, let such joyn with them, here is an Opportunity for generous publick spirited Men, to distinguish and signalize themselves in behalf of the publick; for that other kind of Men dare not venture their Estate in the Improvement of a publick Trade. Men may talk of doing great for the publick, but who will venture their Money in a publick Stock, except virtuous and noble Men? If the Cause be not good produce strong Reasons, let us consider the Practice of the Nation, the Principles of politick States, let us consult Reason and not fancy, if *New-England* never saw it; yet if old *England* has proved it, methinks it might be allow'd of. We may raise Scruples & Doubts against the best Schemes, but methinks we need not be very curious, when we can't readily go into a worse Way than we are in of Course.

Indeed the meer possibility of miscarrying or being unfortunate, is a slender Reason to forbid a good Proceeding. What we ask is but a rational thing to ask for, and what every rational Man would wish to succeed, and no more than what free Subjects might rationally be indulged with. Do any mistrust the Privileges and Benefits too great to be monopolized, let such join and take Part; the Cause groans for want of Undertakers, the more the better; does any mistrust that the emitting of Bills are not favoured by our Rulers at Home, then why does the more depending kingly Governments so freely emit large Banks as some does? Or does any mistrust that to increase the Quantity of our Medium of Trade must needs sink the Credit of it? Let these exercise Reason and they'll know better; however, I have heard them that should be wise Men argue, that only the advancing *three* or *four thousand Pounds* in *Connecticut,* to pay their Agent, caused the Bills of Credit to sink evidently the faster in *New-England;* then what a sorrowful Drugg would they become, if *ten* or *twenty thousand Pounds* should be advanced to encourage a publick Trade? but alas! this would scarcely be perceived, for that I presume that no less than *five hundred thousand Pounds,* in our Money is wanting of a competent Supply for our ordinary Commerce, which gradually emitted as it might be received in Exchange with Time for the Business of the Country to recruit, would but maintain, rather than sink the Credit of Money. Could I but think of any rational Objection against our Cause, I would rationally solve it, or I would give over the Cause, but I can't find one, and so I can't tell what to say farther. Indeed there may be many frivolous Scruples made against the best Projections, & in matters of temporal Profit Men are apt to be Wary and Skettish, rather chusing to remain as they are, than run the venture of a new Project, especially those that can make the best of the Times, but this Disposition will never stand *New-England* in stead; we must be more generous & charitable in our thinking and look with Sympathy upon reasonable Proposals, as if they come from Men, and not from Fools, for when Projectors must be treated with Frowns and Disdain, it discourages the most necessary kind of Men from shewing their Faces.

One necessary Principle more I have to urge, and that is publick Bounty in carrying on publick Affairs.

In Times of Peace and Tranquility it is not only convenient but very necessary, to undertake great and notable Works for publick Benefit, as building Fortifications, Castles, Bridges, State-houses, Colleges or any other great Works of a publick Nature. The common or ordinary demand for Labour is not sufficient to prevent the prevailing of Idleness, especially among a People that are not in the Way of advancing their worldly Grandeur in the Expences of Labour.

So Weak and Feeble as *New-England* is, or any Part of it, they might carry on such Works to an eminent Degree, and yet the Common-Wealth should flourish never the less. We might spare abundance of Labour from our ordinary Occasions; only to say we are an idle, prodigal, lavish People proves it; for our Prodigality enlarges the Business of Labour, and if Idleness will maintain us at a prodigal Rate, then surely we have Labour to spare.

It signifies but little for every one to try who shall do most of the little there is to be done, for he that can with the most advantage gain the Business, will certainly supplant the other of his Profit, and put him out of the Way of Business; and the Extravagancy of some must make a Demand for the Prudence of others. I can't suppose that King *Solomon*'s great Buildings in the least impoverished the People, tho' his Burthens might seem heavy; for as soon as the great Undertakings were finished, the Business scanted, and the Kingdom faded, and the manners of the People corrupted. It is a certain Truth that great Undertakings upon the publick Account, if regularly managed never hurts the Common-Wealth, but rather inures a People to Principles of Virtue, when otherwise Principles of Licentiousness will prevail. But Men must be drawn gradually into publick Service, as others may have Time to lay out their Business accordingly as they find the Demand for their Produce increases; for sudden drawing Men out of the common Business might occasion great Wants and Scarcities. Now it would be much better for the State of *New-England* if such great and notable Works, as aforesaid, might be carried on upon the publick Account. If we should advance largely to the encouraging of Colleges and Schools &c. it would but be our Glory and Interest, for we may well spare the Labour, but then Learning would be encouraged, and we might have many the more well accomplished States-Men bred up among us. In many Cases the seeming advance of Burthens is but the giving of Strength to bear them. But then in the first Place, It is very necessary that we be in a Way of Exchanging a considerable Quantity of our Labour either for Money or for Bills of Credit, to some convenient Degree to set us beforehand, that we may have Money to pay the Labourer, and not that we should remain plunged with only our necessary Provisions for a current Stock being discouraged down to very Scarcity to make them current, and consequently to meer Poverty: Besides, Men will work for Money, when they won't work for other Species: Therefore I say that it is necessary there should be a good large Stock of Currency, that instead of spending our Time seeking Money, waiting for our Dues, suffering Damages & Perplexities, we might be plying our Work and Business to Advantage like able Men.

But some may object that such publick Liberalities would tend to lay Burthens on the poor Widows &c. to help the Rich. To this I answer, that the Polls of Widows and helpless kind of People, such as are not able to labour, does but little to publick Charges, nor do the Poor pay Taxes upon what they don't possess, so that this can be but an inconsiderable Wrong to them.

Or if others with more Reason object, that it would lay the Burden upon prudent, industrious Men. To these I would answer, That to advance Money to support a rich Farmer in raising Victuals & Cloathing to supply the common Demand for Labour, or for the publick Money to be improved to any such Purpose or End, as to uphold a private producing for the common Market, would indeed be a Burthen and a Disadvantage to Men of Business that must advance the Money; but for the Money to be proportionably advanced to the Support and Enlargement of Schools, to the carrying on of any great and publick Buildings, enabling Men employed in publick Service to build and furnish for themselves largely, as becometh a publick Station, does but make so much more Profit in the ordinary Business of the Country in the natural Tendency of it besides the publick Intent or End of the Business carried on. Therefore I say, that to undertake largely in such publick Affairs contributing liberally to carry on the same, is no Hindrance to the Common-Wealth but very necessary, under our Circumstances of Business, to promote Principles of Industry, by enlarging the Demand for Labour.

A stingy closehanded Disposition is not good for the Common-Wealth; Men of that Disposition may do much to supply the common Demand for Labour, drawing others to stoop to them; but that which makes for the Common-Wealth is for Men to carry on Business industriously, and lay out and expend largely, making good Business for others as well as for themselves, and thus by a generous and friendly Commutation in Business, the Common-Wealth may wax and flourish, and this would encourage Men of Business to come in and settle among us, which with the Advantage of an enlarged Commerce, and a suitable increasing Stock of Money or Bills of Credit, to carry it out ably and freely, we might advance our selves in the Interest of the Crown and Kingdom.

THE END.

· 28 ·

"A Sincere Lover of Virginia" [Sir William Gooch], A Dialogue (Williamsburg, 1732)

IN THE 1720S AND 1730S, Virginia producers suffered declining tobacco prices, and a frequently cited cause was the common inclusion of trash tobacco in the hogsheads sent to Britain. In the early 1730s, the Virginia legislature sought to deal with this problem by establishing an inspection system that required public inspectors to examine all containers of tobacco and burn whatever did not meet an established quality. Although the system turned out to be a great success in the long run, the initial reaction to it was ambivalent, with angry mobs burning several inspection houses. In an effort to nip the public outcry in the bud, Lieutenant Governor William Gooch, who governed Virginia successfully from 1727 to 1749 and was the author of the plan, wrote and published the pamphlet reprinted in this selection. Using the form of a dialogue between a county justice, Love-Country, and two modest-sized producers, Thomas Sweet-Scented and William Oronoco (sweet-scented and oronoco being the two principal varieties of tobacco produced in Virginia), Gooch sought to educate planters on the expected benefits of the new system. Explaining that the colony's laws were "the People[']s Direction in moral Actions" and that justices like Love-Country were duty-bound to give them "all the Light they can, into the Intent and Meaning of them," Gooch used Love-Country to explain why and how the execution of the inspection law would benefit them by raising the quality of shipments, bringing higher prices in overseas markets, and removing the incentive of local merchants to raise prices for their goods to compensate for whatever tobacco turned out to be unsalable.

This *Dialogue* is remarkable, first, as an illustration of how in the consensual political worlds characteristic of the colonies provincial leaders could not simply run roughshod over their constituents but had to speak to broader public concerns and, second, for its articulation of a model of the way political relations were supposed to be conducted in Virginia, with ordinary planters deferring to the superior knowledge of local leaders. (J.P.G.)

A

DIALOGUE

BETWEEN

THOMAS SWEET-SCENTED,

WILLIAM ORONOCO, Planters,

both Men of good Understanding, and Justice

LOVE-COUNTRY, who can speak for himself.

RECOMMENDED

To the Reading of the Planters.

By a sincere Lover of *VIRGINIA*.

WILLIAMSBURG:

Printed by WILLIAM PARKS.

M,DCC,XXXII.

A Dialogue, &c.

Tom. How d'ye, how d'ye, Neighbour? Well, how goes the World?

Will. I am pretty well I thank you, only troubled a good deal in Mind.

Tom. Why what's the Matter, Man?

Will. Matter! Matter enough: I have been at the Warehouse, to have some of my Tobacco inspected.

Tom. Ah! Well, pray how is it? I want sadly to know a little: How do you like these new Officers?

Will. By my Troth, *Tommas,* I can't tell what to say to it; I am really nonplust.

Tom. Prithee tell me how it fared with you: Let me hear a little.

Will. Hear a little! You shall hear a great deal, if you go to that. Can any Body say, that it is not very hard upon a poor Man, to have Part of his Labour burnt by these Inspectors, because, forsooth they don't like our Tobacco? when at the same time, for aught I can see, they are no better Judges of it than any of us.

Tom. 'Tis very hard indeed Neighbour: For my Part, I can't by any manner of Means approve this new Law.

Will. Approve it! No, who can? For they tell me, that if our Tobacco is not 800, they won't pay us for the Cask.

Tom. How so?

Will. You may depend upon what I tell you, and something worse: For, when I was at the Warehouse, Neighbour *Seconds* brought Two Hogsheads of Tobacco to be viewed, which, to please these Men, he had made above 800: But so it fell out, the Tobacco not having been well handled in the Curing, by pressing it hard to make it that Weight, it turn'd black, (as you know Tobacco will do that is not well lookt after;) and what do you think these unmerciful Officers said to him—Why truly, that it was such black Stuff, unless he would pick it, they must burn it all.

Tom. What, and so if our Tobacco is not 800, they won't pay us for the Cask; and if, to make it that Weight, it turns black under the Press, which, as you say, all Tobacco will do that is'nt well handled, they'll burn it, will they? Things are come to a fine Pass indeed.

Will. Burn it! Ay, up it goes in a Funk, unless you'll pick it; I must say for them, they'll suffer a poor Man to do That. But there's another Circumstance harder than what you've heard: If our Casks are not exactly of such a Gauge, be our Tobacco never so good, they won't pass it: What think you of that? This seems to me to exceed all the rest.

Tom. No, there's nothing new in that, d'ye see: There has been for some Years a Law ord'ring us not to make our Hogsheads above such a Size.

Will. Indeed! Well that's what I never knew before: One of our Neighbours, sometime since, did say that's the Truth on't, that we must make them so and so, and luckily I did, but I never knew there was a Law for it; and till this Year, I am sure we never minded it; every Body made their Casks as big as they pleased.

Tom. That can't be denied, but we—

Will. What then, this that I thought so very hard, is come to Nothing?

Tom. Not to be charged to this new Law, it being—

Will. It signifies Nothing to talk of it then.

Tom. Nothing, d'ye call it? I always thought we were obliged to con—

Will. Alas, I mean 'tis not material, not worth Noticing in this Case, in this new Law, where there are so many other Things that punch us.

Tom. There I agree with you: I wish with all my Heart *Will,* I could but once understand what our Assembly meant by making such a Law.

Will. Find that out if you can: 'Twould puzzle a Philosopher, I believe: Ud's *{blotted}*xcant younder comes Justice LOVE COUNTRY, they say he is a mighty Man for this Law, thinks it a very good Law; and I must confess I have heard other Gentlemen say so, particularly, that 'tis a good Law for the poor Planters; but, for my Life, I can't see in what.

Tom. We have lost the Justice, he is turned out of the Road to a Plantation on the Left Hand.

Will. I am sorry for it, he is a right honest Man; and if we could have got him into Talk, would have told us all. However, let's stay here, perhaps he may come this Way anon.

Tom. Then, as we were saying,—oh—Notwithstanding what so many Folks say, I can't discover One good Thing in the Law.

Will. Folks say! Why Man, tho' some Folks say as I told you, there are other Folks that say quite contrary: I am sure I have heard a great many Speeches against it at the Race-Grounds, and at the County-Courts, when the Courts were over, and Men were got together in the Ordinary, speaking their Thoughts freely, without any Liking to it, nay, they have publickly curs'd it: And sure we can't all of us be mistaken.—Why, pray is it not a clear Case, don't we see our Tobacco burnt by the Humour of the Inspectors? Who can bear such Usage?

Tom. Far and softly, *Will:* Don't fly into Passion; that avails nought, you know; for, bear it we must: What can we do? Nothing but quietly submit:

Will. Quietly submit! Hast thou lived to these Years to be so tame a Creature, as to cry out on such an Occasion, What can we do?—Yes, Yes, something might be done, if we could but confide in one another.

Tom. As how, pray? What wou'd thy wise Head propose, ha?

Will. My wise Head! Why, my wise Head tells me, that there are a Power of People in some of the *Upper Counties,* and abundance in the *Northern Neck,* that complain as heavily against this Law as we do; and certainly, 'tis as easy as 'tis to jump over a Fence-Rail, for us to get together, and think of something or other that might be done, to force—

Tom. A pretty Fellow indeed! To force! To force what? Art thou such an Oaf as to talk after this Rate? To force! Force your self headlong into Rebellion, be hanged, lose your Land, and ruin your Family, rather than submit to a Law, the Great Ones and the Rich Ones must submit to as well as we; a Law, whatever at present we may think of it, was undoubtedly designed by our Burgesses for the Good of the Country.

Will. But hark you *Tom:* What did you talk of Rebellion for, and all that? No, I ask your Pardon there, I did not mean That neither.

Tom. Not mean, No verily I believe thee: Though whatever you meant, would have signified but little; your Meaning woudn't have procured you a Pardon, woudn't have sav'd you from the Gallows: And I must needs say, all our Disturbances are owing to such Wiseacres as you. You pretend to fly in the Face of the Government? I charge you on my Friendship to talk no more in this Strain.

Will. Indeed *Tom.* I did not consider—But *Tom,* the Justice is coming.

Tom. Ay, Young Man, if he should hear what you have been talking of, I woudn't be in your Coat for—

Will. Pray *Tom.* be pacified; and since you have declared your self my Friend, advise me seriously how to behave.

Tom. Behave! If you are really One of the impatient Crew, and can't wait the Event of this new Regulation, send your Grievances to the Assembly; they say they are to meet in *May.*

Will. In *May!* That's a good one indeed: In *May!* If we carry our Tobacco to the Warehouse, Part of it will be burnt before *May* comes; and if we don't, by what I can learn, no Body will buy it of us.

Tom. Why then you must be contented, that's all that I know, I am sure, I'm resolv'd to be so: I am as uneasy, it may be, as some others are, but not quite so fierce; for tho' I can't tell how, in what, nor when, I comfort my self with the Hopes that this Law will help us, that it was not made in vain.

Will. Say no more, here's the Justice.

Justice. Good Day to you, Neighbours.

Will. The like to your Worship.

Tom. The same to you, Sir,—Let me speak, *Will.*

Will. Do so then, since you are so fond on't.

Justice. What News d'ye hear? All the Discourse now, I suppose, is about our new Law: Pray how goes Tobacco at the Warehouses?

Will. Go, Master! Some of it goes into the Fire.

Justice. Thrown into the Fire, say'st thou? I am very glad to hear it, exceedingly rejoiced.

Tom. But why, Master, are you so glad?

Will. Ah, Master, why so rej——

Tom. Be quiet, can't you. What makes you so glad, Sir?

Justice. 'Tis a certain Sign the Inspectors are honest Men, and do their Duty.

Tom. Their Duty! 'Tis very hard upon us in the mean Time.

Justice. No such Thing, I promise you: In the first Place, don't you know good Tobacco as well as they?

Tom & Will. To be sure we do.

Justice. Then why do you carry such Tobacco to them, that you know they must burn? But however, since I have happened with you, and we are entred upon the Subject, if you are willing to be informed, and are resolved to govern your selves accordingly, be patient, speak one at a Time, and you'll both of you be made easy, never fear.

Will. We shall do as you desire, Sir, and think our selves much obliged to you.

Tom. We want, may it please your Worship, to hear what may be said on the Side of this same Law, and what Good it will do us poor Planters; for we are strangely pestered with odd Notions about it.

Justice. I don't wonder at it; the best Things are the most liable to be abused: Though it astonishes me, that so plain a Law as this is, should have so many Enemies: A Law, not only the best that ever was made for the Country, for our Trade in general, but the best for the poor Planters.

Tom. Your Worship said, for the poor Planters?

Justice. I did so; and that You may comprehend me the better, tell me the Parts of it You dislike, and I'll explain their Meaning to You.

Tom. Dislike!

Will. Dislike! Dislike! Sir.

Justice. Ay, tell me what you grumble at.

Tom. Grumble at!

Will. Burning, *Tom.*

Tom. Grumble at! Why, Sir, don't they burn our Tobacco; and is not that enough to make any Man grumble?

Justice. I own they do burn Tobacco, and this Year they'll burn a great deal of Tobacco; for a worse Year for Tobacco we have not had these 20 Years: But what then? If they burn Yours, they'll as readily burn mine, and some of every Man's they'll burn, if we don't sort it carefully before we carry it to them. And now let me ask you a Question, answer me honestly? Is the Tobacco the Inspectors burn, fit for any thing else? Can either of you say, 'tis fit for any Market? If not, then such Trash ought to be destroy'd.

Tom. Why Master, since you have put it so very home to us, we must own, the Tobacco they burn, is not good for much; but then, as bad as it is, we always got something for it, and so, I don't doubt, we should this Year, were we at Liberty; which, we confess, has been a very indefferent Year for Tobacco.

Justice. Therefore pray consider: The Accounts we have had for several Years past, from every Port in *Great-Britain* our Tobacco is carry'd to, are full of Complaints, that we make more than all *Europe* can consume, and a great Part of it such Trash, as no Purchaser will meddle with.

Tom. If this be true, Why then, Master, don't they stint us?

Justice. Stint you! It has been tried, and found ineffectual: And no wonder; for tho' it lessen'd the Quantity, it did not mend the Quality; there was Trash still in Proportion to clog the Markets; and so there would be, reduce the Number of Plants as low as you please: Let us be restrained never so much, we find Ways to make it up, and you own you can sell all.

Tom. I do: But Burning, Master! That's the terrible Article.

Justice. Not a Bit; 'tis no such terrible Thing. Isn't the Country almost ruined? And let me tell you, this very Year our Ruin had been compleated, had not this excellent Law interposed, which destroys all bad Tobacco, and suffers none but good to be exported to the Markets in *Europe.*

Tom. But spare me, Sir: What have we, who sell our Tobacco in the Country, to do with the Markets Abroad?

Justice. If you don't send any Home, you must know all of it goes Home; and that a great many of us ship our Tobacco on our own Venture to the Markets: Thousands of Hogsheads are every Year consigned upon Freight to the Merchants in *London, Glascow, Bristol,* and other *Ports:* And can you be such a Simpleton, as not to consider, that the better the Markets are in *Europe,* the more Money you'll sell your Tobacco for here: Or, that when all Trash is destroyed, and our Staple gets a Reputation, the Price for it will advance, and in all Likelihood the Consumption of it increase.

Will. There seems to be some Sense in that, Master; the better the Commodity, the better it will sell, to be sure.

Justice. Thou hast hit it, *Will:* The Lowness of the Markets, I have been long since convinced, is not altogether occasion'd by the Quantity: Therefore, if under the Direction of this Law, we lessen the Quantity, and mend the Quality, by destroying the Trash, we drive the right Nail.

Tom. Do you in Earnest conceit so, Master?

Justice. No less, my Word for it: If, when your Tobacco is well cull'd, you get as much for 800 that is Clean and Neat, as you could do before this Law for 1200 Tag-rag and Bob-tail, what Injury or Injustice pray will this Law do you? The naked Truth, *Tom,* is this, *Bad Tobacco destroyed, stamps a Value upon the remaining Good,* which will for ever be depreciated by a Mixture.

Tom. I grant it, Sir; but I fear we must wait some Time to see all this come to pass.

Justice. If you were to wait, you would be no Loser at the Long Run; but there is no Room for such Fears: Have but Patience, and this very Year you'll see it come to pass. Send 2000 Weight of Tobacco to the Warehouse, if the Inspectors pass but 1200 of it, I will engage to give you more, in Money or Goods, for the 1200, than you could sell the 2000 for.

Will. Engage to give us more! Will you so?

Justice. Yes, tho' I am no Dealer, only to shew you what you may do.

Tom. But, Sir, after we have been at the Trouble, and perhaps some Expence, in carrying our Tobacco to the Inspectors, that they should have Authority to burn it, That is what galls us.

Justice. A pretty Business indeed! Don't both of you boast that you know good Tobacco as well as they? Is it not, therefore, unreasonable to complain of what you may prevent, by carefully Sorting of it before you carry it to them? And then, the envious and designing Men would not have that Handle for Clamour and Noise, nor would it be so much in their Power to raise foolish Stories against the Law, because they see Tobacco burnt, that a right honest Man, tender of the Welfare of his Country, would not offer to Sale.

Tom. What your Worship says is very right.

Justice. A Man with half an Eye might see it: 'Tis your Impatience that spoils all: You eagerly catch up every idle Story that artful Men, for private Interest, propagate among you; and then you impute them to the Law: When, lack-a-day, the Sense and Meaning of the Law is no way concerned; all your Uneasiness arise from their wicked Insinuations. Let me tell you, 'tis much easier to raise a Dust than to lay it.

Will. 'Tis but too true, I have seen enough of that, Master.

Justice. What, you begin to be convinc'd, do you? Let us then next reflect upon the great Advantage of these Inspectors Notes, which they give you for your Tobacco after they have pass'd it; Notes full as good as so much ready Money, the same as so much Cash, and as such will be received in Payment at any Store, for what Goods you want: Your Tobacco you may parcel out, into as many of them as you please, so as to be able to pay this Man 50 Pounds of Tobacco, another 100, and another 200; in short, make Payment of any Debt: And thus, according to the Price of Tobacco, these Notes will answer 10, 20, 30, or 40 Shillings in Money, in any Part of the Neck you live in.

Tom. We were told that we were to have Notes, but never dreamt of this good Accompt they are like to turn to; that Thing of Burning was always uppermost.

Justice. Did'st thou never read the Law?

Tom. Not I, Sir.

Justice. Have you, Neighbour?

Will. No truly, I can't say I have.

Justice. Has it been read to you?

Will & Tom. No.

Justice. I thought as much; clever Fellows indeed! you have been finding Fault with a Law you never read, never heard read, a Law you know nothing of, but from the Reports of lawless Mouths, who meant, by what they said, to impose upon you.

Tom. As I am inclined to think what your Worship has told us is the Truth, I must acknowledge the Imposition.

Justice. Imposition with a Witness. But as I was saying, by Virtue of these Inspectors Notes, I dare to promise you Goods much cheaper than hitherto you have had them: So that by this Law, you'll not only get more Money for your Tobacco, but you'll pay less for your Goods.

Tom. Ah Master, that's rare News indeed: But how, Sir, how is that to be?

Justice. Every Man must say, that knows any thing of your way of Dealing in these Upper Parts of the Country, nay, the Storekeepers will own it, that they were always obliged to be very sharp in the Sale of their Goods, on the Score of the Badness of the Tobacco they were generally paid in, and the Risque they run of being Losers by it at Home; and therefore they valued their Goods, raising the *per Cent.* upon them, not from the prime Cost, but by the Quality of the Tobacco: Insomuch, that when you have had the Name of selling your Tobacco for 10, 12, 15 Shillings per Hundred, in Reality you had not above 4, 5, or 6 Shillings.

Will. What have we been thus used?

Justice. Yes, marry have you: I have known in a scarce Year, one of these Gentlemen give 3 l. 2 s. 6 d. per Hundred for Tobacco, in Goods, the first Cost of which Goods was not above 20 s. if so much.

Tom. If so, we have paid through the Nose.

Justice. Yes; but it was with Tobacco not fit to be put there.

Tom. But Sir, the Season is far advanced, and I don't hear that any Price is set upon Inspected Tobacco, or, that many Goods are in the Stores.

Justice. The Ships are very late in this Year, they came out late; those that sailed the first, have had long Passages; they are but just arrived, and few Goods are yet imported: But assure your selves, in a little Time the Face of Affairs will be much changed for the better.

Will. We should rejoice to see it.

Justice. Rest satisfied: *Rome* was not built in a Day: Laws are never made to oppress People, but to relieve them: And this very Law against which there is so much Cavil, is calculated to redress all our Grievances in Trade. The Clamours that oppose it, only shew how corrupt Men are, nothing else.

Tom. Indeed!—Well, but Master, woudn't a Stint do all these fine Things as well; and then, mayhaps, the Country would be easy.

Justice. A Stint, Noodle! *Tom.* you are enough to provoke me: Are we not now under a Stint? And let me tell you, the most indulgent Stint that could be propos'd for us.

Tom. How's that, Sir! Clear that same Indulgence, if you please.

Justice. It wants no Clearing, it speaks its self: But if I must tell you my Story over again, and beat into your Head by Repetition, you shall have it. You remember, before this Law, we were limited by an Act of Assembly to 6000 Plants per Taxable, and some were for reducing us lower, to a less Number; but did that, or will such a Method, remedy the Mischiefs the Country lay under?

Tom. I can't say it did.

Justice. Say it did! No, it would not do: And therefore I tell you again, we must mend our Staple, as well as lessen the Quantity. But answer me faithfully, Did you make more Tobacco under a Stint, than what, by this Law, in a favourable Year, you may get pass'd by the Inspectors? If you did, then this Law lessens the Quantity, and mends the Quality: If you did not, you have no Reason to complain.

Tom. I can't say any thing to it one Way nor t'other; but by your Leave, Sir, under the Stint Law, I could sell all that I made, and that I can't do now: There's the Grievance.

Justice. For my Part, I must think, if any Law may be called grievous, 'tis that which cuts us short in the Management of our own Land.

Tom. Nay, but Sir, where's the Difference between cutting a Man short in his Labour, and in the Fruit of his Labour; these Laws considered together, the Stint appears the more favourable of the Two, for by That I reap some Advantage from all my Labour.

Justice. If you were the only Person concerned in making of Tobacco, and carried on the whole Trade by your self, it would then be cruel, not to say unjust, to restrain you either Way; because, the Consequence of your Management would advantage no other Man, neither would it injure any other; but when the Public is taken into the Account, 'tis quite another Argument; and as the whole Country is engaged in the same Trade, every Man in the Country will be more or less affected by the Contrivances of unfair Dealers. This was the Reason why the Assembly, the Guardians of our Trade and Property, entred into these Measures, to prevent, if possible, in this general Commerce, all Fraud and Deceit, by making every Man honest.

Tom. This is what our Assembly meant, is it Sir? In troth, I think they're honest Gentlemen.

Justice. But let me answer the Bounce you made of Advantage from all your Labour, by which, you declare the Stint the more favourable Law: Don't you know, that the Reward of your Labour depends upon the Profit you make at the Winding up of the Bottom? For Instance, suppose now you had 100 Bushels of Wheat in the Ear, in several Stacks in your Yard, which you might sell for 2 Shillings the Bushel; and that by the Accident of Fire, half of it was destroyed. Now, only suppose the like Misfortune had befallen every Man in the Country, and that the Price of Wheat by this Casualty advanced, as no Doubt it would, and you could sell the remaining 50 Bushels at 4 Shillings; what's become of the Produce of all your Labour, as you term it? Have you any Reason on the Account of Interest to bewail Burning?

Tom. No, I think not.

Justice. The Case is the same in Tobacco, with this Difference, Tobacco is made better by Part of it (the Trash) being destroied; and for that one Reason, will fetch a better Price: So that, to the extraordinary Labour you are at, in making more Tobacco than you are allow'd to sell, be pleased to place the Advantage you will reap by mending the Quality; and rest assured you'll be well paid for your Pains.

What, perhaps you are resolved not to be convinced.

Will. Sir, we are not obstinate; but you must needs think, we have been strangely prepossest: For, notwithstanding 'tis so very plain, to shew you the Roguery of some that shall be nameless, 'twas confidently buzzed about, as if, by this Law, the Rich intended to ruin the Poor.

Justice. None but the worst of Villains could suggest such a Reflection: No such Thing, upon my Honour: Consider the Persons concerned in making this Law; Are they not all of them Gentlemen of Probity and great Integrity? And have they not, by this very Act of theirs, sufficiently testified their Regard for the Public, and their tender Concern for the poor Planters?

Tom. Well, for my Part, I am resolved never to quarrel for the future with what I don't understand: And whenever they din any idle Reports against Laws in my Ears, that are beyond my Capacity, if your Worship will give me Leave, I'll wait on your Worship with them.

Justice. Do so and welcome, either of you: Don't suffer your selves to be debauched by ne'er a He that wears a Head: 'Tis the Duty of every

Magistrate, as the Laws are the Peoples Direction in moral Actions, to give them all the Light they can, into the Intent and Meaning of them.

Will. We thank you, Master.

Justice. Have you done with Objections?

Will. Tommas has said nothing, Sir, about the Charge of the Warehouses, and the Inspectors Salaries.

Justice. What of them, pray?

Tom. Nay, it may be, this is a Rout about Nothing too: But the Thing *Will.* means, is the Charge the Country is put to on those Two Accounts, the Houses, and Officers Salaries.

Justice. The Country put to! Why the Whole is defray'd out of the Money paid by the Shippers, for Passing their Tobacco.

Tom. But we poor Men don't ship any Tobacco.

Justice. Then you are not concerned in it one Way nor t'other; it rests upon the Merchants. But, if Charges and Expences are drawn in to make the Cry the louder, let what follows make a thankful Impression upon your Minds, to the Assembly; who, by this Law, have released us from the Tax we paid, under the Stint-Law, to Tellers, for Counting our Plants; from the One Shilling per Hogshead we paid to Rolling-houses; and from the Expence of Receivers.

Tom. These Things were nothing to us.

Justice. If you did not pay them, they did who purchased your Tobacco; and if they are relieved from these Charges, and are to be paid by the Captains of the Ships, 4 *s.* per Hogshead, for the Trouble and Expence of Shipping their Tobacco themselves, can't they for this Reason afford to give you the better Price?

Tom. Cry-mercy: But, Sir, the Shipping of the Tobbacco occasions great Murmurings; they say the Country is not able to do it.

Justice. Willing Minds would go a great Way towards it: In the Lower Parts of the Country, where the Rivers are broad, and the Navigation difficult, they may not be able; but towards the Heads of the Rivers it might be done: But this Complaint is Nothing; for, if the Publick are not in a Condition to comply with That Clause of the Law, they may depend upon Relief, when the Assembly meet; who, without any Question, will make such Alterations and Amendments, as they find, in the Execution of it, are wanting, to make all Parties concerned in it, easy. And we shall deserve to be branded for the maddest People on the Face of the whole

Earth, not to acquiesce; but by malicious and ignorant random Judgments, endeavour to defeat such good Purposes.

Tom. These Hopes, Master, as much a Convert as I am to Truth, do administer more Comfort; for, who can be discontented, that knows what the Assembly aim'd at by this Law, and that they'll leave no Stone unturned, to secure to us the good Things contained in it; most especially, more Money for our Tobacco, and less for our Goods; that we mayn't pay away so much as we receive.

Will. There are one or two Particulars more I must trouble your Worship with, that I have heard discoursed of, as Grievances.

Justice. Well, let me hear them; make Dispatch; it grows late.

Tom. Why one is, That tho' they are at no Charge for Rolling-Houses, they say they are strangely hamper'd, having no Place to lay the Goods in, they import: Indeed this is no Concern of ours who buy our Goods in the Country. Then they cry, that many of them had Wharfs and Landing Places, which are become useless.

Justice. As to convenient Places for lodging their Goods, Are not the former Storehouses still in Being, where they may put their Goods? No Man that imports Goods, is destitute of Friends that live on the River, where so many Wharfs and Landing Places, you say, are become useless, but he may have the Benefit of the most commodious in Situation near his Dwelling, to lodge his Goods, since the Captains of the Ships are so obliging to put them on Shore where-ever they are desired. As to their Uselessness on other Accounts, 'tis of no Weight; if it doth deprive some People of any Profit they were formerly to them, 'tis a private Stake, and must be given up to the Good of the Publick. This is all you have to say, I presume?

Tom. Yes, Master, we thank you; we had been sadly on't, if we had not had the good Fortune to meet with your Worship.

Justice. Since you esteem it so, I am glad, for your Sakes, that we were so fortunate.

Tom. Ay, Master, 'tis very lucky for Neighbour *Will.*

Will. Hush, *Tom,* Hush.

Justice. Why for *Will,* more than for your self?

Will. Nothing in the universal World, only *Tommas,* now your Worship has made him light-heel'd, now your Worship has made it out that 'tis a good Law for the poor Planters, has a Mind to be jocose.

Justice. Upon my Conscience 'tis a good Law for every Body: I have not told you half the good Things contained in it; I have confined my self, for your better Information, to the Trade in the Country; when alas, if I was to launch out, into the Effects of it Abroad, 'tis impossible to say when I should have done.

Tom & Will. Indeed, Sir!

Tom. We are obliged to your Worship, for this seasonable Instruction: We shall expect to find what your Worship has told us; and in the mean Time, shall do our Endeavours to reconcile Neighbours to so beneficial a Law.

Justice. Do so: But before we part, since we have conversed so much on this Subject, and I have taken so much Pains with you, I can't think of leaving you without a Word or two of Advice, which, on all Occasions, remember to put in Practice. Live as become honest Men, minding only your own Business: Fear God, honour the King, and meddle not with those that are given to Noise and Violence: Submit your selves to every Law: Keep from Race-grounds, those Schools of Gaming and Drunkenness. Never go near the County-Courts, unless Business calls you thither; and when it doth, return Home as soon as it is done: Make it your principal Employment, this coming Summer, to look well to your Crops, especially your Tobacco, which ought to be tended with the same Care that Annuals are in a Garden: And, since you are indulged the Privilege of making as much Tobacco as you can, make it as good as you can. The Inspectors don't take Pleasure in burning of Tobacco; 'tis what the Law requires of them, and they are under the Obligation of an Oath, a very great Penalty, to destroy all that is bad.

Will. But, Master, out of Spite and Malice they may burn ones Tobacco, and I don't see how we can help it.

Justice. Prove that, and you have your Remedy against them; and you may be assured, such a One wou'd be turned out of his Office, with Infamy.

Tom. But then, they may be more nice in Transfer-Tobacco on Account of the Penalty, if, upon a second View, 'tis not found good; and most of That belongs to poor Planters.

Justice. The Inspectors are bound by Oath, to take Care of the Goodness of the Crop-Tobacco, as well as the Transfer; and, I don't question, they perform their Duty in both: But the Cause why the Transfer-Tobacco is more found Fault with, is, Many more are concerned in That than the

Other; and, as 'tis generally carried to the Warehouse in Parcels, People think it hard to see so much of each Parcel rejected, as is often done, and as this Year it deserves: But, at the same Time, they should consider, that the Crop-Tobacco undergoes as strict an Examination, and has as much in Proportion, condemned to the Fire. The Truth is, The great Noise that's made, about the Strictness used in Transfer-Tobacco, proceeds from a malicious Insinuation, as if the Inspectors only regarded their own Interest, lest the Transfer-Tobacco should be refused, and turned upon their Hands by the Publick Creditors, if found faulty; but I can see no manner of Reason to apprehend any ill Consequence to any Planter, from this Observation.

Tom. If we are under no Hardship from hence, I must say, No Man living, and dealing in Tobacco, has any Fault to find with this Law.

Justice. Well, let me end with you: And, if under this Regulation, we send Home more good Tobacco than can be consumed, fear not, my Lads, with this Method we may expect a Stint; there is no other Way to recover our Trade, which, This Year, had it not been for This Law, would have demolish'd us all. God be with you. Farewell.

Tom and Will. Good Night, Sir: We are much obliged to you.—Huzza! God bless the King, the Governor, Council, and House of Burgesses.

Tom. 'Tis high Time for us to part too: Good by to you, *Will.*

Will. Adieu: The Justice is a good Man; he gave us very good Advice: But I must go to see a Race sometimes, for all that.

Tom. Well, Well: Good Night to you.

FINIS.